LET'S **KILL** GANDHI!

Tushar A. Gandhi (b. 1960) is a great-grandson of Kasturba and Mohandas Gandhi, and the grandson of their second son, Manilal, and his wife Sushila. In 1996, he discovered an urn containing the ashes from Gandhi's funeral pyre, forgotten in the strong room of State Bank of India's Cuttack branch. He secured permission from the Supreme Court and immersed them in the Triveni Sangam on 30 January 1997. In the same year, he founded the Mahatma Gandhi Foundation, of which he is currently the founder-president. Tushar is the president of Lok Seva Trust, Mumbai, and a director of the Gandhi Research Foundation, Jalgaon.

In 2005, he commemorated the seventy-fifth anniversary of the Dandi Kooch by organizing a re-enactment of the 241-mile-long walk. He walked the entire stretch and was instrumental in getting the prime minister to declare the route from Sabarmati Ashram to Dandi, India's only historic heritage route.

Tushar currently lives in Mumbai with his wife Sonal and children Vivan and Kasturi.

LET'S **KILL** GANDHI!

A CHRONICLE OF HIS LAST DAYS, THE CONSPIRACY, MURDER, INVESTIGATION, TRIALS AND KAPUR COMMISSION

TUSHAR GANDHI

RUPA

Published by
Rupa Publications India Pvt. Ltd 2021
7/16, Ansari Road, Daryaganj
New Delhi 110002

Sales centres:
Bengaluru Chennai
Hyderabad Jaipur Kathmandu
Kolkata Mumbai Prayagraj

Copyright © Tushar A. Gandhi 2021

The views and opinions expressed in this book are the author's own and the facts are as reported by him which have been verified to the extent possible, and the publishers are not in any way liable for the same.

All rights reserved.
No part of this publication may be reproduced, transmitted, or stored in a retrieval system, in any form or by any means, electronic, mechanical, photocopying, recording or otherwise, without the prior permission of the publisher.

P-ISBN: 978-93-90918-03-4
E-ISBN: 978-93-90918-11-9

Sixth impression 2025

10 9 8 7 6

Printed in India

This book is sold subject to the condition that it shall not, by way of trade or otherwise, be lent, resold, hired out, or otherwise circulated, without the publisher's prior consent, in any form of binding or cover other than that in which it is published.

*Dedicated to victims of violence and hate
and
my brother Kush, who was one*

CONTENTS

Foreword   xi

BOOK 1
Murder, Murderers, the Conspiracy, Investigations and the Previous Failed Attempts

1. 'He Ram': Another Crucifixion   3
2. The Murderers   14
3. The Plot   45
4. Bungling the Investigation Facilitating Gandhi's Murder   120
5. Discarded Mentor   141
6. Attempts that Failed   157

BOOK 2
The Last Years
Years of Tumult, Triumph, Tragedy and His End

7. The Last Years   171
8. Violence Erupts   208
9. Bihar: An Orgy of Hate   269
10. Alone, Isolated and Abandoned   297
11. City of the Dead   366

BOOK 3
Red Fort Trial, Appeals, Execution and Kapur Commission

12. Red Fort Trial   407
13. Appeals and Execution   471
14. Kapur Commission   487

Epilogue 657

APPENDICES

Appendix 1: Chargesheet 665
Appendix 2: The Judgment 670
Appendix 3: Translation of Urdu Diary Entry of Briefing to Nagarvala 691

Acknowledgements 693

A good man never dies.

> —JAMES WHITCOMB RILEY
> from 'A Good Man'

He lives, he wakes—'tis Death is dead not he.

> —JOHN KEATS
> from 'Adonias'

'Unto each man his handiwork, unto each his crown,
The just Fate gives;
Whoso takes the world's life on him and his own lays down,
He, dying so, lives.
Whoso bears the whole heaviness of the wronged world's weight
And puts it by,
It is well with him suffering, though he face man's fate;
How should he die?
Seeing death has no part in him any more, no power
Upon his head;
He has bought his eternity with a little hour,
And is not dead.
For an hour if ye look for him, he is no more found,
For one hour's space;
Then ye lift up your eyes to him and behold him crowned,
A deathless face.
On the mountains of memory, by the world's wellsprings,
In all men's eyes,
Where the light of the life of him is on all past things,
Death only dies.'

> —ALGERNON C. SWINBURNE
> from 'Super Flumina Babylonis'

FOREWORD

'My life is my message.'

−M.K. Gandhi

In the early evening of 30 January 1948, Mahatma Gandhi, father of the newly liberated and partitioned Indian nation, Bapu to us, his descendants, was murdered by a Hindu fanatic.

The world remembers Gandhi and pays homage to him on this day since then, but the story of his murder has been forgotten. Every 30 January, the heads of the Indian government visit Raj Ghat and lay wreaths at his Samadhi. Although Gandhi was murdered at 5:17 p.m., a siren used to sound at 11:00 am, reminding the people of India that Gandhi, the apostle of peace, had been murdered on that day. The practice was to observe silence as a homage to the Father of the Nation, a practice long since abandoned. In New India, his sacrifices have been forgotten; now his murderer is worshipped. India today is hurtling down that very path of intolerance and hate, which led to its division in 1947 and the murder of the man it once revered as the Father of the Nation. In New India, they worship and eulogize his murderer and make a public spectacle of it; they enact his murder to glorify the murderer; they worship the weapon used to murder Gandhi. Intolerance has become our creed, bigotry a virtue, violence and murder our method. Killing has become acceptable and is often celebrated; hate has become institutionalized and is purposefully planted in our minds and hearts; silence is patriotic; Hindutva is the official policy. If this hate and fragmentation is not arrested, India will cease to exist. Bapu is no longer in our midst to save us; his martyrdom will have been in vain if we do not desist.

Since 30 January 1948, various groups have circulated their own unfounded theories about his murder. Many lies have been passed off as truths; half-truths have been mixed with true incidents and passed off as whole truths. The murderer Nathuram Godse's act has been glorified by the claim that he did it from a sense of outrage at Gandhi's pro-Muslim stance which harmed Hindus. 'Gandhi was responsible for Partition'; 'Gandhi was pampering Muslims and was discriminatory towards Hindus'; 'If Gandhi was allowed to live he would harm Bharatmata'; 'Gandhi forced the Indian government to pay Pakistan ₹55 crores (₹550 million)'; 'Gandhi turned a blind eye to the sufferings of the Hindu refugees and pampered Muslims who had stayed back at the time of Partition'; 'Killing Gandhi was the only way to save Bharatmata'; 'Gandhi was detrimental to the cause of a Hindu Rashtra'; 'Nathuram was a patriot, deshbhakt, he murdered Mahatma Gandhi to save the Rashtra': these were, and even today are, some of the lies propagated by the followers of Godse and his patron Savarkar and the Hindu extremist organizations, the Rashtriya Swayamsevak Sangh (RSS) and Hindu Mahasabha, to justify Gandhi's murder.

Are these allegations true? Not at all, but a few generations of Indians have grown up believing these lies to be true because they have not been told the truth. The silence of Gandhians, who kept turning the other cheek whenever Gandhi was attacked and slandered, has strengthened this belief further. Too few know that there were four recorded attempts on Gandhi's life, before the last two on 20 and 30 January 1948. Four of the five failed attempts were at a time when Pakistan was not even on the agenda of the Muslim League. All the four attacks were by the extreme right wing, from amongst the uppercaste Hindus of Poona, by fanatic followers of V.D. Savarkar; three of these four attempts were made by the Narayan Apte–Nathuram Godse gang, ultra fanatic disciples of Savarkar. Nathuram was caught red handed in two of these attempts.

On 20 January, a crude bomb was exploded by a Punjabi refugee, Madanlal Pahwa, during the evening prayer meeting at Birla House. Immediately after his arrest, Madanlal confessed to being a part of a gang conspiring to kill Gandhi. He confessed that the leaders of the gang were from Poona and that one of them was the editor and the other the publisher of the extremist periodical *Hindu Rashtra* and *Agranee*, Marathi periodicals published and printed by Godse and Apte and funded by Savarkar. Madanlal led the police to Room No. 40 of Marina Hotel in Connaught Place, New Delhi, where the gang leaders had stayed before the failed attempt on 20 January 1948 and where all gang members had gathered before the attack. The police found unclaimed laundry from the room, which bore the initials 'N.V.G.', Nathuram Vinayak Godse. They also found a copy of the then-not-yet-released press statement of the secretary of the Delhi Hindu Mahasabha, Ashutosh Lahiri.

After the failed attempt, on the evening of 21 January, Morarji Desai, the home minister of the Bombay Province, was informed by J.C. Jain, a professor of Hindi at Ruia College, Bombay, about the conspiracy and about Savarkar's association with the gang members and his involvement. Madanlal Kashmirilal Pahwa had boasted to Jain about being part of a gang which had set out to kill Gandhi in Delhi. Desai did not pay much heed to Jain's warning but claimed to have mentioned it to Sardar Patel, the then Union home minister, when Desai met him at Ahmedabad. According to Desai, Patel confessed to having information about a conspiracy but dismissed Jain's story as being too farfetched. Later, during the Kapur Commission's investigation, both Sardar Patel's secretary and his daughter Maniben denied that Desai had briefed Sardar Patel about the information given by Jain.

Even with all this information available to them, the police were not able to track down the culprits or establish their identities in time. Ten days later, Nathuram Godse, Narayan Apte and Vishnu Karkare met at the Delhi railway station's retiring room and proceeded to Birla House. They mingled freely with the crowd gathered for the evening prayer meeting. At seventeen minutes past five on the evening of Friday, 30 January 1948, Godse blocked Gandhi's path and pumped three bullets from a 9 mm Beretta pistol into Gandhi's chest from point blank range. Gandhi collapsed with the chant of 'Ram' on his lips and died.

Godse finally succeeded in doing what he had failed to do on at least three previous occasions and may be several more. What was the police doing? Were they negligent? Complacent? Or was it a case of turning a convenient blind eye? The Delhi Police had a signed confession from Madanlal which said that the gang was fanatical enough to try again. '*Woh phir ayega!*' (He will come back!) was often repeated by Madanlal during his very intense interrogation. Both the Poona and Bombay police were aware of *Hindu Rashtra* and *Agranee*, their staff and the people behind them. Surprisingly, the Poona Police was never informed or asked for help. A very senior officer of the Poona Police was given Madanlal's statement and asked to take it to Bombay post haste. The officer decided to travel by train via Allahabad, breaking journey there to perform post-death rites for his departed ancestors at the holy Triveni Sangam, instead of taking a plane or a more direct route to Bombay. By the time the officer reached Bombay, Nathuram Godse, Narayan Apte and Vishnu Karkare had already left and were on their way back to Delhi. When questioned later about his slow travel mode, the assistant commissioner replied that he suffered from a fear of flying. His explanation was accepted.

One of the crucial factors in the success of the murder plot was that the police—who were hampered by Gandhi's decision not to allow additional security and frisking of his visitors—did not think of deploying constables or inspectors from Bombay, Poona or Ahmednagar at Birla House, who would have been able to identify Godse, Apte and Karkare, known history-sheeters with police records in their hometowns. After the murder, Anna Gadgil the veteran Congressman from Poona, was the first person to identify Nathuram Godse, the murderer.

The Union government or at least some of the members of the Cabinet were fed up of the interventions of the meddlesome old man. To them, a martyred Mahatma would be easier to live with. According to a secret report submitted to Home Minister Sardar Patel, many in the police and defence force and many bureaucrats at that time were secret members of the RSS and the Hindu Mahasabha, and were actively supporting and promoting the ideology of the Hindu extremist organizations; they continue to do so even today, now with official patronage. The gang members were storm troopers of these extremist organizations and personally aligned with V.D. Savarkar. Could there have been a tacit cooperation between them all?

The way the investigation was carried out, and the lackadaisical approach of the police in trying to protect Gandhi's life, leads one to believe that the investigation was meant to hide more than it was meant to reveal. The measures taken by the police between 20 and 30 January 1948 felt as if they were more to ensure the smooth progress of the murderers than to try and prevent Gandhi's murder. I have extracted a few mentions from Anil Nauriya's article 'Writings on Gandhi's Assassination: A Critique of the Sectarian Narrative'. Nearly a month after Mahatma Gandhi's assassination on 30 January 1948, Sardar Patel, the then-home minister, wrote to Prime Minister Jawaharlal Nehru on 27 February 1948 pointing to Vinayak Damodar Savarkar and his group: 'It was a fanatical wing of the Hindu Mahasabha directly under Savarkar that (hatched) the conspiracy and saw it through.' However, a few months later, on 18 July 1948, Patel wrote somewhat differently to his Cabinet colleague, Syama Prasad Mookerjee (1901–1953), a past president of the Hindu Mahasabha: 'As regards the RSS and the Hindu Mahasabha… as a result of the activities of these two bodies, particularly the former, an atmosphere was created in the country in which such a ghastly tragedy became possible.' Even in his February letter to Nehru, Patel had said that Gandhi's assassination was 'welcomed by the RSS and the Mahasabha'. In a letter dated 11 September 1948 to the RSS ideologue and supremo M.S. Golwalkar, Sardar Patel remonstrated with him over the fact that 'RSS men expressed joy and distributed sweets after Gandhiji's death.' It is a fact that the RSS cadres were prepared to celebrate because they had preknowledge about Gandhi's murder and instructions to celebrate it. This is a pointer towards the organization's involvement in Gandhi's murder.

Gandhi had succeeded in driving out the British, but his ethics and morality were difficult to follow for his political heirs. To them, he was a patriarch who had outlived his usefulness and was now proving to be a nuisance. He had suggested that the Congress be disbanded: what he meant was that a coalition of persons subscribing to disparate political ideologies could no longer survive, now that freedom had been won and India was turning towards becoming a democratic republic, so it would be best to disband the coalition and the constituents must freely form more homogeneous political parties in the newly formed Indian democracy, which is what happened eventually. He had threatened to go to Pakistan to reverse the process of partition. He forced the cancellation of politically motivated short-term measures in his pursuit of establishing an ideal society. He threatened to launch a social reform movement. He opposed the move to rapidly industrialize India, preferring the slow and sustainable Gramudyog and Gramswaraj model. He ordered the ministers to live as servants of the people and to convert the opulent bungalows they had inherited from the departing British into shelters for homeless refugees. He had asked Mountbatten to vacate the Viceregal Palace and convert it into a hospital for refugees. Such an unbearable pain this old man had become!

How could the political heirs of Gandhi cope with such an impractical old man? If somehow he could be removed from the scene, where was the harm? There was anger against him from certain quarters, why not fan that anger and let it conveniently consume the apostle of peace? The RSS and Hindu Mahasabha were angry with him as he had foiled their plan of a clean and absolute partition of the country, achieving a Muslim-free Hindu Rashtra. When the transfer of populations was taking place, these organizations tried their best to ensure a complete exchange of population, to first achieve a Muslim-free north India. Once that was done, it would be easy to drive Muslims out from the rest of India and then a pure Hindu Rashtra would be formed. The Muslim League had already demonstrated this method by efficiently terrorizing the Hindu population of West Punjab, Sindh, North-West Frontier Province and East Bengal into leaving or murdering them. But Gandhi, with his non-violent methods, ensured that this did not happen in Free India. The Muslims, who were on the verge of fleeing, felt reassured by his efforts and promise, and stayed put. The angry Hindu extremists felt that since Pakistan had been created, Muslims had lost the right to remain in India. They blamed Gandhi for not letting them achieve this goal, and they still do so. Many Congress politicians, too, secretly felt the same way. Very cleverly, the RSS and Hindu Mahasabha fanatics camouflaged their real anger under the guise of outrage about the vivisection of the motherland and the slaughter of Hindu brethren in East and West Pakistan and conveniently blamed Gandhi for this. The Congress leaders were happy that someone else was being crucified for blunders they had committed.

Brahmins dominated both the RSS and Hindu Mahasabha, and they were angry with Gandhi for having started the movement for a classless, caste-less Indian society. The resurgent lower castes, liberated and empowered by Gandhi, newly acquainted with their democratic rights, were threatening the dominance of the upper castes, and in particular the Brahmins, who, under the British, had monopolized the bureaucracy and judiciary. In enslaved India, there had been only one Brahmin empire—the Maratha empire of Poona, which was the last to fall to the British Raj. Poona Brahmins considered themselves to be the heirs of the Peshwas, the rightful claimants to the Indian crown, and they believed that the day the British left India, the reins of the land would be handed back to them, the chosen ones. They had even served their colonial masters loyally and they deserved to be rewarded, just like the other collaborator, Jinnah and his Muslim League. This dream of the self-proclaimed descendants of the Peshwas was shattered by Gandhi and his movement to empower the downtrodden and, till then, disenfranchised millions and make them aware of their rights.

The first attempt on Gandhi's life took place in Poona, when a hand grenade was thrown at his car in 1934. This was at a time when Pakistan, or even the giving of ₹55 crores to Pakistan, had not even been envisioned. The RSS and Hindu Mahasabha members used to paste Gandhi's photographs on the soles of their footwear as an insult to him. His photographs were used as targets in weapon training camps organized by Hindu extremist organizations to train their cadres in the use of firearms. These were the people who helped Godse and Apte in planning the murder, provided them with support, funds and equipment; they were the ones who celebrated Gandhi's murder by distributing sweets and bursting crackers. They refer to Gandhi's murder as Vadh, a Sanskrit word used to describe the forces of good slaying Rakshasas, the demons in Hindu mythology. They considered Gandhi to be a demon, and they still do so today.

The trial of the murderers was conducted in a specially constituted court in an unused military barrack in Red Fort, New Delhi. The prosecution was lackadaisical; it felt as if the trial was predecided, five people were being offered to the prosecution to be proven guilty and convicted. Savarkar was to be exonerated and acquitted. The defence was given a free hand in expounding their vicious propaganda of Hindu–Muslim hatred. The most surprising aspect was that Nathuram Godse was allowed to make his hate speech in court twice, once at the Red Fort trial and again during the appeal in the Punjab High Court. It was only after his statement was filmed in court and widely transmitted that the Indian government realized the damage that statement was causing to the already fragile fabric of India in its infancy. Then, in a knee-jerk reaction, they banned it and provided the Hindu extremists with a martyred propaganda tool. Godse's statement, published in a book titled *May It Please Your Honour* by his brother and co-accused Gopal Godse, was finally freed of the ban by the Supreme Court of India, but not before the Hindu extremist right had used it in its underground propaganda to build a huge force of fanatics and sympathizers who hated Gandhi and worshipped his murderer!

The statement is definitely not written by Godse, who never displayed such a masterly command over language: his writing style was loud, crass, abusive and threatening. The document has been very cleverly written to emotionally exploit and influence even the most liberal of minds. V.D. Savarkar, a co-accused in the Gandhi murder and Nathuram's mentor and patron, had absolute mastery over such hypnotic use of language. He was a firebrand writer and orator beyond compare. Godse had free and private access to him during their incarceration and trial at the Red Fort Special Court and, later, prison for the accused for the duration of the trail. The statement attributed to Godse was without doubt penned by Savarkar to justify Gandhi's murder and further the cause of the Hindu extremists and was definitely an afterthought to the deed.

It has now been more than seventy years since Gandhi's murder, yet many truths have remained unknown and many untruths popularized. The partition of India and the slaughter of humanity in its aftermath are still very volatile and sensitive issues. The Hindu extremists have very successfully spread their version of Gandhi's role in the tragedy of Partition. Gandhians and Congressmen, by silence on the part of the former and complacence on the part of the latter, have reinforced the lies of the Savarkarites and Sanghis, who now rule India.

The ideology of murder is thriving in India today. To silence divergent opinions, opinion-makers, influencers and social reformers like Dr Dabholkar, Comrade Pansare, writer Kalburgi and journalist and activist Gauri Lankesh were murdered by the present-day practitioners of the ideology of murder preached by Savrakar and the Sangh. Many years have passed since these murders, but the culprits are yet to be arrested and prosecuted. No wonder, practitioners of the ideology of intolerance and murder today rule India and many of its states.

Recently, another attempt has been made to sow the seeds of confusion and doubt about the murder itself. A claim has been made of unearthing evidence to suggest that there was a fourth bullet fired at Bapu, from a different gun, by another gunman, which actually killed Gandhi. Fourth and fifth generation photographs, crudely retouched many times over, are being flouted to suggest that forensic analyses of them will prove the existence of a fourth bullet wound on his chest. There is no fourth bullet wound since there was no fourth bullet fired at Bapu. It is alleged that an autopsy/post-mortem was not carried out on Bapu after his murder and this was done to hide the fourth bullet wound and the true cause of his death! It is true that an autopsy/post-mortem was not performed, but immediately after he was shot, Bapu was examined by three doctors, both his personal physicians and government doctors. They, after individually inspecting his wounds and recording them in detail, had pronounced him dead immediately after the attack. The next morning, the Surgeon General of India, the highest ranking doctor in medical service at that time, had again carried out a detailed examination of Gandhi's body and ratified the cause of death. There is an aversion in the Indian psyche to a dear one's body being vivisected and cut up, and even today, relatives beg that their dear one's bodies not be subjected to such indignity after death. Gandhi was the most respected and revered person in India at that time and it is very understandable that since there was no doubt about the cause of his death, the powers that be, the two most influential ministers of the government and his most ardent disciples, Sardar Patel, the home minister, and Pandit Jawaharlal Nehru, the prime minister, would not have wanted Bapu's body to be thus desecrated, and so an autopsy was deemed not necessary. There is no sinister motive. There were hundreds of people who had seen the murderous attack on Gandhi from close quarters, the reason for his death was not in doubt, it had been confirmed after examination by three doctors independently, immediately after the attack.

It has been alleged that although the murder happened at 5:17 p.m., it was only announced forty-three minutes later, so something sinister happened in those intervening forty-three minutes. It must be remembered that from the moment Godse shot Bapu till the announcement was made on All India Radio's news bulletin that evening, Bapu's body was in the midst of his close associates, aides and family, so if the allegation was to be believed even momentarily, it means that not only the prime minister and home minister of India at the time of the murder, but Bapu's closest associates and aides and his son and his family were involved in the sinister plot that is alleged to have been executed in the intervening forty-three minutes. Only depraved minds and pathological liars would have the audacity to suggest this.

The announcement of Gandhi's murder wasn't rushed because they wanted to establish the identity of the murderer, and more so his religion, before an announcement was made, since a malicious rumour was being spread that a Muslim had murdered Gandhi. Nathuram wasn't revealing his identity, either. His identity and the religion he belonged to were only revealed when Anna Gadgil, a veteran Congressman from Poona and a minister in the Union government identified the murderer and revealed that the murderer was a Hindu Brahmin from Poona. Those weren't days of news 24×7 and there was no mania of 'Breaking News'. There were fixed news bulletins and so, on 30 January 1948, Gandhi's murder was announced in the scheduled 6:00 p.m. news bulletin on All India Radio. There was no sinister motive here either, as is being alleged by purveyors of lies and propagandists of the Sangh.

Recently, a plea was made to the Supreme Court of India, seven decades after Gandhi's murder, to order a new investigation into it. The objective was malicious: to sow disinformation and mix lies into the facts of Gandhi's murder. There is a sinister ulterior motive too, that of discrediting the Kapur Commission of Inquiry's investigations and getting its report discredited and abrogated. The Kapur Commission's investigation report is the only document that reveals the existence of a much larger and sinister conspiracy to murder Gandhi and to overthrow a democratic government and replace it with a Hindu Rashtra, the involvement of the RSS and Hindu Mahasabha, both uppercaste Hindu supremacist and extremist organizations in the plot, and the complicity of Savarkar, who was acquitted in the Gandhi murder trial, not because of evidence of his innocence but because the prosecution failed to submit sufficient evidence in court to convict him. Once the Kapur Commission's inquiry is discredited and its report discarded, the history of the Gandhi murder can be falsified and rewritten to suit the current ruling dispensation. Then, the inconvenient truth of the Gandhi murder can be buried for eternity and replaced by convenient and more comfortable lies. Then, their ambition to create a New India, a Hindu Rashtra, where lies rule and truth is discredited, discarded, and those who dare tell the truth, persecuted, will be realized.

In 2014, after assuming office, in one of his first acts, Prime Minister Modi ordered the immediate destruction of over 40,000 till-then-classified documents stored in the National Archives by declaring them 'of no consequence'. There is no record to say which documents were destroyed. We will never know the information contained in them. There was no justifiable reason for their destruction. A part of history has been obliterated; some of those papers could have been related to the Gandhi murder conspiracy—we will never know now. Those involved in Gandhi's murder may have destroyed evidence of their involvement in the plot. In Gujarat, the laboratory of the Hindu Rashtra, students in schools are being asked questions to explain why Gandhi committed suicide. Elsewhere, Sanghis celebrate Gandhi's murder, re-enacting it by firing on Gandhi's photographs and performing poojas of the photograph and replicas of the gun used to murder Gandhi. Godse worship is becoming mainstream and is patronized by the organizations involved in Gandhi's murder. *Let's Kill Gandhi!* is a compilation of verified facts gleaned from verbal history, books earlier published, records of the investigation and murder trial, books written by the defence lawyers and judges, newspaper reports of that period, startling and shocking revelations made during the Kapur Commission of Inquiry and what I grew up hearing in the family and witnessing the bewilderment of Gandhi's loved ones. It reveals nothing new, but for the first time, everything related to the Gandhi murder has been compiled in one book.

During my childhood, I had an experience that left a very distinct impression on me. I must have been barely ten years old when my grandmother, Sushilaben, came to stay with us from South Africa. She expressed a desire to meet Gopal Godse, Nathuram's younger brother and a co-accused in the murder. He had just finished serving a life sentence for his part in the murder of my great-grandfather. Father drove all of us to Poona. For us, Poona meant going to the samadhis of Kasturba and Mahadevkaka, Mahadev Desai, Gandhi's secretary and close associate, who had both died while incarcerated at the Aga Khan Palace prison along with Bapu. Thus, we first visited Aga Khan Palace and prayed at the samadhis of our ancestors. Then, we went to the home of my great-grandfather's murderers. For Gopal Godse, our action was like an acceptance of their deed by the family of their victim. He manipulated the episode to imply that we had endorsed their dastardly deed and expressed approval of their evil act. To me, it was all very confusing. I was too young to understand that my grandmother was trying to convey that the Gandhi family had forgiven the Godses and held no ill will against them. It was like Priyanka Gandhi meeting Nalini, a convict in her father Rajiv Gandhi's murder, in prison. I still can't understand why we needed to do that. How can one forgive someone who is unrepentant? I can never forgive them, nor can I forgive the ideology that created Nathuram Godse the murderer, the Hindu supremacists, the fascist and fanatic RSS and Hindu Mahasabha and Savarkar, who were involved in my great grandfather's murder but escaped being convicted and punished or were let off.

I had another opportunity to interact with Gopal Godse in the last years of the 1900s—a frail old man but still as rabid and as adept at passing off blatant lies as truth. Gopal and I were on a talk show hosted by my dear friend, the late Priya Tendulkar. After the shooting wrapped up, Gopal Godse tried to rise unsteadily to his feet. He stumbled and was about to fall, so I automatically extended a hand to steady him and helped him disconnect the lapel mike. Press photographers caught this moment and the next day the photograph was splashed on the pages of national papers. My act had been one of common courtesy to a frail old man, but Gopal flaunted the photograph as a proof of my admiration of him and approval of his deed!

On 30 January 1997, I immersed an urn containing the ashes from my great-grandfather's funeral pyre. This was the closest I have been to him physically. After performing the ritual at the holy Triveni Sangam at Allahabad, I went to the Gandhi National Museum at Raj Ghat in Delhi, where the bloodstained clothes worn by Gandhi at the time of his murder are preserved. For the first time, I saw and handled the 9 mm Beretta semi-automatic pistol that Godse had used to murder Bapu. As I held the gun, I felt extreme rage inside me; at that moment, I felt like firing the gun at a Sanghi. I was repulsed and appalled by this emotion of virulent hate and immediately put the gun down. I realized that a lot of hate and anger lay dormant within me and I had to get rid of this corrosive venom before I succumbed to it. This book is a result of that rage that has been bottled up in me for far too long. My great-grandfather said, 'Anger is an acid which corrodes the vessel in which it is stored.' This book is my attempt to expel the acid bottled up within me, but even after having written it, I realized that I haven't been able to expunge the anger and the hate entirely. What I have learnt is to hate the sin more than the sinner.

India is today going through a similar phase as it was during the mid-1940s. The democratic process has been made a mockery of by power hungry, opportunist politicians who have fragmented the electorate on the basis of castes and sub-castes, religion and region. The Hindu extremist elements, aided by the acts of exploitative Muslim clergy and opportunistic political leadership, have grabbed power. They have accelerated their drive to rid India of its Muslim citizens or to terrorize them into living as serfs in the country of their birth. Autocrats have cleverly used the democratic process to grab power and are now busy subverting democracy and its institutions. The Constitution, the soul of India, is being trampled. The socialism and secularism enshrined in our Constitution are being systematically demonized and forsaken. The Hindu extremists want to establish a Brahmin-dominated nation as it was before Gandhi and Ambedkar, a Hindu Rashtra for the upper castes, by the upper castes and of the upper castes. They are succeeding even beyond what they could imagine: in New India, bigotry, hate and intolerance are virtues, and murder and dumb silence, patriotic.

We will not survive another partition. We do not want caste supremacy; we do not want another war between religions. Profiling is the first step towards ethnic cleansing; we cannot live through the ages of Hitler and Milosevic again. Democracy must not become subservient to autocrats. We must fulfil Gandhi's unfulfilled dream of reuniting India, Pakistan and Bangladesh, a reunification of hearts and not of a landmass, but first, we will have to start at home. India cannot survive the RSS and Hindu Mahasabha's version of a Hindu Rashtra. We do not want another partition, neither of hearts nor of territory. Babri Masjid has been demolished, a 'grand' Ram Temple will soon stand in its place. It will act as a reminder to Muslims that in New India, they are no longer equal citizens, it will signify the same to all minorities and the lower castes. This cannot be allowed to succeed; humankind must be saved from fanatics and extremists but unfortunately, we do not have a Gandhi to save us from this madness.

I have updated, edited and corrected this new edition of my book to make it more up to date and timely. This book puts the facts straight, lest we forget.

Tushar A. Gandhi
18 January 2021

BOOK 1

MURDER, MURDERERS, THE CONSPIRACY, INVESTIGATIONS AND THE PREVIOUS FAILED ATTEMPTS

1

'HE RAM': ANOTHER CRUCIFIXION

It shows how dangerous it is to be too good.

—George Bernard Shaw,
reacting to Gandhi's murder

It was 4:55 p.m. on Friday, 30 January 1948. Gandhi was going to be late for the evening prayers. To him, being late was a sin.

Abha was worried, but the atmosphere in the room was electric. Gandhi was engrossed in a very important conversation with his dear and long-standing friend and associate Sardar Vallabhbhai Patel, home minister of the Indian Union and number two in the Union government. The meeting had begun at 4:00 pm; Patel had come accompanied by his daughter Maniben. The intense dialogue between the mentor and his protégé was on the growing rift between Sardar Patel and Pandit Nehru, the threat it posed to the party and government and the consequences for the fledgling nation. The dialogue went on with no sign of an end. To catch Gandhi's attention, Abha put his evening meal in front of him, comprising some cooked vegetables, 12 ounces of goat milk, some carrot juice and a decoction of ginger, sour lime and aloe juice mixed together in a bowl. But that day, Gandhi ignored his meal too.

'Today he will be late for prayers and he will be very angry with himself,' Abha thought. She could do nothing to divert his attention, overawed into silence by the sheer intensity of the discussion and the charisma of the two leaders. Finally, she mustered up some courage and held up the clock in front of Gandhi so that he could see the time, but even that failed to distract him. Seeing Abha's predicament, Maniben interrupted the conversation and reminded Bapu that he was getting late for his tryst with God, his evening prayers.

'I must now tear myself away, Sardar Saheb but please do consider my earnest appeal. I am going to make the same appeal to Jawahar, later today,' Gandhi told Patel. After partaking of the frugal meal, he bid adieu to Sardar and rose to get ready for the evening prayers. It was ten minutes past five. People had already gathered on the rear garden lawns of Birla House. Bapu stepped out of the room he was occupying in Birla House and after going around the other wing of the house he walked towards the place of his evening prayers.

As he walked accompanied by his 'walking sticks' Abha and Manu, Gurbachan Singh, a Sikh veteran of Netaji Subhas Chandra Bose's Indian National Army (INA), informed him that two brothers from Kathiawad wanted to meet him. 'Tell them to come after the prayers,' Gandhi replied. 'I will see them if I am alive.' This was the second time that he had mentioned death that day. It was thirteen minutes past five.

Gandhi slowly walked towards the prayer ground, still weak from his last fast, his hands resting on the shoulders of Abha and Manu. He laughed and exchanged jokes with them. Gurbachan Singh usually walked a few paces in front of Gandhi, clearing a path for him through the crowd. That day, he lagged behind, since he had gone to convey Gandhi's message to the brothers waiting to meet him. Gurbachan Singh was hurrying, trying to catch up, still more than a dozen steps behind Gandhi.

He teased Abha about the raw carrot meal that she had served him, saying that it was cattle food.

Abha replied, 'Ba (Kasturba) called it food fit only for a horse!' 'Is it not grand of me to relish what no one else would care for?' Gandhi responded.

'Bapu, your watch felt neglected today,' Manu complained, 'you ignored it.'

'Why should I care, since you are my time-keepers?' Gandhi wondered.

'But you ignored your time-keepers too,' Manu replied and Gandhi laughed heartily.

As they climbed the three steps leading to the terraced garden where the prayers were held every evening, Gandhi became serious. 'I am late by fifteen minutes. I hate being late, it is a sin. I like to be punctual for my tryst with God, at the stroke of five.'

All conversation stopped; there was a tacit understanding between Gandhi and his 'walking sticks', that as soon as they stepped on to the hallowed prayer grounds, all jokes and conversation stopped. Nothing but thoughts of prayer would now occupy their minds.

The crowds parted, forming a passage through which Gandhi walked towards the low platform, his day bed, on which he sat during the prayer meeting, occasionally greeting people. He took his hands off the shoulders of the two girls and walked with his hands joined in greeting. He had hardly taken two or three steps forward when a young man dressed in a blue-grey shirt elbowed his way through the crowd and blocked his path.

The young man folded his hands and said, 'Namaste Bapuji.' Manu tried to get the young man to let them pass; she said, 'Brother, Bapu is already late for prayers...' But before she could complete the sentence, the man pushed her out of his way, and Manu stumbled and fell. The rosary and spittoon that Manu was carrying fell from her hands. Before anyone in the tightly packed crowd could realize what was happening, the man whipped out a snub-nosed semi-automatic pistol and fired three shots in quick succession, point blank, from less than two feet away, at Gandhi.

The bullets pierced Gandhi's chest, two going through his seventy-eight-year-old frail body, one remaining lodged in his still-living flesh. The killer was so close to him that one of the ejected bullet casings was later found in the folds of the shawl Gandhi had draped on his upper body. The first shot entered his upper abdomen on the right, 2.5 inches above the navel and 3.5 inches to the right of the mid-line. The second penetrated the seventh intercostal space one inch on the right of the mid-line, and the third on the right side of the chest, one inch above the nipple and four inches from the mid-line. The first and the second shots passed right through him and came out from Gandhi's back; the third remained embedded in his lung. As the first bullet hit Gandhi, his foot, suspended mid-stride, came down. He was still on his feet when the second and third bullets pierced his body. 'R...a...m,' Gandhi sighed, and then, the father of a fledgeling nation fell, never to rise again.

As life ebbed away, his face reflected inner peace. With his last few breaths, the devout Hindu chanted the name that Rambha Ma, his childhood maid, had taught him, 'Ram... R...a...m... R...a...m... R...a...' The time was seventeen minutes past five on the evening of Friday, 30 January 1948. Mahatma Gandhi, my Bapu, the Father of the Nation, born Mohandas Karamchand Gandhi, had been murdered. Abha, in whose lap Gandhi died, realized that he was no more when the fading chant of Ram stopped.

The crowd was stunned. They had heard three shots fired, they saw Gandhi collapse and they saw a man holding a gun. There was a murmur, a few voices rose in shock and anger, there were a few muffled sobs, rage was building and the situation was volatile. A gardener, Raghu, from the Birla household staff, rushed up to the gunman and hit him on the back of his head with the blunt side of his sickle, and then grabbed him from behind. A shoulder flap of the killer's shirt was torn off. Passions threatened to run amok as volunteers carried the limp and bleeding Gandhi back into the room he had emerged from just a few minutes back. They tried to administer a few drops of honey mixed with warm water, but it was futile. Gandhi was dead.

On the rear lawns of Birla House, the situation was turning ugly; the enraged mob was threatening to lynch the killer, '*Miya lagta hai, Musalman ne Bapu ko mar dala!*' (He looks like a Muslim. A Muslim has killed Bapu!) someone screamed, most likely Narayan Apte. This was the plan, to create confusion and sow seeds of hate to enrage the mob, to ignite an inferno of hate and violence. The crowd immediately took up the chant 'A Muslim has killed Bapu, kill all Muslims!' Pyarelal Nayyar, Gandhi's personal secretary since 1942, rushed out on to the lawn and took control of the situation. 'Calm down, we are Bapu's children, we will not seek revenge,' he attempted to pacify the crowd. Volunteers took hold of the murderer, who did not divulge his identity or his religion, aware that a rumour was spreading that he was a Muslim, that it was all going according to their plan. His accomplices, mingling with the crowds, were busy creating more mischief. The murderer was taken to a room on the ground floor of Birla House and held there.

Dr B.P. Bhargava was urgently summoned to attend to Gandhi. His regular medical caretaker, the diminutive Dr Sushila Nayyar, the younger sister of Pyarelal, was away in West Pakistan on a mission assigned to her by Gandhi to rescue refugees and ensure their return and welfare and to seek the Pakistan government's cooperation for the same. Sardar Patel had just reached his home when he was informed about the tragedy; he rushed back to Birla House and was the first senior minister to arrive. Grief stricken, he picked up the limp wrist of his leader, with whom he had been talking just a few minutes ago; his face suddenly lit up with hope, he thought he felt a faint pulse. He shouted for Dr Bhargava, 'He lives! There still is life! Attend to him, save Bapu!' Dr Bhargava felt for a pulse and checked for eye reflexes; there were none. He held a mirror close to Gandhi's face, there was no condensation, no breath. Dr Bhargava looked up at Patel and mumbled, 'Dead for ten minutes, very sorry.'

Abha and Manu burst into tears, but soon everybody gathered their composure and started chanting Bapu's favourite hymn, Ram Dhun, '*Ishwar Allah Tere Naam Sabko Sanmati de Bhagwan*'. Pandit Nehru arrived and rushed to Gandhi's side. He clutched at Gandhi's bloodied clothes and sobbed uncontrollably. Patel consoled him, their differences melting away in the face of the tragedy. Speaking to Pyarelal a little later, Patel commented, 'Others can weep and find relief from their grief in tears, I am unable to do so.'

Lord Mountbatten, who had returned from Madras that afternoon, was informed about the tragedy and rushed to Birla House. As he entered, he heard someone shout, 'A Muslim has killed Bapu, kill all Muslims!' Instinctively, Mountbatten turned around and shouted, 'You fool, everybody knows the murderer is a Hindu!' Later, when questioned by his aide as to how he could be certain it wasn't a Muslim, he replied, 'I pray it is not a Muslim. If a Muslim has murdered Gandhi, humankind will witness a carnage such as I cannot bring myself to even imagine!'

Mountbatten realized that he would have to take control. He took Patel and Nehru aside and requested them to calm down. Patel told Nehru what Gandhi had asked of him; they both embraced each other and vowed to work unitedly.

The police arrived and took charge of the situation. At the spot where Gandhi had fallen, a young boy was handing out fistfuls of the blood-soaked soil. Gandhi's glasses and handmade leather slippers, which had slipped off when he fell, were never found. The police cordoned off Birla House, vacated the garden and started searching for clues. N.V. 'Anna' Gadgil, another 'N.V.G.', a veteran Congressman from Poona, looked inside the room where the murderer was being held and immediately recognized him. He said in Marathi, '*Are Nathya, he tu kay kela?*' (Nathya [as Nathuram Vinayak Godse was known in Poona] what have you done?) The worst nightmare of the leaders of India had ended: it was now established that Gandhi's killer was a Hindu, in fact a Hindu Brahmin from Poona. When the police took Godse into custody, the first thing he demanded was medical aid for a minor wound on the back of his head and a few scratches. After the first aid, he was taken to the Tughlaq Road police station and locked up in a cell there, where the First Information Report (FIR) of Gandhi's murder was filed.

Gandhi's youngest son Devadas and his family were the first from his immediate family to reach Birla House. Devadas tenderly took the lifeless hand of his father and caressed it as tears rolled down his face. For his family and that of his siblings—Harilal, Manilal and Ramdas—there would be no opportunity for private grief. Gandhi belonged to the nation in death as he had in life.

Mountbatten, Nehru and Patel discussed the funeral arrangements in an adjoining room. Mountbatten's suggestion was to embalm Gandhi's body and preserve it and display it like Lenin's has been in Red Square. Pyarelal and Devadas vehemently rejected the suggestion. 'Bapu would not want it. What is more, he would want his funeral to take place at the earliest,' Devadas said firmly. It was decided that the funeral would take place the next evening at an appropriate place on the banks of the river Yamuna. The armed forces would be in charge and Mountbatten would oversee the arrangements. After consultations with doctors and legal experts, it was decided that there was no requirement for an autopsy to be performed; the cause of death had been established beyond doubt and corroborated by witnesses and doctors who had examined the body. Devadas, with the help of other male members of the family, took the body for the ritual bath. While removing the bloodstained clothes, they recovered one of the bullets that had passed through Gandhi's body and a spent shell in the folds of the shawl draped over his upper body. The three entry wounds were small and had not caused a lot of bleeding, but the two bullets which had passed through his body had torn out much larger chunks of flesh on his back and caused severe haemorrhaging. After bathing the body, the doctors closed the bullet wounds after recording their position on his body and measuring each one of them. Then, Gandhi's body was draped in a fresh set of clothes.

The doctor's report mentioned the cause of death as, 'Death…caused by shock and internal haemorrhage due to…injuries inflicted…by bullets fired from a pistol at close range.' In the meantime, a mixture of cow dung, mud and water was spread on the floor to form a square on which a Khadi sheet was spread, Gandhi's body was placed on this sheet, a shawl was spread covering it and drawn up to his neck, leaving only the face uncovered. Devadas folded back the shawl to leave the chest bare; he said, 'The bullet wounds on Bapu's chest are medals of gallantry awarded to a non-violent warrior, the world must see them.'

All India Radio's six o'clock English news bulletin began that evening with the announcement, 'A Hindu Brahmin shot Mahatma Gandhi, the Father of the Nation, this evening. Gandhiji is no more.' The nation came to a halt as the news rode the airwaves to every corner of the world. While the nation mourned, there were some who rejoiced and celebrated by distributing sweets. The Shakhas, centres of the RSS and Hindu Mahasabha, bore a festive look. Lamps were lit, flowers showered, firecrackers burst and sweets distributed to celebrate Gandhi's murder: they were prepared to celebrate; they knew, they had been told. What the Sanghis had failed to do in the past had been done at their bidding by one of their cadre. In Alwar, a principality in Rajasthan, a handbill announcing Gandhi's murder was distributed five hours before his murder.

Meanwhile, the roads leading to Birla House on Albuquerque Road were getting choked. VIPs, Cabinet ministers, Congress leaders, diplomats, senior bureaucrats and others jostled for space with the common people for a last glimpse of Gandhi; all of them wanted to enter Birla House to pay their respects to their Bapu. The police were finding it difficult to control the crowds as well as to carry out investigations at the crime scene. Senior officers requested Devadas and Pyarelal to shift the body to a place where people could see it from the road. The Birla family was consulted and it was decided that the body would be kept on an elevated platform, on the first floor terrace, facing the road. The makeshift platform was slightly tilted so that the body could be seen by all. When Gandhi's body was placed in sight of the people gathered on the road, a hush fell over the crowd. The sight of Gandhi calmed them. The group of Sikh refugees who, during his fast, had shouted slogans of 'Let him die!', now sat on the kerb and chanted verses from the Granth Sahib, tears streaming down their cheeks; anger was replaced by grief.

Late that evening, Prime Minister Jawaharlal Nehru addressed the nation standing on a stool placed at the gate of Birla House; All India Radio broadcast it to the entire nation, live. In a voice choked with grief and overwhelming sadness, he said, 'Friends... The light has gone out of our lives and there is darkness everywhere and I do not quite know what to tell you and how to say it. Our beloved leader, Bapu as we called him, the Father of the Nation is no more... We will not see him again as we have for these many years. We will not run to him for advice and seek solace from him. The light has gone out, I said, and yet I was wrong. For the light that shone in this country was no ordinary light. The light that has illuminated this country for these many years will illuminate this country for many more years and a thousand years later that light will still be seen in this country and the world will see it and it will give solace to innumerable hearts. For that light represented the living truth, and the eternal man was with us with his eternal truth reminding us of the right path, drawing us from error, taking this ancient country to freedom...'

At midnight, the body was brought down from the terrace; it was once again bathed and anointed with sandalwood paste and then placed in the centre of a room filled with flowers. Next morning, at 11:30 a.m., the bier, with Gandhi's body covered with the tricolour, was placed on a gun carriage. Dr Sushila Nayyar arrived just as the funeral procession was about to start. She bid a tearful adieu to him, whose medical well-being had been her responsibility in the past few years. The cortège started, with Devadas and his elder brother Ramdas, Gandhi's third son, who had rushed to the national capital from Nagpur in central India, standing on either side of Gandhi's head. Nehru, Patel and other Cabinet ministers stood around the body on the gun carriage. Others walked alongside.

The gun carriage was pulled by two hundred soldiers from the three wings of the armed forces. Three aircraft of the Indian Air Force passed over the cortège and showered flowers. If the people passing by Birla House the evening before had resembled a river in spate, the people lining the route and following the funeral procession resembled an ocean of humanity. By a rough estimate, the number of people accompanying the funeral procession was more than a million. People lined the route, stood on balconies and terraces of buildings. Others climbed onto trees and some daredevils took refuge on top of light and telephone poles. Many climbed on to the War Memorial, others clung to the pillars of the canopy over King George V's statue. Passing through the roads of New Delhi, the procession reached the cremation ground on the banks of the river Yamuna at 4:20 p.m. People had started gathering there since morning. Somewhere in that crowd, Gandhi's eldest son Harilal,* a derelict vagabond, tried to get close to his father's body. Being the eldest son, it was his right to perform the last rites of his father, but unkempt and dressed as he was in rags, no one was going to allow him to come anywhere near the funeral pyre. That privilege was for the elite. In death, Gandhi had been put beyond the reach of the common people with whom he had been one throughout his life.

---

*Harilal had been very close to his father in South Africa. During the Satyagraha for equal rights in that country, he had come to be known as 'Chota Gandhi' or 'Little Gandhi'. He was the first to use fasting as a form of protest during the South African Satyagraha, when he forced his jailers to treat him in a humanitarian manner, as prescribed in the jail manual, by going on a protest fast. However, he then fought with his father and left. One of the issues between them was Harilal's desire to study further, while Gandhi preferred for him to become an activist. Another issue was Harilal's early marriage to Gulab; Gandhi felt that both were too young to get married. Harilal's several attempts to establish a business failed. He lost his wife in the influenza epidemic and, due to his wayward ways, his children were taken away from him by Kasturba and were brought up in her care in the ashrams. Then, he became a derelict destitute and drunk. He was patronized by some Muslims, who intended to use him to embarrass Gandhi. They endeared themselves to Harilal by encouraging and financing his drinking habits and other vices and, after gaining his confidence, they induced him to convert to Islam. After a much-publicized conversion to Islam as Abdulla Gandhi, Harilal's Muslim name, his patrons publicly invited Gandhi to accept his son's adopted religion. Throughout his life, Gandhi had always expressed very strong views against conversions. He criticized his son's conversion and termed it inconsequential and something that would not bring glory to Islam. Realizing that they had failed to humiliate Gandhi, their vested interests abandoned Harilal. In a fit of depression, Harilal went on a drinking binge and was arrested by the Madras Police on charges of causing public nuisance. When his identity was established, Gandhi was informed. Gandhi publicly disowned Harilal; in private, he admitted his defeat for not being able to save his firstborn from ruin.

At 4:30 p.m., the body was placed on a funeral pyre made of 600 kilos of sandalwood, 160 kilos of ghee, 80 kilos of incense, 40 kilos of coconuts and 15 kilos of camphor. It was ironic that Gandhi, who had voluntarily embraced poverty all his life, was being accorded a funeral befitting a king. Finally, the tricolour was removed; Devadas sprinkled water from the Ganga on the body, a final act of purification. Bapu's disciples chanted verses from the Gita, Koran and Bible as sandalwood logs were placed on his body. The pyre was lit by Bapu's third son Ramdas, while it is alleged that his eldest son Harilal watched from afar, denied his rightful duty. Gandhi's second son Manilal lived in South Africa and was unable to attend his father's funeral.

As the flames grew in intensity, so did the chants of '*Mahatma Gandhi amar rahe*!' (Mahatma Gandhi is immortal!) When the all-consuming fire was reduced to embers, some people sat down by the smouldering pyre on an all-night vigil, while the entourage returned to Birla House. At last, Harilal got the chance to approach his father's funeral pyre. He had fought with Gandhi throughout his adult life and yet he felt compelled to grieve at his father's funeral pyre. (This is an unverified account because another account places Harilal in Bangalore, where he is said to have walked into a newspaper office and placed his obituary to his father and a severe condemnation of the forces behind his father's murder on the editor's desk and walked away.)

It was twenty-four hours after Gandhi's murder that people began to ask questions. How could this have happened? Who could have committed such a heinous deed? Why Gandhi? Could this not have been prevented? What were the police doing? But, in fact, the events that led to Gandhi's murder had been set in motion long ago.

There had been a few attempts on his life in South Africa. The only attempt to murder him, ordered by an Englishman, occurred in Champaran during Gandhi's Satyagraha there. The first documented attempt on his life—in India by Sanatani Hindus—had occurred as far back as 1934 in Poona. After that, there were four more, all of which had some connection with Poona Brahmins, Sanatani Hindus and Savarkarites. In three of them, the involvement of the Apte–Godse gang, his eventual killers, had been recorded. The last unsuccessful attempt had taken place at Birla House just ten days earlier, on 20 January 1948.

The police had arrested the bomber and received many tips about his accomplices and their identities and affiliations, and yet three members of the gang—the leaders—had reassembled, arrived at Birla House at the same time as on the 20th, carrying a deadly weapon. The murderer had gotten within handshaking distance of Gandhi and had pumped hot lead into his chest from point blank range, killing him. How was this possible?

Despite the police knowing of the previous attacks on Gandhi and the common factor in all of those, how was it possible that the same people could so easily have murdered him?

It was believed that on several occasions, the prime minister of United Kingdom, Churchill, had reprimanded the British Secret Service and Directorate of Military Intelligence for not having carried out operations to 'eliminate' Gandhi. What the English never accomplished was successfully carried out by their Indian allies, the Hindu extremists. But how could they do it so easily? There were many questions but no answers.

II

THE MURDERERS

Bachche hain, abhi yeh samajhte nahin hai. Maroonga to yaad karenge ke bodhha theek kehta tha.

(They are children. They do not understand the situation now. After I die, they will remember that what the old man was saying was right.)

—M.K. Gandhi,
20 January 1948

All the accused in the Gandhi murder, although very diverse in nature, shared a common characteristic—they were all Hindu bigots and fanatics and all of them were fiercely loyal to Savarkar. One was a pathological woman hater, Nathuram Vinayak Godse; another a debonair womanizer, Narayan Dattatreya Apte; an orphaned street urchin who had made it big and become a bigot, Vishnu Ramkrishna Karkare; a revolutionary turned collaborator, V.D. Savarkar; a doctor who believed in taking, rather than saving lives, Dr Dattatreya Sadashiv Parchure; a rogue arms merchant and mercenary, Digambar Ramchandra Badge; his servant, Shankar Kistayya; a homeless refugee hothead, bristling with anger and thirsting for revenge, Madanlal Kashmirilal Pahwa; a hero-worshipping kid brother, Gopal Vinayak Godse. The murder weapon was a 9 mm Beretta semi-automatic pistol, serial number 606824, popularly called 'The Fascist Special', which travelled across three continents, Europe, Africa and Asia before finally reaching the hands of Gandhi's assassin in Gwalior, just two days before it was used to murder Gandhi.

For fourteen years, the right-wing Hindu extremists had been plotting to kill Gandhi, and the participation of Poona-based Narayan Apte and Nathuram Godse, both fanatic, devoted followers of Savarkar, has been reported in a majority of these attempts. For most of this period, Narayan Apte was the leader of the gang. Nathuram Godse, Gandhi's eventual murderer, was his subordinate. They were as unlike as chalk and cheese but their friendship was forged by their fanaticism.

Nathuram was born into a economically lower-middle-class Chitpavan Brahmin family. The term 'Chitpavan' literally means 'purified by the holy fire'; the Chitpavans are believed to be of pure Aryan lineage. Another opinion is that they are Jewish descendants of one of the lost tribes of Egypt. Among the many illustrious Chitpavan Brahmins were Gandhi's political guru Gopal Krishna Gokhale and the firebrand leader of the hawks in Congress, 'Lokmanya' Bal Gangadhar Tilak, as well as Gandhi's murderers.

The Godses originated from a small village called Uksan in western Maharashtra. Uksan is about 10 km from Kamshet, a railway station town on the Bombay–Poona line. Vinayak Godse, Nathuram's father, worked as a junior worker in the government-run Indian Postal Services. Vinayak was married in 1892 to a ten-year-old girl from the Chitpavan Brahmin community. Their first three sons, born in rapid succession, died in infancy. Only a daughter, their second born, survived. The elders of the family consulted a soothsayer who told them that the family was suffering the ill effects of a curse, and no male child would survive. The only way to negate this curse was by appeasing the family goddess and cheating fate: they would have to bring up their next male offspring as a girl. Vinayak and his wife performed rituals to appease the goddess and seek protection for their unborn sons. They swore an oath that, at birth, they would get their next born son's left nostril pierced and make him wear a nose ring, a common practice for newborn girls. A boy was born to the couple on 19 May 1910. At birth, he was named Ramchandra, later shortened to 'Ram'. As promised, the boy's left nostril was immediately pierced and he was made to wear a nose ring (called 'nath' in Marathi). Thus, the boy came to be called Nathuram, 'Ram who wears a nose ring'. For the first few years of his life, Nathuram was brought up as a girl. His hair was allowed to grow long and braided into plaits. He was made to wear a blouse and petticoat, like a girl. His parents had promised to bring him up as a girl to cheat fate. Finally, after all the subsequent boys survived, Nathuram's nose ring was removed, his long braids cut and he was allowed to dress as a boy, but the name Nathuram stuck for the remainder of his life. Nathuram was followed by Dattatreya, Gopal, Govind, and another daughter.

Because his job involved frequent transfers, Vinayak spent many years away from the family during the formative years of his children's life. The meagre salary of a very junior worker in the postal department meant that the Godse family had to live in perpetual poverty. Nathuram grew up largely without the protective presence of his father. The boy was mercilessly teased and became traumatized by having to live as a girl. Young Nathuram soon turned into a brooding loner, who would sit, lost in a world of dreams, dark moods and fits. Soon, he was branded 'different'. As was prevalent in those days, people with personality traits other than normal were either branded 'idiots' or, if lucky, said to possess divine powers; Nathuram was lucky, it was believed that he had the ability to communicate with the family goddess and could see the future. The Godse family believed that he went into a trance when made to look at a black spot painted on a copper plate using lantern soot; they believed that he saw figures and heard divine messages. They also claimed that, during the trance, the family deity spoke to them through Nathuram, with the goddess answering their questions through him. Nathuram could never recollect what he said during these trances. He was known to suffer from migraines and was prescribed medication for it. Finally, at the age of sixteen, the trances stopped. Gopal Godse writes that Nathuram gave up being a medium for his family voluntarily.

Nathuram was initially educated in the village primary school in Marathi, his mother tongue. After completing primary school, he was sent to Poona for his matriculation. Nathuram was not academically inclined, but loved to read mythologies and scriptures in Marathi. However, as he was unable to master the English language, he could not complete his matriculation. He was a healthy youth who was known to be the best swimmer in his village. A metric or eleventh-grade pass was the minimum requirement to get a job as a junior clerk, the bottom rung in government service. Vinayak was now nearing retirement age and was keen that his eldest son get a job in his department, so that the family would be provided for. But Nathuram could not cross the matriculation hurdle. He tried to take up carpentry but gave up after learning the rudiments of the craft. When he was nineteen, his father was transferred to the scenic but sleepy seaside hamlet of Ratnagiri on the west coast of Maharashtra.

Ratnagiri had been the place of confinement of Vinayak D. Savarkar and, before him, the deposed and exiled king of Burma, HRH Theebaw Min.

Nathuram had heard about Savarkar living in Ratnagiri and one day, he visited the Savarkar residence. His life was never the same again.

Nathuram soon became a regular visitor to the Savarkar home. His political indoctrination had begun; Nathuram had finally found a surrogate father, a guru. In Savarkar, he saw the father who had never been there for him. Savarkar's desire for Hindu resurgence and avenging militant version of Hinduism appealed to the youngster and he soon became an ardent devotee. As a consequence of the agreement with the British, Savarkar had pledged not to indulge in political activities, not to deliver political speeches in public, and even his books could be published only if the publishers certified that they were devoid of any political message. But Savarkar gave vent to his feelings in private; there were no restrictions on what he said within the four walls of his home provided by the British and visitors were free to come and go. Most of what was said in the Savarkar home was not anti-British but anti-Congress, anti-Gandhi and anti-Muslim. Nathuram absorbed this outpouring of hate by his master like a sponge absorbs fluids.

Impressed by Nathuram's devotion, Savarkar appointed him his secretary. Nathuram picked up the rudiments of English by listening to Savarkar and started mimicking his style of speaking. He soon became proficient in writing and speaking English.

In 1931, Vinayak Godse finally retired from the postal department. He decided that they would have to shift to a small town where his meagre pension would be sufficient to sustain his large family. The Godses settled down in the small town of Sangli in southwest Maharashtra. To supplement his father's pension, Nathuram learnt tailoring and set up a shop. This too was insufficient, so to add to the family income, he started selling fruits.

Some Brahmins inspired by Savarkar's ideology got together in Nagpur, the geographical centre of British India, to establish a Hindu Sangathana or organization. This was the precursor to the RSS and the Hindu Mahasabha. The Sangathana was of Brahmins, by Brahmins and for Brahmins. The idea was to forge a militant uppercaste Hindu organization, which would espouse, under the guise of Hindu unity, uppercaste Hindu supremacy. They opposed the Gandhian policy of uniting all Indians, equality for Muslims and the absolutely abhorrent policy, to the Brahmins, of equality for the untouchables, to bring them to the same level as the rest of Hindu society. Gandhi was their main enemy. Their call to the Hindu upper castes was to forsake Gandhi's non-violence and take up arms in the service of their colonial masters. The idea of such an organization was first mooted by Savarkar, as was the two-nation theory—the ideology that conceived Pakistan.

Nathuram faithfully served his master in Ratnagiri while the idea of the Sangathana was being discussed. He knew that Savarkar had blessed the birth of the militant Hindu right-wing organization. So, when a branch of the Sangathana was opened in Sangli, Nathuram was the first to join and was soon appointed its secretary. He was now in his twenties and his parents wanted him to marry a girl from their caste. However, Nathuram was still not over the trauma of having been forced to live as a girl in his childhood, so he vehemently refused marriage.

In 1937, the first provincial Congress government of Bombay released Savarkar. The Hindu Sangathana and other Savarkarites got together and took him on a tour of the Marathi-speaking province. He delivered lectures in various towns and cities; one of the places he visited was Sangli. Nathuram, as the secretary of the local branch of the Sangathana, was in charge of all the arrangements for Savarkar's stay and public programmes in Sangli. Savarkar trusted him due to his close acquaintance with him in Ratnagiri. Nathuram joined Savarkar's entourage and accompanied him on the rest of the tour. Nathuram decided that living in Sangli was stifling his growth. He had to shift to a more centrally located place close to Bombay and Savarkar; he shut his shop in Sangli and moved to Poona. Although he did open a tailoring shop there, most of his time was spent in the activities of the Hindu Sangathana.

Nathuram now worked twenty-four hours a day as a member of

the Hindu Mahasabha. The training he had received in Ratnagiri came in handy. He became a passionate preacher of the Hindu supremacist cause. In 1938, the Mahasabha launched a march on the princely state of Hyderabad, ruled by the Nizam. Nathuram was entrusted the leadership of the first batch of marchers; as soon as they entered the Nizam's territories, he was arrested and imprisoned for a year. By the time he was released, the Second World War had broken out.

After his release, Nathuram returned to Poona. In 1940, Nathuram met someone with whom he was going to develop a life-long bond. Narayan D. Apte had just returned from Ahmednagar, where he had been working for the Mahasabha. The two young men were as different as chalk and cheese, but as it usually happens, they instantly formed a bond which was to last them for the rest of their years. In 1942, Savarkar mooted the idea of forming a Hindu Rashtra Dal, members of which would be the stormtroopers of the Hindu Mahasabha. Nathuram Godse and Narayan Apte joined the Dal and at its peak, the Dal had a couple of hundred members. Its members were given martial training and were indoctrinated in Savarkar's philosophy of intolerance, bigotry, violence and murder. It's only visible activity was disrupting Congress meetings, heckling Congress leaders and hounding Gandhi. Nathuram and Apte were leaders of the Dal.

In 1944, Nathuram broached, to Apte, the idea of starting a periodical, a mouth piece for Savarkar, Hindu Mahasabha and their Dal. Savarkar blessed their endeavour and gifted ₹15,000 for it. The inaugural issue of *Agranee* was published on the Hindu new year, Gudi Padva, celebrated in Maharashtra. The front page, like all the subsequent issues, carried a portrait of Savarkar on its masthead. Nathuram was its editor and Apte, publisher.

Nathuram and Apte, now inseparable, were at the forefront of the activities of the fanatics. Nathuram had accepted the more dynamic and extroverted Apte's leadership. Their joint venture *Agranee* was barely managing to survive. Savarkar, however, kept them afloat with frequent and much-needed infusions of funds. *Agranee* faced continuous prosecution for infringements of the Press Act from the Bombay provincial government because of its violent and abusive language and its campaign of hate. This continuous persecution increased the anger

Nathuram felt for the Congress and its leaders. Finally, just before the government issued orders to close it down, in an effort to keep it going, Apte and Godse renamed their periodical *Hindu Rashtra*.

On the personal front, Nathuram was still rejecting every proposal of marriage brought by his parents. The only habit he cultivated was an addiction to coffee. Apte and he would frequent the tea rooms of Poona, and one of their favourite haunts was the cafe/restaurant at the Poona railway station. Throughout his life, Nathuram was able to form relationships and close bonds only with men. He was instantly attracted to men with dynamic and extrovert personalities; thus, he was bound in a hero–disciple relationship with Savarkar in his formative years and then formed a bond of subordination to the extrovert and flamboyant Narayan Apte, who was actually a year younger than him. Nathuram hated with equal passion, and the target of his pathological hatred was another very strong and dynamic man, Mohandas Gandhi.

◆

The second accused in the Gandhi murder case was Narayan Dattatreya Apte, a Chitpavan Brahmin from Poona. Apte, born in 1911, belonged to a family of scholars. He was flamboyant, an extrovert and an incorrigible womanizer. Wine, women and all the luxuries of life were his weaknesses. He smoked and drank and, unlike a Brahmin, even relished meat; he loved to wear western clothes like a pucca gentleman of the Raj, a wannabe Brown Sahib. Apte was blessed with looks most women found attractive. He had a way with them and exploited this to flit from one relationship to another. While Nathuram was repulsed by the mere shadow of a woman, Narayan was attracted to them like a moth is to a flame.

Like Nathuram, Narayan was the firstborn of his parents; like Nathuram, he also headed a large brood of siblings, three sisters and four brothers. But unlike the less-educated Nathuram, Narayan had completed his graduation. Narayan passed his matriculation from Poona and then graduated from Bombay University in 1932 with a bachelor's degree in science. Later, he also earned a BEd degree.

As was customary in Indian families, Apte's parents arranged his marriage immediately after his graduation to a girl from a family of

Brahmins of the same caste. Champa Fadtare was from an old and influential Brahmin family of Poona. The Fadtares were better off than the Aptes and influential to boot. To Narayan's parents, Champa was a perfect match for their son; her family, with their influence and wealth, would be able to arrange an appropriate job for their out-of-work son-in-law. With the help of his in-laws, Apte secured a job as a teacher in the American Mission High School in Ahmednagar, run by an American nun.

Apte worked hard at his job. He also venerated Savarkar and subscribed to his fanatic ideology of hate and murder. While in Ahmednagar, Narayan established a rifle club with a shooting gallery that was allowed to use only .22 calibre guns that fired slugs instead of bullets, due to a restriction on the use of firearms by Indians imposed by the British rulers after the uprising of 1857. The Government of Bombay Province issued a license to Narayan Apte for the first civilian shooting club, which became very popular and was soon replicated in Poona and many towns of Maharashtra.

In 1939, Narayan Apte joined the Ahmednagar branch of the Hindu Mahasabha headed by its founder Vishnu R. Karkare, a hotelier. Apte did not respect Karkare, an illiterate self-made man. The cool vibes were reciprocated by Karkare, a Hindu zealot, who could not bring himself to respect a person working at a Christian missionary organization. It was during this time that Apte met Nathuram and they became close friends, soon to become inseparable.

While Apte was in Ahmednagar, Champa bore him a son. Narayan was overjoyed, he adored his firstborn male child and affectionately called him Pappan. However, tragedy was round the corner for the Aptes. They soon discovered that things were not quite right with their son: he did not show any milestones of intellectual development. It was initially dismissed as the anxiety of young parents, then brushed off with the explanation that some babies were slow, but by the time Pappan was two years old, it was painfully apparent that he suffered from a very debilitating mental ailment. Narayan was shattered; he wanted to give up Ahmednagar and also his fledgling career. The grief of fathering a severely intellectually impaired child drove him away from Champa and, very soon, into the arms of other women.

At the outbreak of the Second World War, Apte took a job as a wartime recruiter in the Royal Indian Air Force (RIAF), as their idol Svarkar had ordered them to help the British War effort. He was given a Wartime commission; his stint with the RIAF would last the duration of the War. He was posted in Poona with a temporary rank of flight lieutenant. This entitled him to wear an officer's uniform with the insignia and all the accoutrements of the RIAF, a handy tool for seducing young women. At last, Apte could leave Ahmednagar and a job he was getting bored of. His only consolation in the job had been the many young women he had taught and charmed. There were many tearful farewells when he quit his job at the mission school. One of the grieving girls was Manorama Salvi, a seventeen-year-old shy Christian girl from Bombay. Apte gave his female students his Poona address and told them that they were always welcome to visit him. One of the students who carefully preserved and later used the address to re-establish contact with Narayan was Manorama.

Eventually, Narayan was offered a permanent commission by the RIAF. Apte was overjoyed: a career as a commissioned officer was respectable and secure. It brought along with it many perks: a home, subsidized goods, quality education for children and a life-long pension, but it also meant transfers and possible posting to the War front. Apte decided not to accept it. His excuse was that the condition of his son Pappan had worsened. Champa too had begun showing signs of emotional distress. She considered Pappan to be her only responsibility, her life revolved around him, excluding even her husband. Narayan had been advised to commit Pappan to an asylum, but he knew that Champa would not be able to bear the loss of her son. So, Apte chose to keep his temporary Wartime commission as long as he was stationed in Poona.

With time to spare, Apte and Nathuram devoted an increasing amount of time to Mahasabha work. It was then that Savarkar launched the Hindu Rashtra Dal. Both Apte and Godse were soon given responsibilities and were rewarded with official positions of leadership. When Godse broached the idea of starting a periodical, Apte agreed and so the two of them became partners in *Agrani* with Savarkar's blessings and funding.

This was also the time that the Apte–Godse gang began the systematic hounding of Gandhi. A series of attacks were carried out on Gandhi, and the involvement of Godse and Apte and their Dal was confirmed in several of these.

After his release from imprisonment in the Aga Khan Palace, Gandhi spent a month at the cool mountain resort of Panchgani, very close to Poona, to recuperate. Narayan Apte and Nathuram Godse led a gang of Dal members to Panchgani and for a week they took out processions, shouting slogans abusing Gandhi and the Congress. Apte was detained and interrogated by Deputy Superintendent (DSP) N.Y. Deulkar, who was to later play a key role in the investigation into Gandhi's murder. The *Times of India*, in its edition dated 23 July 1944, reported the incident at Panchgani, stating that Gandhi was heckled by a group of young men led by a journalist from Poona, N.D. Apte.

While holding down two jobs, one as a commissioned recruitment officer for the RIAF and the other as the manager of *Agranee,* along with his activities in the Hindu Mahasabha, Narayan found time to start an illicit liaison with his former student Manorama Salvi. She was studying in Wilson College in Bombay and stayed in the Ramabai Hostel for Girls, which was attached to the college. She wrote to Apte, and a few days later, resplendent in his air force officer's uniform, Apte presented himself at the hostel matron's office. The usually very strict Mrs Hewat was charmed by the dashing young officer, and when he asked to meet Manorama and a couple of other girls who were his ex-students, permission was granted immediately. Apte took the three young women out for a film and snacks. Soon, Narayan became a regular visitor to the hostel, but now he asked only to meet Manorama, and very soon the two became lovers. Manorama would fabricate stories and get permission from the hostel warden to stay out all night. The two checked into hotels in South Bombay as husband and wife. Narayan had bought a motorbike and thought nothing of riding a hundred and thirty miles between Bombay and Poona to meet his lover, Manorama, while he was still married to Champa.

At the end of the War, Narayan's commission in the RIAF ended. Now, both Nathuram and Narayan were solely dependent on *Agranee* for their livelihood.

Meanwhile, Hindus and Muslims were being politically polarized. Fanatic Islam was taking hold amongst the Muslims and extremist zealots were gaining a hold on Hindus. This helped the duo to resuscitate the dying *Agranee*. As circulation increased, revenues began to flow in, and they were able to get funding from moneyed, bigoted Hindus for many of their schemes to attack Muslims. In pre-Independence India, it became easy for both Muslim and Hindu fanatics to get funds and radicalized foot soldiers for their campaigns.

Nathuram and Narayan soon started looking to expand their publication. They acquired a plot of land to build an office, which would house their newly acquired printing press. A shed was built at 495 Shanwar Peth, an old locality of Poona from where *Agranee* was published and the Shivaji Printing Press functioned.

It was 1946; India was to be torn asunder by the massacres of Hindus in the riots during the Muslim League orchestrated 'Direct Action Day'. The League was hellbent on terrorizing the colonial administration and the Congress, to get them to agree to their demand for a separate Muslim homeland. If innocent Hindus had to be sacrificed, so be it. And if there was a Hindu backlash against the Muslims, resulting in a massacre of Muslims, it would further their demand for a separate Pakistan.

♦

Vishnu Ramkrishna Karkare was born to Brahmin parents. His father died while Vishnu was very young, leaving the children with no memories of their father. His mother was forced to abandon him and his siblings soon after his father died. Like many children of his time, Vishnu did not even know his date of birth, not unusual in India even today. Fatherless and abandoned, Vishnu initially grew up at the Northcote Orphanage run by Christian missionaries in Bombay. The records of the orphanage show that Vishnu was born sometime in 1910.

Vishnu received only very rudimentary primary education. When he was ten, he ran away from the orphanage and started working as a 'Chaivala', serving tea in a small tea room. He did not last too long but he did learn the trade. One day, he ran away to Poona. Very little is known about Vishnu's life in Poona, but he learned to read and write Marathi and speak a smattering of Hindustani, a mixed dialect of Hindi and Urdu spoken in north, northwest and central India. For the next fifteen years, Vishnu survived in Poona by doing odd jobs. Judging from what he became as a young man, Vishnu learnt much more than how to survive in Poona. As a young man, he became an ardent subscriber to Hindu extremist ideology and a fanatic follower of Savarkar.

Perhaps somewhere along the way, the orphaned street urchin must have developed a deep-rooted resentment for the way life had treated him. Whatever the trauma he suffered in childhood, Vishnu grew up a very angry young man, and the target of his hatred was Muslims.

After spending fifteen years in Poona, Vishnu, now a young man of twenty-five, decided to move on. With his life's possessions packed in a gunnysack, he caught a bus to Ahmednagar. Here, the young man opened a small tea stall near the bus depot. Along with hot cups of chai, Indian brewed and spiced tea, Vishnu served puri, fried flatbread, and thecha, a fiery relish of coarsely ground green chillies, garlic and crushed roasted peanuts tempered in hot oil. Soon, Vishnu's tea stall became popular and he moved to an unused cowshed. Karkare eventually expanded it into a hotel which offered lodging and boarding, and after a few years, built the Deccan Guest House in the Kapda Bazaar area of Ahmednagar where it still stands. The orphaned, abandoned urchin, who had lived most of his childhood and youth on the streets, had become a moderately prosperous hotelier.

Karkare was now called 'Seth', a colloquial equivalent of 'boss'. He got married and decided to indulge in his fondness for theatre by funding a theatre group which regularly performed shows as a travelling entertainment company. In those days in rural Maharashtra, these touring companies were the only source of entertainment and were very popular. Vishnu, after achieving a certain social status, decided to start doing 'social work'. He provided shelter to uppercaste Hindu students from villages free of charge and established the Ahmednagar branch of the Hindu Mahasabha.

In 1939, Karkare met Narayan Apte at a Mahasabha meeting. They did not interact much at the first few meetings, as both were indifferent towards one another; in fact, Karkare suspected the integrity of a person who worked for Christian missionaries. When elections were held for the Ahmednagar municipality, Karkare filed his nomination and was elected unopposed. The street urchin had indeed come a long way. At thirty-two, he was married, owned a profitable business, was a patron of the performing arts, headed a political organization and was an elected councilman.

It was during this phase of his life that Karkare came in contact with a person who sold weapons in Poona, Digambar Badge. Whenever Karkare visited Poona, he would purchase some legal and a lot of illegal arms and explosives, like homemade crude bombs and hand grenades, from the Shastra Bhandar Weapons Store, owned by Badge. Karkare learned that Badge specialized in chain mail vests which protected the torso of the wearer from knife and sword attacks, so he had a couple made for himself, which he would wear under his shirt or jacket whenever he went on 'missions'.

When the Muslim League gave a call for 'Direct Action', mass rioting, murder and arson erupted, as Calcutta and East Bengal indulged in an orgy of violence and beastliness. In the first phase in Calcutta, Hindus were massacred by Muslims; then the Hindus avenged the massacre in an even more savage manner. This was avenged by unimaginable savagery in the isolated interior districts of East Bengal. The savagery of East Bengal was retaliated by a brutal massacre of Muslims in Bihar: the vicious cycle continued.

Karkare joined a band of avenging Hindus and claimed to have travelled through the riot-ravaged districts of East Bengal. On his return, he visited branches of the Hindu Mahasabha and recounted exaggerated accounts of the atrocities committed on the Hindus in the riot affected districts and fanned the flames of Hindu anger in Maharashtra. Nathuram injected venom into the stories with his acid pen and made them more inflammatory while publishing them in *Agranee*. An association was, thereby, formed.

◆

Dada Maharaj (Maharaj is used as a title and denotes him being a priest) was head of a sect of Hindus based in Bombay, and he had also visited some parts of Noakhali in an attempt to reconvert Hindus who had been forcibly converted to Islam. He was keen to help anybody who wanted to seek revenge for the atrocities committed on the Hindus in East Bengal. Dada Maharaj was a wealthy man and keen to fund attacks on Muslims.

The supply of arms and funds to Hindu extremists, whom Dada Maharaj financed, was looked after by his younger brother Dixit Maharaj. Dada decided whom to help and sanctioned funds; Dixit Maharaj made the arrangements and bought and supplied the weapons. One of Dixit Maharaj's regular suppliers was Digamber Badge of Poona.

A Brahmin living in Poona, Digambar Ramchandra Badge was a colourful character with a penchant for theatrics. Due to his mismatched features and a squint, Badge had a face that was not easily forgotten. He had a luxurious flowing beard and shoulder-length hair, which he kept heavily oiled. Badge fancied himself to be a master of disguise but his disguises were often so loud that instead of helping him blend into a crowd or his surroundings, they would attract attention. His favourite getups included those as a sadhu, a fakir, a butcher, a Sikh farmer, a folk musician and so on. Once, he landed at Dixit Maharaj's house dressed as a folk musician with his servant behind him, carrying a big drum. Badge dramatically ripped the drum open to reveal neatly packed daggers and short swords inside.

Badge was a very resourceful and effective salesman, and his clients rarely left empty-handed. The success of his arms business stemmed from the fact that there was nothing he could not procure for his customers—those willing to pay the price he quoted. He had sources working in the arms depot in Poona Cantonment, so when required, he could even supply genuine British-manufactured arms, ammunition and explosives. Post the Second World War, British troops returning home had hidden caches of arms, ammunition and explosives at several places in India, with the intention of profiting from their sale. Badge knew these caches and the people who owned them.

Badge was famous for his stabproof vests made of knitted chain mail and his tiger claws which were knuckledusters with razor sharp metal tiger claws which were used to slash and disembowel opponents.

Badge ran his business on a minimum expenses–maximum profit principle. He employed workers at the lowest salaries and treated them like slaves. Sometime in 1945, Badge visited Sholapur, a town near the border of Maharashtra and Andhra Pradesh, which had a reasonable Telugu-speaking population. Here, he hired a poverty-stricken youth, Shankar Kistayya, to work for him.

♦

Shankar Kistayya was an illiterate youth who lived in a slum in Sholapur's Yellama Nagar locality with his widowed mother. The youngster worked as an apprentice to a carpenter. Badge was looking for someone who would make and fix wooden handles on the dagger blades he bought at discounted rates and sold at a premium. Shankar was the right choice. Badge offered him the job at a salary of five rupees a month plus boarding and lodging. For the poverty-stricken Shankar and his mother, this was a sudden windfall. What Shankar did not know was that, along with his official duty, he was supposed to act as rickshaw puller, delivery boy, sweeper, washerman, cook, masseur and do anything else that Badge ordered him to do. He had to do the same chores for Badge's sister, too. Shankar was becoming Badge's slave.

Badge was a bad paymaster and never paid Shankar his full salary. At one time, Badge owed him six months of wages, and every time Shankar asked for his overdue wages, Badge would beat him up and deny him food. Having had enough of this inhuman treatment, Shankar ran away to Sholapur. Using his contacts with the police, Badge filed a false complaint of theft against Shankar and got him arrested. After receiving a 'special' treatment at the hands of the police, Shankar decided that he was better off serving Badge. He meekly resumed his duties.

♦

In Poona, Narayan Apte was preoccupied; his domestic life was in shambles. Pappan, his son, had become progressively more unmanageable, forcing Apte to finally commit him to an asylum. Champa became hysterical on losing her son and blamed Apte for it. He had to relent and bring Pappan back home, but this drove Narayan out of his home.

In Bombay, Manorama told Apte that she was pregnant. She had moved out of the hostel and was living with her parents. Her father, Daulatrao Salvi, lived in police quarters next to the Northcote Police Hospital in Byculla where he worked as a male nurse. Manorama was in her final year of BA, a few months away from graduation. Her pregnancy was a matter of great worry for her, as her family was a part of a very orthodox and close knit Roman Catholic community. She feared her parent's response and the scandal that her pregnancy would cause in their community. She required that Apte make their relationship official by marrying her before her pregnancy was discovered.

Nathuram had no such worries. His family had moved back to Poona; his sisters were married off and two of his brothers were working and had their own homes. He lived in a tiny one-room tenement at 334, Shanivar Peth, very close to the office and press of the *Hindu Rashtra*. He edited *Hindu Rashtra* from a tent pitched behind the building that housed the printing press. He accepted Apte as his leader in all their schemes and actions on behalf of the Mahasabha as a loyal Savarkarite and member of the Hindu Rashtra Dal.

Apte was worried; the people who had readily funded his harebrained schemes were now demanding results. Apte needed money to sustain his lavish lifestyle, while Nathuram had to keep their publication going. Discussing this over cups of hot tea and coffee at one of their regular haunts, the cafeteria attached to the Poona railway station, Apte suggested, 'Let's kill Gandhi!' Nathuram's eyes lit up, but immediately doubts crept in. 'We have made several attempts on his life but failed, now no one will trust us,' he expressed his doubt. Apte was desperate and he needed Nathuram to believe in this. 'Times have changed. There are many who are willing to support us. Tatyarao (Savarkar) has blessed the scheme. Many who worship him will help us. We have supporters in influential places, even amongst the police. Trust me. Let's kill Gandhi! Our time has come!' Nathuram nodded. An attempt on Gandhi's life was sure to generate a lot of publicity; it would be easy to convince their financiers and the funds would come pouring in. At a very secret meeting in Alwar where Nathuram was present, it was decided by a handful of princes, Savarkar and the head of the RSS that Gandhi would be murdered as a signal for a nationwide mutiny by Hindus. At that meeting, Nathuram accepted the task of murdering Gandhi.

In the core team, Apte and Nathuram were close friends. Badge and Kistayya were master and servant. Karkare was the odd man out. Soon, he too would meet someone he could befriend. Ahmednagar was one of the many destinations for refugees of Partition. Karkare started working to make life a bit easier for these unfortunate victims and provided them temporary shelters and unlimited meals. Ahmednagar had a sizeable

Muslim population that had good homes and flourishing businesses and was generally well off. This infuriated the refugees; they wanted to drive out the Muslims and take over their businesses and homes, just as had been done in their homes and towns. Their anger was heightened by news from across the border: the Nizam's cadre of thugs, called the 'Razakars' or 'volunteers', led by a ruthless fanatic Kassim Rizvi, had not only terrorized the Hindus living in Hyderabad but also often crossed borders to raid isolated villages and Hindu hamlets. The backlash of these actions was borne by the innocent Muslim residents of Ahmednagar. The situation became so volatile that the administration prohibited carrying any weapons by civilians in the entire district.

At that time, Karkare was busy collecting weapons and ammunition and recruiting men for Apte's proposed raid on the Nizam's border tax post. They needed grenades, but Badge had hiked his price and was now asking for ₹200 apiece. Karkare heard that grenades could be bought much cheaper in Bombay from one of the many illegal factories. He went to Bombay and visited the refugee camp in Chembur. Here, the Maharaj brothers introduced him to a young refugee hothead, Madanlal Pahwa, who promised Karkare that he would get him very cheap hand grenades.

◆

Madanlal came from Pakpattan, a small village in Montgomery district of West Punjab, now in Pakistan. He was twenty-one days old when his mother died. The boy was a troublemaker since childhood and was severely disciplined by his father and stepmother, and frequently beaten mercilessly. When Madanlal turned seven, he was sent to a gurukul where he got into scrapes and violent fights with fellow students, and was soon expelled. As a youth, Madanlal joined a militant RSS shakha. His father was a dedicated Congressman and his son's antics displeased him. On one occasion, after receiving a sound thrashing, Madanlal ran away from home. He reached Rawalpindi and enlisted in the Royal Indian Navy. Madanlal served in Lahore, Rawalpindi, Jhelum and Bombay, where he was discharged in 1946.

The partition of India, which also meant the division of Punjab and Bengal, was already on the cards, and sectarian violence had erupted all over. Madanlal decided to go back to his village and organize Hindus. He led attacks against the Muslims in Lahore; once, while trying to set off a bomb, he lost the first phalange of his index finger. Speaking to writer Manohar Mulgaonkar, Madanlal recounted a more glamorized version, claiming that while working in a clandestine bomb factory, he had slipped and his finger had been crushed in the teeth of a gear wheel. He said, 'My assistant immediately shut off the machine and wanted to call a doctor, but the factory was littered with grenades, and to call a doctor then would have meant that the illegal operation would be exposed. I just picked up a knife and hacked it off!' The first story seems far more plausible.

Madanlal crossed over to India with the first wave of refugees. He reached Gwalior, where he joined a gang of marauders who attacked and murdered many Muslims fleeing to Pakistan. They would board trains at smaller stations in the princely state of Gwalior, identify the Muslims, pull them off the train and massacre them. They often abducted Muslim women and after raping them, sold them off. The maharaja of Gwalior, Jiyajirao Scindia, and his administration ignored these activities, as the maharaja was favourably inclined towards the Hindu extremists. Soon after reaching Gwalior, Madanlal received news that his father was admitted to the Ferozepur Hospital. He had been severely mauled in the post-Partition riots in Punjab while trying to flee to India. Madanlal, who had never cared about his father, now vowed to avenge the injuries suffered by his father by inflicting ten times more on Muslims.

When things became too hot to handle for Madanlal in Gwalior, he moved to Bombay and started living in the Chembur refugee camp. To sustain himself, Madanlal looked for employment and came in touch with Prof. Jagdish Chandra Jain, who offered him a means of income by selling books written and published by him for a commission. However, to sustain himself, Pahwa had to look for other work and joined the Vassen Puspasen Fireworks factory. The real business there was making hand grenades clandestinely, and Madanlal was employed as a grenade maker. To supplement his income, Madanlal pilfered some hand grenades and sold them to revenge-seeking refugees and others in the camps. It was through this activity that he came in touch with Dixit Maharaj. Under the pretext of selling Jain's books, Madanlal sold hand grenades to the Maharaj brothers.

When Karkare came to Bombay to buy hand grenades, Apte referred him to the Maharaj brothers, who in turn introduced him to Madanlal. There was an instant bonding between the two. The garrulous small town hotelier and the lonesome hotheaded young refugee formed a relationship of patron and ward. Karkare persuaded Madanlal to move to Ahmednagar; he promised him shelter, plenty of opportunities for revenge and business. Madanlal was at a loose end and decided to take up Karkare's offer. He took his pending wages in kind, packed a few dozen hand grenades, his meagre belongings and followed 'Karkara Seth', which is how the Punjabi Madanlal pronounced Karkare's name, to Ahmednagar.

A few hours after Madanlal left for Ahmednagar, police raided the Vassen Puspasen Fireworks factory. The illegal grenade manufacturing was discovered and its owners and workers were arrested. Madanlal had escaped by the skin of his teeth, but the police came to know about a refugee bombmaker who had got away.

In Ahmednagar, Madanlal gathered a group of young hotheaded refugees and formed a band of avenging vigilantes. Under Karkare's patronage, the gang started terrorizing Muslim residents of Ahmednagar. Madanlal forcibly took over a fruitseller's stall in the market by driving away its Muslim owner. Karkare funded the start of his own fruit business. Now Madanlal was indebted to 'Karkara Seth' and was willing to do anything for him. Karkare expanded his business by driving away Muslim merchants and taking over their businesses. He found managers for these newly commandeered businesses from among the many refugees; besides providing them with employment, it also earned Karkare their gratitude, loyalty and wealth. Madanlal also found a girlfriend, Shevanta, eventually.

Sometime in December 1947, Madanlal visited Bombay. He met Jain, who was rather angry with him for not having settled his accounts. Madanlal pacified him and squared up the account. Soon, he was boasting about his life in Ahmednagar and about his exploits. He talked about his benefactor 'Karkara Seth' and how he was not only financing his business but also their campaign against Muslims. He mentioned how he had attacked many Muslim establishments and processions with hand grenades and boasted about how 'Karkara Seth' depended on him to provide muscle power whenever required.

Karkare took Madanlal to Poona, where they met Apte and Nathuram.

The plans for raiding the border post were again discussed. Karkare recounted Madanlal's exploits with hand grenades in Ahmednagar. Apte was pleased; at last they had found someone who was proficient with explosives, fanatically committed to their cause and, most importantly, someone who could be easily manipulated. The RSS had launched a campaign of disrupting Gandhi's prayer meetings in Delhi. They made it look as if refugees from West Punjab found it offensive when Ayats from the Koran were recited at Gandhi's public prayers and were demonstrating against it. As the days progressed, the protests became more and more intense and angry, threatening to turn violent. It was all orchestrated to show as if anger amongst the aggrieved refugees was intensifying and one day they would violently attack Gandhi. They needed a refugee hothead to perform the task. In Madanlal, Apte had found his scapegoat. Apte told the group to be ready for another mission at short notice and that they may have to stay away for a long time. He informed them that a training camp for use of arms and explosives had been organized in Alwar and Gwalior. Madanlal boasted that he was proficient in using arms and explosives and could organize a skilled instructor for the training, if required.

On 5 January, Karkare learnt that Congressmen were organizing a public meeting for communal harmony. An eminent Congress leader, Raosaheb Patwardhan, was going to address the meeting. Karkare ordered Madanlal and his men to disrupt the meeting and drive away the Congressmen. Madanlal and his stormtroopers reached the venue armed with daggers; their stock of explosives and grenades had been confiscated and the rest hidden to evade being seized by the police. As soon as Raosaheb Patwardhan started speaking, Madanlal and his men started heckling him and shouting anti-Muslim and anti-Congress slogans to disrupt the meeting. When Raosaheb Patwardhan ignored them and continued to speak, Madanlal rushed on to the stage, pulled away the mike, grabbed the senior Congress leader by the scruff of his neck and dragged him off the stage. Before he could act further, a couple of police constables pulled him away. There was complete pandemonium. A dagger was found on Madanlal's person, which was confiscated, and after a reprimand, surprisingly, Madanlal was let off. Later, in court, during the Gandhi murder trial, Madanlal stated that the constables were sympathizers to their cause and therefore lenient towards him.

It was at this time that Karkare and Madanlal were urgently summoned to Poona. Apte wanted them to drop everything else and get there immediately. Just as they were about to leave on 9 January, Karkare's source in the police department informed them that a warrant for their arrest was being prepared. Now it became imperative that the two of them leave Ahmednagar immediately. At the railway station, Madanlal bumped into Inspector Joshi, who knew him as Karkare's man. He asked Madanlal what he was doing there and Madanlal told him that he was on his way to Delhi to get married, and in a few minutes he boarded a train for Poona. Inspector Joshi did not inform his department about Madanlal's departure.

All the gang members assembled at Nathuram's office at Shivaji Printing Press. The plan was discussed and it was decided that since Badge had hiked his rates, they needed to find a cheaper source for weapons. Madanlal knew that his old factory had been closed down by the police but claimed that he had other sources in the Chembur refugee camp. Apte told Karkare and Madanlal to leave for Bombay immediately and to procure as many hand grenades and explosives as they could. Bombay was home to the supreme leader of the Hindu Mahasabha, Vinayak Damodar Savarkar, the man who had instilled an intense hatred for Gandhi in his followers. Savarkar was the inspiration behind the plan to kill, and the several failed attempts on Gandhi's life had been initiated and inspired by Savarkar, if not directly by issuing orders, then through his vitriolic outburst of the need to save Hinduism from its arch enemy, Mohandas Gandhi. Gandhi's ascendancy in India had stymied Savarkar's political career. For all his efforts to be a national leader of the Hindus, Savarkar had been confined to being the leader of a few uppercaste Brahmins of Maharashtra. This rankled the intrinsically hate-filled and bitter man, who had, all his life, preached the doctrine of revenge, murder and violence.

◆

Vinayak Damodar Savarkar was born on 28 May 1883 in Bhagur, a tiny village near Nasik, in a Maharashtrian Chitpavan Brahmin family to Damodar and Radhabai. Since his childhood, Savarkar had a distinct hatred for Muslims which intensified with age. That part of Maharashtra, comprising Savarkar's village among others, had, for centuries, been inhabited by Muslims, with almost every village in the surrounding areas having an evenly matched population of Hindus and Muslims. Savarkar formed a gang of children from his village and regularly attacked Muslims and got into brawls with Muslim ruffians. Over a period of time, this grew into stabbings and planned attacks on mosques and Muslim processions and religious functions. To his credit, Savarkar was a brilliant student, but everything he did had an undercurrent of hate and violence. He wrote, with equal expertise, prose and poetry that could bring tears to the eyes of the reader. He used this talent to incite passion and hate in people.

During his teenage years, Savarkar, who had an affinity for violence, was influenced by the revolutionary anti-colonial movement in India. When he was fifteen, a sensational killing took place in Maharashtra. The Chaphekar brothers of Poona, incensed by the very strict and perceived to be heartless methods used by the British to contain the plague epidemic in Poona, murdered W.C. Rand, a British officer who had very strictly enforced measures to contain the spread of the plague. The Chaphekar brothers were arrested, tried and hanged by the colonial British administration. A whole generation of Maharashtrian youth were greatly influenced by their sacrifice. Savarkar was one of them.

In 1901, he secured admission to Fergusson College in Poona. This was the time when Bal Gangadhar Tilak, 'Lokmanya', a very eminent leader of the hawks in Congress, held sway. His fiery speeches were responsible for influencing many young people joining the anti-colonial movement. Savarkar was influenced by Tilak, and led many student agitations against the British, exploiting his oratory skills to the hilt. He organized a movement of undergraduates and graduates and called it Abhinav Bharat, 'Innovative India'.

Savarkar paid a heavy price for his anti-colonial activities and was stripped of his degree. Undeterred, with the help of eminent Indian leaders, he set sail for England to study and be called to the bar.

In London, Savarkar was, like other Indian students, exposed to a lot of revolutionary influences. He joined Gray's Inn, qualified four years later and was admitted to the bar. During these years, he was influenced by the anarchist movement in Europe. He met and fell in love with a young British lady, Margaret Lawrence. He started the Free India Society which met once a week; from the members of this society, he selected those who, like him, believed in a violent revolutionary movement. They secretly got in touch with other revolutionaries in France and contacted Russian anarchists to learn the science of bomb-making and use of arms.

During his stay in England, Savarkar wrote prolifically, and many of his manuscripts were smuggled into India and published. He wrote regularly for a nationalist periodical called *Talvar* (Sword), published in Paris by Bhikaji Cama and edited in Berlin by Virendranath Chattopadhyay. He wrote a romanticized account of the Sepoy Mutiny of 1857, the uprising of the Indian soldiers against the British East India Company.

Two chapters of Savarkar's book were stolen by British Secret Service agents and despatched to the colonial administration in India, which banned it even before it was fully written. It was finally published in 1907 by underground publishers. Before the Marathi original could be printed, the British raided the publisher in Sholapur. The manuscript was smuggled out of the country by Savarkar's friends from Poona and an English translation was published in Holland, many copies of which were smuggled into India. The colonial administration in India, alarmed by its tone and contents and to a large extent misinterpretation by inept translators, served an order prohibiting Savarkar from returning to India.

In 1909, in London, Madanlal Dhingra a member of Savarkar's Free India Society, murdered Sir Curzon Wylie, the government prosecutor who had secured the penalty of death against Khudiram Bose and many other revolutionaries from Bengal. Savarkar organized a fund for Dhingra's defence in London and opposed the statement issued by some Indian expatriates in London condemning his violent act. He also lobbied for a fair trial for Dhingra. In Nasik, a revolutionary shot and killed the British collector, A.M.T. Jackson, to avenge Baburao's prosecution. The British administration alleged that the gun used in the killing was sent by Savarkar from London. Sensing that his arrest was imminent, Savarkar escaped to Paris. There was a small community of Indians living in Paris, and Savarkar tried to foment revolutionary fervour amongst them. However, he began missing his British beloved and tried to sneak into London for a secret rendezvous. He was not destined to meet her ever again.

Savarkar was arrested at Victoria Station and imprisoned at Brixton prison where he was served an order of deportation to India. The colonial administration had decided to prosecute Savarkar on the charge of waging war against the king. Deputy Superintendent of Police C.I. Power from the Bombay Police went to London, accompanied by a posse of constables, to accompany Savarkar. Scotland Yard also deputed Detective Inspector Edward Josh Parker to accompany Power on the journey back to India. The group embarked on a journey on the *SS Maurea*. A storm forced the ship to make an unscheduled stop at Marseilles. Savarkar knew he had to escape; he was sure that he would either be sentenced to death or imprisoned once he reached India. Early in the morning, he requested to go to the toilet. Two constables stood outside the door while Savarkar went in unshackled. He bolted the door and covered the spy hole with his tunic. He squeezed himself out of the porthole, jumped into the sea and swam ashore, but his captors spotted him.

Savarkar reached French soil before the British police did. He was hoping to seek refuge with his friends in Paris, but that was not to be. He was caught by a gendarme and handed over to his British captors. Savarkar's revolutionary life was over. On his return to India, the British colonialists sentenced him to an unprecedented fifty years of incarceration in Cellular Jail in Port Blair, Andaman Islands, Kala Pani.

Nobody was known to have survived Kala Pani. Savarkar, the revolutionary firebrand, did not survive it either. After serving ten years, his health and spirit were broken and he made his peace with the British government. He wrote several letters, the first of these as early as a mere six months into his sentence, apologizing for his inadvertent crimes against the British Crown and promised to be a loyal collaborator for the rest of his life in return for clemency. Many other Kala Pani detainees at Port Blair endured daily floggings, torture, starvation, unhygienic conditions and solitary confinement, but refused to be broken. They served their sentences with their heads held high, their bodies ravaged but their spirits unbroken by their tormentors. Savarkar was not made of the same stuff. He meekly surrendered to the British after only ten years of his sentence and never in the rest of his entire life opposed them again. He emerged from Cellular Jail a bitter religious zealot. Neither his bitterness nor his desire for revenge was directed towards the British, his tormentors; it was aimed at the Indian Muslims and Gandhi, who by then had emerged as the undisputed leader of the freedom movement.

Ironically, after his abject surrender to the British, his supporters hailed him with the honorific title 'Swatantra Veer', the brave warrior of freedom. In one of his several pleas for mercy, Savarkar wrote: 'I hereby acknowledge that I had a fair trial and just sentence. I heartily abhor the methods of violence resorted to in days gone by and I feel myself duty bound to uphold law and constitution (added by the British) to the best of my powers and am willing to make the "reforms" (initiated by the colonialist British) a success in so far as I may be allowed to do so in future.' This is a verbatim excerpt from a facsimile of Savarkar's several apology letters to the British authorities. After his acceptance of the government's terms for his release, he was brought to the mainland and kept in confinement in Ratnagiri. He was forbidden from attending any public or private political activity. Publishers had to guarantee that his manuscripts did not contain any political message or any anti-British comment before publishing them. In return, the British provided him with a comfortable bungalow and a pension which continued till Independence in the picturesque seaside town of Ratnagiri in western Maharashtra, where he stayed till 1937 when he was released by the provincial Congress government.

During one of his journeys to emancipate Harijans in the Konkan, Gandhi expressed a desire to visit Ratnagiri to meet Savarkar, but the colonial administration refused permission. Gandhi sent Kasturba instead. On her return from the visit, Ba confessed that she did not like either the man or the people who surrounded him; she felt that they had a menacing, evil aura about them. It was in Ratnagiri that Nathuram Godse came under the spell of Savarkar. The seeds of Gandhi's murder were sown there.

Amidst his loyal inner circle, Savarkar kept playing the hate Gandhi card, accusing Gandhi and the Congress of Muslim appeasement and criticizing the Satyagraha movement. Thus, amongst the fanatics that comprised Savarkar's inner circle, some of whom commanded units of extremist Hindu commandos, the message was loud and clear: 'If you want to establish a Hindu Rashtra, get rid of Gandhi and subvert the Congress and their Satyagraha.' It was after 1934 that the numerous attempts on Gandhi's life occurred, all in some way or the other associated with Poona and a group of Brahmins of Poona, particularly Apte and Nathuram Godse, both fanatic Savarkarites.

Till two days before Gandhi was murdered, Godse and Apte lacked one of the most vital necessities to carry out the murder—a reliable firearm. It was provided to them by Dr Dattatreya S. Parchure of Gwalior, another fanatic Savarkar loyalist. It was Savarkar who pointed them in the direction of Gwalior and Dr Parchure.

◆

Parchure was born into a family of Brahmin teachers. Originally from Poona, the family had moved to the princely state of Gwalior. Dattatreya did his schooling and graduation from Poona and after a medical degree from Bombay University, he settled in Gwalior. Although a qualified allopathy doctor, he practised ayurveda and homoeopathy from a dispensary in the Patankar Bazaar locality of Gwalior. His main activity was as the extremist leader of the local Hindu Mahasabha and as the self-styled dictator of the Hindu Rashtra Sena, which he established on orders from his idol Savarkar. They were very active during Partition in attacking, looting and murdering fleeing Muslims. The forty-seven-year-old doctor was a colourful character. His skeletal face sported flowing hair that cascaded on to wiry shoulders, and a long flowing beard that hung to his chest. Dull black eyes peered at faces from behind thick glasses that made his eyes look disproportionately magnified; his intense stare intimidated people subjected to its scrutiny.

Parchure had built up the Mahasabha and his Hindu Rashtra Sena to make the former a formidable political force in Gwalior politics and the latter a means to terrorize and subjugate opponents. He enjoyed the patronage of the ruler of Gwalior, who turned a blind eye towards their acts of fanaticism and terror. Madanlal Pahwa, who had also started his quest for revenge from Gwalior, had, on several occasions, partnered with Parchure's Sena in attacking and murdering fleeing Muslims.

Parchure was a quite a braggart. He liked to impress people with highly exaggerated accounts of his exploits, many of which he had just heard about! As soon as word of Gandhi's murder reached Gwalior, Parchure publicly claimed to have been involved in the plot, saying that he had armed the murderer and that the murderer was one of 'them'. He was arrested when reports of his public boasting and celebrations after Gandhi's murder were reported to the newly formed provincial government of the Congress.

Parchure had previously interacted with Godse often as an office bearer of the Mahasabha and as a fanatic Savarkar loyalist. In November 1947, they had attended a Hindu Mahasabha–RSS summit in Alwar as well as a secret training camp to train in the use of handguns and other firearms. At one time, they had been on the verge of merging Godse's Hindu Rashtra Dal and Parchure's Hindu Rashtra Sena; the negotiations had ended in acrimony and bitterness when the two fought over the issue of the leadership of the unified entity. But at a time when failure threatened the credibility of Nathuram Godse and Narayan Apte, they heeded the advice of their idol Savarkar and approached Parchure for help in procuring a reliable firearm, and due to his loyalty to Savarkar, Parchure obliged.

In January 1948, Parchure was a bitter and angry man. At the time of Independence, it had been known that the days of the princely states were numbered. In Gwalior, there were two contenders for democratic administration, the Congress and the Hindu Mahasabha. The Mahasabha leadership had assumed that they would be invited to form the government by King Jiyajirao Scindia, but for reasons best known to the ruler and his equation with the Union government, Scindia invited the Congress to form the government. Parchure, who, as the leader of the Mahasabha, had dreamt of becoming the chief minister of Gwalior, was left out in the cold. When Godse confided in him about their intention to kill Gandhi, Parchure found a release for his hatred. It was also alleged that Parchure had received ₹60,000 from the king of Gwalior; Parchure claimed that it was to fund agitations to destabilize the Congress government and Nathuram claimed that it was to fund Gandhi's murder as was promised by the princes at the secret meeting in Alwar, and they fought over this issue too. But it was Parchure who provided the murder weapon to Nathuram just two days before he fired three bullets from it point blank at Gandhi, killing him instantly.

The last member of the gang who murdered Gandhi was another fanatic follower of Savarkar and a fanatic hero-worshipping younger brother of Nathuram Godse, Gopal Godse. Gopal was twenty-seven years old at the time of the murder. Unlike his brother Nathuram, he was married and was the father of two daughters. Gopal hero-worshipped his elder brother and had followed in his footsteps since childhood. After completing his matriculation, he joined the Military Ordinance Service as a civilian clerk. At the outbreak of the Second World War, he volunteered for overseas service. In 1941, he was sent abroad along with the British Column to Iran and Iraq. He served with the Persia and Iraq Force for the next three years and returned to India at the end of the War in April 1944. After being demobilized, he went back to his old job, and was promoted to the post of assistant storekeeper in the Ordinance Depot at Kirkee on the outskirts of Poona. But one rather unusual action by this person of very regular habits and a stickler for rules confirms that he was a part of the conspiracy hatched by his elder brother since a long time. While being demobilized from the Wartime commission, Gopal did not surrender his military issue .38 Webley Scott revolver. The meek and obedient Gopal would not have done this unless someone he trusted and respected had asked him to do so. Not wanting to keep the now-illegal weapon with him, Gopal made a trip to their ancestral home in Uksan and buried the gun, wrapped in an oil skin, under a guava tree in the courtyard, to be retrieved for future use when ordered by his elder brother.

Gopal lived with his family in a small two-room apartment he had rented behind the bazaar in Kirkee. At work, he was meek, but when summoned by his elder brother, he was ready to do anything. In January 1948, he agreed to go to Uksan to fetch the revolver for the Apte–Nathuram gang. He dug up the Webley Scott from its shallow hiding place and carried it to Delhi, making him an accomplice in the bomb attack on Gandhi on 20 January. After that failed attempt, Gopal developed cold feet and returned to Poona and resumed duty at work. On hearing that his elder brother, Apte and Karkare were regrouping, Gopal made a trip to Thane and delivered a gun to his brother Nathuram, after which he severed all contact with the gang and returned home.

Speaking to author Manohar Mulgaonkar after his release from prison, Gopal gave a very theatrical account of his commitment to the Apte–Godse gang and their goal to murder Gandhi. 'After seeing Badge and Shankar running away without accomplishing the task of murdering the Mahatma on 20 January, the first thought that crossed my mind was to escape. But when I reached the taxi, I found that the driver was not at the wheel. When I opened the rear door I found the guns hidden by Badge on the back seat.

'I was filled with uncontrollable rage. I decided that this was my chance to complete the task we had planned. I picked up the gun and rushed back to the servant's quarters. I entered Choturam's room and bolted the door from inside. It was then that I realized that the window covered by the lattice work grill was too high. I pulled a cot under the grill and climbed on it. I pulled out my .38 Webley Scott service revolver and prepared to shoot Gandhiji. But even after climbing on top of the bed and standing on the tips of my toes with my hands stretched overhead, I was barely able to reach the bottom edge of the grill. There was no way I could have aimed the gun and shot at Gandhiji through the grill. I pulled myself up to the grill but to do this I needed both my hands and realized that I could not fire the gun in that position. Gandhiji was still addressing the assembled audience. Finally, I gave up the attempt. When I tried to open the door, I forgot that I had bolted it and kept trying to push it open, but the door would not budge. I could hear loud voices from the prayer ground and from the courtyard of the servant's quarters. I was terrified and thought that this was it. I broke into a cold sweat. Then, I felt new energy and superhuman strength coursing through my limbs. I aimed a kick at the door, at the second kick the door flew open and I was free. Gathering my wits, I calmly walked up to the taxi and got in.'

This story is very farfetched. That this foolhardy antic of Gopal went unnoticed is not likely. Immediately after the bomb explosion, the servants, some people attending the prayer meeting and the police constables had all rushed to the spot and arrested Madanlal. The eyewitnesses who had pointed out Madanlal as the bomber were standing in the courtyard of the servants' quarters. A woman, Sulochana Devi, who had seen the taxi arrive and the gang members alighting from it, had also seen them talking to Madanlal. All this was happening in very close proximity to where Gopal claims to have attempted to murder Gandhi. If nobody noticed him going into the room, they would have definitely heard the banging on the door, it crashing open and a stranger emerging from the servant Choturam's quarter. This clearly was a figment of Gopal's imagination.

◆

Till two days before he murdered Gandhi, Nathuram Godse did not possess a reliable firearm to conduct his deed. Once again, his plan was in danger of flopping. But on the advice of his patron Savarkar, and with the help of Parchure, Nathuram acquired one of the most popular European close range killer guns of that time, the 9 mm Beretta semi-automatic pistol, the Fascist Special.

The 9 mm Beretta semi-automatic, serial number 606824, was in excellent working order, almost brand new. It was the perfect weapon for the murder. It had travelled an improbable route, traversing three continents, to reach Birla House on 30 January 1948. Specially manufactured in Italy in 1934 for the fascist officers of Mussolini's army, the gun was carried by an officer of Mussolini's invading army into Abyssinia. When Mussolini's army was defeated in Abyssinia and surrendered to the British forces, the Beretta was taken from its owner as a trophy of victory by the commanding officer of the 4th Gwalior Infantry, Lt Col V.V. Joshi. He carried it home to Gwalior.

On his return, Joshi served as a military Aide De Camp to Maharaja Jiyajirao Scindia of Gwalior. How it came into the possession of Jagdishprasad Goel, a trader in the illegal weapons market in Gwalior, is a mystery which has remained unresolved. Did Joshi sell it to a gunrunner? Why would Joshi sell a gun which he had taken as a souvenir of a famous victory in battle? He was working for the ruler; he could not have been hard-pressed for money. How Goel got hold of it has remained an unanswered mystery. Goel sold the gun to Dandavate, an associate of Parchure who purchased it on behalf of Nathuram Godse on Parchure's order. Dandavate gave the fully loaded gun and seven additional rounds of ammunition to Nathuram on the evening of 28 January at Parchure's home, just two days before Nathuram used it to murder Gandhi.

On 30 January 1948, at 5:17 p.m., the Fascist Special was fired for the last time by Nathuram Vinayak Godse. Three 9 mm bullets emerged out of its short barrel in quick succession and hit Gandhi, traversing a distance of less than two-and-a-half feet. After the murder, the gun was fired twice by forensic investigators to match the bullets recovered from the murder site. Till today, the gun remains locked up in a sealed steel cabinet at the National Gandhi Museum opposite Raj Ghat in Delhi.

◆

Three more people were listed as accused in the Gandhi murder case: Gangadhar Sukhram Dandavate, Gangadhar Jadhav and Suryadev Sharma, all three from Gwalior, but the police was not able to capture them till the very end of the Red Fort trial. These three fugitives had a very minor role in the conspiracy, largely of being witnesses to the purchase transaction of the murder weapon in Gwalior and witness to Parchure's public claims in Gwalior about his involvement in the Gandhi murder. The police had established a very sound case against all the accused and, according to them, the three absconders did not really matter. The three were arrested sometime towards the end of the trial but the government did not prosecute them, which was very strange in a case involving the murder of the Father of the Nation. This part of the investigation was left incomplete and no wonder, since they were conducted in Gwalior by the bungling U.H. Rana. How the murder weapon travelled from the Gwalior Palace to the hands of a black market weapon's dealer and then ended up in the hands of Gandhi's murderer Nathuram was never investigated. Could it have been because the gun had been acquired through the involvement of Savarkar and investigating it would have implicated Savarkar in Gandhi's murder? We will never know.

III

THE PLOT

Murder consists in making others suffer unto death, so that a murderer, or those others for whom he murders, may benefit.

—M.K. Gandhi,
21 May 1925

For all his harebrained schemes, Apte used to purchase weapons from Badge. In July 1947, Apte visited Shastra Bhandar, accompanied by Karkare. Apte told Badge that he wanted a STEN gun for some influential clients. Badge jumped into their car and told them to drive towards Yerawada Central Jail, picking up a Sikh former soldier, Gurdayal Singh, on the way. Parking the car behind the jail, Gurdayal got out and returned a few minutes later, holding a packet containing a gleaming STEN gun. Till then Apte had always scoffed at Badge, but the ease with which Badge had produced the gun established his credentials with Apte. After dropping off Gurdayal Singh, they returned to Shastra Bhandar, where Badge asked for ₹1,200 for the STEN gun and, flush with funds from his financiers, Apte paid him the amount and purchased the gun. Very soon, Apte realized that neither he nor any member of his commando unit could even hold the gun properly, let alone load, aim and fire it. They realized that they would need a lot of ammunition to train people, but they had none. Just like the mortars and flame thrower scheme, the STEN gun was yet another one of Apte's follies.

In November 1947, Narayan Apte again asked Badge for arms and ammunitions. Looking at the list, Badge stated that he did not have the weapons right then but would arrange for them soon. A few days later, Badge informed Apte that his order was ready. In the last week of

December, Apte went to the Shastra Bhandar to ask Badge if the weapons that he had listed were available. On being told that they were, Apte told Badge that their mutual acquaintance, Vishnu Karkare, would collect them in a couple of days. It was only in the second week of January 1948, however, that Apte sent Karkare to the Shastra Bhandar.

The events that followed from that day, from 9 to 30 January 1948 would reshape the future of the newly independent nation.

Friday, 9 January 1948

In Poona, Apte told Badge that Karkare and his companions would inspect and take delivery of the arms and explosives.

At about 8:30 p.m., three people including Karkare came to Shastra Bhandar. One of them was Madanlal Pahwa, who, after inspecting the cache, told the others that he knew how to handle the explosives. After inspecting the weapons and explosives, they left, asking Badge to hold on to them.

Saturday, 10 January 1948

In Poona, Apte went to Shastra Bhandar, and at about 10:00 a.m. he took Badge to the *Hindu Rashtra* office. There, in the presence of Nathuram, Apte asked Badge to supply them with two revolvers, two gun cotton slabs with primers and fuses and five hand grenades. Badge said he did not have revolvers but could immediately supply the gun cotton slabs and hand grenades. It was agreed that Badge would try and get the revolvers and deliver everything to the Hindu Mahasabha office at Dadar in Bombay, on the evening of 14 January.

Sunday, 11 January 1948

In Bombay, Madanlal Pahwa and Vishnu Karkare visited the residence of Prof. J. C. Jain. Madanlal knew Jain since the time he used to live as a refugee in the Chembur refugee camp in northeast Bombay. After spending a few minutes catching up with each other, Madanlal told Jain that he was going to leave for Delhi soon on an important mission.

Without elaborating, they left, and Madanlal promised to meet the professor before leaving for Delhi.

Monday, 12 January 1948

In Delhi, Gandhi had a meeting over tea with the Governor-General of independent India and its last viceroy, Lord Louis Mountbatten. The latter was very worried about the deteriorating communal situation in the whole of north and west India. As more and more refugees from West Punjab poured into Delhi and its outskirts, the government was finding it increasingly difficult to meet the demands for housing, warm clothing, food and potable water.

Muslims, driven out of their homes, had taken refuge in overflowing refugee camps in Chandni Chowk and Jama Masjid areas, compounding the crisis. Hindu and Sikh refugees were demanding that the homes vacated by the Muslims should be given to them. Persons left behind to guard the homes of fleeing Muslims were either driven out or killed by Hindu and Sikh refugees and their homes forcibly occupied. Mosques were captured, idols of Hindu deities were installed in them and declared to be 'liberated' Hindu temples. This is an old Hindu Mahasabha–RSS tactic which is still in use; even in the recent communal riots in Delhi in 2020, these tactics of 'liberating' mosques was utilized. The situation in Delhi was becoming more volatile by the telling of highly exaggerated and many a times completely fabricated stories of the atrocities committed in the newly formed West Pakistan.

The RSS and Hindu Mahasabha, both of whom had done nothing to prevent Partition, now swung into action to spread exaggerated and fabricated stories of torture, rape, abduction, murder and forcible conversion of Hindus in Pakistan. Not that such reprehensible incidents did not happen: Partition saw some of the most brutal atrocities committed on both sides of the new border by whichever community that was a majority there. The Muslim League was equally active in spreading hatred and igniting passions. Ever since 'Direct Action Day' called by Jinnah on 15 August 1946, the chain of violence and brutality continued to intensify at every subsequent instance.

Mountbatten was worried. He knew that if Delhi was to go up

in flames, India would be lost. He had witnessed Gandhi, whom he affectionately called 'little sparrow' and admiringly referred to as his 'One-Man Boundary Force', perform a miracle in Calcutta and East Bengal. He hoped that Gandhi would repeat the miracle to save Delhi and, as a consequence, India. To achieve this objective, he had decided to recruit Gandhi's services at this meeting. However, another problem had cropped up. Under the terms of partition, India and Pakistan were to receive a proportional share of the cash balance of undivided India. Of the cash balance of ₹3,750 million, ₹200 million was paid to Pakistan on the day of the transfer of power on 14 August 1947. After hectic negotiations by the Partition Committee, of which both Nehru and Patel were members, it was agreed that Pakistan would be paid a further ₹550 million; this was ratified by a treaty signed by Nehru and Patel with their Pakistani counterparts, a bilateral agreement between two independent nations. Now Pakistan, on the verge of bankruptcy, was demanding the balance payment. The public sentiment was against this. Patel and Nehru felt that the payment should be withheld till all the issues arising between India and Pakistan were resolved, including Pakistan's invasion of Kashmir. One populist thought was that the money not be paid at all and be used instead to resettle refugees.

Refusal to part with the balance amount was unethical and illegal. It would have also branded India an untrustworthy nation which did not honour its treaties and commitments. If Pakistan dragged India to an adjudicator, India would be sure to lose. Mountbatten was India's Governor-General, but he was a representative of the British Crown; as the head of the government, he would be party to any act by the Indian government. He did not want to be responsible for this deceit.

At the meeting with Gandhi, Mountbatten started by discussing the deteriorating communal situation in the capital and his fears of the situation deteriorating into a civil war. Gandhi had realized that he would have to offer himself as a sacrifice if he wished to save his fledgling nation. Since it was his day of silence, Gandhi wrote his replies to Mountbatten. He assured Mountbatten that he would do something to avert the disaster. As Gandhi rose to leave, Mountbatten voiced his concern over the issue of withholding the promised payment to Pakistan. Gandhi listened to what Mountbatten had to say about India's stand and its legal unsustainability and immorality. He shook his head in displeasure and left without commenting.

That evening, at his prayer meeting, Gandhi's message was read out to the gathering. He dwelt on his concerns over the situation in the capital and the plight of the refugees. He sympathized with the homeless refugees and reiterated that it was the duty of the government to provide them housing. Muslim homes were being forcibly occupied; mosques were also being occupied and Hindu idols were being installed in them. He feared that this would harm Hinduism. This was not the way he wanted his countrymen and co-religionists to behave, he said, and declared that he would be starting a fast unto death from the next day at noon.

◆

In Poona, the news of Gandhi's decision to fast was heard on the radio news bulletin by two men sitting in the office of *Hindu Rashtra* in Shaniwar Peth, a cramped and crowded locality of old Poona—the editor and publisher of *Hindu Rashtra,* Nathuram Godse and Narayan Apte. The two Savarkarite hotheads, affiliated to both the RSS and Hindu Mahasabha, decided that Gandhi's interference in the working of the Government of India was the perfect excuse to murder him. If this man was not killed now, they decided, he would do irreparable damage to the establishment of the Hindu Rashtra of their dreams and as visualized by their leader Savarkar. Apte looked at Nathuram and said, 'This is a good excuse for murdering Gandhi. The atmosphere is conducive and since we have Tatyarao's blessings, we are assured of getting financial backing and support. Our people are everywhere and ready, we have widespread support, this time we will definitely succeed.' Nathuram looked up at Apte, his eyes reflecting no emotion, and said, 'We must kill Gandhi this time! I had accepted the task in Alwar, now we must deliver on the promise.' They had tried earlier on several occasions and failed—this time they would not. This time they had support. It had been decided at the secret meeting at Alwar that the signal for the coup d'état, to overthrow the government and establish a Hindu Rashtra, was to be Gandhi's murder. Nathuram had accepted the responsibility of murdering Gandhi, in the presence of his leaders. The time had come to make good that promise.

Tuesday, 13 January 1948

At Birla House in Delhi, Gandhi started his fast at 11:55 a.m. with the singing of '*Vaishnava jana to tene kahiye*' (Call him a true man of God who...). He was surrounded by members of his entourage and the Birla family.

This was the first time in the long history of his fasts that Gandhi did not insist on his close aides leaving to take up their predetermined responsibilities. It was as if he knew that a crisis would occur when he would require the presence of those he could trust. Nehru and Patel were not going to insist on him abandoning the fast. Sardar Patel was upset with Gandhi's decision and Nehru was reluctant to take the lead in trying to help meet Gandhi's conditions for ending the fast.

When a Sikh friend asked Gandhi to name the one who was responsible for making him fast, Gandhi answered he blamed no individual or community in particular, but he did feel that if the Hindus and Sikhs insisted on turning out the Muslims from Delhi, they would be betraying India and their own faith. His was an 'all-inclusive fast', directed against nobody in particular and yet addressed to the conscience of all. 'If all groups or even one of them responds fully,' he said, 'I know the miracle will be achieved.'

Sheikh Abdullah, the prime minister of Kashmir, was visiting Delhi with his deputy, Bakshi Ghulam Mohammed. They requested Gandhi to end his fast 'for the sake of Kashmir. Kashmir needs you now more than ever', they appealed. Gandhi told them that his fast was intended to cover Kashmir too. Maulana Azad, a friend and associate, intervened and said, 'Even if we are to dash our heads against a stone wall, his resolve, once taken, won't be given up. To argue further with him is only to prolong his agony. The only thing for us to do is to begin thinking what we can do to fulfil his conditions which alone will induce him to give up his fast.'

On the day Gandhi started his fast, Lord and Lady Mountbatten were hosting a reception at Government House. Some members of Gandhi's retinue were also invited. They were unsure whether to go, but Gandhi convinced them otherwise. 'Mountbatten will probably want to discuss the fast with you,' he told Pyarelal. 'It would be worthwhile getting his reaction first-hand. In any case, you will be able to report to me whether any alcoholic drinks were served at the function!'

On meeting Pyarelal at the function, Mountbatten immediately said, 'I have only one criticism to make: he should have discussed it first with Pandit Nehru.' During the evening, shocking news came from Pakistan: that a train carrying Hindu and Sikh refugees from the North-West Frontier Province had been attacked and looted at the Gujrat railway station in West Punjab. A number of passengers and the entire company of Indian soldiers guarding the train were massacred and some women were abducted. Referring to this incident, Mountbatten remarked, 'It makes Mr Gandhi's task more difficult. But his victory will be all the greater for it.' When Pyarelal reported the conversation, Gandhi said, 'Have I not often said that one must be a great warrior to fully appreciate the power that is non-violence?' Quoting the Gujarati poet Pritam he said, '*Harino marag che shoorano, nahin kaayarnu kaam jo.*' (The path of the Lord is for the brave, not for cowards.)

At the evening prayers, he declared that he would break his fast only when conditions in Delhi permitted the withdrawal of the military and the police without any danger to peace.

◆

In Poona, Nathuram Godse made changes to his life insurance policies. He nominated Champa Apte, Narayan Apte's wife, as the beneficiary on a policy of ₹2,000. Apte signed it as a witness.

Wednesday, 14 January 1948

In Delhi, as in other parts of the country, the festival of Makar Sankranti, falling on the winter solstice, was being celebrated. In Maharashtra, people exchanged sweets made from Gud (jaggery) and Til (sesame seeds), and wished each other '*Tilgul ghya ani goad goad bola*!' (Have this sweet made of jaggery and sesame, and say sweet things!) Prema Kantak, a Congress socialist from Maharastra, sent some homemade Tilgul to Gandhi on the second day of his fast, who distributed it amongst the people present at Birla House. Gandhi was being criticized for his fast which the critics claimed to be partial towards Muslims. He answered that in a way they were right. All his life he had stood up for the rights of minorities. But his fast was against the Muslims too, in the sense that it should enable them to stand up to their Hindu and Sikh brethren and demand their safety and well-being from their co-religionists in Pakistan. To some maulanas from Delhi, who, a few days back, had said that they should be given a safe passage to England, he said, 'I had no answer to give you then. I can now face you. Shall I ask the government to arrange a passage for you to England? I shall say to them: "Here are the unfaithful Muslims who want to desert India. Give them the facility they want."' The maulana apologized and Gandhi retorted, 'That is like the Englishman, who kicks you and at the same time says "I beg your pardon!"' On a more serious note, he added, 'Do you not feel ashamed asking to be sent to England? And then you said that slavery under British rule was better than independence under the Union of India. How dare you, who claim to be patriots and nationalists, utter such words? You have to cleanse your hearts and learn to be cent per cent truthful. Otherwise India will not tolerate you for long, and even I shall not be able to help you.' In times of crises, Gandhi preferred to be brutally honest.

The Union Cabinet met outside Gandhi's room at Birla House that afternoon and decided to reconsider their decision to withhold payment of the balance amount of ₹550 million to Pakistan. This angered certain sections of Indian society. Gandhi's fast provided a convenient foil for the government to deflect people's ire away from them and towards Gandhi.

During that evening's prayer meeting, Gandhi spoke about the massacre of refugees at Gujrat in West Punjab, and of Hindus and Sikhs in Karachi. 'How long can the Union put up with such things? How long can I bank upon the patience of the Hindus and Sikhs in spite of my fast? Pakistan has to put a stop to this state of affairs. They must pledge themselves that they will not rest till the Hindus and Sikhs return and live in safety in Pakistan. Pakistan will only then become *Pak* (pure) ... Then and only then shall I repent that I ever called it a sin, as I am afraid I must hold today, it is. I want to live to see the Pakistan not on paper, not in the oration of Pakistani orators, but reflected in the daily life of every Pakistani Muslim. Then the inhabitants of the Union will forget that there ever was any enmity between them and the Union will proudly copy Pakistan and if I am alive I shall ask her to excel Pakistan in well-doing. This fast is a bid for nothing less. Then we shall have real *Swaraj*. Then though legally and geographically we may still be two states, in daily life no one will think that we are separate. I remember to have read ... in the Delhi Fort ... when I visited it in 1896, a verse on one of the gates which when translated reads: "If there is paradise on earth, it is here, it is here." I would love to see that verse with justice inscribed on the gates of Pakistan.'

Ever since the Calcutta killings of August 1946, Gandhi had been telling Muslims who had remained in India that if they continued to sit on the fence instead of courageously denouncing the excesses of their co-religionists, even at the risk of their lives, or if they harboured secret sympathy with the perpetrators of those excesses, it would bring down upon them the wrath of those with whom—Pakistan or no Pakistan—the bulk of them must live. At the commencement of his fast, he told a group of maulanas who came to request him to reverse his decision that if happenings like the recent massacre of the Hindu and Sikh refugees on the train, continued unchecked, 'Even ten Gandhis will not be able to save Indian Muslims!'

Late that evening, some Sikh refugees from West Punjab held a demonstration outside Birla House. They were angry that Gandhi was demanding that they vacate the homes they had captured by driving out Muslim inhabitants. They shouted in anger, '*Khoon ka badla khoon se lenge!*' (Blood will be avenged with blood, an eye for an eye!), '*Marta hai to marne do, hame ghar do!*' (If he is dying, let him die, give us homes!) and '*Gandhi ko marne do!*' (Let Gandhi die!) Nehru, while leaving Birla House after a meeting, heard the slogans and jumped out of his car. Trembling with rage, he rushed at the demonstrators shouting, 'Who dares to shout "Let Gandhi die!"? Let him who dares, repeat those words in my presence. He will have to kill me first!' The demonstrators dispersed in the face of Nehru's ire.

Inside his darkened room, Gandhi asked, 'What are they shouting?'

'They are shouting "Let Gandhi die!"'

'How many are they?'

'Not many, Bapu.'

Gandhi sighed and, as was his habit since childhood, started chanting, Ram Nama. Very soon, he was fast asleep.

♦

In Poona, Nathuram made changes to his second life insurance policy. He nominated Sindhu Godse, younger brother Gopal Godse's wife, as the beneficiary to a policy of ₹3,000. Apte signed this one too as a witness.

That afternoon, Apte and Godse left for Bombay by the Deccan Express. The train left Poona at 4:30 p.m. They were seated in the second-class compartment. Badge, disguised as a sadhu, accompanied by his servant Shankar Kistayya and carrying the explosives and detonators, travelled by the same train, sitting in the crowded unreserved general coach.

Apte saw an attractive lady looking for a window seat walking towards them. He chivalrously offered her his seat and shifted to the one opposite her, next to Nathuram. The young lady was Shanta Modak, a Marathi film and stage actress popularly known as 'Bimba'. Narayan was in his elements, he chatted with her throughout the four-hour trip to Bombay. Nathuram maintained a stony silence.

Narayan mentioned that they were going to alight at Dadar and go to a place in Shivaji Park. Shanta replied that she was also alighting at Dadar and going to Shivaji Park. Apte offered to drop Shanta. Shanta had arranged for her brother to pick her up at Dadar Station, so she offered Apte and Godse a lift, in her brother's Jeep. On learning that they were going to Savarkar Sadan, V.D. Savarkar's home, Shanta told them that her home was down the road.

Badge and Shankar Kistayya alighted at Dadar and proceeded straight to the Hindu Mahasabha office to deliver the goods, while Apte and Godse drove down to Savarkar Sadan with Shanta and her brother, where Apte waved goodbye to Shanta. After they drove off, Godse and Apte entered the home of their mentor and patron. After a while, they left and proceeded to the Hindu Mahasabha office. There they met Badge and Kistayya on the stairs. All of them then proceeded back to Savarkar Sadan with the explosives. Badge was carrying the bag containing the explosives and detonators. Apte and Godse went in with the bag of explosives. They came out after a few minutes, still carrying the bag; Savarkar had approved of their cache of weapons but refused to keep them in his home. All of them got into a taxi and proceeded to Dixit Maharaj's home in Bhuleshwar next to Mota Mandir, an old business district in south-central Bombay.

Dixit Maharaj's real name was Mahant Shrikrishna Jeevanji Maharaj. He was the younger brother of Dada Maharaj, the Mahant or head priest of the Mota Mandir.

When they reached his home, Dixit Maharaj was asleep, so Apte gave the bag of explosives to a servant, telling him to keep it in a secure place. They wanted to show the 'goods' to Dixit Maharaj the next day and then they would take the bag.

The four then drove to the Hindu Mahasabha office. Apte gave Badge ₹50 towards travel expenses and asked Badge and Kistayya to stay at the Hindu Mahasabha office premises. Apte was eager to get rid of the two so he could keep his date with his beloved, Manorama.

Apte and Godse had checked into the Sea Green South Hotel on Marine Drive, on the fringe of the business and government district of Bombay, along one of its famous promenades. Apte would occupy a room with his beloved and Nathuram would occupy another.

When Badge and Kistayya entered the Hindu Mahasabha office, they saw Madanlal Pahwa there. After greeting each other, Badge enquired about Karkare. Pahwa told him that Karkara Seth was visiting a friend in Thana, a town and district headquarter near Bombay, and would be back either late that night or the next morning.

Pahwa had visited Prof. Jain that afternoon and told him about the work he and his group had done in Ahmednagar. At this point Angad Singh, a friend who was visiting Prof. Jain, got up to leave and Pahwa went on to boast that he was part of a gang who were going to Delhi on an important mission. On being coaxed, he said that their mission was to 'deal' with a very important leader for which they had procured bombs and weapons. He said that Karkara Seth, who had accompanied Pahwa on his previous visit, was the financier. Pahwa claimed that he was entrusted the job of exploding a bomb at Gandhi's prayer meeting to create confusion and panic. Taking advantage of the ensuing chaos, the rest of the group would 'overpower' Gandhi. Pahwa told Jain that they were doing this on the orders of Savarkar, that Savarkar had personally commended him for his work in Ahmednagar and told him to associate with the group and its mission. Jain did not take Pahwa seriously as he believed Madanlal was just a hothead and braggart.

Thusday, 15 January 1948

At Birla House, on the third day of his fast, Gandhi's condition was deteriorating. He was weak and had to be carried to the bathroom. A medical bulletin issued by three physicians attending on him, Drs B.C. Roy, Jivraj Mehta and M.D.D. Gilder, who had examined him individually, stated: 'Gandhiji is naturally losing weight, weakness has increased, his voice is feeble. Acetone bodies have appeared in his urine.' This implied that the disintegration of the body tissue as a result of starvation had begun to fill his blood with toxins, and his kidneys were not being able to flush the toxins out efficiently. In short, his kidneys were failing.

But Gandhi's spirit was still lively. In a letter to Miraben, Gandhi joked: 'I am taking my meal such as a fasting man with prescribed food can take. Don't be shocked. The food consists of eight ounces of hot water sipped with difficulty. You sip it as poison, well knowing that in result it is nectar. It revives me whenever I take it. Strange to say, this time I am able to take about eight meals of this poison-tasting but nectar-like meal. Yet I claim to be fasting and credulous people accept it! What a strange world!'

He was unable to walk to the prayer ground that evening, so a microphone was hooked up in his room by his bedside. Gandhi's voice was barely audible as he spoke to the people gathered there to hear his daily evening speech. His cot was placed on the veranda from where he could be seen by the people gathered outside. He lay on his side, covered by a white woollen shawl, his hands folded, his face sad, pensive and serene at the same time. When the people saw him, they realized that they would have to act fast. Deputations of Hindus, Muslims and Sikhs and others assured him that they would live in peace and harmony; a deputation of refugees from the Frontier Provinces assured him that, in spite of having suffered immensely, they would not retaliate, not seek revenge.

Addressing a rally of more than 10,000 Hindu, Sikh and Muslim refugees, Nehru said, 'The loss of Mahatma Gandhi's life would mean the loss of India's soul, because he is the embodiment of India's spiritual power... Like a prophet, he has realized that communal fighting, if not checked immediately, would bring about the end of freedom.'

In many of his prayer meetings after the carnage that followed the Muslim League's Direct Action Day on 14 August 1946, Gandhi had held the Muslim League responsible for spreading hatred and igniting communal passions in both parts of India. Shuaib Qureshi, a close friend of his, protested that this criticism was unjustified, but Gandhi felt that in these trying times, he must not sugarcoat the issue for diplomatic niceties. He told Qureshi that he was unrepentant about blaming the Muslim League for the present state of affairs. 'I cannot in all honesty absolve it. Nor must I in this crisis, mince words or keep back things which might displease. Those who cannot appreciate this side of my nature cannot associate themselves with the prayer for the successful termination of my fast. It is the privilege of friendship to speak nothing but the truth even though it might sound unpleasant to the ear.'

On the third morning of Gandhi's fast, the Government of India, in a communiqué, announced that it had decided to immediately pay Pakistan the balance sum of ₹550 million. 'The Government has shared the worldwide anxiety over the fast undertaken by ... the Father of the Nation. In common with him they have anxiously searched for ways and means to bury the hatchet of ill will, prejudice and suspicion, which has poisoned the relations of India and Pakistan. Impelled by the earnest desire to help in every way open to them in the objective which Gandhiji has at heart, the Government has sought for some tangible and striking contribution to the movement for ending the physical suffering of the Nation's soul and to turn the Nation's mind from the present distemper, bitterness and suspicion to constructive and creative effort. The Government is anxious to remove as far as possible, without detriment to the national good, every cause which leads to friction between India and Pakistan...'

Gandhi's fast had also come on the eve of the crucial meeting of the United Nations (UN) Security Council which was to discuss the Kashmir issue. He was asked if his fast would not have the effect of overshadowing the refugee train massacre and the Karachi riots in which a large number of Sikhs and Hindus had been killed. The representatives of Pakistan would not be worth their reputation if they did not seize the opportunity with both hands to prejudice India's case in the eyes of the UN. Gandhi answered that he was not in the habit of allowing himself to be deflected from the pursuit of truth by such considerations. His fast was intended to embrace and purify even the UN. 'For all I have known of the powers and people outside India, I make bold to say that the fast has created only a healthy impression. Outsiders who are able to take an impartial and unbiased view of what is happening in India cannot distort the purpose of the fast ... the United Nations know that my fast aids them to come to a right decision and to give the right guidance to the newly made two Dominions.'

◆

In Bombay, at about 9:20 a.m., Apte and Godse reserved two seats on the afternoon Air India flight to Delhi on 17 January under the assumed names D.N. Karmakar and S. Marathe. The Apte–Godse gang was not short of funds and the leaders stayed and travelled in comfort and luxury, unlike other members of the gang. After booking their flight tickets, they went to the Hindu Mahasabha office in Dadar and met Madanlal, Kistayya and Badge. Apte asked them to come with him; since Pahwa was not ready, he was left behind. The four proceeded to Shivaji Printing Press, where they met Karkare. The press belonged to G.M. Joshi of Thana, a family friend of Karkare and a Savarkar loyalist with whom he had stayed the previous night. Apte, Godse and Karkare went into Joshi's office cabin. The meeting's agenda was to seek funds from Joshi, and it lasted thirty minutes. The five then came back to the Hindu Mahasabha office. Karkare asked Pahwa to pick up his bedding and accompany him. Apte got a taxi and all of them, except Kistayya who was asked to remain at Hindu Mahasabha Bhavan, drove to Dixit Maharaj's home, in Bhuleshwar.

They were all ushered into the sleeping quarters where Dixit Maharaj was resting. The bag containing the explosives was called for. Badge showed the grenades and explosives to everybody and demonstrated the use of hand grenades. Dixit saw that Badge was making a mistake and demonstrated the proper method: '*Aise karoge toh khud bhi ud jaoge!*' (If you use it thus, you too will be blown up!) Apte handed the bag to Karkare and told him and Madanlal to proceed to New Delhi immediately, carrying the 'goods' with them.

Apte asked Dixit if he could provide two revolvers, Dixit replied that he did not have any just then but would try and get them. Apte, Godse and Badge then came out of Dixit's home and stood in the courtyard of the Mota Mandir. Apte asked Badge if he would accompany them to Delhi along with Kistayya: 'Tatyarao has decided that Gandhi, Nehru and the Muslim League leader from Bengal, Huseyn Shaheed Suhrawardy must be eliminated. He has entrusted the work to us. Will you join us and help us carry out Tatyarao's command?' Badge agreed to accompany them, but wanted Tatyarao's blessings in person.

The Apte–Godse gang had now recruited a shooter.

Badge wanted to return to Poona before leaving for Delhi, as he had unfinished business to attend to. Nathuram also wanted to visit Poona to meet his younger brother. Gopal was supposed to fetch a gun for him, and Nathuram wanted to make sure that he did. Apte, Godse and Badge then drove down to the Cotton Exchange Building near Pydhonie, an old trading district of south-central Bombay. Apte and Godse went in, leaving Badge outside. The Apte–Godse gang was raising funds from known sympathizers and financiers. Next, they proceeded to the Hindu Mahasabha office. Badge got off there; Apte told him to definitely meet them at the Victoria Terminus railway station on the morning of 17 January, they would wait for him in the concourse.

When Badge went to the Mahasabha office to pick up Kistayya and their luggage, he met Madanlal there, who told him that they had missed the Punjab Mail to Delhi that afternoon. Karkara Seth was organizing tickets for them to travel by another train to Delhi, departing later that evening. They eventually managed two third-class seats on the Peshawar Express, a train that used to run from Bombay to Peshawar in the North-West Frontier Province of undivided India. The train departed from Victoria Terminus at its scheduled time, 9:30 p.m.

Badge and Kistayya left for Poona by the Madras Mail, which left an hour later from the same station. Nathuram Godse had also left for Poona that evening.

Apte stayed back in Bombay. He wanted to spend a few days with his beloved Manorama. Apte told her that he was about to leave on a secret mission from which he may possibly not return. Manorama was shattered: the man whom she had trusted was abandoning her for some mysterious mission. Her family would be dishonoured and ostracized, she would have to face the shame of being an unwed mother all by herself; she was inconsolable.

Friday, 16 January 1948

In Delhi, Gandhi had reached a critical state. His vital signs were slowing down; doctors attending to him were worried about his failing kidney function. His weight, which had dropped by two pounds on the first two days of the fast, now remained steady at 107 pounds. Their worry was not about a sudden collapse but long-lasting and irreparable damage to his vital organs. But Gandhi was resolute. 'My sole guide, even dictator, is God, the infallible and omnipotent Ram Nama... If he has any further use of this frail body of mine, he will keep it, in spite of the forebodings of the medical men and women. I am in His hands. Therefore, I dread neither death nor permanent injury... But I do feel that the warning of the medical friends should, if the country has any use of me, hurry the people to close their ranks. Like the brave men and women that we ought to be under hard-won freedom, we should trust even those whom we may suspect to be our enemies. Brave people disdain distrust.'

Reacting to a suggestion that, since the government had agreed to pay the balance amount to Pakistan immediately, he should withdraw his fast, he said that the reasons for which he had started the fast remained unresolved. The killings and violence had not stopped. Much more needed to be done before he would even think of breaking his fast. 'The hearts have not changed, the hatred is still there.'

That evening, addressing the prayer congregation from his bed, Gandhi said that his vow would be satisfied if the Hindus, Muslims and Sikhs of Delhi achieved a union of hearts. 'The fittest answer to this fast should be a complete friendship between the two Dominions such that members of all communities should be able to go to either Dominion without the slightest fear of molestation... It will be wrong for the rest of the two Dominions to put too heavy a strain upon Delhi. Our government has taken a liberal step without counting the cost. What will be Pakistan's counter gesture? The ways are many if there is the will. Is it there?' he asked.

Sardar Patel, back in the capital, had to leave for Saurashtra on an important engagement that day, but was reluctant to do so. Gandhi insisted that he go, which led to the speculation that the home minister was leaving Delhi to show his displeasure with the decision of the government and the fast undertaken by Gandhi.

◆

Badge and Kishtayya arrived in Poona early in the morning. Badge took the last of his stock of weapons and handed them over for safe keeping to his regular customer and friend Ganpat S. Kharat. Badge had sold his property in his native village, Chalisgaon, near Jalgaon. He wanted to collect the money before leaving for Delhi.

Nathuram had also reached Poona. He went to Shastra Bhandar looking for Badge twice. On his return that evening from Chalisgaon, Badge went to the *Hindu Rashtra* office and met Nathuram, who took out a small calibre pistol and requested Badge to exchange it for a bigger and more effective handgun. Badge had recently sold a .32 calibre revolver to Sharma, a member of the Hyderabad State Congress, who agreed to exchange his gun for the small calibre gun and money. He gave Badge four cartridges along with the gun. The revolver was of .32 calibre, but the cartridges were of a smaller calibre, most probably meant for a magazine-loading gun. Badge was unaware of the mismatch.

At the Kirkee Arms Depot, Gopal Godse had put in a fresh application for casual leave from 17 to 23 January 1948; the leave was granted.

Gopal promised his brother that he would retrieve his military issue revolver from their ancestral home in Uksan. Nathuram gave Gopal ₹250 for the gun and for his journey to Delhi, and told him to meet him and Apte at the Delhi railway station on 18 January. Gopal assured his brother that he would retrieve the revolver from Uksan and reach Bombay on Saturday, in time to catch the Punjab Mail to Delhi that afternoon.

The gang was now armed and ready to strike.

Saturday, 17 January 1948

In Delhi, Hindu and Sikh refugees met Gandhi, followed by Nehru, who implored him to give up his fast since the situation in the capital was rapidly improving. Gandhi told them not to be in too great a hurry.

'Whatever you do should ring true. I want solid work.'

That day, Gandhi received a telegram from Karachi. Muslim refugees, who had been driven out of their homes from Delhi, wanted to know if they could now come back and reoccupy their homes. 'This is the test,' Gandhi said on reading the telegram. His representatives fanned out with copies of the telegram to every Hindu and Sikh refugee camp and explained to the people what they had to do to convince Gandhi to end his fast.

By evening, 10,000 refugees had signed a declaration that they would welcome the Muslims, even if they had to suffer Delhi's biting cold winter in ill-equipped refugee camps. They gave their full assurance to Gandhi that they would welcome the returning Muslims and would work for peace, goodwill and communal harmony. They pleaded with Gandhi to break his fast.

Their hope was further strengthened when the Delhi administration announced that within a week's time, every non-Muslim refugee in Delhi would be provided some kind of shelter. Nehru and some of his Cabinet colleagues threw open the gates of their official bungalows to refugees. Gandhi had suggested that the palatial bungalows vacated by the British and now occupied by Union ministers and bureaucrats be used to house refugees and that Government House, the former viceroy's palace, be converted into a hospital for refugees.

The maharaja of Patiala assured Gandhi that he had met all the Sikh leaders of Delhi, who had given him their word that they would spread the message of communal harmony and brotherhood in the city. The nawab of Maler Kotla visited Gandhi and told him how, during the disturbances, when some of the Muslim refugees in his state had begun to threaten the local Sikhs, he had announced that for every Sikh killed in Maler Kotla he would shoot ten Muslims. 'Not a single incident occurred after that.' One of his ancestors had courageously defied the Mughal emperor Aurangzeb when he had ordered the execution of the sons of a Sikh guru, and since then Sikhs all over had always given asylum to Muslims from Maler Kotla and vice versa. The nawab said that during the post-Partition riots, Maler Kotla had remained a safe sanctuary for Sikhs and Hindus. When Muslims travelling anywhere through Punjab, during the troubled times, declared that they were from Maler Kotla, they were protected by Sikhs. Gandhi replied, 'So my dream for India has come true in Maler Kotla!'

During his prayer meeting that evening, Gandhi said that the number of telegrams he was receiving was increasing. There were many telegrams from Pakistan too. They were good so far as they went. But as their friend and well-wisher, he was bound to tell those who were moulding Pakistan's destiny that if they failed to see and admit the wrongs for which it was responsible, they would not be able to make that country permanent. He had reluctantly accepted Partition as a *fait accompli* and added that he would not mind all of India becoming Pakistan if Pakistan meant what its name implied, land of the pure. That did not mean he approved of Partition or an involuntary reunion but that he wished 'to remove and resist the idea that Pakistan should be reunited by force of arms. Whilst I am lying on what is truly a deathbed, I hope all Pakistanis will realize that I would be untrue to them and to myself if from a sense of weakness and for fear of hurting their feelings, I failed to convey to them what I truthfully feel. If I am wrong ... I should be told and, if I am convinced, I promise that I shall retract what I have said here.'

He warned the people of India as well that they should not act under the pressure of the fast. What a spiritual fast does 'is a cleansing of the hearts. The cleaning, if it is honest, does not cease to be when the cause, which induced it, ceases... It ceases only with one's death.... Neither the Rajas and Maharajas nor the Hindus and Sikhs or any others would serve themselves or India ... if at this, what to me is a sacred juncture, they mislead me with a view to terminating my fast. No one need disturb this happy state, unless he can honestly claim that he had turned from Satan towards God.'

Gandhi had become increasingly restless since the afternoon, and towards evening, nausea set in. One of the doctors in attendance suggested that he should add an ounce of orange juice to the water he sipped. Gandhi responded that in that case he would have to fast for another twenty-one days, commencing from the day he started adding orange juice to his water. Another doctor suggested cupping the kidneys to induce them to function but Gandhi refused, 'I appreciate your affection but let me die if die I must.'

'But is not cupping, too, a kind of fomentation which you have not ruled out under nature cure?' the doctor persisted. 'That is how we slip from our resolve,' replied Gandhi. 'Rama Nama alone is now my nature cure.'

Even during his fast Gandhi did not deviate from his routine, which began with the first prayer at 3:30 a.m. That morning, he had dictated a letter to Richard Symonds, whom he had nursed through an attack of enteric. After his daily practice of the Bengali alphabet, he had the morning papers, important letters and telegrams read out to him, followed by a medical check up, massage and bath till 10:30 a.m. He then dictated his statement to Pyarelal on the Government of India's decision to release Pakistan's share of the cash balances while lying in the bathtub. Between 10:30 a.m. and midday, he received seven visitors, including three ruling chiefs of states. Between 12:30 p.m. and 3:35 p.m. he rested, followed by his regular nature cure routine, and held serious discussions with ten visitors, including Nehru, Maulana Azad and four maulanas of Delhi. After the evening prayers, he received a big crowd of people, including a maharaja, a chief minister and nearly half a dozen ministers of the central Cabinet.

His doctors' bulletin that day sounded a grim warning: 'In our opinion, it would be most undesirable to let the fast continue. Therefore, it is our duty to tell the people ... to take immediate steps to produce the requisite conditions for ending the fast without delay.'

That evening, breaking tradition, Lord and Lady Mountbatten paid an impromptu visit to Gandhi; he greeted them with a quip, 'It takes a fast on my part to bring the mountain to Mohammed!' It was more than a personal visit: Mountbatten later said that apart from the natural anxiety he felt for the health of a friend, he was anxious to give an indication to the world, and to Gandhi, that he was with him in the object of his fast.

Non-Muslim shopkeepers visited Gandhi to assure him that they had lifted the boycott of Muslims; now Muslims were welcome to purchase from their shops and reopen their shops which had been forcibly shut. Subzi mandi, the vegetable market of Delhi, had witnessed some of the worst atrocities: Muslim vendors had been murdered or driven away and surviving Muslims in the area had been subjected to a total economic and social boycott.

Addressing a rally, Maulana Azad said that Gandhi had laid down seven conditions which had to be fulfilled. His fast would end when responsible people from all the concerned parties, who could guarantee their proper implementation, signed a peace pledge to fulfil these conditions. 'He must not be given false assurances,' the Maulana warned.

'If we can perform what he calls upon us to do, then alone can we go to him and ask him to give up his fast. Otherwise it would be better that we leave him in the hands of God.'

A Central Peace Committee, consisting of 130 members representing all communities, was formed under the chairmanship of Dr Rajendra Prasad, who had succeeded Acharya Kripalani as Congress president. The committee held its first meeting that evening at Dr Prasad's residence and adopted a resolution, assuring Gandhi that they would do all that was in their power 'to create, establish and maintain the spirit of peace, harmony and brotherhood between all communities'. Representatives of the Hindu Mahasabha and RSS, known for their extreme communal stance and their role in inciting communal hatred, did not attend. Their friends gave a guarantee on their behalf. This sounded rather suspicious but some felt that as time was running out, an attempt should be made to persuade Gandhi to end his fast on the basis of the committee's resolution without waiting for those absent to sign. Pyarelal, who represented Gandhi at the meeting, knew that time was short but also knew that Gandhi would not accept a resolution that was not guaranteed by all. The meeting ended with a decision that emissaries would be sent to convince the absentee members to sign the resolution. Gandhi was putting the commitment of his people to peace to the test, his people were in turn testing his resolve.

When Pyarelal returned to Birla House, the mood was gloomy. Gandhi's condition had worsened during the latter part of the evening, he had frequently slipped into a delirium, and doctors attending on him were anxious. After failing to wake him up by calling out to him, Pyarelal gently shook him several times. Gandhi finally opened his eyes and very attentively listened to the report of the meeting. He refused to accept an incomplete assurance. He warned that the penalty for a breach of the undertaking given to him would be nothing less than the voluntary forfeit of his life, on his part. He was in no hurry to end his fast, neither should they be.

◆

Meanwhile, Nathuram, Badge and Kistayya had arrived in Bombay that morning. They had travelled separately; Godse had taken an earlier train and Badge and Kistayya had travelled together later. Badge, having asked

Kistayya to get off at Dadar and wait for him at the Hindu Mahasabha office, alighted at Victoria Terminus. Apte and Godse were waiting for him at the entrance of the terminus. They were delighted to know that Badge had managed to exchange the small calibre pistol for a bigger handgun.

The trio took a taxi and first proceeded to the Sea Green South Hotel to pick up a tearful Manorama Salvi. They dropped her off near her home in Byculla in central Bombay.

In order to raise funds for their mission, the gang proceeded to visit several known sympathizers who had previously funded them.

Some of the people they approached, who had financed them on previous occasions, were Charandas Meghji, an industrialist and businessman; Ganpatrao Afzalpurkar; and Mahadeo G. Kale. The gang then met Dixit Maharaj to try and convince him to give them his revolver. Dixit Maharaj demanded payment for his gun; the gang left empty-handed.

Apte, Godse and Badge next went to the Hindu Mahasabha office and picked up Kistayya. They then went to meet their patron and inspiration V.D. Savarkar. On reaching Savarkar Sadan, Kistayya was told to wait in the taxi, while Apte, Godse and Badge entered the house. Badge was left in the hall on the ground floor; Apte and Godse went up to the first floor room to meet with Tatyarao V.D. Savarkar.

After about ten minutes, the duo came down accompanied by Savarkar, who looked at Badge and nodded his head and conveyed his blessings by gestures. After taking his blessings, the trio left. Outside, a beaming Apte told Badge that Tatyarao had blessed their mission and said, '*Yashasvi houn ya!*' (Come back successful.)

The four of them then proceeded to the Juhu airport in the waiting taxi. Apte mistakenly thought that their flight to Delhi would leave from there, but their flight actually was to depart from Santa Cruz airport at Kalina. The taxi driver tried telling them this but was rebuffed by Apte. On the way, Apte proudly told Badge in Marathi, '*Tatyarao ni ase bhavishya kele ahe ki Gandhiji chi shambhar varsha ata bharli, aple kam nishchit honar yat kahi sanshay nahi.*' (Tatyarao has predicted that Gandhiji's hundred years will now end. There is no doubt that our mission will be accomplished successfully.)

On reaching Juhu airport, they realized their mistake and rushed to

Santa Cruz domestic airport, arriving just as the flight was preparing to leave. Before parting, Apte gave Badge ₹350 and asked him to proceed to Delhi with Kistayya by the evening train. Apte told Badge that they would meet him at the Delhi railway station, but if they did not, the two were to proceed to Hindu Mahasabha Bhavan in Delhi and wait for the others there. Badge and Kistayya continued to travel by Kotian's taxi to Kurla, an eastern suburb of Bombay, to collect some money from a friend. Then they drove to Kurla suburban station. Badge insisted that Kotian, the driver, sign a receipt for the taxi fare, ₹55. It was a princely sum from a single client for a taxi driver those days. Also, because of their behaviour, Kotian remembered all the passengers who travelled with him that morning and the places they went to.

At Santa Cruz, Apte and Godse were the last to board their flight, which travelled to Delhi via Ahmedabad. To their surprise, they found Dada Maharaj travelling by the same flight. At the Ahmedabad airstrip, Dada Maharaj chided Apte saying, '*Tumne baatein badi badi ki par kabhi kuch kiya nahi*.' (You talked big but never did anything.) Apte replied, '*Amhi jya mohime var nighloy, te par padu tevha tumhala kalel*.' (When we succeed in the mission we have embarked upon, you will come to know.)

The gang leaders were on their way to Delhi.

At noon that day, Karkare and Pahwa, carrying the explosives and hand grenades, reached Delhi. They had got talking to a fellow traveller during the train journey, Shantaram A. Amchekar, a Maharashtrian refugee who was going to Delhi to get his government job reassigned to the Government of India. Before Partition, he had held a government post in Karachi.

In his zeal to help refugees, Karkare took Amchekar under his wing and offered him hospitality in Delhi. From the station, they first went to Hindu Mahasabha Bhavan but could not find accommodation there. They got into a tonga and went to Chandni Chowk in Old Delhi, where they checked into Sharif Hotel at Fatehpuri and took a room with three beds. Karkare signed the guest register under the assumed name B.M. Bias in Hindi. Amchekar, who signed after him, did not notice this. Madanlal signed his real name in English. They were assigned Room 2 with three beds.

Karkare then went looking for the gang leaders, leaving Pahwa and

Amchekar at the hotel. That evening Pahwa took Amchekar to meet his relatives, as he was to see a prospective bride there. On the way back, they stopped at a public meeting being addressed by Jayprakash Narayan. Pahwa shouted slogans heckling J.P., demanding to know why, since he had not been allowed to address meetings in Bombay, J.P. was being allowed to address refugees here. Before the police could catch him, Pahwa melted into the crowd and, along with an alarmed Amchekar, reached Sharif Hotel and retired for the day. Karkare did not return that night.

Apte and Nathuram reached Delhi that evening. They drove to the Marina Hotel in Connaught Place and checked in under the assumed names M. Deshpande and S. Deshpande. They were assigned Room 40 on the third floor of the hotel. In K.L. Gauba's book *The Assasination of Mahatma Gandhi*, it is stated that during their stay in Delhi, Nathuram and Apte met with their patrons and contacts. The meetings were held in Room 39 of Marina Hotel which was assigned to the two. No one else knew about these ultra-secret meetings, not even the investigating police. Gauba writes that he was told about this by his unnamed contact and the information was confirmed by the owner of Marina Hotel. After checking in, they went to Hindu Mahasabha Bhavan, where Karkare was waiting for them. Returning to the hotel, Karkare ordered a whisky from room service and, after dinner, they parted ways. Karkare wanted to meet an influential sympathizer in the capital and planned to spend the night at his home.

In Bombay, Badge accepted the hospitality of his hotelier friend Navare, owner of Aasra Hotel, in Dadar. Aasra was famous for its vegetarian food, and as a friend of the proprietor, Badge and Kistayya were given a special room and treated to a lavish feast. After the frenetic activity of the past few days and after gorging on a feast, the opportunity of siesta on a comfortable bed was too much for Badge to resist. He and Kistayya overslept and missed that evening's Frontier Mail to Delhi. The shooter had not adhered to the prescribed travel schedule.

Sunday, 18 January 1948

At Birla House, when the doctors came to examine him, Gandhi complained of pain in the stomach. His weight, measured by Nehru that morning, still registered an ominous 107 pounds.

The Peace Committee met that morning at Rajendra Prasad's residence. This time, representatives of the Hindu Mahasabha and RSS, along with members of all important organizations and representatives of the refugees from Sabzi Mandi, Karol Bagh and Paharganj—the three worst affected parts of the city—were present. All of them accepted the conditions set by Gandhi and signed the peace pledge, individually and on behalf of the organizations they represented:

'We wish to announce that it is our heartfelt desire that Hindus, Muslims, Sikhs and members of other communities should once again live in Delhi like brothers in perfect amity. We take the pledge that we shall protect the life, property and faith of the Muslims and that the incidents which have taken place in Delhi will not happen again.

1. We want to assure Gandhiji that the annual fair at Khwaja Qutub-ud-Din's mausoleum, at Mehrauli, will be held this year as in previous years.
2. The Muslims will be able to move about in Sabzi mandi, Karol Bagh, Paharganj and other localities just as they could in the past.
3. The mosques which have been left by the Muslims and which are now in the possession of Hindus and Sikhs will be returned. The areas which have been set apart for the Muslims will not be forcibly occupied.
4. We shall not object to the return to Delhi of the Muslims who have migrated from here if they choose to come back, and the Muslims shall be able to carry on their business as before. We give the assurance that all these things will be done by our personal efforts and not with the help of the police or the military.

We request Mahatmaji to believe us and give up his fast and continue to lead us as he has done hitherto.'

While the pledge was being signed, news came from Birla House that Gandhi's condition had dramatically deteriorated. Dr Prasad rushed to Birla House with some members of the committee to report the progress to Gandhi and to explain the slight delay in getting all the committee members to Birla House. Soon, all the members were assembled in Gandhi's room, which was packed to capacity. Those present included Nehru, Maulana Azad, Zahid Hussain, the high commissioner of Pakistan, representatives of Delhi Muslims, the RSS, Hindu Mahasabha and various Sikh organizations. The Delhi administration was represented by Chief Commissioner Khurshid and Deputy Commissioner M.S. Randhawa.

Dr Prasad recounted the proceedings of the meeting. He said that those with reservations about signing the pledge the previous evening had today done so without any hesitation. It was decided to set up various committees to oversee the implementation of the promises made in their pledge. Others recounted how that morning, a group of 150 Muslims were taken to Sabzi Mandi, where they had been greeted with fruits and refreshments by Hindu merchants. In view of this, they all pleaded with Gandhi to give up his fast.

Replying to this, Gandhi said that they would have to realize the implications of their pledge. What they had achieved in Delhi had to be realized in the whole of India. If things in Delhi were set right, it would set things right in Pakistan too. He reminded them that he was not a man to shirk going on another fast if he later discovered that he had been deceived or had deceived himself into breaking this fast prematurely. They should, therefore, be extremely wary and act with full sincerity. He invited the representatives of the Muslims who had been frequently meeting him to tell him whether they were satisfied that the conditions in Delhi were now such as to warrant his breaking the fast.

He referred to a book given to him by a friend in Patna, which mentioned that according to the Koran, kafirs or Hindus were worse than poisonous reptiles, fit only to be exterminated. He was sure that no God-fearing Muslim could subscribe to that creed. He added that if they fully accepted the implications of their pledge, they should release him from Delhi so that he might be free to go to Pakistan. Maulana Azad, speaking after Gandhi, said that he could not leave unchallenged the observation made in the book as it pertained to the teachings of Islam. He had no hesitation in calling it a libel on Islam.

Listening patiently to all the leaders who stood before him with folded hands and moist eyes, Gandhi relented, and said, 'I shall break my fast. Let God's will prevail.' He accompanied this with the recitations of holy passages from Hindu, Islamic, Parsi and Buddhist scriptures. A glass filled with 8 ounces of orange juice mixed with an ounce of glucose was brought into the room. Maulana Azad held the glass to his lips. It was 12:45 p.m. Gandhi had repeated the miracle of Calcutta in New Delhi as Lord Louis Mountbatten had hoped he would.

It was an auspicious day, the Sikh guru Gobind Singh's birthday, and soon after breaking the fast, Gandhi dictated the following message: 'The Sikhs have shown true courage in eschewing anger. This is the true teaching of Guru Gobind Singh Maharaj. That one single Sikh is stronger, braver than one and a half lakh, one hundred and fifty thousand others, bears this very meaning. Victory to the Sikhs!'

After the much-relieved gathering dispersed, Nehru revealed to Gandhi that he too had been fasting for the past two days, a fact kept secret even from his household. After Nehru left, Gandhi scribbled a note and dispatched it to his home: 'Now break your fast… May you live for many long years and continue to be the Jawahar (jewel) of India. Bapu's blessings.'

Later, Gandhi called Pyarelal and asked him to meet Zahid Hussain, the Pakistani envoy, to check when he could visit Pakistan. Zahid was effusive in his praise of Gandhi's fast and said his wife admired him, having read his works in their Urdu translations. He added that he had received telegrams every day from all over Pakistan enquiring about Gandhi's health. 'You do not know how deeply Gandhiji's latest act of sacrifice has stirred the hearts of the people of Pakistan,' Hussain said. But when asked whether this meant that the Government of Pakistan would now welcome Gandhi's visit to Pakistan, he said, 'No, not yet. But I hope that conditions will have changed for the better sufficiently before long.' The Pakistani government was not quite satisfied with the conduct of the authorities on the Indian side. In the Simla High Court, Muslims were still not allowed to practice. Zahid sounded less and less sincere with every passing minute, Pyarelal informed Gandhi on his return to Birla House.

'There seems little chance of my completing the full span of one hundred and twenty-five years,' Gandhi replied with a deep sigh on hearing the report of Pyarelal's meeting with the Pakistani high commissioner.

◆

At Marina Hotel that morning, Karkare had joined Apte and Nathuram for breakfast. The three then took a tonga to Albuquerque Road to reconnoitre Birla House. The lanes running parallel to the low brick compound wall afforded an unhindered view of the house and the compound, and the room occupied by Gandhi was clearly visible from there. The servants' quarters at the rear entrance provided easy access to the compound and to the prayer lawns and there was a side entrance too from the lane to the rear gardens of the Birla House, where the prayer meetings were held. The servants' quarters were at a level lower than the garden, but its back wall and the rear wall of the lawns were the same height. There were small ventilation windows in the rear walls of each of the servants quarters, opening on to the prayer lawns; these windows were covered by fixed carved stone grills, and one of them was directly behind where Gandhi sat on the wooden cot for the evening prayers.

Since all the gang members had been told that if they missed each other at the railway station in Delhi, they were to proceed to Hindu Mahasabha Bhavan, it was decided that Karkare would be stationed at Mahasabha Bhavan during the day to receive other members of the gang as they arrived. The gang leaders had gathered in Delhi but the one carrying the gun and their shooter were yet to arrive. Without Badge, their plan would be doomed. Although Godse, Apte, Pahwa and Karkare had all received small arms training at Alwar and Gwalior as preparation for the plot to murder Gandhi and Gopal had been trained to use weapons when he enlisted in the army during the Second World War, none of them was ready to be the trigger man of the gang; for that, they depended on a mercenary.

That evening, the three, Godse, Apte and Karkare, attended Gandhi's 5:00 p.m. prayer meeting. They mixed freely with the crowd and went around the grounds; they were sure that as Gandhi had ended his fast, he would address the meeting from his regular spot, with his back to the wall of the servants' quarters, within a day or two. While they were surveying the prayer grounds, Apte pointed to the platform, a low wooden cot, on which Gandhi sat during prayers and addressed the crowds. Right behind him, about ten feet away, was the ventilation grill of a servant's room. Anybody standing inside the room and looking out through the grill would be able to fire a shot, point blank, at Gandhi. Why, he may even be able to push a hand grenade through the grill's openings, to ensure that Gandhi did not survive. They needed to organize access to the room.

Pleased with how simple it was going to be for them to execute their plan, they went to Delhi railway station to receive Gopal, who was scheduled to arrive on the Punjab Mail, and Badge and Kistayya, who were to reach by the Frontier Mail. Both the trains reached Delhi within an hour of each other. The three of them pushed through the crowds searching for Gopal, Badge and Kistayya but found none of them. Unknown to them, Badge and Kistayya had missed their train. Gopal had jumped off the train as it was entering the platform at Delhi and had rushed out of the station, afraid that if police checked arriving passengers, he would be caught carrying a gun. The leaders, seeing that the gun and the mercenary had failed to arrive, started feeling despondent. On that miserable, cold winter evening in Delhi, the most ambitious of their plans also seemed to be doomed. The three downcast men reached Marina Hotel. Nathuram ordered hot coffee for himself; Apte and Karkare, feeling more miserable than usual, ordered a double peg of whisky each. As in every hotel, orders for alcoholic drinks left a record. Every peg served had to be accounted for, so the name of the customer and room number was recorded in a separate 'Liquor Register' maintained by the hotel.

Gopal, caught in the icy rains, returned to the station and lay down on the platform amongst the hundreds of refugees who had made it their temporary home.

In Bombay, Badge and Shankar Kistayya reached Victoria Terminus and boarded the Punjab Mail at 2:30 p.m. The train would reach Delhi the next evening after twenty-four hours, chugging through the entire central Indian plains and across the Vindhyas.

Finally, the most vital member of the gang, the shooter, was on his way, carrying with him the other gun.

Monday, 19 January 1948

At Birla House, Gandhi observed his daily routine. The fatigue of his fast and the resulting weakness had no effect on his daily rituals.

The fast had taken its toll on Gandhi's seventy-eight-year-old body. The damage to his kidneys worried his doctors, but Gandhi had proved many a doctor wrong in the past. His regular and frugal habits and abstemious nature had endowed on him phenomenal healing powers. He had absolute command over sleep. 'When I lose command over sleep,' he said, 'I shall be finished. It will be a sign not merely of physical decay but of the deterioration of the spirit as well. All deterioration begins with the spirit; next, it affects the body and finally, one's environment.'

Since he had started eating his regular meals, he insisted that he had to earn them by doing what he termed 'bread labour', a proportionate amount of physical labour to justify the intake of food; every day, all his life, he had lived with this belief and had performed bread labour without fail. So, that day, although weak and tired, Gandhi insisted on spinning his Rentio, the portable compact spinning wheel developed in Sabarmati Ashram to spin and pull one thousand metre-length handspun strands of Khadi yarn. The yarn he spun would annually be woven into cloth used to clothe him. Bapu joked that it did not require too much effort on his part to make clothing for himself due to the minimal amount of clothing he wore!

He wondered out loud, since his presence was now not required in Delhi, if he should leave for Pakistan even if the government and officials there were inimical to the idea. If he was able to achieve in Pakistan what he had in Calcutta and Delhi, it would remove the biggest hurdle to the development of a healthy atmosphere in the subcontinent. It could well bring about a reunification of the two countries, eventually. He also wanted to go to Kashmir to heal its wounded psyche. His heart told him that Kashmir, if left untreated, would become a festering wound and eventually destroy his beloved India.

◆

At the Hindu Mahasabha office, things were hectic. Ashutosh Lahiri had come under fire from the extremists in the Mahasabha who criticized him for his association with Gandhi's seven-point peace pledge. He was forced to prepare a statement, denying that any representative of the Hindu Mahasabha had signed the pledge on behalf of the Mahasabha; his statement was to be released to the press that evening.

Apte and Godse were at the Mahasabha office, worried about the non-appearance of the three members and the most vital cogs of their plan: the guns and the shooter. An agitated Lahiri finished a draft of the press release, signed it and gave a copy to Nathuram to read. Nathuram did not pay heed to either the press release or to a whining Lahiri and absent-mindedly stuffed the copy of the statement in his jacket pocket. Later, back at the hotel, he read it and left it in one of the drawers in a cupboard in the room.

Apte requested Lahiri to allow him to make a call to Bombay. Lahiri asked that a suitable amount to cover the charge of the call be deposited first. Apte handed over ₹15 and booked a call to Bombay number 6020, the number of the phone at Savarkar Sadan. Apte asked for Kasar or Damle in particular: he wanted to find out if either Gopal Godse or Badge had gone to Savarkar Sadan and left a message for him. This was also the agreed upon signal to their patron that all was going according to plan. The call was tried at 11:30 a.m., but neither Kasar nor Damle were available. Just then, Karkare, who was standing near the door, saw Gopal enter Hindu Mahasabha Bhavan. '*He kay Gopal alaa!*' (There, Gopal has arrived!) he said. Apte cancelled the call and was told that the charge was one rupee and fifteen anna, a little less than two rupees. In those days, not many people booked an urgent call and then cancelled it and so the call, booked on 19 January at 9:20 a.m., stuck in the minds of the operators on duty in the exchange, Kulwant Kaur in Delhi and G. Phurness in Bombay. In the days of manually connected calls, the operators would note the phone numbers, booking time and booking ticket number on chits, which were later recorded in a register and the chits were preserved for auditing. Many a times, the bored operators doodled on these chits too, so there was a lot of erasing, scratching off and over writing on them.

Nathuram rushed to embrace his younger brother. '*Sukh rup phonchla. Pravasat tras tar nahi zala na? Saman anala?*' (You have arrived safely. Hope your journey was comfortable. Have you got the goods?) Gopal patted his bag and said, '*Chinta naka karu, Dada, aramat alo. Saman pan anala.*' (Don't fret, brother, the journey was comfortable. I have brought the goods too.)

Karkare and Gopal left for Sharif Hotel, where a relieved Pahwa met them. Karkare did not introduce Gopal to Amchekar, but rather brusquely told him that they had to leave for Jullundhar to finalize Madanlal's marriage that afternoon and so he would have to vacate the room. Amchekar, who had already registered with the Government Transfer Bureau and was keen to return to Bombay to be with his family, said it was fine with him and thanked Karkare for his generosity. The three then collected their luggage—as usual Madanlal carried his and 'Karkara Seth's' baggage—and checked out. They hired a tonga and went to Hindu Mahasabha Bhavan, and Amchekar left for the railway station.

Later that afternoon, Karkare and Apte went to Birla House to arrange access to the servants' quarter. They had now finalized the plan: Badge would get into the room in the servants' quarters and as soon as the gun cotton bombs exploded, he would fire at Gandhi and push a hand grenade through the grill to ensure Gandhi did not survive. The rest of the gang would position themselves in a semicircle facing Gandhi and toss a couple of grenades into the crowd to create panic and chaos. Taking advantage of the chaos, the gang members would flee.

Apte and Nathuram would be responsible for directing and coordinating the actions of all the gang members. Very cleverly, they had ensured that neither of them would be caught armed or participating in the act of Gandhi's murder. Nathuram had also shielded his younger brother Gopal. For all their anger and commitment to rid the nation of the Duratma or evil soul, Gandhi, they were effectively not taking any risk that would implicate them. Karkare found out who lived in the room they required access to and talked to Choturam to grant his friend access to his room to photograph Gandhi during the prayer meeting the next evening. He offered Choturam ten rupees for the use of his room for a few minutes. Choturam wondered why the sahib wanted to take photographs of Gandhi from the back, but the servants at Birla House had become used to the crazy antics of photographers wanting to take photos of Gandhi from all sorts of angles. The French photographer Henry Cartier Bresson was the craziest of the lot: Choturam had seen him climb trees, position himself on rooftops, lie flat on the ground, perform all sorts of contortions while taking photographs, so he wasn't too surprised by this request to photograph Gandhi from the back. Ten rupees for a few minutes of access was also incentive enough, so he agreed.

That evening, Apte, Nathuram and Karkare went to Delhi railway station to look for Badge. Not finding him amongst the arriving passengers, they returned to Hindu Mahasabha Bhavan, dejected and despondent. There they found, to their great relief, Badge and Kistayya sitting and chatting with Pahwa. Karkare and Gopal shared a room at Hindu Mahasabha Bhavan that night. The adjoining dormitory was also allotted to them, so Pahwa, Badge and Kistayya slept there.

All the gang members had gathered in Delhi less than twenty-four hours before their planned attempt on Gandhi's life.

Tuesday, 20 January 1948

After the winter showers, Delhi had become extremely cold. At Birla House, the day began as usual. Gandhi had been restless all night due to a wracking cough, but he refused to take any medicine for it.

No appointments were scheduled for that day. Gandhi spent the entire morning and the better part of the afternoon catching up on correspondence. Since the previous evening, Gandhi had started attending the prayer meeting, but due to weakness, he was carried to the prayer place on a chair. That evening, the prayer meeting was delayed as the public address system had developed a snag. It took some time before it was repaired.

◆

At Marina Hotel, Nathuram and Apte ordered breakfast in their room. In those days, hotels had dhobis, washermen who would visit the occupied rooms every morning, take the laundry for washing and ironing and deliver the clothes the same evening or the next morning. Nathuram gave his soiled clothes for washing, not realizing that his clothes were marked in indelible ink with his initials 'N.V.G.'. The dhobi listed ten clothes given for washing and ironing by occupants of Room 40.

At Hindu Mahasabha Bhavan, Apte reached Karkare's room at 8:30 a.m., and asked Badge and Kistayya to accompany him to Birla House. They were stopped at the gate by a sentry; Apte told him that they had come to meet one of Gandhi's secretaries. He scribbled a name on a piece of paper and asked the sentry to take it inside. While the sentry went in, a heavily built man dressed in a suit walked out of the gate. Apte pointed at him and told Badge that he was Shaheed Suhrawardy.

'He will be sitting next to Gandhi at the prayer meeting. You must kill both of them or at least one of them as per Tatyarao's command.' The sentry came back and let the three of them in.

Apte, Badge and Kistayya walked into the Birla House compound and proceeded towards the rear, where the prayer grounds were situated. Apte showed Badge the wooden bed on which Gandhi and Suhrawardy would be seated. Then he showed Badge the lattice work grill barring the window of the servant's room and told him that access to the room had been arranged. Pahwa and Karkare would light the two slabs of gun cotton on the walls on both sides of the low cot; as soon as they exploded, Badge was to shoot Gandhi and toss the hand grenade at him. Kistayya was to stand in front of Gandhi and fire on him from the front and also toss a grenade at him to ensure he was killed. Karkare and Madanlal would also throw the grenades they were carrying.

The plan was an amateur's exercise in overkill. They were so desperate to kill Gandhi that they did not realize they were going to unleash a barrage of shots and explosives in a densely packed crowd. The effect it would have on the people assembled there did not bother them. They gave no thought to the loss of innocent lives their attack would cause. The average attendance at Gandhi's prayer meetings was between four and five hundred men, women and children, but after the fast, the crowds had swelled to over a thousand daily. The garden measured 8,000 square feet, and women and children occupied the front rows near Gandhi. According to their plan, that was where the maximum damage would be done when their explosives and hand grenades exploded. But to Apte, Godse and Karkare, this loss of innocent lives was acceptable collateral damage. If, while murdering Gandhi, they killed or maimed innocent women and children, it was acceptable to these Savarkarites.

The stage, a wooden cot, was measured; the distance from the cot to the ventilator window of the servant's quarter was measured; the apertures of the stone grill were measured using a string. The distance between the two spots where the gun cotton bombs were to be exploded was paced off and measured. People noticed the three men hovering around the prayer grounds, but no one bothered to find out what they were up to.

Apte pointed out where Nathuram, Gopal and he would stand. He asked if Badge was sure he would hit the target from the distance that separated him from his victim. Badge assured him that he would be able to do so with ease.

Finally, at 11:30 a.m., the three returned to Mahasabha Bhavan where they learnt that Nathuram was suffering from a migraine and was resting at Marina Hotel. Pahwa was waiting for them with Gopal. Apte suggested that they should go some place where they could test the guns.

The grounds behind the Mahasabha Bhavan were a thick forest. Apte led Badge, Kistayya and Gopal into the forest. After walking for about fifteen minutes, they came to a tiny clearing. It was the perfect spot to test the guns. Apte paced off the exact distance between the grill and where Gandhi would be sitting and asked Kistayya to give him the revolver. Apte loaded four rounds into the gun, not noticing that the bullets were smaller than the chamber and did not fit snugly. He then handed the gun to Kistayya and told him to fire at a spot on a tree that he had marked as a target. To their horror, when the gun was fired, the bullets did not reach the target which was barely ten feet away! The bullets popped out of the gun barrel and fell to the ground hardly three feet away. That was when they realized for the first time that the gun and the ammunition were mismatched and would not work together. Gopal opened the oilskin packet and took out his service revolver, the .38 Webley Scott. The moist soil had rusted and jammed its firing mechanism. Gopal had some lubricating oil and a penknife in his trunk with which he could clean the gun; he asked Shankar to go back to Mahasabha Bhavan and fetch the materials.

While they were waiting for Shankar, they saw three forest guards walking towards them. They quickly hid the guns under a blanket they had spread. One of the guards, Meher Singh, asked the group what they were doing there. Gopal, who could speak a smattering of Punjabi, explained that they were on a picnic with friends. After ordering them not to hang around for too long, the guards left. The gang members hastily scurried back to Mahasabha Bhavan.

Karkare and Pahwa were waiting for them there. The gang was again in a fix. Both their guns were useless—how on earth were they going to execute the plan? Putting up a brave front, Apte asked Karkare and Pahwa to proceed to Marina Hotel. Gopal carried the canvas bag with the explosives and the useless guns. The four got into a taxi and were driven to the hotel. They found Nathuram stretched out on a bed in the hotel room. Badge and Kistayya went down for lunch in one of the dhabas outside the hotel.

When they returned, they found Gopal repairing his military-issue gun. Badge and Pahwa went into the bathroom to fix primers and fuse wires in the gun cotton slabs and detonators to the hand grenades. Nathuram and Kistayya stood at the door and watched the preparations. Nathuram addressed Badge, speaking in Marathi, 'Hi aapli shevatchi sandhi ahe, kam yashasvi zalech pahije Tatyarao na shabda dila ahe, sagla vayvasthit ahe hyachi kalji ghya, Bandopant.' (This is our last chance; our task must succeed, we have promised Tatyarao, ensure that everything is properly prepared, Bandopant.) Gopal, by then, had cleaned and reassembled the revolver. On firing the unloaded revolver, it seemed to function properly. To test the time it would take for the fuse to burn, they decided to cut a similar length of fuse wire and light it. There was a loud crack and the room filled with smoke. A waiter, alarmed by the sound, came to investigate. Apte stopped him at the door and convinced him that a mattress had accidentally caught fire while they were smoking on the bed and reassured him that there was no need for concern.

Apte then assigned duties to the various members. He suggested that Pahwa carry one gun cotton slab and one hand grenade. Kistayya would carry the other set. Nathuram, Karkare and Gopal would carry a hand grenade each. Badge would carry a revolver and the last hand grenade, and Apte would carry the other revolver. Badge intervened and said that one gun cotton slab was enough to create a commotion. He suggested that Pahwa should carry a gun cotton slab and a hand grenade. Pahwa would light the fuse and move away; he would have sixty seconds before the explosion. Gopal and Karkare should have one hand grenade each, while Kistayya and he would carry a revolver and hand grenade. He would shoot Gandhi using Gopal's gun. Apte and Nathuram would oversee every detail and coordinate everyone's actions. The shooter had come up with a perfectly workable plan. It would also conveniently keep Apte and Nathuram safe and unnoticed.

Karkare suggested that as soon as Madanlal exploded the gun cotton bomb, Badge should shoot Gandhi and those carrying grenades should throw them at Gandhi and in the crowd to create chaos. Apte said that he would signal Madanlal and Nathuram would signal Badge to synchronize their actions. The others would mix with the crowd and wait for the moment to carry out their assigned tasks. They were sure that in the ensuing commotion, they would escape from Birla House and regroup at Hindu Mahasabha Bhavan before escaping back to Poona. To them, their plan was so simple it felt like a school picnic.

Apte then gave each of them an assumed name to be used at Birla House that evening if they needed to communicate. Nathuram became Deshpande, Karkare was Bias, Apte was Karmakar, Kistayya was Tukaram and Badge was Bandobhau. Since Madanlal was to be the fall guy, he was not assigned a code name and Gopal was to be a mere observer, so he did not require a code name either. Nathuram wore a dark blue half-sleeved shirt and khaki shorts. Apte wore a dark blue jacket and trousers similar to his old RIAF uniform. Karkare wore a dhoti, Nehru shirt and a Gandhi topi. Madanlal wore a jacket given to him by Apte and trousers, both with extra large pockets. Gopal dressed like Nathuram. Shankar wore a shirt, coat, dhoti and a cap. Badge wore a dhoti, shirt and a Nehru coat. In a vain attempt to hide his identity, Karkare painted on a false moustache, darkened his eyebrows and painted a large vermilion tilak on his forehead, his loud getup attracting attention.

Apte distributed arms to the gang members. Badge carried both the revolvers and hand grenades in a canvas bag, along with the gun cotton bomb. He had pilfered a couple of towels from the hotel bathroom, he stuffed those on top in his bag. The others hid the items given to them on their person.

Karkare and Madanlal were the first two to leave the hotel for Birla House, followed by Apte, Badge, Kistayya and Gopal. Nathuram complained of a headache and said he would leave later. Badge disclosed the identity of their victim to Kistayya as they were leaving the hotel. 'We have to kill Gandhi according to the orders of Tatyarao, just do what I do, when I tell you to do it, nothing else,' he said. Kistayya had learnt to obey his master's orders to the letter.

The four of them hired a taxi driven by Surjit Singh, a Sikh driver, near Regal Cinema. They first went to Hindu Mahasabha Bhavan, and while the taxi was kept waiting, three of them went to the rooms they were occupying. Gopal stored his trunk in the cupboard. They were then driven to the rear entrance of Birla House. A service lane opened into an open plot of land behind the servants' quarters. As the taxi neared the rear gate, an off-duty watchman of Birla House, Bhursinh, an ex-army sepoy, got up to stop it from entering the compound. When he saw that the car had pulled up by the kerb and stopped, he went back to where he was sitting, chatting with Choturam, a car cleaner working for the Birla family. They both noticed that four people stepped out of the car, the Sikh driver remained seated behind the wheel. Two people from the compound walked up to the four and chatted for a few minutes, later one more joined the group. By this time, Bhursinh left for his duty at the side gate, from where people wanting to attend the prayers entered. After a few minutes of chatting, the group broke up into ones and twos and entered the prayer grounds. A woman who lived in the servants' quarters of 9, Albuquerque Road—Sulochana Devi—also saw the gang arrive by car and enter the compound of Birla House. Often, her children, aged seven and four, came to the grounds to play with other children of the neighbourhood. Sulochana had, as was her habit, come to check on her children when she saw the taxi driving up and the four men getting out and talking to two people who had been standing in the courtyard of the servants' quarter of Birla House. As usual, Sulochana stood chatting with her friend near the rear gate of Birla House.

Karkare had arranged access for Badge to Choturam's quarter the previous day. He approached Choturam. Choturam was curious the sahib's friend wanted to take photographs of Gandhi from his room, but how was he going to take photographs since neither of them was carrying a camera? Karkare replied that the camera was in the car.

After confirming with Choturam, Karkare walked back to the car. Badge, Kistayya, Gopal and Nathuram had gathered around. Karkare told Badge that the room had been arranged. Badge saw several people sitting outside the servants' quarters and three men sitting just a few feet outside the door of the room he was supposed to enter. He realized that it was going to be impossible for him to escape after firing from inside the room. It also dawned on him that, post the murder, Kistayya and he would be left holding smoking guns, while the rest of the gang would make good their escape without being noticed. Badge was developing cold feet. He refused to enter the room, saying that Choturam had only one eye and it was a bad omen which would bring bad luck. He said that he would stand in front of the cot, as close as he could get to where Gandhi sat. As soon as Madanlal detonated the gun cotton slab, he would fire at Gandhi and lob a hand grenade at him. The others realized that there was no way they were going to convince Badge to do otherwise. Badge had also realized that the trellised grill had openings which were big enough for the hand grenade to be pushed through, but it was not possible to hurl it at any distance from the window. As a result, the grenade would explode just beyond the grill, so while it may kill the victim, the one who hurled the bomb could also be maimed or killed.

Thus, the plan was changed at the last minute. By this time, Gandhi had begun addressing the gathering after the Sarva Dharma Prarthana was recited. They had missed the appointed time for the bomb blast, when the prayers from the Koran were being recited, as per the ongoing protest at Gandhi's prayer meetings since one year. The gang walked into the compound to take up their positions. Pahwa sauntered up to them and whispered that he had placed the gun cotton slab on the wall behind Gandhi. Karkare asked Pahwa if he was ready. Madanlal replied in affirmative and walked back towards the spot where he had placed the gun cotton bomb on the rear wall, less than seventy feet from where Gandhi sat. The spot was visible from the rear gate; Sulochana saw the young man walk up to the wall. She noticed the brick-like object kept on the wall too. She saw the young man put a cigarette in his mouth and light it up. 'No one should be smoking at the time of the prayers,' she thought, so she took a closer look at the brash young man.

In the meantime, Badge caught hold of Kistayya and took the gun and grenade from him and ordered him to do nothing till he was instructed otherwise. Badge placed the guns and grenades in the bag he was carrying and ran to the car; he placed the bag under the towel on the rear seat. The taxi driver had walked up to the prayer ground. Badge walked back to the grounds with his hands in his coat pocket, pretending that he was carrying the gun and grenade in his pockets, and took up his assigned position. None of the others realized what Badge had done.

Badge signalled to Apte that he was ready. Apte signalled to Pahwa, who lit the fuse of the gun cotton bomb with a lit cigarette and walked away. Sulochana saw him light the fuse and hastily move away. Madanlal signalled that the slab would explode at any instant. Sulochana saw this too.

Gandhi was addressing the gathering, '*Ab ek akhri baat keh ke mein meri baat khatam karunga...*' (Now with these last words I will end...). A loud explosion shattered the peace of the prayer meeting. There was a lot of smoke and dust; a chunk of the wall had been blown off. A few people got up and rushed towards the spot where the explosion had occurred; the gang members waited for the next action to take place. Nothing happened. No shots were fired. Inexplicably, neither Karkare nor Gopal threw the grenades they were carrying.

All India Radio used to broadcast the prayers and Gandhi's talk live, as was the practice since Independence. In the recording of that evening's prayer meeting, at seventeen minutes and a few seconds, one can hear the explosion and then Gandhi calming the audience.

'If we panic like this over nothing, what will be our plight if something really happens? ... Listen! Listen everybody, nothing has happened, listen to me. Sit down quietly.' The panic that the gang had hoped for did not happen. Gandhi's words calmed the crowd. The gang members were the only ones left standing, very conspicuously, but circumstances helped them avoid attention. They saw a few people who looked like the security staff of Birla House rushing towards the spot where the bomb had exploded. They saw a lady pointing towards Pahwa and the next moment he was grabbed and marched off towards the police picket, just outside the gate in a tent.

The gang panicked, sure that they would be caught any minute. Apte, Nathuram and Gopal rushed out off the rear gate and got into the taxi shouting, '*Gadi chalu karo, gadi chalao, jaldi, jaldi!*' (Start the car, start the car! Drive, drive away, fast, fast!) Sulochana saw the three men rush out of the rear gate, get into the car and shout for the driver, the driver came out, got into the car and drove off. Several others saw this too; a young boy noticed the number plate and gave the car's number to the police, but on checking the number proved to be wrong.

Karkare melted into the crowd and made his escape. Walking past the police post and looking into the tent, he made eye contact with Madanlal and signalled him to remain calm, then he walked away. Badge caught hold of Kistayya and, avoiding the police constables, walked out of Birla House.

They hired a tonga and proceeded towards Hindu Mahasabha Bhavan. Badge saw Nathuram, Gopal, and Apte there in a state of panic. A blazing row ensued between Badge, Nathuram and Apte, each accusing the other of betrayal. Badge was livid that the others had all planned their escape with no consideration for him. Although Nathuram and Apte had themselves not done anything that evening, they blamed Badge for the failure. Apte told Badge that they did not require his services any more and that he should go back to Poona. Badge told Shankar to dispose of the remaining explosives and hand grenades immediately. Shankar buried the cache in the woods behind the Bhavan. Karkare arrived at the Hindu Mahasabha Bhavan and joined the others.

Gopal was told to leave for Poona immediately, taking the useless guns with him. Nathuram and Apte also decided to flee from Delhi, their plans once again in shambles. Karkare said he was going to stay in Delhi and try and organize legal help for Pahwa. All of them picked up their bags and hurriedly left. Apte and Nathuram went to Marina Hotel and checked out. Nathuram forgot to pick up the copy of the press release that Ashutosh Lahiri had given him and the laundry that he and Apte had given for washing that morning. They fled to the railway station in panic.

Nathuram and Apte were devastated. Their well-laid-out plan had once again failed at the last minute. Like all their previous endeavours, they had once again failed. Who would believe them now? How would they face Tatyarao? They had let their mentor down, had betrayed his command. The Apte–Godse gang had once again lived up to their reputation of being incompetent failures.

On reaching the station, Badge and Kistayya bought tickets for Bombay on the 11:00 p.m. train and decided to stay put on the platform. Badge saw a couple of police constables walking along the platform, and fearing that they would be arrested, they left and went to the Old Delhi railway station. A train was leaving for Bombay within the hour, they boarded it. From Bombay, they headed to Poona. Their part in the conspiracy to murder Mahatma Gandhi was almost over, but Badge was still to play a major part, post Gandhi's murder.

Nathuram and Apte left for Old Delhi station and travelled first class on an overnight train to Kanpur, from there they would board another train to Bombay. After their failed attempt, Apte noticed that Nathuram had become very quiet and distant. Apte knew that, at such times, it was best to leave him alone. According to Apte, sometime during that night on the train, Nathuram woke him and said, '*Apan Gandhiji cha vadh karnya cha tharavla hota, apan Tatyarao na shabda dila hota, aapan ata pathi jau shakat nahin, Tatyarao na dilela shabda palay lach pahije, apan punha prayatna karu, pan ata meech kareen, ata dusryan vaar avalambun rahaycha nahin, bas ek vyavasthit bandook milvayla havi, mag parat yeu ani je tharavla te karu. Ata Gandhiji cha vadh meech karin!*' (We had decided to slay Gandhiji, we can't give up, we must fulfil the promise we made to Tatyarao. We must achieve what we have planned. We will try again, but this time I am going to do it myself. No relying on others. Let's get an efficient gun, then we will go back to Delhi and finish what we had planned to do. I will slay Gandhiji myself.) Having said this, Nathuram seemed to calm down. He then dozed off. Till that moment, Apte had been the leader of the Apte–Godse gang, and Nathuram his faithful follower. At that moment, the mantle of leadership changed hands. Now for a short while, Nathuram would be the leader. Apte would merely be a hanger on.

After spending some time at a tea shop, Karkare and Gopal went to Old Delhi and checked into a cheap hotel close to the railway station. The Frontier Hindu Hotel was mainly used by travellers staying overnight or people in transit. Gopal checked in as Rajagopalan and Karkare as G.M. Joshi. They stayed for one night.

At Birla House, immediately after the blast, Madanlal was caught by Bhursinh, Sgt Ram Chander and Rattan Singh, a police constable. He was taken to the main gate and handed over to the police on duty there. K.N. Sawhney, a magistrate from Karnal and the district officer for refugees, who was attending the prayer meeting and was sitting three to four feet away from Gandhi when the explosion took place, frisked Pahwa. He found a hand grenade in the right hand pocket of the coat Madanlal was wearing. The hand grenade was defused, packed in a tin and sealed as one of the first pieces of evidence in what was then called the 'bomb attack case' and would later become the 'Gandhi murder case'. A little while after the bomb explosion, Nehru arrived at Birla House. Gandhi called Sawhney and said, 'The boy was brave', and compared him to Bhagat Singh, the revolutionary martyr. He added, 'They are children.

They do not understand the situation now. When I am dead, then they will remember that what the old man said was true.'

Madanlal was taken to the Tughlaq Road police station. Initially, it was assumed that he had acted alone, a crazed refugee giving vent to his anger as had been happening since the past ten months, but when the statements of Choturam and Sulochana were recorded by the police, they realized that a larger conspiracy was at work and that more than one person was involved.

Senior police officers rushed to the police station and Pahwa's interrogation began in earnest. Severe third degree methods were used to make Madanlal speak. Very soon he began confessing to the police. He named 'Karkara Seth', a hotelier from Ahmednagar, as the financier from Ahmednagar; he talked about the editor and publisher of *Hindu Rashtra* and *Agranee* from Poona and the editor's younger brother; he talked about a bearded weapons supplier from Poona and his servant. He also said that a Raja Sahib was involved in the plot and gave details of the meeting at Marina Hotel and the entire plan. Throughout his interrogation, Madanlal repeated over and over again, '*Woh phir ayega!*' (He will come back!)

Choturam and Sulochana told the police about the people accompanying Pahwa; she also provided their physical descriptions. A young boy gave them a car number, DLH 9435, but it was found to be that of a bus. Late in the evening, Madanlal took the police to Marina Hotel. He led them to Room 40 on the third floor of the hotel, indicating that the gang leaders had stayed there and that the gang members had gathered there before leaving for Birla House. The manager of the hotel, C. Pacheko, was summoned and asked to open the room, which was searched thoroughly. In one of the drawers of the dressing table, the police found the press release typed on the Hindu Mahasabha letterhead, signed by Ashutosh Lahiri. This should have alerted the police to the fact that Madanlal's accomplices were affiliated to the Hindu Mahasabha. They checked the hotel registers and found the occupants registered under false names. A waiter told the police of the strange explosion in the room that afternoon and being told that a mattress had caught fire. When the police checked the mattresses in the room, they found no sign of any burning. The police was also shown the unclaimed laundry, some of which bore the initials 'N.V.G.'. By the time the police finished their work, it was past 11:00 p.m. They proceeded to Hindu Mahasabha Bhavan and searched Room 3 there, but did not find any clues. Surprisingly, the police did not question either the staff or Ashutosh Lahiri. Back at the police station, Pahwa's interrogation continued through the night.

Wednesday, 21 January 1948

At Birla House, the morning papers arrived, all of them featuring the bomb attack on Gandhi. Many, including Hariram, a servant of G.D. Birla who attended on Gandhi, thought of him as God and wondered why anyone would want to harm or kill him. 'How could they?'

After the evening prayers, Gandhi said, 'When I first heard the noise of the explosion, I thought it was the military carrying on their routine target practice. I did not realize till after the prayer that it was a bomb explosion and the bomb was meant for me.' He added that no one should harbour any resentment against the misguided youth who had exploded the bomb. He probably regarded Gandhi as an enemy of Hinduism and himself as an instrument for his removal. He could not ask the police to let off the culprit but appealed to the police not to harass the young man, instead suggesting that they should put him on the path of true action.

Early in the morning, the police took Madanlal to Old Delhi station from where the first two trains for Bombay would be departing within an hour of each other. Gopal, carrying the revolvers, was travelling by Punjab Mail. Karkare had come to the station to see him off. Gopal had stashed his bedding and the canvas bag with the guns under his bunk in the third-class compartment. As there was some time before the train left, Karkare and he went to the railway canteen for breakfast in the concourse of the station. While they were having tea, they saw two policemen escort a handcuffed man with a blanket covering his face, with just two holes to look out of, being brought towards the canteen. Gopal suspected that the police had brought Madanlal to identify his accomplices. The blood drained from Gopal's face. 'Fortunately, we were sitting in the far corner of the room so Madanlal did not see us,' Gopal recalled later. After marching up and down the platform several times, the policemen walked off with Madanlal. Gopal heaved a sigh of relief, rushed across the platform and boarded the train.

After Gopal left, Karkare stayed in the canteen till he was certain that the police had left with Madanlal. He went across to the Frontier Hindu Hotel, collected his bag, and went to a waiting room at the station, venturing out only in the afternoon. Later, in his statement to the police after his arrest, Karkare said that he had parted with Gopal on the evening of 20 January. He claimed that he had spent that night on the footpath outside Birla Dharamshala. He made his way to the Hindu Mahasabha Bhavan to see if he could muster up some help for Madanlal, but nobody was willing. A dejected Karkare decided to go to Madanlal's relatives, there too he was rebuffed. He tried to get help from his influential contacts in the capital for the next two days, but he was rebuffed by all.

The director of the Intelligence Bureau and inspector-general of police, T.G. Sanjeevi Pillai, was given charge of investigating the bomb attack case. That evening, Sanjeevi ordered two officers from the Delhi Police, DSP Jaswant Singh and Inspector Balkishen, to go to Bombay with a brief extract of the information provided by Madanlal. They were instructed to brief J.D. Nagarvala, the deputy commissioner of police in Bombay and chief of Intelligence Bureau, about Madanlal's confession, and then proceed to Poona and hand over a copy to the deputy assistant inspector-general of police, Criminal Investigation Department (CID), Raosaheb Gurtu, to find out if any of those alluded to in Madanlal's statement were from Poona or known to the police. Madanlal's statement, as was the practice in those days in north India, was in Hindustani written in the Urdu script. No policeman in Bombay could read Urdu, and no translations were provided by the Delhi Police.

In Bombay, Prof. Jain saw the headlines in the morning newspaper, and when he read the name of the bomber who had been arrested by the police, he was shocked. There were no reports of the arrest of the other members of Madanlal's gang, but Jain remembered that Pahwa had introduced 'Karkara Seth of Ahmednagar' to him as the financier of the plot to 'overpower' Gandhi on the orders of Savarkar and also that he was part of a group involved in the attempt. After seeing the reports in the papers, Jain felt that he should report Pahwa's conversation but was apprehensive and feared for his life as he lived in Shivaji Park, a Hindu Mahasabha stronghold. He contacted the then premier of Bombay Province, B.G. Kher, but as Kher was going out of town, he asked Jain to meet his home minister, Morarji Desai. At 4:00 p.m. that evening, Prof. Jain reported the conversations that Madanlal had with him on 11 and 14 January to Morarji Desai in his chambers. He informed Desai about 'Karkara Seth' of Ahmednagar, Madanlal's meeting with Savarkar, his boast that they were acting on Savarkar's orders and about the involvement of a group of accomplices. He requested Desai not to divulge his identity as he feared for his life. Inexplicably, Desai did not ask any police officer to be present while Jain made his statement, nor did he record or make notes of the statement.

After Jain left, Desai called Deputy Commissioner of Police Jamshed Dorabjee Nagarvala, 'Jimmy', who headed the Intelligence branch. Jimmy Nagavala was busy, so Desai requested a meeting at the Bombay Central railway station later that evening, as he was going to Ahmedabad by the Gujarat Mail departing at 8:30 p.m.

At Bombay Central, Desai informed Jimmy Nagarvala about what Jain had told him without revealing the professor's identity, and asked him to investigate the matter. Desai asked Nagarvala to arrest 'Karkara Seth' of Ahmednagar at the earliest and to place a round the clock watch on Savarkar. Desai mentioned that he was meeting Union Home Minister Sardar Patel in Ahmedabad and would brief him too.

One of the first things Jimmy Nagarvala did was to post two plainclothes policemen to watch Savarkar Sadan at Shivaji Park round the clock. Nagarvala was sure that if there was a larger conspiracy, then Savarkar would definitely be involved. And if Savarkar was involved, the gang members would definitely check in with him. Nagarvala also alerted his men to bring him information about any plots by radical Savarkarites. For some strange reason, Nagarvala refused to believe that the plot was to murder Gandhi. He believed that it was a plot to kidnap Gandhi, to hold him hostage.

Nathuram and Apte reached Kanpur that morning and checked into the first-class retiring room at the station. Nathuram signed the register using his real name. They glanced through the newspapers and were relieved to see that the police were not looking for any accomplices of the Birla House bomber. They took the 11:30 a.m. Lucknow–Jhansi Mail to Jhansi, from where they got on to the Delhi–Bombay Punjab Mail to Bombay.

Thursday, 22 January 1948

At Birla House, Gandhi had returned to his regular routine. He was keen to dispense with all his pending work before he took up his next task. Recovery of the abducted women in both dominions, the persecution of Hindus in Sind, and the evacuation of those who wanted to cross the border into India were some of the issues that demanded his attention. The plight of the non-Muslim refugees in Bhanwalpur State in Pakistan, waiting to be evacuated to India, was worrying. Gandhi decided to send two emissaries. He asked Leslie Cross of the Friends Service Unit and his personal physician Dr Sushila Nayyar to leave for Bhanwalpur immediately.

That evening, Gandhi walked to take his place at the prayer meeting, which was held as per schedule at the same spot where the bomb attack had taken place. The damaged wall had been quickly repaired. He had rejected Patel's suggestion of deploying more police at Birla House and of frisking all those who attended the prayers or limiting their numbers. 'My faith does not allow me to place myself under any kind of human protection at prayer time,' he said; if he did, it would reduce his profession of faith to a mockery.

♦

Early that morning, at the police headquarters in Bombay, the two officers from Delhi met Nagarvala and gave him a copy of Pahwa's confession. Nagarvala brushed them off, asking them not to interfere with the investigations he was conducting without bothering to even glance at Madanlal's statement given to him. Later, he was to deny even having received it.

Gopal Godse reached Bombay in the early afternoon. He alighted at Dadar station and waited on the platform to board a train to Poona. He was eager to reach home and be with his family. A police constable walked up to him and demanded to search his luggage. Gopal was petrified, thinking that now he would surely be caught when the revolvers in his shoulder bag were discovered. Slowly, he unrolled the bedding. After probing and poking the bedding, the constable left without checking Gopal's shoulder bag. Gopal heaved a sigh of relief. He had barely escaped this time. He did not want to be caught.

On reaching home at six that evening, the first thing he decided to do was to immediately get rid of all the incriminating evidence that could link him to the conspiracy. Gopal went to his friend Pandurang Godbole's home in Sadashiv Peth. Godbole used to work at Gopal's brother's company, Udyam Engineering. He gave Godbole a parcel containing the .38 Webley Scott revolver and requested him to hide it. He planned to ask Badge to exchange the useless .32 for the .22 calibre pistol that Nathuram had originally given him.

Friday, 23 January 1948

At Birla House that morning, Gandhi wrote a letter to his grandson, Dr Kanti Gandhi, Harilal's son: 'The fast seems to have done some harm to my body. To that extent I may be said to be deficient with regard to Rama Nama, that faith requires ceaseless practice, which I have not been able to manage. If God wants my faith to bear fruit, He will grant it. Even if I do not get that experience in this life, I think my faith will remain unshaken.' To an ashram associate, he wrote: 'My giving up the fast has not lessened my responsibility. It has added to it. It will count for something if I show some achievement in Delhi. On the 20th I might have died. But Rama saved me because he has to take some more work from me. If I can die with a smile on my lips, it will be a great mercy... This morning I had a long frank talk with Manu. I am a servant of Rama. I shall work as long as He commands me to work. I shall go when He commands me to go. I am prepared for both. My only prayer is that I may realize non-violence and make others to realize it, too. You should join me in that prayer.'

Gandhi attended the first session of the new Congress Working Committee (CWC) constituted by Dr Prasad, the Congress president. The members congratulated Gandhi on achieving peace in Delhi and expressed relief that he had escaped unscathed from the bomb attack. It was Netaji Subhas Chandra Bose's birth anniversary. The two had their differences: Netaji had relinquished the post of Congress president as Gandhi was opposed to him continuing in that post, and had gone on to form the Forward Bloc. That evening Gandhi paid glowing tributes to Netaji, 'Subhas Babu was a votary of violence, while I am a devotee of Ahimsa. But what does that matter? The most important thing is that we should learn from other people's virtues. Subhas was a great patriot. He laid down his life for the country. The soldiers of his INA included Hindus, Muslims, Sikhs, Parsis, Christians and others. He had no use for parochialism and caste distinctions. In his eyes, all were Indians and servants of India. Let us, in remembering Subhas, think of his great virtues.'

◆

The Punjab Mail, carrying Nathuram Godse and Narayan Apte, reached Bombay's Victoria Terminus at noon. The two took a taxi to Sandhurst Bridge near the Harkisondas Hospital in central Bombay. They planned to stay at the Arya Pathik Ashram, a cheap lodge patronized by Apte and Manorama on several occasions. The manager of the lodge, Gaya Prasad Dube, regarded Apte as a loyal customer and offered him special treatment. Apte always demanded and paid for a double room for himself to ensure privacy for him and his beloved. This time, unfortunately, no two-bed rooms were available. All Dube could offer was two beds in a dormitory, to be shared with six other lodgers, but he promised to allot the first available double room to Apte. Apte signed under his real name and wrote 'friend', as was his practice when he stayed there with Manorama.

Leaving their luggage at the hotel, Apte called Manorama. She was both surprised and relieved to hear from him. After talking to Manorama, Apte and Nathuram rushed to Thana, G.M. Joshi's home. Both Karkare and Apte knew him. Before leaving for Delhi they had met at the Shivaji Printing Press owned by Joshi, and he had given the gang some funds. The two wanted to find out whether Joshi had heard from Karkare. When Joshi replied in the negative, they asked about Karkare at a couple of other places, but drew a blank everywhere.

Although Nathuram had declared that their new plan would be a one-man effort and they would not be regrouping, the two seemed desperate to reassemble the gang. They sent a message to Gopal, informing him that they were in Bombay and that Manorama knew their whereabouts.

Karkare had meanwhile left Delhi dejected and aprehensive. To escape being arrested by the police, he jumped off the train at Mathura and took a bus to Agra.

At the police headquarters in Bombay, the two officers from Delhi Police were ushered into Nagarvala's office. He ordered them both to immediately leave for Delhi and not waste time in Bombay.

Surprisingly, the two officers chose not to comply with the orders given to them in Delhi to also pursue investigations in Poona; instead, the two boarded a flight and were back in Delhi after wasting two days in Bombay, achieving nothing.

Saturday, 24 January 1948

At Birla House, even as he was planning ahead for various activities in February, Gandhi sensed a great doubt somewhere deep inside him. In a letter to his nephew and Manu's father Jaisukhlal Gandhi, he wrote: 'You should come to Sevagram in February. It is possible that I may have to go to Wardha for Jamnalal's* death anniversary on 11 February. But it is not certain. It does not seem likely that I can get away from Delhi. I am dictating this letter immediately after prayer. There is a heap of letters to be attended to. If God wills, we shall be meeting in a few days, and then we can talk about the rest.'

In another letter he wrote: 'I am a servant of Rama. I will do His work as long as He wills. I shall have won in my mission if I am granted a death in which I can demonstrate the strength of truth and non-violence. If I have been sincere in their pursuit, and acted with God as my witness, I shall certainly be granted that kind of death. I have expressed my wish at prayer that, should someone kill me, I should have no anger in my heart against the killer, and that I should die with Rama Nama on my lips.'

Gandhi had sent Dr Sushila Nayyar to Bhanwalpur and Lahore as his

---

*Jamnalal Bajaj, the patriarch of the Bajaj family, whom Gandhi considered his fifth son.

personal representative to meet Ghazanafar Ali Khan, Pakistan's minister for refugee rehabilitation, and take steps to evolve a viable policy to help rescue and return abducted and hostage women and help resettle other destitute persons, preferably in their homes and to ensure the welfare of the refugees in the transit camps at Bhanwalpur while they waited to cross the recently drawn border. Dr Nayyar sent Gandhi a message from Lahore saying that she had had useful discussions and a mechanism would soon be put in place to achieve the goals he desired. In the evening, a deputation of Karnataka Congress leaders called on him. They wished to form a state on the basis of the mother tongue of the majority living there. Gandhi was not averse to the idea; he believed in giving more importance to India's vernacular languages.

♦

At the Delhi Police headquarters, Jaswant Singh and Balkishen filed the report of their trip to Bombay. They hadn't been able to arrest 'Karkara Seth', nor had they established the identity of the editor and publisher of *Hindu Rashtra*, they said, and complained to their superiors about the cavalier treatment they had received in Bombay at the hands of DCP 'Jimmy' Nagarvala.

Meanwhile, the person the Delhi Police was looking for, Karkare, boarded a train from Agra, continuing his convoluted journey back to Bombay. During the night, he changed trains at Itarsi in the Central Province, now Madhya Pradesh, and then at Kalyan, an industrial town northeast of Bombay, and finally reached Thana.

In Bombay, Dube allotted a double occupancy room to Apte. A delighted Apte immediately left to fetch his beloved Manorama. Nathuram had gone to the Elphinstone Annexe Hotel on Carnack Road, close to the Victoria Terminus, next door to the Bombay police commissioner's office and police headquarters; there, he booked a room in the name of N. Vinayakrau and friend. Apte returned to Arya Pathik Ashram at noon with Manorama. She stayed the day and spent the night there with Apte. Nathuram stayed away and watched a double bill of English films.

Sunday, 25 January 1948

At Birla House, planning his movement for Gram Swaraj, self-reliant villages and ridding India of the evil caste system, Gandhi wrote to Prabhudayal Vidyarthi, a village worker living in Sevagram. He said that he expected several difficulties in the tasks of rural reconstruction, so the workers committed to this cause must be resolute, hardy and also tactful change makers. That afternoon, he attended the second session of the CWC. He supported the proposal for provinces to be created on the basis of languages spoken and insisted that thereafter citizens should all live together with love and cooperation without any preferential treatment based on mother tongue, religion or caste.

That evening, at the prayer meeting Gandhi said, 'I will not ask how many Muslims there are at this meeting. I shall only ask everyone to treat them as their brothers. More and more people have been coming to the prayers. If each one of you makes it a point to bring a Muslim friend, it will be a great thing. The Urs at the shrine of Khwaja Syed Qutub-ud-Din Bakhtiar Sahib in Mehrauli is starting tomorrow. Earlier, the shrine was partially damaged. Now it has been repaired, I have been assured that the Urs will take place as usual. Formerly, a large number of Muslims and an equal number of Hindus and Sikhs used to go there. The Hindus and Sikhs should go there with peace and reverence in their hearts this year too.'

Referring to his plans for the month of February, Gandhi said, 'I will leave for Wardha on 2 February with Rajendra Babu. But I shall try to return to Delhi as soon as I can. The report that I shall be staying in Wardha for a month is not correct. I will go only if you bless me and assure me you will not start fighting as soon as I leave! Later, I want to visit Pakistan too, if its government permits me.'

◆

At the police headquarters in Delhi that morning, the two police officers' report reached Sanjeevi's desk. He did not want to take up his subordinates' complaints with Nagarvala. He believed that the conspirators were from the Bombay Province and thus he required the cooperation of Bombay Police. U.H. Rana, deputy inspector-general

(DIG), CID, Poona, was in Delhi. Sanjeevi summoned him, briefed him about the case and gave him a copy of the information gleaned from Madanlal till then, this time with an English translation. He ordered Rana to take it to Bombay post haste, hand it over to the Bombay Police and get them working to identify and arrest the people mentioned in the statement and also to look for them in Poona himself.

Rana left for Bombay that day, but surprisingly, he chose to travel a convoluted route, making the journey so long that it rendered the mission entrusted to him redundant. Rana decided to go to Bombay by train and not by air since, he later claimed, he had a fear of flying. Instead of a direct train to Bombay, he chose to travel via Allahabad, a big detour. At Allahabad, he stopped to perform post-death rituals for the eternal peace of his departed ancestors' souls at the holy Sangam. He was in no hurry. He was not bothered about the urgency of the task assigned to him.

At Thana, Karkare went straight to Joshi's house, Shanta Sadan, in the Navpada Enclave. Joshi told Karkare that Apte and Godse had come looking for him two days back but had left without giving any information about their whereabouts. Karkare decided to send a telegram addressed to Apte in Poona, but being a cautious man, he sent Joshi's eighteen-year-old son, Vasant, to the Central Telegraph Office in the Fort area of Bombay, round the corner from Flora Fountain. It was a 20 mile journey one way. As it was a Sunday, only express telegrams were booked. The message in the telegram was: 'Apte, Anandashram, Poona. Both come immediately, Vyas.' 'Vyas' is another way of spelling 'Bias' which was Karkare's assigned code name in the gang.

In Poona, Gopal had been a regular visitor to Apte's house, enquiring about Apte from Champa. When he received the message from Nathuram, that he and Apte were in Bombay, Gopal duly informed Champa.

That morning, Champa received a telegram addressed to her husband from somebody named Vyas. She could not make any sense of it, so she sent it to Gopal, who recognized the sender. Gopal rushed to the station and boarded the first train leaving for Bombay. He had to reach Bombay, find his brother, give him the message and get back to Poona by the next morning as he was to resume duty. He took the .32 revolver with him. He had tried to give it to Badge to get it exchanged, but Badge had become angry and abusive, so Gopal had kept the gun with him. Now he wanted to give it back to his brother, who may have some use for it. Gopal's fear of arrest had lessened with the passing of days. He got off at Thana and from a pay phone at the station, he called the Northcote Police Hospital and requested Manorama to inform Apte that Vyas was waiting for them in Thana. Then he went to Joshi's home and met Karkare.

At the Elphinstone Hotel that morning, Apte and Godse visited a wealthy supporter of extremist Hindu ideology, Paranjape, a banker and co-owner of the Silver Bank Company. They asked him for a loan of ₹25,000 for their paper.

Paranjape promised to give them ₹10,000 if they came to his office the next day. Knowing that they would get less than what they asked for, Apte had asked for an inflated amount, hoping to get at least ₹5,000. What Paranjape promised was a windfall. The duo rushed to the Air India office in Fort and booked two tickets to Delhi on the noon flight on Wednesday, 28 January. The tickets were booked under the assumed names of D. Narayanrau for Apte and N. Vinayakarau for Nathuram; they gave their address as Sea Green South Hotel on Marine Drive.

When they returned to the Elphinstone Annexe Hotel, they found Manorama waiting for them with the message from Gopal. Apte and Nathuram immediately left for Thana.

The gang was regrouping.

At Joshi's home, they requested him for some privacy. Then, Nathuram revealed his plan to the group. Karkare and Gopal looked towards Apte for approval, but realized that something had changed after their last debacle. Apte had been deposed; the new leader was Nathuram Vinayak Godse.

Apte and Karkare declared that they would accompany Nathuram on the mission. Gopal handed the .32 revolver to his brother. His part in the conspiracy to murder Gandhi was over. He was going back to his family and job.

The gang of seven was now reduced to three. Gopal enquired from Joshi what time the next train for Poona would leave. On being told that the next train for Pune arrived at Thana at 10:00 p.m., Gopal made for the railway station and boarded the train to go back home.

Monday, 26 January 1948

At Birla House, it was Gandhi's day of silence. He held talks with Dr Gopichand Bhargava, Prafulla Chandra Ghosh and others, giving his remarks and replies in writing. He followed the same procedure when he attended a session of the CWC.

At the evening prayer meeting, his written speech was read out by Pyarelal Nayyar: 'Today, 26 January, is India's Independence Day.* This observance was quite appropriate when we were fighting for independence, and we had not seen or handled it. Now that we have seen and handled it, we seem to be disillusioned. What are we celebrating today? Surely not our disillusionment! What we are entitled to celebrate is the hope that the worst is over, and that we are on the road to showing the lowliest of India's villagers that independence means their freedom from being a serf, and that they are no longer slaves born to serve the cities and towns of India, but that they are entitled to use city-dwellers for the finished products of their well thought-out labours. They are the the salt of Indian earth.'

◆

In Bombay, Nathuram and Apte went to see Dada Maharaj with the hope of persuading him to give them an efficient handgun. Dixit Maharaj was also present at the meeting. At their last meeting, Apte had boasted to Dixit Maharaj that they had procured a truckload of weapons and explosives and were going to take it to Kashmir to fight the Kabalia invaders from Pakistan. Dixit Maharaj now asked Apte about this shipment to Kashmir. Apte replied that the shipment was ready and they were looking for a revolver for their own defence, since it was very dangerous to travel north of Delhi. Dada Maharaj declined, saying that he could not help them. He had lost faith in the duo: when they had met Dada Maharaj on the flight to Delhi, he had taunted them about their chronic failures. Apte then asked for financial help, but the Maharaj brothers refused.

---

*In 1930, the Congress had declared 26 January as Independence Day. Bapu held on to that significance, although 15 August had supplanted it in reality.

Later that morning, Apte and Nathuram went to the Silver Bank Company to meet Paranjape to collect the promised funds. They were to meet Karkare at nine that evening for a final briefing before the three of them made their way to Delhi. With a lot of cash in their pockets, Apte and Nathuram decided to spend the afternoon indulging in personal pleasures. Apte had invited Manorama for an afternoon of lovemaking, so Nathuram decided to watch another English film. Apte also planned to use Manorama to provide him an alibi later, to prove that he had not been with Nathuram in Delhi at the time of the murder. Apte instructed Manorama that as soon as she heard news of Nathuram's actions in Delhi, she must send a telegram addressed to the secretary of the Hindu Mahasabha in Delhi: 'Arriving Delhi to arrange Godse's defence. Narayan D. Apte.' He made her memorize it and promise him that she would do as instructed. Manorama was willing to do anything for the man she loved earnestly, even though she realized that he was abandoning her.

That evening, after an early dinner, Nathuram and Apte caught a train to Thana. Karkare was waiting for them on the platform. The three crossed the railway tracks and squatted under a lamp in a secluded area of the yard, where Nathuram briefed Karkare about their plans. They told him that they were leaving for Delhi by air on 27th, but before that, they would meet Tatyarao one last time. They planned to request Tatyarao to help them get a gun. Once they got a gun they planned to return to Delhi by the morning of 29th. Nathuram asked Karkare to definitely reach Delhi latest by 28th night. On 29th morning, Karkare was to wait for them near the stone fountain of the Queen's Garden outside the Old Delhi railway station. Karkare promised that he would wait all of Thursday for them. By now, Karkare had run out of money, so Apte gave him ₹300 for his travel and stay in Delhi. Before leaving for Delhi, Karkare instructed his friend Joshi to get two used tickets of local trains of Mumbai dated 30 January and keep them safely.

The three then walked back to the main platform and sat at a tea stall, waiting for the last local for Bombay. After Godse and Apte boarded the train, Karkare walked back to Joshi's home.

U.H. Rana, to whom Sanjeevi had entrusted Madanlal's statment, was still travelling by train from Allahabad to Bombay—a journey which would take him another twenty-four hours.

Tuesday, 27 January 1948

At Birla House, Gandhi had an important appointment that day. Set amidst idyllic surroundings, 7 miles south of Delhi is Mehrauli, historically renowned as the ancient capital of Prithviraj Chauhan. It is the seat of the Dargah Shareef, the mausoleum of Khwaja Syed Qutubuddin Bakhtiar Kaki, a Sufi saint. The shrine ranks second in importance to the dargah of Khwaja Moinuddin Chishti at Ajmer. During the riots that had ravaged Delhi, the shrine had been desecrated and vandalized. Every year an Urs, a fair, was held during the feast of the Peer or saint, which was attended not only by Muslims but, in the true Sufi tradition, by Hindus, Sikhs and Christians too. Gandhi had demanded holding of the Urs as a pre-condition to breaking his fast, so the Delhi administration had cleaned up the shrine and its surroundings, and the vandalized portions of the dargah had been repaired and restored.

Hindus and Sikhs vied with each other to welcome visitors with flowers and steaming cups of tea from the tea stalls they had set up near the dargah. Gandhi was accompanied by Abha, Manu and another lady from his entourage. Women were not allowed inside the sanctum sanctorum. He suggested that they wait outside 'preferably under the protection of a Muslim friend', but his hosts insisted that the ladies must accompany Gandhi as they were his daughters. On seeing the damage done to the intricately carved white marble screen around the dargah, Gandhi lamented, 'I am afraid that Hindu and Sikh shrines in Pakistan must have suffered similar damage.' News had appeared in the press, quoting a statement issued by the Pakistan government, that 130 Hindu and Sikh refugees had been slaughtered in Parchinar refugee camp at Peshawar by raiders from the tribal territories. The actual casualties were much higher. Unlike in the past, the news did not trigger retaliatory attacks on the Muslims in the capital. 'I must say,' Gandhi remarked as he came out of the shrine, 'the response of the Sikhs to my call to non-violent courage has exceeded my expectations.' Speaking about the carnage at Parchinar, Gandhi said, 'I want you all to take a vow that you will never again listen to the voice of Satan and abandon the way of brotherliness and peace. The news from Parchinar has shocked me but you must not allow even such provocations to rekindle in your hearts the sentiments of retaliation and revenge. You should tell yourself and all concerned that they were out not to demand blood for blood but to meet with love even the murderer.'

Talking to his companions on his way back from the shrine, Gandhi expressed his utter disappointment with the way the UN Security Council was dealing with the Kashmir issue. Instead of considering India's complaint and getting the aggression negated, the stage was being set to ask India to withdraw its troops from Kashmir as a preliminary condition to the holding of a plebiscite which would decide the future of Kashmir. The UN seemed to have become a body where falsehood and prevarication enjoyed a high premium. 'Today they are preparing to put Pandit Nehru's government in the dock,' he remarked. 'Unless we are extremely wary, we shall come out with our name tarnished.' Once again his concern was coming true.

In the afternoon, Gandhi was interviewed by Kingsley Martin, a British journalist. Gandhi reiterated his growing conviction that India's struggle for freedom from foreign rule had not really been non-violent at heart, and that the fatal difference between word and deed had been the root cause of all the violence seen in the country after Partition. He saw India's passive resistance to have been expedient, undertaken only because the freedom fighters had no military strength with which to battle the British Empire. True non-violence, in his view, had to be an attitude of the strong who commanded power but would use it due to their faith in Dharma, and not because they were powerless.

Speaking at the prayer meeting that evening, Gandhi referred to raiders in Kashmir having abducted a number of women and children from Mirpur. 'I must ask the raiders and the government of Pakistan, for the sake of humanity, and for the sake of God, to return all the abducted women with due respect. It is their duty to do so. I have enough knowledge of Islam, about which I have read a good deal. Nowhere does Islam teach people to carry away women and keep them in such disreputable conditions. This is worship of Satan, not of God.'

Vincent Shean, an American writer, interviewed Gandhi after the prayers. They talked about the influence of religion and the philosophy of ends and means. Speaking on his objection to the use of force, Gandhi said that his objection to the use of force was not because force could as well be used to support unrighteous wars; it was fundamental. 'I do not know what is intrinsically good. Hence, I do not go by results. It is enough if I take care of the means. If evil does seem sometimes to result from good, the inference would be that the means employed were probably wrong. Good action to produce good results must be supported by means that are pure.'

◆

In Thana, Karkare left Joshi's home that afternoon after making all arrangements as requested by Apte, reaching Bombay Central station three hours before his train to Delhi was scheduled to leave. Karkare got a seat in the third-class compartment of the Frontier Mail.

In Bombay, on their way to the airport, Godse and Apte stopped and met their mentor V.D. Savarkar at Savarkar Sadan. (This came to light much later when Damle and Kasar deposed before the Kapur Commission.) They spent nearly forty minutes with him and briefed him about their plan. They requested his help in procuring an efficient gun, and Savarkar advised them to meet Parchure in Gwalior and to seek his help in procuring a reliable gun. *'Te aaplech ahet, nakki madad kartil.'* (He is one of us, he will surely help.) Godse and Apte then took a taxi to the airport and boarded the flight to Delhi. They occupied seats almost at the rear of the plane. Apte drew attention to himself by flirting with the air hostess, Lorna Bainbridge. She remembered Apte and his friend because Apte continuously asked for coffee and sweets as a pretext to speak to the strikingly beautiful Anglo-Indian air hostess. While on the one hand, he was creating alibis to prove he wasn't with Nathuram at the time of Gandhi's murder, on the other hand, Apte was leaving a trail of witnesses who would later help confirm his involvement in the murder.

On reaching Delhi, the two went directly to the Old Delhi railway station and boarded the Grand Trunk Express to Gwalior, a princely state which had been recently amalgamated into the Indian Union.

The train chugged into Gwalior station a little after midnight. There were very few passengers alighting at Gwalior at that hour. Outside the station, Nathuram and Apte asked a few tongawallahs if they knew Dr Parchure's home. One of them, Gariba, agreed to take them there for one rupee. On the way, the reins of the carriage broke and they had to hail another tonga, driven by Jumma, who then dropped them off at Parchure Wada.

Dr Dattatreya Sadashiv Parchure was the founder of the Hindu Mahasabha in Gwalior and the head of a private army of thugs, the Hindu Rashtra Sena. Nathuram hoped that Parchure would be able to get him a reliable gun, now that Savarkar had suggested it too.

The Parchures were a big clan; all the brothers and their families lived in a large family mansion, a Wada, on Station Road in the Lashkar or cantonment area of Gwalior.

When Nathuram knocked on the doors of Parchure Wada way past midnight, he was met by Parchure's son Neelkanth, who told them to wait while he informed his father of their arrival. Parchure had retired to his sleeping quarters only a few minutes back and was irritated by this unannounced visit at such a late hour. He came down after a few minutes and told Nathuram and Apte to leave, almost banging the door on their faces. Nathuram told Parchure that they were there on a mission for Savarkar and had come to him for help as suggested by Savarkar. Parchure was an ardent disciple of Savarkar so he relented and ushered Godse and Apte into his home. In a surprisingly frank manner, which suggested that Nathuram had absolute faith in Parchure or that Savarkar had assured him of Parchure's reliability, Nathuram told him that they were on a mission to murder Gandhi on Savarkar's command, and he needed Parchure's help in getting an efficient gun for that purpose. Without batting an eye, Parchure asked the two to stay the night at his home and promised to do whatever he could after daybreak.

In Bombay, late in the afternoon of the 27th, Rana finally reached his destination after travelling through more than half of India at a leisurely pace. By the time he reached Bombay, the three leading members of the gang of conspirators had already left on their assigned mission to murder Gandhi. Rana went directly to Jimmy Nagarvala's home and spent a pleasant evening with him over drinks and dinner; Nagarvala was known for his lavish and generous hospitality amongst his colleagues in the force. Rana briefed Nagarvala about the investigation, but for some unexplained reason, decided to keep Madanlal's statement to himself. After a couple of drinks, the two called Sanjeevi in Delhi, assuring him that they were on the job and would keep him informed about any progress in the investigations. Nagarvala informed Sanjeevi that he believed that the real conspiracy was to kidnap Gandhi, not to murder him, and claimed that there was a core group of twenty persons, each assisted by twenty dedicated volunteers, who were involved in the conspiracy, and he would soon expose the entire plot and arrest all the ring leaders in one fell swoop. Nagarvala warned Sanjeevi to be extra careful about protecting Gandhi. Sanjeevi did not order Nagarvala to abandon chasing his wild, unsubstantiated theories and to act on the leads provided by Madanlal.

Wednesday, 28 January 1948

At Birla House, Gandhi was busy chalking out a blueprint for the future of the Congress. He was giving finishing touches to a new constitution for the organization. It was almost as if he was drawing up a testament for the party he had nourished and converted from a debating society of urban intellectuals into an all-encompassing national movement for freedom.

He had meetings with R.R. Diwakar, Acharya Jugal Kishore and members of the Congress's constitution subcommittee, followed by talks with Rajendra Prasad, Pandit Nehru and Rajkumari Amrit Kaur. Now that freedom had been won for India, Gandhi wanted the people to turn their attention to constructive activities. In them he saw a rationale and the means for a government to be run well, keeping as its compass the welfare of the people, and by putting the controls in the hands of constructive workers.

Continuing his interview with Vincent Shean, Gandhi said that the functions of the government could not be carried on without using force; he reiterated his conviction, that a man who wants to be good and to do good in all circumstances must not hold power.

'Is all government to stand still then?' Shean asked. Gandhi, always practical in thought and deed, replied, 'No. He, the man of non-violence, can send persons to the government who represent his purpose and will. If he goes there himself, he exposes himself to the corrupting influence of power. But my representative there holds, as it were, a power of attorney only during my pleasure. If he falls prey to temptation, he can be recalled. But I cannot recall myself! All this requires a high degree of intelligence on the part of the electorate. There are organizations of constructive work. I do not want to send their workers to Parliament. These workers I want to stay outside and keep Parliament under check. The constructive workers will do so by educating and guiding the voters.'

Shean, who had read the Bhagvad Gita, asked, 'The whole of it is in defence of a righteous war. The Second World War was fought as a righteous war. Yet, violence is more rampant after it. What do you think?' Gandhi replied, 'See what is happening in India, in Kashmir. Yet, I have faith. If I live long enough, my followers will see the futility of it (employing force), and come round to my way.' He explained that though the Gita was presented in the physical setting of a battlefield, the righteous war in its text referred to the eternal duel between right and wrong that was constantly waged within the human heart and mind. The thesis of the Gita was neither violence nor non-violence: it advocated right, detached action pursued with truthful means, leaving the fruits of every action to the care of Almighty God.

The call of duty kept him going, but Gandhi seemed to be troubled by presentiments as well. In a letter to a Gujarati friend, Gandhi said, 'I am still knocking about in a dark world. I do not intend to stay here for long. Whatever has to be decided will be decided within the next four days.'

At his prayer meeting that evening, the conversation steered towards South Africa, where Gandhi's social and political career had begun long decades ago and where Indians were still fighting for their rights. He said, 'In South Africa, our people are fighting. In India, we have no laws depriving the people of the right of owning land or living wherever they please. That is so in South Africa. Indians there struggle to safeguard their rights and defend the honour of India. Their struggle has taken the form of Satyagraha. The Indians are few in number, but if they are true Satyagrahis, their victory is certain. I shall ask the government of South Africa not to be too severe with the Satyagrahis who carry on their legitimate struggle with such decency. The government should understand their grievances, and come to a settlement with them.'

◆

On board the Frontier Mail, Karkare was sitting in a crowded third-class compartment. The hotelier and Hindu Mahasabha activist was heading to Delhi on a mission which would bring him momentary notoriety.

But, as previously, Karkare was going to be remembered briefly and then remanded to a life of ignominy and oblivion.

In Gwalior, at Parchure's home that morning, Parchure sent his son Neelkanth and bodyguard Roopa to fetch Gangadhar S. Dandavate, who knew gun dealers in Gwalior. When Dandavate arrived at Parchure Wada, he found Parchure in conversation with two men who were introduced to him as Nathuram Godse and Narayan Apte of Poona. Parchure asked Dandavate to procure a good and reliable gun for his friend Godse, who would pay for it. Dandavate asked Parchure to give them his own weapon but Parchure angrily replied, 'I am not a fool to give my own gun which can be easily traced back to me. You do as you are told!' Dandavate promised to do his best and left. Parchure then left for his clinic.

In the afternoon, at about 12:30 p.m., Madhukar K. Kale, a Hindu Mahasabha activist, visited Parchure's home. He found Parchure in conversation with two strangers and Dandavate. One of the strangers was holding an old revolver. Neither Nathuram nor Apte could fire the gun. Dandavate offered to demonstrate, so they went out into the backyard of Parchure Wada. Here, Dandavate aimed at a tree and fired a round easily, but when Nathuram tried, he was unable to pull the trigger. Nathuram requested Dandavate to get them a more reliable gun. He told Dandavate that he was in a hurry as he wished to board the 3:00 p.m. train to Delhi. Dandavate said that he could only manage to get a gun by the evening and suggested that they should take the night train. Nathuram agreed.

After Dandavate left, Parchure and his guests retired to the first-floor guest rooms of his home. Kale had witnessed the entire conversation and the trial of guns that morning.

Dandavate went to Jagdish Prasad Goel, a gun dealer, who showed him a gleaming 9 mm Beretta semi-automatic pistol that he had recently acquired. He asked for ₹500 for the gun with a full clip and seven rounds of extra ammunition; there were nine rounds already in the magazine. Dandavate told him that he would give him the cash after his clients approved of the firearm.

Nathuram and Apte were delighted to see the gun. Although they had ample cash and were desperately in need of a gun, they haggled over the price. They offered ₹300 in cash and the country-made revolver Nathuram had in exchange for the Beretta. Goel was furious and demanded the entire amount in cash or his gun back. Nathuram managed to convince Parchure to guarantee the balance amount and got to keep the gun for a down payment of ₹300 and the revolver. After dinner with Parchure, they left for the station at 10:30 p.m. to catch the Bombay–Amritsar Express for Delhi. That night, the train was delayed by three hours. They finally boarded the train at 1:30 a.m.

The murderer and his accomplice were on their way, armed with an efficient gun.

Karkare arrived at the Old Delhi station late in the evening of 28 January. This time he did not look for a hotel. He was running out of money, so he spread his bedding on the platform amidst hundreds of refugees and slept there.

Thursday, 29 January 1948

At Birla House, Gandhi woke up soon after 3:00 a.m. He finished his ablutions and prayer in the cold, dark hours. The ice cold wind outside howled bitterly. He set himself to spinning Khadi yarn on his Rentio and dictated letters.

To a friend Sankaran, who had lost his daughter, he wrote: 'What comfort can I give? Death is a true friend. It is only our ignorance which causes us grief. Sulochana's spirit was yesterday, is today, and will remain tomorrow. The body, of course, must die. Sulochana's body has gone, taking her failings with her, leaving only her good behind. Let us not forget that or her. Be even more diligent in the discharge of your duty.'

That afternoon, some refugees from Bannu came to meet Gandhi. They were survivors of the train massacre at the Gujerat station. They wanted to express their anguish and anger towards Gandhi. One of them said, 'You have done enough harm, old man. You have ruined us utterly. You ought to now leave us alone and retire to the Himalayas!'

Gandhi replied, 'I cannot retire at anybody's bidding. I have put myself under God's sole command.'

The man persisted, 'It is God who is speaking to you through us. We are beside ourselves with grief.'

Gandhi patiently replied: 'My grief is no less than yours.' With sympathy and honesty, he pacified the grieving refugees.

That evening, speaking at the prayer meeting, Gandhi narrated the incident and said, 'I cannot run away from you and enjoy the peace of the mountains. But if all of you were to go to the Himalayas, I might follow you as your humble servant.'

It had been a hectic day, and by the evening, Gandhi was exhausted. 'My head is reeling. And yet I must finish this,' he remarked to Abha, pointing to the draft of the constitution of the Congress, which he had undertaken to prepare for the CWC, and added, 'I am afraid I shall today have to keep late hours.'

At 9:15 p.m., he finally rose to go to bed. It was his practice to have some casual and often lighthearted banter with those who sat around. That day, he said, 'I allow the girls to be my walking sticks, but really I have accustomed myself to not depend on anybody for anything. Girls come to me as to their father. Personally, it means nothing to me.'

Commenting on the political scenario, he wondered why some Congressmen, who had toiled and sacrificed for the country's freedom and on whom now rested the burden of independence, were succumbing to the lure of office and power. 'Where will this take us? How long will this last? Shall we be able to maintain our prestige in the world? Where do I stand? What must I do to realize unruffled calm and serenity in the midst of disquiet?' he wondered. Then, in a tone of infinite sadness, he repeated the well-known verse of Nazir, the celebrated Urdu poet from Allahabad:

> *Hai Bahare Bag Duniya Chand Roz, Dekh lo Iska Tamasha Chand Roz.* (Shortlived is the splendour of spring in the garden of this world. Watch the show while it lasts.)

A wracking cough that had plagued him for the past few days started bothering him again. He had been advised to suck Penicillin lozenges to subdue the cough, but he reiterated, once again, his resolve to be cured by the power of Rama Nama alone. He told Manu, 'If I die of a lingering illness, nay even by as much as a boil or a pimple, it will be your duty to proclaim to the world, even at risk of making people angry with you, that I was not the man of God that I claimed to be. If you do that, it will give my spirit peace. Note down this too, that if someone were to end my life by putting a bullet through me—as someone tried to do with a bomb the other day—and I met his bullet without a groan, and breathed my last taking God's name, then alone would I have made good my claim.'

♦

At the Old Delhi railway station, Karkare got up and made his way to one of the public lavatories and then had some tea and biscuits at a tea stall. He was in a hurry to take up his vigil by the water fountain in the Queen's Garden across the road from the station.

The park had been occupied by homeless refugees. After a while, Karkare decided that he was too conspicuous rooted to one spot and started walking round the periphery of the garden. He sat down to chat with a tea seller, who had set up a little tea stall on a stool. Karkare learnt that he was a refugee who had lost his home and family during the riots but had managed to escape to Delhi with less than what could be stored in a small trunk; he was determined to put the tragedy behind him and restart his life. After spending time walking and chatting, Karkare was getting anxious: would his associates be successful in their quest for a reliable weapon or would they once again fail?

The duo for whom Karkare was waiting was still travelling to Delhi from Gwalior. En route, the train had been further delayed, and instead of reaching Delhi as per schedule in the early hours of the morning, they reached at midday. Nathuram went to the booking office to get a retiring room. The booking clerk, Sundarilal, asked him to come back later. Godse went back at around 1:00 p.m. and Sundarilal allotted him a first-class waiting room, Room No. 6, at the Delhi main station; Godse gave his name as N. Vinayakrau. Apte and Godse then had a hot meal at the railway restaurant and rested in the room. Surprisingly, they did not bother to look for Karkare. At about 6:00 p.m. that evening, Nathuram rang for the room attendant Hari Kishan and gave him some clothes to be washed and ironed. Hari Kishan called Jannu, a shoeshine boy, and told him to wash and press the clothes and deliver them to Room No. 6.

Karkare kept up his vigil till the late evening. He had survived by drinking innumerable cups of tea and puffing on several bidis. He was chilled to the bone and weary from the prolonged wait when, at last, in the evening, he saw his two accomplices emerge from the railway station and walk up to the fountain.

The three of them then rushed back to the retiring room. Behind closed doors, Nathuram rummaged through his trunk and brought out a gleaming blue-black pistol. Karkare had never seen such a strange firearm.

'*Golya Kuthe jatat, Bharaychya kuthun*?' (Where do the bullets go? Where does one load them?) he asked, bewildered.

Nathuram showed him the magazine which fitted into the grip of the pistol, and held up a small bundle tied in a piece of cloth, which contained seven extra bullets.

The three then left to walk down to Chandni Chowk. On an impulse, they stopped at a roadside photographer's kiosk, where Nathuram had his picture taken. He ordered three copies; the photographer promised to have them ready within an hour. After dinner, Apte and Karkare went to see a film, while Nathuram said that he wanted to retire early. On his way back, he collected the photographs.

After the film, Apte excused himself since he wanted to visit Delhi's red-light area. The casanova could not wait to get his hands on Delhi's famous tawaifs.

Karkare reached the station well past midnight. Not wishing to disturb Nathuram, Karkare lay down on the platform just as he had done the previous night.

Friday, 30 January 1948

At Birla House, the day began as an ordinary winter day. The inmates went about their routine chores. The Birla family, one of India's leading industrial families, occupied a major part of the house. For the past few months, the traditional Marwari household awakened every morning to the drone of spinning wheels. Seth Ghanshyamdas Birla and his family had become used to this and many historic events happening in their family home.

For the subject of everyone's attention, Mohandas Gandhi, this was a day like all the others in his life of seventy-eight years, three months and twenty-eight days. Ever since Ba's death, his personal needs were taken care of by young Abha, his grandniece-in-law, and Manu, his grand-niece. Manu begged to be excused from accompanying him on his morning walk, since she wanted to powder some cloves for his jaggery and clove-powder lozenges, which he took to relieve his cough. Gandhi, who did not approve of anyone missing their duty in the present to anticipate and provide for the unknown future, admonished Manu. 'Who knows what is going to happen before nightfall or even whether I shall be alive? If at night I am still alive you can easily prepare some.'

Gandhi still had to finalize the draft of the new constitution for the Congress party. He had to give finishing touches to the vision he had dreamed for India, his last will and testament for his beloved country. Pyarelal Nayyar, his secretary ever since the death of Mahadev Desai, was to check and correct the final draft which Gandhi would complete after his morning walk. Congressmen were not going to like his suggestion of disbanding the party and forming the Lok Sevak Sangh, a force of volunteer workers who would take up the work of rural development and social reforms. The ever-increasing piles of correspondence needed to be answered. Margaret Bourke White, the photographer for *Life* magazine, wanted to shoot a photo feature with him. The French photographer Henri Cartier Bresson was continuously ambushing him with his camera; Gandhi had told him to stay away when he was to meet Sardar Patel and later Pandit Nehru—he did not wish to be distracted or disturbed.

Just before midday, Gandhi, as was his habit, took a brief nap on a cot outside his room, soaking the warmth of the winter sun. Manu noticed a young man moving around in the rooms occupied by Gandhi and his entourage. She did not pay much attention to him but felt that he seemed to be there for a reason other than Gandhi's darshan. He started to question Manu about where Gandhi sat, where he worked, when he ate, when he slept. Finally, she excused herself. People often came to see how Gandhi lived and so on, so this was nothing unusual, Manu convinced herself. A few minutes later, she looked out to see if Gandhi had woken up. She saw that he was still sleeping, and hovering above him was the same hawk-eyed young man, staring down intently at him. When she looked at his face, Manu felt a chill go down her spine; he looked as if he were in a trance, a strange, menacing expression frozen on his face. Fearing that he would disturb Gandhi's sleep, Manu walked up to him and whispered, 'Bhai, Bapu is resting, please come back later.' The young man seemed to snap out of a trance, and without uttering a word, he turned around and walked away. Manu was not going to forget his eyes and the expression on his face in a hurry: it reminded her of a cobra ready to strike.

After he woke up, Gandhi discussed the situation in Noakhali with Pyarelal, who was living with volunteers as a peacekeeper there. Just the previous day, Gandhi had sent a message to Dr Syama Prasad Mookerji, one of the ideologues of the RSS, who was also a minister in the Union Cabinet, requesting him to use his influence over the more fanatical elements of his party. The press and sources close to Gandhi had reported that many of these fanatics had been making increasingly rabid hate-filled communal comments in their public speeches, which were inciting violence. Of late, they had been openly issuing threats to kill Congress leaders. Gandhi felt that there were other ways of voicing their grievances and Dr Mookerji, as a member of the Congress-led government, should silence these fanatics in the interest of national unity and in an effort to bring peace to a nation which was being torn apart by hate. Dr Mookerji was hesitant and showed his disinterest in the matter. The extremist fringe had hijacked the party, the moderates had no say in its running or control over the ongoing campaign of hate.

Amidst all this, Gandhi also planned to visit Sabarmati Ashram, which he had abandoned when he left on the Dandi Kooch in 1930. Sevagram had become their home and the nerve centre of activities. He was planning on leaving for Wardha the very next day, accompanied by Dr Prasad and some members of the CWC. Prior to that, there was a very important task for him. Lord Mountbatten had briefed him about the growing rift between his two protégés, Patel and Nehru. Their ego clashes threatened to split the Congress and throw the functioning of the interim government into total disarray; only Gandhi could bring about a rapprochement, he said. Gandhi assured Mountbatten that he would meet and request Patel to be magnanimous and work unitedly with Nehru. Patel was headstrong, but as the elder statesman of the two and one with greater experience, he would understand the need for two of India's most powerful leaders to remain united.

Nehru was known to be impetuous and impatient with criticism and divergent views. He could be difficult to work with, but Patel would have to handle him carefully and be a stabilizing influence on the government in these trying times. If everything else failed, then one of them would have to resign in the interest of the smooth functioning of the government and for the sake of unity. Gandhi decided to talk to the two prior to and post his prayers. Gandhi knew that Patel was smarting over the fact that he had sided with Nehru in the leadership of the Congress party. He was also aware that, in the recent past, Patel had displayed his displeasure at the influence exerted by Gandhi over the functioning of the government, but he trusted Sardar Patel enough to be sure that he would listen to him, so he had kept his afternoon free for Sardar.

It was nearing 4:00 p.m., and Sardar Patel was expected any moment.

◆

At the Old Delhi railway station waiting room, Nathuram got up early. When Karkare entered the room, Apte had returned after his night of debauchery. After a bath, the three of them went to the non-vegetarian cafeteria at the station, run by Brandon & Co. Why they went to a non-vegetarian restaurant is a mystery, as both Nathuram and Karkare were strict vegetarians. As they sat down, a waiter walked up to them and said in Marathi, 'Namaste Saheb, lamb pravas kelay vat ta.' (Sahibs, you have come a long way from home.) For a split second, the three panicked. Nathuram, regaining his composure, replied, 'You too are far from home. The last time I saw you at the Poona station restaurant.' The waiter had often served Nathuram and Apte there. The last time they had visited the restaurant at Poona station, Apte had suggested that they should try once more to kill Gandhi; the same waiter had served them that day, too. The waiter, recently transferred to Delhi from Poona, was delighted to meet folks from home. For the three gang members, it was an ill omen to be recognized so easily on the day they planned to murder Gandhi.

They ordered three plates of buttered toast, tea for Apte and Karkare and English coffee for Nathuram. While they were waiting for their order to arrive, Nathuram brought his hands together and crossed them at the wrist, indicating being handcuffed, the fear triggered by being so easily identified by someone from back home. After breakfast, they went back to their room and locked themselves in. Nathuram wrote three letters. He addressed one each to Apte's home and office addresses in Poona and one to Karkare's Ahmednagar address. He enclosed copies of the photograph taken the previous night and wrote to explain his actions to his friends.

Nathuram was creating an alibi for his co-conspirators to establish that they had not been with him in Delhi when he murdered Gandhi. Then, they got down to discussing the plan for that evening. They were aware that the police presence at Birla House had been doubled since the 20th and feared that if policemen from Poona or Ahmednagar were deployed at Birla House, they would be recognized and held before accomplishing their task.

Apte suggested that Nathuram should impersonate a photographer and carry a tripod and camera with a black hood, under which he could shoot Gandhi unnoticed. This was rejected as impractical as they may not be allowed to get too close to Gandhi with cumbersome photography equipment. Nathuram would have to take a shot from far but no one was confident about his marksmanship. Apte's next suggestion was immediately accepted. He suggested that Nathuram hide under a burqa, which would also create the false impression that Gandhi's murderer was a Musalman. This way, another round of retaliatory violence could be triggered post the murder. Apte and Karkare immediately rushed to Chandni Chowk where many shops sold pre-stitched burqas. They purchased one for fifty rupees that would fit Nathuram.

In the meantime, on an impulse, Nathuram left for Birla House. He wanted to have a last look around. Surprisingly, he was neither stopped nor questioned. He walked into the rooms occupied by the Gandhi entourage, where he met Manu and questioned her about Gandhi's routine. He saw Gandhi sleeping on a cot on the lawns adjoining the room. Nathuram walked up to his prey. This close to the man he was determined to kill, he went into a semi-trance, till he was shaken out of it by Manu. He snapped out of it, turned around and rushed out of Birla House. He took a tonga to the railway station and reached a few minutes before his companions came back. He did not tell them about his little excursion.

Nathuram tried on the burqa; it was a perfect fit but he got entangled in its voluminous folds. His hands became ensnared and he could not locate his pant pocket, pull out the gun from it or aim it. When he tried to walk, he tripped and fell. The idea was a non-starter. Nathuram discarded the burqa. Apte, who had not thought once before spending money to buy sex the previous evening, grumbled about the waste of money.

With no workable plan for the evening's attempt, they took a taxi to Birla Mandir, a temple built by the Birla family, very close to Hindu Mahasabha Bhavan. They walked into the woods behind the temple, and almost at the same spot where they had tried out the guns ten days ago, set up a target on a tree trunk, Gandhi's photograph cut out of a newspaper. Nathuram measured twenty odd paces from the tree and, taking up position, squeezed off two shots. Both the shots hit the target. According to Karkare's statement to the police later, Nathuram practised shooting from various distances and positions. This could not have been true. They had been given only seven extra rounds of ammunition in Gwalior. Also, the noise of repeated gunfire would have definitely attracted the attention of forest guards. After the murder, when the gun was examined by forensic investigators, they found most of the rounds in the magazine unfired. Nathuram told the others that the idea of disguising himself was not working. Instead, he would wear something loosely resembling a uniform, which was devoid of a religious identity. On the way back, they bought a blue grey shirt with large pockets and shoulder flaps. They also bought a khaki cap the ensemble resembled an armed forces uniform.

They were back at the retiring room by 1:00 p.m. Nathuram tried on the shirt; it fitted him well. It was finally time for them to vacate their room. Nathuram requested Sundarilal to extend the booking for another twenty-four hours, but the clerk said that he could do that only on the orders of the station superintendent. An argument ensued between the two. An infuriated Sundarilal insisted that Nathuram, whom he knew as N. Vinayakrau, immediately vacate the room. He stood around till the three walked out with their baggage. Sundarilal ordered Hari Kishen to lock the room.

This incident stayed with Sundarilal. Hari Kishen, Jannu and the waiter at the non-vegetarian cafeteria had also had a good look at them. Nathuram's amateurish attempt to create alibis for his accomplices had been rendered ineffective by their own actions. Right from 9 January, they had left a mile-wide trail of clues and witnesses, which would eventually lead the police to all the gang members and their accomplices.

The three then went to the third-class waiting room where all passengers were allowed to stay. This was a bare hall with a few wooden benches and tables and was crowded with families and their baggage. Luckily, they found a just-vacated bench. Nathuram stretch out on it, while the other two sat on the floor next to him. Apte suggested that they should go to Birla House once and see if there were any familiar faces amongst the policeman patrolling there. Apte and Karkare took a taxi to the intersection of Akbar Road and Albuquerque Road and walked down the entire length of the road twice, keeping a close watch on the gate. They were relieved that there were no familiar faces, no one who could recognize them.

They took a taxi from near the Edward Road Officer's Mess and headed back to the Old Delhi railway station, reaching at about 3:00 p.m. There they found Nathuram reading a novel. That morning Nathuram had expressed a desire to eat peanuts roasted in their shells. On their way back from Birla House, the two found a hawker selling these near India Gate; they bought a packet to give to Nathuram. They sat talking about inane things while Nathuram relished the peanuts. The trio was gripped by the emotions of those embarking on a momentous mission. They knew that their actions would change the history of the world; they knew that Nathuram would be a condemned man but hoped that with the help of their influential patrons in Delhi, the other two would escape. At a quarter past four, Nathuram got up and said, '*Ata nighayala pahije.*' (Must leave now.) He patted his pocket to reassure himself that the gun was there. '*Amhi barober Yeu?*' (Should we come along?) Apte asked. After coming all the way from Bombay, it was a very surprising question. If they were not going to act as Nathuram's wingmen while he took position to murder Gandhi, why had they accompanied him?

'Why not?' Nathuram replied. '*Ata ith paryant allat tar shevat paryant barobar raha.*' (After having accompanied me so far, you might as well remain with me till the end.) Saying this, Nathuram walked off.

After ten minutes, Apte and Karkare took a tonga to Connaught Place. They left their bedding and bags in the waiting room at the station. After walking a few paces they got into another tonga and got off a couple of hundred yards away from the gate of Birla House. The two then mixed with the crowd and walked into the gardens at the rear of Birla House, where the prayers were held. They found that the lawns were packed to capacity. Some people were sitting and some were standing, while many others were pacing around. Everybody was looking towards the corner of the house around which Gandhi emerged every evening to attend the prayer meeting. It was 5:00 p.m.; Gandhi was late. There was a murmur in the crowd: 'He is never late for prayers. Has something happened? Will he not attend the prayers this evening?'

Apte and Karkare found Nathuram waiting on the lawns between the low platform where Gandhi sat during prayers and the steps that led up to the terraced garden where the prayers were held. Gandhi would climb up these steps; he would have to go past them on his way to where he sat. Apte and Karkare positioned themselves on both sides of Nathuram, a few paces behind him; they would ensure that he was not jostled or obstructed. None of them showed any signs of recognition to one another.

The time was fifteen minutes past five. Suddenly, there was a murmur; Gandhi had come into view around the corner of Birla House and was slowly making his way towards the prayer lawns.

Nathuram, flanked by Apte and Karkare, now very close behind him, moved to a spot from where it would be easy for them to move directly into Gandhi's path.

Gandhi had reached the steps; the crowd surged towards him. It was threatening to engulf him. They were lucky: the big Sikh companion of Gandhi, who normally always preceded Gandhi and cleared a path for him through the crowed, wasn't there today. He was following Gandhi, trying to catch up. The crowd was disciplined: a path opened up for Gandhi to walk through.

Gandhi had taken his hands off the shoulders of Abha and Manu and was returning the greetings of the crowd with folded hands while making his way towards the dais.

Nathuram made his move. He moved in from the right and stepped directly into Gandhi's path. Manu saw the young man blocking their path. Nathuram stood with folded hands bowed and said, 'Namaste, Bapuji.' Manu requested the young man to move away, saying, 'Brother, Bapu is late for the prayers...' Before she could finish her sentence, the young man pushed her aside; she stumbled; the spittoon and rosary fell from her hands; she fell to the ground too. As she fell, she recognized Nathuram. She had seen him that day at noon, the man in a trance, with a menacing expression on his face. In the next instant, Godse whipped out a gun, pointed it at Gandhi and squeezed off three shots one after the other in rapid succession.

Three gunshots rang out. Manu heard Gandhi utter, 'Ram...Ram...R...a...m...R...a...,' and then she saw him fall.

It was seventeen minutes past five on the evening of 30 January 1948.

The history of India had been rewritten. The world would never be the same.

IV

BUNGLING THE INVESTIGATION FACILITATING GANDHI'S MURDER

My faith does not allow me to put myself under any human protection at prayer time, when I have put myself under the sole protection of God.

—M.K. Gandhi,
21 January 1948

I draw the attention of the Union government to the shocking inefficiency and the lack of initiative displayed by the police in investigating the matter between 20–30 January 1948. After the arrest of Madanlal, the Delhi Police had detailed information about the existence of a conspiracy to murder Gandhiji, in a very comprehensive statement made by Madanlal. Dr J.C. Jain had informed the Honourable Minister, Morarji Desai, about the existence of a conspiracy to murder Mahatma Gandhi, the Bombay Police were immediately given all the information. On the basis of these two statements, contact was immediately established between the Delhi and Bombay Police. But the Police failed in extracting any benefit from these two statements. If at that time investigations were carried out with due diligence and a bit of enterprise, it is possible that this tragedy could have been averted.

—Judge Atmacharan,
ICS, in his judgment in the
Gandhi murder case

It is difficult to protect someone who refuses to be protected by mere mortals. Gandhi was such a person.

After the failed murder attempt on the 20th, Union Home Minister Sardar Patel had suggested that more police be deployed to protect Gandhi; the number was increased from five to twenty-five policemen in plain clothes. Patel's suggestion of frisking everyone who attended the prayer meetings was outright rejected by Gandhi. He refused to have armed police present during the prayers and refused to restrict the number of people attending his prayers. 'My faith does not allow me to put myself under any human protection at prayer time, when I have put myself under the sole protection of God,' he said.

After Madanlal's arrest, it was initially believed that he had acted on his own—the act of an angry refugee. But from Choturam's and Sulochana Devi's statements, the police realized that there were more than one person involved in the attack. During his interrogation, Madanlal kept repeating: '*Woh phir ayega!*' (He will come back!) The Delhi Police came under immense pressure to arrest Madanlal's accomplices fast.

◆

Since colonial times, it has been mandatory in India to register newspapers and periodicals under the Press Act; the information lists each publisher, editor and printer, along with their addresses. One visit to the department of the registrar of newspapers would have revealed the identities of those associated with *Agranee* and *Hindu Rashtra*. In the next ten days, neither Sanjeevi nor Nagarvala did this. Due to its rabid and hate-filled editorial content, the two periodicals had been fined on many occasions. Since 1946, *Agranee* had been under observation by the Bombay provincial government. Thus, a detailed report, containing its editorial record and office details, name and address of its editor, publisher and owners, was prepared by the local intelligence department of Poona. A copy was sent to the provincial home department, another to the Union home department and a third to the Intelligence Bureau, the department headed by Sanjeevi, the chief of investigation in the bomb attack case. This came to light eighteen years after Gandhi's murder, during the Kapur Commission's investigations. All three main accused in the murder were history-sheeters and were known to the police in their towns and provinces.

In the days after the 20th, the gang leaders freely moved around Bombay city and province, visiting their regular haunts and their supporters to source funds and look for weapons. Yet the police could not activate their network of informants and get any information about the killers. Nagarvala had evolved his own theory about the conspiracy: he believed that there was a core group of twenty to twenty-five people, actively conspiring to attack and kidnap Gandhi. This core group, he believed, was assisted by a team of twenty people for each of the leaders, and they had access to a huge cache of arms and explosives hidden all over the country; their objective was to destabilize the government. Nagarvala was confident that, given time, he would expose the entire plot and arrest all the members of this sinister organization in one fell swoop. He had ordered surveillance on the Hindu Mahasabha offices, but what good was surveillance when the watchers did not know who they were looking for? It was the same for the surveillance on Savarkar Sadan: the watchers did not know who they were looking for.

The surprising bit was that although he had heard about Karkare's involvement from two different sources, Morarji Desai and the Delhi Police, Nagarvala did not attach any importance to it. He merely brushed it away as a planted attempt to throw him off the scent of the real plot. Instead of asking the Ahmednagar Police for information about Karkare, Nagarvala contacted his brother, an honorary magistrate in Ahmednagar, and asked him. The next day, Nagarvala's brother informed him that Karkare was not in Ahmednagar and also told him that the Ahmednagar Police were on the lookout for Karkare. Neither did Nagarvala pay heed to this information, nor did he bother to inform his superiors in Delhi. Later, during the Kapur Commission's inquiry in Ahmednagar, it came to light that the police in Ahmednagar knew not only about Karkare's association with Madanlal but also about his close ties to Apte and Godse.

To the Delhi Police officers, Nagarvala's orders were that they should not advertise their presence in Bombay. He ordered them not to wear their uniforms and asked them to check out of the hotel they were staying in. On their return to Delhi, the officers claimed that they had more than three meetings with Nagarvala during their two-day stay in Bombay, but at every meeting, he was extremely rude and abrupt with them, insisting that they leave the Bombay Police alone and go back to their home base. On the afternoon of 23 January, the officers met Nagarvala again, who told them to leave immediately and dismissed them. The officers had been ordered to go to Poona and hand over a copy of Madanlal's confession to the police there, but they did not go to Poona and immediately returned to Delhi. It wasn't as if constables had been sent from Delhi: these were fairly senior officers, a DSP and an inspector, but they behaved like incompetent junior constables disinterested in the task assigned to them. If the Poona Police had been informed about *Agranee* and *Hindu Rashtra*, they would have immediately revealed the identity of Nathuram Godse, Narayan Apte and the weapons merchant Badge.

Sanjeevi read the report filed by his officers on their return from Bombay and their complaint about how Nagarvala had treated them. He did not confront or reprimand Nagarvala, his junior, deciding that he should not antagonize him since he required his cooperation in the investigation. Sanjeevi rightly believed that the conspirators belonged to Bombay Province, so he would require the cooperation of the Bombay Police in the investigation, but there was no coordination between the two departments and no communication either. Three days after the attack on Gandhi and Madanlal's arrest, although Madanlal's interrogation continued and he further divulged clues about the identities of his accomplices, the police made no headway in the investigation. Truly shocking was the complete lack of coordination between the Delhi and Bombay police departments. Nagarvala was not informed about the recovery of unclaimed laundry bearing the initials 'N.V.G.', and Sanjeevi was not briefed about information provided by Jain or what Nagarvala had learnt about Karkare from Ahmednagar. This information, when tallied with Madanlal's confession, would have proved invaluable. On the evening of the 27th, Nagarvala and Rana spoke to Sanjeevi from the former's residence. Nagarvala told Sanjeevi that he was not going to act on the confession as he was very close to exposing the real conspiracy and promised to send a detailed report. Sanjeevi did not reprimand Nagarvala for pursuing an uncorroborated line of investigation and ignoring a confession backed by the statements of three eye witnesses. Surprisingly, he agreed to wait for Nagarvala's report. The promised report was on

Sanjeevi's desk on the morning of 31 January 1948, more then twelve hours after Gandhi was murdered.

On returning to Poona, Rana claimed to have fever, so he did not attend office on 28 January and also did not summon any of his officers home to brief them.

Finally, on the evening of the 29th, Rana briefed his subordinate Rao Saheb Gurtu about the information provided by Madanlal. Gurtu immediately recited from memory the names of Nathuram V. Godse (N.V.G.) and Narayan D. Apte as the editor and publisher of *Agranee* and *Hindu Rashtra*, respectively, and Badge as the proprietor of Shastra Bhandar. Gurtu gave photographs of everyone alluded to in the confession to Rana and their history-sheet records made by the police. Rana, however, did not divulge this information to Nagarvala or Sanjeevi. Later, he told the Kapur Commission that he did not trust the telephone system as the operators were known to listen in. He did not use the secure police communication lines to transmit this crucial information to his superiors in Bombay or Delhi. When asked why he did not rush an officer with the information to Delhi, he replied that he did not think it necessary.

When questioned later about his slow journey to Bombay, Rana said that Sanjeevi had asked him to travel discreetly, so he decided to travel via Allahabad. The other excuse he gave was that he was afraid of flying, so he travelled by train. His irrational explanation was accepted. Why Sanjeevi asked Rana, head of CID, Poona, to act as a messenger boy and not carry out independent investigations based on the confession is also a mystery. Nagarvala never revealed the reason for his obstinate belief that the conspiracy was to kidnap, not murder, Gandhi. He was never asked to explain, till the Kapur Commission of Inquiry raised the issue twenty years later. Surprisingly, Sardar Patel appointed him overall in-charge of the investigations after Gandhi was murdered. The man who had totally bungled the investigation between 20 and 30 January, and in doing so, made it easy for the conspirators to succeed, was rewarded by being put in charge of the murder investigation.

Another major lapse on the part of the police was regarding the press release they had found in Room No. 40 of Marina Hotel. It established that the occupants, who were suspected to be Madanlal's accomplices, had connections with the Hindu Mahasabha in Delhi. A casual questioning of its office bearers would have revealed the identities of the conspirators and their call to Savarkar. If the Delhi Police had questioned Ashutosh Lahiri, he would have revealed the identities of Nathuram, Apte and Karkare and their association with Savarkar. In an affidavit submitted to the Kapur Commission, Lahiri complained that the police did not bother to question him between the 20th and 30th. If they had, he could have provided a lot of information about all those who were eventually accused of murdering Gandhi.

That the police must have gathered a lot of information about the identities of the gang members and their sympathizers is apparent from the speed of the arrests of the accused and the identification of all the witnesses in the Gandhi murder case post 30 January. Within fifteen days of the murder, the entire gang was behind bars. Even the identities of their sponsors and suppliers were established and many of them were detained and questioned. It is unlikely that Nathuram would have revealed information to the police as willingly as Madanlal. The police did not use third degree methods on him. Nathuram, who complained about every imagined and actual infringement of his rights or about ill-treatment by the police in court, never accused the police of harassment or torture.

There was another glaring lapse on the part of the police. No policemen from Bombay Province, especially from Poona and Ahmednagar, were brought to Delhi to help in investigations and to act as watchers and spotters at Birla House to ensure that known troublemakers from their home province were apprehended before they got near Gandhi. Nathuram, Apte and Karkare were apprehensive about this and had gone to Birla House on the 30th to see if any police officers from their province were positioned there. The murderers had thought of this possibility but the police had not. The Bombay city and provincial police claimed that it was up to the Delhi Police to ask for such help. Yet, on 1 February 1948, four police constables from Poona were sent by air to Delhi to look for Apte and Karkare and to ensure that they created no further mischief. What isn't known is whether this was done on a request from the Delhi Police or if it was an initiative of the Poona Police.

Nagarvala had, in the only act of intelligent police work, ordered the arrest of Badge on 24 January. Not that he had any evidence to order the arrest: a hand grenade had been found in the pocket of the coat worn by Madanlal when he was searched after his arrest on the 20th. He had confessed that the conspiracy had been hatched in Poona and divulged that an arms trader from Poona was involved. The Bombay Police were also investigating bomb attacks in Poona where hand grenades were used. Badge was known to the police to be a weapons and explosives dealer from Poona. However, this order of Nagarvala too became a victim of inter-departmental non-cooperation. Poona Police fell under the Bombay provincial police department, but was independent of the Bombay City Police. For the next seven days, they sat on the order; Badge was eventually arrested on the morning of the 31st. The Poona Police claimed that Badge had gone into hiding in the forests surrounding Poona, so they could not find and arrest him. After his arrest, Badge told the police that after arriving from Delhi on the 22nd, he had been in Poona at his home all along.

On 9 January, Inspector Razak of Ahmednagar Police had recommended that Karkare and Madanlal be detained and questioned. It took the department three days to process the recommendation and issue warrants; by then, both had fled Ahmednagar. Karkare was an influential person and it would not be surprising if a friend or sympathizer in the department had tipped him off about the impending arrest. Inspector J.N. Joshi, a stenographer with Ahmednagar Police, had run into Madanlal at the railway station on 9 January 1948 and had spoken to him. He later recalled that Madanlal had mentioned that he was going to Delhi to approve of a prospective bride. Razak's recommendation must surely have passed Joshi's desk. Karkare was an elected member of the Ahmednagar municipality, well known in Ahmednagar, and it was also common knowledge in Ahmednagar that Madanlal was a member of Karkare's gang. Joshi did not bother to tell his superiors or his subordinates that at least one of the persons they wanted to detain, had already flown the coop.

After reading the newspaper reports about the bomb attack at Gandhi's prayer meeting on 20 January and the subsequent arrest of Madanlal Pahwa by the Delhi Police, Sub-inspector Balakundi of Ahmednagar Police informed his DIG that he suspected that the Madanlal arrested by the Delhi Police was the same Madanlal who had been active in Ahmednagar and was an associate of Karkare, both of whom the Ahmednagar Police wanted to arrest. Inspector Razzak of Poona Police and Sub-inspector Deshmukh of Ahmednagar Police also expressed the same suspicion to the DIG, who told them to keep the information to themselves; if the Delhi, Poona or Bombay police wanted the information, they would ask them for it. The DIG told Razzak that on his return to Poona, if he wished, he could inform the DIG CID there. He told Sub-inspector Deshmukh that if he wished to go to Delhi to look for Pahwa and Karkare there, he could do so on his own. The DIG did not think it important to inform his counterparts in Poona, Bombay or Delhi about the information his subordinates had given him regarding Madanlal and Karkare.

A report about Pahwa's and Karkare's subversive activities was sent to the home department of Bombay Province on 8 January. S.M. Dalal of the home department signed the report on 11 January and sent it to his boss, V.T. Dehejia, secretary in the home department, Government of Bombay Province. Dehejia signed the report on 12 January and recommended that both Karkare and Pahwa be arrested. He forwarded the report to Home Minister Desai, who signed it on the same day and ordered that both Pahwa and Karkare should be immediately arrested. Yet, less than ten days after the bomb attack, when Prof. Jain informed him about Pahwa and his accomplice Karkare, Desai did not remember that he had signed the order for their arrests only a few days ago.

Inspector Balakundi knew that Apte and Godse were associated with Karkare; he and his men had watched all four every time they met in Ahmednagar. He suspected that Karkare bankrolled the Apte–Godse gang's activities.

Around the 28th, Sub-inspector Deshmukh went to Poona and then Bombay looking for Karkare, and he took Sub-inspector L.N. Joshi with him. L.N. Joshi knew Karkare and Apte very closely. He claimed that he had set Karkare up in his business when he first arrived in Ahmednagar. Joshi used to regularly have lunch at Karkare's lodge, and many a times, he had seen Madanlal eating there. When they reached Poona, they first went to Shivaji Printing Press, and not finding Karkare there, they went looking for him to Anand Ashram, Apte's home. There, Champa told them that she did not know about Karkare's whereabouts and that Apte too had been away from home for the past several days. She thought that he had gone to Nagpur to get Savrakar's articles published in a book and from there he was going to Gwalior. Champa let slip that her husband was planning to go to Gwalior.

On 30th morning, Deshmukh and Joshi reached Bombay and searched for Karkare in Lalbaug, Byculla and Naigam. Karkare's brother worked in a textile mill in central Bombay. They searched for him till 9:30 p.m. that evening, when they heard the news of Gandhi's murder. The Ahmednagar Police were aware of the association of Apte, Godse, Karkare and Pahwa, but they kept the information to themselves.

There were grenade attacks in Poona on Muslim establishments and processions during Muharram. The premier of Bombay Province was aware that the police had arrested a close associate of Apte in such an attack and suspected that the publisher of *Agranee* Narayan Apte was involved in the attack too. He had written to his home minister asking him why Apte had not been arrested so far. All this transpired around 20 January 1948, but strangely between 20 and 30 January, during those fateful ten days, everyone seemed to have suffered from memory loss.

♦

After the Gandhi murder, the Union home ministry launched an investigation to find out the extent of infiltration of RSS and Hindu Mahasabha cadres and sympathizers in government services, police forces and armed forces. The presence of a large number of active members was found in all wings. Apart from active members, there were numerous sympathizers who subscribed to the intolerant, fanatic ideology, and supported and encouraged Hindu extremist groups.

Pyarelal, in his book *Mahatma Gandhi: The Last Phase, Vol. 10, Part II*, has written about this unexplained lethargy on the part of the police.

'What, however, surprises one is that in spite of the definite and concrete information of which the authorities were in possession, they should have failed to trace and arrest the conspirators and frustrate their plan. The failure was an index of the extent of the rot that had permeated many branches of the services, not excluding the police. In fact, later it was brought to light that the RSS organizations had ramifications even in government departments, and many police officials, not to mention the rank and file, gave their sympathy and even active help to those engaged in RSS activities. Even before the bomb explosion, some of the refugee camps in Delhi were known to be buzzing with loose talk about the assassination of Gandhiji and other Congress leaders who enjoyed the reputation of being opposed to communalistic ideologies. A letter which Sardar Patel received after the assassination from a young man, who according to his own admission had been gulled into joining the RSS organization but was later disillusioned, described how members of the RSS at some places had been instructed beforehand to tune in their radio sets on the fateful Friday to hear the good news. Immediately after the news of Gandhi's murder, sweets were distributed in RSS and Hindu Mahasabha Shakhas, branches. When on 31st evening it was decided to ban the RSS and official orders given, the local police chief in one of the Indian states, according to the Sardar's correspondent, sent word to the organisers to close their office "for thirteen days" as a sign of mourning, and disperse but not to disband. The rot was so insidious and widespread that only the supreme sacrifice could arrest or remove it.'

Judge Atmacharan, the presiding judge hearing the Gandhi murder trial in the special court at Red Fort, was extremely critical of the police's role in abetting Gandhi's murder. He passed severe strictures against the police in his judgment. 'I may bring to the notice of the Central Government the slackness of the police in the investigation of the case during the period between 20-1-1948 and 30-1-1948. The Delhi Police had obtained a detailed statement from Madanlal K. Pahwa soon after his arrest on 20-1-1948. The Bombay Police had also been reported the statement of Dr J.C. Jain that he had made to the Hon'ble Mr Morarji Desai on 21-1-1948. The Delhi Police and the Bombay Police had contacted each other soon after these two statements had been made. Yet the police miserably failed to derive any advantage from these two statements. Had the slightest keenness been shown in the investigation of the case at that stage, the tragedy probably could have been avoided.' Short of holding the police guilty of assisting in Gandhi's murder, the presiding judge had passed one of the most adverse comments on record against the police.

The J.L. Kapur Commission of Inquiry, instituted in 1965 to look into the allegations that many people had information about the planned attempt on Gandhi's life, also passed many adverse remarks against the negligence and ineptitude of the police in general and the sheer inefficiency of some of the senior officers in particular.

Deputy Prime Minister Sardar Patel's letter dated 27 February 1948 to Prime Minister Nehru says: 'It was a fanatical wing of the Hindu Mahasabha directly under Savarkar that (hatched) the conspiracy and saw it through' (*Sardar Patel's Correspondence*, Volume 6, p. 56). This also indicates the involvement of Savarkar and those fanatically loyal to him in Gandhi's murder. If the police had been even slightly more efficient during the investigation of the bomb attack, Gandhi could have been saved.

◆

Murder Investigation and Arrests

After the 30th, the police was very quick in arresting the accused. First, Nathuram was taken to the Tughlaq Road police station and formally charged and arrested for the murder of Mohandas Gandhi. An FIR, was recorded and filed at the Tughlaq Road police station.

At 5:30 a.m. on 31 January, Inspector Oak of the Poona district police arrested Badge from his home in Poona. When asked where Madanlal had got the explosives, Badge confessed to having supplied them. However, he denied that he was part of the conspiracy to kill Gandhi. Later, after getting a conditional pardon, Badge made a confessional statement to Nagarvala, recounting the events from day one in great detail. Nagarvala led a raid on Savarkar Sadan in the afternoon on the 31st. When they reached there, Savarkar met them outside his first floor room. On seeing Nagarvala, he immediately asked, 'So you have come to arrest me for the murder of Mahatma Gandhi?' Nagarvala was surprised that Sarvakar should preempt him in such a way and replied that they were there only on a routine search and seizure operation. While Nagarvala was searching Savarkar's home, it came under attack from an angry mob. A large posse of police was called for and the rioters dispersed. Incriminating documents were seized from his residence, establishing the close relationship Savarkar had with the gang members in general, and Nathuram and Apte in particular. Savarkar was detained in the Gandhi murder case on 5 February and was formally arrested on 11 March 1948.

Nagarvala went to Poona looking for Apte, Gopal Godse and Shankar Kistayya on 5 February. At Apte's home, he was told that they had not seen or heard from him for the past twenty days. Shankar had gone to Sholapur to meet his mother and hadn't returned. He walked into the Bombay Police headquarters on 6 February, looking for his master Badge, and was greeted with a tight slap by Nagarvala and arrested.

Gopal was hiding at his ancestral home in Uksan. Inspector Charles Anthony Pinto of Bombay Police had staked out the Godse home in Uksan. On the afternoon of the third day, Pinto saw Gopal arrive there. After ensuring that Gopal had settled in, Pinto confronted and arrested him and immediately brought him to Bombay. On being interrogated, he told the police that he had given his revolver for safe-keeping to Pandurang Godbole, his friend who used to work in his elder brother Dattatreya Godse's company, Udyam Engineering, a fabrication workshop. Pinto took Gopal back to Poona on the 8th to Godbole's home.

After Godbole learnt that Gandhi's murderer was Gopal's brother, Nathuram, he panicked. He had agreed to hide the gun that Gopal had given him and was certain of now being implicated in the murder case. He spoke to his friend, Kale, who agreed to dispose of the gun. After sustained interrogation, Godbole admitted that he had handed over the gun to his friend. Kale was immediately picked up and questioned. He admitted that he had thrown away the gun the night Godbole had given it to him, in the bushes opposite the gate of Fergusson College in Poona. The gun wasn't found even after an extensive search was conducted by the police. Kale and Godbole were detained and kept in custody for questioning for six weeks.

By now Nagarvala, acting on Badge's confession, had picked up almost all the accused except Apte and Karkare. After Nathuram's arrest, a diary was recovered from him, which proved to be a valuable source of information. Godse had kept very detailed accounts of the money spent by them. Details like '250 to Gopal'; '50 to Bandobhau'; '305 Bombay–Delhi aeroplane'; '300 Karkare' were all neatly noted down. Although Nathuram claimed that he was acting on his own, from his notes, the police surmised that there was a larger group at work. Nathuram and Apte called Badge 'Bandobhau', Gopal could only be Nathuram's brother Gopal Godse, and 308 for 'Bombay–Delhi aeroplane' meant that two one-way tickets for Delhi had been purchased, since one ticket cost ₹154 in those days. Not only this, the diary also had an account of Nathuram's movements between 20 and 30 January. He had mentioned staying at Elphinstone Hotel in Bombay from the 24th to the 27th. On 5 February, two CID officers visited Elphinstone Hotel on Hornby Road but found no record of their stay in the guest register. The manager asked them if they meant Elphinstone Annexe at Carnac Road. He spoke to the manager of the Annexe, Kashmirilal, and asked about the persons the police were looking for. The Annexe is a small hotel; the gallery which doubles up as its lobby could be clearly seen from where Kashmirilal was speaking on the phone. Apte and Karkare were standing just outside their room when the call came through. Kashmirilal noticed them. Govinda, a room attendant, was standing close to Kashmirilal; overhearing the conversation, he mentioned that one of the occupants of Room 5 had also stayed with them from 24th to 27th. Hearing vague references to 24 January, Apte asked Kashmirilal what was going on. After reassuring him that it was nothing, Kashmirilal hurriedly left for Elphinstone Hotel with the guest register, where the two cops were waiting for him. Suspicious, Apte and Karkare immediately picked up their bags and left. They beat the police by thirty minutes.

◆

On the evening of the 30th, after starting the rumour that the assailant was a Muslim and raising slogans like 'Kill all Muslims!' and '*Khoon Ke badle Khoon!*', Apte and Karkare had slipped out of Birla House using a side gate and made their way to Old Delhi railway station. They spent the night on the platform there and saw the police arrive at the station and carry away Nathuram's luggage from the retiring room. Apte and Karkare planned to meet some sympathetic politicians in Delhi, who they knew were supporters of the Hindu right wing, to get funds and help organize their escape. However, when they tried to reach their benefactors the next day, they got caught in the million-strong crowd accompanying Gandhi's funeral procession. They later discovered that no one was willing to help them; doors were slammed on their face. They made their way back to the station and caught an express train to Allahabad as they suspected that the trains to Bombay were being watched.

As per Apte's instructions, on hearing of Gandhi's murder, Manorama Salvi had faithfully sent a telegram on the morning of 31st, addressed to the secretary of the Hindu Mahasabha in Delhi. It read: 'ARRIVING DELHI ARRANGE FOR GODSE's DEFENCE Stop N Stop D Stop APTE Stop'. After a roundabout route, Apte and Karkare reached Bombay on 2 February. They first went to the Sea Green (North) Hotel. Satyavan Rele, the manager, was unable to give them a room but offered them two beds in different rooms occupied by other people. On the 3rd, they checked out and got a double room at the Elphinstone Annexe Hotel.

On hearing the manager's conversation, the duo hurriedly left the hotel and took a taxi to Arya Pathik Ashram at Sandhurst Bridge. Apte was sure the manager, G.P. Dube, would accommodate them, but they were out of luck. Later, Dube told the police that he had been put off by their dishevelled look. After being turned away from there, Apte and Karkare, for the first time, experienced what it felt like to be on the run. They went straight to the Victoria Terminus station and caught a local train to Thana. In the late afternoon, they turned up with their bags at Joshi's house, who knew of their involvement in Gandhi's murder, but Joshi was a staunch Savarkarite and Karkare's friend, so he stuck his neck out for them. The two were keen to escape to a foreign territory or country to evade arrest. Joshi volunteered to meet some people to seek help for them. The first person he approached was M.G. Ghaisas, who was asked to go to Poona to assess the situation there and find out if the police was looking for Apte. Ghaisas returned on the 9th morning with encouraging news, so Apte and Karkare left immediately for Poona. According to their statements, in Poona, they were offered hospitality by their friends and were able to hide in their homes; other friends brought news and clothes for Apte from his home, while some offered to help them escape.

However, Poona was becoming dangerous for them: the police were closing in. Karkare and Apte decided to leave for Bombay. They were certain that friends in Bombay would be able to help them escape to Goa, then a Portuguese colony, and from there, they would escape to a foreign country. Apte and Karkare returned to Bombay on the morning of 11 February and went straight to Thana. They stayed with Joshi for two days. Joshi's son had got them used suburban railway tickets that had been purchased on 30 January. In the event of their arrest, they hoped to fool the police into thinking that they had been in Bombay on that day. After Apte's arrest, police found ticket number 05891 dated 30 January 1948 from Dadar to Vile Parle on his person. It could not have been too difficult a task for organizations like the Hindu Mahasabha and RSS to procure a used ticket. For accounting purposes, all the tickets collected at stations from passengers are recorded; their numbers are noted in a recovered ticket register at the station and then sent to the central office and from there, to the divisional office. Once the ticket numbers are recorded and tallied, the tickets become useless and are disposed of. It is possible to siphon off a couple of tickets anywhere during this process. After investigation, the police were able to prove that the ticket had been collected by the ticket checker at Vile Parle Station and entered in the used ticket register the same day they had been issued. Like the telegram sent by Manorama, the possession of the ticket also proved to be a worthless alibi.

On 13 February, Apte and Karkare checked into Pyrke's Apollo Hotel behind Regal Cinema in south Bombay. Apte and Manorama had checked in here several times as Mr and Mrs Apte. Claudio Pinto, a clerk at the reception counter, checked in N. Kashinath and R. Bishnu and gave them the keys to Room 29 on the second floor. At about ten the next morning, Apte called Manorama, asking her to meet him at six that evening at the hotel. Unknown to him, the police knew about their liaison due to Badge's confession. Since Manorama's father was working as a male nurse in the police hospital, he lived in police quarters and their phone was an extension number from the general police exchange. For the past few days, Nagarvala had ordered surveillance on the Salvi home, and their phone conversations were monitored. The police listened into Apte's conversation with Manorama that morning. After setting up a love tryst with Manorama, Narayan Apte and Vishnu Karkare went their separate ways.

At 11:00 a.m., Inspector B.A. Haldipur arrived at the hotel and enquired about the occupants of Room 29. He was told that they were not in. Haldipur decided to wait for them to come back. He took up a vantage position in the lobby; he knew that Apte had asked Manorama to come at six that evening. Inspector Haldipur was fond of sketching people, and on many of his vigils, he would draw sketches of those he saw or those he was investigating. While waiting for Apte and Karake to turn up, Haldipur sat and indulged in his hobby of sketching. After a long vigil, at 5:30 p.m., a taxi pulled up in front of the hotel and Apte got out. Pinto, the reception clerk, nodded, a prearranged signal, and Haldipur pounced on Apte. He was arrested and whisked off to the police headquarters.

Karkare had gone to Thana to meet Joshi to check on the arrangements for their escape out of the country. He came back to the hotel at 8:25 p.m. Haldipur was waiting for him, and he arrested Karkare too. Now most of those named by Badge were in the hands of the police.

On 11 February, Shankar Kistayya led a police party to the spot in the woods behind Hindu Mahasabha Bhavan and the South Indian School in New Delhi, where he had buried the hand grenades and the unused gun cotton slab before escaping from Delhi on the evening of 20 January. He showed them two spots, about 45 yards apart, from where the police recovered three live hand grenades, twenty-five cartridges and a gun cotton bomb with an attached fuse wire.

The register at Old Delhi railway station's retiring room showed that Nathuram had booked it after producing a ticket from Gwalior to Delhi dated 29 January and one from Poona to Delhi. Godse had confessed that he procured a gun in Gwalior with Parchure's help. On 14 February, DSP of Bombay CID, N.Y. Deulkar, arrived in Gwalior to arrest Parchure. He discovered that Parchure was being held in the Gwalior Fort in military custody.

Parchure had celebrated Gandhi's murder by distributing sweets and boasting that he knew the killers. He had publicly referred to Gandhi as the reincarnation of the Mughal emperor Aurangzeb, who was known to be a religious fanatic and was alleged to have ill treated Hindus during his reign. Parchure had told his elder brother on 29 January (after Nathuram and Apte had left for Delhi) that the people staying at their home the previous day were on a mission to murder Gandhi and that he had helped them to acquire a gun on the recommendation of Savarkar. After Gandhi's murder, he told Ram Dayal Singh that a good deed had been done; 'The enemy of the Hindu Dharma has been killed.' He added that the killer was one of their own men. When all this was reported to

Home Minister Dhule of the newly appointed Congress government in Gwalior, he immediately ordered Parchure's arrest under the Maintenance of Public Security Ordinance.

The bungler U.H. Rana also got into the act. He arrived in Gwalior and, along with Deulkar, demanded that Parchure be handed over to them.

On 17 February, Nagarvala received an order from Delhi, appointing him the officer heading the investigation of the Gandhi murder case. Inefficiency did fetch rewards. But Nagarvala was ordered to investigate the murder immediately. Sardar Patel had summoned him to Delhi on 1 February itself. As Nagarvala was preparing to leave for Delhi to take charge of the Gandhi murder investigation, one of his junior officers informed him that an undertrial detainee at Arthur Road Jail was insisting on meeting him urgently. When Nagarvala went to the Arthur Road Prison, Limaye, an undertrail detainee and known Savarkarite, was brought to meet him. As was his habit, Nagarvala greeted Limaye with a tight slap and asked him why he wanted to speak to him. Limaye asked Nagarvala if it was true that Gandhi had been murdered and the murderer was Nathuram Godse. Nagarvala confirmed this. Limaye told him that if Nathuram Godse was the murderer then Narayan Apte was sure to be his accomplice; the two always did things together and both would have definitely acted on the orders of Savarkar since they were fiercely loyal to Savarkar and faithfully obeyed his orders.

On 18 February, Parchure expressed his intention to make a voluntary confession. R.B. Atal, a first-class magistrate, was summoned to Gwalior Fort, which was under the command of the army. Access to Parchure was only possible after getting permission from the military commandant of the Fort. Atal was accompanied by senior superintendent of police, Gwalior, Dinkar P. Thorat Patil.

On reaching the Fort, they were first taken to the office of Commanding Officer Major Chhatrey. Accompanied by Chhatrey, Atal proceeded to the cell where Parchure was detained. The cells were situated at a higher level in the fort, which had been built by the Mughals to hold their prisoners in solitary confinement. On meeting Parchure, Atal asked him if he wanted to make a confessional statement voluntarily. Parchure replied in the affirmative. Atal then took Parchure to the rear veranda of the cell and asked for a table and two chairs to be placed there. He also asked Chhatrey to post two armed soldiers as sentries in the back compound abutting the veranda, who should stand at a distance of 50 yards from them.

For the next hour, Atal explained to Parchure the legal ramifications and implications of making a sworn confession. Under the prevalent laws, the conviction of a person making a sworn confession was certain. Atal informed him that nobody could force him to make a confession. Parchure insisted that he was making a confession voluntarily, and only after he was convinced did Atal ask Parchure to begin. For the next forty-five minutes, Parchure revealed all that had transpired, from the night of 27 January, when Nathuram and Apte had come to his home, till they left in the evening of the 28th. After listening to Parchure, Atal gave him half an hour to make up his mind and then asked him a few questions. After this long drawn-out process, Atal wrote down, verbatim, Parchure's confession in English.

Atal then read out the statement to Parchure, made him sign every page and ensured that he very diligently performed every legal procedure of recording a confession so that it would not be dismissed due to any technical or procedural mistake in court.

Parchure's confession was more than enough to nail him for his role in the Gandhi murder conspiracy. Based on information provided by Parchure, had the police thoroughly investigated how the gun had come into Goyal's possession and why the maharaja's Aide De Camp had parted with a prized war trophy, evidence of Savarkar's involvement in the murder conspiracy could have been proved. But the purchase of the gun was never investigated.

On 26 February 1948, Apte and Karkare led a police party to the woods behind Hindu Mahasabha Bhavan in Delhi. Apte pointed out the spot where a pistol had been test fired in the early afternoon on the 30th. He pointed out a tree which had four bullet holes. Three portions of the bark were cut and taken as evidence, as well as an empty cartridge case that was found near the spot. The next day, Apte went along with the police to Parchure's residence in Gwalior. Here, he pointed out the wall where a pistol had been test fired. A number of bullet marks were found on the wall; a spent bullet found embedded in the wall was dug out and taken as evidence.

By the time Nagarvala was appointed the chief investigating officer, the police had the prime accused in hand. His job now was to tie up the loose ends, which comprised going over the legal procedures of conducting identification parades, matching the handwriting samples and building up an ironclad case which could not be demolished by defence lawyers. A number of identification parades of the accused were conducted in Delhi and Bombay, which were supervised by magistrates: in Delhi, they were conducted by Magistrate First Class Kishen Chand, and in Bombay, by Chief Presidency Magistrate Oscar H. Brown. One of his first tasks was to collect evidence and witness statements that would link the bomb attack case with the murder case.

Nagarvala, shuttling between Delhi and Bombay, built up a massive dossier of evidence against each of the accused over the next two months. The one person against whom he could not find much hard evidence, other than the confession of Badge, was Savarkar. Just the fact that a phone call had been made to Savarkar Sadan from the Hindu Mahasabha office in Delhi on the morning of 19 January was not enough to nail Savarkar. There was no reason for anybody from the Delhi Mahasabha office to call Savarkar that morning. Apte had a reason and he was at the Mahasabha office at the time the call was booked. But, inexplicably, the Hindu Mahasabha in Delhi was not investigated.

Among the documents seized from Savarkar Sadan during the raid on 31 January, many letters written by Nathuram and Apte to Savarkar were found, confirming the close relationship between the three. After 14 January, Apte had bragged about meeting the actress Shanta Modak 'Bimba' in the train and befriending her to his fellow accomplices. Badge told Nagarwala about this in his confession. The police interviewed 'Bimba' and recorded her statement, which revealed how she met Apte and Nathuram on the Deccan Express on 14 January and that she had given them a lift in her brother's Jeep and dropped them off at Savarkar Sadan in Shivaji Park.

Prof. Jain had also mentioned Madanlal telling him about Karkare taking Madanlal to meet Savarkar and the latter congratulating and blessing him.

However, despite all these efforts, there was a lacunae in the murder investigations. The procurement of the gun was never investigated efficiently. No wonder, since the bungler Rana was heading the investigations in Gwalior. This led to a weakness in the prosecution's case in the trial, and allowed Savarkar to escape punishment.

Before arresting Savarkar, Nagarvala, accompanied by his boss, Commissioner Bharucha, and the premier of Bombay Province, B.G. Kher, had briefed Sardar Patel in Delhi and asked for his permission to detain and question Savarkar. Sardar Patel had told them that they should not arrest Savarkar thinking that it would please the Union government. If they were to arrest Savarkar and charge him with being involved in the Gandhi murder, they should have sufficient evidence to get a conviction. All the three assured Patel that they had more than enough irrefutable evidence to convict Savarkar in the Gandhi murder. It was only after getting this assurance that Sardar Patel approved the request to detain and question Savarkar. However, in the court, the evidence produced against Savarkar by the prosecution was weak and easily discredited by Savarkar's defence, leading to Savarkar being acquitted by the judge. Even though the approver Badge had provided solid evidence against Savarkar, for an approver's evidence to be upheld in court, it had to be backed by at least two pieces of independent corroborative evidence. Savarkar's defence was successful in raising sufficient doubt about both the evidences presented in court by the prosecution to support Badge's testimony: the record of the call by Apte from the Hindu Mahasabha office in Delhi to the Bombay phone number listed as being Savarkar's and Shanta Modak's account of dropping Apte and Nathuram at Savarkar Sadan. If the procurement of the gun in Gwalior had been thoroughly investigated, Savarkar would have been convicted.

The police filed the chargesheet in the Gandhi murder case on 27 May 1948.

By the time the trial started, Nagarvala and his team of investigators had gathered enough evidence to prove the involvement of each of the accused. If they had shown half the speed and skill while investigating the failed attempt of 20 January, as they showed in investigating the murder, the history of India might have been different.

The main accused in the Gandhi murder case, according to the chargesheet, were: 'Accused No. 1' Nathuram Vinayak Godse; 'Accused No. 2' Narayan Dattatreya Apte; 'Accused No. 3' Vishnu Ramkrishna

Karkare; 'Accused No. 4' Madanlal Kashmirilal Pahwa; 'Accused No. 5' Shankar Kistayya; 'Accused No. 6' Gopal Vinayak Godse; 'Accused No. 7' Vinayak Damodar Savarkar; 'Accused No. 8' Dattatreya Sadashiv Parchure; 'Accused No. 9, 10 and 11' Gangadhar S. Dandavate, Gangadhar Jadhav and Suryadeo Sharma (declared absconders). The last three were not apprehended by the police till the end of the trial. Badge had been granted a judicial pardon in return for the deal he had struck with the court by becoming an 'approver' in the case.

The detailed chargesheet is reproduced in Appendix 1.

V

DISCARDED MENTOR

They were the ones, the word went round, with whom business could be done. The impossible old man was put on a pedestal, admired for his genius and unerring hunch, consulted, listened to with respectful attention and bypassed.

—Pyarelal Nayyar,
in *Mahatma Gandhi:
The Last Phase, Vol. 10, Part II*

If the Godse–Apte gang and the bungling policemen were instrumental in Gandhi's murder, the role of the politicians was no less nefarious. Whether intentional or circumstantial, they played a vital role in making it easier for the murderers to succeed. Others made the act possible by discarding Gandhi's ideals and publicly distancing themselves from him. After the murder, Apte and Karkare were confident that they would escape with help from some powerful politicians in Delhi, both in government and otherwise. After the murder, a lot of criticism was directed towards the Iron Man of India, Sardar Vallabhbhai Patel, the home minister. He has been credited with having successfully convinced and coerced all the princes and kings of the princely states to merge into the Indian Union. Credit for the rebuilding of the Somnath temple in Kathiawad, very close to Porbandar, the birth place of Gandhi, and earlier destroyed by the invader Mahmud Ghazni, also goes to him. But Gandhi's murder remains a great blemish on his otherwise illustrious record.

As home minister, he was in charge of the police and intelligence departments, but as stated in the judgment of the Red Fort trial, the police were responsible for the ease with which Gandhi was murdered.

J.C. Jain had provided vital clues to the home minister of Bombay Province, Morarji Desai, a staunch Gandhian and a very close confidante of Sardar Patel. Desai claimed that he passed on the information to Patel immediately on meeting him in Ahmedabad on 22 January. However, the Delhi Police never acted on that information. Jain was never called in for questioning by the police. The Delhi Police maintained throughout that they were never told about the information that Jain had provided. Why did Patel not see the necessity of informing Sanjeevi, who was overseeing the bomb attack investigation and Madanlal's interrogation in Delhi? This remains a mystery. Testifying before the Kapur Commission, Sardar Patel's daughter Maniben and his secretary Shankar denied that Morarji Desai had informed Sardar about the information given to him by Prof. Jain. Morarji insisted even in his testimony to the Kapur Commission that he had briefed Sardar Patel about the information given to him by Jain when he met him at Ahmedabad on 22 January.

Another startling revelation made by Sardar's daughter during the Kapur Commission's hearings was that she remembered that about a fortnight before the murder, two very agitated men had come to meet her father at their residence one early morning. Her father had later told her that they were the editor and publisher of a Marathi publication from Poona, who were complaining about the unjust prosecution they were subjected to by the provincial government of Bombay. This could only have been Nathuram and Apte. Madanlal, in his confession, had stated that his accomplices were an editor and owner of *Hindu Rashtra* and *Agranee* periodicals from Poona. If Sardar had been kept informed about the investigation into the bomb attack case, he should have recollected the visit by the angry editor and publisher from Poona and connected the two.

Patel did report the threat to his life to Gandhi and advised that his security be increased and all who came to meet him should be frisked. It was a foregone conclusion, however, that Gandhi would refuse any such request. Surprisingly, Patel gave in and left the matter of Gandhi's safety in the hands of destiny. One can understand that all the ministers were scared of the fact that if any action of theirs displeased Gandhi, he could go on another fast, but Patel did not show much interest in overseeing the investigation of the bomb attack case.

Recent events had upset Patel. One was that Gandhi had commenced a fast which had embarrassed and angered Patel. As home minister, he was responsible for providing security to the citizens of the country, but Gandhi had gone on a fast because he felt that the Muslims of India were not receiving their deserved share of security. Patel's detractors in the Congress had launched an attack on him for failing his duties as home minister and providing a reason for Gandhi to go on a fast. Patel had made his displeasure known in no uncertain terms. At a time when the entire Cabinet of independent India operated from Birla House during Gandhi's last fast, Patel left New Delhi to visit Bombay and Ahmedabad.

When the Union Cabinet decided not to withhold the balance payment of ₹550 million to Pakistan, Patel was annoyed. According to Pyarelal, this was the proverbial last straw that broke the camel's back. 'Increasingly, he had had to defer to his Cabinet colleagues on matters of importance and although Gandhi differed on many issues with the stand taken by Patel, he had defended the latter in the face of attacks from the pro-Nehru factions of the Cabinet. Patel did not like to be defended by anybody, not even Gandhi,' writes Pyarelal.

Patel had a very monochromatic view of things, black or white, and was very extreme in his actions. A famous story about his strength and willpower throws light on his attitude towards vexing issues. In his early youth, Vallabhbhai Patel had developed an abscess in his armpit. As the treatment failed to provide relief, he picked up a knife, heated it over the glowing coals on his mother's kitchen stove and plunged it into the abscess and drained it!

He used the same kind of reasoning for being the first to accept Partition.

◆

Released from prison after the Quit India movement, Congress leaders had lost the resolve to fight; they now wanted to negotiate, cut deals, compromise if required but get power at any cost. Only the obstinate old man was still willing to fight for truth. At the conference called by Wavell in Simla, it was apparent that the colonial government was partial towards Jinnah and his Muslim League. Despite being cautioned and warned by Gandhi, the Congress leadership continued negotiating with the government and allowed the colonial government and Jinnah to dominate and gain an advantage. On many occasions, Gandhi threatened to withdraw from the negotiations but then they would mollify him and force him to stay. They needed him because they needed someone who could be blamed when things went wrong. This happened during the talks with Wavel, where Jinnah managed to manipulate the nominations for the interim government. The same situation continued during the Cabinet Mission negotiations. Gandhi was forced to be present but no one listened to him. Gandhi issued warning after warning, but they fell on deaf ears. Gandhi understood the situation but was helpless because he had been isolated. Major decisions were taken disregarding his advice, and later on, when realization dawned about the error in those decisions, the blame was cleverly apportioned to Gandhi since they knew he would not contradict them. As was his habit, he always blamed mistakes on a weakness or flaw in his own character or in his adherence to truth and punished himself for everything that went wrong, even when he had warned everyone about it. Jinnah, along with the colonial administration, had recognized this isolation of Gandhi and they made the most of it.

Finally, when Mountbatten arrived with the partition plan, it was too late. Gandhi was preoccupied with riots in various parts of India and saddened by what he saw happening to his country. When negotiations were going on about the transfer of power, although he was present physically, Gandhi's heart and mind were burdened by the suffering of the victims of the insanity that had gripped his people and was tearing his nation apart. Thus, at that crucial time too, his lone voice, warning against the dangers of partition under British rule, was drowned out by the clamour for power, leading his own people to accuse him of groping in the dark and being impractical and abandon him at crucial junctures. Jinnah took full advantage of the situation and the partial disposition of the colonial administration and the British government towards him and walked off with much more than he had ever imagined he would get.

He used the strategy of terrorizing and belligerence to achieve his objectives. His masterstroke was 'Direct Action'. The Congress leadership had no answer to it. The Hindu extremists also helped by unleashing counter violence against the Muslims, legitimizing Jinnah's demand for a separate homeland for Muslims. Gandhi's was the lone voice against this, but it was drowned out by the cacophony of hate and anger mixed with opportunism and lust for power.

After the Simla Talks, right up to the transfer of power, Gandhi was treated as a nuisance to be tolerated, exploited whenever required but not to be listened to, discarded betrayed even.

Finally, when the time came to decide between an undivided India and the formation of Pakistan, Patel and Nehru immediately opted for partition for several reasons, including the desire to just be rid of the harassment of the Muslim League.

Sardar Patel wasn't the only leader to opt for partition; almost the entire Congress leadership, with the exception of Maulana Abul Kalam Azad and Khan Abdul Gaffar Khan, opted for partition and abandoned Gandhi. Acharya Kripalani, the then-Congress president, had justified his support for partition saying, 'The Hindu and Muslim communities have vied with each other in the worst orgies of violence. I have seen a well where women with their children, 107 in all, threw themselves to save their honour. In a place of worship, fifty young women were sacrificed by their menfolk for the same reason. These ghastly experiences have no doubt affected my approach to the question. Some members have accused us that we have taken the position out of fear. I must admit the truth of their charge. The fear is if we go on like this we will reduce ourselves to a state of enslavement and worse. I have been with Gandhiji for the past thirty years. Why then am I not with him? It is because I feel that he has as yet found no way of tackling the problem on a mass basis.' Patel said, 'I agreed to Partition as a last resort when we would have lost it all.' There was a tone of defeat in their excuses too.

If it can be said that Patel was angry with Gandhi and let his anger cloud his judgement, the 'Jawahar' of Gandhi's eye, Nehru, as prime minister, also failed to support and protect Gandhi.

Nehru was known to be ambitious, a man eager to become the first prime minister of independent India. Post Independence, he was bogged down by seemingly insurmountable problems: the transfer of power, the tragedy of Partition, the resettlement of millions of refugees, the Pakistani invasion of Kashmir and his rivalry with Patel in the Congress. But as prime minister of India, and as one who enjoyed that privilege due to the fact that Gandhi had favoured him, Nehru failed to protect Gandhi.

He was also guilty of blatantly discarding Gandhi in the decision-making process while policies were framed for independent India.

Nehru had been drifting away from Gandhi's vision for India and Gandhi in matters of state. For a long time, he had considered Gandhi as a role model and father figure, but since the advent of the Mountbattens, Nehru was more influenced by the last viceroy and more so by his vicerine. The shrewd couple had sensed the distance between Nehru and Gandhi and the rift and rivalry between Nehru and Patel, which they exploited fully. This has been summed up in the following extract from *Mahatma Gandhi: The Last Phase, Vol. 10, Part II* by Pyarelal. 'But whether they knew it or not, the whole galaxy of the Old Guard, like the galactic system in outer space, were imperceptibly being drawn into a different sun orbit—the orbit of Lord Mountbatten, the coming Viceroy. The different settings in which they and Gandhiji had been functioning of late had differently conditioned their thinking, outlook and approach. Gandhiji's was the redemptive way. He represented the non-violent approach which has its own logic. Unless true repentance manifested itself in Bihar, irrespective of what was happening in other parts of India, the hearts of Hindus and Muslims could not be united and partition of India would be the inevitable result. Sardar Patel, surveying the scene from his orthodox political plane, thought in terms of reciprocity—uniform action in Bihar and Bengal and elsewhere. The League would come to its senses only when it realized that violence was a game "at which both parties can play". Pandit Nehru's was an idealistic approach, but it lacked the sanction which Gandhiji's leadership during the non-violent freedom struggle had provided and which alone could make that idealism effective. Sardar Patel the matter-of-fact realist, was at times very critical of what appeared to him as the disjointed idealism of his colleague. But however much they disagreed with each other, neither of them could agree with Gandhiji. They had willy-nilly to obey the dynamics of the machine of which they had become a part—an administration based ultimately upon force—and the inexorable logic of their own policies since coming into power in the Provinces and at the Centre. A widening gulf separated them from their erstwhile oracle, Gandhi. Sardar Patel was the first to recognize it. The recognition came late to Pandit Nehru, and he continued to struggle against it almost to the last.'

Pyarelal also writes: 'But Lord Mountbatten found in Congress Leaders apt pupils, who hung on his lips, when he discoursed to them on the problem of defence in the event of India being partitioned or otherwise. They were the ones, the word went round, with whom 'business could be done'. The impossible old man was put on a pedestal, admired for his genius and 'unerring hunch', consulted, listened to with respectful attention and by-passed. But the more they drifted away from him, the more they needed him. For in the last resort he alone could deliver the goods. Wanting nothing for himself, he was anxious only to give and to serve, knowing no jealousy, giving himself no airs, never resentful ... never rude, claiming no rights for himself, loath to brood over an injury ... slow to expose, eager to believe the best, always hopeful, always patient.'

At one point, Gandhi had blamed Nehru for sabotaging his dream of a united India. In a very emotional statement to Jayprakash Narayan, the leader of the Congress Socialists, in Panchgani in 1946, Gandhi said, 'Jawaharlal has destroyed my dream of an undivided India.' What prompted this statement? As it implies, this was one of the greatest betrayals faced by Gandhi. This is alluded to in the memoirs of Maulana Azad and in a book written by Minoo Masani *Bliss Was It In That Dawn*. It is a historic fact that Mountbatten first convinced Patel to accept the partition plan; he then convinced Nehru to accept it, since Patel had already approved of it. Mountbatten took the partition plan to Gandhi last, when Gandhi was left with no choice but to accept it.

Gandhi had tried to avoid partition. When all his efforts had failed, he had broached the idea that partition be considered after independence, without any interference from the British. But it was an exercise in futility. Jinnah, who knew he was dying, an ageing Patel and an impatient Nehru, all wanted power fast. It was a statement made by Nehru, as the president of the Congress in Bombay on 10 July 1946, that gave Jinnah and the Muslim League the excuse to unleash violence to achieve Pakistan. Addressing journalists, Nehru had said, 'The Congress will enter the National Government unfettered by any previous pact or understanding. The Congress will be free to frame its policies and actions according to the situations and ground realities. The Congress has agreed to be a member of the Constitution Committee. The Congress will be free to change and alter the Cabinet Mission Plan according to its requirements.' The Congress, like the Muslim League, had previously agreed to abide by the Cabinet Mission plan and this statement by the Congress president came out of the blue. To be fair to Nehru, it must be said that this outburst, which would have very serious ramifications, had stemmed from the constant harassment by Jinnah and the Muslim League and their constant changing of the goal to thwart the Congress leaders. As expected, Jinnah and the Muslim League reacted vehemently and called an emergency session. There, Jinnah declared, 'In the wake of the Congress President's statement, the only option available to the League is to revive vociferously the demand for Pakistan.' At the end of the session, the League backtracked on its previous acceptance of the Cabinet Mission plan and rejected it. The Congress was caught in a bind. It had previously accepted the Cabinet Mission plan, but its president had publicly declared his intention of subverting it. Finally, they reacted to the resolution of the Muslim League and issued a face-saving but ambiguous statement and appealed to the League to cooperate with the Congress in drafting the Constitution of India and in the transfer of power talks. Jinnah rejected the CWC's statement and said that what had been implied by its president was the Congress's real policy.

When the CWC met to approve of the Mountbatten Plan to divide India, Jayprakash Narayan and Dr Ram Manohar Lohia were special invitees. In his book *Guilty Men of Partition*, Lohia describes the meeting: 'Gandhi, the Frontier Gandhi Khan Abdul Gaffar Khan,* Jayprakash Narayan and I were the only four to oppose the plan to partition India, no one else uttered a word of protest against the plan to divide India.' He further writes: 'Gandhiji interrupted the discussion, he lamented that before approving the Partition Plan neither Nehru nor Sardar Patel had briefed him. He had been kept in the dark. An angry Nehru interrupted Gandhiji and said that he had been informing Gandhiji about the developments. When Gandhiji reiterated that he had been kept in the dark about the Partition Plan before it was accepted by Sardar Patel and Nehru, Nehru demurred and admitted that since at that time Gandhiji was touring the riot affected district of Noakhali it was not possible for them to inform him about the Partition Plan.'

---

*Khan was also known as Frontier Gandhi or Sarhad Ke Gandhi.

D.G. Tendulkar, in Volume 7 of his biography of Gandhi, *Mahatma*, has described the meeting and it tallies almost entirely with the version given by Dr Lohia. Tendulkar writes: 'At the meeting, Gandhiji further said that since the Congress Leaders had pledged their acceptance of the Partition Plan, it was binding on the party to accept the Partition as a face-saving exercise for their leaders. After the acceptance of the Partition Plan by the Congress and the Muslim League, the Viceroy and the British Government should step aside and the Congress and the League should without outside influence or pressure chalk out a plan for the partition of India.' Here, the words 'since the leaders had given their word' and 'as a face-saving exercise' become very important. It proves that Patel and Nehru had, without consulting or briefing the party or Gandhi, unilaterally agreed to the partition of India. Yet, the RSS and Hindu Mahasabha blamed Gandhi for the vivisection of India and used it as an excuse to murder him.

Gandhi first heard of the Congress resolution demanding the division of Punjab on communal basis through a press report in March 1947, while he was touring riot-ravaged Bihar. Pyarelal writes in *Mahatma Gandhi: The Last Phase, Vol. 10, Part II*: 'It was the month of March, 1947. Gandhiji had been in Bihar nearly a week, battling with all his strength to bring together the sundered hearts of Hindus and Muslims in that riot torn Province so that they could once again live together as brothers in the land of their birth, when by a stroke of irony he saw in the papers the Congress resolution demanding the partition of the Punjab on communal lines. It was as if the abyss had suddenly opened under his feet. He had not been consulted or even forewarned, "I think I did not know the reason behind the Working Committee resolution," he wrote to Nehru on 20th March. "I cannot understand it," he wrote to Sardar Patel, too. The Congress resolution on the demand for dividing the Punjab stated:

> During the past seven months India has witnessed many horrors and tragedies which have been enacted in the attempt to gain political ends by brutal violence, murder and coercion...

'The Punjab ... became six weeks ago the scene of an agitation, supported by some people in high authority, to coerce and break a popular Ministry which could not be attacked by constitutional methods. A measure of success attended this, and an attempt was made to form a Ministry dominated by the group that had led the agitation. This was bitterly resented and has resulted in increased and widespread violence...

'The tragic events have demonstrated that there can be no settlement of the problem in the Punjab by violence and coercion, and that no arrangement based on coercion can last. Therefore it is necessary to find a way out which involves the least amount of compulsion. This would necessitate a division of the Punjab into two Provinces, so that the predominantly Muslim part may be separated from the predominantly non-Muslim part.'

By formally asking for a division of Punjab on religious lines, the Congress awarded legitimacy to the Muslim League's demand for a separate Muslim homeland, Pakistan. The British administration and the Muslim League had been waiting for just such an opportunity. Gandhi immediately realized the danger behind the Congress's demand, but unfortunately learnt of it only when it was too late. This was how the country was divided: by a mix of political terror, chicanery and a conniving colonial power on one side, and a morally exhausted and cowardly political leadership on the other.

To Nehru, Gandhi wrote: 'I would like you ... to tell me what you can about the Punjab tragedy. I know nothing about it save what is allowed to appear in the Press which I thoroughly distrust. Nor am I in sympathy with what may be termed by the old expression of "hush hush policy". It is amazing how the country is adopting almost the very measures which it criticized during British administration. Of course, I know the reason behind it. It makes no appeal to me.' Gandhi was subtly warning the Congress leadership that they were adopting the colonial policies of withholding information from citizens and the dangerous divide and rule policy too.

The Congress passed the resolution demanding the partition of Punjab on religious lines in the first week of March 1947, without informing or consulting Gandhi. Even after passing the resolution, neither Nehru nor Patel saw it fit to inform him. After a fortnight of the resolution being adopted, on 20 March, Gandhi wrote to Nehru: 'I have long intended to write to you asking you about the Working Committee resolution on the possible partition of the Punjab. I would like to know the reason behind it. I have to speak about it. I have done so in the absence of full facts, with the greatest caution. Kripalani said in answer to a question in Madras that it was possible that the principle might be applied to Bengal also. I was asked by a Muslim Leaguer of note ... if it was applicable to the Muslim-majority Provinces, why it should not be so to Congress-majority Provinces like Bihar. I think I did not know the reason behind the Working Committee's resolution. Nor had I the opportunity. I could only give my own view which was against any partition based on communal grounds and the two-nation theory. Anything was possible by compulsion. But willing consent required an appeal to reason and heart. Compulsion or show of it had no place in voluntariness.'

On the same day, he wrote to Patel: 'Try to explain to me your Punjab resolution if you can. I cannot understand it.' Patel replied on the 24th: 'It is difficult to explain to you, the resolution about Punjab. It was adopted after the deepest deliberation. Nothing has been done in a hurry or without full thought. That you had expressed your views against it, we learnt only from the papers. But you are, of course, entitled to say what you feel right.' The former mentor was being put in his place.

'The situation in the Punjab is far worse than in Bihar.... The military has taken over control. As a result, on the surface things seem to have quietened down somewhat. But no-one can say when there may be a burst-up again. If that happens, I am afraid, even Delhi will not remain unaffected. But here of course we shall be able to deal with it.' But Patel was going to be proved wrong even in Delhi. They required Gandhi to ensure peace in the national capital.

Nehru responded to Gandhi's letter the day after Patel wrote: 'About our proposal to divide Punjab, this flows naturally from our previous discussions. These were negative previously, but now a time for decisions has come and mere passing of resolutions giving expression to our views means little. I feel convinced and so did most of the members of the Working Committee that we must press for this immediate division so that reality might be brought into the picture. Indeed, this is the only answer to Partition as demanded by Jinnah. I found people in the Punjab agreeable to this proposal, except Muslims as a rule. For the present it means an administrative decision without any change in law.'

How could both Nehru and Patel fail to recognize that any demand for division on the basis of religion only legitimized the League's demand for a separate Muslim nation and emboldened the Hindu fanatics to demand a 'Muslim-free' India? But Gandhi's protégés had emerged from his shadow, and now considered their mentor to be a burden they were very reluctantly carrying along. Pyarelal writes: 'Such a thing would have been inconceivable in olden days. Even when he was ranging over the length and breadth of India, they did not fail to consult him before taking any vital decision.' But things had changed.

Speaking at a prayer meeting, Gandhi had said, 'If Partition is unavoidable, it should not be at the hands of the British, the division of the country should not be considered while the British still rule over India. Let the British grant Independence and then the Congress and Muslim League will sit together and decide about the division of the country. I suggested this to the Viceroy; Pandit Nehru and Sardar Patel did not like my suggestion. Let them do what they wish, but let nobody say that Gandhi was a partner to the division of the country. Everyone is in a hurry to achieve independence at any cost.'

The Congress high command had discarded Gandhi and they would regret it. After Independence, when the horrors of the post-Partition massacres blew up in their face and the enormity of the transfer of populations and the tragedies that happened due to it hit them, all the top leaders of the Congress wrung their hands in despair and cried themselves hoarse, saying that they had not expected such horrifying consequences. Two years later, on 16 October 1949, Nehru declared before an audience in New York that, if they had known the terrible consequences of Partition, they would have resisted the division of India. 'It was a big mistake on our part not to have listened to Gandhi at that time,' confessed Maulana Azad. 'If we had only known!' exclaimed Dr Rajendra Prasad. Acharya Kripalani, president of the Congress at the time of Partition, had earlier accused Gandhi of groping in the dark as there was no alternative to Partition. Later in his life, he reserved the choicest epithets for those in the Congress high command whom he blamed for the partition of India, conveniently forgetting his own advocacy of the Partition plan at the All India Congress Committee (AICC) convention.

It has been over seventy years since Gandhi's murder. The principal players of that time are no more. For the past seventy years and more, many lies have been propagated to justify and legitimize Gandhi's murder and about Gandhi's role in the tragic events during the last year of his life. Followers of Gandhi and the subsequent leaders of the Congress have failed to counter the malicious disinformation campaign of Hindu right-wing organizations. The Hindu extremists have recently adopted Patel as their icon, perhaps unaware that he was the one who first accepted the British plan to partition India. He was also one of the signatories to the treaty which agreed to unconditionally give Pakistan ₹550 million.

Patel had been upset by Gandhi's stand on this issue. At the time of Independence, the cash balance of undivided India had to be divided between the two countries according to the size of their territory and population; the debt was also thus divided between them. The cash balance of undivided India was ₹3,750 million. It was decided that Pakistan would be paid ₹200 million on the day it came into being, i.e., 14 August 1947. After negotiations, a bilateral treaty was signed between the two independent nations and Pakistan's share was set at ₹750 million. Deducting the ₹200 million already paid, India owed Pakistan ₹550 million. According to the bilateral treaty, India agreed to pay Pakistan the balance amount at a later date or when Pakistan demanded payment. Patel and Nehru were signatories to this treaty. In Pakistan, the Muslim League ministers went public about having signed this treaty to garner popularity. In India, the news caused a lot of resentment. Worried about the backlash, Congress leaders publicly stated that they had mentioned that the balance amount would be paid when all the unresolved issues between India and Pakistan were sorted out. The treaty was signed when the incursion into Kashmir had already started, but neither did the Muslim League ever accept this 'when all issues are resolved' condition, nor were the Congress leaders ever able to prove that this condition had been included in the treaty. In fact, the treaty document did not mention any such condition.

When the refugees poured in from East and West Pakistan and the atrocities committed on them there became known, the Indian Cabinet decided that India would withhold the payment of the balance amount of ₹550 million, but this was in violation of the treaty. If challenged—and Pakistan would definitely have challenged India's stand—it was not defensible. They had signed a treaty with another independent nation and the treaty did not have any clause for withholding the payment. Not only would India have been branded an untrustworthy nation, but also be guilty of breach of contract. The Indian Cabinet was trying to take a populist stance but were jeopardizing the reputation of the country internationally. When news of the decision made by the Cabinet reached Governor-General Lord Mountbatten, he was worried. Since he was technically the head of the government, he would be party to any decision taken by the Cabinet, and he was loath to be a part of such chicanery.

On 12 January, Gandhi went to meet Mountbatten to understand the situation in Delhi. As Gandhi was leaving, Mountbatten mentioned the decision of the Cabinet to withhold the balance payment, adding that it was legally not defensible and morally dishonest. Gandhi criticized the decision, but left without making any commitment.

That evening, at the prayer meeting, Gandhi announced his decision to go on a fast unto death to bring about peace in the capital. By now the Indian Cabinet had realized the futility of their decision to withhold making the balance payment to Pakistan. Mountbatten had been working feverishly to influence the senior members of the Cabinet to reverse the decision. With the realization that their decision was unsustainable, they were now faced with a dilemma: if they went back on their earlier stand, they would be exposed to public wrath. Patel said, 'The Muslims are already angry with us, we cannot afford to anger the Hindus too.' The Congress was afraid that it would lose popular support and, as a consequence, power.

The Cabinet realized that if they reversed their decision during Gandhi's fast, it would appear as if they had done so under pressure from him. Whatever their thoughts were, when the Cabinet announced their decision to pay the balance amount, it was popularly believed that Pakistan was given the money due to Gandhi's tactics of blackmail by fasting because Gandhi was partial to the Muslims and to Pakistan. This is something that is believed even today. The Cabinet's decision was announced on the second day of the fast, but Gandhi's fast continued for four days more. Today, the campaign has created a belief that Gandhi gifted ₹550/- million to Pakistan because of his 'loyalty' to Pakistan.

The anger against Gandhi was fanned by the RSS and the Hindu

Mahasabha, who campaigned amongst aggrieved refugees, saying that Gandhi was responsible for their miseries. There were many in the Congress who also secretly harboured the same kind of feelings. On several occasions, Gandhi had criticized communal comments publicly made by prominent Congress leaders. Pyarelal writes in *Mahatma Gandhi: The Last Phase, Vol. 10, Part II*: 'Gandhiji viewed with growing uneasiness and alarm the prospect of counter-communalism that was being bred in the Indian Union by continued ill-treatment of the minorities on the other side. Already some ugly symptoms had begun to appear. The President of a Provincial Congress Committee was reported to have said in a public speech that if any harm befell the Hindus in Pakistan the Congress would "resort to reprisals in India after 15 August". Gandhiji immediately wrote to him: "You are enunciating the doctrine of an eye for an eye and a tooth for a tooth. Only, you will wait till the 15 August. Has the Congress policy changed? Congressmen have changed, I know, but I am not aware of any change in the Congress Constitution. Secondly, if Congress policy or practice has changed, who compels you to wait till 15 August? Who will be responsible for the incalculable harm that will have overtaken the people of India as well as Pakistan in the meantime? Who can control the people if they go mad and launch on a course of retaliation?"' One wishes that present day leaders, who have made hate their creed, would realize the harm it does to the nation.

The Direct Action Day riots had terrorized the Hindu populations of Punjab and Bengal and instilled a fear of its recurrence in the hearts of the Congress leaders. In one of his outlandish demands, Jinnah had demanded not only the Punjab and Bengal, but also a 1,000-mile corridor across northern India linking the two Pakistans! The RSS and Hindu Mahasabha did not publicly condemn any of these demands. They were happy if Muslim homelands were created, for then they could then launch a movement to drive Muslims out of Hindustan. But when Partition really happened, the two organizations were thwarted in their plan to purge Hindustan of non-Hindus. They would never forgive the one man who stood between them and their dream of a communally cleansed Hindustan—Gandhi. Even after they succeeded in murdering him, they could not erase his memory and have continued their campaign of lies and hate against him.

After Gandhi's murder, in a letter that Sardar wrote to Pandit Nehru, it is very clear who he blamed for Gandhi's murder: 'It was a fanatical wing of the Hindu Mahasabha directly under Savarkar that (hatched) the conspiracy and saw it through' (*Sardar Patel's Correspondence*, Volume 6, p. 56).

When Nathuram pulled the trigger, he not only accomplished something he had tried and failed on several occasions before, but he also did an immense favour to the now estranged political heirs of Gandhi. A martyred Mahatma was so much easier to live with. Now, they could exploit his name and the very special place that he held in the hearts of the majority of the people of India, when and in whatever manner they wanted, without having to bear with his meddlesome ways and the burden of his 'impractical' ideology. However, Gandhi had once said, 'If my faith burns bright, as I hope it will even if I stand alone, I shall be alive in the grave and, what is more, speaking from it.' He continues to do so even today; the din of Godse worship hasn't been able to drown out Gandhi's voice.

VI

ATTEMPTS THAT FAILED

By the grace of God I have been saved from the proverbial jaws of death, seven times. I have not ever hurt anybody. I consider no one to be an enemy, so I fail to understand why there have been so many attempts on my life. The attempt on my life yesterday failed. I am not ready to die just yet. I am going to live till I reach 125 years.

—M.K. Gandhi, on 30 June 1946 in Poona,
after surviving one more attempt on his life

Pan Tumhala Jagu Denar Kone?! *(But who will allow you to live that long?!)*

—A mocking retort from Ramchandra 'Nathuram'
Vinayak Godse, Gandhi's murderer

Gandhi was assaulted many times in South Africa. Several attempts on his life and threats to do him harm were made there.

The first known attempt on Gandhi's life in India and the only one involving an Englishman occurred during the Champaran Satyagraha in 1917. There was a lot of resentment against Gandhi amongst the British zamindars and indigo factory owners of Champaran due to the success of Gandhi's Satyagraha in Champaran. On the afternoon of 15 April 1917, thousands had gathered at Motihari railway station in Bihar's Champaran district to wait for the man who they hoped would lift their lives out of despair: after all, he was the hero of South Africa. Rajkumar Shukla had promised them that he was bringing a saviour, a messiah who would free them from slavery and oppressive poverty.

Gandhi alighted at the station from a train coming from Muzaffarpur at 3:00 p.m. He had come to probe the appalling conditions under which local farmers were being forced by landlords to grow indigo and the cruel Tinkathia system. Tinkathia was a barbaric system under which the native peasants of Champaran, Bihar, were forced to cultivate indigo on 3 katha of land out of every 20 katha of land they cultivated. (A katha is a land measure, little less than an acre.) Inhuman taxes was levied and extorted from the poverty-stricken farmers, to add to their misery. Nobody knew it then, but Gandhi's fact-finding mission would snowball into the first successful Satyagraha in the country and begin a new chapter in India's fight for independence.

According to the account in the book *Champaran ke Swatantatra Senani*, towards the end of this visit, Gandhi was invited to have dinner by Erwin, a notorious British manager of an indigo factory in Motihari. Angered by Gandhi's interference and successful abrogation of the exploitative Tinkathia system, the Englishman planned to murder Gandhi. Under the guise of making friends, he invited Gandhi to dinner. Gandhi accepted the invitation but declined dinner, since it was his day of weekly fasting. Rajendra Prasad was accompanying Gandhi on this occasion. Erwin persuaded Gandhi to accept a glass of milk. Erwin had ordered his cook Batak Miya Ansari to mix poison in the milk before serving it to Gandhi. He warned Batak Miya that obedience would be handsomely rewarded but disobedience would attract severe punishment, penury and even death. When the time came, the pious cook could not be part of the evil scheme. He did bring the poisoned glass of milk to Gandhi, but pretending to be clumsy, he spilled the milk before Gandhi could drink it. The plot came to light when a cat lapped up the spilt milk, collapsed and died. Gandhi ignored the attempt on his life and refused to file a complaint against Erwin.

Batak Miya paid a heavy price for defying Erwine; he and his family were reduced to penury. Rajendra Prasad, independent India's first president, was a witness to the incident, and on a visit to Bihar post Independence, he recalled the incident and praised Batak Miya's valour. Independent India did not honour or reward Batak Miya despite its first president acknowledging his heroism. Recently, the Bihar government celebrated the centenary of the Champaran Satyagraha, but Batak Miya remains forgotten. This was the first recorded attempt on Gandhi's life in India and the only one made by an Englishman.

Prime Minister Winston Churchill is known to have, on many occasions, castigated the British Secret Service for their failure to 'deal' effectively with Gandhi. There is no record of the British government agencies or the colonial administration making an attempt to 'deal' with Gandhi or any other Indian leader. What the British never did was done by their longtime supporters, the Hindu extremists.

Of the seven attempts on Gandhi's life in India, five are well-documented and involve the Pune branch of the Hindu Mahasabha and fanatics loyal to Savarkar. Three of these point specifically to the involvement of Narayan Apte and Nathuram Godse. The last of these was when a bomb was exploded at a prayer meeting on 20 January 1948. It was immediately after this failed attack that Madanlal Pahwa was arrested.

Godse and Apte, the Hindu Mahasabha as well as its offshoot, the RSS, have always claimed that Gandhi was murdered because he was partial to Muslims, because he was responsible for the partition of India, because he was an enemy of Hindus and if allowed to live would cause Hindus great harm. They claim that the last straw was when he forced the Government of India to pay Pakistan ₹550 million. However, most of the failed attempts on his life took place at a time when Gandhi had not displayed any 'partiality' towards Muslims and the country was yet to be divided, and, therefore, there was no question of paying Pakistan anything. Yet the Hindu Mahasabha, Sanghis and the Godse–Apte gang had made him their target. Was it Gandhi's campaign to eradicate untouchability that offended these caste supremacist Hindus?

◆

The First Attempt

25 June 1934, Poona

Gandhi was passing through Poona while on his historic Harijan Yatra, his movement for emancipation, equality and dignity for the untouchables. He was to deliver a speech at the Corporation Auditorium and receive a citation from the city council. There are many versions of this story. An eyewitness account was written by Shripad Joshi in his book *Mahatma, My Bapu*. The following is an extract from the fourth chapter titled 'From Death's Jaws'. There are other recorded versions which have slight variations, those have been described too. 'Like men, towns and cities also have their individuality, their virtues and faults, their peculiarities. Some are primarily business towns, some are known for their fighting spirit and some for their interest in learning. Poona is no exception. It is known as the seat of learning. Poona has played a vital role in creating the national spirit and the reformist movements in Maharashtra. At the same time, side by side with these, there has been a strong current of reactionary thought, opposed to all progressive thought and action in Poona, like the serpent in the forest of sandalwood. It was Poona which led the strongest opposition to Gandhiji and his thoughts. Perhaps Poona was afraid that the leadership of India brought to it by Lokmanya Tilak would be taken away by Gandhiji. But it seems that Gandhiji had, inexplicably, a strong fascination for Poona. It is possible that he was secretly fascinated by Poona, which was sanctified by social reformers, workers and patriots like Ranade, Phule, Gokhale, Tilak, Agarkar, Shinde, Karve etc. He had stayed in and taken vital decisions at various places in Poona, like the Yerawada Jail, the Aga Khan Palace, Dr Dinshaw's Nature Cure Clinic and Panchgani. I wonder if he knew that it was Poona which was going to make him a martyr!

'On 30 January 1948, it was a Poonaite who assassinated the Father of the Nation and became the centre of world's anger and loathing. What peace can this give to his soul! But even before obtaining this distinction, Poona had tried its hand at a similar attempt on 25 June 1934. Indian terrorists (revolutionaries) had tried their hand at throwing bombs at men attending a reception in honour of some British dignitary and had often gained the admiration of people because in those cases they reflected the feelings of the people. But the unknown person who threw a bomb (grenade) at Gandhiji in the Poona Municipal Hall was never honoured thus... Even today I recall the terrible blast of that bomb. The Municipal Hall was chockfull of the people of Poona and the crowd had spilled out into the streets outside. Our Boy Scout Band was awaiting his arrival in the southern balcony on the first floor of the building. I was the flute-player in that band. Our Boy Scout Band was patronized widely in those days. We used to feel somewhat embarrassed when called upon to play during ceremonies like marriages etc., but were glad to be called in for functions like the one in the Municipality. We were happy that we were participating in a welcome to Gandhiji and would see him that day... Shortly we heard shouts of "Gandhiji has arrived!", "Mahatmaji has come!", "That is his car!" etc., from the crowds outside and struck up a tune. A car stopped under the balcony. We thought that Gandhiji would alight and all of us would be able to see him. I leaned over the balcony while continuing to play the flute. Suddenly, a deafening noise was heard, drowning out the music of the band. Alarmed, we looked at each other. We could not guess what it was but felt that something evil had happened. However, we continued to play. After some time, we were told that it was not Gandhiji but Annasaheb Bhopatkar who had arrived. Gandhiji arrived after some time and we saw his frail figure. The function went through without a hitch. After he had left, we began to collect our instruments for departure when we were surrounded by the CID. We were searched thoroughly. But the real culprit had already run away. The government announced a big award for his apprehension but he was never found. As a result, it was never found out whether the terrorist was some opponent burning with jealousy at Gandhiji's popularity or was some fanatic orthodox Hindu who thought that his religion would be destroyed by the removal of untouchability.'

Writing about this incident in Gandhi's biography, Acharya Shankar Dattatreya Jawdekar mentions: 'When Gandhiji was on his way to receive the address, some fanatic Hindu, enraged at his devotion to the cause of the untouchables, threw a bomb at him. Fortunately, it went astray and Gandhiji was unharmed. The police have been unable to catch the terrorist... The protection of righteousness, and righteous conduct, was the essence of Gandhiji's eternal religion. But some of those who called themselves the real followers of the eternal Hindu religion thought that it could be saved only through the murder of Gandhiji. When this stupid and evil orthodoxy was embellished with politics, militant Hindu nationalism was born, which resorted to terrorist conspiracy. In the end, a blind follower of this perverted Hindu terrorism assassinated Gandhiji. But Gandhiji had already accomplished his mission of freedom for India.'

'I cannot believe,' Gandhi said about the attack, 'that any sane

Sanatanist (fundamentalist) Hindu could ever encourage the insane act that was perpetrated this evening. However, I would like the Sanatanist friends to control the language that is being used by the speakers and writers claiming to speak on their behalf. The sorrowful incident has undoubtedly advanced the Harijan cause. It is easy to see causes prosper by martyrdom of those who stand for them. I am not aching for martyrdom, but if it comes my way in prosecution of what I consider the supreme duty in defence of the faith I hold in common with millions of Hindus, I shall have well earned it and it will be possible for the historian of the future to say that the vow that I have taken before the Harijans that I would, if need be, die in the attempt to remove untouchability was literally fulfilled. Let those who grudge me what yet remains to me of this earthly existence, know that it is the easiest thing to do away with my body... What would the world have said, if the bomb had dropped on me and my party, which included my wife and three girls who are as dear to me as daughters and are entrusted to me by their parents? ... I have nothing but deep pity for the unknown thrower of the bomb. If I had my way, and if the bomb-thrower was known, I should certainly ask for his discharge even as I did in South Africa, in the case of those who successfully assaulted me. Let the reformers not be incensed against the bomb-thrower or those who may be behind him. What I should like them to do is to redouble their efforts to rid the country of the deadly evil of untouchability.'

A description that is slightly at variance with the one above says that the hand grenade bounced off the bonnet of the car in which Gandhi was travelling and rolled some distance away before exploding and injuring some officials. In another version, it is said that there were two cars in which Gandhi and his entourage were being brought to the venue. At a railway crossing, they got separated, so the car bringing Gandhi to the venue reached a minute after the first car. When the first car arrived, it was assumed that Gandhi was in it; the band started playing the welcome tune and the welcoming committee rushed towards the car. The assassin assumed that his victim had arrived and dropped the grenade from his perch on the roof. The hand grenade landed on the bonnet of the car and rolled on to the middle of the street where it exploded. The car in which Gandhi was travelling reached the venue a moments after the explosion. Gandhi saw the damage caused by the explosion, but decided to go ahead with the programme.

In yet another version, a number of people are claimed to have been injured: the chief officer of the municipal corporation, two policemen and seven others.

The grenade was reportedly thrown by anti-Gandhi Hindu extremists, as mentioned by Pyarelal in his book and by Gandhi's biographer B.G. Tendulkar. Pyarelal writes: 'This time their attempt was very well planned and executed to perfection...' This implies that there had been prior attempts on Gandhi's life and that the people responsible for the previous attacks were involved in this one too. Pyarelal's remark also implies that the attempts before 25 June 1934 had failed due to lack of planning and coordination and that the murderers were getting better with each attempt.

Pyarelal continues: 'These people kept photographs of Gandhi, Nehru and other Congress leaders in their shoes. They were trained to shoot using Gandhiji's photograph as the target. These were the same people who later murdered the Mahatma while he was striving to bring peace to a riot ravaged Delhi, in 1948.'

This was the first documented attempt on Gandhi's life in India. Many historians have alleged that this could have been the work of the Nathuram Godse–Narayan Apte gang. The gang was involved in several other bomb attacks on those critical of their brand of Hindutva and those working against the dominance of upper castes. This was also the time when the Hindu Mahasabha was extremely active and Savarkar, confined to Ratnagiri, was spreading his doctrine of Hindu supremacy, Muslim hatred, and anti-Congress and anti-Gandhi venom.

Sanatani Hindus were enraged by Gandhi's movement of assimilation of the untouchables as equals in the Hindu fold, and began a nationwide hate campaign against Gandhi.

♦

The Second Attempt

July 1944, Panchgani

Gandhi had contracted malaria during his imprisonment at Aga Khan Palace prison. On his release in May 1944, he was advised rest by his physician. He retired to Panchgani, a mountain resort near Poona, where he stayed at Dilkhusha Bungalow. A group of eighteen–twenty men reached Panchgani by a chartered bus from Poona and carried on a week-long protest against Gandhi. When Gandhi was told about this, he invited the leader of the group, Narayan Apte, for a discussion. Apte rejected the invitation and his group continued with the demonstration.

During a prayer meeting one evening, Nathuram Godse rushed towards Gandhi. He was brandishing a dagger—Jambhiya—in his hand and shouting anti-Gandhi slogans. Godse was overpowered and disarmed by Manishankar Purohit, proprietor of Surti Lodge of Poona, and D. Bhilare Guruji of Satara, who later became a Congress member of the state legislature from Mahabaleshwar. The other young men accompanying Godse ran away. Godse's attack caused a minor panic in the prayer meeting, but Gandhi remained calm. He asked Godse to spend eight days with him so that they could understand each other. Godse rejected this invitation and was allowed to go free by a magnanimous Gandhi.

Before leaving Poona, Godse had boasted to his journalist friends that some important news concerning Gandhi would soon reach them from Panchgani. Joglekar, a reporter working for Godse's periodical *Agranee*, corroborated this fact. A. David, the then editor of the *Poona Herald*, stated under oath, while deposing before the Kapur Commission, that Godse had made an attempt on Gandhi's life. He had heard of Godse's boast to fellow journalists about the planned attack. In a small news item, the *Times of India* reported that a Poona-based editor had attempted to assault Gandhi at Panchgani.

Police records show that there were day-long demonstrations against Gandhi at Panchgani. The records also mention that Godse was held for trying to rush at Gandhi shouting slogans but do not mention whether he was armed. Dr Sushila Nayyar, Gandhi's physician and close associate, testified before the Kapur Commission that one of the protesters was found to be carrying a dagger but could not confirm whether it was Nathuram Godse. However, the two men who overpowered Godse, Manishankar Purohit and D. Bhilare Guruji testified to this attack at the Kapur Commission's inquiry, and stated emphatically that they had caught and disarmed Nathuram Vinayak Godse that day at Panchgani and saved Gandhi's life.

I had the opportunity to meet Bhilare Guruji on 13 January 2007 at Sangli. He was in his late eighties, a very strong and active man with a razor-sharp memory. In his youth, Bhilare Guruji had been a wrestler of renown. Asked to narrate the happenings of that fateful day sixty-three years ago, Bhilare Guruji firmly stated that Nathuram Godse had tried to attack Gandhi. According to him, Nathuram was brandishing a Jambhiya. Describing how he stopped Godse with the help of Manishankar Purohit, Bhilare Guruji recollected that when they grappled with Nathuram and wrestled him to the ground and disarmed him, Gandhi hailed them and instructed them not to be rough with the attacker. He wanted them to bring Nathuram to him so that they could talk. Bhilare Guruji also mentioned that Vishnu Karkare, Thatte, Badge and Gopal Godse were in the group of protestors too. Most of them were involved in Gandhi's murder four years later.

Bhilare Guruji attended my book launch in Mumbai in 2007. He narrated the incident, describing how he had save Bapu's life in Panchgani and lamented the fact that he had not been at Birla House on the fateful evening of 30 January 1948 to save Bapu's life one more time.

◆

The Third Attempt

September 1944, Sevagram

Gandhi was preparing to hold talks with Jinnah to wean him away from the demand for Pakistan. The Hindu Mahasabha and RSS were opposed to any dialogue with Jinnah or his Muslim League. Nathuram Godse and L.G. Thatte had publicly threatened to do whatever was required to stop Gandhi from meeting Jinnah.

Gandhi travelled from Sevagram to Bombay for the talks. Godse and Thatte led a gang of men to stop Gandhi and were joined by another group from Bengal. The gang picketed the gate of Sevagram Ashram to ensure that Gandhi did not leave for Bombay and shouted slogans against Gandhi. Dr Sushila Nayyar testified before the Kapur Commission that Nathuram Godse was stopped and detained by Ashram residents as he rushed towards Gandhi brandishing a Jambhiya. He was disarmed and handed to the police. The police report of the assault also corroborates this fact. The report adds: 'It wasn't certain whether they meant to harm Gandhi, but they were armed and determined to stop him from meeting Jinnah at any cost.'

Pyarelal, in a letter to Tej Bahadur Sapru, wrote: 'The leader of the protestors at Sevagram, an extremely bitter and fanatical die-hard, was ready to go to any lengths to stop Gandhiji from meeting Jinnah. The arresting officer who recovered the dagger from the leader of the band asked him mockingly whether he wanted to become a martyr. The leader replied that when Gandhi was eventually killed, one of them would become a martyr. The officer again asked him why they were wasting their time and lives in the fight between their leaders and Gandhi. If Gandhi was to be stopped, why didn't they leave it to Savarkar, their leader? The leader of the gang replied, "If Savarkar talks with Gandhi, it will be an honour for Gandhi. The time will not come for Savarkar to have to talk to Gandhi. Gandhi will be dealt with by this Jamadar."' Pyarelal wrote that the person indicated by the group leader as 'Jamadar' was Nathuram Godse.

No information is available about the others in the gang. After the train carrying Gandhi departed from Wardha, the police let the detained gang members go.

◆

The Fourth Attempt

29 June 1946, en route to Poona

On his way to Poona, the train carrying Gandhi—known as the Gandhi Special—met with an accident between Nerul and Karjat stations on the night of 29 June. The engine driver in his report stated that he saw boulders placed on the tracks in front of the train with the intention of derailing it. The engine crashed into the boulders, but a tragedy was averted because the driver, Pareira, was alert and had applied the emergency brakes in time, which considerably slowed down the train before impact. The wheels and axle of the engine were severely damaged. Another engine was sent and the Gandhi Special was taken to Poona. Gandhi slept through the entire episode.

The Poona Police claimed that the boulders had been placed by looters to stop goods trains, but the railway records showed that no goods trains were scheduled to travel on that route before or after the Gandhi Special. The police had not discounted sabotage, and clearly the Gandhi Special had been the target.

On 30 June, speaking at a public prayer meeting in Poona, Gandhi said, 'By the grace of God, I have escaped from the jaws of death seven times. I have not hurt anybody nor do I consider anybody to be my enemy, I can't understand why there are so many attempts on my life. Yesterday's attempt on my life failed. I will not die just yet, I aim to live till the age of 125.'

'*Pan tumhala tevdha jagu denar kon*?!' (But who will allow you to live that long?!) came Nathuram Godse's mocking reply a few days later, at a public meeting organized by the Poona branch of the Hindu Mahasabha. This was mentioned after Gandhi's murder, by people who were present at that meeting.

◆

The Fifth Attempt

20 January 1948, New Delhi

A bomb was exploded a few metres behind where Gandhi sat while conducting his evening prayer meeting at Birla House. Madanlal Pahwa was arrested from the crime scene immediately after he detonated the bomb. According to his confession, the bomb explosion was part of an attempt to murder Gandhi.

◆

Apart from these recorded attempts on Gandhi's life, information is also available about other incidents. In one, Prabodhankar Thackre, father of Shiv Sena supremo Bal Thackerey and grandfather of the present chief minister of Maharashtra, Uddhav Thackerey, is know to have warned Sanatani Hindus to stop their repeated attempts on Gandhi's life. He wrote about how his warning had stopped a planned attack on Gandhi's life when he was visiting Akola in Vidarbha.

On 30 January 1948, at 5:17 p.m., ten days after the last failed attempt, Nathuram Godse walked up to Gandhi, pulled out a semi-automatic pistol and pumped three bullets into Gandhi's chest from point blank range. Finally, Godse succeeded in killing Mahatma Gandhi.

◆

In writing this, I have referred to Pyarelal's *Mahatma Gandhi: The Last Phase*, Tendulkar's *Mahatma*, and *Mahatmya Chi Akher* (The End of the Mahatma), a book in Marathi by the late Jagan Phadnis.

BOOK 2

THE LAST YEARS
YEARS OF TUMULT, TRIUMPH,
TRAGEDY AND HIS END

VII

THE LAST YEARS

There go my people and I must follow them for I am their leader.

—Rev. Dr Martin Luther King Jr

I believe in walking alone. I came alone in this world, I have walked alone in the valley of the shadow of death and I shall quit alone, when the time comes.

—M.K. Gandhi, addressing the
AICC Convention in Bombay on 7 July 1946

The last years of Gandhi's life were tumultuous. He was to achieve the greatest triumph of his life, freedom for his country and people, but at the same time, he would stand by helplessly and watch his dream be betrayed and turned to dust. The unity of his people that he had forged would crumble, non-violence would be discarded and his people would indulge in bloodcurdling orgies of violence. He would implore, beseech, plead but no one would listen to him, neither his own people nor those opposed to him. In the last few years, Gandhi was left to tread a lonely tragic path, all by himself.

Gurudev Rabindranath Tagore had written a poem much earlier, and it seems as if Gurudev had written it for Gandhi in the winter of his life. It is titled 'Ekla Chalo Re' ('Walk Alone'):

Jodi Tor Dak Shoone Keu Na Ashe Tobe Ekla Cholo Re
Tobe Ekla Cholo, Ekla Cholo, Ekla Cholo, Ekla Cholo Re…
If they answer not to thy call, walk alone;
If they are afraid and cower mutely facing the wall,

O thou of evil luck, open thy mind and speak out alone.
If they turn away and desert you when crossing the wilderness,
O thou of evil luck, trample the thorns under thy tread,
and along the blood-lined track travel alone.
If they do not hold up the light when the night is troubled with storm,
O thou of evil luck,
with the thunder-flame of pain ignite thine own heart and let it burn alone.

In the last years of his life, apart from a small band of loyal followers, Gandhi trudged a lonesome path, unmindful of the obstacles and pitfalls in his path, braving the thorns and the stones, forlorn and discarded.

British Intrigue

Gandhi was released, earlier than expected, on 6 May 1944, twenty-one months after his detention on the eve of 9 August 1942, after giving the clarion call of 'Quit India!' and 'Do or die!'. His last imprisonment, at Aga Khan Palace Detention Centre, was personally traumatic. He had lost two of his closest companions: his associate, confidante and secretary of twenty-five years, Mahadev Desai, whom he had come to love as a son, and then his wife and companion since they were both thirteen, Kastur. He had cremated them on the grounds of the prison camp and then lovingly built two small shrines from stone and mud with his own hands at the site of their cremation.

As the car carrying Gandhi out of the prison camp reached the gates, he glanced out of the window and caught a fleeting glimpse of a pile of wood in a corner of the compound. Enough wood and sandalwood had been stocked by his colonial jailers for his funeral in case he died while in prison. Twice during his last incarceration, the administration had assumed that he was on his deathbed. Once, when he went on a fast, the guard around the detention camp had been doubled and the armed forces and police were put on high alert throughout the Raj to suppress any uprising caused by the news of Gandhi's death. The second time was when he had been suffering from dysentery and malaria. This time, the

Foreign Office even issued a guideline to all its embassies worldwide on how his obituaries should be written, which was signed by the foreign secretary, Anthony Eden. The Chungking Office received a copy while the Indian savant and philosopher, Dr S. Radhakrishnan happened to be there and he read it. The instructions in the despatch were: 'In case of Gandhi's death do not diminish his moral stature, acknowledge his uncompromising allegiance to unworldly ideals, express regret that his unrivalled influence was not at the service of the Allied Nations, especially China and India.'

Gandhi would not die that easily though, not while his work remained incomplete. As the car carrying him proceeded towards Parnakutir, the mansion of Lady Premlila Thackersey, Gandhi was thinking about Kasturba and Mahadevbhai. 'She had been so eager to get out of prison. Yet I know that she could not have had a better death. Both she and Mahadev laid down their lives at the altar of liberty. Martyrs both, they have become immortal.' It was Netaji Subhas Chandra Bose who had called Ba a martyr first; in his obituary, he accused the colonial administration of murdering Ba to break Gandhi's spirit.

In memory of Kasturba, Gandhi wrote to the Government of Bombay Province on the day he was released, 'I wish to put on record ... that by reason of the cremation of the corpses of Shri Mahadev Desai and then my wife Kastur, the place of cremation ... becomes consecrated ground... I trust that the plot will be acquired by the Government... I would like to arrange for the upkeep of the sacred spot and for daily prayers.'

The British released him when the Allies swept across the English Channel and landed on the beaches of France to reclaim Nazi-occupied Europe and finally crushed the Nazis in their citadel, Germany. This eventually led to the surrender of the Axis powers in Europe and the suicide of the Nazi Führer, Adolf Hitler, and ended one of the most devastating wars of the twentieth century in Europe.

After his release from prison, the British continuously tried every ploy to get Gandhi to retract the 1942 resolution of the Congress, demanding that the British 'Quit India' and declare independence. Gandhi insisted that the resolution was passed by the CWC and only they could withdraw it. The leadership of the Congress was imprisoned; Gandhi demanded that they be released or he be allowed to meet them in prison to decide on the future course of action. To Lord Wavell, the viceroy, he wrote asking him to 'find the keys to Aurangabad Fort' where most of the members of the CWC were imprisoned.

To his bitter critic, the British prime minister, Sir Winston Churchill, he wrote seeking permission to allow him to meet with the CWC in prison. Below is the letter reproduced from *Mahatma Gandhi: The Last Phase* by Pyarelal Nayyar.

Dilkhusha, Panchgani
17th July, 1944

Dear Prime Minister,

You are reported to have the desire to crush the 'Naked Fakir' as you are said to have described me. I have been long trying to be a fakir and that too naked—a more difficult task. I, therefore, regard the expression as a compliment though unintended. I approach you then as such and ask you to trust and use me for the sake of your people and mine and through them those of the world.

Your Sincere Friend,
M.K. Gandhi

The letter to Churchill went astray. Two months later, another copy was sent. Churchill responded indirectly, thanking Gandhi for his letter via the viceroy's office. It was quite clear that the British were not willing to listen to any demand from Gandhi or the Congress. They had their own game plan. In his reply, Viceroy Lord Wavell wrote that he did not see anything constructive either in Gandhi asking to be allowed to meet and confer with the CWC members or by arriving at a settlement. Gandhi expressed his disappointment at the stance taken by the viceroy and submitted a 'concrete proposal': 'I am prepared to advise the Working Committee to declare that in view of changed conditions, mass Civil Disobedience envisaged by the resolution of August, 1942, cannot be offered and that full cooperation in the war effort should be given by the Congress if a declaration of immediate Indian Independence is made and a National Government responsible to the Central Assembly be formed subject to the proviso that during the pendency of the war, the military operations should continue, as at present but without involving any financial burden on India.' This proposal was made on 30 July 1944. He concluded with the message: 'I shall continue to knock so long as there is the least hope of an honourable settlement.'

But the British were in no mood for an 'honourable settlement'. After raising their pet bogeys 'their duty to safeguard the interests of the racial and religious minorities and of the depressed classes, and their treaty obligations to the Indian states' which came in the way of acceding to Gandhi's demand, and reminding him that the British offer made by Sir Stafford Cripps of unqualified freedom after the cessation of hostilities was 'conditional upon the framing of a constitution agreed by the main elements of India's national life', Wavell further reiterated that 'it was the most pious desire of His Majesty's Government to settle the vexed Indian problem'. He concluded, 'But proposals such as those put forth by you are quite unacceptable to His Majesty's Government as a basis of discussion.'

The reply was from Wavell, but the language was that of Prime Minister Churchill. Gandhi commented that the viceroy's reply meant that 'unless all the main parties agree to the constitution of the future, and there is agreement between the British Government and the main parties, there is to be no change in the constitutional position, and the Government of India as at present is to be carried on... It is as clear as crystal that the British Government do not propose to give up the power they possess over the 400 millions, unless the latter develop strength enough to wrest it from them. I shall never lose hope that India will do so by purely moral means.'

Finally, the War ended in 1945. The Allies were triumphant, but the British Empire was crumbling. India was one of the most important colonies which they would soon be forced to free. The British were not going to let go that easily. If they were to lose the jewel in their crown, they would extract a dear price for it. They knew that when they left, they would have to hand over power to the Congress, their bitter enemy, which had extracted a great price from them. The non-violent fight for freedom had made the British lose face like never before. They would use their allies, the newly revived Muslim League led by Jinnah, their collaborators, the Hindu extremists headed by Savarkar, the RSS and India's princes, all of them their trusted allies, to divide India in such a way that the shape of independent India would resemble the tattered remains of a once glorious tapestry.

Gandhi–Jinnah Talks

Gandhi knew that India could only thrive and prosper as an independent nation if all the religious groups, the caste divisions amongst Hindus and other minorities and the princely states came together to form a single united nation. He was willing to go to any lengths to achieve this, even to further delay independence, for the sake of forging unity. He had realized that the steepest hurdle he would face in this task was Jinnah. Gandhi had made great efforts to win over Jinnah before he was arrested in 1942 on the eve of his 'Quit India' call. On 4 August, Gandhi made an offer to Jinnah, through a common friend, Meklai, to forge a united front against the British. The terms he offered were, 'Provided the Muslim League cooperated fully with the Congress' demand for immediate independence without the slightest reservation … the Congress will have no objection to the British Government transferring all the power it today exercises to the Muslim League on behalf of the whole of India. And the Congress will not only not obstruct any Government that the Muslim League may form on behalf of the people, but will even join the Government in running the machinery of the free state.' Gandhi assumed that Congress leaders would accept this.

Jinnah reacted by saying that this was not what he had expected to hear from Gandhi. He replied after Gandhi was arrested: 'This letter of Mr Gandhi can only be construed as a move on his part to embroil the Muslim League to come into a clash with the British Government solely for the purpose of his release.'

C. Rajagopalachari, a close associate of Gandhi, had opposed Gandhi and Congress's stand on the Quit India resolution and disagreed with the policy of non-cooperation with the British War effort. Consequently, he had not been arrested by the British in 1942. Like Gandhi, Rajaji (C. Rajagopalachari) believed that if the Congress agreed to the right to self-determination for the Muslim-majority areas as demanded by the Muslim League, it would join hands with the Congress in demanding India's independence.

When the gates of the Aga Khan Palace Prison Camp were briefly thrown open by the British—who feared that as a result of the fast undertaken by Gandhi and the various ailments he was suffering from, he was close to death—Rajaji availed of the brief respite to visit him and put forth a formula he had evolved to bring about a settlement between the Congress and the Muslim League. The formula became popularly known as the 'Rajaji Formula' and stated that: (1) the Muslim League should endorse the Indian demand for independence and cooperate with the Congress in the formation of a provisional interim government for the transitional period; (2) the Congress would agree, after the termination of War, to the appointment of a commission to demarcate contiguous districts in the northwest and northeast of India, wherein the Muslims were in absolute majority; (3) in the areas thus demarcated, a plebiscite of all the inhabitants would be held on the basis of adult franchise or some equivalent device would decide the issue of separation from India. If the majority decided in favour of forming a sovereign state separate from India, such a decision would be given effect to; (4) in the event of separation, mutual agreement would be entered into for safeguarding defence, commerce, communications and other essential matters and finally (5) these terms would be binding only in case of transfer of full power and responsibility for the governance of India, to Indians by the British.

Gandhi endorsed the Rajaji Formula. Rajaji then presented the plan to Jinnah who summarily rejected it and described it as offering 'a shadow and husk, of a maimed, mutilated, and moth-eaten Pakistan'.

Gandhi revived his efforts to bring Jinnah back into the fold of the national movement after his release. On 17 January 1944, he wrote to Jinnah, this time intentionally using their common mother tongue, Gujarati. 'Brother Jinnah, there was a time when I was able to induce you to speak in the mother tongue. Today I venture to write to you in the mother tongue. I have already suggested a meeting between you and me in my invitation from jail. I have not yet written to you since my release. Today, I feel prompted to do so. Let us meet whenever you wish. Do not regard me as an enemy of Islam or of Indian Muslims. I have always been a servant and friend to you and mankind. Do not disappoint me.'

By writing in Gujarati, Gandhi was subtly reminding Jinnah that Hindus and Muslims shared many vernacular languages and regional cultures, which negated one of the reasons put forth by Jinnah and the Muslim League to buttress their demand for Pakistan: that two distinctly separate nations existed in India, one Hindu, the other, Muslim. Jinnah replied from the houseboat *Queen Elizabeth* anchored on Dal Lake in Srinagar: 'Dear Mr Gandhi, I will be pleased to receive you at my home in Bombay, on my return from Kashmir some time in the middle of August.'

When Gandhi left Sevagram to meet Jinnah, a gang of Hindu Mahasabha and RSS fanatics attempted to stop him, but unmindful of the attack on his life, Gandhi continued his journey to Bombay. The atmosphere in Bombay on the eve of the talks was electric. The police was on full alert; many of the streets and roads in the vicinity of Malabar Hill—where the two principal players were staying and were to meet— were blocked off. The entire city was placed on red alert. Gandhi took up residence at Birla House, which stands halfway up Malabar Hill towards the Nepean Sea Road. The talks were held at Jinnah's home, which was at 10, Mount Pleasant Road.

This was one of the rare occasions when Jinnah referred to Gandhi as Mahatma Gandhi, appealing to him to promulgate a period of political truce, saying, 'It has been the universal desire that we should meet. Now that we are going to meet, help us. We are coming to grips. Bury the past.'

The talks began on 9 September 1944 and continued for eighteen days, but they were an exercise in futility. Jinnah's only objective, perhaps, had been to try and convert Gandhi to his way of thinking.

'The more our arguments progress, the more alarming your picture appears to me,' Gandhi wrote to Jinnah on 15 September, 'as I ... imagine the working of the Lahore Resolution in practice, I see nothing but ruin for the whole of India.' After this, the correspondence entered a phase of acrimony. At one stage, Jinnah once again questioned Gandhi's claim of representing the aspirations of all the downtrodden of India and demanded that he accept the Lahore Resolution. Gandhi insisted that if at all there was to be a separation, it should be like a break-up in a family between two brothers who, although separated, continued to remain part of the larger family. Gandhi said that he would accept the division of the country if, after independence, the majority of the adult population residing in the regions that were to be divided voted for the division. On 27 September, addressing a well-attended prayer meeting, Gandhi declared that the talks had failed to reach a satisfactory or mutually acceptable conclusion, as neither of the parties had been able to convince the other.

'All the parties and especially the members of the Muslim League should ask the Qaid-i-Azam to revise his opinion,' Gandhi said in a press statement the next day. 'If Rajaji and I have stultified the Lahore Resolution, we should be educated.' In an interview to Stuart Gelder from the *News Chronicle*, he remarked, 'I believe Mr Jinnah is sincere, but I think he is suffering from hallucination when he imagines that an unnatural division of India could bring either happiness or prosperity to the people concerned.'

Thus, the talks between Gandhi and Jinnah ended or stalled, and were never revived again. Jinnah's obstinacy ensured that no positive outcome was possible.

The Simla Conference

As the Second World War drew to a close in Europe, public opinion in Britain and the Western world became increasingly critical of the continued denial of self-determination leading to independence for the people of India. Great Britain had faced a very embarrassing situation at the Commonwealth Relations Conference, when its own nominee, the leader of the Indian delegation, demanded dominion status for India by a fixed date and told the British statesmen that they could not prevent India from achieving freedom.

Lord Wavell, a former soldier and viceroy of India, had time and again pressed Whitehall to resolve the Indian deadlock to enable India's active cooperation in the prosecution of the war in the Far East. In March 1945, Wavell was called to England by His Majesty's government (HMG) for consultations on the situation in India and the road ahead. While he was in London, the War in Europe ended with the unconditional surrender of Italy and Germany. The Labour Party withdrew from the Wartime coalition and the government fell on 23 May. A caretaker government took charge and the next general elections were fixed for 5

July. As the date neared, even the Tory diehards, who had till then refused to even consider a change in HMG's policy towards India, realized that the situation could not be ignored any longer. Soldiers who had returned home after serving their Wartime duties in India had brought back with them horrifying stories of the brutal colonial regime and the total failure of the administration in providing humanitarian relief during the great famine in West Bengal. Public opinion in Great Britain was increasingly critical of their country's role in India. The tremendous goodwill that Gandhi enjoyed amongst the British people was another factor that made it imperative for the politicians seeking re-election to show that they were willing to bow to the winds of change.

On 14 June, with the concurrence of HMG, Lord Wavell made a public announcement explaining the intended constitutional amendments 'within the framework of the 1935 Government of India Act'. The viceroy would attempt to form a national government which would replace the existing Viceroy's Executive Council, with equal representation of caste Hindus and Muslims, selected in consultation with the Indian leaders. Simultaneously, all the members of the CWC, detained since August 1942, were released, in accordance with what Gandhi had been requesting since his release.

A Simla Conference, chaired by the viceroy, was announced, to be held from 25 June 1945, which would include invitees from all political parties and groups selected by the viceroy. Twenty-one invitations were sent out, eleven to the premiers of the provinces, leaders of the Congress party and the deputy leader of the Muslim League in the Central Assembly, leaders of the Muslim League in the Council of States, leader of the Nationalist Party and the European Group in the Central Assembly, one representative each from the scheduled castes and the Sikhs and to Gandhi and Jinnah as the recognized leaders of the two main political parties. Initially, no invite was sent to the president of the Congress, Maulana Azad.

Gandhi was convalescing in Panchgani when he was informed about the viceroy's broadcast by a press correspondent and the invitation extended to him to attend the conference. Gandhi immediately commented on the Congress president not being invited and wrote to the viceroy: 'I represent no institution formally. I am not even a primary member of the Congress since 1934, as an individual I can only tender advice. My presence in the Conference will change the official colour, unless I become an official representative of the Congress. The Congress president is the proper authority to represent the Congress' point of view'. An invite was immediately despatched to Maulana Azad. Gandhi agreed to go to Simla as an experienced advisor and stay there as long as the viceroy and the other invitees needed his services. In his broadcast, the viceroy had not mentioned a word about Indian independence and, ominously, for the first time, the term 'caste Hindu–Muslim parity' was used as a basic condition in the formation of national government. Gandhi commented: 'Personally, I can never subscribe to it, nor the Congress, if I know its mind. In spite of having overwhelming Hindu membership, the Congress has striven to be purely political. I am quite capable of advising the Congress to nominate all non-Hindus and most decidedly non-caste Hindus.' He stressed this point further by saying, 'Congress has never identified (itself) with caste or non-caste Hindus and never can, even to gain independence, which will be one-sided, untrue and suicidal.'

Gandhi refused to travel by the air-conditioned coaches provided for the Congress contingent, choosing to travel by his favourite third-class coach. Preston Grover, a correspondent with the United Press of America, was travelling by the same train. Concerned about Gandhi's physical well-being, he requested him to retire to the air-conditioned coach. Gandhi replied: 'Many thanks for your considerate note. But let me melt myself in this natural heat. As sure as fate, this heat will be followed by refreshing coolness which I shall enjoy. Let me feel just a touch of real India.'

On arriving in Simla, Gandhi had a hurried bath and meal at Rajkumari Amrit Kaur's residence and left for a meeting with the viceroy. At the Viceregal Lodge, greeting Lord Wavell he said, 'I, too, am a soldier like you, though I bear no arms.' After exchanging pleasantries and a few moments of casual talk, Gandhi rose to leave, expressing his compliments to Lady Wavell. He spent the next thirty minutes talking with her and the viceroy's son. Gandhi stayed with Rajkumari Amrit Kaur for the entire duration of the Simla Conference. He had a favourite seat on one of the raised terraces, from where he gazed at the scenery, the pristine, eternally snow-covered Himalayan mountain range and the fir-clad hills and valleys. The azure blue skies formed a breathtaking backdrop for the pearly white brilliance of the Himalayas, carpeted by the vibrant multihued greens of the valleys. 'The world has nothing to equal it,' murmured Gandhi.

The viceroy was eager that Gandhi attend the conference as a delegate, but he declined, saying that in a representative conference, there was no room for an individual, however eminent. He offered to stay in Simla for the duration of the conference and agreed to give advice when required.

In his opening address to the delegates, Wavell sounded genuinely eager and honest. 'I said in my broadcast that on all sides there was something to forgive and forget... You must accept my leadership for the present... I will endeavour to guide the discussion of this conference in what I believe to be the best interest of the country.'

Commenting on the opening address, Gandhi said, 'It is a good and dignified expression that Lord Wavell has used. He thus acts in the conference as its leader and not as the agent of Whitehall.' The viceroy navigated the conference through the predictable shallows and rapids of disagreements and conflicts. The Congress objected to having been classified as a Hindu party in the viceroy's address, and he denied having called them thus. Jinnah jumped into the fray, branding the Congress a Hindu party, and there followed a sharp exchange between Jinnah, the viceroy and Congress members.

Viceroy Wavell: 'There is nothing in my proposals which characterizes Congress as a communal body.'

Jinnah: 'We have met here as communities and Congress does not represent anybody but the Hindus.'

Viceroy Wavell: 'Congress represents its members.'

Dr Khan Saheb: 'What does he mean? I am a Congressman. Am I a Hindu or a Muslim?'

Viceroy Wavell: 'Leave it at that. The Congress represents its members.'

India's history would have chartered a different course if the viceroy had been firm about his utterances. The hollowness of his opening statement was to be proven before the conference ended. From then on, it was all downhill, and the end was predictable: the conference ended up achieving nothing. But one thing was evident, that now, unlike earlier, Gandhi could not get the Congress leaders to follow him.

On the 29th, when the conference reconvened, the viceroy announced that since none of the parties could come to an agreement, instead of wasting time, the delegate parties could send him their suggested lists of nominees for the national government he proposed to constitute. He would add some names himself and after consultation with the concerned parties, arrive at a generally acceptable final list. The Congress submitted a panel of fifteen names, attempting to give proper representation to all the minority communities. The list comprised:

Maulana Abul Kalam Azad (Congress Muslim), Asaf Ali (Congress Muslim), Pandit Jawaharlal Nehru (Congress Hindu), Sardar Vallabhbhai Patel (Congress Hindu), Dr Rajendra Prasad (Congress Hindu), M.A. Jinnah (Muslim League), Nawab Mohammad Ismail Khan (Muslim League), Nawabzada Liaquat Ali Khan (Muslim League), Dr Syama Prasad Mookerji (Hindu Mahasabha), Gaganvihari Mehta (Hindu), Rajkumari Amrit Kaur (woman, Indian Christian), Muniswami Pillay (scheduled caste), Radhanath Das (scheduled caste), Sir Ardeshir Dalal (Parsi), and a Sikh member, whose name they would submit later.

Jinnah wrote to Wavell: 'With regard to your suggestion for submitting a panel of names ... the Working Committee (of the League) desires to point out that when a similar proposal was made by your Excellency's predecessor, Lord Linlithgow ... the Working Committee opposed it, when its objections were brought to the notice of Lord Linlithgow, he dropped the proposal and suggested another alternative.'

On 14 July, when the conference met for the final sitting, Wavell revealed that even without receiving a list from the Muslim League, he had formed a list of Executive Council members which he was certain would be acceptable to the conference. The viceroy did not place the list before the conference for consideration and debate. In his concluding remarks, he said that the conference had failed and he was holding himself responsible for the failure.

'It grieves me to think,' Gandhi wrote to the viceroy, 'that the conference which began so happily and so hopefully should have ended in apparent failure—due exactly, as it would seem, to the same cause as before. This time you have taken the blame on your own shoulders, but the world will think otherwise. India certainly does.' Probing into the cause of the failure he continued: 'I must not hide from you the suspicion, that the deeper cause is perhaps the reluctance of the official world to part with power, which the passing of virtual control into the hands of their erstwhile prisoners would have meant.'

The result of the conference was to introduce the formula of 'caste Hindu–Muslim parity' into politics and to adopt officially the principle of religious division on the eve of independence. Commenting on the intentions of Lord Wavell, Francis Sayer of the United Nations Relief and Rehabilitation Administration said in an interview with Gandhi, 'You will admit, that Wavell did make an honest attempt to break the deadlock.'

'An honest attempt should have ended honestly,' Gandhi replied.

Confirmation of the less-than-honest intentions of the British administration came in the form of a letter received by Pandit Nehru from London: 'It is now known that the Wavell offer was maintained as part of election necessities. Also, that the final termination of the talks by Wavell, without taking the obvious course of forming a government without Jinnah, was dictated from here.'

Cabinet Mission

After the failure of the Simla Conference, India was in a continuous state of ferment. Demand for self-determination and freedom was gaining momentum. Congress cadres were restive; another showdown was imminent.

Gandhi took the brief lull after the Simla Conference to tend to the needs of his colleague: Sardar Patel's health had been ruined during his incarceration. He suffered from a spastic colon. Doctors advised a major surgery, but the risks were too great. Gandhi suggested that Patel put himself under his care and allow him to nurse him back to health with nature cure. Thus, the two of them checked into the Nature Cure Clinic, run by Dr Dinshaw Mehta in Poona, in the third week of August 1945. They stayed there for three months, with Gandhi personally supervising Patel's treatment.

An incident occurred there, which had a connection to Gandhi's murder. Gandhi's second daughter-in-law Sushila and grandson Arun, my grandmother and father, were also accompanying him. One morning, a young man came visiting carrying a nicely wrapped basket. He insisted on meeting Gandhi to give him the present he was carrying. Sushila told him that he would have to wait since Gandhi was busy and was not to be disturbed. The young man made her promise that the present would only be opened by Gandhi and then he left. Arun was excited and eager to find out what the present was, so as soon as Gandhi was free, he carried the basket to him. Gandhi asked Arun to open it. When the basket was opened, it was found to be full of old and torn footwear. This was not a present, it was an insult. Gandhi smiled and asked Arun and his elder cousin to go and sell the contents of the basket to a scrap dealer. They got three rupees for the lot. Gandhi instructed them to deposit the amount as a gift from an anonymous benefactor in the Harijan Fund. That evening, at the public prayer meeting, Gandhi narrated the incident and thanked the 'friend' for the gift. The young man was attending the meeting and became very angry that Gandhi had sold the gift he had given and demanded that the money be returned to him. Gandhi thanked him and said that since he had accepted the gift, it was his to do as he wished. The young man became abusive and when it was feared that he may turn violent, he was removed from the scene. Sushila and Arun eventually returned to South Africa after Gandhi's murder. When the photograph of his murderer was published in newspapers there, Sushila recognized him to be the same young man who had presented the footwear in Poona.

◆

The election results in England showed that there was an overwhelming majority in Britain in favour of ending British rule in India. The Labour Party swept the polls and formed the government. Lord Pethick-Lawrence, the new secretary of state for India, was an old friend of Gandhi. Congratulating him on his appointment, Gandhi wrote: 'If the India Office is to receive a decent burial and a nobler monument is to rise from its ashes, who can be a fitter person than you for the work?', to which Lord Pethick-Lawrence replied: 'I greatly hope that our personal friendship, which has existed for so many years, may bear fruit in harmonious cooperation in achieving the lasting good of India and her people.'

The viceroy was invited to confer with the new Labour government in London in the last week of August to review the Indian problem *de novo* and find a solution. At the same time, the long-postponed elections to the central and provincial legislatures were announced to be held during winter. On 19 September 1945, after the viceroy's return from London, a statement was issued in India announcing the intention of both HMG and the viceroy, immediately after the elections to the Central Assembly and in the provinces, to (1) invite the resumption of ministerial responsibility in the provinces, (2) convene a constitution-making body as soon possible and (3) reconstitute the Viceroy's Executive Council with the support of the main Indian parties.

Gandhi was touring the cyclone ravaged province of Bengal at that time.

◆

The viceroy kept HMG in England briefed about the situation in India. His reports were becoming grimmer with every passing month. The situation in India was rapidly deteriorating. Sustaining British rule in India was becoming increasingly difficult and unjustifiable. The colonial government was becoming increasingly unpopular with almost all sections of Indians. A showdown with the 'caste Hindu Congress' was looming large. In a despatch sent to Whitehall in December 1945, the viceroy pointed out that if the Congress was suppressed, it would create a vacuum, as no other organization could replace it. After the elections, the Congress was sure to present its demand in a more extreme form, and if some action to solve the deadlock was not taken in the meantime, it would become very difficult to resist it. The Congress might even resort to 'direct action' to enforce its demand, and in that eventuality the government would find itself without any support, not even from the princes.

The armed forces were also not left untouched by the anger and nationalistic fervour. There were outbreaks of violence in Jubbalpore and some other cantonments. A similar outbreak in Poona was only averted by the advice against such a move, given by Gandhi to the representatives of the Indian troops, who had secretly met him. The INA under-trials, Indian soldiers who had fought the British in Burma under the leadership of Netaji Subhas Chandra Bose, were lionized all over India. In February

1946, Calcutta had erupted for three days, and the police had resorted to firing on student-led processions and protests fourteen times.

The results of the elections of the provinces and the Central Assembly came in. The Muslim League, due to its head start over the Congress, which was severely repressed between 1942–45, and the patronage it received from the British administration, predictably managed to win almost all the Muslim seats in the Central Assembly, as well as all the provincial legislatures with a sizeable Muslim population, except the North-West Frontier Province where a Congress ministry led by the Khan brothers swept the polls, not only capturing the Assembly but defeating the League on the majority of the Muslim seats too. The Congress formed ministries in eight of the eleven provinces; in Punjab it formed a coalition with the Unionist Party, which cut across communal alignments. The Muslim League formed ministries in Bengal and Sind in a coalition with the Hindu Mahasabha.

♦

On 19 February 1946, the new government announced in the British Parliament that a mission comprising three Cabinet ministers would shortly be sent to India. There, in association with the viceroy, they would proceed to give effect to the programme outlined in the Viceregal announcement of September 1945. Announcing this, the Labour prime minister, Clement Attlee, made some very pertinent remarks in the House of Commons, on 15 March 1946: 'India must choose what will be her future constitution. I hope that the Indian people may elect to remain within the British Commonwealth... But if she does so elect, it must be of her own free will... If, on the other hand, she elects for independence, in our view she has a right to do so... I am well aware, when I speak of India, that I speak of a country containing a congeries of races, religions and languages... We are very mindful of the rights of minorities, and minorities should be able to live free from fear. On the other hand, we cannot allow a minority to place a veto on the advance of the majority... There is the problem of the Indian States... I do not believe for a moment that the Indian princes would desire to be a bar to the forward march of India. But, as in the case of any other problems, this is a matter that Indians will settle themselves.'

For the first time, the three principal hurdles that had tripped up the process of settling the Indian question till then seemed to be dismantled: the veto of the minority on political advance, the obligation towards the princes and the denial of the right to unqualified independence. But, as the proverb says, there are many a slip between the cup and the lips, and these assurances were also proven to be false. However, other hurdles 'arising out of past circumstances' still threatened the process. India was to pay a terrible price for these 'past circumstances'. Gandhi, observing the process, was a worried man. It was the hour of the country's destiny. Would the India of his dreams acquit itself in a manner worthy of its glorious past? 'The British Cabinet Delegation will soon be in our midst,' he declared, 'to suspect their bona fide in advance would be a variety of weakness. As a brave people, it is our duty to take at its face value the declaration of the British ministers that they are coming to restore to India what is her due. If a debtor came to your house in contrition to repay his debt, would it not be your duty to welcome him? Would it not be unmanly to treat him with insult and humiliation, in remembrance of an injustice?'

◆

In March 1946, while Gandhi was staying at the Nature Cure Clinic, he received a personal invitation from the British Cabinet delegation to meet them in Delhi in the first week of April to discuss with them how the British could most expeditiously 'Quit India'. The special messenger bearing the invitation from Delhi, Sudhir Ghosh, almost did not make it to Poona. The car sent to take him to the airport was delayed, so he missed the Royal Air Force flight which was to take him to Bombay and then on to Poona. Half an hour after take-off from Delhi, the plane crashed, killing everyone on board.

Gandhi accepted the invitation and left for New Delhi. Reading Road, New Delhi, is where the magnificent Birla Mandir is situated. Just a stone's throw away from this magnificent edifice in red stone and marble is a humble temple to the Saint Valmiki, author of the epic Ramayana and the patron saint of the Valmiki community of north India. Members of the Valmiki community predominantly worked as sweepers and traditionally were shunned as untouchables because of the caste hierarchies in Hinduism. A low wall separated the temple from the municipal sweepers' colony, known then as 'Bhangi Colony'. On his trip to New Delhi to confer with the Cabinet Mission, Gandhi camped in a two-room tenement next to the Valmiki temple. For the next few months, this became a hub of activity. The CWC regularly met here. Pandit Nehru, Sardar Patel, Maulana Azad, Jayprakash Narayan and Sarojini Naidu were daily visitors; the bureaucracy, foreign guests and world press corps all made a beeline for the humble abode next to the temple. Anybody who had anything to do with India eventually ended up at the humble doors of the 'half-naked fakir' at his Bhangi Colony camp.

In the summer of 1946, the obscure little colony rivalled the Viceregal Palace in importance. It was here that the final chapter of the dramatic last days of the British Raj were written. Many meetings with the Cabinet Mission were held here, which eventually led to the demise of the 150-year-old British Raj, the birth of independent India, the tragedy of Partition and Gandhi's murder. Bhangi Colony was situated adjoining a playground, where Gandhi held his evening prayers. A band of militant Hindu youth also used the ground for physical training and weapon drills. They ended their daily preparation with a salute to their version of Mother India, which was intolerant of the Paradharmi, or people of other religions and faiths, i.e., Muslims. They were members of the RSS, a fascist organization of uppercaste Hindus. The RSS was creating an atmosphere where, after Gandhi's murder, they could deny their involvement by showing how they or their cadre weren't involved: had they wanted to, it would have been so easy for them to get rid of him. It was during Gandhi's subsequent stay at Bhangi Colony that protests began to be staged during his prayer meeting, staged to look as if the protesters were angry refugees. They were orchestrated by the Hindu extremist organizations and its leadership as a build-up to their ultimate objective to murder Gandhi.

♦

Meanwhile, the INA prisoners were being held in Red Fort and their court martial was in progress. The attention of the nation was focused on them. The British had tried to keep the whereabouts of the INA detainees a secret, but Sardar Patel had got information about them and brought it to Gandhi's notice. Some of the patriots had already been court martialled and executed. As soon as this was reported to Gandhi, he wrote to Lord Wavell: 'This I write in fear and trembling, lest I may be overstepping my limit. I am watching the progress of the trial of the members of the corps raised by or under Shri Subhas Babu. Though I can have nothing in common with any defence by force of arms, I am never blind to the valour and patriotism often displayed by persons in arms... India adores these men who are on trial. No doubt the government have overwhelming might on their side, but it will be a misuse of that power if it is used in the teeth of universal Indian opposition. It is not for me to say what should be done, except that what is being done is not the way...'

Next, Gandhi met General Auchinleck, comander-in-chief of India, to convince him to stop the court martial proceedings against the INA prisoners. He expressed his pleasure at the reassuring reply from the general.

Gandhi, accompanied by Patel, visited the imprisoned INA detainees once in Kabul Lines, Delhi Cantonment, and once at Red Fort. At Red Fort, the prisoners told them how, in the INA, they had totally obliterated the barriers of religion and caste, and Hindus and Muslims ate in the same mess. However, as prisoners of war, their British captors had resorted to segregation. They were served 'Hindu tea' and 'Muslim tea' separately by the camp authorities. This was a prevalent practice in the Indian Armed Forces in British India.

Gandhi told them that they should overcome this by, 'mixing the two together half and half and then sharing!'

'That is exactly what we have been doing!' they replied.

General Mohan Singh, one of the founders of the INA, preferred separate quarters in the detention camp due to the cracks that were dividing the INA leadership after Subhas Chandra Bose's death. Gandhi visited him next and then went to the field hospital where the injured prisoners of war were confined. He met Major-General Chatterjee, Major-General Loganathan and Colonel Habib-ur Rehman here. Until Gandhi met the INA prisoners, he refused to believe the reports of Bose's death in a plane crash. Colonel Habib-ur Rehman, who was with Netaji on the plane, recounted an eyewitness account of the crash. He told Gandhi, 'Netaji had received extensive burns on the hands and other parts of the body. But unmindful of them, he asked me how I was. I told him I felt all right, and hoped to pull through. He told me that he did not expect to survive and gave his last message: "I am going, but tell my countrymen and all concerned, the fight for Indian Independence must continue till the goal is attained." The crash occurred at 9:30 a.m. At half past three in the afternoon, Netaji breathed his last, retaining consciousness almost till the end. Not a groan escaped his lips in spite of the agony he suffered.' In his post-prayer speech that evening, Gandhi announced that, contrary to his previous belief, he was now convinced that Netaji Subhas Chandra Bose was no more.

♦

The Cabinet Mission comprised three members of the British Parliament—Lord Pethick-Lawrence, Sir Stafford Cripps and Albert V. Alexander. Gandhi admired Pethick-Lawrence. Sir Stafford Cripps had come to India in 1942 to explore the possibility of granting it dominion status after the War, if India cooperated in the British War effort, but the offer he had brought was unacceptable to almost all Indian parties. Gandhi had dismissed the Cripps Mission as 'a post-dated cheque drawn on a failing bank'.

The members of the Mission arrived at Karachi Airport on 23 March 1946 and reached Delhi the following day. From 1 to 17 April, they connected with various 'representatives of Indians', meeting 472 leaders in the course of 182 sittings in an effort to arrive at the greatest common measure of agreement among the various parties'. After the first week, the expectations of the people of India began to rise.

The Cabinet Mission's negotiations were held against a backdrop of communal trouble. The Muslim League was livid that the British prime minister had threatened to take away its power of veto. Jinnah denounced this attempt to 'bypass the League' as a 'flagrant breach of faith'. True to its creed, communal fires were lit in many places and the hand of the Muslim League was evident in the mischief. On 2 April, during a meeting with Pethick-Lawrence, Gandhi had suggested a couple of acts of confidence building. One of these was the release of all political prisoners, including those who had been arrested in cases of sabotage during the 'Quit India' movement: 'They could not be a danger to the state, now that the pursuit of freedom has become a common cause.' Gandhi's recommendation was gradually implemented. The socialist leaders Jayprakash Narayan and Dr Ram Manohar Lohia were released on 12 April. The INA under-trials were released two days later.

Woodrow Wyatt, a staff member of the Cabinet delegation, met Gandhi in the second week of April. 'Do you think we are getting off your back?' he asked.

'I feel that you will. But you must have the strength.'

Wyatt referred to the hurdles created by the League's demand for Pakistan: 'What if we imposed what we considered to be a just solution and went?'

'All would be upset,' Gandhi replied.

'So it must be left to India's decision?'

'Yes, leave it to the Congress and the League. Thanks to Jinnah's genius and British cooperation, he has built up a powerful organization, comprising not all but the major part of the Muslims. I will advise you to try him and if you feel he cannot deliver the goods, take the Congress into your confidence... But in any case, the British occupation must end forthwith.'

'And what happens after the British leave?'

'Probably, there will be arbitration... there might be a bloodbath. It will be settled in two days by non-violence if I can persuade India to go my way, or the ordeal may last longer. Even so, it would not be worse than what it is under the British Rule...'

There was an opinion gathering strength amongst some influential Muslim supporters of the League that Jinnah's obstinacy on Pakistan was harming the cause of the Muslims. Sir Stafford Cripps agreed that Jinnah's Pakistan was an 'impossible idea, even the League had realized it. When I find a person getting louder and more violent in his denunciation of his opponents, I get the feeling ... that he is beginning to recognize that the extreme case for which he stands is becoming desperate.'

On 27 April, Pethick-Lawrence wrote to the presidents of the Congress and Muslim League suggesting that they make 'one further attempt to obtain agreement'. They suggested certain fundamental principles for agreement: there should be a Union government dealing with foreign affairs, defence and communications and there would be two groups of provinces, one of predominantly Hindu provinces and the other of Muslim provinces. These groups would deal with all other subjects which the provinces desired; the provincial governments would deal with all other subjects and would have all the residuary sovereign rights. If the League and Congress were prepared to enter into negotiations on this basis, Pethick-Lawrence went on to suggest in his letter, arrangements would be made for them to meet in a conference, together with the Cabinet Mission.

But the Cabinet Mission's talks were also destined to fail, just like the ill-fated Simla Conference. The contradiction between what they said and their actions was the reason. While the British prime minister had declared in Parliament that minorities would no longer be permitted to exercise veto over majority, in practice, the British kept pandering to Jinnah. The Congress was continuously pushed into a corner and forced to compromise. The Congress had objected to groupings on a communal basis but between the Mission, the viceroy and the colonial department, that's what was being implemented, and the Congress was left with no option. On the question of paramountcy of the pact between the British Crown and the Indian princes too, the Congress wanted that the paramountcy should be transferred to the Indian government, but the British were happy to just let it lapse and let the Indian government and the princes decide the fate of the various kingdoms and principalities of India. The Congress too was inconsistent: after first opposing communal groupings, they internally passed a resolution to divide the Punjab and Bengal on communal basis.

Another worrying development in the Congress was that, more and more frequently, its leadership was talking in multiple voices instead of one united voice. Gandhi was informed that the Cabinet Mission had received a letter with a proposal from a very senior Congress leader in his personal capacity and not as a party representative. Gandhi was alarmed at this act of indiscipline.

The Congress and the Muslim League differed on the issue of funds for the Union government. The Congress wanted the Union government to raise the necessary finance for the discharge of its functions by taxation. The Muslim League insisted that the federal union should in no event have the power to raise revenues in its own right but only by contribution.

The League also wanted that no decision—legislative, executive or administrative—should be taken by the Union. On 'controversial matters', a decision should be taken by a vote in its favour of three-fourths. The Muslim League was adamant on achieving Pakistan and if they failed, since there were dissenting voices amongst their ranks too, then they would emasculate the Union government.

While the Cabinet Mission continuously refused to accept partition or division and termed Jinnah's vision of Pakistan as an unrealizable 'pipe dream', they continued to encourage the separatist agenda of the Muslim League. The Congress leaders, in their haste to get independence and power, kept slipping into the trap that had been so efficiently laid for them by the League and their friends in the colonial administration, from where the only escape was to accept partition.

The Cabinet Mission had also begun to sink into the quagmire of British colonial policies and practices, and was unwilling to take bold decisions. Gandhi's appeal to Sir Cripps much earlier, hoping that 'this time there is determination to do the right thing in terms of India', had failed to break through the diplomatic balancing act and the so-called British 'responsibilities' towards 'all' their Indian subjects. The British refused to see India as a whole and insisted that there were several Indias. If they could not rule it, the British were determined to fragment India.

◆

As was fated, the conference was a failure: what was acceptable to the Congress was rejected by the Muslim League and the demands of the Muslim League were acceptable to none. The Cabinet Mission kept trying to please all, and behind the scene, the viceroy and his colonial department kept playing their games. Finally, on 12 May, it was announced that the conference had failed to bring about an agreement between the Congress and the League. Admitting failure, the members of the Cabinet Mission returned to Delhi.

On 16 May, the Cabinet Mission, with the 'full approval of His Majesty's Government in the United Kingdom', published their recommendations for the speedy implementation of a new constitution. Their plan envisaged two stages: the long-term plan for the setting up of a constitution-making body and the short-term plan of the formation of an 'interim government having the support of the major political parties'. On the question of the partition of India, the Cabinet Mission's recommendations were quite emphatic—they were strongly averse to it. Apart from this, the recommendations were very ambiguous and convoluted. Many were at total divergence with previous clauses. In all, it was a most confusing document, trying desperately to please all. To the Congress, it offered a common centre and the freedom of choice to the provinces to form groups or not. To the Muslim League, it offered the prospect of 'Muslim zones' to be formed in the northwest and northeast of India by making it obligatory for the representatives of the provinces to sit in sections to settle the provincial constitutions. To the princes, it offered release from paramountcy, which was not to be transferred to the successor government, giving them the ability to declare independence or bargain for deals to join the Union. To the Sikhs, it held out the prospect of preserving intact the integrity of their homeland.

Gandhi studied the document in detail and gave his interpretations in an article published in *Harijan* on 26 May 1946: 'After four days of searching examination of the State Paper issued by the Cabinet Mission and the Viceroy on behalf of the British government, my conviction abides that it is the best document the British government could have produced in the circumstances. My compliments, however, does not mean that what is best from the British standpoint is also best or even good from the Indian. Their best may possibly be harmful... It is an appeal and an advice. It has no compulsion in it. Thus, the Provincial assemblies may or may not elect the delegates. The delegates, having been elected, may or may not join the Constituent Assembly. The Assembly having met, may lay down procedures different from the ones laid down in the statement. Whatever is binding on any person or party arises out of the necessity of the situation. Therefore, when Lord Pethick-Lawrence, Secretary of State for India, said to a press correspondent, "If they do come together on that basis, it will mean that they will have accepted that basis, but they can still change it, if by a majority of each party they desire to do so," he was right in the sense that those who become delegates, well-knowing the contents of the statement, were expected by the authors to abide by the basis, unless it were duly altered by the major parties... This is perfect so far, but what about the Units? Are the Sikhs, for whom the Punjab is the only home in India, to consider themselves against their will, as part of a Section which takes in Sind, Baluchistan and the Frontier Province? In my opinion, the voluntary character of the Statement demands that the liberty of the individual Unit should be unimpaired. Any member or section is free to join it. The freedom to opt out is an additional safeguard. It can never be a substitute for the freedom retained in Para 15(5).'

The three main parties involved in the Cabinet Mission's deliberations ended up interpreting the recommendations as was convenient and beneficial to them.

On 28 May, the members of the CWC dispersed. Gandhi accompanied some of the members to Mussoorie for a short rest and respite from the scorching Delhi summer. There was nothing to do since the Muslim League was going to make known its response to the 16 May Plan only after the meeting of the Council of the Muslim League on 6 June. On the 7th, Gandhi returned to Delhi. The car carrying him covered the 175 miles almost entirely at night. The car was stopped on the Yamuna bridge as it entered Delhi. The sentry on duty peered through the window and asked the Sikh driver to identify himself and his passengers. The driver replied, '*Gadi mein Hindustan ke garibon ka badshah savaar hai!*' (I carry the king of India's poor.) The sentry stood at attention and let the car pass.

The CWC met on 8 June. It later came to light that Cripps had met Jinnah and the latter was agreeable to the formation of a coalition interim government consisting of the fittest persons, without any reference to parity. During the course of an interview, the viceroy suggested to Gandhi that representatives of the Congress and the League should meet and jointly finalize a list of people to be nominated to the coalition government. Welcoming the viceroy's suggestion, Gandhi replied that the nominees should be persons of proven ability and incorruptibility; 'there should be no talk of parity, they should agree to be closeted in a room, and no one should leave till an agreement was reached. In the absence of an agreement in spite of all the efforts, the Viceroy should examine the merits of the respective lists submitted by both the parties and accept one or the other, not an amalgam of the two.'

Just as people began to feel that the new formula would succeed, Jinnah refused to sit at a negotiating table with Congress President Maulana Abul Kalam Azad, a non-League Muslim. According to Jinnah,

Hindus were the enemies, but non-League Muslims were traitors and he would not 'treat with traitors'! The Congress refused to backtrack on this matter. Fearing another breakdown in talks, the viceroy suggested that the Maulana, as the Congress president, nominate Nehru to represent him at the proposed meeting. Gandhi advised the Congress to accept this proposal for the sake of a settlement, but with a clear understanding that at the meeting, Nehru would only act as the Maulana's mouthpiece.

Nehru reached the viceroy's office for the meeting at noon on 12 June. Jinnah did not turn up for the meeting. Nehru showed the viceroy the Congress's list of proposed nominees for the interim government. Now, it was Wavell's turn to change colours. At the meeting, he raised the issue of Hindu–Muslim parity. The next day, Gandhi wrote to Wavell: 'You are a very great soldier, a daring soldier. Dare to do the right. You must make your choice of one horse or the other. So far as I can see, you will never succeed in riding two at the same time. Choose the names submitted either by the Congress or the League. For God's sake do not make an incompatible mixture and in trying to do so produce a fearful explosion.'

In a personal letter addressed to Cripps, Gandhi wrote: 'You are handling the most difficult task of your life as I see it. The Mission is playing with fire. If you have the courage you will do what I suggested from the very beginning... you will not be able to have your cake and eat it too. You will have to choose between the two—the Muslim League and the Congress, both your creations... Coquetting now with the Congress, now with the League and again with the Congress, wearing yourself away, will not do. Either you swear by what is right or by what the exigencies of the British policy may dictate. In either case, bravery is required. Only stick to the programme. Stick to your dates even though heavens may fall. Leave by 16 June 1948, whether you allow the Congress to form a coalition or the League. If you think that the accumulated British wisdom must know better than these two creations of yours, I have nothing to add. But I have fancied that you are not cast in that mould.' The letter ended with the advice: 'Bury yourself in private life, unless the brave British announcement made is fulfilled to the Indian hope. A word to the wise.'

Sir Stafford Cripps replied: 'I can assure you, neither I nor my colleagues lack courage to act but we want to temper our courage with prudence.' Referring to the advice given by Gandhi, he continued: 'Certainly, I shall never put my desire to return home and rest before my determination to leave nothing undone which may help a solution of the difficult problems here... I shall have great hope that before we leave India, we may have helped towards the settlement of the problem.'

In his post-prayer speech on the 16th, Gandhi pleaded for patience. He said, 'You should bear with the Mission, too. They have inherited the tradition of imperialism which they cannot outgrow all at once... We must not blame them for not throwing it overboard overnight. Let us trust their bonafides. Let us not act upon mere suspicion.' That night, he woke up at half past one and dictated a draft of a letter from the CWC to the viceroy in response to the unilateral announcement about the interim government. He emphasized four points: (1) the League being avowedly a Muslim organization could not include any non-Muslim representative in its list; (2) the Congress as a nationalist organization must have the right to include a Congress Muslim in its list; (3) the League could have no say in the selection of any name outside those belonging to its quota of five Muslims. This meant that, in the event of a vacancy occurring among the seats allotted to the minorities, the Congress alone would have the right to select names to fill up the vacancies as it claimed to represent all sections by right of service and (4) in action, the interim government should be regarded as being responsible to the elected representatives in the Assembly.

The CWC ignored Gandhi's draft and, in the afternoon session on 17 June, decided on their reply: the CWC was not 'enamoured' of the viceroy's proposal but they did not want to say 'no' to it. The non-inclusion of a nationalist Muslim from the Congress would be dealt with by nominating a nationalist Muslim in place of a Hindu from the Congress quota, even though this would effectively give the majority Indian community a minority representation in the interim government.

After having denied that he had ever assured the Congress that the interim government would enjoy the same powers as a dominion Cabinet, in a letter addressed to the Congress president on 30 May, the viceroy went on to assure that 'His Majesty's government would treat the new interim government with the same close consideration as a dominion government; most liberal intentions may be almost unrecognizable when they have to be expressed in a formal document. I have no doubt that if you are prepared to trust me, we shall be able to cooperate in a manner which will give India a sense of freedom from external control and will prepare (it) for complete freedom as soon as the new constitution is made.' The Congress surprisingly cowed down to the bullying tactics of the Muslim League and the partisan behaviour of the viceroy, and decided to accept the viceroy's plan for the interim government. It was decided that, since the inclusion of Abdur Rab Nishtar's name directly affected the Khan brothers of the North-West Frontier Province, the CWC would wait for the arrival of Khan Abdul Ghaffar Khan from Uttmanzai the next day.

The CWC now realized that the viceroy was not only behaving in a partisan manner towards the Muslim League and Jinnah, but actually in alliance with them. This feeling was further strengthened when, on 22 June, the viceroy, in a letter to the Congress president, asked the Congress not to press their demand for the inclusion of a nationalist Muslim from their party in the interim government: 'For reasons of which you are well aware, it is not possible for the Cabinet Mission or myself to accept this request.' This was at variance to his reply rejecting the objections raised by the Congress to the Muslim League's nominee Abdur Rab Nishtar. The viceroy had, on 15 June, reasoned that 'I cannot accept the right of the Congress to object to names put forward by the Muslim League, any more than I would accept similar objections from the other side.'

To Gandhi, the intricacies of maintaining a balance of power were meaningless. He refused to accept a change of role for the Congress for the mere success of a power-sharing formula. To him, the Congress was rightfully and duty-bound to portray its role as a nationalist organization representing all communities and classes. The Congress would be committing political suicide if it accepted any other role. Similarly, it must not discard, for any political gains, its friends. Such opportunism would be the cause of its downfall and would eventually prove fatal. 'To gain the world at the cost of one's soul' was a bad bargain for Gandhi. The CWC, however, thought differently.

The Cabinet Mission had asked for the final decision of the Congress and the League on their proposals to be conveyed to them by 2 o'clock.

At noon, someone from the viceroy's house rang up Pandit Nehru to say that the Working Committee's reply should be sent at once. Pandit Nehru rang up Sardar, who replied that he saw no reason for the hurry and asked Sudhir to contact Mr Blaker of the Cabinet Mission staff and say that such impatient insistence would needlessly spoil matters. Gandhi, on being informed of it, drafted a short interim reply to be sent straight away and suggested that the Cabinet delegation should be informed that a detailed letter would follow. This was done.

Pyarelal writes: 'In the afternoon meeting of the Working Committee, Bapu asked me to read out a note which he had written for them. In it, he pointed out that the Constituent Assembly had no *de jure* authority, as it did not bear the imprimatur of the Parliament. It was based only on a recommendation of the Cabinet Mission. "Their recommendation will remain in their mouth or on the printed paper. We shall have no authority even to order a constable if there is a row in the Constituent Assembly. This is a dangerous situation. There must be the imprimatur of the Parliament and real power in the Central Government before we can make anything of the Constituent Assembly. The imprimatur of the Parliament would clear the way for the Chairman of the Constituent Assembly (by making the issue adjudicable) in case he wants to refer a point of major importance to the Federal Court for decision." In the course of the discussion that followed, Sardar pressed with great vigour his view that the explanation given by the Cabinet Mission in regards to the Reforms Office was quite adequate and the Congress could not postpone giving its decision forthwith without damaging its prestige. Bapu scribbled: "My mind is in a fog… It centres round the insertion of reference to para 19 … and the meaning of 'scrapping the whole plan' (of the Interim Government)." Sardar lost patience. Bapu asked Sarat Bose and Rajendra Babu to give their legal opinion as to whether the declaration that had been issued to the Speakers of the Assemblies left the members, who might go into the Constituent Assembly after signing it, freedom of action in regard to para 19 of the 16 May Plan. The opinion of Sarat Bose was that the reference to para 19 in the instructions did not take away from the members' liberty of action, since their acceptance of the State Paper was subject to the legal interpretation of the clauses in dispute. Rajendra Babu's opinion was that para 19 did not make grouping compulsory. It only gave Provinces freedom to form groups as was clear from the language of the document itself. In regard to having the imprimatur of the Parliament on the State Paper, Pandit Nehru felt that it would be a "limiting process" and restrict the scope of interpretation. For once, fear has proved a liar. The Cabinet Mission issued an elucidation in the evening that the form which the members of the Constituent Assembly were required to sign did not bind them to frame a constitution in terms of para 19. The pledge they had to sign required them only to cooperate in framing a constitution for India. At 8:00 p.m., when Bapu's silence ended, he and Sardar met the Viceroy and the members of the Cabinet Mission at the Viceroy's House. On returning from there, Sardar again asked Bapu: "Were you satisfied?" Bapu replied: "On the contrary my suspicions have deepened. I suggest that hereafter you should guide the Working Committee." Sardar replied: "Nothing of the sort. I am not going to say a word. You yourself tell them whatever you want."

'At 10:00 p.m., Bapu wrote a letter to Cripps: "I would rather not write this note... In spite of the readiness ... of the Working Committee to go in for the Constituent Assembly, I would not be able to advice the leap in the dark... There is nothing but a vacuum after you throw all the commitments on the scrap heap, if you really do intend to do so... The instructions to the Governors (issued by the Reforms Office), innocuous as they have proved to be, have opened up a dreadful vista. I, therefore, propose to advise the Working Committee not to accept the long term proposition without it being connected with the Interim Government. I must not act against my instinct..." At 8:00 a.m. on 23 June 1946, Bapu went to attend the Working Committee meeting. He asked me to read out the note which he had written to Cripps last night. He then addressed them very briefly: "I admit defeat. You are not bound to act upon my unsupported suspicion. You should follow my intuition only if it appeals to your reason. Otherwise you should take an independent course. I shall now leave with your permission. You should follow the dictates of your reason."

'A hush fell over the gathering. Nobody spoke for some time. Maulana Saheb with his unfailing alertness at once took in the situation. 'What do you desire? Is there any need to detain Bapu any further?' he asked.

Everybody was silent. Everybody understood. In that hour of decision, they had no use of Bapu. They decided to discard the pilot. Bapu returned to his residence.

'The Working Committee again met at noon and addressed a letter to the Cabinet Mission, rejecting the proposal for the formation of the Interim Government at the Centre and accepting the long-term plan with its own interpretation of the disputed clauses.' In spite of it, they made Bapu attend the afternoon session of the Working Committee. At noon, the Cabinet Mission invited the members of the Working Committee to meet them. Bapu not being a member was not sent for and did not go. On their return, nobody told Bapu a word about what had transpired at the meeting.

The final phase of negotiations with the Cabinet Mission also saw a phase when the growing distance between Gandhi and the CWC, and between him and some of the Congress stalwarts, became very apparent. There were many issues on which he did not see eye to eye with the Congress leaders. More often than not, the Congress and its leaders were abandoning Gandhi and turning a deaf ear to his advice. Yet, they needed him to endorse their decisions, to make them acceptable to the people of India; the masses in the country's fields and villages would accept anything that their Bapu had blessed. And so, after disagreeing with him, after ignoring his advice, after sidelining him, they would run to him to endorse their acts, and he dutifully obliged.

They did not agree with him when he insisted that the differences between the Muslim League and the Congress be resolved only after the British left. 'Independence first,' he insisted; 'power soonest and at any cost' was their refrain.

Referring to an incident in the Working Committee on his last day in Delhi, Gandhi wrote to Patel from Poona on 1 July 1946, saying, 'I did not like our conversation today. It is nobody's fault. The fault, if at all, is of the circumstances. What can you or I do for it? You go by your experience, I by mine. You know I have been at a loss to understand a number of things which you have done… You speak in the Committee with much heat. I do not like it. On top of it, today came the question of the Constituent Assembly… All this is not by way of a complaint. But I see, we are drifting in different directions.'

Patel replied: 'What can I say after your letter? I must be at fault. Only, I cannot yet see it and that makes me feel unhappy. I do not want to take a different path... My own instinct was to the contrary but if I had not done what I did, the Congress would have been held to blame afterwards... I do betray some heat when I speak in the Committee... That is a temperamental defect ... but there is nothing in it.'

Gandhi had realized that his political heirs had come of age and it was time he let them go, let them make decisions because independent India would rely on their ability to govern and take decisions independently, so he voluntarily withdrew.

The Working Committee's decision conveyed to the Cabinet Mission on 25 June did not solve the matter. The Cabinet Mission adhered to its own interpretation of the disputed clauses; they decided to shelve any effort to resolve them for the time being. The Cabinet Mission decided that the responses of both the Congress and the Muslim League were in accordance with their 16 May Plan and so both the parties were qualified to be invited to form the interim government. They called a short recess in the negotiations, and on 29 June, the three-member Cabinet Mission left Delhi for London.

Gandhi's instinct was alerted to the hidden pitfalls due to various reasons. He was suspicious of the mechanizations of the British administrative machinery in India. He had realized that there was disagreement over many matters, between the members of the Cabinet Mission and also between them and the viceroy and the British colonial administration. Finally, he was worried about the way the viceroy's reform office was functioning. He had time and again expressed his conviction that India would come into its own only when it broke the 'Indian Steel Frame'. Srinivas Sastry's words, spoken after the Second Round Table Conference in London, came back to his mind: 'Many good intentions emanating from Whitehall have been assassinated in the dark corridors of the Delhi Secretariat.'

On 27 May, Gandhi wrote to Cripps: 'Trust put on is worse than useless, trust felt is the thing that counts... Trustworthy action on the part of the Cabinet Mission will dispel all mistrust or distrust, as the sun dispels the morning mist.'

The AICC met in Bombay on 7 July 1946 to ratify the decisions taken by the Working Committee. The Socialist elements in the Congress were opposed to the CWC's acceptance of the long-term proposals of the Cabinet Mission. A large part of the speech Gandhi delivered endorsed the Working Committee's decision.

'You know my relations with the members of the Working Committee… I could have asked them to turn down the proposal about the Constituent Assembly … but I could not adduce any reason for it… Their decision which … is unanimous is before you… The members of the Working Committee are your faithful and tried servants; you should not lightly reject their resolution.

'I am willing to admit that the proposed Constituent Assembly is not the parliament of the people. It has many defects. But you are all seasoned and veteran fighters. A soldier is never afraid of danger. He revels in it. If there are shortcomings in the proposed Constituent Assembly, it is for you to get them removed. It should be a challenge to combat, not a ground for rejection. I am surprised that Shri Jayprakash Narayan said yesterday that it would be dangerous to participate in the proposed Constituent Assembly and they should, therefore, reject the Working Committee's resolution. I was not prepared to hear such defeatist language from the lips of a tried fighter like Jayprakash… A Satyagrahi knows no defeat.

'Nor would I expect a Satyagrahi to say that whatever Englishmen do must be bad. The English are not necessarily bad. There are good men and bad men among the English people as among any other people… We ourselves are not free from defects… Some people say that Satyagraha is of no avail against a person who has no moral sense. I join issue with that. The stoniest of hearts must melt if we are true and have enough patience. A Satyagrahi lays down his life, but never gives up. That is the meaning of "do or die"…

'This is no time for dalliance or ease… The Constituent Assembly is going to be no bed of roses for you, but a bed of thorns. You may not shirk it…

'If you asked me whether in the event of your rejecting the proposed Constituent Assembly or the Constituent Assembly failing to materialize, I would advise the people to launch civil disobedience, individual or mass, or undertake a fast myself, my reply would be "No". I believe in walking alone. I came alone in this world, I have walked alone in the valley of the shadow of death and I shall quit alone, when the time comes. I know I am quite capable of launching Satyagraha even if I am alone. I have done so before. But this is no occasion for a fast or civil disobedience. I regard the Constituent Assembly as the substitute of Satyagraha. It is constructive Satyagraha.

'The alternative is constructive work to which you have never done justice... But a Satyagrahi cannot delay action till perfect conditions are obtained. He will act with whatever material is at hand, purge it of dross and convert it into pure gold...

'Let us not be cowardly in our approach, but face our task with confidence and courage. Let not fear of being deceived dismay us. No one can deceive a Satyagrahi. Never mind the darkness that fills my mind. God will turn it into light.'

The decision of the CWC with regards to the Cabinet Mission's proposal was ratified by the AICC by 204 votes for and 51 votes against.

Gandhi left for Panchgani to rest and recuperate but the anxiety about the direction in which his beloved country was heading and his inability to understand the doubts that kept needling him made his stay in Panchgani uneasy. He decided to cut short his stay and head for Sevagram. He spent a few days at the Nature Cure Clinic in Pune. However, instead of resting, there, his schedule became very hectic, with a lot of people meeting him.

◆

The CWC met again in Delhi in the last week of June. The discussions centred around the Congress's acceptance of the long-term plan of the Cabinet Mission while rejecting their short-term plans. In another part of the city, the Working Committee of the Muslim League was continuously in session, impatiently awaiting the Congress's decision. Jinnah and the League usually practised the strategy of holding back their hand till the Congress's cards were on the table. The League had already accepted the Cabinet Mission's proposal of 16 May. Their interpretation of the grouping clause had been endorsed by the Cabinet Mission and Jinnah had secured further assurances from Viceroy Lord Wavell. He assumed that the Congress would never accept such a lopsided plan and thus the League would be invited to form the interim government.

On the evening of 25 June, having received the Congress's reply, to his surprise, the Cabinet Mission sent for Jinnah and informed him that they were satisfied by the replies of both parties and both had qualified to be part of the interim government. The Congress had expressed its inability to be part of this government in accordance with Paragraph 8 of the 16 June proposal which said 'that, if either of the two parties was unwilling to join the formation of the coalition government on the lines set up in that statement, the Viceroy would proceed with the formation of an interim government which would be as representative as possible of those willing to accept the statement of 16 May.'

Jinnah was furious. He asked the Cabinet Mission to give him in writing what they proposed to do, and then rushed to the Working Committee of the League, where he had them pass a resolution accepting the 16 June proposal for the formation of the interim government. He felt that, after the Congress's stand, the viceroy was honour-bound to invite the Muslim League to form the interim government. However, the Cabinet Mission maintained that, according to them, 'If either the Congress or the Muslim League would not consent to come into the Coalition Government, then the scheme for Coalition Government went and we would have to find some other Interim Government of those who accepted the scheme of 16 May.' Accepting the 16 May statement entitled the Congress to be invited to be a constituent of the coalition government as the biggest political group in the country. Accordingly, on 26 June, the Cabinet Mission issued a statement to the effect that further efforts for the formation of the interim government would be resumed after a short break while the elections for the Constituent Assembly were taking place.

The Muslim League was angry; it felt that it had been outmanoeuvred, let down, deceived. Jinnah demanded that since the plan for the formation of an interim government was shelved, the elections for the Constituent Assembly must also be postponed. This was rejected by the Cabinet Mission too. A livid Jinnah accused the Cabinet Mission of 'breach of faith'; he termed the Cabinet Mission's interpretation of Paragraph 8 as 'most fantastic and dishonest'. For once, Jinnah was stranded without the help of his traditional patrons, and like a petulant child, he resorted to threats and and arm twisting.

The League Council met on 29 July and withdrew its previous acceptance of the 16 May Plan. It announced its intention to launch 'Direct Action' to achieve Pakistan. 16 August 1946 would be 'Direct Action Day' they declared.

VIII

VIOLENCE ERUPTS

Perhaps the only thing that can be quite positively asserted about this orgy of arson and violence is that it was not a spontaneous uprising.

—Report in *Hindustan Standard*, 6 November 1946

We are not yet in the midst of civil war. But we are nearing it.

—M.K. Gandhi, in *Harijan* after the Great Calcutta Killings

Direct Action Day

To thundering applause in the concluding session of the Muslim League's Council Jinnah declared: 'Today we bid goodbye to constitutional methods… We have forged a pistol and are in a position to use it.' At a a press conference on 31 June, he further clarified that since both the British government and the Congress were armed in their own way, one with firearms and the other with the threat of mass struggle, the Muslim League felt that it was high time it also got ready for a struggle to enforce it's demand for Pakistan. He declined to discuss the details of the proposed 'Direct Action', saying, 'I am not prepared to tell you that now.' Asked whether 'Direct Action' would be violent or non-violent, he replied, 'I am not going to discuss ethics.' Others in the Muslim League were much more forthcoming, and a sinister connotation to 'Direct Action' began to emerge. Khwaja Nazimuddin of Bengal explained, 'There are a hundred and one ways in which we can create difficulties, especially when we are not restricted to non-violence. The Muslim population of Bengal knows very well what "Direct Action" would mean and we need not bother to give them any lead.' Nawabzada Liaquat Ali Khan, Jinnah's right-hand man, explained, '"Direct Action" means resorting to non-constitutional methods and that can take any form and whatever form may suit the conditions under which we live; we cannot eliminate any method, "Direct Action" means action against the law.' Sardar Abdur Rab Nishtar was far more honest in explaining the League's plans for 'Direct Action!': 'Pakistan can only be achieved by shedding blood and if the opportunity arises, the blood of non-Muslims must be shed, Muslims do not believe in Ahimsa!'

As early as April 1946, Sir Feroz Khan Noon, while addressing the Muslim League Legislator's Convention, had warned, 'For placing us under one Central government, the havoc which the Muslims would play would put to shame what Chengiz Khan and Halaku did.' The Muslim League went on a campaign of provocation, and both the Congress as well as the British administration stood by and watched. The League was going to wait till the appointed date to let loose their thugs. Communal incidents had already been reported from Ahmedabad, Bombay, Allahabad, Aligarh, Dacca and various other places. The Muslim League set up a 'Council of Action' to plan and execute the proposed 'Direct Action' programme and their press carried the message to Muslim communities all over. A leaflet containing a special prayer for the crusade announced that 100 million Indian Muslims 'who through bad luck had become slaves of Hindus and the British' would be starting 'a Jehad in this very month of Ramzan'. Another leaflet featuring a picture of Jinnah wielding a sword, proclaimed: 'We Muslims have had the Crown and have ruled. Be ready and take your swords… O Kafir! … your doom is not far and the general massacre will come!'

The Muslim League's boast that they represented all the Muslims was put to one of its most severe tests by the 'Direct Action Day' programme. It was soon apparent that 'Direct Action' would only succeed in the states under Muslim League control, which were mostly the provinces it claimed for its Muslim homeland: in the west, parts of Muslim League-influenced West Punjab, Sindh, and in the east, the Muslim League-ruled Bengal.

Bengal was governed by a coalition of the Muslim League and Hindu Mahasabha. The government was headed by Shaheed Suhrawardy. Suhrawardy had declared that if Congress was in power at the centre, Bengal would raise the standard of rebellion. They would declare independence.

As chief minister, Suhrawardy controlled the law and order machinery, including the police department. He systematically shunted out senior Hindu police officers and replaced them with Muslims. By 16 August 1946, 'Direct Action Day', of the twenty-four police stations in Calcutta, in twenty-two Muslim officers were in charge and Anglo-Indian officers were in charge in the remaining two.

The provincial government declared 16 August a public holiday. Muslim League legislators were active in distributing arms and forming gangs led by professional criminals, so 'Direct Action Day' was in reality 'The Day of the Rampaging Mobs' organized by the Muslim League. Sharif Khan, a Muslim League member of the Legislative Assembly, personally organized gangs of criminals in his locality and armed them. Sharif was a known gangster and was also known to be a trusted goon of Suhrawardy. Mohammed Usman, the Muslim League mayor of Calcutta and secretary of the Calcutta Muslim League, visited Muslim localities of Howrah accompanied by Sharif Khan and incited the local Muslim gangsters and Muslim League stormtroopers to violence. Fuel, which was strictly rationed, was comandeered by the chief minister and distributed among Muslim League leaders.

One of the events planned for 'Direct Action Day' was a mass rally of Muslims at the Calcutta Maidan. Muslims were asked to congregate after marching through various localities. After listening to inflammatory speeches by their leaders, they would disperse.

From the midnight of 15 August 1946, Calcutta was shrouded in a fog of dread and hatred. Bands of Muslims took over the streets and bylanes of Calcutta, and the night was pierced by maniacal shouts of hatred. '*Allah-o-Akbar!*' and '*Ladh ke lenge Pakistan!*' (We will snatch Pakistan by the power of our swords!) were shouted in pockets of non-Muslim minorities living in the midst of Muslim strongholds. The one feature that is common till today in planned communal clashes in India was also apparent in Calcutta on 'Direct Action Day': the total and purposeful paralysis of the law and order machinery. Criminals ruled the streets, there was no one to respond to pleas for help and cries for rescue.

Shaheed Suhrawardy took command of the central police control room, which received law and order reports from all over. He kept the police in check while directing the actions of the marauders, using the law and order machinery. On the evening of the 16th, Inspector Wade caught eight Muslims redhanded, with a lorry loaded with looted goods; he arrested them and sent them to the police station. Suhrawardy reached the police station even before the looters and ordered their release on his 'personal responsibility'. He did this repeatedly, till a complaint was lodged against him with the governor, and the chief minister was politely requested to 'stay away from the control room'.

By mid-day on the 16th, large processions of Muslim hooligans took to the streets, armed to their teeth, and started marching towards the Calcutta Maidan for the mass rally being held there by the League.

While returning from the rally, the inflamed mobs attacked shops and business establishments owned by Hindus and Sikhs and burnt cars, buses and trams. Pedestrians were stabbed. Within hours of the rally, the streets of Calcutta were controlled by the League's goondas. Now, the second phase of terror was launched: armed mobs, shouting pro-League and pro-Pakistan slogans, began attacking, looting and ravaging pockets of Hindu and non-Muslim populations. An unrestrained orgy of violence, murder, rape, arson and looting was let loose, while the police passively looked on, or in certain cases, actively assisted the marauders, guided by the chief minister. The inferno that was lit on 16 August 1946 continued on 17 and 18 August 1946.

After three days of rampage by Muslims, the Hindu backlash took over and the results were equally devastating. The Hindus had also armed themselves and organized their bands of 'defenders'; these were the hotheaded stormtroopers of the RSS and Hindu Mahasabha, some local and many others brought in from other states.

The Hindu mobs attacked small pockets of Muslim settlements with great savagery. The innocent Muslims, who had for centuries lived in peace with their Hindu and Sikh neighbours, were paying the price for the savage acts of their fanatic co-religionists elsewhere.

Soon, Calcutta resembled a slaughterhouse: the stench of decaying bodies filled its streets, human flesh roasted in burning homes and structures, and puddles of blood stained the roads. Bodies of stripped and raped women and young girls were strewn all around. Dead bodies of children and severed body parts were stuffed down manholes, resulting in choked drains and overflowing sewers; sewage began to pool on the streets, adding to the gruesome mess.

The most common and effective method of attack, adopted by murderers from both communities, was to encircle isolated individual homes or small pockets of the minority community and seal off all escape routes. Then, the systematic looting, slaughter and abductions would begin. Men and boys would be targeted first, slaughtered in front of their families. Women of all ages were raped multiple times before being murdered or abducted to be trafficked. The mobs would then loot and set the homes on fire, even ordinary citizens indulging in the looting.

Press reports from that period throw light on the horror of 'Direct Action Day' and its aftermath. Kim Christen of *The Statesman* reported: 'I have a stomach made strong by the experience of a war hospital, but war was never like this.' An editorial in the same paper mentioned: 'This is not a riot... It needs a word found in medieval history, a fury. Yet a "fury" sounds spontaneous and there must have been some deliberation and organization to set this fury on the way. Hordes who ran about battering and killing with eight foot lathis, may have found them lying about or brought them out of their own pockets, but that is hard to believe. We have already commented on the bands who found it easy to get petrol and vehicles when no others were permitted on the streets. It is not mere supposition that men were imported into Calcutta to help in making an impression.'

In the same issue, in an article titled 'Disgrace Abounding', the paper wrote: 'The origin of the appalling carnage and loss in the capital of a great province, we believe the worst communal riot in India's history, was a political demonstration by the Muslim League... In retrospect its conduct before the riot stands open to the inference—not only by political opponents, that it was divided in mind on whether rioting of some sort would be good or bad... The bloody shambles to which this country's largest city has been reduced is an abounding disgrace, which, owing to the Bengal Ministry's pre-eminence as a League Ministry, has inevitably tarnished seriously the all-India reputation of the League itself.'

'The Great Calcutta Killing', as it came to be known, consumed the lives of more than five thousand people; more than fifteen thousand were reportedly injured and hundreds of thousands made homeless.

The Muslim League had launched 'Direct Action Day' to intimidate and terrorize the Congress and the British administration, and in this, they succeeded spectacularly. They had not expected the magnitude of the Hindu backlash but were able to exploit it to their advantage too. Commenting on the carnage in Calcutta, an unconcerned Jinnah called it a Hindu conspiracy to malign the Muslim League and its government in Bengal. He held the Congress, the Cabinet Mission and Gandhi responsible for the tragedy of Calcutta. His lust for power had turned this once liberal individual into a fanatic zealot.

Gandhi heard about the Calcutta carnage when he was at Sevagram Ashram. Speaking after the evening prayer on 24 August, he asked the Ashramites to think what their duties were in the face of the conflagration which had overtaken the country. 'Let us be humble and confess that we have not got the strength today to meet all the expectations that the people entertain of us,' he said. 'If they had realized fully the principles for which the ashram stood, they should have rushed into the blaze and offered the purest sacrifice which might have "conceivably quenched the flames." A pure sacrifice did not mean the thoughtless annihilation of the moth in the flame. Sacrifice to be effective must be ... willing and ... made in faith and hope, without a trace of ill will or hatred in the heart... There is nothing that such sacrifice cannot achieve.'

'We are not yet in the midst of civil war. But we are nearing it,' he wrote in a series of editorials in the *Harijan*. 'At present we are playing at it... If the British are wise, they will keep clear of it. Appearances are to the contrary.'

The hour had come for the people to make their final choice between Pax Britannica and freedom. He predicted that the British authorities, having decided to quit, would show greater weakness. 'The parties will find that it is ... a broken reed. If the fratricidal strife extended to the whole of India and it was the British gunpowder that kept the two from stabbing one another,' he warned, the inevitable result would be that 'the British power or its substitute will be in possession of India for a long time to come. The length will be measured by the period required by the parties coming to sanity. It will come either after an exhausting mutual fight, independent of the foreign element or by one party eschewing violence in spite of the heaviest odds. Let Hindus and Muslims ... realize that if India is to be an independent nation, one or both must deliberately cease to look to British authority for protection… My advice is Satyagraha first and Satyagraha last…'

After the rejection of the Cabinet Mission's plan by the Muslim League and their call of 'Direct Action', the British Cabinet instructed the viceroy to invite the Congress to form a national interim government which would replace the Viceroy's Council. Nehru, recently appointed president of the Congress, was invited to take charge as vice-president and to form a government of his nominees to be sworn in on 2 September. Jinnah declared that the Muslim League would boycott the interim government and would observe 2 September as a day of protest, staging a black flag demonstration outside the Delhi Secretariat. This was a green signal to Muslim Leaguers to once again go on a rampage. This time, they targeted those whom Jinnah called traitors and hated virulently, nationalist Muslim leaders who supported the Congress. Sir Shafat Ahmed Khan, a nationalist Muslim who had accepted Nehru's invitation to join the interim government, was stabbed by Muslim League fanatics and left for dead by the roadside in Simla. Shafi Ahmed Kidwai, brother of Rafi Ahmed Kidwai, a nationalist Muslim minister in the Government of United Provinces, was murdered in Mussoorie.

Calcutta continued to smoulder; there was violence throughout August, September and October. The Muslim League was happy with the unfolding events. When the plight of Hindu victims was reported, they called it a conspiracy to malign the League, and when the Hindus retaliated, they used it to buttress their demand for Pakistan. Meanwhile, the RSS and Hindu Mahasabha used the attacks on Hindus to consolidate their hold on the Hindu community. They claimed to be their protectors and recruited new cadres. They instigated them to slaughter innocent Muslims and intimidate the survivors.

On 2 September 1946, Congress ministers of the interim government took oath of office with Gandhi's blessings. Gandhi had returned to Delhi and was again staying at his camp in a tenement in Bhangi Colony. In the early hours of the morning, he scribbled a short message for the members of the new government, to remind them that they must not forget to redeem the pledge which they had made when the Congress was in the wilderness. His 'instrument of instructions' was brief and included this sentence: 'You have been in my thoughts since the prayer. Abolish the Salt Tax. Remember the Dandi March. Unite Hindus and Muslims. Remove untouchability. Take to Khadi.' He gave them a message which came to be called his talisman: 'I will give you a talisman. Whenever you are in doubt, or when the self becomes too much with you, apply the following test. Recall the face of the poorest and the weakest person whom you may have seen, and ask yourself, if the step you contemplate is going to be of any use to him. Will he gain anything by it? Will it restore to him control over his own life and destiny? In other words, will it lead to swaraj, freedom for the hungry and spiritually starving millions? Then you will find your doubts and your self melt away.'

Gandhi wanted to return to Sevagram Ashram as soon as the interim government was installed, but the newly sworn-in ministers prevailed upon him to stay in Delhi and guide them. So he stayed on in Delhi through the hot September month when the city is prone to duststorms and sweltering heat. Watching all that he had fought for frittered away, corrupted and destroyed, unfortunately by those whom he had trusted the most, Gandhi prepared himself to face the storm which his unfailing instinct warned him was coming.

◆

While the political scenario in Delhi was becoming more and more complex, the newly appointed Cabinet found that they were systematically being obstructed in their work by the colonial administration. Wavell was still desperately trying to woo Jinnah to get him to participate in the interim government. He asked the Congress to keep some of the Cabinet posts vacant for the League. One of the posts he wanted to retain for his favourites was the home ministry. This almost led to the resignation of the Congress government, as Sardar Patel had always made his preference for the home ministry known, and asking him to vacate it was akin to asking for his resignation. But hanging on to their favourite ministries cost the Congress, and subsequently the nation, dearly. It was thus that the finance ministry fell into the lap of the Muslim League when finally Wavell managed to convince Jinnah to allow the Muslim League to join the interim government. The Congress had given the treasury of the nation into the hands of a party which wanted to break the nation at any cost. The harassment that the Congress ministers subsequently faced was one of the reasons for their ultimate capitulation on the issue of the partition of India.

After the interim government was sworn in, Wavell's partiality towards the League became very apparent; he kept cajoling Jinnah to agree to join the interim government and kept entertaining their demands. Finally, Gandhi expressed the opinion that the time had come when the viceroy needed to be counselled by a more competent constitutional expert. This mildly worded advice was an undisguised rebuke. After prolonged negotiations and many concessions, the Muslim League finally agreed to join the interim government.

Events, meanwhile, were unfolding rapidly in other parts of the country. The ghost of 'Direct Action Day' and the retaliatory violence in its wake were coming back to haunt the nation. As the Muslim League joined the interim government, the first reports about the horror unleashed in Noakhali, the marshy district of Bengal, started trickling in. The reports were several days late, but when they were published, they horrified the entire country. The Muslim League had systematically carried out a vicious campaign in the interiors where Muslim majorities existed: Hindus were depicted as enemies and the Muslim populace was exhorted to prepare to take Pakistan by force. The Muslim National Guard was reorganized and armed, and preparations for avenging Calcutta were on on a military footing.

Reports of lawlessness and near anarchy in eastern Bengal appeared in the newspapers with alarming regularity. A letter published in *The Statesman* on 12 September, ostensibly written by a Muslim said: 'When I was travelling on 14 August (two days before 'Direct Action Day'), I saw some Muslims freely selling long knives at the railway stations. When after the events in Calcutta I was again travelling by train on 26 August, a Muslim gentleman occupied a first class compartment next to my second class. At every stop he incited the Muslims to butcher the "Mirjafri" (traitors) non-League Muslims and Hindus alike and illustrated this advice by gestures; the fanatic was a high ranking Leaguer.'

Kamini Kumar Dutta, a member of the Legislative Council from Komilla in East Bengal, issued a press statement, published in the *Amrit Bazar Patrika*'s edition of 19 September 1946: 'What has alarmed us and the minority community in East Bengal, is the perilous, narrow margin which now divides order from anarchy in East Bengal. Muslim League propagandists are spreading exaggerated stories of alleged brutal atrocities said to have been committed by the Hindus upon the Muslims in Calcutta and this propaganda ... is making the situation perilous to the maintenance of law and order. To our knowledge, a highly placed Muslim official was heard declaring that thousands of dead bodies will be seen ... strewn over the country in no time. Once there is a large scale outbreak in any part of East Bengal, conflagration will spread throughout.' Another report in *The Statesman* dated 30 September said: 'Life and property are unsafe in Eastern Bengal. Gangsters operate on railway lines, stop trains at places of their choice, rob and carry away the booty by boats or bullock carts before the news reaches the next station.' Huseyn Shaheed Suhrawardy, the premier of Bengal, admitted that his government was aware of the situation in eastern Bengal. 'Yes, I have seen reports of this unfortunate communal tension in East Bengal. We must all deplore it,' he said. But just as it happens in India even today, neither he nor the government did anything to prevent the tragedy.

Pyarelal writes in *Mahatma Gandhi: The Last Phase, Vol. 13, Part I*: 'The Frankenstein of communalism had burst its bonds but its keeper's concern was not that it had escaped but that its first performance was not up to the mark.'

Gandhi's intuition proved accurate, once again. An inferno of hate and violence had been lit. Only time would tell how much of the country and its people it would consume and the price it would extract before it was doused. The scars of the pre- and post-Partition massacres are still festering more than seven decades later.

Noakhali Set Afire

Perhaps the only thing that can be quite positively asserted about this orgy of arson and violence is that it was not a spontaneous uprising of the villagers. However many goondas may live in Bengal, they are incapable of organizing this campaign on their own initiative.

—Muriel Lester's report from
Noakhali in *Hindustan Standard* on 6 November 1946

Noakhali district lay in one of the most remote and inaccessible parts of the Gangetic delta, in the southwestern part of the Chittagong Division in East Bengal, initially East Pakistan, Bangladesh, since 1971. It is crisscrossed by an intricate network of canals called Khal. These waterways were the only means of transport; land transport was mainly over narrow footpaths and Shanko, small rickety bridges built of bamboos over the Khal. The region experiences heavy rainfall during monsoon and in the cyclone season. Floods were an annual occurrence. Messages from remote villages would take long to reach the authorities. The soil was fertile, with an abundance of coconut and beetlenut palms, which formed a canopy through which sunlight struggled to penetrate. Banana, papaya, litchi, pineapple, citrus fruits and mangoes grew in abundance. The waterbodies teemed with fish. But behind the enchanting facade lurked a beast, the beast of communal hate. The hamlets were widely scattered and isolated from one another by thick jungles, fields of tall jute reeds and cut off by crisscrossing water canals.

In East Bengal, the Muslim majority largely comprised poor artisans and impoverished farm labourers, while the Hindu minority consisted of educated middle class, rich traders, zamindars, landlords and moneylenders. Thus, there was an economic division to the already vitiated religious divide that led to what was, till then, one of the most brutal, systematic and planned communal massacres.

It started on 10 October 1946, but for nearly a week, there were no reports of the calamity in Noakhali. The first reports of disturbances in East Bengal were released to the press by the Bengal Press Advisory Committee on 14 October: 'Reports of organized hooliganism in the district of Noakhali have reached Calcutta. Riotous mobs with deadly weapons are raiding villages, and looting, arson and murder are continuing since ... 10 October, on a very large scale. Forcible mass conversion, abduction of women and desecration of places of worship are also reported. Areas affected so far are reported to be over 200 square miles of the Sadar and Feni subdivisions. Approaches to the affected areas are being guarded by armed hooligans.

'Among the large number of people reported to be murdered or burnt alive are the president of the District Bar with family, and a prominent zamindar of the district. Inquiries with official sources in

Calcutta revealed that military and armed police have been rushed to the affected areas, which comprise the entire Ramganj, parts of Begamganj, Lakshmipur, Raipur, Senbagh, Feni, Chagalanaiya and Sandwip thanas, police precincts.'

Another message informed that all movement to and from the affected areas was being restricted 'by hooligans, armed with deadly weapons'. The telegram also referred to 'the planned organization behind this terrible carnage, arson and loot'. After a show of concern over the planned calamity orchestrated by him and his party, Suhrawardy pleaded his inability to visit the affected areas since he had to rush to Darjeeling where the Governor was holding a Cabinet meeting. 'It seems odd,' commented *The Statesman* on 18 October, 'that, despite evidence of administrative breakdown in a part of the Province for weeks, notoriously menaced by just this sort of catastrophe, there should have been no movement yet of the Governor or Chief Minister to the point of catastrophe. The one remains in Darjeeling, the other has gone to join him there.'

Within ten days, the trouble spread to the northern parts of Noakhali and the neighbouring district of Tipperah. A reporter from *The Statesman* mentioned that for thirteen days 'about 120 villages in Ramganj, Lakshmipur, Begamganj and Senbagh thanas in Noakhali district, with a population of 90,000 Hindus and nearly 70 villages in Chandpur and Faridganj thanas in Tipperah district, with a Hindu population of about 40,000 remained besieged by hooligans'. Inspector-general of police, Taylor, stated that the hooligans 'were armed with guns and various types of other weapons and they were still defiant and not afraid to face the police and the military'. As the mob proceeded, 'they cut telegraph wires, demolished bridges, dammed canals and damaged and barricaded roads, making ingress and egress to and from the invaded localities impossible'.

The newly elected president of the Congress, Acharya Kripalani, accompanied by Sarat Chandra Bose and other Congress leaders, flew over the affected areas on 19 October. The plane flew at almost tree-top level to enable the leaders to get a clear view of the situation on the ground. They saw a mob demolishing a bridge, while groups of people could be seen gathered at strategic places. The chief minister, who flew with the group on their return, did not seem to be moved by the plight of citizens of the state he ruled; he was busy taking photographs of the burning villages, proof of his very efficient organization of the League's agenda of hate and violence.

A clear picture of what was happening in the remote districts of east Bengal was emerging from reports of various official, unofficial and press sources. The military intelligence branch in New Delhi received dispatches, according to which an ex-member of the Bengal Legislative Council, Mian Ghulam Sarwar, was the kingpin of the riotous mobs. He had systematically carried out a propaganda of hate, had provided arms and monetary inducements to the rampaging mobs and was still spearheading the campaign against the Hindus in the districts of Noakhali and Tipperah. The authorities claimed that a warrant had been issued for his arrest but he had gone underground, while local eyewitnesses claimed that Sarwar was openly leading the campaign of genocide.

Some villagers did manage to escape the pogroms, either by buying their way through or with the help of their neighbours. These refugees from the affected districts began arriving in Calcutta and other safe places in west Bengal and east Bihar, carrying horrifying stories of the devastation. The country suddenly woke up to the situation in Noakhali. Now the Hindu fanatics got into the fray: cries for vengeance were heard at every Shakha of the RSS and Hindu Mahasabha. The revenge seekers were not going to the rescue of their co-religionists in Noakhali, but were headed for Bihar and Calcutta to wreak vengeance on the unsuspecting Muslim population there. But this was still some time in the future.

What happened in Noakhali can be illustrated by a couple of accounts of survivors. A young girl, the sole survivor of a well-known landowner's family from a village in Noakhali under the Ramgunj police station, narrated the incident where her whole family was slaughtered. On the morning of 11 October, she said, a group of village people came to their house and threatened that if the householders did not contribute ₹500 to the fund of the local Muslim League, they would be murdered, their property looted and their houses burnt. The money was immediately paid. After a short while, a huge menacing crowd surrounded the house. One of the members of the family tried to pacify the mob, but before he could utter a word, the leader who was wielding a Dao, a heavy curved long knife, beheaded him. Then they attacked the oldest man of the family. After butchering him, they seized his second son and placed him on the body of his father. His hysterical mother threw herself on her son and pleaded with the mob to spare him. The men beat the woman till she fainted and then attacked the son. The girl rushed out, clutching ₹400 in cash and gold ornaments, hoping to buy her father's life. The leader snatched the money and ornaments from the girl and chopped off her father's head.

An editorial in *The Statesman* published on 25 October commented: 'Arson, looting, murder, abduction of women, forced conversions and forced marriages are everywhere and by every investigator spoken of as the characteristics of the lawlessness. After the Calcutta catastrophe of August, there had been ample cause for strong precautions, particularly on that very part of the map where renewed catastrophe has now occurred. Arrests of the miscreants seem to have been few. Energy has been miserably wanting somewhere.' Referring to the plea that a complete breakdown in communication was a major factor leading to a delay in restoring law and order, the report further added: 'It is not an adequate explanation for the public mind. It is bad country, but the hooligans manage to move about and the police have the general public to help them with information, they are not operating in Japanese-occupied country during wartime.'

Muriel Lester, the English pacifist, was in India at that time. On hearing about the catastrophe, she rushed to establish a relief centre in Noakhali. She sent back a report in the first week of November which was published in the *Hindustan Standard* on 6 November, which said: 'The worst of all was the plight of the women. Several of them had to watch their husbands being murdered and then be forcibly converted and married to some of those responsible for the killings of their husbands and family. These women had a dead look. It was not despair, nothing so active as that. It was utter blankness… The eating of beef and declaration of allegiance to Islam has been forced upon many thousands as a price for their lives… Perhaps the only thing that can be quite positively asserted about this orgy of arson and violence is that it was not a spontaneous uprising of the villagers. However many goondas may live in Bengal, they are incapable of organizing this campaign on their own initiative. Houses have been sprayed with petrol and burnt. Who supplied this rationed fuel? Who imported stirrup pumps into this rural area? Who supplied the weapons? ... The goondas seem to think that they really are the rulers of this beautiful area of Bengal. One sees no sign of fear among those who had stood by and watched destruction, tyranny and aggression; anxiety as to the future punishment does not seem to exist.' Shah Sayed Ghulam Sarwar Hussaini, Pir Saheb of Daria Sharif, Village Shampur, Noakhali, as he was known among his followers, became the de facto dictator of Noakhali. He initiated some of the most barbaric attacks and massacres in the region. A thorn in his flesh was Rai Saheb Rajendralal Chowdhury of Chowdhurybadi, Karpara, president of the Noakhali Bar Association, who had organized local defences against the growing lawlessness and thus earned the wrath of Sarwar. A few days prior to the outbreak of violence, a hermit from Bharat Sevashram, Trayambakananda, had come to Chowdhurybadi and stayed with Rai. The sadhu wanted to revive the practice of Sitala Pooja in Hindu Badis, households. The puja was performed by anointing the idol of the goddess with the blood of a freshly sacrificed goat. However, a rumour was spread throughout the surrounding villages that the blood of a Muslim would be offered at the next puja. On hearing this, Sarwar was a like a man possessed.

On the morning of the 10th, Sarwar summoned Rai Bahadur, but suspecting foul play, the latter refused to go. At 8:00 a.m. that morning, Sarwar addressed a mob of several thousand gathered in Shampur Bazaar, and declared that he wanted the heads of Rai Saheb Rajendralal of Karpara and Sadhu Trayambakananda. He instigated the mob and let them loose in the bazaar. All the Hindu shops in the bazaar were looted and burnt and a temple was completely ravaged. The mob now divided itself into three gangs and went off in different directions. One group attacked Ramganj Bazaar, the other went towards Dasgharia Bazaar and destroyed the Thakur Mandir there. The third group attacked the Kaccheri, office of Suren Bose, zamindar of Narayanpur. Suren Bose had been warned by a local police officer of the danger and advised to flee to safety that very morning, but he refused, saying, 'I do not want to leave my brethren behind... I must ... face death with them.' When the mob reached his house he opened fire on the mob, but he was soon captured and hacked to death, along with five other members of his family. The house was then torched and their bodies were thrown into the inferno.

The next morning, on the 11th, at about 8:00 a.m., Chowdhurybadi was attacked by a gang of forty to fifty rioters shouting '*Allah-o-Akbar!*', and in Bengali '*Hindur Rakta Chai!*' (We seek the blood of Hindus). Chowdhury was well prepared for an attack. He, along with his son and some young men of the Badi, confronted the mob some distance away from the main house. In the fight that ensued, three or four attackers were killed and the rest fled. But within a few hours, they returned, accompanied by a ten-thousand-strong mob armed and baying for the blood of the Chowdhurys. Rajendralal's family members and other residents took refuge on the roof and barricaded themselves. One of his bodyguards, Kali Prasanna Raut, had positioned himself on the roof. He opened fire on the approaching mob from there, killing nearly thirty to forty attackers. When he ran out of ammunition, the attackers returned and set the house on fire. The men were stripped, stabbed and tied to trees. Then, in full view of their families, they were hacked to death. Rajendralal was led to the backyard where he was forced to lean over a butchering block. His head was severed and triumphantly presented to Ghulam Sarwar. The women were led to different locations and molested and raped. Some of them were brought back and given shelter in a neighbouring Badi. Rajendralal's wife and a group of other women took refuge in the house of one his Muslim servants, from where they were rescued on 18 October by Abdul Gofran, the minister of civil supplies.

Two daughters of the Chowdhury family were abducted by a gang of ruffians. They were taken to the Shahpur high school and repeatedly gangraped. One of them was then taken to the still-burning Shahpur Bazaar and murdered, and her body was thrown into the raging inferno. The other one escaped, lost her way, and after pleading with strangers for help, was directed by a kind Muslim shopkeeper to Rajbadi in Shahpur, where she took refuge with a Hindu family. Her abductors surrounded the home and threatened them with death if they did not hand over the girl. The terrified hosts pushed the girl out into the hands of her abductors. Finally, one of them, a Muslim teacher, showed mercy and took her away. He betrayed her later, however, and kept her confined. She was taken out in a boat into a flooded rice field and murdered near Khalispara, a village about half a mile from Shahpur Rajbadi. Her corpse was thrown into the water to rot.

The attack on Chowdhurybadi resulted in the deaths of twenty-four people, sixty-nine were wounded and ninety-three were reported missing, feared dead. A five-year-old girl of the Chowdhury family, who had miraculously escaped, was presented before Gandhi when he took up residence in Dattapara refugee camp.

The mysterious sadhu Trayambakananda, according to his own version, escaped from Chowdhurybadi after the first attack and hid in the surrounding forests. Making his way through the Khals and jungles, he reached Ramganj, from there with a police escort he reached Noakhali and then on to Calcutta. There he became an instant hero, reveling in the attention showered on him while narrating exaggerated colourful tales of his escape.

The charred barrel of Kali Prasanna Raut's muzzle-loader was picked up from the debris of Chowdhurybadi by one of the looters and was used to create mischief two years later in 1948, after Gandhi's murder. One of Ghulam Sarwar's men planted the barrel in the camp run by the Gandhi Peace Mission, which was under the charge of Pyarelal Nayyar. The idea was to spread the news that a weapon used to massacre Muslims was found in the camp, thus pressurizing the authorities to close down the camp and drive out the Gandhians. The allegations against the Gandhi Peace Mission were investigated by a minister of the East Pakistan government. An honest local Muslim revealed the insidious plot.

A day after leading the massacre at Shahpur Bazaar and Chowdhurybadi, Sarwar sent a report to the authorities that 'goondas from outside' were responsible for the carnage and that the lives of people were in danger. He provided relief from the loot accumulated by his gangs to his victims, who, having been forcibly converted to Islam, were now considered a part of his flock. Sarwar was finally arrested by the military on 22 October.

A notable case of forced conversion was that of Harendra Ghosh, secretary of the Congress committee of Raipur. After escaping the attack on his village, Harendra took refuge with two Muslim workers who agreed to spare him if he converted to Islam. When Harendra finally consented, a pamphlet was produced and he was made to sign it. On 15 October, Harendra was taken to a mosque at Raipur and confined there. Here, he was made to sign another pamphlet, which was printed in the local press and circulated amongst Hindus to convince them to convert. He was confined in the mosque for twelve days. In his written statement to Gandhi later, Harendra recounted his days of horror: 'My daily diet was beef and rice, which I was forced to eat. I was taught Namaz and had to give lectures on Fridays in front of thousands of Muslims on Islamic creed and culture. Among the leaders who took part in this barbarity and met daily in the mosque morning and evening to issue directions to the gangs of murderers and arsonists, were a local member of the Legislative Assembly, secretary of the Thana Muslim League, two secretaries of the Union Peace Committee, two presidents of Union Boards and a zamindar.'

The local Harijans too were not spared, even though Jinnah tried to win them over by successfully getting the Congress classified as a 'caste Hindu' organization and then nominating a Harijan from Bengal as a member of the interim government from the Muslim League's quota. In Noakhali, if the Harijans did not convert to Islam, they were murdered.

However, there were instances of the two communities helping each other too. At Bhatialpur, a Muslim stood between a Hindu doctor and a mob out to lynch him. He finally managed to save Dr Chandrashekhar Bhowmik, who later joined the Gandhi Peace Mission and served as a translator for Pyarelal Nayyar. The same Muslim later saved Pyarelal Nayyar, who was once waylaid by a gang while he was rushing to diffuse a volatile situation in a village under the jurisdiction of his peace camp.

In Delhi, Gandhi was troubled by the events in Bengal and the repercussions it would have all over the country. He knew that India would only survive if Hindus and Muslims lived amicably. Day after day, he pleaded for sanity to prevail, first from Sevagram and then from his camp in New Delhi. On 24 October, just as the evening prayers were about to commence in the courtyard between Valmiki temple and the rooms occupied by Gandhi, a band of RSS workers disrupted the meeting and refused to allow verses from the Koran to be recited. They pushed through the audience and advanced threateningly towards the spot where Gandhi was sitting, holding anti-Muslim placards and shouting anti-Gandhi slogans. After returning to Poona, Narayan Apte and Nathuram Godse boasted about participating in the protest and terrorizing Gandhi. The plot to murder Gandhi was under way.

In consultation with Nehru and Patel, Gandhi decided to leave for Calcutta and then to Noakhali on 28 October. At the prayer meeting on that day, Gandhi said that he was going to Bengal to try and bridge the gap between the two communities. He wanted to console the women and children. He also wanted to meet the governor and the chief minister, and then proceed to the riot torn district of Noakhali. The next morning, he left with a small band of handpicked followers on his pilgrimage of peace.

Peace Pilgrim

Gandhi was travelling on this route after a gap of thirteen years; thousands of people thronged the stations and stood dangerously close to the tracks passing through their villages to catch a glimpse of their Bapu. The railway authorities tried every means at their disposal to disperse the crowds, even using improvised water cannons to drive them away, but to no avail.

While Gandhi was travelling towards Calcutta, violence erupted in Bihar. Hundreds of refugees from East Bengal had reached the northeastern parts of Bihar. Almost all Biharis in that area had family in Calcutta and East Bengal who had suffered during the pogroms, many had been killed, and this exodus and stories about the plight of Hindus in Noakhali inflamed the passions of the Biharis. Hindu fanatics from all over India added fuel to fire. The Muslims of Bihar bore the brunt of the fury. Bihar was a predominantly impoverished agrarian state; villages and settlements were traditionally divided on lines of religion and caste. Hindu hordes identified isolated Muslim settlements and villages and ruthlessly butchered the residents, not sparing even a single inhabitant. Violence rapidly spread to the larger towns, and finally to the capital Patna, within a week.

On reaching Calcutta, Gandhi and his group were taken directly to Satish Chandra Dasgupta's Khadi Pratishthan Ashram at Sodepore. A gathering of several hundred people had been patiently waiting for Gandhi. Addressing them, he said that he had come with a blank mind to do God's will.

Suhrawardy suffered from delusions of grandeur. He had styled his office on the lines of the private courts of Mughal emperors, and received guests into his court, stretched out on a mattress like an emperor. He made no exception for his meeting with Gandhi. 'How is it Shaheed Saheb, everybody calls you the chief of the criminals? Nobody seems to have a good word to say about you!' Gandhi asked. Suhrawardy replied insolently, 'Mahatmaji, don't people say things about you, too, behind your back?'

'That may be,' replied Gandhi with a smile. 'Still there are some who call me Mahatma. But I have not heard a single person calling you, Shaheed Suhrawardy, a Mahatma!' Suhrawardy shamelessly replied, 'Mahatmaji, don't believe what people say about you in your presence!'

After this opening exchange, the two sat down to hammer out a peace plan for Bengal. The document that emerged envisaged a peace maintained by mutual cooperation and trust without the fear of external force or under duress from the British. Both Muslims and Hindus would be equally responsible. The Government of Bengal would guarantee the peace, a peace not imposed by military and police but by bringing about a mutual change of heart in both the communities: 'It is our certain conviction that Pakistan cannot be brought about by communal strife nor can India be kept whole through the same means. It is also our conviction that there can be no conversion or marriage by force; nor has abduction any place in a society which has any claim to be called decent or civilized.' A committee comprising an equal number of Hindus and Muslims would be formed under the chairmanship of the chief minister, who gave a guarantee that his government would implement the recommendations of the Peace Committee.

Meanwhile, Nehru, Patel, Liaquat Ali Khan and the infamous Sardar Abdur Rab Nishtar rushed to Patna to take stock of the situation there and nip the trouble in the bud. They assured Gandhi that they would bring Bihar back to normal soon, but their assurances proved to be futile; the poison of hate had spread too deep. It could only be countered by Gandhi. Before leaving for Noakhali, Gandhi informed his associates and the people of India that he would henceforth consume only the barest minimum food necessary to survive, and if the situation did not improve in Noakhali and Bihar, he would give up food totally until peace was established. To Nehru he wrote: 'The news from Bihar has shaken me. My own duty seems to be clear... Although I have striven hard to avert a fast, I can do so no longer... My inner voice tells me, "You may not live to be a witness to this senseless slaughter. If people refuse to see what is clear as daylight and pay no heed to what you say, does it not mean that your day is over?" The logic of the argument is driving me irresistibly towards a fast. I, therefore, propose to issue a statement that unless this orgy of madness ceases, I must go on a fast unto death... You can strive with me, if you think differently. Whatever you say will carry weight with me. But knowing as you do my temperament, I am sure you will approve of my proposed step. In any event, you will go on with your work without a moment's thought about my possible death and leave me to God's good care. No worry allowed.'

Before departing for Noakhali, Gandhi issued an appeal addressed to the people of Bihar, titled 'To Bihar': 'Bihar of my dreams seems to have falsified them... It is easy enough to retort that things under the Muslim League government in Bengal were no better, if not worse, and that Bihar is merely a result of the latter. A bad act of one party is no justification for a similar act by the opposing party... Is counter communalism any answer to the communalism of which Congressmen have accused the Muslim League? Is it nationalism to seek barbarously to crush the fourteen per cent of Muslims in Bihar?

'I do not need to be told that I must not condemn the whole of Bihar for the sake of the sins of a few thousand Biharis ... I am afraid, if the misconduct in Bihar continues, all the Hindus in India will be condemned by the world. I am in no way ashamed of my Ahimsa ... But I do not want in this letter to talk of Ahimsa to you. I do want, however, to tell you that what you are reported to have done ... is worse than cowardice. It is unworthy of nationalism, or any religion.... What you have done is to degrade yourselves and drag down India.' Gandhi could very well have been referring to present-day India.

On 6 November, Gandhi and his band of peacemakers, accompanied by representatives of the Bengal government, left by a special train for Noakhali. Accompanying him were the Bengal government's minister of labour, Shamshuddin Ahmed, and two parliamentary secretaries, Nasrullah Khan and Abdur Rashid; they were entrusted with ensuring the cooperation of the local officers during Gandhi's peace mission to Noakhali. Initially, the daughters of both Suhrawardy and Nasrullah Khan were to accompany Gandhi, but the plan was abandoned after Suhrawardy was 'advised' that two unveiled Muslim girls travelling through Noakhali would 'offend' the sensibilities of the fanatical mullahs of Noakhali.

Large crowds greeted Gandhi at Khustia and Goalando, where he told the crowds that he hoped to reawaken the Hindu–Muslim unity that was achieved during the Khilafat Movement of the early 1920s through his present tour. Goalando was the last stop on the railhead, the onward journey of over a hundred miles would be by boat down the Padma river. They reached Chandpur late at night, where a telegram from Patel was delivered to Gandhi. He wanted to reply to it immediately but none of the phone or telegraph lines were working. The night was spent on the boat anchored midstream. The next morning the entourage alighted to continue the journey by train to Chaumuhani in Noakhali. As they disembarked, two delegations waited on Gandhi: one Muslim, the other Hindu. The Muslim delegation comprised prominent Muslim Leaguers who were very resentful about the peace delegation. Their contention was that the news about the happenings in Noakhali were hugely exaggerated, that it was a motivated campaign to tarnish and discredit the Muslim League. They claimed that in the districts of Noakhali and Tipperah, only fifteen Hindus had been killed, whereas in the indiscriminate firing by the largely Hindu army, more than thirty innocent Muslims had been killed. Even today such excuses are made, as recently as the 2002 riots in Gujarat and Muzaffarnagar in 2013.

The district magistrate of Noakhali, McInerny, had issued an official notice, which was shown to Gandhi. The notice said 'that, unless proved to the contrary, it would be assumed that everyone who accepted Islam after the disturbances was forcibly converted and in reality remained a Hindu'. Reading the notice, Gandhi said that if all the Muslims endorsed the notice it would go a long way to settle the question. 'Why should there be a public show of it, if anybody genuinely felt inclined to recite the Kalima?' The members of the Muslim delegation had come with prejudiced minds. Thinking that Gandhi would severely reprimand and accuse them, they had come prepared with strategies of counter-attacking every accusation and condemnation. But although Gandhi was severe in his criticism, he refrained from condemning the entire community.

The second delegation meeting Gandhi was a group of about twenty Hindus, comprising eminent Congress workers of the area and former revolutionaries who had taken part in the famous Chittagong armoury raid. They demanded that the Muslim police officers, constabulary and Muslim members of the military be removed and replaced by Hindus. To this Gandhi said: 'I come from Kathiawad—the land of petty principalities. No woman's honour is safe in some of these principalities and the chief is no hooligan but a duly anointed one.'

And so they argued. The Hindus wanted all sorts of protection. They maintained that since they were in a minority in Bengal, they were not in a position to defend themselves. Gandhi replied that even if there was only one surviving Hindu in Bengal, he wanted him to possess the confidence and courage to live in the midst of Muslims and die fighting, if he must, like a hero.

'The proportion of Muslims and Hindus here is six to one. How can you expect us to face such heavy odds?'

'When India was brought under British subjugation, there were only 70,000 European soldiers against 330 million Indians.'

'We have no arms. The hooligans have the backing of government bayonets.'

Describing the Satyagraha in South Africa, Gandhi gave the example of a minute Indian community rising to demand equal rights from an overwhelming armed European community with all the might of the government behind them. 'The Europeans had arms. We had none. So we forged the weapon of Satyagraha. Today an Indian is respected by the white man in South Africa, not so the Zulu with all his fine physique.'

'Would you permit Hindus to take the offensive?'

'The people of Bihar did that and brought disgrace upon themselves and India. I have heard it said that the retaliation in Bihar has "cooled" the Muslims down. They mean it has set the clock of Indian independence backwards. The independence of India is today at stake in Bengal and Bihar. The British government entrusted the Congress with power at the Centre not because they were in love with the Congress but because they had faith that the Congress would use it wisely and well. Today Pandit Nehru finds the ground slipping from under his feet. But he will not let that happen. That is why he is in Bihar. Use your arms well, if you must, but do not ill use them. Bihar has not used its arms well... The best succour that Bihar could have given to the Hindus of East Bengal would have been to guarantee with their own lives the absolute safety of the Muslim population living in their midst.'

At the next railway station, Laksham, a large crowd of refugees had gathered to plead their case with Gandhi. He assured them that he would not leave Bengal till peace was restored and added, 'Why should you be afraid of the cry of "*Allah-o-Akbar!*"? The Allah of Islam is the same as the Rama of Hindus. To run away from danger instead of facing it is to deny one's faith in man and God and even oneself. It is better far to drown oneself than live to declare such bankruptcy of faith.'

Gandhi and his entourage reached Chaumuhani on the afternoon of 7 November. Sucheta Kripalani, who had come to the area as a relief provider along with the advance party, had extensively travelled in the region, and she reported her findings to Gandhi. She was shocked by what she had witnessed in the interiors. She told him that the peacemakers' task was not going to be easy. There was rot all around; water sources had been polluted due to the rotting cadavers, there was an acute shortage of foodgrains. Due to the rift in the two communities, it was difficult to find casual labourers to do menial tasks. Kripalani reported that a new way of creating mischief was being practised to discredit the volunteers; rumours had been spread that Gandhi was bringing an army of Hindu criminals to let lose on Muslims and that the military and police personnel accompanying Gandhi were going to harass and persecute 'innocent Muslims'. But the rumours did not work. More than 15,000 people came to hear Gandhi speak, and the crowd largely comprised Muslims.

That night, the League's minister Shamshuddin Mohammad, accompanied by his colleagues and representatives of local Muslims, came to meet Gandhi to discuss ways of bringing about peace in the area.

On the morning of 9 November, Gandhi started his journey into the interior villages of the district of Noakhali. He was accompanied by the two parliamentary secretaries, the district magistrate and the superintendent of police. A majority of the farmers had been killed in these districts, while others had fled to refugee camps. A Fatwa had been issued, ordering Muslims not to work for Hindus. A social, cultural and economic boycott of Hindus was strictly enforced in the two districts.

Even though there was a bountiful harvest, the districts were faced with a manmade scarcity of food.

Gopairbag was the first village Gandhi and his entourage visited. Here, amidst thick groves of arecanut and betelnut palms, were five clusters of homes of Hindu families surrounded by nearly fifty times as many Muslim families. One of the Hindu homes belonged to a rich Patwari, a government official from feudal times who maintained land records. The Patwari had an estate valued at several hundred thousand rupees. This estate had witnessed the most barbarous massacre, rape, pillage and arson. The Patwari's family had been singled out for 'special treatment'; twenty-one male members out of twenty-three had been rounded up and murdered during the attack. The two survivors who escaped were eyewitnesses to the entire episode. The perpetrator and leader of the massacre was a neighbour, Qasim Ali, an ex-RIAF man, who had been absconding since the attack, and no one dared to testify against him.

The next day Gandhi shifted his camp from Chaumuhani to Dattapara to visit more affected villages in the interiors. That evening, he addressed the prayer gathering, where over 80 per cent of the people present were Muslims. He said, 'I want to assure you that I am a servant of both the Hindus and the Muslims. I have not come here to fight Pakistan. If India is destined to be partitioned, I cannot prevent it. But I wish to tell you that Pakistan cannot be established by force... I ask my Muslim brethren to search their hearts and if they do not wish to live as friends with the Hindus, to say so openly. The Hindus must in that case leave East Bengal and go somewhere else. The refugees cannot stay on as refugees forever. But even if every Hindu of East Bengal goes away, I shall still continue to live amidst the Muslims of East Bengal. If, on the other hand, you want the Hindus to stay in your midst, you should tell them that they need not look to the military for protection but to their Muslim brethren instead.'

The effects of the partial fast were telling on the seventy-seven-year-old Gandhi. His food intake was less than 600 calories per day. Finally, to conserve his strength, after much deliberation, he allowed himself to be carried to and from the prayer grounds on a chair slung on bamboo poles and carried by two members of his party. His voice had become feeble and his face was deeply lined with anguish. But when he spoke, there was neither any trace of anger nor did he become impatient. His speeches were brutally honest, hiding nothing, holding back nothing, suppressing nothing. On 11 November, Gandhi visited Noakhola, Sonachak and Khilpara, all of them under Ramgunj police station. They travelled by car and then by small dugout boats that were poled through the waterways. Noakhola had witnessed the murder of eight members of a Hindu household, including a fifteen-year-old boy. At Sonachak, Gandhi saw that a settlement of more than a hundred households had been systematically looted, burnt and partially razed. The next day, while he was addressing a prayer meeting attended mostly by refugees, a Maulvi declared that the Muslims were feeling 'unhappy and even frightened' by the prospect of their Hindu brethren leaving East Bengal. He assured the gathering that the Muslims 'in their thousands' would welcome them back in their midst. Gandhi reminded him that he wanted only sincerity and not empty talk. 'The return of the refugees was not an easy task,' he said, and added that no scheme of repatriation would work unless the Muslim League sincerely cooperated.

After visiting Gomatoli and Nandigram, the first phase of the pilgrimage through Noakhali district was completed. The next phase was to be a new experiment in the armoury of Ahimsa and its most dexterous exponent, Gandhi. The same devastation greeted Gandhi at Nandigram, a village of nearly 600 homes, where a school, hostel and hospital had been reduced to ashes. On 14 November, Gandhi shifted his camp from Dattapara to Kazirkhil, moving into the heart of the devastated areas. On the way, he stopped at Shampur, the epicentre of the violence. Shampur was the stronghold of the self-styled supreme commander, Mian Ghulam Sarwar. Before Gandhi's arrival, Sarwar had spread a rumour that Gandhi was accompanied by a large posse of police and his entourage comprised plainclothes police who would utilize the planned public meeting to identify and arrest Muslims. This led to a partial boycott of the meeting by the local Muslims.

At Kazirkhil, Gandhi's camp was in a partially destroyed home of a prosperous local Hindu. An advance party of volunteers had cleaned the place and made it habitable. Speaking after the evening prayers, Gandhi observed that he found peace in his surroundings, but not on the faces of the people. He had carried on a grim struggle against the government for twenty years in South Africa and for the past thirty years in India, but he had resolved not to leave Bengal empty-handed. Four miles to the southeast of Kazirkhil was the village of Dasgharia. Bibi Amtus Salam, a devout Muslim woman, follower of Gandhi and an inmate of his Ashram, had established a relief camp here. Practically all the abducted women who had been forcibly converted to Islam had been rescued by Bibi.

One positive transformation that Gandhi's peace mission brought about in Noakhali was that, before long, all those who had been forcibly converted were able to revert to his or her original religion. Gandhi then decided that he would disperse his band of peacemakers. Each one would be sent to one village where they would establish camps for rehabilitation and peacemaking. He told them that this was the supreme test of his faith in Ahimsa. 'Either Ahimsa is the law of life or it is not,' adding that if 'Ahimsa disappears, Hinduism disappears.' One wishes today that the self-proclaimed militant protectors of Hinduism would understand this. One of the members of his party remarked, 'The issue is not religious but political. It is not a movement against the Hindus but against the Congress.'

Gandhi replied, 'Don't you see that they think that the Congress is purely a Hindu body? And do not forget that I have no watertight divisions such as religious, political and others. Is the tangle to be solved violently, or non-violently—that is the question.' In a letter to a friend he wrote: 'The work I am engaged in here may be my last act. If I return from here alive and unscathed, it will be like a new birth to me. My Ahimsa is being tried here through and through as it was never before.' Gandhi declared that for the duration of his stay in East Bengal, he would live in the home of a Muslim, preferably a Muslim Leaguer approved by the Bengal ministry. During his talks with Abdul Gofran, he made the request and the minister was taken aback. How would he live in the house of a complete stranger? Who would look after him? 'I will look after myself; I shall need nobody's attention,' Gandhi replied. 'Then, I am afraid,' Gofran replied. 'No Muslim family will be prepared to receive you!' But Gandhi's mind was made up. He knew that if the Hindus saw him living alone with a Muslim League friend, it may bring about a change of heart. The Muslims, too, would be able to examine him from close quarters.

'When I was in detention in the Aga Khan Palace,' Gandhi remarked, 'I once sat down to write a thesis on India as a protagonist of non-violence. There are, as we know, two aspects of Hinduism. On the one hand is the historical Hinduism with its untouchability, superstitious worship, animal sacrifice and so on. On the other hand, we have the Hinduism of the Gita, the Upanishads and Patanjali's Yoga Sutra, which is the acme of Ahimsa, oneness of all creation, pure worship of one immanent, formless, imperishable God. Ahimsa, I believe, is the way of life and India has to show it to the world.'

On 20 November, Gandhi took leave of his entourage. Accompanied by his stenographer Prof. Nirmal Kumar Bose, who doubled as his interpreter, they embarked in a canoe made of split bamboos. In a statement, Gandhi said: 'I find myself in the midst of exaggeration and falsity. I am unable to discover the truth. There is a terrible mutual distrust. Truth and Ahimsa by which I swear, and which have, to my knowledge, sustained me for 60 years, seem to fail to show the attributes I have ascribed to them. To test them, or better to test myself, I am going to a village called Srirampur, cutting myself away from those who have been with me all these years, and who have made life easy for me... The other workers, whom I have brought with me, will each distribute themselves in other villages of Noakhali to do the work of peace, if it is at all possible, between the two communities... Many friends from outside Bengal have written to me to allow them to come for peace work but I have strongly dissuaded them from coming. I would love to let them come if and when I see light through this impenetrable darkness. In the meantime... I have decided to suspend all other activities in the shape of correspondence, including the heavy work of *Harijan* and the allied weeklies...'

After travelling for two-and-a-half hours down the Khal, the canoe docked at Srirampur, a tiny village falling under the Ramgunj police station. Gandhi alighted from the craft and carried his personal effects to the small tin hut that had been arranged for his stay. The hut was an abandoned dwelling of a Hindu family which had fled due to the riots. Before the violence, Srirampur had been home to 382 Muslim and 200 Hindu families. Now, only three Hindu families remained; the rest had fled in terror. Gandhi spread his mattress on a wooden plank, which was to be his bed at night and office during the day for the next six weeks. He arranged his books and writing material and other personal paraphernalia neatly in the room. The hut was in the midst of a clearing, surrounded by pools and lush green paddy fields.

For the past few years after Ba's death, Abha, Gandhi's grand-niece-in-law, had been taking care of him; he had come to depend on her ministrations. She had accompanied him to Noakhali too, but he had sent her away to work in a rehabilitation camp established by Thakker Bappa in the Char Mandal area of Noakhali district. 'I must own that I was getting accustomed to her service almost as a matter of habit,' he wrote. 'But the habit of taking service from a particular individual is inconsistent with austerity.' His daily diet here consisted of a pound of goat's milk diluted with an equal volume of vegetable soup for lunch, for dinner he had the same combination with the addition of a grapefruit.

We get an idea of his daily activities in Srirampur from his diaries which I have excerpted here from Pyarelal's book *Mahatma Gandhi: The Last Phase*.

'*Srirampur, 21 November 1946:* Conducted the Morning Prayer myself with the exception of the Gita chapters. After prayer wrote letters to X. Y. and Z. A Maulvi attached to the Howrah Mosque of Noakhali had a talk with me during the morning walk. A. and B. (two Hindu workers) came afterwards and had a long talk. Told them that people had to take their courage in both hands and return to their villages, especially where there is a good Hindu with a good Muslim to give guarantee of safety and protection...

'Massaged the body with my own hands but had to forgo a shave (for lack of time). Had curdled milk with vegetable soup for mid-day meal. Some Muslims ... saw me before the evening prayer; some more followed after the prayer. Made enquiries about local Muslims... Had a two hour talk with M. and his friends. Diet the same as yesterday but without the grapefruit.

'*Srirampur, 22 November 1946:* Rose at 4:00 a.m. The Gita recitation took two hours. Pronunciation of the reciter was very unsatisfactory.

'Wrote to R. that his son (who recently lost his wife) should not remarry, or marry a widow if he must.

'Visited a Muslim badi at 7:30 a.m. The way was long. It took a full

20 minutes to get there—55 minutes coming and going.

'Gave myself massage like yesterday... At 10:30 a.m. a number of visitors came. After they had gone, had a short nap with mud-pack on the abdomen. Spun for one hour. Abdullah (the superintendent of police) with some others came for the meeting at Ramgunj in the evening. Started at 4:00 p.m. with them for Ramgunj. Reached Ramgunj at 5:20 p.m. The meeting continued till 10:30 p.m. Addressed a few words at the end... Had evening prayer on the boat on the return journey and then some sleep. Had milk while proceeding to Ramgunj; hot water on return. Reached Srirampur at midnight.

'*Srirampur, 23 November 1946:* Recited the Gita chapters (during the morning prayer) also myself. In future P. is to recite the Gita only when he has sufficiently mastered the pronunciations. Had an English hymn sung at the prayer.

'Completed the statement on the death of Malaviyaji. Visited a Muslim house at 7:30 a.m. talked about the Koran to the inmates. Later they sent a present of coconuts and oranges.

'Massage was given by N. so that I was able to have a forty minute nap on the massage table. Leafy vegetable served at mid-day was very bitter. Took it with 1 oz. of coconut milk ... next unsuccessfully tried to have a doze of sleep, nausea and griping. Dozed off with mud pack on the abdomen while proceeding to Ramgunj... Had to stop the boat on account of violent diarrhoea and vomiting ... felt relieved... Reached Ramgunj at 5:00 p.m. Had another motion during the recess but was able to address the meeting at the end without difficulty. Started on the return journey at 8:15 p.m. ... Reached Srirampur at 11:00 p.m. ... Completed the daily quota of spinning, partly on the boat while proceeding for the meeting and partly at the meeting itself.'

After a day's gruelling work on 1 December, Gandhi wrote: 'The back aches. Revised an article for *Harijan* lying in bed. Dozed off in the middle.'

Gandhi was ambidextrous; the entry of 2 December reads: 'Must stop. Even the left hand now aches and has struck work. To bed 9:30 p.m.'

On 8 December, his diary records the following with reference to a slip in the observance of his weekly silence: 'I see my discipline of silence is only skin deep. Silence is a great art, not easy to master.'

On 20 December, Gandhi completed one month at Srirampur. 'He is (now) a friend of both the communities here', ran a press despatch. 'Muslims and Hindus of the village do not hesitate to come to him to seek his help. He is their friend, philosopher and guide… In his lonely life he tries to do everything himself … cooking his own food … arranging his own things, massaging his own body and acting as his own doctor.' 'Mahatma Gandhi is spending most of his time in attending the poor and the sick', ran another despatch. 'Yesterday morning he visited a Muslim's house where he saw patients treated by Dr Sushila Nayyar. In the afternoon he visited another Muslim's house to give medical aid. In the evening he paid a visit to the Press camp and attended to a bedridden journalist.' 'He walks fast', said one report. 'Last Saturday he walked with excellent speed through the narrow village road, crossing two precarious bridges and covering about 2 miles in 40 minutes. He has also increased his evening and morning walks…' Another report said: 'Gandhiji does not like to be surrounded by workers or other people. None is allowed to stay in his camp for the night except in cases of emergency. One man travelled all the way from Nagpur but he was immediately sent back after his special job here was finished. One woman who had been on fast came here yesterday and broke her fast before Gandhiji… She also was sent back straight away.'

On a visit to a local Maulvi's house, Gandhi learnt that of a total population of 1,400, there was only one matriculate, and only forty could read and write. One thousand of them could recite the Koran, but none of them understood what they were reciting. Gandhi noted in his diary: 'It is awful to keep them (Muslims) in darkness as to the meaning of their scripture.' This practice still persists. Thereafter, whenever he spoke to Muslims, he discussed the Koran with them and explained the meanings of the Ayats, verses, to the best of his ability. This angered many mullahs as they felt he was encroaching on their territory.

Gandhi decided to learn Bengali so that he wouldn't have to depend on an interpreter. Like everything else, he took to learning the language diligently. A note in the diary of one of his contemporaries shows Gandhi's earnestness: 'To practice Bengali character writing, he drew squares in his exercise book like a lower form schoolboy. When I twitted him for it, he replied, "That is how my teacher used to teach us to draw characters of the alphabet. It is an excellent method. People think that one ceases to be a student when his schooldays are over. With me it is the other way about. I hold that so long as I live, I must have a student's inquiring mind and a thirst for learning." After having his fruit juice he began to pore over his Bengal primer. While doing so, he dozed off for about ten minutes, waking up at 7:15 a.m. At 7:25 a.m. we started on our day's march, reaching ... at 8.25 a.m. after full one hour's walk. Immediately on his arrival there, he again sat down to do his Bengali lesson.' This diligence continued till the last day of his life. He completed the last exercise a few hours before his murder on 30 January 1948.

A conference comprising thirty Hindus, Muslims and government representatives was held at the Ramgunj Dak Bungalow on 22 November. A plan for the establishment of peace according to the suggestions submitted by the Bengal government was hammered out and a nucleus for a peace committee for Ramgunj Police Station was formed. The peace committee, according to the unanimously adopted formula, would comprise an equal number of Hindus and Muslims. Peace committees, village unions and a police station were also formed for the villages. In the case of any disagreements, it was decided that the district magistrate would be the final arbiter with full powers. The peace committee was to work extensively to restore confidence amongst the victims. They were to restore the dwellings of returning refugees; provide food, provisions and clothing to the refugees; draw up lists of criminals and get them arrested and prosecuted.

The first meeting of the peace committee was held at the Ramgunj Police Station on the evening of the 25th. Shamsuddin Ahmed, a minister of the Bengal government, announced that seven Union peace committees had been recently formed and were functional in restoring peace in East Bengal. He assured that the Bengal government was sincere in its desire to win the confidence of its minority citizens. Speaking last, Gandhi remarked that the success of the scheme would depend on the people in the committee. He was troubled by some Muslims scrambling for a place on the peace committees. It filled him with a sense of fear, as he felt that in some parts of the state, trouble was still brewing. He had recently received a telegram from Sandwip Island reporting grave trouble there. Hindu women, fearing molestation, had stopped wearing vermilion on their foreheads.

Early on the morning of 24 November, Sarat Chandra Bose, accompanied by a few friends and colleagues, met Gandhi at Srirampur. He voiced his doubts about the sincerity of the ministers and the chief minister of Bengal towards restoring peace. Gandhi agreed with Bose that the ministers had indeed sunk to the lowest possible levels and yet one had to work with them.

On being challenged that his opposition to conversion was identifying him with the Hindu right wing and the Hindu community exclusively, he replied that he personally had no issue with the religion a person chose. However, such conversions could not in their very nature be on a mass scale and never for saving one's life or property, or for temporal gains. What had happened in Noakhali was a travesty and negation of all religion.

There was an opinion that pockets should be carved out of Bengal where exclusive colonies of the minorities could be established. Gandhi opposed this demand and said it would pose a threat to a united India in future. A delegation of Hindu Mahasabha members, headed by their leader N.C. Chatterjee, met Gandhi and argued for the creation of such colonies. Gandhi told them that this was a dangerous and unworkable solution, since a concentration could always be overwhelmed by superior numbers. 'Whether they are many or few, the Hindus of East Bengal have to learn the art of being brave. What if the Muslims of Bihar wanted to create Muslim sanctuaries in Bihar? It would be looked upon by the Hindu population of Bihar as a potential menace. By the same token, the creation of pockets can bode no good for the Hindus of East Bengal.'

Gandhi's mission of one worker per village was now operational in twenty villages. Aid was pouring in from all over. He feared that with all the aid and volunteers, the government would ease off on their responsibilities. The demobilized and recently freed men of the INA had come to Noakhali to assist Gandhi. Their leader, Sardar Niranjan Singh Gill, approached Gandhi to ask him to assign them duties in Noakhali. The Muslim League had expressed concern at the presence of the large number of INA men in their midst. Gandhi advised Singh to obtain permission from Suhrawardy before starting on their relief work. Suhrawardy had been facing increasing criticism from his Cabinet colleagues and Muslim League members for allowing Gandhi and his band of workers a free hand in Noakhali. Suhrawardy pleaded with Niranjan Singh not to make his situation worse. However, at that time, the central leadership of the Muslim League was desperately trying to woo the Sikhs of Punjab to join their grouping in the northwest. Suhrawardy was ordered not to antagonize the Sikhs, thus Niranjan Singh was granted permission. Instead of a thousand, Gandhi allowed only a hundred volunteers. Ultimately, the bulk of the INA volunteers were sent back; only a batch under Col Niranjan Singh continued to be in charge of Gandhi's camp in Srirampur, and accompanied him on his village-to-village march on foot through the riot-torn districts. Finally, even this group was sent back when Gandhi left for Bihar in March 1947. Niranjan Singh, however, continued to work in Noakhali along with other volunteers in the Gandhi camps, even after freedom and parition.

Soon, Gandhi's work began to show results. Muslim families began to break the shackles of mistrust and suspicion and see him as their friend. They began flocking to his prayer meetings and gathered around him during his daily walks; Hindus did not remain untouched either. 'Gandhiji's continued presence in Noakhali is resulting in a slow but steady restoration of confidence among the affected people', reported a correspondent, in the third week of December. 'Evacuees are now returning to their homes'; 'The Mahatma's method of solving the communal problem has been found to be a super-method', reported another. 'It may take time to yield its fullest results, it does always when it is an appeal to the soul but it is always a sure and more lasting method... It is not a peace dictated from above but worked up from within'. The change was also felt by people in other parts of the country. However, there were many sceptics, one of them was C. Rajagopalachari. In a letter written on 19 November, on the eve of Gandhi's departure for Srirampur, he wrote to Pyarelal: 'When is Bapu coming back? What is the good of remaining there so long?... All the good that can result has already resulted... What is the good of under feeding? It is dangerous.' Two weeks later, Rajagopalachari wrote to Gandhi: 'I have been silently watching and reading the reports that appear about your work there. I agree with you that the work you are on is great in every way and all else must give way. My note to you was wrong. You are now—I think for the first time in some respects—putting into the field, positive Ahimsa. And you will win. God willing our problems may be solved.'

The suspicion Gandhi had about the sincerity of the Cabinet Mission's intentions with regards to the grouping clause proved to be right. The British Parliament rejected all the objections raised by the Congress and promulgated a law which made it a *fait accompli* for the minority groups to compulsorily tag along with the dominant factions while voting on or opting out of a grouping. After a failed conference in London, where the Congress was represented by Nehru, the possibility of the Sikhs and Hindus in Punjab and the non-Muslims in Assam having to remain within the grouping dominated by the Muslim League, in other words, having to break away from India, became a reality. The Congress leaders were once again realizing their folly in disregarding Gandhi. Patel was rattled by the terror tactics of the Muslim League and began to publicly advocate a tit-for-tat policy. He wanted to deal with the Muslims the way some of them were dealing with the Hindus. The 'Iron Man of India' did not realize it then, but was later to admit that this was just the response the Muslim League was hoping to invoke. Not paying heed to Gandhi and abandoning his methods during times of crises was going to cost India and the Congress dearly.

While correspondence between Gandhi and Patel remained warm and honest, the thoughts expressed in the letters accentuated the drift between the two. While disagreeing with his opinions and disapproving of some of his actions, Gandhi encouraged Patel to act according to his beliefs.

Speaking of his inner turmoil to Dr Amiya Chakravarty of Calcutta University, who was visiting him in Srirampur, Gandhi commented: 'I am in the midst of a raging fire, and will not leave till it is put out; life in these parts must be made liveable for sorely affected men and women. The work of organization must go on, and physical as well as moral rescue achieved.' Dr Chakravarty asked him what technique could be used to approach the wrongdoers so that their resistance could be dissolved, 'as they are not only unrepentant but defiant and even jubilant over their misdeeds.' Gandhi replied, 'The only way to meet their attitude is not to succumb to it but to live in their midst and retain one's sense of truth.

I am groping for light. I am surrounded by darkness—but I must act or refrain as guided by truth. I find that I have not the patience and the technique needed in these tragic circumstances—suffering and evil often overwhelm me and I stew in my own juice. Therefore, I have told my friends that they should bear with me and work or refrain as guided by wisdom, which is now utterly demanded of us. This darkness will break and if I see light even those will see it who enacted the tragedy of the recent communalism in Bengal.'

The antagonism that the Muslim League rank and file felt towards Gandhi's peace mission in Noakhali was summed up in a press statement issued by one of the Muslim League parliamentary secretaries, Hamiduddin, who had accompanied him. 'Mr Gandhi does not intend to go to Bihar... Will it be wrong if one feels that Mr Gandhi is in Noakhali only to focus the attention of the world on the happenings there and to magnify the same for keeping the Bihar happenings in the background?... Mr Gandhi may conveniently ask all the outside volunteers both male and female to quit, while advising the refugees to return to their homes... No more sermons or instructions seem to be necessary for the Hindus there and the Muslims never required it ... Free from outside propaganda, they will begin to repose faith in their Muslim neighbours with whom they have been living peacefully for centuries.' Hamiduddin denied that any forcible conversions had taken place. He alleged that by not refuting the exaggerated reports about the casualties and carnage in Noakhali, Gandhi had lent credibility to them. He ended his open letter saying, 'Gandhiji should now leave Noakhali and utilize his valuable time and energy for something else, if not for the Bihar sufferers.'

Srirampur soon became a beehive of activity. Nehru, the newly appointed president of the Congress, was coming to meet Gandhi. Accompanied by Acharya Kripalani and a small group of Congress workers, they reached the Gandhi camp at midnight. The next day there were crowds of locals who had gathered to catch a glimpse of Gandhi and the leaders from Delhi. Joking with his mentor, Jawaharlal commented, 'So, this is your lone sojourn!' 'You forget I am a Mahatma, too!' replied Gandhi with a hearty laugh.

Verbal and written complaints against Patel's alleged anti-Muslim attitude were constantly being registered with Gandhi. Nehru was accompanied by Mridula Sarabhai, an ardent follower of Gandhi. She complained to him about Patel's speeches, which, from being critical of the Muslim League, were now becoming anti the entire Muslim community. The harassment suffered by the Congress members of the interim government was a result of the Muslim League's sustained and well-thought-out strategy; to blame all Indian Muslims was not a correct response. However, due to his speeches, the perpetrators of the Bihar massacre were emboldened by their misplaced notion that they had Patel's support. By no stretch of imagination could anyone allege that Patel was communal or a Hindu supremacist. As a minister holding the home affairs portfolio in the interim government, Patel lacked the ability of 'diplomatic speech'. This enabled the Muslim League to spread the canard amongst the Muslims that their interests would be jeopardized in an undivided India with leaders like Patel at the helm. Gandhi wrote to Patel and he responded, saying that if Gandhi wished, he was ready to step down from the Cabinet.

Nehru updated Gandhi about the goings-on in New Delhi over the past two months. He talked about the obstinacy of the League and the duplicity of the viceroy Lord Wavell and his bureaucrats who kept capitulating to the League each time it resorted to arm-twisting. Wavell was even forcing the Congress to form coalition governments with the League in provinces where the Congress had won clear-cut majorities. Nehru admitted that the Congress had been betrayed over the issue of the interpretation of the clauses relating to the grouping. His Majesty's government put an end to the controversy about the interpretation of the grouping clause by an Act of State. A declaration was made in both the Houses of Parliament that HMG had legal advice which confirmed that the statement of 16 May meant what they had always stated was their intention, namely, that voting in the Sections should, in the absence of an agreement to the contrary, be taken by a simple majority vote of the representatives and that part of the statement so interpreted should, therefore, be considered as essential part of the scheme of 16 May. The Constituent Assembly was free to refer the matter to the Federal Court if it so wished, but if the Muslim League could not be persuaded to come into the Constituent Assembly and a constitution came to be framed without the participation of the League, parts of the country in which the Muslim League was in a majority would not be bound by the results. His Majesty's government would not, therefore, undertake to submit to Parliament for acceptance a constitution so framed, as they could not contemplate 'forcing such a constitution upon any unwilling part of the country'. 'That position,' commented Sir Stafford Cripps on the floor of the House of Commons on 12 December, 'had always been realized by the Congress, which had repeatedly said that they would not coerce unwilling areas to accept the new constitution.'

The Congress was pushed into a corner. Many Congress leaders were now expressing regret for not having listened to Gandhi. Patel was one of them. His guilt was more so because it was on his insistence and in defiance of Gandhi in June 1946 that the Working Committee hurriedly accepted the Cabinet Mission's plan of 16 May, going against Gandhi's instincts. In a letter to Sir Stafford Cripps, written on 15 December 1946, Patel wrote: 'When the invitation to go to London came, our first instinct was to decline. But the Prime Minister's appeal and his assurance created a feeling in Pandit Nehru's mind that refusal to accept the invitation may be regarded as an act of discourtesy; he left India full of hopes, but he returned sadly disappointed... You called the League delegation there at a time when there was some realization that violence is a game at which both parties can play... Just when the time for settlement was reached, Jinnah got the invitation and he was able to convince the Muslims once again that he had been able to get more concessions by creating trouble and violence... In London, the stage was set against us... Your interpretation means that Bengal ... can draft the constitution of Assam. It is amazing. Do you think such a monstrous proposition can be accepted by ... Assam, particularly after the sad experience of wholesale forcible conversions, arson, looting, rape and forcible marriage? You can have no idea of the resentment and anger caused by your emphasis on this interpretation. If you think that Assam can be coerced to accept the domination of Bengal ... If they frame the constitution of Assam in such a way as to make Assamese opting out impossible, what is the remedy in your statement? You know that Gandhiji at the age of 77 is spending all his energy in the devastated Hindu homes in Eastern Bengal and trying to recover the lost girls and bring back those forcibly converted to their old faith. But he is working against heavy odds... He is surrounded by a very hostile atmosphere. In the event of his death there in these circumstances, what will happen no one can say. I shudder to think of the consequences… You know, when Gandhiji was strongly against our settlement, I threw my weight in favour of it. You have created a very unpleasant situation for me. All of us here feel that there has been a betrayal. The solution has now been made more difficult, nay almost impossible. The Viceroy would not give us peace. We have to work through this. It is an impossible situation.'

The British government's declaration of 6 December raised a life-or-death issue for Assam and the North-West Frontier Province. Assam, where the Hindus and Congress constituted the majority, and North-West Frontier Province, where an elected Congress government was in power, would pass into the control of the Muslim League-headed government in Bengal and in Punjab, respectively. On the other hand, if they refused to abide by the decision of the Congress, it would be construed as a betrayal of the Congress, and would wreck the Constituent Assembly and thereby play into the hands of the Muslim League. As always, whenever they were caught in a bind, Congress leaders ran to Gandhi for advice. This time, they wished to bring him back to Delhi to guide them in the negotiations. Gandhi's advice was clear. Rightly or wrongly, the Congress had come to the decision that it would stand by the decision of the federal court. 'The decision of the Federal Court will go against the Congress' interpretation of grouping as far as I can make out, for the simple reason that the British Cabinet says it has got legal advice which upholds their decision. The Federal Court is the creation of the British. It is a packed Court.

'No one can force Assam to do what it does not want to do. It should lodge its protest, retire from the Constituent Assembly, and frame its own constitution as an autonomous unit. Not only a Province but even a single individual can rebel against the Congress and by doing so serve it, assuming that the individual or the Province is in the right. I have done so myself. That would be the kind of Satyagraha against the Congress for the good of the Congress… For the independence of India, it is the only condition. Each unit must be able to decide and act for itself.'

Nehru and his party continued to hold consultations with Gandhi and tried their best to convince him to return to Delhi with them, but he was firm in his decision. An entry in his diary on 30 December 1946 mentions: 'Jawaharlal had about ten minutes talk before leaving. It was to the effect that I ought to be with them at Delhi.' In a note to Nehru, he wrote: 'Your affection is extraordinary and so natural! Come again, when you wish, or send someone who understands you and will faithfully interpret my reactions ... when in your opinion consultation is necessary and you cannot come. Nor is it seemly that you should often run to me even though I claim to be like a father to you, having no less love towards you than Motilalji. Do not depart from the spirit of the draft you showed me yesterday. Somehow or other I feel that my judgement about the communal problem and the political situation is true. I have no doubt now about the wisdom of what I had said in Delhi when the Working Committee accepted the Cabinet Mission's statement. This does not mean that what was done by the Working Committee should not have been done. I could not support with reason what I had felt so vaguely. This time it is quite different. My reason wholly supports my heart. I notice daily verification. So, I suggest frequent consultations with an old, tired servant of the Nation.'

On the morning of 30 December, at half past seven, Pandit Nehru and the accompanying party left Srirampur. Gandhi walked with them to the extent of his daily morning walk. Addressing the press on his return, Pandit Nehru remarked: 'It is always a pleasure and an inspiration to meet this young man of 77. We always feel a little younger and stronger after meeting him and the burdens we carry seem a little lighter.'

As the last day of 1946 dawned, Gandhi began to feel restless again. He felt that he had achieved all that he could by staying in Srirampur. To spread the hope of Srirampur to other areas of Noakhali, he would have to launch the next phase of his campaign for peace. He wrote to Patel about the darkness that seemed to engulf him in Noakhali: 'I am being tested through and through. My truth and Ahimsa are being tested in a balance more delicate than any a pearl merchant ever used... Truth and Ahimsa are perfect. They can never fail. But I, their exponent, may. This much I do hope that before that happens, merciful God will take me away from this world and send a worthier instrument to carry out His will... Do not call me away from here. If I myself run away from here like a coward, defeated, it may be my fate, not India's fault. But I have no such fear. I am out to do or die...'

In another letter to Patel, after Nehru's visit, Gandhi wrote: 'I heard many complaints against you... Your speeches are inflammatory... You have left behind all distinction between violence and non-violence; you are teaching the people to meet sword by sword; all this is harmful if true. Whatever I have heard I have passed on to you for your consideration. This is a very delicate time. If we deviate from the straight path by ever so little, we are done for. There is not that unison in the Working Committee that there should be. Send some trustworthy and intelligent person, if you think fit, to explain things to me and understand my mind. There is no need whatsoever for you to come yourself. You are no longer physically fit to run about. You seem to take no care of your health; that is bad.'

Patel's hurt was evident in his reply: 'I have your letter. It has pained me. Naturally you have written on the basis of the reports that you have received and the complaints that you have heard. It is news to me that my speeches are made with an eye to the gallery. It is my habit to tell people the bitterest truths. The remark about meeting sword by the sword has been torn out of a long passage and presented out of context. If there are divisions in the Working Committee, they are not today's growth. They have been there for a long time. At present, on the contrary, there is a very large measure of accord in most matters. The confidential reports which the Bengal government and the Governor of Bengal are sending regarding your continued stay in Bengal are very bad. They wish to push you out from there.'

Pyarelal writes: 'Sardar's reply was perfect so far as it went. The charge of personal ambition was beneath contempt. But Gandhiji's worry was deeper. True, Sardar did not want office for himself, but obviously prized it for the power it gave to the Congress. If the Sardar had shared his belief that "non-violence is the mightiest force" on earth, he would have prized more highly his formidable role as the Sardar of Bardoli than that of the Minister for Home Affairs in the interim government.' In his next letter to Sardar Patel, Gandhiji expressed only his concern about Sardar's health: 'Your health makes me feel anxious. You must get well. There is yet so much to do... The situation here is delicate. Watch what happens here.'

On 1 January 1947, Gandhi announced that he would be leaving the following day. 'Those who had once looked upon him with suspicion and distrust, now come here with reverence and gratitude. These are some of the indications that Gandhiji's ethical approach to the bitter problem is working at a slow but steady pace,' said a press despatch from Srirampur. A local Muslim was reported to have said, after a visit to Gandhi's prayer meeting, 'We have great regard for Gandhiji and we want him to stay on here.' A remark made at a press briefing by Shaheed Suhrawardy was even more significant, 'I hope Mahatma Gandhi will succeed in his mission not merely in Bengal but also in other parts of India.'

Early on 2 January, Gandhi broke camp. Describing the last morning of his stay in Srirampur, Dr Chakravarty wrote: 'The stars were still shining in the sky and the village of Srirampur lay quiet, waiting for the new day, when after the morning prayer Gandhi settled down to work. One could see him wrapped in white, his forehead shining as he went on writing in the light of a hurricane lantern. After 7:00 a.m., he came out for his morning walk in the village, crossing precarious bridges and grassy lanes wet with the morning dew. He greeted Muslim peasants as they proceeded to their fields and to work in the farms.' Hindus and Muslims alike stood and watched Gandhi pass. Superintendent of police, Abdullah, who had developed a deep attachment to Gandhi, accompanied him from Srirampur to Chandipur. He had assigned a party of twenty military police, armed with guns to provide security for Gandhi. Gandhi requested that no one was to walk with him. He wanted to be by himself.

Chandipur was three miles away from Srirampur; Gandhi reached there at 8:50 a.m. He requested Abdullah to remove the armed guards accompanying him, 'I appreciate the vigilance with which the Bengal government is trying to protect me but I need no other protection save God's.'

Gandhi stayed in Chandipur for five days. Those who had fled from their homes to escape death were now returning in large numbers. Speaking at a prayer meeting, he likened his mission in Noakhali to a pilgrimage.

Gandhi now realized that he would have to reach out to every corner of the devastated regions of Bengal. He had to replicate what happened in Srirampur and the only way he could do this was to embark on a walking expedition. For the next two months, the seventy-seven-year-old would walk, part of it barefoot, covering a distance of 116 miles, visiting forty-eight villages in two stages. He started on the morning of 7 January 1947. After his morning rituals, he enquired if all his instructions for the march had been carried out. At exactly half past seven, Gandhi was bid farewell by his followers who sang Tagore's *'Aekla chalo re...'* (Walk alone...).

The route Gandhi followed was through very scenic landscape. After an hour and a half, the party reached Mashimpur, their halt for the day. Satish Chandra Das had designed a portable hut made with panels of split bamboo, cane and grass. The hut had shelves for books and utensils and two small cubicles attached to the hut had a provision for a toilet and massage room. Gandhi took one look at it and pronounced it to be 'too palatial'. He instructed that the cabin be utilized as a travelling dispensary for the poor. 'I can make myself comfortable anywhere and everywhere. If there is no-one to receive me under his roof, I shall be happy to rest under the hospitable shade of a tree,' he told Gupta. The cabin was sent to the medical camp run by Dr Sushila Naiyyar to be used as a portable clinic.

The next morning, there was a chill in the air as Gandhi left for Fatehpur. As Manu applied oil to his feet, she discovered that his soles had cuts and were bleeding. Gandhi's host in Fatehpur, Maulvi Ibrahim, was a remarkable person. He was a committed social reformer and had, for the past fifty years, tried to change the attitudes of the local populace. He was working towards abolition of any job from being labelled as 'low-class work'.

The next day, Gandhi moved to Daspara. A poor Muslim villager had offered to host Gandhi but retracted his invitation at the last moment, fearing the wrath of his fellow Muslim neighbours. That evening, less than half a dozen Muslims attended the prayer meeting. Some of them sent word saying that there could be no harmonious relationship between the two communities as long as Gandhi continued to move under armed protection. Gandhi had time and again asked the police and the government to withdraw the armed escort. Gandhi wrote to Suhrawardy: 'All my attempts at bringing about real friendship between the two communities must fail so long as I go about fully protected by armed police or military... The fright of the military keeps them from coming to me and asking all sorts of questions for the resolution of their doubts. I do see some force in their argument... I do not need it. It certainly interferes with my Sadhana. I suggest you make a declaration that on a satisfactory assurance being given to you by the Muslims in the area through which I may pass regarding my safety, you will withdraw the escort. If this happens, it will be a dignified procedure, and it will produce a good effect all round.'

The next day, Gandhi left for Jagatpur where he was to address a meeting of local women. Many of them wept as they narrated their stories. That evening some local Muslims tried to instigate Gandhi by making hateful statements and questioning his motives. Pyarelal writes: 'As he contemplated the scene around him, once more the feeling came upon him that there was not likely to be an early end of his mission in Noakhali. "The signs are all against it," he remarked. To be able to command heart unity between Hindus and Muslims, he would have to make still further progress.'

The next day, 11 January, waking up at 2:00 a.m., Gandhi was kept busy with work till the last moment before his departure for Lamchar. A large group of local Muslims, including women and children, had gathered around the path at the crossing; many of them accompanied Gandhi to Lamchar. He was welcomed warmly even by the Muslims there; they were beginning to understand and appreciate his efforts. At Lamchar, Gandhi realized that a major cover-up had taken place immediately after the riots: the local people, politicians and police had all been involved in the riots but the victims did not have the courage to inform the administration.

The next day, Gandhi reached Karpara, where Sushila Pai was running a relief and rehabilitation centre. He advised the workers to begin by providing the people with basic requirements like clean drinking water; he along with Satish Gupta, devised a natural filter, which cost ₹50, which was sufficient to provide pure and safe drinking water for twenty-five families. At the next destination, Shahapur, Muslims came out in large numbers to greet Gandhi. The next morning, the walk to Bhatialpur took nearly eighty-five minutes, with several stops on the way. The local Muslims and Hindus of Bhatialpur had formed a peace committee. The Muslim members had signed a manifesto condemning the barbaric incidents during the riots and had assured their Hindu neighbours of all possible help in rehabilitation. The Muslims appealed to those who had robbed and plundered Hindu homes to return the stolen property to the rightful owners.

The next morning, a thick mist shrouded the woods as Gandhi resumed his march. His destination was the hamlet of Narayanpur. Before taking leave of his hosts and the people of Bhatialpur, Gandhi visited the family temple which he had reopened and consecrated the previous day. The next two stops on Gandhi's pilgrimage was Narayanpur, and Ramdevpur-Dasgharia. Kanu Gandhi, Gandhi's grand-nephew and official photographer, had established a relief camp here. Many Muslims gathered along the route to welcome Gandhi.

A constant demand of some Muslims, ever since Gandhi had arrived in Noakhali, was the immediate release of Mian Ghulam Sarwar, who had been arrested only after a lot of pressure had been put on the government. His henchmen issued 'warnings' to those who had registered complaints against him. A delegation of Sarwar's 'deputies', comprising twelve local Muslims, met Gandhi at Ramdevpur; a threat of a violent agitation for his release was cloaked thinly in their petition. However, Gandhi dismissed their demand.

On the morning of 19 January, just as the party was to leave Badalkot for Atakora, they realized that heavy dew had rendered the footpaths very slippery. The path was narrow and they could only walk in a single file. Twice, Col Jiwan Singh slipped and fell, and Gandhi offered him the end of his walking stick to pull himself up. Atakora was only two miles from Badalkot but it took them a whole hour to reach. The next day, the party left for Sirandi where Bibi Amtus Salam, a devout Muslim follower of Gandhi, had been working. She had been on a fast for the past twenty-five days to protest against some local Muslims. Bibi was a strict Muslim and held the unity of the two communities as the supreme goal of her life. During the recent riots, she had rushed to many troubled spots in Delhi, Calcutta and Dacca and succeeded in bringing the situation under control. She had rescued many abducted girls and women from their captors and restored them to their families. Gandhi arrived at Sirandi, where a large gathering of local Muslims met him and pleaded with him to convince Bibi Amtus Salam to give up her fast. Gandhi was aware that she only craved for peace between the Hindus and Muslims and if that was guaranteed, she could be convinced to end her fast. Gandhi prepared a declaration for their signatures, which was signed by eleven leading Muslims from four villages. The twelfth member was absent. He had gone to attend a meeting several miles away. He signed the declaration the following morning. Gandhi then explained the significance of the signed pledge to Bibi Amtus Salam. After the recitation of Al-Fateha, Bibi Amtus Salam broke her fast by sipping 3 ounces of diluted orange juice from a glass held by Gandhi.

After Sirandi, Gandhi moved to Kethuri on 22 January. He was exhausted, physically and mentally drained, after the hectic activities at Sirandi. The next morning, while going through a sheaf of papers after the morning prayers, he dozed off. It was time to leave on the day's journey, a large number of people were waiting outside, but Manu could not get herself to wake him. Finally, when Gandhi woke up, he was annoyed with himself that, due to a moment's weakness, the day's schedule had been delayed by a few minutes. He had always believed that every moment of one's time was a sacred trust from God, to be used strictly in His service. 'When people have been told we are to start at seven, it must be at the stroke of seven. Unpunctuality is a sin.'

During the march to Paniala, the next halt, Manu sang a new Ram Dhun, '*Raghupati Raghava Raja Ram Patita pavan Sita Ram, Ishwar Allah Tere naam sabako sanmati de Bhagawan...*', which she had heard as a little girl, sung in a Vaishnava temple in Porbandar, her hometown. It had stayed with her and spontaneously surfaced that morning. From then on, Gandhi insisted that this version of the Ram Dhun was to be recited in his prayer meetings. Today, Hindu extremists condemn him for desecrating a traditional chant to Rama by adding Allah to it and advocate reviving the old 'pure' version of the Ram Dhun. However, it wasn't Gandhi who 'polluted' a Hindu chant but Manu, who remembered it from her childhood. The Pranami sect amongst Vaishnavas traditionally combined verses from all religious scriptures and sang them as prayers, and this version of the Ram Dhun had come from that Pranami tradition which the Gandhi family practiced.

A large number of the survivors of the riots attended that evening's prayer meeting. After the prayer at Paniala, Gandhi was subjected to a barrage of angry questions from a group of Muslim League hecklers which he handled deftly to pacify them.

Assam was in a dilemma; being clubbed with the Muslim League-ruled Bengal and majority Muslim East Bengal would prevent it from having any say on which side it would remain with and in the drafting of the constitution. Gandhi's advice to Assamese constituents in the Bengal Assembly was to walk out of the section in the Constituent Assembly unless there was a guarantee that a constitution unacceptable to Assam's representatives would not be sought to be forced upon it by the representatives of the other provinces in the section. Leaguers heckled Gandhi for what they called his 'double standards'.

The hecklers also brought up the situation of Muslim trespassers in Assam. The Muslim League government of Bengal had launched an invasion of Assam to alter the communal ratio of the state's population. Muslim immigrants, and specifically Muslim League National Guards, were infiltrating Assam in organized groups. They illegally occupied vacant government lands in Assam and refused to vacate them. This forced the Congress government there to forcefully evict the illegal encroachers. It was purely an administrative issue and the measures taken by the Assam government were well within the purview of maintaining law and order, but the Muslim League used the issue to whip up communal frenzy and accuse the Congress government in Assam of perpetrating atrocities on the Muslim population. Gandhi was accused of remaining silent on this by the Muslim League's hecklers in Paniala. He calmly replied that illegal trespassers, merely because they happened to be Muslim or Bengalis, could not claim exemption from the operation of the common law. The Muslim League accused Gandhi of being partial towards Hindus.

Gandhi's next stop was the village of Muraim. Some of the women who attended Gandhi's prayers were veiled. The village Maulvi gently rebuked them saying: 'We are blessed today to have a man of God like him in our midst. Our community today suffers from the stigma of shedding the blood of our Hindu brethren. He has come to free us of this stain. It is absurd to observe Purdah in his purifying presence.' The next morning, the Maulvi walked half-way with Gandhi to Hirapur. In Hirapur, there were only two Hindu families. The prayer gathering that evening was the biggest during Gandhi's entire pilgrimage.

On 26 January, which had been celebrated as independence day for the past seventeen years since the Congress had taken the pledge of Swaraj on 26 January 1930, Gandhi and his tiny entourage reached Bansa, where he hoisted the national flag. After stopping in Palla, the party headed towards Panchgaon. As was her practice, Manu went to visit Muslim women in their homes. She was refused entry; doors were slammed in her face. An old Muslim woman came out and, pressing a roti into her hands, she asked Manu to eat it. To her horror, Manu saw that she had been given a piece of fish wrapped in the roti; she told the old woman that she was a strict vegetarian, so she could not eat fish. The woman exclaimed bitterly, 'A Hindu is after all a Hindu,' referring to the practice of orthodox Hindus not eating food offered by a Muslim. 'How can we then believe that Gandhi has come here to establish Hindu-Muslim unity!' To reassure her, Manu tore off a piece of the roti without touching the fish and ate it. Only after this did women from other homes step out and meet Manu. When Manu reported the incident to Gandhi, he was saddened at the extent to which distrust had spread.

The campaign continued at Jayag. The new Ram Dhun, which was revived at Paniala, underwent further modifications.

'Thou art the purifier of the fallen,
Ishawar and Allah are Thy names,
Do Thou grant right understanding to all humans,
Krishna, Karim are Thy names, So are Rama, Rahim,
Do thou grant right understanding to all humans.'

The new version gave the Muslim hardliners another excuse to attack Gandhi. They objected to the clubbing together of the names of Hindu gods with various names of Allah. They warned him not to recite Ayats from the Koran. Today, Hindu bigots criticize Gandhi for this, equally vehemantly.

Gandhi reached Amki on 30 January. His faith in Rama Nama was put to a severe test here. As goat's milk was not available, he agreed to have coconut milk and coconut oil substituted for goat milk butter. Accordingly, he had 8 ounces of coconut milk. However, this change in diet brought on a severe bout of diarrhoea and colic. By the evening, he was totally drained and exhausted. Manu noticed that he was perspiring profusely and she thought he had fainted. She called out to Prof. Nirmal Bose for help. Together they lifted and placed him on his bed. She hurriedly scribbled a note summoning Dr Sushila Nayyar and was about to give it to Prof. Bose, when Gandhi opened his eyes. 'I did not like your calling Nirmal Babu,' he said to her. 'You are yet a child. I can, therefore, excuse you. But what I had really expected of you was that on an occasion like this, you would do nothing but take the Lord's name. I was chanting his name all this while. Do not inform anybody about it, not even Sushila. Rama alone is my true doctor. He will keep me alive so long as He wants to take work from me, otherwise he will take me away.' Manu tried to hide the note she had scribbled for Dr Nayyar but Gandhi noticed it. 'So, you have already written?' he asked and Manu nodded. He said, 'Today God has saved both you and me. Sushila would have left her work in her village and rushed to me. It would have made me angry with myself and with you. I have today been put to the test. If His name has really established dominion over my heart I shall not die of illness.'

At the next stop, Amishapura, a large crowd greeted him. An ex-airman, who had deserted the air force and taken on an assumed identity, had joined Gandhi's entourage. The man had been accepted into the 'family' on the condition that he was to remain with Gandhi and work under his direct supervision. On reaching Amishapura, he broke away and declared that he would work independently of the peace workers. Gandhi immediately alerted the authorities as the man was from Malabar and his unsupervised activities could be dangerous.

Gandhi arrived at his next destination, Sadhurkhil, on the morning of 3 February. It had now been one month since Gandhi had embarked on his barefoot peace pilgrimage through riot-torn Noakhali. His pilgrimage had instilled confidence in the riot-affected community and had, to a large extent, helped it to rid itself of the fear and distrust towards the majority community.

After a day's halt at Dharampur and another at Prasadpur, Gandhi reached Nandigram on 8 February, where he was welcomed by a large crowd. 'What hospitality can we offer you?' asked a Muslim whose home Gandhi visited. 'The hospitality of giving me a place in your love and affection,' Gandhi replied.

The next day, Gandhi reached Bijoyanagar after walking for an hour and a half. Relief and peace workers who had accompanied Gandhi to

Noakhali, and were now working in various villages in the district, were faced with a dilemma. He had given strict instructions that they were to involve local workers in their relief work and keep away from local politics and factions. However, every village was divided and the workers were finding it difficult to find local help. Gandhi's message was emphatic though: 'I have not known a single village which is devoid of an honest worker. I can categorically say to the principal worker: If you have any outside help, get rid of it. Work singly, courageously, intelligently, with all the local help you can get and if in the end you do not succeed, blame yourself only and no one else and nothing else.'

Raipur had witnessed the worst carnage in the area, next only to Shahapur. Gandhi found plenty of evidence that trouble was still brewing in the districts. A Muslim man who had come all the way from Punjab to meet Gandhi had been robbed of all his belongings on the way. Another Muslim from Gujarat had been threatened by some local Muslims for wanting to meet Gandhi. There were two Jama Masjids in Raipur. The Imam in charge of one took him around to see the mosque, but the other refused, saying that he needed written permission from the trustees of the mosque. While returning to his camp after the evening prayer, Gandhi visited a temple which had been seized by local Muslims during the riots and converted into 'Pakistan Club'. It still bore that tell-tale signboard, four months after the riots. The local Muslims assured Gandhi that they would take all the necessary steps to restore the temple.

Meanwhile, the Karachi resolution of the Muslim League had put an end to any hope of the Muslim League joining the Constituent Assembly. On 9 February, Nehru wrote to Gandhi: 'The League resolution was about as bad as it could be. Perhaps there was a virtue in it, for it makes the position quite clear. After this resolution it is even more difficult than before for us to carry on in the old way in the interim government. We are moving in the matter.' He wrote again the next day: 'We have informed the Viceroy that in view of the Muslim League resolution passed at Karachi, the League members cannot continue in the government. There is really no answer to our charge and demand and the Viceroy realizes it. He is awaiting instructions from London.' The *London Times* commented: 'The League, while apparently relying on the British declaration that a constitution framed by the Constituent Assembly, not fully representative, cannot be enforced upon unwilling parts of India, may perhaps have lost from sight the not less significant undertaking that a minority cannot be suffered indefinitely to impede the progress of the majority.'

In a press interview on 15 February, Patel revealed that the Congress members of the interim government had asked HMG either to implore the Muslim League to share in drafting a new constitution or to leave the Cabinet. If they didn't, he said, the Congress would. The step, which had been contemplated for a long time, was precipitated by the refusal of the Muslim League members in the interim government, who sat in the Lower House, to support the government on an important decision. The issue was a delicate one of taking punitive action against some troublemaking elements in the North-West Frontier Province. To deal with such a vital issue of law and order upon purely communal lines was a danger signal which no responsible body could ignore. Even the conservative *London Times* was forced to observe that the behaviour of the two League Ministers was 'in fact indefensible'.

In a letter written in December 1946, Gandhi had said: 'In my opinion, for the British not to leave India till there is perfect peace in the land seems to me to be an impossible dream. What they can and must do is to transfer the whole power to the willing and capable party and at the earliest moment to withdraw the British part of the army and disband the rest. They should not think of keeping any part for the protection of the British interests. These must be left to the goodwill of the people of India. This is the royal road to peaceful transfer and no other.'

The British government was driven to very nearly the same conclusion. On 20 February 1947, Attlee made a statement in Parliament that it was HMG's definite intention to take necessary steps to effect the transfer of power to responsible Indian hands by a date not later than June 1948. Under the State Paper of 16 May 1946, they had agreed to recommend to Parliament the adoption of a constitution that might be framed by the Constituent Assembly. But if a constitution in terms of the Cabinet Mission plan was not worked out by a 'fully representative Constituent Assembly by that time', Attlee went on to say, 'HMG will have to consider to whom the powers of the Central Government in British India should be handed over on the due date, whether as a whole to some form of Central Government for British India, or in some areas to the existing Provincial Governments or in such other way as may seem most reasonable and in the best interest of the Indian people.'

The British prime minister announced the termination of Lord Wavell's appointment as the 'Wartime' viceroy and the appointment of Lord Mountbatten as his successor and last viceroy of India. Although formal compliments were paid to him on the termination of his services, Lord Wavell was being dismissed for his inept handling of the situation. Wavell was leaving behind a political deadlock worse than ever: communal violence which threatened to turn into a raging inferno, organized lawlessness which had already taken over three provinces and threatened to convert the entire country into a battlefield, a vertically split Central Secretariat divided between the viceroy's personal staff and the brown Gora Sahibs of the British Administrative Service and a crumbling administrative service into which communalism had infiltrated.

Giving his first reaction to HMG's announcement, Gandhi wrote to Nehru on 24 February: 'Evidently I had anticipated practically the whole of it. My interpretation of (Attlee's) speech is this, Independence will be recognized of those parts which desire it and will do without British protection; (1) The British will remain where they are wanted; (2) This may lead to Pakistan for those Provinces or portions which may want it. No-one will be forced one way or the other. The Congress Provinces, if they are wise, will get what they want; (3) Much will depend upon what the Constituent Assembly will do and what you as the interim government are able to do; (4) If the British Government are able to remain sincere the declaration is good. Otherwise it is dangerous.'

The future would depend on India's capacity to take up the challenge of independence in terms of the Quit India resolution for which Gandhi had been trying to prepare them, and the British government's willingness to retire unconditionally, leaving India to its fate, and its capacity to get the services to implement that decision loyally and impartially in letter and in spirit.

Devipur, the last village in Noakhali district where Gandhi would camp for the night, was very scenic. The path leading to the village meandered along the Dakatia river. He sent for the principal worker as he was unhappy with the excess money that had been spent on decorating his route. Where did they find all the material? Surely it could not be from the village! The poor worker tried to explain: they had raised a subscription to accord him a fitting welcome. Gandhi said, 'Did you realize that by indulging in this vain display you would acerbate communal passions? This display means nothing to me ... but it will leave a legacy of ill-will behind which will continue to poison the communal relations in this village for a long time to come. You are a Congressman. Did it not occur to you, knowing my strong views on Khadi, that ribbons and buntings made of mill cloth would only hurt me?'

Gandhi personally supervised the unravelling of the garlands and wreaths and had every yard of yarn rewound so that it could be reused to weave cloth. He salvaged almost twenty cones of yarn. 'While he was pouring out his soul like this,' Manu wrote in her *Diaries from Noakhali*, 'he looked the very picture of a volcano in eruption. But there was no trace of anger or reproach in his voice. From his face one might as well have thought that it was some terrible lapse of his own that he was confessing. And, indeed, he has often told us that a lapse on the part of his men should be regarded as his failure, the failure of his teachings'.

On 18 February, Gandhi crossed into the adjoining district of Tipperah, reaching the first village in the district, Alunia, at 8:30 a.m. The district was marked by a considerable change in scenery and nature of the soil. It was soft alluvium in Noakhali but loam in Tipperah. The areca nut gardens were there but the coconut groves grew scarce. The verdant stretches of emerald green rice fields which abounded in Noakhali were missing here. In order to simplify his meals, Gandhi concocted some very strange and unappetizing dishes at Alunia. Pyarelal writes: 'As part of his midday meal, he had a thick sticky stew of lady's fingers (Okra), bitter gourd and greens, without spice or salt. Into this he poured boiled goat's milk and took it after stirring it with a spoon. As I watched him, I wondered how on earth anybody could swallow that horrible stuff! I had to pay dearly for it. Guessing perhaps what was passing in my mind he twitted me, "What do you know of these things! When you feel really hungry whatever is set before you is a treat!" Out of his overflowing affection, he offered me two spoonfuls of the concoction which I swallowed with as brave a face as I could!'

Although his mind and body were exhausted, Gandhi was far from being spent. 19 February was Mahashivratri, a festival of Lord Shiva. Gandhi was in Birampur that day. For him, the festival brought back painful memories; he had lost his wife Kastur on that day three years ago in the Aga Khan Palace Prison Camp. Since then, he had observed Kasturba's death anniversary by fasting and praying. To all outward appearances, it was like any other day, which began as usual at four in the morning and continued without a break. The only allusion to the event which meant so much to him personally is contained in a solitary sentence in his diary: 'On this day, and exactly at this time (7:35 p.m.) Ba quitted her mortal frame three years ago.'

At 7:35 p.m., the party gathered around a tiny oil lamp lit in front of a portrait of Kasturba, which was adorned by a garland of yarn, hand spun by Gandhi. The yarn would later be retwisted and sent for weaving; nothing was to be wasted. Gandhi sat through the recitation of the first six chapters of the Gita, then, due to fatigue, he lay down to rest. He later mentioned that while he lay listening to the rest of the recitation, he felt at one with his dear departed partner. He felt her presence. 'During the Gita recitation, the whole scene of Ba's last moments three years ago came back and stood before my mind's eye in all its vividness. I felt as if her head was actually resting in my lap. This was particularly so after the sixth chapter, when I laid myself down to rest and for a moment fell into a gentle sleep. I must own,' he wistfully remarked. 'Without her, I could not have succeeded in my striving for Ahimsa and self-discipline. She understood me better than anyone else. Her loyalty was matchless. On the last day, I did not know, till the very end, in whose lap she would close her eyes. But she sent for me just before the end and breathed her last in my lap. That was Ba. We can fittingly observe her shraddha (death anniversary) by recalling her virtues and trying to cultivate them in ourselves. I have not known another instance of such guileless faith, selfless devotion and service as hers. Ever since our marriage, she stood by me in all my life's struggles, with an unwavering fidelity and dedicated herself to my life's mission—body, soul and all—in a manner that has few parallels.'

Birampur was situated on the banks of the river Meghna, a mercurial river which often changed its course. It now flowed almost 6 kilometres away from the village. The fishermen had also suffered greatly in the riots. Looking at their plight, it was for the first time that Gandhi mentioned that the only option for them was a voluntary and total translocation.

Opposition by Muslim radicals and the Muslim League's campaign against Gandhi reached a crescendo at the next village, Bishkatali. This small village had a Hindu population of 306 people in the midst of an overwhelming Muslim majority of 4,694. Hindu survivors had left the village; none of them had returned. Many posters had been pasted on the trees on both sides of the path leading to Bishkatali, warning Gandhi.

'Remember Bihar and leave Tipperah immediately. We have warned you many times, still you are here. Go back; otherwise it would be the worse for you!'

'Go where you are wanted. Give up your hypocrisy and accept Pakistan!'

'Muslim League zindabad! *Quaid-i-Azam zindabad*! Let there be Pakistan! Down with the Congress!' Gandhi ignored these attempts to intimidate and provoke him.

Gandhi left Kamalapur the next day for Char Krishnapur, in the heart of the Char region. 'Char' literally means an island formed in the riverbed due to the shifting of the river. The Char area in Noakhali and Tipperah is a gift of the river Meghna, its lazy, silt laden, ever shifting flow contributing to the formation of a network of Chars. The bulk of the population of Char Krishnapur consisted of Namashudras, Harijans, while the Muslims numbered only 200. The Namashudras had suffered terribly during the riots and the reign of terror had continued long after other parts had been relieved. As a local Muslim who was to host Gandhi backed out due to immense pressure from his community, an improvised shed was erected using charred and blackened corrugated tin sheets, salvaged from the burnt-down remains of a homestead.

Gandhi had begun to get reports from his workers spread over the two districts about how Hindus were being intimidated. Muslims, those aligned to the Muslim League, the perpetrators of the recent violence, were secretly meeting to plan a new campaign of terror. The Hindus were being threatened with further attacks unless they withdrew their complaints. A large number of Hindu fishermen, betel-leaf growers, weavers, petty shopkeepers, etc., who had for generations served both communities, were being reduced to penury due to a boycott of their services and businesses. Hindu agriculturists were facing a similar boycott. Muslim agricultural labourers who had worked their fields for centuries were not being allowed to work on Hindu owned farms, a situation that could possibly cause an acute shortage of foodgrains.

The objective of the organizers of this campaign of isolation and intimidation was to force an exodus of the Hindus from the district and then from the whole of East Bengal. Already, the survivors of the riots and the victims of the boycott campaign had started talking in despair about an impending partition of Bengal. Gandhi said, 'Those who talk of separation must know where we stand. If boycott is the policy of the government, we must know about it. A community cannot take action by itself. Bengal as well as other Provinces must understand this. Even if I fail, truth will not have failed. I must strive and carry this issue towards light. I may live or perish in the attempt. Noakhali and Tipperah are not an isolated problem, but it is a problem which India must solve for herself and humanity. Fortunately or unfortunately, I have had success in the most difficult ventures of my life. But I do not know what will happen this time. The greatest trial is given to us but it is never beyond our power to overcome it.'

Meanwhile, the continued hardship to which Gandhi was subjecting his body had begun to take its toll. Pyarelal describes Gandhi's condition in *Mahatma Gandhi: The Last Phase, Vol. 9, Part I, Book Two*: 'The dead-set at me is growing fiercer,' ran a letter by Gandhiji. 'But to face such attacks joyously and unflinchingly has been my business in life. My present yajna is one of utmost purification. It may be my last.' In the course of a conversation with a friend, who had come with some important despatches from New Delhi, he remarked: 'I do not want to die ... of a creeping paralysis of my faculties—a defeated man. An assassin's bullet may put an end to my life. I would welcome it. But I would love, above all, to fade out doing my duty with my last breath.' One of his letters to a friend described him as 'trekking over unfurrowed tracks in stormy weather'. He might have, in this way, gone on forever. But flesh and blood have their limits and nature has put a wise check on man's striving. For some time, he had been complaining of a 'drumming sound' in the ears, a red flag of high blood pressure, to which he was prone. Under the advice of friends, at last he agreed to make a prolonged halt at Haimchar to recoup himself. The rest at Haimchar lasted for six days, which helped Gandhi regain much-needed energy for his task ahead.

Thakker Bappa, who was conducting the relief and rehabilitation operations in Haimchar, had briefed Gandhi about the situation in the Char areas. The destruction of the Namashudra villages in the Char area had been on an unprecedented scale. The recently launched mass economic boycott of non-Muslims had further worsened their situation. The plight of the Harijans of Noakhali debunked Jinnah's assurance to the Indian Harijans that they would be better off throwing their lot in with the Muslim League.

Nuruddin Chowdhary, the relief commissioner of Chittagong Division, had outlined a grand plan to rehabilitate and uplift villages, in an elaborate speech delivered at a meeting of the local peace committee. Gandhi reacted by saying that, to him, they seemed like grand words with no substance, since the plan ignored the 'issue of issues' which stared all of them in the face, namely, the worsening relations between the Hindus and the Muslims of Noakhali. Personally, Gandhi concluded, he would give top priority to the establishment of unity between the two communities, the lack of which had vitiated the entire atmosphere so that even in the meeting of the peace committee, where the relief commissioner had unveiled his ambitious plan, very few non-Muslims were to be seen participating.

Speaking at the first prayer meeting at Haimchar, attended by a large number of Namashudras, Gandhi said that they should not regard themselves as fallen or as 'untouchables'. Referring to the British prime minister's statement, he observed that whatever might have been in the history of British rule in the past, there was not a shadow of doubt that the British were going to quit India in the near future. The prime minister's statement put the burden on the various parties of doing what they thought was appropriate. It was up to them to make or mar the situation. Nothing could overturn their united wish. So far as he was concerned, he was emphatically of the opinion that if the Hindus and Muslims closed their ranks and came together without external pressure, they would not only effect the future of India but probably the whole world. The alternative was a civil war which would only serve to tear the country to pieces.

On 28 February, Nehru wrote: 'The Working Committee is meeting here soon and all of us were anxious to have you here on the occasion. We considered the question of sending you a joint telegram appealing to you to come. But though we are not sending the telegram we feel very strongly that your advice during the coming critical weeks is most necessary. At present it is exceedingly difficult for any of us to leave Delhi and if you will not come how are we to meet?' On 24 April, Nehru again wrote to Gandhi: 'You must have seen my statement on the new declaration made by the British government. The statement was considered carefully by all our colleagues in the interim government minus, of course, the Muslim Leaguers... Mr Attlee's statement contains much that is indefinite and likely to give trouble. It meets our oft-repeated demand for quitting India... Matters will move swiftly now or at any rate after Mountbatten comes.... The Working Committee is meeting on 5 March... If you could convey to us your ideas on the subject, we would be grateful.' Gandhi believed that what he was doing in Bengal was his duty; he could not leave his task unfinished. In a letter to Patel, he wrote: 'I may not be able to prove it to you, but I am convinced that my work here is of supreme importance. All of you veterans are there, putting your shoulder to the wheel... I am the only figure among ciphers here. Allow me, therefore, to continue here. If I can achieve something worthwhile, the whole country will be benefited; if I fail none will be any worse for it.' To Maulana Azad, who had suggested to him to make Calcutta his headquarters if he could not come and stay in Delhi, Gandhi replied: 'If the Ahimsa about which I have written so much and which I have striven to realize in practice all these years does not answer in a crisis, it ceases to have any value in my eyes. The truth however is that so long as I cannot make good here, I can be of no use anywhere.'

'My walking pilgrimage,' he wrote to a friend in Europe, Mrs Edmund Privat, 'gives me immense peace of mind. The upshot I do not know nor do I care to know. Man has no control over results. That is the sole prerogative of God. Hence I can sing with Cardinal Newman:

"I do not see the distant scene;
one step enough for me."'

Gandhi's refusal to leave Noakhali till his mission had borne fruit, created a dilemma for the Congress leaders. It was vividly expressed in one of the letters written to him by Nehru: 'I know that we must learn to rely upon ourselves and not run to you for help on every occasion. But we have got into this bad habit and we do often feel that if you had been easier of access, our difficulties would have been less.' But Gandhi was firm: 'I feel that I should be useless unless I could do something here... We are all in the hands of the Power which we call God.'

In the end, it was neither his desire, nor the persistent demand of the Congress leaders that prevailed. What Gandhi had referred to as 'the Power we call God' made him decide. It was neither to stay on in Noakhali, nor to rush to Delhi where there was a clamour for his presence, but it was to answer a desperate cry that rose from Bihar that took Gandhi away, never to return to what he referred to as his 'unfinished business' in East Bengal.

A letter received from the president of the district Muslim League from Monghyr in Bihar said: 'The atrocities committed by the Hindus in Bihar have no parallel in history. But not a word of sympathy for the Muslim sufferers of this province, and not a word of rebuke and reproach for the criminals could come from your mouth. Still you ask the Muslims to have faith in the nationalism advocated by you, in the "national" Congress supported by you and "national" leaders patronized by you. I would request you therefore, to come to Bihar at your earliest if you really want to serve humanity.' To this bitter and vastly exaggerated missive, Gandhi replied: 'Your letter is hysterical. I would like you to tell me how I can serve the Muslims better by going to Bihar. Whilst I do not endorse your remark that the atrocities committed by the Hindus in Bihar have no parallel in history, I am free to admit that they were in magnitude much greater than in Noakhali. I would urge you, as president of the Monghyr District Muslim League, to confine yourself to proved facts which, I am sorry to say, you have not done.'

Suhrawardy jumped into the fray and in his incorrigible way made a frivolous reference to Gandhi's 'inner voice'. Gandhi replied, 'I have seen in the newspapers a statement attributed to you which reads like a jibe at me. I would not expect that from you. Therefore, I give you the credit of believing that I have the inner voice to which I listen. My belief is that all mankind has it. But the outside din and noise have practically deadened it for the vast majority of people. When my voice speaks, I shall find myself in Bihar without any further prompting.'

While refusing to be goaded into taking a hasty step, Gandhi made all efforts to get at the truth. He sent Col Niranjan Gill to Bihar to send him a report of the situation there. Gill's report exploded the myths propagated by the Muslim League, but what it said was damaging enough for the Government of Bihar too.

During his week-long stay in Haimchar, Gandhi began to plan the next phase of his peace pilgrimage on foot through the district, which was to begin on 2 March. He had drawn up an elaborate itinerary across the Charmandal area, covering parts of Noakhali and Tipperah districts. It then led back to Srirampur, from where he had originally started two months ago. From there, he planned to start again and cover the other portions of Noakhali and Tipperah. However, this was not to be.

That evening, Gandhi informed Satish Chandra Das Gupta of his intention to proceed to Bihar immediately. He described how, till the previous day, he had been planning to set out on the third phase of his pilgrimage, but at the appointed hour, found himself preparing to set out for Bihar instead. He referred to the report which he had received about the atrocities that were said to have been committed by the Hindus of Bihar, before which the happenings of Noakhali seemed to pale into insignificance. He was as concerned about the welfare of the Muslims as of the Hindus. His mind made no distinction between the two. He had sent an urgent wire to the chief minister of Bihar.

Till 1 March, however, he received no reply from Sri Krishna Sinha (Sri Babu), the chief minister of Bihar. Before retiring, he left instructions that his luggage was to be kept packed and ready for departure the next day. Although he lived with very few possessions and personal items, Gandhi had collected a vast number of books and correspondence. Among the things he would take with him to Bihar were a Bengali dictionary and a notebook in which he did his daily Bengali writing exercises.

2 March was a gloomy day. Thakkar Bappa had taken it upon himself to supervise the winding up of Gandhi's camp and ensure that all the baggage was properly loaded on the Jeep. The fog finally lifted at 11 a.m. and the sun shone through. For the first time in two months, Gandhi was wearing his sandals. It was difficult for him to walk through the surging crowds to the waiting Jeep. He was accompanied by Prof. Nirmal Kumar

Bose, Manu Gandhi, Dev Prakash Nayar and Hamid Hunar. All the others who had originally accompanied him, he left behind to continue peace building and rehabilitation work at the various centres. Satish Chandra Das Gupta was authorized to represent him in dealing with authorities during his absence. He intended to come back, but that was not to be.

The party reached Chandpur at 3:20 p.m. Huge crowds surrounded the residence of the late Hardayal Nag, the grand old man of Chandpur, where arrangements had been made for Gandhi's stay. His last public prayer meeting in East Bengal was attended by over 30,000 people.

Addressing the gathering, Gandhi said that he was going to Bihar with the purpose of trying to establish peace there. He expected to return to his chosen scene of service, Noakhali, as early as possible.

At 9:30 p.m., the party boarded a steamer. The last to take leave was Col Jiwan Singh. As Gandhi scribbled out his final orders that he should send away his men, Jiwan Singh felt hurt and unhappy, thinking it was a dismissal for him. He was about to bid goodbye with a heavy heart when Gandhi wrote on another slip of paper: 'I do not want to lose you personally.' Jiwan Singh stayed on in Noakhali even after Gandhi's murder.

The following day, 4 March 1947, from 8:45 a.m. to 10:00 a.m., Gandhi was closeted with the chief minister of Bengal. Gandhi admitted that things in Bihar were not as well as he had been led to believe. That gave Suhrawardy his chance. With a note of bitterness mixed with triumph in his voice, he told Gandhi that Nehru and Dr Rajendra Prasad had betrayed him. This hurt Gandhi deeply. When asked later if there was a likelihood of anything fruitful coming out of his talk with the chief minister, Gandhi replied in the negative. 'He is past master in the art of gab; he went on talking round and round; would not give me a chance to get even a word in edgewise concerning what was uppermost in my mind.'

As the train carrying Gandhi chugged towards riot-torn Bihar, the apostle of peace was lying on his third-class bunk preparing for the ordeal ahead. Of one thing he was sure, as soon as he was assured that Bihar was on the path of peace, he would rush back to Noakhali. He knew that his work there was incomplete. The clouds of suspicion and hatred had still not been dispelled.

Destiny, however, had other plans for him.

IX

BIHAR: AN ORGY OF HATE

I hate to hear these 'jai!' shouts, they remind me of the Hindus who massacred innocent Muslim men and women accompanied by the cries of 'Jai Shree Ram!' and 'Har Har Mahadev!', just as the Muslims murdered Hindus while shouting 'Allah-o-Akbar!' I know of no greater sin than to oppress the innocent in the name of God! Stop it!

—M.K. Gandhi,
29 April 1947

Bihar was where Gandhi had cut his political teeth in India on his return from South Africa in 1915. Gandhi had been moved by the plight of the indigo farmers of Champaran, who were forced to grow indigo and pay heavy rent and tax to British landlords, which turned them into virtual slaves. Gandhi had championed their cause and forced the colonial government to implement agrarian reforms and liberate the farmers from the tyranny of landlords and indigo factory owners. Success in Champaran had catapulted Gandhi into a position of leadership in India's fight for freedom. Ever since, Gandhi felt a special kinship with Bihar.

Reporting on the situation in Bihar, Nehru, in a note to Gandhi on 6 November 1946, wrote: 'Bihar is an impoverished agrarian state. Most of its landless rural populace seasonally immigrate to work in the fields of Punjab and other states. At least one member of every rural Bihari family immigrates to other states in search of work. More than a million Bihari immigrants live and work in Calcutta as labourers, domestic help, rickshaw pullers, artisans and small traders. This was the segment which suffered the most during the riots in Calcutta. They lost their meagre belongings, their small businesses and many of them were slaughtered on the streets of Calcutta. Till 1911–12, Bihar was a part of Bengal Province. A large number of Bengali Hindus lived in Bihar, and relatives of these people were killed in the riots in Calcutta and then in Noakhali and Tipperah. The Calcutta and Noakhali survivors who had managed to flee poured into Bihar and with them came tales of their suffering and gruesome descriptions of the massacres, forced conversions and the most passion-rousing details of crimes against their women. The abductions, rapes, forced conversions and marriages under duress to their abductors: this was a new development and it created a huge outrage amongst the Hindu population countrywide. A large number of Biharis were plunged into sorrow at the plight of their relatives and co-religionists. A wave of anger began to form in Bihar and the rest of India as the stories, embellished with each narration and many a times fabricated to suit the teller's political motives, began to spread. The time was right for those who saw an opportunity for political gains in this human tragedy.'

Nehru was referring to the Hindu right-wing extremists and the Muslim League. The Hindu right wing, which had been largely marginalized because of its collaborationist role during the freedom movement, desperately needed an opportunity to reinstate itself in the political arena in an India which was rapidly moving towards freedom. This was their opportunity. They had their cadre well entrenched in the civil services and the police force. Now, they were activated to support and encourage the agenda of their political and ideological parent organizations—the Hindu Mahasabha and RSS. Both organizations got actively involved in spreading religious hate amongst the aggrieved peasantry of Bihar. They convinced the Biharis that their existence depended on whether they would allow the Muslims to live in their midst or drive them out. If allowed to stay, the Muslims would one day do a repeat of Calcutta and Noakhali in Bihar. Meanwhile, the Muslim League also vitiated the atmosphere by instilling fear amongst the Muslims of Bihar, that they were susceptible to sudden attacks by the majority community. Both the communities were systematically armed. The campaign of hate reached a crescendo; all that was required to ignite the inferno was a spark.

The spark was provided in September 1946 in the village of Benibad in Muzaffarpur district. A local Muslim was reported to have abducted a Hindu girl from Calcutta and was holding her hostage. The Hindu community demanded that the girl be handed over to them, and the man agreed to do so in a couple of days. On the promised day, a crowd of Hindus reached his home, only to find it deserted: there was no sign of the girl or the man. The enraged Hindus gave vent to their anger and the Muslims in the neighbourhood bore the brunt of it. The police did not reach the spot in time to prevent the tragedy, since the van carrying them broke down on the way. However, the guilty Hindus were prosecuted by the Congress party. In response, a pamphlet titled *Present Miseries of the Hindus of Bihar* was issued by the provincial Hindu Mahasabha, claiming that there was enough evidence to show that the Muslims in Bihar were planning an organized attack on the Hindus. The latter would be taken unawares and slaughtered like they had been in Calcutta and Noakhali. The 'nationalist, wise and brave act of the Hindus' was being repaid with extreme severity by the Congress government. The Hindus must, therefore, make it clear to the Congress that they would not allow the power they had given to be abused!

A faction in the Congress believed that an equally brutal response to the Muslim violence in Noakhali was necessary and justified. During the Bihar massacre, many of them believed that this was a justified reaction; they were convinced that it was the strong response in Bihar that kept the 'aggressive' Muslims in check nationwide. Even today, in many a case of communal strife, Congress leaders have been known to behave similarly. The glaring example was in 2002 in Gujarat. The administration and police were deeply infiltrated by active members of the communal extremist organizations. They, along with officers that supported the organizations, effectively sabotaged the government's attempts to bring the situation under control. In many places, they encouraged the acts of violence against the other religious groups and participated in them. 'It is curious,' wrote Nehru to Gandhi, 'how these very officers during the British regime carried out policies against India's national interests.'

Another incident that provoked communal violence occurred in Chapra, headquarters of the Sarna district, a town almost evenly populated by Hindus and Muslims. The festival of Diwali fell on 24 October that year. Due to the losses suffered by almost every family, the celebrations were very subdued. The Hindu Mahasabha instigated the Hindus to celebrate the day by seeking vengeance upon those who had turned their Diwali 'dark'. A prominent Muslim League leader congratulated a gathering of Muslims and asked them to rejoice as they had forced the Hindus to observe a joyless festival, '*Aaj Hinduon ke ghar mein maatam manaya ja raha hai. Hum logon ko aaj jashan manana chahiye.*' (Today there is mourning in Hindu homes. Let us celebrate it by feasting and rejoicing.)

On 25 October, public meetings to condemn the massacres of Hindus in Bengal were held in many towns in Bihar, further aggravating an already tense situation. The government had permitted the meetings hoping that by doing so, the pent-up rage would be purged. Instead, it led to igniting an out-of-control inferno. By late afternoon and early evening, riots erupted at nine places in Chapra. Heavily armed mobs took to the streets. Overall, fifty communal incidents were reported. Police opened fire on three occasions at three different places. Several instances of stabbing and rioting were reported. Rioting continued on the 26th; the superintendent of police stopped a large Hindu mob from attacking Muslim Bastis in Chapra by firing thirty rounds. He was successful in dispersing this particular mob, but trouble rapidly spread to the rural areas of the district and continued in a planned manner for the next five days before it was stopped.

The Bihar carnage is graphically described by Pyarelal in *Mahatma Gandhi: The Last Phase, Vol. 10, Part I, Book Two*:

'The local Congress leaders began to arrive in the town from 26 October. They started touring the interior. On their way, they encountered mobs sometimes numbering 50,000. The mobs turned back when they were told that what they were doing might cost them Gandhi's life. By 27 October, all the Congress leaders of the district had arrived and after forming themselves into batches penetrated into the villages. From 28 October onward, no planned attack was reported at any place in the district. The chief minister, Sri Babu, arrived in Chapra on 28 October, in company of his colleague Dr Syed Mahmud. What they saw flabbergasted them. "We started (by plane from Ranchi) on 28 October and reached Chapra the same night. About hundred houses had been burnt in the town. About six thousand people had taken refuge in the district school and were in a very bad plight. The next day we went to Paigambarpur. It is a big village. About fifty houses had been burnt here. A similar number of men, women and children had been murdered and burnt in these houses. The police were there. The Muslims said that the Sub-Inspector had joined the rioters. As soon as we reached Chapra, we sent some Congressmen. These people reached Paigambarpur by 3:00 a.m., even then they extricated three people from the fire and saved their lives. The police by that time had disappeared. When Sri Babu, the chief minister, and I went there, we saw some frightened women sitting under a tree crying. Skulls and bones met our feet as we trod through the lanes. A man, who had been burnt to charcoal, was found in a sitting posture in one house. In another house the fire was still smouldering. The door outside had been locked. One woman caught hold of our feet and began to cry. She said that the village watchman had snatched her baby from her lap and cut it into two. Sri Babu could not check his tears. He mentioned the incident next day in his speech at Muzaffarpur. Another woman said that she had given all her savings amounting to some thousands in order that the rioters might spare her two little children. The money was taken, and then the children were slaughtered in her presence. Most of the villagers were middle class people. Many Muslims complained that the Hindu collector of Chapra had played an important part in the riot. Some of the things that he was reported to have done and said were beyond description." (From Dr Mahmud's report to Gandhi, 17 February 1947.) On 31 October they returned to Patna. Reports of disturbances in Patna district and town were sent in. "We sent for the Brigadier in charge of the military to provide military assistance. He said it was unnecessary. In the evening, news came that a large number of wounded, including a proportion of old men, women and children, had arrived at Patna and Taregna stations. Two of the wounded women were pregnant, about 50 bodies were lying on the Taregna station even two or three days after." The next day, they went to Ranchi to see the General in command of the military forces. From the air, they saw below a big village in flames. A mob of ten thousand was surrounding it. "People were literally imprisoned in their homes. Women and children had assembled on their thatched roofs weeping and wailing piteously. They frantically waved their arms to draw our attention as our plane passed overhead. Sri Babu could not stand it. He wept." On 2 November, while returning to Patna after meeting the General, they again saw several villages burning and mobs engaged in looting. Some villages were completely deserted; others were besieged by mobs. In the afternoon, they made another flight over Patna district and saw several more villages burning.

'All this took place within a distance of ten to fifteen miles from Patna, the capital of the province. "The indifference and negligence of the district officers," reported Dr Mahmud to Gandhi, "seemed to beggar description." In the words of Nehru, "even if they had walked, they could have reached the sites of occurrence in time."

'Dr Mahmud's report continued: "About three and half lakh (three hundred and fifty thousand) Muslims are said to have fled from Bihar to different places after selling their gold ornaments at a ridiculous price and their homes and property for a song. In one village alone of Tilhari, I saw five wells full of dead bodies and another ten to twelve wells similarly choked with the dead in Dharla village. Where there was a river in the vicinity, the dead bodies were thrown into it. Their numbers cannot be ascertained. Those killed include a high proportion of old men, women and children. There was a large number of infants in arms among the wounded in hospitals. Some women told me how their little ones were murdered in their laps."'

From Chapra (Saran district), the trouble spread to Monghyr, Bhagalpur, Santhal Paraganas, Patna and Gaya districts. On 25 October, a procession was taken out in Patna to observe 'East Bengal Day'. It terminated in a big meeting at Bankipur Maidan, presided over by Prof. Abdul Bari, the Muslim president of the provincial Congress committee. Highly objectionable slogans were shouted by a section of the procession, in spite of the assurance of the organizers that this would not happen. Attempts were made at the meeting to pass a resolution calling on Hindus to avenge Noakhali. These were resisted by the president and some other prominent persons present. This happened the following day also. But unlike Chapra, with the exception of one stabbing incident, trouble was averted as a result of elaborate precautions taken by the authorities.

Muslim Leaguers also played their part in inflaming the situation in Patna. On the night of 27 October, they took to the streets armed with lethal weapons. The mob ran down the streets of Muslim dominated areas of Patna shouting the battle cry *Allah-o-Akbar!* Gathering Muslims from these areas, they brought them to pre-designated centres; here, they were supplied with arms and ammunition and instructed to be prepared for the signal to launch attacks. A railway line separated the Muslim-dominated areas from the Hindu areas of Patna. The frenzied sloganeering of the Muslim extremists brought out the Hindu mobs from the adjoining localities in thousands. The two mobs now faced each other, across the railway tracks. The Patna police, assisted by many Congress leaders, rushed to the spot and took up position on the railway tracks, right in between the mobs. After a lot of persuasion, the mobs retreated. A section of the Hindu mob regrouped at Kumarhar village near Patna city, while another mob gathered in another village close by. The police intercepted both the mobs before they could go on a rampage. This was on 28 October; thereafter, the trouble spread to the rural areas of Patna district, which then became the worst affected. Reports of large-scale rioting and arson were received from the Phulwari Sharif and Poonpoon police stations on 29 and 30 October, followed by the news of the first terrible massacre at Masaurhi. The riots then spread in the south-east towards Biharsharif and the northern border of the Jehanabad subdivision in the district of Gaya.

As early as 27 October, the local authorities at Patna, after consultations with the commissioner, had requested for military assistance to control the situation. But until the 31st, the inspector-general of police, Creed, was of the opinion that the situation was well under control. On 31 October, the request for immediate military assistance was made again. The Brigadier in charge of the military garrison dismissed the request saying that it was not necessary as the situation was not 'nearly so bad as that of 1942', referring to the stray incidences of violence that had erupted during the Quit India movement. Magistrates accompanied by troops finally took up positions in the interior of the Patna subdivision on 3 and 4 November. By the 5th, Gandhi's partial fast as a penance for the Bihar disturbances had commenced. Thousands of leaflets carrying the news about Gandhi's partial fast and his resolve to go on a fast unto death were distributed all over.

Nehru and Patel, accompanied by Liaquat Ali Khan and the infamous Sardar Abdur Rab Nishtar, arrived in Patna on 3 November. Dr Rajendra Prasad, Maulana Azad and Acharya Kripalani joined them soon after, followed by the viceroy. Addressing a big gathering in Patna on the 6th,

Nehru said, 'It is a matter of shame for me to come down here and ask you to observe the basic principles of civilized conduct when so many problems, national and international, are facing us and need solution. By no standard of civilized conduct can acts of lawlessness and killing of neighbours be justified. There can be no justification for stooping to bestiality, simply because some fellows have lost their heads elsewhere. What is happening in the Province is pure and simple hooliganism and it is your first and foremost duty to stop it at once at all costs. You cannot shift the responsibility by simply saying that you did not take part in it individually.' Dr Rajendra Prasad told people that his district was being tainted. The government was determined to handle it with the use of force. Kripalani remarked, 'By indulging in such acts, you have only helped your enemies inside and outside the country and have proved traitors to the country's cause.'

On the night of 6 November, Nehru sent a report to Gandhi in which he described how the poor were suffering the brunt of the disturbances. He also mentioned a change in the Bihar situation. 'On the whole the situation is quietening down,' he said. During their flight over Patna, Monghyr and Gaya on the 7th, they found 'the general outlook to be very peaceful, with peasants tilling the field'. By the 8th, Nehru wrote: 'As far as one can judge, the mass movement against the Muslims is over.' There was a new tendency visible, which was hopeful: 'Muslims suggested that the evacuees should return to their villages where they still existed, so as to look after their property which they had left in a hurry, and to cut their paddy crops which were ripe. There was a danger otherwise of these being cut and taken away by others. Thus, the primary instinct of self-preservation was giving place to the love of property. This in itself was indication of the return of some measure of normality.'

Of the sixteen districts, six had been affected by the riots. According to government figures, 9,869 homes were damaged or destroyed; 2,186 rounds were fired by the police and military, killing 393 people and injuring 100. Although it was difficult to estimate the exact number of those murdered, the government said the number of Muslims killed in the riots was in the region of 5,400. The Friends Services Unit estimated that the number killed was 10,000. The truth lay somewhere between these two figures.

The Bihar killings ultimately partitioned India. After this, there was no looking back: events spiralled out of control, finally leading to the division of India and the massive exchange of population which till then was harped on only by Jinnah and his Muslim League, but was considered impractical and unnecessary by both the Congress and the colonial administration. Bihar was the opportunity the Muslim League was waiting for.

The Bihar Muslim League published a report on the riots on 1 December, which was widely publicized by the Muslim League-sponsored press all over India. The leaders of the Congress party and the government were accused of having formed 'an underground council of war against the Muslims which planned and executed the massacres of Muslims and worked as the High Command of the campaign of mass killing'. The premier of the province, Sri Krishna Sinha, who was considered even by the Muslims as their true friend and benefactor, was branded a murderer and accused of having issued 'written orders under his own signature to government officers that no help is to be given for evacuation and rescue work and that this order is to be strictly followed'. Jayprakash Narayan, the socialist leader who had severely criticized the Congress and had publicly accused many Congressmen of having participated in the riots, was himself targeted by the League and labelled an 'ultra communalist'. The League's accusations were so reckless and farfetched that Nehru was forced to denounce them emphatically: 'The report is so wild and irresponsible that it becomes impossible to attach importance to what they say.'

The Muslim League's effort was ably helped by the Hindu extremists comprising the Hindu Mahasabha and RSS, as well as by the Congress's follies. Syed Abdul Aziz, a prominent Muslim League leader and bitter critic of Gandhi, compiled a very damaging report which showed how far the police and civic administration was guilty of aiding and abetting the rioters and their criminal inaction. His research showed that although Muslims were murdered, raped and mutilated and their properties pillaged, in many cases within a few yards of but no more than two miles from a police station or a magistracy, no action was taken for days to save the lives or property of the victims. For instance, Poonpoon and Hilsa were within a hundred yards of a police station; Masaurhi and Taregna railway stations within 300 and 400 yards, respectively; Chistipore and Palawapore within half a mile; Attasarai and Manaura within one mile and Kaila within a mile and a half from the police station. In all these places, Muslims were systematically murdered and their properties looted. Abdul Aziz concluded his damaging statement saying: 'If the officials and police had any sense of their duty and determination to protect the Muslims, at least 100 constables, 15 sub inspectors, 10 inspectors, 2 District Superintendents of Police, 10 Magistrates and 2 District Magistrates should have allowed themselves to be killed or injured before they allowed thousands of men, women and children under their direct charge to be slaughtered mercilessly.'

Relief measures and compensations announced by the government reached the survivors at a criminally slow pace. In Benibad, ₹45,000 was sanctioned to be distributed amongst the Muslim survivors, but it was disbursed only after six months, when Gandhi reached the village. *The Statesman*, in a series of articles on the Bihar riots, was severely critical about the way the riots were handled. An article appearing on 8 November, titled 'Disgrace Also', stated: 'A pogrom of such magnitude could hardly happen without premonitory signs. Yet the local administration seems to have been caught unawares.' Another article published on 13 November said: 'Not only does Bihar's tragedy resemble Bengal's worse one in severity, there can be found dismal similarity in other particulars. Governors slow moving or not on the spot; Ministers apparently at the outset divided in mind whether some rioting would not be good or bad, and later, amidst the crises of carnage, quite incapable of disciplining the mob… The Governor's absence at the critical time has indeed evoked remark.'

After the riots were brought under control, the Congress committed a grave blunder. It was a foregone conclusion that there would be a mass movement of Muslims fleeing the riot-torn regions. The government immediately set about establishing refugee camps. To blunt the virulent attack launched by the Muslim League, the shell-shocked Bihar government handed over the responsibility of establishing and running the camps to the Muslim League. Systematically, the League started establishing the camps in such a way that they could segregate the Muslim victims and concentrate them in regions in a manner whereby they could claim maximum territory in the cause of establishing a Muslim homeland. The camps were virtually closed to the Congress. The relief material sent by the Bihar government was claimed to have been sent by Jinnah. Many camps were taken over by bands of Khaksars, volunteers and other fanatic elements; they commandeered a major part of the relief material and rations for their own use. The resulting scarcity was blamed on the Bihar government, thus further aggravating anger amongst the victims. They were made to believe that they would find safety only when they had their own country.

Khan Abdul Ghaffar Khan, the Baluchi leader and Pathan chieftain who had, along with his tribe, given up the path of violence and formed the brigade of Red Shirts—the Khudai Khidmatgars, servants of God—was prevailed upon by the Congress and several non-Congress people to visit Bihar after the riots. Such was the respect that he had earned from one and all by virtue of his selfless service, sincerity and moral fervour that he could speak with authority to both Hindus and Muslims alike. He did not mince words, and the Bihar ministers listened to him without rancour.

'India today seems an inferno of madness and my heart weeps to see our homes set on fire by ourselves,' Badshah Khan, as he was also known, remarked at a joint gathering of Hindus, Muslims and Sikhs held at Gurdwara Har Mandir Sahib, the birthplace of the tenth and last guru of the Sikhs, Guru Gobind Singhji, in Patna city. 'I find today darkness reigning over India and my eyes vainly turn from one direction to another to see light.' He was fed up of power politics, he said, and was deeply pained at the hatred which he saw being preached all over India. As a 'servant of God', he was eager only to serve suffering humanity. Reporting on the occasion, a press correspondent wrote: 'The sincerity of the man which shows so transparently in every word he says has left a deep impression on his audiences. There was nothing new in what he said. Nevertheless, the few simple words coming from a heavy heart struck an answering chord in many of his hearers. The scenes of fraternization which marked one of Frontier Gandhi's (another name Khan Abdul Ghaffar Khan was known by) meetings and the coming together of all communities in places of worship are reminiscent of the Khilafat days.'

Pyarelal has perfectly described the situation: 'The scene to which Gandhi was coming was thus chaotic and full of violence. He had to lead people to introspection and self examination; to turn hardened hearts to genuine repentance; to steady friends and win over foes even against what they mistook for their self-interest; to bring love where hatred and cunning ruled; and finally, to call a mighty organization that had forgotten itself, back to the path of duty, and thereby steady the foundations of democracy, shaking at its very inception. His non-violence was called to the supreme test. Bihar became another outpost in his "do or die" mission.'

Gandhi arrived in Bihar on 5 March 1947. He immediately beckoned Dr Syed Mahmud and Prof. Abdul Bari, the Muslim president of the provincial Congress committee, both of them old colleagues and staunch nationalists. 'So, you are still alive,' he remarked with joyless humour. Dr Mahmud's home was on the banks of the Ganga. During the following weeks, the Ganga played an integral and important role in Gandhi's life. It was his constant companion when he sat down by its bank after the evening prayer to write out his daily post-prayer address or received people for interviews during his evening walks.

Dr Rajendra Prasad, the former premier of Bihar, along with his party colleagues and members of the provincial Congress committee, met him at Dr Mahmud's residence. Gandhi sat surrounded by his old and trusted lieutenants, but his head was bowed with grief and anxiety.

The next morning, two workers, whom Khan Abdul Ghaffar Khan had left behind in Patna, came to meet him. Their report of the situation in the interiors deeply affected Gandhi. The vice-chancellor of Patna University, C.P.N. Sinha, came to meet him next and expressed great relief at his presence in Bihar. Gandhi informed him that he had requested Khan to join them. Sinha asked Gandhi what Khan had thought of the work being done there. Gandhi replied that the ministry was happy with everything, but it was the people, rather than the officers, who would be capable of dealing with the problems. Gandhi said that Khan had further suggested that there be a non-political committee for the purpose and he himself thought it was a good idea. Dr Rajendra Prasad joined them next. In his earlier meeting with Gandhi, he had mentioned that the Muslim League with its National Guard had been preparing for the fight. Arms had been imported into the province from Aligarh even after the outbreak of disturbances. To Gandhi, these statements sounded like a justification of the Hindu violence and was incompatible with genuine repentance. Rajendra Babu went on to say that an economic boycott of Muslims had been called by the Hindu Mahasabha and RSS combined, and was being imposed in many areas. To tear the two communities apart when their lives were so closely interlinked was totally unacceptable to Gandhi.

Late in the afternoon, he had a long meeting with the Bihar ministers. He suggested that a commission of inquiry be appointed. 'If we are not quick about the matter, it will lose its effect; we shall be held to have admitted the League's case.' Chief Minister Sri Krishna Sinha expressed the fear that the League would make political capital out of it. Gandhi admitted that it was a possibility, but it was a chance they had to take.

Many Congressmen were annoyed with Dr Mahmud for having called Gandhi to Bihar without consulting them. Gandhi tried to clear this misunderstanding, saying, 'Dr Mahmud's letter which has brought me to Bihar was in reply to my peremptory inquiries; he has not acted disloyally towards you.'

On the 7th, Gandhi received many delegations who wished to report on the Bihar situation. The first to do so were representatives of the Muslim Students' Federation, a student's group aligned to the Muslim League.

They told him that the only way Muslims could continue to live in Bihar was by either dividing the state or resettling the Muslim refugees in contiguous settlements. Gandhi refused both the demands, saying that he wanted to bridge the gap between the two communities and not widen it. The next to meet him was a delegation from the Jamiat-ul Ulema, a group representing Muslim religious leaders. Their complaint was that the Muslims were being threatened and intimidated. The Majlis-i-Ahrar, council of elders, reiterated the complaint. Jayprakash Narayan's testimony was extremely critical of the government and the Congress party. An even worse indictment of the Bihar government and the Congress came from the Momin community. They were traditional Congress supporters, yet they too alleged that many senior Congressmen were actively involved in the rioting incidents.

On 8 March, Mohammad Yunus came to meet Gandhi. He had been chief minister in the stop-gap ministry of Bihar before the Congress finally agreed to accept office in 1937. He said that those who had promoted or participated in the riots could be no friends of the Congress, even though they may carry the Congress badge. He complained that the Congress was responsible for the League's belligerence. If the Congressmen had displayed vision and broadmindedness earlier, things would not have come to this pass. Yunus was an old friend and Gandhi felt that he could be candid with him. He said, 'Could Jinnah be left out of the picture? Was it not up to those Muslims who thought that he was going the wrong way to try to correct him?' To this, Yunus replied, 'That cannot be. Either you follow Jinnah or you get out of the Muslim League.' Hearing this, Gandhi remarked, 'Then the future is dark indeed for Islam and for India; more for Islam than for India.'

On 11 March, the round of interviews continued. All the Muslim delegations that came to meet him pressed upon Gandhi to accept the idea of a division of Bihar on communal lines. Even the Jamiat-ul-Ulema, which claimed to be a nationalist organization, now advocated the implementation of the separatist solution. All the Muslim groups who met Gandhi in Bihar condemned the Congress most severely.

On 12 March, Gandhi began his tour of the interiors. The first village he visited was Kumarhar, barely three miles from Patna junction railway station. The mobs had neither spared the madrasa, the religious school, nor the masjid. It was the same in the next village Gandhi visited, which was Parsa. On the way, his car was stopped by villagers of Sipara, who presented a purse to him, which Gandhi discovered had some coins and a letter of repentance. Speaking that evening at Abdullah Chak, Gandhi remarked that he wanted every Indian to feel that he had a share in every evil deed committed anywhere in India, no matter by whom and against whom, and upon all lay the burden of undoing it. There were only two paths before the country, he remarked at Khusrupur, the next place he visited: the path of returning blow for blow, and that of unadulterated non-violence. The Champaran Satyagraha of 1917 was an education in the latter, but recent happenings in Bihar had forced him to the conclusion that their non-violence was that of the weak.

When Gandhi arrived in Patna, Badshah Khan was travelling in the interiors. From there, he wrote to Gandhi: 'You are right. Our Ahimsa is on test. When I see politicians surrounding us wrongly using the name of God and religion to propagate hatred, I begin to hate politics.' Immediately on learning about his whereabouts, Gandhi sent for him. From then, he became a constant companion, Gandhi's silent shadow, his rock-like support, till almost the very end.

16 March was Gandhi's day of weekly silence. He requested Badshah Khan to speak on his behalf after the evening prayers. In deep anguish, Badshah Khan said that he found himself surrounded by utter darkness, which increased the more he thought of the future of India. He could see no light despite his best efforts. If India was burnt down, all of them would be losers. He was a Khudai Khidmatgar, thus he was in their midst. He reminded them that their responsibility had greatly increased, especially after the British declaration that they would quit India in fifteen months. They had to remember that what could be achieved through peace could never be achieved through hatred or force. They had Europe as an example to learn from. Addressing the Muslim Leaguers in general, he added that if they desired Pakistan, they could have it only through love and willing consent, not by coercion.

The next phase of his tour through Bihar would take Gandhi through one of the worst affected areas, Masaurhi, where entire villages had been wiped out. When trouble broke out in other parts, the Muslims of Masaurhi began to congregate in their strongholds, strengthening the suspicions of an eminent attack that the Hindu Mahasabha and RSS had warned Hindu villagers about. On the night of 30 October, loud cries of '*Allah-O-Akbar!*' rent the air. What set off this sudden outburst of provocative sloganeering was never discovered, but it spread panic amongst the Hindus. The siren of a cloth mill owned by a local Hindu Mahasabha leader was sounded, Hindu 'volunteers' took to the streets shouting '*Mahabir Swami Ki Jai!*', a slogan in praise of Lord Mahavir, the Jain saint who had founded a religious sect devoted to non-violence. The Muslims quietened down. Some Congress workers interceded, ensured a temporary peace and both sides withdrew. The next day, some Muslims panicked and fled to the railway station to board any trains going to Patna. The mill owner spread a rumour that Muslims had attacked the railway station and in the skirmish that followed, some Hindus had been killed. A large mob of Hindus proceeded towards the railway station, where Muslims, mostly old men, women and children, were waiting to board trains to Patna. Over the next few hours, the station turned into an abattoir. Almost all the Muslims trapped at the station were caught and butchered. Some survived because of the presence of mind of an engine driver. His goods train was preparing to leave just as the attack began. The engine driver detached the engine from the wagons and headed towards the next junction, where he contacted the authorities and brought back a large troop of armed forces to Masaurhi. The mob set the ticket office on fire and the armed forces arrived just in time to save some of the Muslims who had taken refuge there.

When Gandhi arrived in Masaurhi four months later, only twenty-five Muslims from the original thousand inhabitants remained. Gandhi remarked that in a report that had been handed to him, it had been stated that the initial aggression in Masaurhi had come from the Muslims. However, he was not concerned as to how the trouble actually started or who started it. What he was concerned to know was how the Hindus, who were in such overwhelming majority, could indulge in the killing of innocents. The Muslims complained that the government was indifferent to their suffering. Gandhi added that he was not there to adjudicate; his was the humble role of a reformer and humanitarian.

On his way to the prayer meeting that evening, Gandhi visited Andari and Gorraiakhari, two villages in Masaurhi. Andari had a population of 462 Hindus and 168 Muslims before the riots. Muslims from the surrounding villages had congregated in Andari on 30 October 1946. When news of the Gorraiakhari massacre had reached the village, they were advised by the military to evacuate. But the Muslims were confident that, armed with a gun and a pistol, they could repel any attack. The attack came on 2 November; the three constables posted there for the protection of the Muslims opened fire, killing seven attackers, but were later forced to flee in the face of a large mob, according to a government report. When Gandhi visited the village, he did not find even one Muslim there. The government reports stated that till date, one case had been filed; of the twenty-nine accused, one had been arrested, another had surrendered in court, processes had been issued against the others, and thirteen persons in the area had been detained under the Bihar Maintenance of Public Order Ordinance of 1946. The Gorraiakhari village had a population of 400 Muslims and 20 Hindus. The government report stated that 119 Muslims were killed, 11 injured and 12 were missing. The village was completely deserted. Gandhi moved through the eerily silent lanes with a heavy heart. That evening, Gandhi was so grief-stricken he could not bring himself to speak. Instead, he utilized the meeting to collect donations for the Muslim victims from the congregation, as a mark of penance for the grave sin they had committed.

The following day, Gandhi camped at Bir, from where he undertook visits to the surrounding riot-ravaged villages. On 20 March, he returned to Masaurhi. Speaking after the evening prayer, he said, 'I am scared to describe the kind of devastation I have seen in the past few days, for fear of breaking down with grief. It is your duty to rebuild what you have so ruthlessly destroyed. You have committed a crime and it is for you to do penance for it.' He said that he would accept names for a volunteer corps for relief and rehabilitation for all the ravaged localities.

While Gandhi was trying to soothe the people, news of further trouble started pouring in from Punjab and Noakhali. The Muslim League, emboldened by the tacit support of the colonial administration, had launched 'Direct Action' in Punjab, in a similar manner as in Calcutta, with similar results. Agitated by the horrifying tales filtering through from Punjab, the Hindu Mahasabha and RSS began organizing their cadres to observe 'Punjab Day' as a day of revenge for the events in Punjab in an already volatile Bihar. The Muslim League announced its intention of observing 'Pakistan Day' in Bengal; the more the polarization, the more the hatred and suspicion, the better the political prospects for both the set of fanatics.

On 21 March, Gandhi shifted to Hasadiha village, where he met several Muslim refugees from surrounding villages; in the afternoon he met with village representatives. He advised them that normal relations would only be re-established if the Muslims withdrew all the criminal cases against the Hindu rioters.

On his return to Patna on 22 March, Gandhi spoke about his experiences over the six days he had travelled through the devastated villages at the evening prayer meeting. Patel had written to Gandhi that some peace seemed to have been established in the Punjab through military measures.

Gandhi arrived at Jehanabad station on 26 March 1947, to be welcomed by a huge crowd. Of the three subdivisions affected during the riots in Gaya district, Jehanabad was the worst. Two gangs were known to be the chief troublemakers. Some areas had managed to ward off the troublemakers with the help of locals. One such person was Sakal Babu, a local headmaster. With the help of his students and some locals, he had patrolled the surrounding villages of Daulatpur, Nagma and Rasalpur day and night until the entire Muslim population had been safely evacuated to Jehanabad. Nine months later, the Hindus of Daulatpur were still guarding Muslim homes. One Muslim told a member of Gandhi's entourage that his property had been so well protected that on returning home after he was reassured of his safety nine months after the riots, he found that the plate containing the half-eaten meal he had left hurriedly during the riots was still lying undisturbed!

When Gandhi reached Jehanabad, Mridula Sarabhai, who was travelling with him, without consulting him, asked the authorities to make appropriate arrangements for Gandhi and his entourage. When Gandhi realized that his promise to the Muslim Leaguers, that he would live with local Muslims in every village, would be broken due to this arrangement, he tried to send a message to them explaining the situation. But the Leaguers had already taken affront, and without giving him a chance to explain, condemned Gandhi for breach of promise. This was released to the press and widely publicized amongst the Muslims of Jehanabad. Gandhi was saddened; he felt that they should have allowed him to apologize and explain the situation before condemning him.

After resting for a bit, Gandhi visited the refugee camp at Kako village, which had about five hundred Muslims. Some of them were from Saistabad in Ghosi police station, the worst affected police station in the subdivision.

The next day, Gandhi visited the refugee camp at Amathua village, a predominantly Muslim village: they had escaped an attack due to the arrival of the military in the nick of time.

At Ghosi, a representative of the Muslims came to meet Gandhi and said that Muslims had faith only in him; they trusted no one else. He expressed the worry that the Muslims would suffer again once Gandhi left Bihar. Gandhi said that he had conferred with the government and had met almost all the leaders of the provincial Muslim League; he would see that justice was done to the Muslims. There had been a constant demand that at least 50 per cent of the policemen and officers in charge of new police stations that were being established to create confidence should be Muslims. Gandhi refused to support any such demand here, 'Therefore, I say, there is no other course to Hindus and Muslims than to be friends one of the other.'

The Muslim League alleged that by repeatedly referring to Noakhali in his public speeches in Bihar, he was likely to make the Hindus think that what they had done was a justifiable reaction to Noakhali. Gandhi said that the inference was incorrect, for he had not spared the Hindus. In fact, there was a time when he used to be equally plain spoken with the Muslims, too. The Muslims did not then regard him as their enemy. But of late, he had to confess, that when he spoke about Muslims, he did so very guardedly. 'I avoid references to Noakhali as much as I can. But to avoid it altogether would not be right. I must not remain silent in the face of the disturbing news that keeps coming in from Noakhali and the Punjab, if only for the sake of the Bihar Muslims. The two are so interlinked.'

During the latter part of March 1947, Bihar Police went on a lightning strike. This added to the crises in Bihar. Ever since his arrival in Bihar, Gandhi had realized that the infiltration of communal elements in the police was one of the main reasons for the success of the rioters and the extent of the carnage.

A special train brought Gandhi's party back to Patna on 28 March at 10:00 p.m. Some members of the entourage left immediately by car, taking a shorter route to reach the camp earlier than the main party. They were greeted at the camp entrance by a couple of grave-faced Congressmen. Prof. Abdul Bari, the Muslim president of the Bihar provincial Congress committee, had been shot dead by a Gorkha sentry of the anti-smuggling force that evening. While returning from a trip to the rural areas, Prof. Bari's car had been stopped and challenged by the sentries of the anti-smuggling force. The sentry pointed his gun at Prof. Bari, when he failed to respond. Prof. Bari was known for his short and volatile temper, and on seeing a gun pointed at him, he jumped out of the car and rushed forward to snatch the rifle from the sentry. The other sentry, without waiting to ascertain the identity of the person, shot him at point-blank range. In losing Bari, Bihar had lost one of its most noble and illustrious sons and an astute nationalist Muslim. Gandhi grieved the loss of Prof. Bari at such a critical juncture.

On 30 March 1947, Gandhi left for Delhi in response to an invitation from the new viceroy, Lord Mountbatten. He planned to return to Bihar after a fortnight. The viceroy had extended an invitation to both Jinnah and Gandhi. He had offered to send his personal York aircraft to pick Gandhi up from Patna, but the offer was declined. Gandhi would travel by a regular train in his favourite third-class coach. Mridula Sarabhai had booked two compartments on both sides of the one in which Gandhi was travelling to provide a buffer between him and other passengers. But nothing escaped Gandhi's eye. At midnight, when the train halted at a station, he called for the station master and told him to open the adjoining compartment to the general public.

Arrangements had been made for him to disembark at a small station near Delhi. As he was being driven to his residence in the Harijan Colony, he requested the driver to stop, saying it was time for his morning walk; he got out of the car and walked the rest of the way.

At three that afternoon, Gandhi met the new viceroy for the first time. Very little or almost no politics was discussed. The viceroy asked Gandhi about his early life and education in England, about his fight for equal rights in South Africa and the early years of Satyagraha. Gandhi was equally eager to meet Mountbatten and discover the man behind the title. They both knew that this was their last chance to hammer out a peaceful settlement of the Indo-British question. Gandhi was greatly impressed by the new viceroy's apparent sincerity, gentlemanliness and nobility of character.

Gandhi woke at three the next morning, his usual time, even though he had retired very late the previous night. At 5:00 a.m., Rajkumari Amrit Kaur came to see him; Maulana Azad followed at half past six. This was followed by meetings with Nehru, Rajaji, Rajendra Babu and lastly Patel, who took him to meet the viceroy. Gandhi's lunch was brought to him in the middle of the meeting by Manu and one of his secretaries,

Brijkrishna Chandiwala. On being introduced to Manu, the viceroy told her, 'You are a lucky girl. My daughter tells me that she feels jealous of you on seeing your photograph with Mr Gandhi. I shall be sending her to attend your prayer meeting.' Gandhi asked the viceroy if Manu could roam the gardens so that they could continue their talks uninterrupted. 'Certainly,' replied the viceroy, 'all this is yours; we are only trustees. We have come to hand it over to you.'

The talks started from where they had been left the previous day. The viceroy told Gandhi that it had always been British policy not to yield anything to force, but Gandhi's non-violence had won. They had decided to quit as a result of India's non-violent movement for freedom. Towards the close of the meeting, Gandhi placed before the viceroy his solution for the Indian deadlock. He reiterated what he had often said: 'He had no objections to Jinnah or the Muslim League turning the whole of India into Pakistan, provided it was done by appeal to reason and not under the threat of violence. But while he had previously held that this could be done only after the British had quit India, and while in principle he still adhered to the view, the crux of his present proposal was that he was now prepared, under Mountbatten's umpireship, not as a Viceroy but as an unbiased individual, to invite Jinnah to form a government of his choice at the Centre and to present his Pakistan plan for acceptance even before the transfer of power. The Congress would give its wholehearted support to the Jinnah government. At the same time, since the Muslim League would now be the government, it would have no further excuse for continuing the movement of organized lawlessness which it had launched in some of the provinces. These must be called off. Further, since the Viceroy had declared that he was out to do justice only and nothing would be yielded to force, if the League did not accept the offer, the same offer *mutatis mutandis* should be made to the Congress. The old policy of trying to please both parties must be given up.'

Mountbatten was faced with a dilemma: he liked the proposal but it went against his duties as viceroy. His preference naturally was in terms of his directive for a solution 'which leaves such good feeling that the Indian parties will want to remain in the Commonwealth'. The British felt that the Congress would be anti-British and their true allies were Jinnah and his Muslim League. The 'anti-British bias' of the Congress was an erronious assumption, but their pet prejudice prevailed and the colonial administration threw its weight against Gandhi's plan. This would force them to choose between the Congress and the League and drop one or the other 'packet', as Lord Morley referred to the two, from the Commonwealth bag. Gandhi told the viceroy, that the 'British policy of divide and rule' had brought about a situation in which the only alternative to a continuation of the British rule, which they had found was no longer feasible, was to accept the logic of the Quit India demand and retire unconditionally, leaving India to its fate. The role of peacemaker in the 'communal triangle' which they had themselves helped create was not for them.

Like his predecessor, Mountbatten too was trying to ride to many horses simultaneously. Although he wished to deliver the best possible solution for the transfer of power plan, he was hampered by the mechanizations of his staff, the colonial political department, Jinnah, and his own divided loyalty towards his cousin the King and His Majesty's government. In trying to please everyone, he ignored Gandhi's continued warnings.

Gandhi's tragedy was that now no one was willing to listen to him or follow his advice; they wanted him to be a decorative figurehead, to be used when required, but they were not willing to travel in the direction he was pointing. Thus, at every stage of the crucial talks leading up to the transfer of power, they ignored Gandhi.

Mountbatten, after having extensive communications and dialogue with Gandhi, claimed that Gandhi had misunderstood him and backtracked on almost every agreement and understanding they had arrived at, be it Gandhi's proposal for transfer of power, Gandhi's warnings about the continuous patronage to Jinnah or even when the initiative was his own, as in the joint peace appeal that Mountbatten had proposed and was issued with the signatures of Jinnah, Mountbatten and Gandhi at his behest. When it was known that Jinnah and the Muslim League continued with their campaign of violence and terror, Mountbatten refused to heed Gandhi's appeal to him to force Jinnah to comply. When Gandhi reminded him that he was a cosignatory, Mountbatten claimed that the responsibility was Gandhi's and Jinnah's; his was merely a representative signature. Thus, at every stage, Gandhi found that he was sidelined and isolated by the viceroy, his colonial administration and his own people.

Gandhi strove with the CWC for the acceptance of the plan he had outlined to the viceroy. There were heated discussions, confused counsels, frayed nerves. Gandhi and Badshah Khan were strongly opposed to any partition under British aegis. To Gandhi's mind, for the Congress to ask for partition of the Punjab and Bengal by the British sounded like a counsel of despair. He was opposed to the entire idea of partition; it would solve none of their difficulties. On the contrary, it would accentuate those that were already there and create fresh ones. But he could not convince them, nor they him. Defeated, he informed the viceroy of his failure to carry the Working Committee with him. His colleagues and he had come to a parting of ways.

The Punjab was burning. The Muslim League had unleashed a reign of terror there too. Hindus were being terrorized, their properties looted and burned, their lands usurped, their women defiled and the minority community massacred. The stories of the atrocities in western Punjab were inflaming the rest of north India. A steady flow of Hindu and Sikh refugees fleeing West Punjab began seeking refuge in New Delhi and its outskirts. Their numbers were increasing by the day. Fanatic Hindu organizations began infiltrating the refugee camps and encouraging people to take revenge. All of north India was waiting to explode. The leaders were busy negotiating the transfer of power. Gandhi was the exception, but he was isolated, abandoned.

Gandhi returned from the penultimate session of the Asian Conference in time for the evening prayer meeting. As soon as the recitation from the Koran commenced, a Hindu Mahasabha–RSS youth stood up and shouted, 'This is a Hindu temple, we will not let you recite Muslim prayers here.' Volunteers tried to remove him from the meeting, but Gandhi intervened. 'I shall not proceed with the prayer so long as there is a single person objecting. I want to ensure the fullest freedom to the dissenting minority.' The young man tried to work his way up to the rostrum but was prevented from doing so. Gandhi moved halfway down to meet him, saying, 'Let no one come between me and this young man.' The same sequence of events occurred the following day as well. On the third evening, as Gandhi was proceeding to the prayer ground, a letter was given to him, supposedly written by the president of the sweepers' union, telling Gandhi to leave as they did not wish him to stay in Bhangi Colony any longer; the letter was found to be fake. That evening, too, three people objected to his reciting verses from the Koran. Thus, each day, his Ahimsa was put to test. The conspiracy to murder Gandhi had moved up a gear.

On the fourth day, he woke up with the thought: 'Why does the opposition at the evening prayer still persist?' He told Manu that his striving for non-violence and truth could be nullified not only by a mistake on his part, but even by flaws in his colleagues. Since she was conducting the prayers, it was for her to ask herself whether the verses she uttered came from the fullness of her faith. The fanatical opposition to the prayers must cease if her prayers came straight from her heart. He was greatly troubled; after a talk with Maulana Azad, he sadly remarked: 'It seems God will not let me live for long.'

After a week of protests at his prayer meetings, a leader of the RSS came to see him and assured him that there would be no more interruptions at his prayer meetings. The RSS had achieved their objective of establishing in the public mind that angry refugees were disturbed by Gandhi's inclusion of prayers from the Koran. It was these angry refugees who were protesting at Gandhi's prayer meeting. The plan to murder Gandhi was to make it look as if an enraged refugee had murdered Gandhi.

'Let no one imagine,' Gandhi observed, in his after prayer discourse, 'that we have had no prayer for the last week. We did not pray with our lips but we prayed with our hearts, which is by far the more effective part of prayer. In this those who have opposed have also helped, though unconsciously. Their opposition has helped me to turn the searchlight inward as never before. You might be tempted to ask what I mean by giving so much of my time and energy to such trifles, when negotiations are in progress with Lord Mountbatten on which hangs the fate of the nation. Let me tell you, for me there is no big, no small. They are all of equal importance. In Noakhali, in Bihar, in Punjab, in Delhi, even in this prayer ground, the battle of undivided India is being lost and won daily.'

6 April marked the commencement of National Service Week. It was on this day in 1919 that Satyagraha against the Rowlatt Act was launched, by observing the day as one of prayer and fasting throughout India.

The spontaneous mass upsurge it evoked was a soul-stirring spectacle, signalling the awakening of India. A week later, the Jallianwala Bagh massacre in Amritsar occurred.

Khwaja Saheb Abdul Majid, a nationalist Muslim leader and a very old friend of Gandhi, came to see him during National Service Week. He was deeply grieved by the impending division of India, but tried to laugh away his sorrow. 'Bapuji is now going to drive us out of India in our old age,' he remarked. 'When India is divided, I shall come to take asylum with you. You won't let the Hindus murder me.' Gandhi interjected, 'If a fanatic should kill you, I will dance with joy! My misfortune is that I don't have many like you who would die bravely and without anger. If I had even half a dozen like you, the flames that threaten to devour us would be put out and peace would reign in India in no time.' Little did Gandhi know then that just nine months later, Khwaja Saheb would recite the Fateha, the Muslim funeral prayer, over Gandhi's bullet-riddled body.

The summer of 1947 was one of the hottest Delhi had experienced in a long time. Gandhi wrapped a wet cloth over his head, his 'air-conditioning', but a far more sinister and volatile wind of hatred was blowing across his beloved land, threatening to consume all in its path. Outwardly, Gandhi appeared calm and serene, but his mind was in turmoil. He was being flooded with hate mail; he was called names like 'Mohammad Gandhi', 'Maulana Gandhi', 'Communalist' and 'Jinnah's slave'. All of them amused Gandhi. He said, 'It is the people who conferred the title of Mahatma, these epithets, too, are a gift from them; they are equally welcome.' Even today, liberal voices in India are targeted by the rabid communal forces with similar abuse and name-calling, similar 'titles' were used to abuse Gandhi, too.

'People's minds are perturbed,' remarked Gandhi on the evening of 10 April. 'They ask me whether Lord Mountbatten would be able to deliver the goods or whether he would be forced to eat his words in the face of organized non-cooperation of the various entrenched British elements in India. Anything is possible in the prevailing circumstances. The dawn of freedom has appeared but we do not feel the glow of its sunrise. We do not know whether what we see is true dawn or false. We are trembling between hope and fear. So far, the British officials and commercial interests have ridden on our backs. Let me tell them, it's now high time that they made up their mind to get off. The Viceroy has declared that the British have decided to withdraw from India by 30 June next year, his declaration is backed by the full authority of the British parliament. Churchill and his party seem determined not to give in without a fight. But fight or no fight, the British power has got to go. I have sounded this note of warning so that if there are any elements again heading for the wrong path, they may pause, reflect and desist. I am told that the British officials and the commercial community are behind the present communal trouble. Lord Mountbatten has become apprehensive, lest what is being alleged against them may after all be true. It is up to the British elements in India to dispel his doubts. The success of Lord Mountbatten's mission is bound up with the loyal cooperation of British commercial interests, the British army and the British civilians in India. If what is being said about them is true, it is a tragedy, they are not being loyal either to the people of India or to their own. I appeal to them to help the Viceroy in the peaceful transfer of power. I hope the Britishers will leave India not as enemies but as friends.'

On 12 April, Gandhi left for Patna.

All of them, Mountbatten, the CWC and the Muslim League, for selfish reasons, differing one from the other, went together into the same cry of 'freedom at any cost'; the 'nation's voice' became a 'voice in the wilderness' in the arena of high politics in the crucial hour of the birth of a nation.

With her motherly instinct, Sarojini Naidu discerned the pathos of the situation, she sensed Gandhi's utter loneliness, the wide gulf that separated him from his friends and opponents alike. This was sending him once again to plough his lonely furrow in Bihar, where over a quarter of a century ago he had made his debut in Indian politics and launched upon a career which, in the course of a single generation, had changed the face of the country. She wrote to Gandhi:

Beloved Pilgrim

You are, I learn, setting out once more on your chosen *Via Dolorosa* in Bihar.

The way of sorrow for you may indeed be the way of hope and solace for many millions of suffering human hearts. Blessed be your pilgrimage.

I am still incredibly weak or I should have attempted to reach Bhangi Colony to bid you farewell.

But even though I do not see you, you know that my love is always with you and my faith.

Your Ammajan,

Sarojini

Back in Bihar, after the stifling heat and even more stifling political atmosphere of Delhi, Gandhi felt ill at ease. He had reasoned with the leaders of all sections and failed. The only thing that could possibly prevent the partition of India now was a radical change in the overall situation. Verbal persuasion alone would not do the trick. However, he would have to set about creating a milieu in which the parties would be compelled to think afresh, but he was running out of time.

Gandhi was to be in Bihar for less than three weeks, but he made a supreme effort for the well-being of the people there. Since the days of the Champaran Satyagraha, Gandhi had always held the people of Bihar close to his heart. The betrayal, by his own, caused him extreme anguish. Two days later, he severely took to task a section of Hindus who had complained against the levying of punitive tax on an area where the locals were not helping the authorities arrest absconders accused of crimes during the riots. 'How disloyal of you to shelter fugitives from justice! You complain that innocent people are being victimized for the misdeeds of the hooligans, but when the government wants to take action to make people cooperate in the arrest of the criminals, you raise a hue and cry. True, those who are harbouring the absconders are few, but the remedy is in your hands. You should bring to light the real culprits so many don't have to suffer for the sins of a few.'

Gandhi's sharpest criticism was reserved for the Bihar ministers, whom he met just before departing for Delhi. He had received a complaint that they were not implementing the rehabilitation policy they had agreed to in his presence. 'I am told that the ministers tell me one thing and do another,' he said to them. 'That is not how we shall be able to attain or to maintain independence. If you nod assent merely to flatter me, you are being unfaithful to me, to your people and to your trust. I do not claim to be infallible. If what I say does not appeal to you, you should straightaway tell me so and try to convince me of my error. By nodding a formal assent when you actually believe me to be wrong, you wrong me and put yourself in the wrong. You must realize that what is happening in the Punjab, Bihar and Bengal is hindering Indian independence.'

That night, he went to bed at half past nine. Due to the tormenting heat, he had reduced his food intake to the barest minimum. As a result, he was feeling weak and his blood pressure had risen. After lying down, he remembered that he had forgotten to do his day's quota of spinning, his 'bread labour'. He got out of bed, prepared the spinning wheel and faithfully spun the daily quota. Only then did he once again lay down and go to sleep, at peace with himself.

29 April 1947 was the last day of Gandhi's stay in Bihar. While bidding farewell to Bihar in his post-prayer speech that evening, he requested the people to show their affection towards him by working for communal unity and not by thronging at railway stations to bid him farewell. 'At this age I cannot stand the shouting of the crowds. Moreover, I hate to hear "*Jai!*" shouts, they remind me of the Hindus who massacred innocent Muslim men and women while shouting such slogans, just as the Muslims killed Hindus shouting "*Allah-o-Akbar!*" I know of no greater sin than to oppress the innocent in the name of God!' This practice continues, even today in India; shouts of '*Jai Shree Ram*!' have become synonymous with the intimidation and subjugation of Muslims.

With this message, Gandhi took leave of Bihar. He was going back to the national capital, where more political intrigue awaited him. He was certain that he would not be able to wean his political colleagues away from the path they had chosen. He had also realized that his influence over them had waned; they had found a new guiding light in Lord Mountbatten. Gandhi was doubtful how effective his stay would be in influencing the course of events, but the eternal optimist was keen to try his best. If his faith in the power of truth and Ahimsa did not waver, he would find a way, and he felt certain that even at the proverbial eleventh hour, he would be able to steer his country away from partition and the resulting human tragedy. Unfortunately, time knew that he would not succeed.

Gandhi addressing worshippers at the dargah of Khwaja Qutub-ud-Din Bakhtiar Kaki at Mehrauli and inside the dargah on 27 January 1948.

News of Gandhi's visit to the Mehrauli urs appearing in the Hindustan Times *on 28 January 1948.*

Gandhi flanked by Abha and Manu, his 'walking sticks', at Birla House.

The route taken by Gandhi as he walked from his room in Birla House to where he was murdered on 30 January 1948.

The spot where Gandhi fell on 30 January 1948. Inset: The stone tablet installed at the spot.

Women from Gandhi's retinue and from the Birla household mourn beside his body.

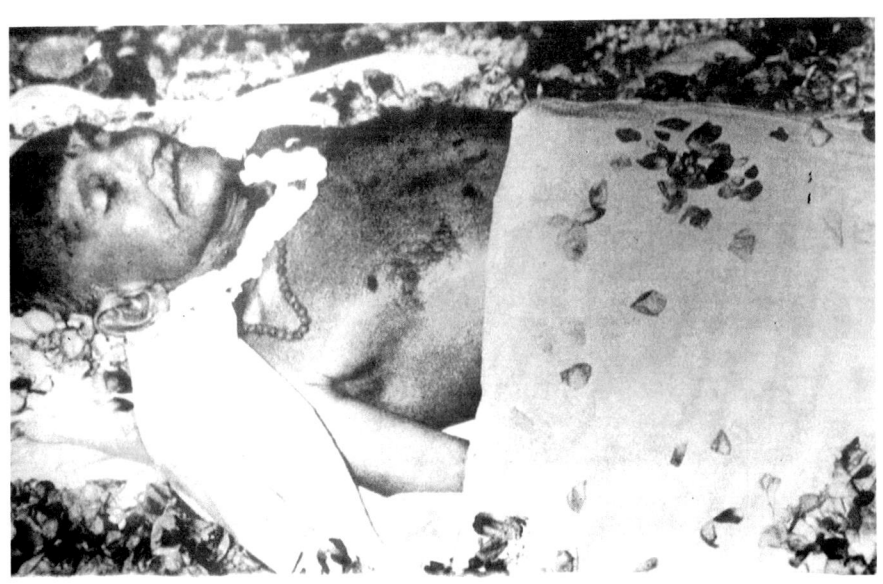

Gandhi's body lying in state, with his chest left uncovered, displaying the gunshot wounds.

Nehru addresses the media from the gate of Birla House on the evening of 30 January 1948.

The flag atop Government House flies at half mast.

Gandhi's body draped in the tricolour, atop the gun carriage outside Birla House.

Gandhi's close aides pray around his funeral pyre.

A forlorn Nehru inspects the preparations for Gandhi's funeral.

Nehru laying a garland on the funeral pyre.

The funeral procession winds its way round the statue of King George.

People perched on electric and telegraph poles to catch a glimpse of Gandhi's funeral procession.

Patel and Ramdas Gandhi console Dr Sushila Nayyar, Manu and Abha as they bid a tearful farewell to Gandhi.

The funeral procession on Rajpath.

The Governor-General's Mounted Guards circle the burning pyre in an effort to prevent people from being pushed on to the funeral pyre.

Prime Minister Nehru speaks with Governor-General Mountbatten.

Rajkumari Amrit Kaur, the Chinese ambassador and Maulana Abul Kalam Azad flank the Mountbatten family.

Royal Indian Air Force planes fly over the flotilla, carrying Gandhi's ashes to the Triveni Sangam.

X

ALONE, ISOLATED AND ABANDONED

One calls himself my Beta (son); the other calls himself my Chela (disciple). Par meri koi sunta nahin. (But neither listens to me any more.)

—M.K. Gandhi,
January 1948

We were willing to cut off the head in order to get rid of the headache!

—Justification for accepting partition

The situation preceding the transfer of power in New Delhi was a hotbed of intrigue and political chicanery. The chief villain in this plot of conspiracies and deceit was the political department of the colonial administration. Along with their allies, the Muslim League ministers in the interim government, they were continuously up to mischief. The Congress had parted with the finance portfolio when the Muslim League joined the interim government. This put the purse strings of the government in the hands of the Muslim League ministers, and they made full use of this gift from the Congress to hinder the functioning of the government, especially the ministries headed by Congress ministers.

Evidence of the complicity of the Muslim League and various wings of the political department and the subversive activities of the withdrawing British troops were reported from all over the country. A group of commandos, who had been working behind the Japanese lines in Burma under Brigadier Wyngate, were found to be engaged in disruptive activities in India; how they infiltrated into India was never explained. Officers in the British Indian Army were known to be active in the efficient trade of arms siphoned off from the military. Secret dumps of illegal arms and explosives were discovered in many places in India. In one instance, a cache of over a thousand STEN guns was discovered at Nagpur, Jabalpur, Kanpur and several other places. Narayan Apte procured a STEN gun in Pune with ease at about this time. The Congress high command had documentary evidence of the complicity of the political department with certain princes, in hatching a conspiracy, to further fragment India. It revealed a well laid out plan to run in large supplies of arms through some of the princely states to organize a D-day all over India. In the face of all this, the Congress leadership, to quote Pandit Nehru, 'became at last willing to cut off the head in order to get rid of the headache!'

On his return to Delhi, Gandhi was confronted with the worsening political and communal situation in the country. On 1 May, he was extensively briefed by Nehru at his camp in Bhangi Colony. Gandhi told Nehru very firmly that the Congress must not allow itself to be dragged into the game of diplomacy with the British to score any advantage over the League. In no case should they barter India's unity for any concession at British hands but should instead demand that the British abandon their middle-of-the-road policy and play straight, strictly enforce the rule of law throughout the country pending the transfer of power and refuse to have parleys with a party that was remiss in that respect or refused to cooperate. If the British were unwilling, he advised that the Congress should go out of the game and bide their time till they quit, leaving the Indian parties to settle it among themselves.

Gandhi refused to accept partition as the only solution and rejected the reasoning that it was a necessary step to avoid chaos. He had previously expressed his views in this regard in a message to a British news magazine, *Cavalcade*, saying that no organic peace was possible without complete independence, including the withdrawal of British troops and influence from India. Imposed peace could only disturb human relations: 'Hence, establishment of organic peace in India inevitably involves senseless strife. This will end quicker when no party is able to look to British power for protection. Forced emasculation of a great nation was bound to have a sad result. No doubt much would depend on Indian wisdom for minimising mischief. I must regretfully say that distrust of British statements has gone too deep and that perhaps legitimately. Therefore, British dealings have to be strictly frank and above suspicion at this critical moment.'

That evening, in his post-prayer speech, Gandhi referred to the joint appeal for peace signed by Jinnah and himself at the behest of the viceroy. It was not open to Jinnah to plead that his followers did not listen to his appeal. It would remove the ground from under his feet because he was the undisputed president of the All India Muslim League, and the League claimed to represent the vast bulk of the Muslim population. Where was the authority of the League if the Muslims resorted to violence to gain its political aim, which was summed up in the word 'Pakistan'? Was the British government to yield to the force of arms rather than the force of reason? The viceroy had solemnly declared that nothing would be yielded to force. There was no meaning in issuing the joint appeal unless it was certain that it meant for both the signatories all that the words thereof conveyed. 'May I ask the Viceroy why he is a silent witness of all this? Why does he not hold me or Jinnah Saheb, whoever is remiss in the implementation of the joint appeal, to account? And if the British cannot make the Hindus and Muslims live in peace with one another, why do they not retire, leaving them to square it out among themselves?' But even if the British did not leave, he went on to say, the answer would not be to take up the sword. 'You are greatly mistaken if you think the British will yield anything to force. And that should be an object lesson to you, too. If you learn to die to the last man, no-one can take anything from you by force.'

However, there remained a basic divergence in their outlook. Gandhi was not able to bring either the Congress leaders or the viceroy to approach the problem of unity and communal harmony in a manner which called for the implementation of the difficult but correct method. While Punjab was burning and the tide of lawlessness and communal frenzy was threatening to engulf the whole of India, trouble erupted again in Noakhali. Gandhi asked Mountbatten whether he should go to Punjab, as was being repeatedly requested by his friends there, or to Noakhali, where he had unfinished business. 'Nehru agrees. Nevertheless I would like you to guide me. This outbreak of violence is not a mere detail. If it cannot be dealt with now, it won't be fourteen months hence.'

Mountbatten replied, 'I quite agree that these outbreaks are not a mere detail. What we have to secure is a settlement between the parties at the Centre and, if possible, a combined front against violence.'

Pyarelal writes: 'The divergence persisted till the end. The policy of trying to please both parties continued and with that the phantom hunt for a "combined front" with the perpetrator of violence, to bring violence under control while the death roll mounted up, converting the country into a vast powder magazine.' Replying to a question posed by Doon Campbell, special correspondent, Reuters, whether he believed that the communal division of India was inevitable, Gandhi said, 'Personally, I have always said "no" and I say "no" even now.' Campbell asked, 'Do you subscribe to the opinion that the British will be morally obliged to stay on in India if the outstanding Hindu–Muslim differences have not been resolved by June 1948?'

This was the first indication to Gandhi that there was a behind-the-scenes lobby working towards prolonging British withdrawal and postponing independence under the pretext of communal strife. Even the new viceroy, Mountbatten, had hinted at such a possibility, provided the Indian parties invited the British power to remain, though personally he regarded this to be a 'most unlikely contingency'. Gandhi made it clear that British withdrawal, 'the noblest act of the British Nation', as he had called it, if it was to be honestly and fully carried out, must take place according to schedule, irrespective of internal conditions. He replied, 'It would be a good thing if the British were to go today, thirteen months mean mischief to India. I do not question the nobility of the British declaration, I do not question the sincerity of the Viceroy, but facts are facts. Neither the British Cabinet nor the Viceroy, however outstanding he may be, can alter facts. And the facts are that India has been trained to look to the British power for everything. Now, it is not possible for India to take her mind off that state all of a sudden. I have never appreciated the argument that the British want so many months to get ready to leave. During that time all parties will look to the British Cabinet and the Viceroy. That being so, the thirteen months' stay of the British power and British arms is really a hindrance rather than a help, because everybody looks for help to the great military machine they have brought into being. That happened in Bengal, in Bihar, in the Punjab and in the North West Frontier Province. The Hindus and the Muslims said in turn: "Let us have the British troops." It is a humiliating spectacle. I repeat: The British will have to take the risk of leaving India to chaos and anarchy. This is so because there has been no Home Rule; slavery has been imposed on the people. And when you voluntarily remove that, there might be no rule in the initial state. The communal feuds you see here are, in my opinion, partly due to the presence of the British. If the British were not here, we would still go through the fire no doubt. But that fire would purify us.'

Patel was becoming increasingly uneasy by reports of the growing Anglo-Muslim bond and the intrigues they were indulging in. At this stage, the colonial administration put forth a proposal: 'Would he convince the Congress to accept Dominion Status as an ad interim arrangement? This would make it possible to anticipate the date of British withdrawal from India. It would also take away from the Muslim League its bargaining power with the British.' Patel was taken in by the argument. On 1 May, the viceroy's secretary reported that Patel was ready to accept an offer of dominion status for the time being. Nehru rejected the proposal out of hand. Officially, the Congress stood committed to the sovereign independent republic resolution of the Constituent Assembly. This did not deter the British government; it realized that all this impasse required was a cleverly worded 'face-saving formula'. It was ultimately found by dropping the words 'King-Emperor' and 'Empire' to spare the conscience of the Congress high command.

The acceptance of the partition of India by the CWC convinced Gandhi that he should be in Bihar and Noakhali rather than in Delhi. Independence would prove to be an illusion if people did not, in the meantime, learn to live in peace with one another. In the meanwhile, disturbing news of the deteriorating communal situation was trickling in from Calcutta and the North-West Frontier Province. Some Pathans from Dera Ismail Khan narrated the lawlessness created by the Muslim League there. On 5 May, Gandhi told Nehru that he wished to proceed to Calcutta post haste.

Commenting on Jinnah's statement during his prayer address on 7 May, Gandhi remarked: 'On bended knee I ask those who want Pakistan, to convince me that Pakistan is for the good of India. Let them put their case before the people and explain to them how it will benefit them. If they succeed in appealing to their reason, well and good, but let them understand that not an inch will be yielded to force.'

'The CWC,' he went on to say, 'has practically decided to concede Pakistan, but demanded that the Hindu majority areas of Bengal and the Punjab must be excluded from it in the event of India being divided. I am opposed to that too. The very idea of breaking up the country makes me shudder. But in that I stand alone.' He told Jinnah plainly that he could not be party to the vivisection of India and would never append his signature to any partition plan. If the Congress high command had resolutely stood by Gandhi and refused to parley on the basis of Pakistan with the British till peace was re-established in the country on the basis of the joint peace declaration and on the basis of the British government's declaration that nothing would be yielded to force, the issue of Pakistan would have been decided by appeal to reason alone. But the Congress high command could not take that firm moral stand, with the result that the ground steadily slipped from under their feet.

Later that day, Gandhi boarded a train for Calcutta. He had a very disturbed journey; the more he thought about the entire reasoning for the acceptance of partition as a prelude to independence, the more he was convinced it was wrong, for which all the parties involved would have to pay heavily. He decided to make another effort to avert, if possible, the disaster. In his letter dated 8 May to Mountbatten, which he posted from a station on the way, Gandhi wrote:

'It strikes me that I should summarize what I said and wanted to say and left unfinished for want of time at our last Sunday's meeting. (1) Whatever may be said to the contrary, it would be a blunder of the first magnitude for the British to be party in any way whatsoever to the division of India. If it has to come, let it come after the British withdrawal, as a result of understanding between the parties or an armed conflict which according to Quaid-i-Azam Jinnah is taboo. Protection of minorities can be guaranteed by establishing a court of arbitration in the event of difference of opinion among contending parties. (2) Meanwhile, the interim government should be composed either of Congressmen or those whose names the Congress chooses or of Muslim League men or those whom the League chooses. The dual control of today, lacking teamwork and team spirit, is harmful for the country. The parties exhaust themselves in the effort to retain their seats and to placate you. Want of team spirit demoralises the government and imperils the integrity of the services so essential for good and efficient government. (3) Referendum at this stage in the Frontier (or any Province for that matter) is a dangerous thing in itself. You have to deal with the material that faces you. In any case nothing should or can be done over Dr Khan Saheb's head as Premier. Note that this paragraph is relevant only if division is at all to be countenanced. (4) I feel sure that partition of the Punjab and Bengal is wrong in every case and a needless irritant for the League. This, as well as all innovations, can come after the British withdrawal, not before, except by mutual agreement. Whilst the British power is functioning in India, it must be held principally responsible for the preservation of peace in the country. That machine seems to be cracking under the existing strain which is caused by the raising of various hopes that cannot or must not be fulfilled. These have no place during the remaining thirteen months. This period can be most profitably shortened if the minds of all are focused on the sole task of withdrawal. You and you alone can do it to the exclusion of all other activity, so far as the British occupation is concerned. (5) Your task as undisputed master of naval warfare, great as it was, was nothing compared to what you are called to do now. The singlemindedness and clarity that gave you success are much more required in this work. (6) If you are not to leave a legacy of chaos behind, you have to make your choice and leave the government of the whole of India, including the States, to one party. The Constituent Assembly has to provide for the governance even of that part of India which is not represented by the Muslim League or some states. (7) Non-partition of the Punjab and Bengal does not mean that the minorities in these provinces are to be neglected. In both the Provinces they are large and powerful enough to arrest and demand attention. If the popular government cannot placate them, the governors should, during the interregnum, actively interfere. (8) The intransmissibility of paramountcy is a vicious doctrine, if it means that the princes can become sovereign and a menace for independent India. All the power, wherever exercised by the British in India, must automatically descend to its successor. Thus, the people of the States become as much part of Independent India as the people of British India.

The present princes are puppets created or tolerated for the upkeep and prestige of the British power. The unchecked powers exercised by them over their people are probably the worst blot on the British Crown. The princes under the new regime can exercise only such powers as trustees can and as can be given to them by the Constituent Assembly. It follows that they cannot maintain private armies or arms factories. Such ability and statecraft as they possess must be at the disposal of the republic and must be used for the good of their people as a whole. I have merely stated what should be done with the States. It is not for me to show in this letter how this can be done. (9) Similarly difficult, but not so baffling, is the question of the Civil Service. Its members should be taught from now to accommodate themselves to the new regime. They may not be partisans taking sides. The slightest trace of communalism among them should be severely dealt with. The English element in it should know that they owe more loyalty to the new regime than to the old and therefore to Great Britain. The habit of regarding themselves as rulers and therefore superiors must give place to the spirit of true service to the people.'

But Mountbatten was not one to swallow the bitter pill. It is possible that he was overtly loyal to his country and the Crown, but he was the one who could have shown sagacity and done what was right by India. Mountbatten's reaction to Gandhi's letter was conveyed to the latter by a colleague a few days later: 'I came up here (Simla) and dined at the Viceregal Lodge last night... He (Mountbatten) said, "I am touched and moved by your Bapu's letter. Though he gives me more headache than anyone else, I admire his instinct. I would love to be able to do what he says, but I can't always see how to do it, and what is more, the Congress members of the interim government do not see eye to eye with him." He was, however, determined not to allow civil war to raise its head. He agreed that Pakistan was a bad thing, but felt that the Congress high command were "now quite anxious for it and for it to happen as soon as possible" in the hope that eventually the League itself would give it up. He (Mountbatten) again said that he was against the whole conception of Pakistan. He was not wholly satisfied with the reaction of His Majesty's government and was struggling to get them to think along your lines. He repeatedly deplored "the legacy that had been left him and the short time he had to do things in".'

Gandhi stayed at the Khadi Pratisthan Ashram at Sodepore ten miles outside Calcutta. A strictly enforced curfew was imposed on the city. The day he arrived was the birth anniversary of Rabindranath Tagore. At his post-prayer meeting, Gandhi told the gathering that when he had appended his signature to the joint peace appeal, he had done so with the utmost sincerity. He had made himself a hostage for the preservation of peace by both the parties. The Hindus of Bihar and the Muslims of Noakhali must, therefore, remember that if they again went on a rampage, they would force him to forfeit his life.

Suhrawardy, the chief minister of Bengal, was a worried man. He had led the faction of the Muslim League which vociferously demanded Pakistan. Now he feared that, with the demand put forth by the Congress, the eastern wing of Pakistan would be a truncated version of what they had assumed it to be. Assam and the industrialized parts of Bengal would, in the new equation, remain with India. In all probability, the port and city of Calcutta would also be lost to the eastern wing of Pakistan. What also worried Suhrawardy was the realization that the eastern and western wings of Pakistan would be separated by a powerful group of intervening Indian Union provinces. He had, for long, cherished the idea of creating a greater Bengal, by amalgamating to it the rich iron and coal belt of Bihar. To realize his ambition, he was prepared even to reinterpret the League's 'two nation' theory. 'The two nation theory,' he said in a press interview, 'has had as its background mainly political considerations. But there are other considerations such as common language, economic ties, interdependence, ethnological and historical ... which directly affect the people... There has been no finality even among eminent professors of politics on the question of what constitutes a nation and different criteria would furnish different answers. Therefore, the two nation theory should be fully capable of being suitably moulded so as to be adaptable to local conditions as the situation demands.'

The Bengali Muslims were different from the Muslims living in the western provinces of India. Both communities of Bengal were proud of their common language, Bengali. The Bengali Hindu was as proud of the poetry of Nazrul Islam as the Bengali Muslim was of Rabindranath Tagore's. These linguistic and cultural bonds had survived the recent shocks of the political divide. The political and ideological divide between the Muslims of Bengal and the Muslims of the western provinces was highlighted by two incidents. The first was when the Muslim League ministers accompanying Gandhi to Noakhali had told him that Bengali Muslims were quite content to have Bengal as a Muslim-controlled province in undivided India; their only quarrel was with the Muslims being assigned the status of underdog. The second was a press report filed by its Delhi correspondent and published on 29 April in the *Hindu*, 'It is significant that while the Punjab Muslim Leaguers are thinking in terms of a separate Constituent Assembly, those from Bengal want to enter the existing one.' There was a band of nationalist Hindus, who saw in the partition of Bengal its ruination. The group was led by Sarat Chandra Bose. One amongst the group was a veteran Congressman, Akhil Chandra Dutt. Soon after the movement for the partition of Bengal was launched by a section of Hindus, he wrote to Gandhi: 'A movement has been set afoot for partition of Bengal and thus "secure a homeland for Hindus". This appears to be the result of a defeatist mentality. In fact, this movement seems to me to be a communal one. Communalism must no doubt be fought, but not by a counter communal movement for a homeland for Hindus. This movement is practically a concession to the principle on which the demand for Pakistan is based. This will not be a solution to the communal problem but will aggravate and perpetuate it. It ignores the fundamental position that communalism is a passing phase and is bound at no distant date to be replaced by political division on economic grounds... Partition will inevitably lead a section of well-to-do Hindus to migrate to West Bengal, leaving the poorer caste Hindus and scheduled caste Hindus to save their life, property and honour by conversion to Islam. Partition will be a wrong step politically, economically, socially, linguistically and culturally... It was my lot in the prime of my life to fight against the partition of Bengal, proposed by Lord Curzon. By an irony of fate I have to fight in the evening of my life against Partition sponsored by my own people. I ... request you to express your views and give a correct lead before further mischief is done.'

There was not the slightest chance that the Hindus would agree to a united Bengal joining Pakistan, or the Muslims consenting to its retention in the Indian Union. So they agreed on a plan of a 'sovereign united Bengal', independent of both India and Pakistan. 'I am amazed,' he remarked to a group of Bengali friends who had seen him in that connection a few days earlier in Patna, 'at the levity with which some people regarded Partition, as if it were child's play. They do not seem to realize that they are gambling with the lives of millions.' Again in Delhi he said, 'It surprises me that we do not see what price we shall have to pay for this third party intervention... I have faith that, when the flood of insanity has subsided, the mud and silt will settle down to the bottom, leaving the waters crystal clear and pure, to bring the blessings of peace to the whole world. For with all its aberrations, our freedom struggle is essentially based on justice, righteousness, non-violence and truth.'

Sarat Chandra Bose, accompanied by Abdul Hashem, secretary of the Bengal Muslim League, met Gandhi the day he arrived at Sodepore Ashram. Hashem, to Gandhi's surprise, based his case for a united Bengal on the grounds of common language, common culture and common history that united the Hindus and Muslims of Bengal alike. Gandhi was surprised by this about turn in one who had staunchly supported the demand for Pakistan just a few months ago. Wearily, Gandhi asked Hashem whether he would have any objections to them joining Pakistan, if instead of incorporation, Pakistan invited them to enter into a 'voluntary federation for the propagation of Islamic culture and religion'. Hashem chose not to reply to his query. Gandhi tried a different approach. 'Since Bengal's common culture, as embodied in Tagore, to which the League's secretary had referred, had its roots in the philosophy of the Upanishads, which was the common heritage not only of Bengal but of the whole of India, would the sovereign Bengal contemplate entering into a "voluntary association" with the rest of India?' Hashem again chose to remain silent.

On 11 May, Suhrawardy, accompanied by Mohammad Ali and Abdul Hashem, met Gandhi to discuss the issue of a sovereign Bengal. Gandhi tried to impress upon Suhrawady the need for a complete and genuine change of heart and absolute honesty.

On 12 May, Suhrawardy met Gandhi again to enlist his support in the demand for a united sovereign Bengal. The latter told him that the only way in which they could prevent the partition of Bengal was by getting Jinnah to implement the joint peace appeal to which he was a signatory. 'Although I represent no community in particular, you see how I am wearing myself out in a supreme effort to bring the Hindus of Bihar to a sense of repentance and wrongdoing. But you are the accredited representatives of the Muslims. Should you not do what I am doing and more, in respect to the Indian Muslim? But you cannot claim to have done that. I am sure that if the Bengal ministry acted with hundred per cent sincerity, Jinnah Saheb and the Muslim League would be compelled to follow suit.'

Suhrawardy complained that no Hindu trusted him; he could not even get a patient hearing, so how could he convince them of his sincerity? In reply, Gandhi made him an astounding offer, which he confirmed later in writing: 'I recognize the seriousness of the position in Bengal in the matter of Partition. If you are absolutely sincere in your professions and would disabuse me of all the suspicion against you and if you would always retain Bengal for all Bengalis—Hindus and Musalmans—intact by non-violent means, I am quite willing to act as your honorary private secretary and live under your roof, till Hindus and Muslims begin to live as brothers that they are.' Suhrawardy was shocked by this offer. 'What a mad offer! I shall have to think ten times before I can fathom its implications,' a visibly shaken Suhrawardy exclaimed as he left at the end of the meeting.

Before leaving Calcutta, Gandhi toured the riot-affected areas of the city. The acting chief minister Mohammad Ali, and the secretary of the Bengal Hindu Mahasabha, the League's coalition partner, accompanied Gandhi. It was a hot late afternoon, when Gandhi returned from the fifty mile drive.

On 10 May, the viceroy showed the revised plan to Nehru to gauge his reaction. Nehru was livid. 'It is a complete betrayal,' he said. 'It means the Balkanisation of India; we can never accept it.' The viceroy hurriedly summoned V.P. Menon, the reforms commissioner. 'The fat is in the fire!' Mountbatten exclaimed. Menon reassured him that he would rework the draft to make it acceptable. The next day, Nehru's reaction to the redrafted plan was reported to be favourable, but he was not quite certain as to how the CWC would respond. Patel was contacted in Delhi and was requested to shepherd it through the CWC; he agreed 'to see to that part of it'. The viceroy and his staff realized that, henceforth, during all delicate negotiations, they must have Patel as a steadying influence alongside Nehru. Once they took care of these two, the Congress high command would be in their pockets. With these two riding shotgun, they did not have to worry about the one Churchill contemptuously called the 'half-naked fakir'!

Gandhi did not have the least doubt that the British would eventually leave, but of late he was worried that what his countrymen would be left holding would be an empty shell that once was a glorious nation. On the morning of 24 May, as Gandhi boarded the train for Delhi at Patna, he told Dr Mahmud, 'The Congress has practically decided to accept Partition. But I have been a fighter all my life. I am going to Delhi to fight a losing battle.' When the train stopped at Kanpur station, his watch was stolen from under his pillow by a souvenir hunter who had entered his compartment. Gandhi was very attached to the watch as it was a present from Indira, Pandit Nehru's daughter. She had gifted it to him twenty years ago when he had gone to Allahabad to see her grandfather Motilal Nehru. Since then it had been his constant companion. Gandhi made an appeal for the return of his watch in the *Harijan*, and fifteen days later, the watch was delivered to his residence at Bhangi Colony in New Delhi by post.

In his post-prayer speech on 26 May, he remarked that independence lay there, right in front of them. It was for them to take it, unless, in their folly, they chose to discard it. Why should they be concerned about what the British Cabinet or the British political parties wanted or desired? 'It is not for them to give us liberty but only to get off our backs. This they are under promise to do. But for retaining our freedom and giving it shape, we have to look to ourselves… We are unable to think coherently, while the British power is there in India. Its function is not to change the map of India, all it has to do is to withdraw and leave India in an orderly manner, if possible. But withdraw in any case on or before the promised date it must, even if it means chaos.'

The next evening, Gandhi directly posed a challenge to Jinnah, the Congress leadership and the British government. Jinnah was a co-signatory to the famous peace pledge issued jointly in their names. Jinnah should have been seen working with him from the same platform, not allowing himself to rest till they had secured peace in the land of their birth or died in the attempt. And yet, while arson and murder were rampant even around the capital itself, preparations for the division of

India were being pushed on. The interim government had unfortunately chosen to follow the negative practice of the British government. 'Its communiqués repeatedly mentioned, in the vaguest of terms, how members of "a certain community" had done the killing, without clearly indicating who had killed whom. Why could not they be bold enough to mention the butcher by his name? Why did not the British power name the guilty party and put it outside the pale?' He maintained that after the joint appeal, Jinnah had left no way open to himself for the attainment of Pakistan, except that of conversation through appeal to cold reason. He had said before that if he had his way, there would be no talk about Pakistan before there was peace, and certainly not through British intervention. Jinnah should first establish peace and, in that effort, he could always command his cooperation, then convene a meeting of Indian leaders of all classes and communities and go on pleading with them the cause of Pakistan till he had carried conviction to them. 'The day we meet together as brothers will be a red letter day in India's annals. For whatever decision we shall then take will be our decision as amongst members of one family.'

'If the Pakistan of his conception was a reasonable proposition,' Gandhi said, Jinnah should have no difficulty in convincing India. Though the events in the North-West Frontier Province, in the Punjab and in Bengal left little room for hope, he was even now prepared to make a sporting offer. Jinnah had claimed that Pakistan would be a state where each would enjoy the fullest security, where there would be no distinction of high and low and where there would be justice for all. If that was really so, he (Gandhi) would himself accompany him and tour with him all over the country and tell the people that they could all live happily in such a Pakistan. 'Let him (Jinnah) not appeal to the British power or its representative Viceroy Mountbatten. The latter's function is only to quit by the end of June next year—peace or no peace. Imposed peace would be the peace of the grave of which all India and the British should be ashamed. Let it not be said that Gandhi was too late on the scene. He was not. It's never too late to mend, never too late to replace the force of the sword with that of reason. Dare the British impose Pakistan on an India temporarily gone mad.'

On 29 May, during his morning walk, a co-worker said to Gandhi:

'You have declared that you won't mind if the whole of India is turned into Pakistan by appeal to reason, but not an inch would be yielded to force. You have stood firm by your declaration. But is the Working Committee acting on that principle? They are yielding to force. You gave us the battle cry of "Quit India"; you fought our battles; but in the hour of decision, I find, you are not in the picture. You and your ideas have been given the go by.'

Gandhi replied, 'Who listens to me today?' to which the co-worker replied, 'The leaders may not, but the people are behind you.' Gandhi replied, 'Even they are not. I am being told to retire to the Himalayas. Everybody is eager to garland my photos and statues. Nobody really wants to follow me.'

The co-worker said, 'They may not today, but they will have to before long,' to which Gandhi replied, 'What is the good? Who knows, whether I shall then be alive? The question is: what can we do today? On the eve of independence, we are as divided as we were united when we were engaged in freedom's battle. The prospect of power has demoralized us.'

That evening, during the prayer meeting, a young man dressed in western clothes got up and began to shout, 'Imprison Jinnah, stop reciting from the Koran, declare war upon the Muslim League!' All this, while a Zoroastrian prayer was being recited. Gandhi interrupted the prayers and requested the volunteers not to be rough on the young man. At this time, All India Radio used to broadcast and record Gandhi's prayer meetings. I have heard a recording of that particular prayer meeting many times over. The man's voice has a frightening intensity, but is matched by Gandhi's calm and reasoned response. These hecklers were very well-trained to garner public sympathy for their cause. Earlier, they raised objections to recitations from the Koran, but this did not go down well. So the Hindu extremists, the RSS and the Hindu Mahasabha changed their strategy. They now demanded Jinnah's arrest and revenge on the Muslim League, while protesting against the recitation of Ayats from the Koran. At that time, there were very few people, if any, in India, who would oppose these demands.

On 2 June 1947, the Indian leaders assembled at the viceroy's house at 10:00 a.m. The Congress was represented by Patel, Nehru and Kripalani; the Muslim League by Jinnah, Liaquat Ali and Rab Nishtar. Jinnah objected to the presence of Kripalani, a ploy to irritate the Congress leaders. When his objection was overruled, since Kripalani, as Congress president, had every right to attend the meeting, Jinnah nominated Rab Nishtar to counter Kripalani. The Sikhs were represented by Sardar Baldev Singh. Mountbatten opened the meeting with the formal offer of the Cabinet Mission plan for acceptance; Jinnah refused to accept it and the offer was withdrawn. Next, Mountbatten unveiled HMG's partition plan which he had brought back from London. It offered: (1) a separate Constituent Assembly for the Muslim majority provinces that were unwilling to join the existing Constituent Assembly, coupled with the partition of the Punjab and Bengal; (2) by the decision of their respective Legislatures voting separately for Hindu and Muslim majority districts. In the event of Bengal being partitioned, there would be a referendum in Sylhet to decide as to which province it would be part of, East Bengal or Assam; (3) referendum to be held in the North-West Frontier Province, without disturbing the ministry in power, to decide which of the two Constituent Assemblies it would join; (4) the Sind Legislative Assembly to decide by a simple majority vote as to which part of India it would belong to; (5) the procedure as to how Baluchistan would decide its future to be left to the viceroy in consultation with the Indian parties, as there was no Legislative Assembly there; (6) the final shape of the partition to be decided by a Boundary Commission appointed for the purpose; (7) no change in the interim government until separation was affected, when two governments would be set up with complete powers in all subjects; (8) to meet the desire of the major Indian political parties for the earliest possible transfer of power: power would be transferred to an Indian government or governments on dominion status basis at even an earlier date; (9) the attainment of dominion status to be, without prejudice, the right of the Indian Constituent Assemblies, to decide in due course whether or not the part of India with respect to which they had authority would remain in the British Commonwealth and (10) the position of the princely states to remain the same as under the Cabinet Mission plan.

Previously, the viceroy had mentioned that the date for independence could be advanced. At the meeting, he dramatically foreshortened the date of departure, bringing it forward to August 1947.

The Congress leaders declared acceptance of the 'partition plan' on the condition that the offer was accepted without alteration by Jinnah and the Muslim League. The Congress and Sikh leaders agreed to convey their final decision in writing by that evening. Jinnah, however, said that only the full council of the League could decide on the partition offer, and that would take some days for the Muslim League's Council to be summoned. The only commitment he was willing to make and that too only on his personal part was that he had 'no desire to wreck the plan'.

At 12:30 p.m., Gandhi arrived for his meeting with the viceroy. This was merely a courteous formality on part of the viceroy; no matter what Gandhi said or suggested, his comments did not matter any longer. Gandhi knew this and was resigned to the fact. 2 June was a Monday, Gandhi's day of weekly silence. He conveyed all he had to by writing on slips of papers which were passed to the viceroy. A section of the British administration and the viceroy's staff had conjured up a phantom threat to the partition plan. They were convinced that Gandhi would dissociate with the Congress and lead a mass movement against the acceptance of the partition plan; this had caused a lot of consternation among the viceroy's staff as well as in Whitehall. This meeting was basically to gauge Gandhi's reaction and ascertain whether their fears had any merit. Such was Gandhi's influence that even after having successfully isolated him from the Congress leaders, the British colonial administration and the British government were still fearful of his ability to thwart their schemes by rousing common Indians to once again fight alongside him. But Gandhi had gauged the mood of his political colleagues and the people of India and knew that at that fateful juncture he stood alone, isolated, abandoned. Allaying the viceroy's fears, he wrote: 'I am sorry, I can't speak. When I took the decision about the Monday silence, I did reserve two exceptions, i.e., about speaking to high functionaries on urgent matters or attend upon sick people. But I know you do not want me to break my silence.'

Responding to the viceroy's guarded enquiry about his fear that Gandhi would foment trouble for the partition plan, Gandhi wrote: 'Have I said one word against you during my speeches? If you admit that I have not, your warning is superfluous. There are one or two things I must talk about, but not today. If we meet each other again, I shall speak.'

The CWC's final decision was communicated that night by a letter addressed by the Congress president to the viceroy. He wrote: 'We accepted in its entirety the Cabinet Mission's statement of 16 May 1946, as well as the subsequent interpretation thereof dated 6 December 1946. We are still prepared to adhere to that plan. However, we are willing to accept as a variation of that plan the proposals now being made. While we are willing to accept the proposals made by His Majesty's government, my Committee desires to emphasize that they are doing so in order to achieve a final settlement. This is dependent on the acceptance of the proposal by the Muslim League and a clear understanding that no further claim will be put forward.'

In view, however, of what had happened at the time of the Cabinet Mission plan, when Lord Wavell had brought the Muslim League into the interim government without obtaining a proper guarantee in writing, the Working Committee's letter added: 'There has been enough misunderstanding in the past and in order to avoid this in the future, it is necessary to have explicit statements in writing in regard to these proposals.'

Jinnah's adamant refusal to give the League's reply in writing precipitated a showdown between the viceroy and him at a midnight meeting, to which Lord Ismay was the only witness. This meeting showed how confident Jinnah was of achieving all his objectives with the tacit support of the British colonial administration and his political patrons back in England that he could remain unflappable in the face of dire threats issued by Mountbatten. Upon his refusal to give a written reply to the partition plan, the viceroy warned Jinnah that if he continued with his intransigence, power may be transferred on the basis of the constitution in force. Jinnah called the viceroy's bluff with a nonchalant 'What must be, must be.' At last, Mountbatten unsheathed his final 'secret weapon'. It was a message from Winston Churchill, to be delivered as a last resort. The message was blunt: 'If Jinnah rejects the plan or tries to place hurdles in its acceptance, tell him it would sound the death knell of his dream of Pakistan.' Jinnah remained nonchalant outwardly, but he was scared as he realized that he had lost his patronage in England, that the one person on whose orders he had resurrected his political career and his demand for Pakistan had abandoned him.

When asked for his acceptance of the partition plan during the leaders' conference the next morning, he nodded, which was taken to be an acceptance. The Muslim League Council then met at New Delhi on 9 June under the chairmanship of Jinnah. While deploring the partition of the Punjab and Bengal, it adopted a resolution accepting the British government's plan 'as a compromise' in the interest of 'peace and tranquillity'!

During his walk on the morning of 3 June, Gandhi asked Rajendra Babu if he might now return to Bihar. But the latter did not feel he should, as his presence was essential in the capital, 'if only for Badshah Khan', cryptically suggesting that the whole process might still degenerate into chaos on the question of the fate of the North-West Frontier Province.

'In all probability,' he said later, 'the final seal will be set on the partition plan during the day. But though I may be alone in holding this view, I repeat that the division of India can only do harm to the country's future. The slavery of 150 years is going to end, but from the look of things, it does not seem as if independence will last as long. It hurts me to think that I can see nothing but evil in the Partition plan. May be that just as God blinded my vision, so that I mistook the non-violence of the weak for true non-violence, He has again stricken me with blindness. If it should prove to be so, nobody would be happier than I.'

After his evening walk, as he sat soaking his feet in a hot water bath, Rajkumari Amrit Kaur came and gave Gandhi the news that all three parties, the Congress, the League and the Sikhs, had signed the plan. The League would not accept anything else; the Congress therefore had no other choice but to accept partition. Gandhi listened to the news without comment; finally, he heaved a sigh of relief. 'May God protect them, and grant them wisdom,' he whispered. That night, the decision was broadcast on All India Radio: 'India will be partitioned!' The announcement was followed by the addresses of Nehru, Jinnah and Baldev Singh. And so ended the suspense about India's future and independence. It also crashed Gandhi's dream of keeping his beloved nation united against all odds. India would be free, but it would be torn asunder and in the process, seeds of hate would be sown at its birth.

At this juncture, there was nobody with Gandhi, neither politicians, nor the people, willing to launch a movement to keep India united, to fight against the League's violence and the Congress's capitulation. Many people claimed that they felt betrayed by Gandhi because he accepted the partition quietly and did nothing to avert it. But no one launched independent agitation against the acceptance of the partition plan either. The Hindu right wing, the self-proclaimed patriots of the RSS and Hindu Mahasabha, did not even once demonstrate against this division which they now, many decades later, call a grave betrayal. The only thing they did was to issue a Firman to all their supporters not to celebrate India's independence and they accelerated their plan to murder Gandhi.

Conditions across the country were deteriorating rapidly. There were daily reports of violence, murder and arson pouring in from Punjab, Bengal and the North-West Frontier Province. The Sikhs, in danger of losing the most as a result of partition, were becoming restive. The minorities in Sind and North-West Frontier Province were becoming increasingly insecure about their future in Pakistan. The trickle of refugees from West Punjab was becoming a steadily increasing flow. The situation around the capital was also grim. There were reports of pitched battles being fought between the Muslim Meos of Gurgaon district and Hindu Ahirs and Jats. Patel, who had agreed to partition to get rid of the danger posed by the League to the unity and stability of India, to his chagrin, found that with the Muslim League's bastion still firmly established in the interim government and in the administration, he could do nothing to cope with the deteriorating situation. They had cut off the head, but the headache refused to go.

On the day after the council of the All India Muslim League adopted their resolution accepting the partition plan, Gandhi once again wrote to Mountbatten to bring home to him the danger of allowing matters to drift: 'The sooner you have a homogeneous ministry, the better. In no case can the League nominees work independently of the whole Cabinet. It is a vicious thing that there is a joint responsibility for every act of individual members... The problem of civil and military services demands the same firm handling. Gurgaon strife is an instance in point, so far as I know, one single officer is responsible for the continuation of the mischief.

'Lastly, may I suggest that the attempt to please all parties is a fruitless and thankless task. In the course of our conversation, I suggested that equal praise bestowed on both the parties was not meant, no praise would have been the right thing. "Duty will be merit when debt becomes a donation." It is not too late to mend. Your undoubted skill as a warrior was never more in demand than today.'

But Mountbatten the political administrator dominated Mountbatten the warrior, and so, the former continued with his own agenda, ignoring the dire warnings of one who, at that time, was the only one endowed with clairvoyance. Gandhi feared that, for all his good intentions, Mountbatten would be bound by his own compulsions and the fetters of the colonial administration, and thus would be unable to avert the looming tragedy unless there was a radical change in the policy pursued since the Cabinet Mission's visit to India. Gandhi belived that the Cabinet Mission's plan for India would have been better than Mountbatten's partition plan. He decided on one last effort to convince the viceroy to see issues from his perspective. On the midnight of 27 June, Gandhi wrote to the viceroy. Because he finished writing when it was past midnight, the letter was dated 27/28 June 1947: 'I sent you a note in the afternoon. The time after the evening prayer and walk I wish to devote to talking to you on certain matters I was able to touch but could not develop when we met. I told the Parliamentary delegation that heralded the Cabinet Mission and the Cabinet Mission itself that they had to choose between the two parties or even three. They were doomed to fail, if they tried to please all, holding them all to be in the right. I had hoped that you were bravely and honestly trying to extricate yourself from the impossible position. But my eyes were opened when, if I understood you correctly, you said that Quaid-i-Azam Jinnah and the League members were equally in the right with the Congress members and that possibly Quaid-i-Azam Jinnah was more so. I suggested that this was not humanly possible. One must be wholly right in the comparative sense. You have to make your choice at this very critical stage in the history of this country. If you think that Quaid-i-Azam Jinnah is on the whole more correct and more responsible than the Congress, you should choose the League as your advisers and in all matters be frankly and openly guided by them. You threw out a hint that Quaid-i-Azam might not be able to let you quit even by 15 August, especially if Congress members did not adopt a helpful attitude. This was for me a startling statement. I pointed the initial mistake of the

British being party to splitting India into two. It is not possible to undo the mistake. But I hold that it is quite possible and necessary not to put a premium upon the mistake. This does not in any way impinge upon the very admirable doctrine of fair play. Fair play demands that I do not help the mistaken party to fancy that the mistake was no mistake but a belated and only partial discharge of an obligation. You startled me by telling me that, if the Partition had not been made during British occupation, the Hindus being the major party would have never allowed Partition and held the Muslims by force under subjection. I told you that this was a grave mistake. The question of numbers was totally untenable in this connection. I cited the classic example of less then one hundred thousand British soldiers holding India under utter subjection. You saw no analogy between the two instances. I suggested the difference was only one of degree. I place the following for you consideration: (a) The Congress has solemnly declared that it would not hold by force any Province within the Union. (b) It is physically impossible for millions of caste ridden Hindus to hold well-knit, though fewer, millions of Muslims under subjection by force. (c) It must not be forgotten that Muslim dynasties have progressively subjected India by exactly the same means as the English conquerors later did. (d) Already there has been a movement to win over to the Muslim side the so-called scheduled classes and the so-called aboriginal races. (e) The caste Hindus who are the bugbear are, it can be shown conclusively, a hopeless minority. Of these the armed Rajputs are not yet nationalists as a class. The Brahmins and the Banias are still untrained in the use of arms. Their supremacy, where it exists, is purely moral. The Shudras count, I am sorry, more as schedule class than anything else. That such Hindu society by reason of its mere superiority in numbers can crush millions of Muslims is an astounding myth. This should show you why, even if I am alone, I swear by non-violence and truth together standing for the highest order of courage, before which the atom bomb pales into insignificance, not to say of a fleet of dreadnaughts. I have not shown this to any of my friends.'

Mountbatten replied the very same day: 'I am glad you wrote because after reading your letter, I feel that almost from first to last I must have failed to make clear to you my meaning. I am glad that you have not shown your letter to others, since I should be very sorry that views should be attributed to me which I did not, in fact, express. I hope you will agree to discuss these matters again at our next meeting.' Unfortunately, there are no records to show that the two ever discussed these matters again. The fact remains that, for all his efforts, Gandhi failed to influence anyone to believe in what he felt was the right thing to do for his country.

During the last week of June and beginning of July, the confrontation between the Congress and League ministers came to a boil. The situation became so volatile that, in exasperation, all Congress ministers threatened to walk out of the government. The question of the continuation of the League ministers in the interim government could no longer be postponed. Uncharacteristically, it was Jinnah who solved the problem rather than, as usual, creating one. He declared that he himself would be the Governor-General of Pakistan. Mountbatten now felt himself free to act. Jinnah again made the surrender of portfolios held by the League ministers a matter of prestige. 'It would be an insult for the League ministers to be asked to surrender their portfolios. The League would not tolerate such humiliation.' When Mountbatten suggested a formula which would satisfy everyone, Jinnah threatened to denounce as 'illegal under the 1935 Government of India Act the Viceroy's plans to reconstitute the interim government'. Legal opinion obtained from London upheld Jinnah's objections. Mountbatten earned a respite. He could say that he had made efforts; he could also justify Jinnah's bullying tactics by citing legal validity. This lasted till the third week of July.

On 19 July 1947, the Indian Independence Bill was passed by the British Parliament and royal assent was given to it. The viceroy reconstituted the interim government, dividing it for all practical purposes into two provisional administrations: one for the Indian Union and the other for Pakistan. The two parts would consult each other only on matters of common concern, but act independent of each other in all other respects. A couple of days after the leaders of the three parties had given their assent to the partition plan, a small high-powered committee, comprising representatives of the Congress, the League and the Sikhs, was set up with the viceroy as chairman. The group would consider various problems arising from the decision of partition and the transfer of power. After the Punjab and Bengal provinces had decided in favour of their own partition, this committee was replaced by a Partition Council, with wider powers and authority to take final decisions. A press release was issued, stating that all the parties in the Council had agreed before the viceroy that partition would be affected in a 'brotherly spirit'. Gandhi was sceptical about the sincerity of the expressed sentiments. 'I am afraid we are deceiving ourselves and the people,' he remarked during the course of a conversation.

It was decided to invite Sir Cyril Radcliffe to serve as chairman of the Punjab and Bengal boundary commissions. His terms of reference were to demarcate the boundaries of the two parts of both provinces 'on the basis of ascertaining the contiguous majority areas of Muslims and non-Muslims'. In doing so, he was to also take into account 'other factors'. This gave hope to both the parties that the Boundary Commission would give them more than could be reasonably expected. The Muslim League hoped that it would give them Calcutta and the Sikhs hoped their property holdings and other qualifications would give them a better chance in the Punjab. The expectations were running high on all sides; it was apparent that not all could be fulfilled, and disappointments arising from unfulfilled expectations further fuelled the existing tension. To add to this was the complete incompetence of Cyril Radcliffe. He was not a cartographer or an anthropologist and was totally ignorant about India; he was the most unsuitable person for the job and yet, in their wisdom, he was chosen to dissect the subcontinent.

Excitement reached a high in the second half of June in the neighbouring cities of Lahore and Amritsar. Both the cities were in the debatable zone in the Punjab; both had predominantly Hindu and Sikh populations and were built up largely by their capital and enterprise. They owned the bulk of the commercial and industrial assets and the moveable and immovable property. Amritsar was the religious capital of the Sikh Panth, Lahore was the capital of the Sikh empire founded by Maharaja Ranjit Singh. The Muslim League demanded the inclusion of both the cities in Pakistan on 'political grounds'. Since the announcement of the partition plan, both the cities were in the grip of absolute anarchy. In Lahore, within the course of a day, more than a hundred homes of Hindus and Sikhs were looted and burned.

As the month of June wore on, the refugee problem increasingly claimed Gandhi's time and attention. Representatives of refugees requested

Gandhi to visit Haridwar, where 32,000 refugees from Rawalpindi and various other towns of West Punjab were huddled together in half a dozen refugee camps. Gandhi promptly visited these camps.

On his arrival there, the official in charge of the camps tried to garland Gandhi. He received a severe reprimand. Gandhi then went on to visit all the refugee quarters and was appalled by what he saw.

A news report filed by Reuters caught Gandhi's attention the day after his visit to the Haridwar refugee camp. It described a grand ceremony planned in London to mark the introduction and acceptance in parliament of the Indian Independence Bill, announcing the birth of two nations. There was a thoughtless levity in England about the impending division of India. It was not as if they were ignorant of the tragedy and the violence that had preceded and threatened to follow independence. Lord Pethick-Lawrence made a rather flippant speech in Parliament during the debate on the Independence Bill. Describing an incident during his student days at Cambridge, he said that their college porter left them one afternoon to go home as his wife was likely to deliver their baby that evening. The next morning he came back with a rather long face and reported that, instead of the single baby that he was expecting, his wife had presented him with twins! 'Something like that has happened in India. Mother India has been in labour for a very long time, and everyone was wondering what would be the character of the infant that would come into being. Lo and behold! Instead of one State emerging from the womb of Mother India, twin states are emerging, as described in the bill.'

The British regarded Indian unity as their proudest achievement and claimed that they deplored its dismemberment. The viceroy had even told the Indian leaders that a clause had especially been incorporated in the Bill to enable the seceder to come back into the Union by mutual agreement. Gandhi felt that if the Reuters report was to be relied upon, the British Parliament was going to set its imprimatur on India's partition with a fanfare which was wholly incompatible with the spirit of what the viceroy had been telling them.

'The papers today talk of a grand ceremony to take place in London over the division of India into "two nations" which were, only the other day, one,' Gandhi remarked during his prayer meeting on 23 June. 'What is there to gloat over in the tragedy? We have hugged the belief that though we part, we do so as friends and brothers belonging to one family. Now, if the newspaper report is correct, the British will make of us "two nations" and that with a flourish of trumpets. Is that to be their parting shot? I hope not. How were the people going to meet this challenge?' he asked. 'This division of India with sub-division of Provinces puts us on our mettle. If the major partner is true to his salt, the foreshadowed wisdom can be confounded not in the shape of avoiding Partition, however distasteful it might be, but by right behaviour on the part of the major partner, by always acting as one nation, by refusing to treat Muslim minorities as aliens in their own home.' Present-day India and its rulers need to be reminded of this.

He wrote to Patel: 'Look at Reuters' wire in today's papers. The bill will create two nations!!! What is the value then of these pompous talks that are going on here? If you have not given your consent to it, you can prevent this crime against the Indian nation. After the bill is passed, nobody is going to listen to you.' A few days later, Gandhi received a note from the viceroy stating that Nehru, Patel and he, all felt that Gandhi should 'unquestionably be shown' the Indian Independence Bill. Accordingly, Gandhi went with the Congress leaders to the viceroy the next morning. His immediate reactions to the draft Bill are on record, scribbled partly in pencil and partly in ink: (1) Some declaration should be made, if it cannot be included in the Statute, that dominion status would be temporary; (2) That it would be equal treatment for the two; (3) There is nothing to show that Pakistan is a seceder and that the entity of India is retained in spite; (4) No province can go over to the other dominion without consent; (5) Pakistan Assembly will not meet before the appointed date; (6) The States' position is uncomfortably weak; (7) May 1946 statement should not be used to block progress.

Although he rejected it on principle, Gandhi was still making sincere efforts to make the Indian Independence Bill more honest and to safeguard his idea of India.

Describing Gandhi's observations on the Bill, Pyarelal writes: 'The irritation had blown off but the steely barb had, if possible, entered even deeper into his heart, when he addressed his prayer meeting on 5 July. He was not disposed, he remarked, like many critics, to read a sinister meaning in the Bill. The fact that there were two Indias instead of one was bad enough in itself. Both had the same status, and the Muslim League was entitled to full credit for bringing about a state of things which seemed to be impossible only, as it were, the day before. They had undone the solemn declaration of the Cabinet Mission. They had succeeded in compelling consent from the Congress and the Sikhs to the division. The thing that was in itself bad, did not become good because the parties concerned had accepted it, no matter that the causes dictating acceptance were different in each case. It was hardly any comfort that Jinnah did not get all he wanted. The difference was not at all in kind. He wanted a sovereign state. That he had in the fullest measure.

'As he read and reread the Bill, Gandhiji went on to say, he saw that the three parties had subjected themselves consciously or unconsciously to public judgement in terms of the Bill. Though the British were divesting themselves of all power, by becoming party to the division and having two members in the Commonwealth family possessing conflicting ideals and interests, they had put themselves to be weighed in the balance. So long as the two parts had any connection with Great Britain, the latter would be judged by action following the Bill rather than by its language, however generous and just it might read. He was afraid it would be a superhuman task to reconcile conflicting interests and treat them equally. What would happen if one decided to go out of the Commonwealth when the Constitution Act was passed? ... The relation to the Princes remained in a most unsatisfactory condition. Here, again, British honour was at stake. The British would certainly be blamed if any mishap occurred.

'Some of the doings of the authorities in Pakistan had given ground for the fear', he went on to point out, 'that there would be an attempt to estrange schedule classes in Pakistan from their Hindu brethren. There had been reports of Muslim League speakers holding forth that the scheduled classes in Pakistan could have separate electorates. (Separate electorates were later forced on the minorities in Pakistan in the teeth of their opposition.) "Was that to be a call for joining Islam of the Pakistani type?" Gandhiji asked. There had been tales of forcible conversions. Was Pakistan a means of converting non-caste Hindus to a special brand of Islam? The world was fast growing out of the dogmas and creeds which had so sickened and confused it that it had begun to deny the very existence of the Maker. Happily that stage of negation was quickly passing and enlightened faith in the Supreme Maker of the Universe was being restored. Was the Islam of Pakistan going to be in the vanguard of that movement for the restoration of universal faith? Or, was it to pass through darkness and denial of God in the name of God? Jinnah, Gandhiji concluded, had thus unwittingly placed Hinduism also on trial. He had said on the previous day that those who believed in India as a nation could have no minority and majority question; all are entitled to equal privileges and equal treatment. The Hindus had the rare opportunity of refining their religion of all dross and showing the strict justness that the brand of Hinduism of the Indian Union was the same as universal religion. Thus viewed, the Indian Independence Bill could be taken as the final examination of all the parties involved in the Bill. It was possible to turn Pakistan, which he had declared an evil, into unadulterated good. If all the forebodings were dispelled and enmities were turned into friendship and mutual distrust gave place to trust'.

With the partition of India came the contentious question of the division of its public assets and wealth and, especially, the division of its armed forces. Between 1 and 11 July, the Partition Council laid down the principles which were to govern division. The fixed assets would naturally belong to the provinces they were situated in, but other assets—down to the blotters in government offices—had to be fairly divided between the two nations. While Sir Cyril Radcliffe drew a line through the map of India, the Partition Council sat in New Delhi day after day, fighting over who would get what. A desk went to Pakistan and its matching chairs remained with India. A magnificent steed remained in India, while its equally magnificent saddle was shipped off to Pakistan. Everything was to be divided and every item was fought over by the two sides. The question of dividing the armed forces between the two nations was, in the words of Lord Ismay: 'The biggest crime and the biggest headache.'

'The army is now being divided into Hindu and Muslim,' Lord Selborne reported to the House of Lords, 'in the manner in which sides are picked before a football match. It is impossible that peace will be maintained.' The division of the armed forces ended up dividing families: two sons of the Navab of Rampur chose differently, one served India and the other, Pakistan. They confronted one another in the battle for

Kashmir where one shot and wounded his brother. Such was the tragedy of the partition.

Gandhi had hoped that it would be possible to write into the treaty of separation itself a provision for joint defence. It was a difficult proposition but not an impossible one, if both the parties were parting as friends and not as enemies, it was feasible. There was something wrong, he remarked at his prayer meeting on 6 July, that they missed the enthusiasm that should accompany such a great event as the imminent advent of full freedom. The reason for the lack of enthusiasm was no doubt to be found in the division of the country into two states which were to be turned into two armed camps. There was to be no common defence force. The army was to be divided; preparations were on to achieve this. They used to talk glibly during the glorious and strenuous days of opposition to British rule of having no army for the suppression of internecine quarrels, which would be non-existent and they wanted no defence force against a foreign enemy. But military expenditure was now to be maintained at a very high level without any near prospect of substantial reduction. In fact, there was the awful prospect of a definite increase in the military expenditure—all for fighting amongst themselves and they would have the spectacle of the two newly created states engaging in a ludicrous race for the increase of armaments, all for mutual slaughter! Was India's freedom a preparation for the abandonment of all they had learnt to prize as dear to them? Instead of self-glorification, he felt it was time for deep self-introspection, self-examination and self-castigation. As the chief actor in the fight for freedom during the past thirty years, he said he was certainly full of searching questions within himself. 'Is the fight, acclaimed as noble, to result in this the approaching inglorious end? In deep anguish I cry with the Vedic seers, "O Lord, Lead us from darkness into light."'

Since India was being divided in two, Gandhi remarked during his prayer meeting on 10 July, they had to consider their conduct accordingly. Unfortunately, it had become the fashion to behave like they were enemies. There were allegations that, in 1944, he had danced in attendance on Jinnah for eighteen days and the Muslim League was now reaping the fruits. Gandhi challenged this aspersion. He had made an offer to Jinnah, he said, which was in the interest of all concerned.

If Jinnah had accepted his offer, he could have been a master in what could have been called 'Pakistan areas'. But they would have had one India before the whole world, without any fear of domination by a third party. But instead, everyone was now baying for the other's blood. He could sense no independence in that barbarous state. He could not be enthusiastic about the impending independence, unless things changed during the next thirty-five days.

'Why could they not,' he asked, reverting to the theme a few days later, 'remain united for the object of facing foreign aggression?' The present mode of division might well lead to internal warfare between the two armies, who might even look upon each other as rivals. That would be a tragedy too deep. For years, they had said that they did not want any army. He still stood by that statement, but others did not. A new generation had arisen. Congressmen were not bound by what they had done during India's bondage. No blame could be imputed to them for the change. Almost every province wanted military assistance. There was a danger of a military dictatorship being established. 'Was this freedom?' he asked. This last warning proved true in the case of Pakistan, which, for a majority of its years as a nation, has been subject to the rule of generals.

As 15 August drew near, Gandhi noted with growing apprehension the portents that were gathering on the horizon. Vivisection of the country was the price that India had paid to avoid chaos and anarchy. But from the look of things, India after Partition was heading for a worse time. Jinnah had once again promised complete freedom of faith, religious worship and full security of life and property to all minorities in Pakistan. But there was a wide chasm between what was professed and what was practised. In Sind, non-Muslims were leaving their homes and fleeing with whatever they could carry on their person. In the meanwhile, nationalist Muslims were being warned by prominent Leaguers that, after Pakistan was established, they would be tried and hanged. Mountbatten had been able to incorporate in a Partition Council statement, a solemn assurance by both parties, a guarantee of civil rights for minorities and former political opponents. But guarantees for the future that were belied by present performance had absolutely no value for Gandhi. He felt deeply worried at the complacency with which those concerned seemed to regard repeated, flagrant violations of solemn guarantees, while they deceived themselves with the hope that ultimately there would be peace. He knew how inexorable was the working of the moral law and how inevitable the penalty when that law is trifled with. He was increasingly apprehensive about the growing tide of counter communalism that was being bred in the Indian Union by the continued ill-treatment of minorities on the other side. He was aware that, in some sections of Hindu society, the creed of revenge was firmly rooted, especially in some of the upper castes who were under the spell of Savarkar and his Hindu Mahasabha, as well as those who believed in religious segregation and Hindu supremacy, as espoused by the RSS. However, he was aware that these organizations appealed to a small percentage of the population. For more than thirty years, he had been able to keep the nation together, but the division of the country was fraying the fragile fabric of unity that he had so painstakingly woven.

Around this time, Arthur Moore, former editor of *The Statesman*, met Gandhi. They had met earlier in 1924, when Gandhi had undertaken a twenty-one-day fast for Hindu–Muslim unity in New Delhi. Moore had then termed the method of fasting as a moral weapon for change as a 'complete failure'. He still had his doubts about its efficacy. 'It does not look like a success so far,' Gandhi said, referring to the 1924 fast, and added, perhaps as an expression of hope rather than an affirmation of faith, 'but there must be some result.' Moore thought Patel's attitude was bellicose but Gandhi corrected him. 'You do not know the Sardar,' he said. 'He is not vindictive or communal. But he does not share my belief that non-violence can conquer everything. He used to be a whole-hogger once. He is so no more.'

'The Sardar is the most popular leader. Perhaps that explains it,' Moore said.

'No,' Gandhi replied. 'The Sardar is a strong man. He will not let any difficulty baffle him. That is the explanation.'

During the Simla Conference in 1945, Gandhi was asked by Preston Grover of the Associated Press of America why he had not asserted himself against his colleagues when, despite his advice, they accepted the 'parity formula'. Everyone, Jinnah, Lord Wavell, the country in general and all the observers at the conference, looked upon Gandhi as the head of the Congress, regardless of the technicality that he was not a member,

Grover said. No settlement would be reached without his consent. 'That is both right and wrong,' Gandhi replied. 'That impression has been created because generally my advice is accepted. But technically and substantially it is wrong.'

Grover insisted that Gandhi's was the controlling voice in the Congress, to which Gandhi replied, 'Not even that. They can shut me out at any time. If I tried to override them, I might succeed for once. But the moment I try to cling to power, I fall, never to rise again. That is not my temperament.'

Finally, at the time of the Cabinet Mission negotiations in June 1946, not only did Gandhi not force the Congress leaders to follow his 'instinct' which was against the acceptance of the Cabinet Mission plan, but also insisted that unless what he told them appealed to their head and heart, the only right thing for them was to follow their own judgement.

If the British had dared to impose the division of India without the approval of the Indian parties, Gandhi—even if all alone—would have fought against it. But the League, as well as the Hindu supremacist parties headed by Savarkar, had already endorsed the two nation theory. Thus, at the time of the agreement to divide India, Gandhi stood alone. Overriding the Congress's decision may not have ultimately prevented partition, and he would have certainly destroyed their political credibility. As a result, the country, looking for astute leadership, would have been faced with a vacuum, the kind Pakistan faced after Jinnah's death.

Since Pakistan was to be an Islamic state, some Congress leaders said, why shouldn't the Indian Union be declared a Hindu nation? The Muslims who, by their very act of not aligning with Pakistan or the Muslim League's political agenda, had proved their loyalty to India, were now being eyed with suspicion and branded as traitors. At one stage, even a leader of Patel's calibre had harboured doubts about the loyalty of the Muslims who had stayed back in India. Gandhi, however, said that no matter what events unfurled, the Congress government could not discriminate against anyone on the grounds of religion. He likened the situation to the tragic life of his eldest son Harilal. 'My eldest son has often come to me saying, "I will be good in future, I will not touch wine." I tell him, "Though I do not trust you, I shall give you a chance." He has not been able to keep his word so far. Yet, if he comes again, I will not turn him out, and I shall hope that he will keep his word, until I know that he has come back only to deceive me. We must trust the Muslims in the same way and at the same time be vigilant.'

Although publicly he did not show the deep hurt he felt about the division of his country and the rejection by his former protégés, the isolation he felt was very apparent in letters he wrote to his colleagues. 'Freedom has come but it leaves me cold,' he wrote to Asaf Ali, the newly appointed Indian envoy to the United States, in the third week of July. 'So far as I can see, I am a back number. I have come to the conclusion that our way was non-violent only superficially, our hearts were violent. It was enough to displace the foreign power. But the violence nursed within has broken out in a way least expected. Heaven knows where it will lead us.' To another co-worker he wrote, 'Where is Swaraj? The British are going but what is there in it to get excited about?'

'I almost despair of seeing peace in my lifetime,' he wrote to Sushila, his daughter-in-law, Manilal's wife. 'What is going on in the country in connection with the transfer of power and Pakistan is putting a heavy strain on me. I have, therefore, lost confidence in my capacity to live for long.'

Gandhi did not like the path his Congress colleagues were taking. At the same time, he did not want to openly criticize them, lest he embarrass them. In the last week of July, he wrote to Patel: 'I do not like much of what is going on here. That does not mean that you should alter your course, but I do not want it to be said that I was associated with it... I also feel that *Harijan* should now be closed. It does not seem to me to be right to give contrary guidance to the country. Think over it at your leisure.' To the manager of *Harijan*, he wrote: 'Perhaps we may have to decide to close *Harijan*. My mind rebels against many things that our leaders are doing. Yet I do not feel like actively opposing them. But how can I avoid it if I am running a paper? You do not want to run it without me, nor does the Sardar.'

Gandhi had mentioned in his letter to Patel that he would like to return to Noakhali, but the Congress leaders wanted him to remain in the capital. With the date for independence fast approaching, the Congress leaders were trying hard to cope with the everyday issues of running a country, including the princely states. Although almost all the princely states fell inside the borders of what was to be India after Partition, Jinnah nursed ambitions of persuading some of the Muslim rulers and as many others as he could to declare independence and then form unions with Pakistan. Many of the princes had accepted that their previous way of life was coming to an end and had more or less accepted the terms offered by the Union of India. Most of them had signed the 'Instrument of Accession' prepared by V.P. Menon, secretary of the state department under Patel. The instrument left the constitutional independence of the states untouched, barring three issues—defence, external affairs and communications, which they surrendered to the Union government. At the time of Independence, three princes remained who refused to surrender—Hyderabad, Junagadh and Kashmir. A standstill agreement for one year was signed with Hyderabad in November 1947, the same being made permanent before the end of the year. Junagadh was successfully dealt with some time later by a popular movement against the nawab's decision to accede to Pakistan. But Kashmir became a bone of contention between India and Pakistan and a festering sore in the body politic of both. 'The more I think over it, the more I feel that as soon as the matter of Kashmir is settled, I should leave Delhi,' Gandhi wrote to Patel on 24 July 1947. Nehru had decided to visit Kashmir in support of the incarcerated pro-democracy leader Sheikh Abdullah, whose trial was scheduled to start on the same date. The maharaja of Kashmir, Hari Singh, warned Nehru that while he was in the Valley, he should confine himself to the defence of Sheikh Abdullah. If he participated in any other political activity, he would have to face the consequences of his actions.

Hari Singh was a Hindu king who ruled over a state with a majority of Muslim subjects. Sheikh Abdullah, leader of the pro-democracy movement, was a Muslim. Hari Singh, in an effort to prolong his sovereignty, parleyed with the Muslim League as well as the militant Hindu groups. With the Muslim League, his plea was that as the head of a largely Muslim population, he deserved their patronage, while to the Hindu fanatics, he appealed to them to rush to the rescue of a beleaguered Hindu king menaced by Muslims.

Based on the report of the goings-on in Kashmir submitted to the CWC by Nehru, it was decided that Patel and Maulana Azad should go on a fact-finding mission to Kashmir. The Congress resolution was sent to Hari Singh. The maharaja responded, saying that he would allow only Patel, and only in his personal capacity, to come to Kashmir and study the situation. The leaders of the Kashmir National Conference, headed by Sheikh Abdullah, wanted Nehru to visit Kashmir, but Hari Singh adamantly refused to allow this. Gandhi wrote to Mountbatten to ask whether Hari Singh would allow him or Patel to visit instead of Nehru. Mountbatten wrote to Hari Singh, advising him to agree to allow Gandhi to visit Kashmir. The maharaja refused to pay heed to the viceroy. On 11 July, Gandhi wrote again to the viceroy: 'I am still without any news from Kashmir. If I was not bound by any promise made to you, of course I would not want any permission to go to Kashmir. I would simply go as any private person.'

By the last week of June, Nehru was thoroughly disgusted by the tactics employed by Hari Singh and his prime minister, Pandit Ramchandra Kak. He declared that he would go to Kashmir at the invitation of the people of Kashmir, disregarding Hari Singh's wishes. This precipitated matters and Kak hastily wrote to Mountbatten that they were now willing to allow Gandhi to visit Kashmir.

Gandhi left for Kashmir on 30 July. He reached Srinagar on the afternoon of 1 August. In the evening, he was taken out for a drive around the capital, which had been lit up to celebrate the restoration of Gilgit to Kashmir, an area so far administered by the Governor-General through the political department. On seeing the capital lit up, Gandhi remarked, 'A great mistake. They should have taken this opportunity immediately to proclaim autonomy for Gilgit within Kashmir.' Almost 100 per cent Muslim by its population, Gilgit was a hotbed of separatist seditious activity, promoted and pampered by the political department.

Gandhi stayed in Srinagar for two days. During this time, he met the prime minister and the maharaja, and had a series of interviews with leaders and workers of the National Conference. On the evening of 3 August, after driving down a dusty road through the crowded bazaar, Gandhi visited the Abdullah residence where he met Begum Abdullah, who had arranged a lavish tea reception in his honour. 'India will be free on 15 August, what of Kashmir?' a deputation of political workers asked him at Jammu. 'That will depend on the people of Kashmir,' Gandhi replied. They also wanted to know whether Kashmir should join the

Union or Pakistan. 'That again,' answered Gandhi, 'should be decided by the will of the Kashmiris.'

After his morning prayers, he resumed the journey to Rawalpindi, stopping briefly at the Wah refugee camp on the way. There were about 9,000 refugees from Rawalpindi and the surrounding areas in the camp on the day of his visit. The situation of the refugees was horrific. Gandhi visited the Panja Saheb Gurdwara on his way back. It had been attacked twice by Muslim mobs during the disturbances. Sikh defenders had managed to repel both the attacks, but they were perturbed about the safety of their shrines in West Punjab. They wanted eastern Punjab to be declared a Sikh state. Gandhi told them that it was unworthy of them to even harbour such ideas. He said, 'I would like every Sikh to be a defender of his faith. I want you to shed all fear about the future and to rely on the plighted word of the Muslim leaders. God is the judge, and the world which is His creation, will judge the Muslim leaders, not according to their pledges and promises, but according to their deeds and those of their followers.' The refugees at Wah camp wanted Gandhi to stay with them till 15 August, but due to pressing engagements, he could not. He said he would leave with them instead, as hostage, Dr Sushila Nayyar, who was like a daughter to him. If anything untoward happened to them, she would be the first to die.

Gandhi boarded the train at Rawalpindi. He intended to travel across the Gangetic plains of north India to Patna, then Calcutta and then on to Noakhali. Halting at Lahore en route, he wrote to Patel from Mrs Rameshwari Nehru's residence on 6 August 1947: 'A lot of useful work has been done in the Wah camp. People ought not to be removed from there. You ought to take up this matter with the Pakistan government. Rawalpindi should again have a Hindu–Sikh population. You should see my speech at Panja Saheb and Wah camp. I have made the suggestion there. I have left Sushila behind at Wah camp. I felt it to be necessary. It cheered up the people. They are in a panic. I see no reason for it.' He also sent a report on his visit to Kashmir to Nehru to be shared with Patel: 'During the two interviews with the prime minister, I told him about his unpopularity among the people. He wrote to the maharaja that on a sign from him, he would gladly resign. The maharaja had sent a message that he and the Maharani were anxious to see me. I met them;

the heir-apparent with his leg in plaster was also present. Both admitted that with the lapse of the British paramountcy, the true paramountcy of the people of Kashmir would commence. However much they might wish to join the Union, they would have to make the choice in accordance with the wishes of the people. How that could be determined was not discussed at that interview.

'Ghulam Mohammad Bakshi was most sanguine that the result of the free vote of the people, whether on the basis of adult franchise or on the existing register, would be in favour of Kashmir joining the Union, provided of course that Sheikh Abdullah and his co-prisoners were released, all bans were removed and the present prime minister was dismissed. Probably he echoed the general sentiment. I studied the Amritsar treaty properly called the "sale deed". I presume it lapses on the 15 instant. To whom does the State revert? Does it not go to the people?' In a letter to Patel he wrote: 'He (the maharaja) wishes to remove Kak… The only question before him is how… In my opinion, the Kashmir problem can be solved.'

Gandhi's mere presence in the Punjab and Kashmir had a positive effect on the communal situation; attacks had stopped, arson and violence had been halted, giving the persecuted population great relief. Gandhi reached Patna on the morning of 8 August and spent the entire day meeting Congress leaders and Bihar ministers. That evening, at the prayer meeting, he asked the people of Bihar to observe 15 August by praying, fasting and sacrificial spinning. 'The charkha has made Bihar. Even today, Bihar leads in spinning. Heaven forbid that Bihar should reduce to ashes all that it has achieved so far.' After his prayer meeting, Gandhi rushed to the station to board the train for Calcutta.

When Gandhi arrived in Calcutta on 9 August, the political scenario had undergone a change. On 3 July, after Bengal had decided in favour of its own partition, a separate Cabinet had been sworn in for West Bengal, headed by the leader of the West Bengal Congress party in the Assembly, Dr Prafulla Chandra Ghosh. In advocating a unified sovereign Bengal, Suhrawardy had upset his central leadership, which had retaliated by selecting Khwaja Nazimuddin as the chief minister designated for East Bengal. The existing Muslim League Cabinet remained in actual administrative charge of the various portfolios for the whole of Bengal till 15 August, but its decisions were applicable only to East Bengal; any decision affecting West Bengal had to be approved by the West Bengal Cabinet.

Calcutta had never quite returned to normalcy since the 'Great Calcutta Killings' of August 1946. Bitter memories of the brutality of the Muslim League's 'Direct Action Day' had embittered relations between the two communities. Additionally, because the partition plan gave government servants the freedom to choose which dominion they wanted to join, all Muslim policemen and officials had opted for Pakistan, and Hindus had been appointed in their place, disturbing the Muslim population. Soon after his arrival at Sodepore Ashram, Dr Ghosh went to meet Gandhi and briefed him about the situation. That evening, Gandhi said that he would not hold an inquiry into what had happened under the Muslim League ministry; he was more concerned with what his friend Ghosh's ministry was doing. If the Muslims of Calcutta were living in terror, it was a severe reflection on the Congress ministry. 'The Government must hold itself responsible also for the acts of the criminals. I will not be a living witness of India's reversion to slavery, which will be her lot, if the Hindu–Muslim quarrel continues, but my spirit will weep over the tragedy even from beyond the grave. My prayer is that God will spare us that calamity.' Announcing his decision to postpone his departure for Noakhali, Gandhi remarked that it was unthinkable that under a government well versed in the art of administration, the majority could for even one moment be permitted to coerce the minority. He had been told that now that the Congress ministry was in power, the Hindu police and officers had become partial in the administration of justice and were doing what the Muslim police and officers were alleged to have done before. He was loathe to believe it. 'If this wretched spirit of communalism enters the police force, the prospect is bleak indeed.' Today, independent India suffers because its policemen have been forced to become partisan and, like the administration, they also have largely become communal.

Suhrawardy was in Karachi and planned to stop for a couple of days in New Delhi on his way back. When he heard that Gandhi was in Calcutta, on his way to Noakhali, Suhrawardy cancelled his stay in Delhi and rushed to Calcutta instead. On 11 August, he called upon Gandhi at Sodepore

Ashram and requested that it would be remiss on Gandhi's part to leave Calcutta while the city was in danger of igniting. Gandhi said that he was willing to stay if Suhrawardy was prepared to work with him in restoring peace and if he guaranteed peace in Noakhali. Gandhi suggested that they live together under the same roof in the disturbed areas, unprotected by the police or the military, and meet people and counsel peace. If Suhrawardy accepted the offer, Gandhi said, he would postpone his trip to Noakhali indefinitely and remain in Calcutta as long as necessary. Gandhi told Suhrawardy to take his time, sleep over it, consult his aged father and his daughter, and then inform him of his decision.

Suhrawardy in 1947 was a chastened man, different from the one who had stormed out of Gandhi's room and termed a similar offer 'mad' just three months back. The next afternoon, Mohammad Usman informed Gandhi that Suhrawardy had accepted his suggestion. At the evening prayer meeting, Gandhi announced his decision of extending his stay in Calcutta. He added that he had been warned not to trust Suhrawardy, but he would trust him and would expect to be trusted in return. Gandhi wrote to Patel on 13 August, informing him of his decision: 'I have got stuck here and am now going to undertake a grave risk. Suhrawardy and I are going from today to stay together in a Muslim quarter. The future will reveal itself. Keep close watch. I shall continue to write.'

The very vigilant and forthright Patel had been observing the goings-on in Calcutta and expressed his concern in a letter: 'So you have got detained in Calcutta and that too in a quarter which is a veritable shambles and a notorious den of gangsters and hooligans. And in what choice company too! It is a terrible risk. But more than that, will your health stand the strain? I am afraid; it must be terribly filthy there. Keep me posted about yourself.'

Gandhi always intimated all the members of his extended family of any major decision or assignment. On the 13th, the day's post contained several handwritten letters informing people about his mission in Calcutta; work carried on till 1:30 p.m. that day.

Pakistan came into being at the stroke of midnight on 13 August 1947: East Pakistan, consisting of the eastern province of Bengal, and West Pakistan, consisting of Punjab, Sind, the North-West Frontier Province and the tribal lands.

On 14th morning, Gandhi sent word to Suhrawardy that he would be starting from Sodepore for his new residence in Beliaghata exactly at half past two in the afternoon; Suhrawardy should arrive in time to join him there. Gandhi, ever the stickler for punctuality, left his room at exactly 2:28 p.m., took his seat next to the driver, and at 2:30 the car carrying him sped off towards Beliaghata.

Hydari Mansion was the old abandoned home of a Muslim in Beliaghata, a congested and filthy locality of Calcutta. In the past twelve hours, however, an effort had been made to clean it up. The crumbling building was open on all sides to the crowds that had begun to gather there. Three rooms had been cleared for Gandhi and his party—one for him, one for his baggage and for members of his party to stay in and the third to be used as his office.

An angry mob greeted Gandhi's and, a little later, Suhrawardy's cars, and the situation threatened to take an ugly turn. Gandhi sent some members from his party to plead with the demonstrators and ask them to remain peaceful as he was willing to listen to their grievances. The situation was described in detail by Pyarelal: 'The demonstration was still going on when Horace Alexander, who had been asked by Gandhiji to come and stay with him at Beliaghata, arrived. The demonstrators tried to stop him too. An Indian friend accompanying Horace tried to reason with the mob. In reply there were even shriller cries of "Gandhi, go back!" Finally, they both got out of the car and walked into the house. The shouting continued. Some young men tried to climb in through the window of the room in which Gandhiji was sitting. Members of Gandhiji's party begged them to desist. It was of no use. Horace began to shut the windows. This, as he himself afterwards put it, proved to be a "most misguided action". Almost immediately, stones were thrown through the glass of the windows and glass was flying in all directions.

'We then realized that there were wooden shutters and these we closed, though stones were still thrown against them for a time. A press reporter came up to me and said, "Are you hurt?" I said, "No, but there is some glass in my hair!" Presently, the representatives of the demonstrators were ushered in to meet Gandhiji. "Last year when Direct Action was launched on the Hindus on 16 August, you did not come to our rescue. Now that there has been just little trouble in the

Muslim quarters, you have come running to their succour. We don't want you here, go back!"

Gandhiji calmly replied, 'Much water has flown under the bridge since August 1946. What the Muslims did then was utterly wrong. But what is the use of avenging the year 1946 in 1947? I was on my way to Noakhali where your own kith and kin desired my presence. But I now see that I shall have to serve Noakhali from here. You must understand that I have come here to serve not only Muslims but Hindus, Muslims and all alike... I am going to put myself under your protection. You are welcome to turn against me and play the opposite role if you so choose. I have nearly reached the end of my life's journey. I have not much farther to go... I have given the same ultimatum to the Muslims of Noakhali too; I have earned the right. Before there is another outbreak of Muslim madness in Noakhali, they will find me dead. Why cannot you see that by taking this step I have put the burden of the peace of Noakhali on the shoulders of Shaheed Suhrawardy and his friends, including men like Mian Ghulam Sarwar and the rest? This is no small gain.'

The evening prayer was held inside the compound of Hydari Mansion. Over ten thousand people squeezed into the tiny place. After the prayers, Gandhi said, 'From tomorrow, 15 August, we shall be delivered from the bondage of the British rule. But from midnight today, India will be partitioned too. While, therefore, tomorrow will be a day of rejoicing, it will be a day of sorrow as well. It will throw a heavy burden of responsibility upon us. Let us pray to God that he may give us strength to bear it worthily. Let all those Muslims who were forced to flee return to their homes. If two millions of Hindus and Muslims are at daggers drawn with one another in Calcutta, with what face can I go to Noakhali and plead the case of the Hindus with the Muslims there? And if the flames of communal strife envelope the whole country, how can our newborn freedom survive?' Many in the crowd began asking agitatedly for Suhrawardy. Gandhi replied that he had asked him to stay away from the meeting as he wanted to avoid even the slightest cause for irritation. He added that as the crowd had shown supreme tolerance, he would ask Suhrawardy to join them the following day.

After the prayer, Gandhi returned to his room and sat down to work. A little later, Gandhi appeared at a window overlooking the street. A group of angry young men had gathered there and were raising slogans against Suhrawardy. Gandhi beckoned Suhrawardy to his side and stood there in full view of the crowd, resting one hand tactfully on Suhrawardy's shoulder and the other on Manu's shoulder. Someone from the crowd shouted, 'Are you not responsible for the great Calcutta killing?'

'Yes, it was my responsibility,' Suhrawardy said, owning up for the first time, publicly, to his role in the massacres during Direct Action Day.

This unequivocal and candid confession of guilt by one who had never known humility, had a profound effect on the crowd. 'It was a turning point,' Gandhi remarked later. 'It had a cleansing effect. I could sense it.'

At Gandhi's request, the armed guards positioned outside the Hydari Mansion were removed from the midnight of 15 August, and young volunteers stood there instead, both Hindus and Muslims in equal numbers.

As the clock struck twelve, a loud cheer went up. India was free! The whole nation erupted with joy, but the man who had spearheaded the battle for independence for the past three decades was fast asleep on the floor of a darkened room in a dilapidated mansion in one of Calcutta's filthiest localities, unaffected by the momentous occasion. In New Delhi, the men he had groomed to take on the responsibility of shepherding India through its infancy were busy with a ceremony which rivalled, in its pomp and pageantry, the great Durbars held by the Raj.

On the morning of Independence Day, Gandhi woke up at 2 a.m., an hour earlier than usual. The day also marked the fifth death anniversary of his close companion and secretary of twenty-five years, Mahadev Desai. Gandhi observed the anniversary in his usual way, by fasting and recitation from the Gita after the morning prayers.

Nearly 30,000 people gathered for the evening prayers on Independence Day. The ground adjacent to Hydari Mansion was choked with people. Gandhi congratulated the citizens of Calcutta on the unity they had achieved and displayed that day. He felt sure that the example they had set would affect the Punjab and other parts of India. He warned the people to use their freedom with wise restraint. They were bound to treat Europeans, who stayed in India, with the same regard as they would expect for themselves.

A letter that Gandhi wrote on 15 August to one of his European admirers, Agatha Harrison, mentioned how he had celebrated that day: 'You know my way of celebrating great events such as today, is to thank God for it and therefore to pray. This prayer must be accompanied by a fast. And as a mark of identification with the poor and dedication, there must be spinning. Hence I must not be satisfied with the spinning I do every day but must do as much as is possible, in consistence with my other appointments.'

In another letter to Rajkumari Amrit Kaur, he wrote: 'I am in a Muslim's house. They are all very good. I have taken no one from Sodepore Ashram. Hence, the help I need comes only from Muslim friends. This is not for me a new experience. It reminds me of old days in South Africa and the Khilafat days here. For the moment I have no enemy. Who knows how long this will last! Hindus and Muslims have become friends practically in a day. Suhrawardy has become transformed, so it looks.'

Rajaji came to meet Gandhi after being freed from the besieged Government House. Apart from being old colleagues who had maintained their friendship though they had differing political ideologies, the two were also bound by marriage: Gandhi's youngest son Devadas was married to Rajaji's daughter Laxmi.

Nearly fifty thousand people gathered for the evening prayers on 16 August, and on the 17th, there was a crowd of nearly a hundred thousand. While addressing them, Gandhi wondered how much of their enthusiasm was genuine. He said, 'Everybody is showering congratulations on me for the miracle Calcutta is witnessing. Let us all thank God for His abundant mercy. But let us not, in this pardonable exuberance, forget that there are isolated spots in Calcutta, where all is not well. I have heard that in one place the Hindus are not prepared to welcome back the Muslim residents who were obliged to leave their homes… I appreciate your overflowing affection, but I hope it will not prove to be a momentary adulation.'

Referring to the large number of Hindus and Muslims at the prayer meetings everyday, Suhrawardy said that no one could have imagined that a meeting of the two communities in such numbers was possible in Calcutta. He said that in the Park Circus area, a predominantly Muslim locality, Hindus were already taking possession of the homes they had fled from.

However, Gandhi could sense that trouble was brewing. The first indication of the trouble Gandhi foretold came that very day. It was the Muslim festival of Eid. A large number of Muslims came to visit Gandhi from early morning. As it was the day of his weekly silence, Gandhi wrote out a short message greeting them. In the afternoon, he got news about trouble breaking out in Barrackpore, fourteen miles north of Calcutta: trouble had erupted over a procession the day before. Gandhi visited Barrackpore late in the afternoon, by which time the trouble had subsided; the episode ended in the two communities embracing each other.

That evening, Gandhi was given a report of another incident that occurred in Kanchrapara, an industrial area twenty-six miles north of Calcutta. The incident was caused by loud music being played outside a mosque while namaaz was being offered. The police had to resort to firing to control the mob, resulting in the death of several people. Gandhi visited Kanchrapara on the 19th.

There was tension in certain areas for another reason. A mix-up had occurred because Bengal was divided twice: once under the notional division and then by the Boundary Commission's award. Under the former, the Hindu-majority districts of Khulna and Chittagong Hill Tracts were included in West Bengal and the Muslim-majority district of Murshidabad, in East Bengal. The Boundary Commission's award reversed this. In these areas, Independence Day had been celebrated according to the notional division. On this being reversed and the border redrawn according to the Boundary Commission's award, the national flags flying in these districts since Independence Day were the wrong ones. This led to hostility in the areas. The matter was referred to Gandhi, who said that there should not be the slightest hesitation in replacing the flags. Personally, he was of the opinion that as the two states were on friendly terms with one another, there was no reason why the two flags could not be displayed side by side. 'Even if they in Pakistan don't, we in the Indian Union should. Let us do the correct thing irrespective of what the other party does.'

With every passing day, the attendance at the evening prayer meeting increased. On 21 August, at the meeting held at Park Circus, more than seven hundred thousand people were present. Flags of the Indian Union and Pakistan were flown alongside each other. Referring to this, Gandhi remarked that he could now proceed to Noakhali.

On 27 August, Gandhi held his prayer meeting at Kidderpur dock area; the presence of a large labour population in this area had converted it into a potential flashpoint for trouble. In his post-prayer speech to the labourers, he observed that the future of labour was closely interlinked with communal harmony. Labour would become invincible when it realized its strength and learnt the art of combination. That could not happen if the workers discriminated against a Hindu employer and a Muslim one, or if the Hindu segment of labour regarded itself as separate from the Muslim segment of labour or both from the Harijan segment.

The 'miracle of Calcutta', as it was being called, was having its effect in other parts of the country. A telephone message from Patna informed Gandhi that the Calcutta miracle was having a profound effect on Bihar too. This news delighted him. On 24 August, the Muslim League party in the Constituent Assembly of the Indian Union passed a resolution expressing 'its deep sense of appreciation of the services rendered by Mahatma Gandhi to the cause of restoration of peace and goodwill between the communities in Calcutta and saving hundreds of innocent lives and property from destruction. By his ceaseless efforts in the maintenance of peace he has shown breadth of vision and large-heartedness. The Muslim League sincerely trusts that Mr Suhrawardy and other Muslims will continue to cooperate with him and show their appreciation of his laudable efforts.'

In an article titled 'Miracle or Accident?', published in *Harijan,* Gandhi wrote: 'Shaheed Suhrawardy and I are living together in Beliaghata, where Muslims have been reported to be sufferers. We are living in a Muslim's home and Muslim volunteers are attending to our comforts with the greatest attention. Here, in the compound, numberless Hindus and Muslims continue to stream in shouting the favourite slogans. One might almost say that the joy of fraternization is leaping up from hour to hour... Is this to be called a miracle or an accident? By whatever name it may be described, it is quite clear that the credit that is being given to me from all sides is quite undeserved; nor can it be said to be deserved by Shaheed. This sudden upheaval is not the work of one or two men. We are toys in the hands of God. He makes us dance to His tune. The utmost, therefore, that man can do is to refrain from interfering with the dance and that he should tender full obedience to his Maker's will. Thus considered, it can be said that in this miracle, He has used us two as His instruments and as far as for myself, I only ask that the dream of my youth is to be realized in the evening of my life.'

People were convinced, however, that the peace in Calcutta was brought about by one man's presence there. Lord Mountbatten wrote to Gandhi: 'In the Punjab we have 55,000 soldiers and largescale rioting on our hands. In Bengal our force consists of one man, and there is no rioting. As a serving officer as well as an administrator, may I be allowed to pay my tributes to the One-Man Boundary Force, not forgetting his Second in Command, Mr Suhrawardy. You should have heard the enthusiastic applause which greeted the mention of your name in the Constituent Assembly on 15 August, when all of us were thinking so much of you.' Ignoring the compliments and seizing the challenge, Gandhi replied to Mountbatten: 'I do not know if Shaheed and I can legitimately appropriate the compliments you pay us. Probably suitable conditions were ready for us to take the credit for what appears to have been a magical performance. Am I right in gathering from your letter that you would like me to try the same thing for the Punjab?'

What Mountbatten had written about the Punjab was tragically true. After its division, both sides of Punjab, the Pakistani West and the Indian East, were in a frenzy of religious hatred and violence. In West Punjab, Hindus were systematically targeted by a campaign of intimidation, abduction, rape, forcible conversion, arson, looting and murder. Survivors were being forced to flee with whatever they could salvage and carry on their person towards India. In the Indian parts of Punjab, a similar fate befell the Muslims at the hands of Sikhs and Hindus. The deeds of either of the savage mobs precipitated an equal, or many times much more severe, retaliation from the other. Hate was feeding on hate and thriving.

On 17 August, Gandhi received a very disturbing telegram from Lahore: 'Since Monday a terrible massacre of the Hindus has been in progress in Lahore city, surpassing Rawalpindi. Hundreds of dead are lying strewn on the roads. Anarkali Bazaar and other business quarters have been burnt down. The greater part of the city is in flames. Water supply to Hindu residential quarters has been cut off. The trapped

Hindus, who tried to escape, were shot down by the military and the police. More than three hundred Hindus were burnt alive. The Hindus are without food and water. They are threatened with destruction. Do something immediately. Your presence in Lahore is necessary.' Gandhi passed the message to Patel with a comment: 'I have not replied to it. It is terrible if true. Let me know the facts.'

Nehru rushed to the riot-ravaged areas of East Punjab on receiving news of the fresh outrage. On his return to Delhi, he wired Gandhi on 21 August, sending him his 'respectful congratulations on the wonderful change in Calcutta' and also telling him that the Punjab needed his 'healing presence'. Gandhi replied the following day: 'I have got stuck here. Noakhali demands my presence. Bihar too will take a few days. Under the circumstances, I do not know when I shall be able to go to the Punjab. You will guide me.' Nehru replied: 'I do not ask you to go to the Punjab immediately. We must face the situation now. Later I might request you to go there.' He enclosed a report about the situation in Punjab, which was most disturbing: 'The southern districts, which had been free from any major trouble, blew up unexpectedly so far as we were concerned. The districts of Hoshiyarpur and Jullundhar especially have witnessed some horrible deeds and large-scale massacre of Muslims. It is quite impossible to form any estimate of people killed. I imagine however, that during the last month the number killed in Eastern Punjab might amount to 7 to 8 thousand. These figures might be completely wrong, as they are guesswork. In Western Punjab, probably the number of those killed is much less, maybe half the other figure. This, of course applies to recent weeks only and not to the previous Rawalpindi and Multan killings. There has been far more arson and looting in Western Punjab than in Eastern… All this killing business has reached a stage of complete madness and vast populations are deserting their habitations and trekking to the west or the east. A large number left Western Punjab in previous months, as you know. Now the process is repeated on both sides… The present trouble started about three weeks ago in Amritsar's rural areas. The Sikhs were the aggressors. Within a week, Lahore retaliated, the Muslims being the aggressors. Since then it has spread on both sides, perhaps more so in Eastern Punjab where well-armed bands, chiefly Sikh, partly Hindu, have been roaming about and attacking predominantly Muslim villages.

Normally Muslims are safe in a village where they are in a minority. Their neighbours do not attack them. Armed bands go specially to Muslim majority villages in Eastern Punjab. Something of this kind happened in Western Punjab too… It appears that most of the petty government officials join in this business, including policemen. Sometimes soldiers also. The whole thing is revolting in the extreme.'

Nehru further added that he had hesitated to write to Gandhi about the situation as he did not wish to add to his worries. But now the stage had come when Gandhi needed to know. 'At present there is no doubt that the Muslim League leaders as well as Sikh leaders are trying to stop the slaughter and arson, having previously lighted the fuse. I have no doubt that we shall put an end to this business within the next few days, at any rate so far as the major events are concerned. But what a terrible legacy! The Punjab will be a ruined province, both west and east, and vast numbers of human beings will be destitute.'

Gandhi was receiving updates on the Punjab situation from other sources too. A deputation of Punjabis settled in Calcutta met Gandhi on 24 August and briefed him about the gory events in Punjab. The same day, Gandhi wrote to Nehru: 'Punjabis in Calcutta have been pressing me to go to the Punjab at once. They tell me a terrible story. Thousands have been killed! A few thousand girls have been kidnapped! Hindus cannot live in the Pakistan area, nor Muslims in the other portion. Add to this the information that the two wings of the army took sides and wreaked havoc! Can any of this be true? … When do you think I should go to the Punjab if at all? I still have work in Calcutta, then in Noakhali and Bihar. But everything can be laid aside to go to the Punjab if it is proved to be necessary.'

Nehru had, in the meantime, gone on his second visit to East Punjab. Immediately on his return on the morning of 25 August, he wrote to Gandhi.

'In my last letter I gave you some idea of conditions in the Punjab. Normally, even after the worst riots, most people stick to their homes. Now with the coming of Pakistan, the urge to get out of it has added to the normal urge to escape from a dangerous zone. On both sides of the border in the Punjab, people are affected this way and mass migrations are taking place on a vast scale. These are largely spontaneous. Inevitably, this is resulting and will result in misery for hundreds of thousands of people. It will mean also a tremendous burden on all governments concerned, provincial and central, on both sides. The Muslims of Amritsar districts, these are the survivors, told me that 50,000 of them had perished in the district. This is certainly wild exaggeration. But we should not be surprised if anything up to 10,000 were killed in Eastern Punjab. There has been widespread killing on both sides; a large numbers of refugees have been massacred. In Eastern Punjab, probably the Akali Sikhs have indulged in killing more than anyone else. Worse than the killing have been the horrible outrages on women on both sides... It is said and rightly that Lahore and Amritsar are quiet. The fact is that there are not many people left there to be killed. That is to say that Lahore has become almost entirely a Muslim city and Amritsar a Hindu–Sikh city. More and more, both in the East and West Punjab, habitually lawless elements are coming to the front, they are not prepared to listen to the leaders. There are internal conflicts also in both the provinces. In Western Punjab there is conflict between Mamdot, the chief minister, and Feroz Khan Noon. Noon appears to be encouraging the wilder elements in the League. In Eastern Punjab there is a good deal of stress and strain between the Sikhs and Hindus. The Akalis, or some of them, do not hesitate to talk in terms of establishing a Sikh state as a result of this turmoil. Their logic is very good, but there is little doubt that many of them have vague hopes that something advantageous to them might happen if trouble continued. Some of these think that they can force India to go to war with Pakistan. In such a war, they imagine that Pakistan is bound to be defeated and then Sikhistan will emerge. Master Tara Singh and Giani Kartar Singh, however, have been trying to get peace restored. Their influence does not seem to go as far as some people imagined. The wilder elements among the Akalis have joined hands with some of the RSS people.'

Nehru was unsure about Gandhi travelling to the Punjab yet. But Mountbatten had realized the significance of the 'One-Man Boundary Force' and the tactical value of the weapon of non-violence. Nehru concluded his letter by saying: 'This morning, at a meeting of the Joint Defence Council, Mountbatten urged me to request you to go to the Punjab, he hoped that you would repeat your Calcutta miracle there. I told him that I was myself not clear about this. I feel you should go but not just yet.'

In the last week of August, Patel received a distress call from Sushila Nayyar, who had been left behind as moral support for the refugees at the Wah refugee camp by Gandhi. She wrote:

'I stayed there, fully convinced that it was wrong for the Hindus and Sikhs to flee from Pakistan. They had inhabited the land for generations and were entitled to live there. If Indians could fight for their rights in South Africa, were they to relinquish their homes in Pakistan? I placed my ideas before the refugees. Some appreciated them, some were resentful. They were not prepared to live the life of hostages, they said. They would rather be beggars in the Indian Union than big landlords in Pakistan, where even the honour of their womenfolk was not safe. I tried to impress upon them that the right thing to do for us would be to die in defence of our honour rather than be bullied out… I visited a few villages from where the people had fled. The deputy commissioner came and assured me that the refugees should be quite safe and soon rehabilitation would become possible. Then the unexpected happened. Trouble again started. East Punjab was reported to be avenging Rawalpindi and the whole of the West Punjab flared up to avenge the happenings in East Punjab. About 10 August, news began coming in of inhuman deeds in the East and West Punjab. Several victims of communal fury from places round about us began to pour into the camp hospital… One of them was a young girl of about seventeen—the sole survivor of a group of seventy-four women, who had jumped into a well to save their honour. Her father Sardar Pratap Singh had come to join the camp earlier. He and his companions had offered armed resistance to the Muslim mobs who had attacked their village. For three days they held the attackers at bay. When at last their ammunition was exhausted, they had to surrender. Several of them, including their leader, were wounded, some others had died. The survivors were told that they would be immediately converted to Islam. They asked for reprieve till the next day. The next day the hooligans came armed with scissors and razors to cut off their victims' hair and shave their beards as a symbol of their conversion to Islam … Some women … were ordered to come out to be converted. An elderly sister speaking for the rest answered that they wanted leave to say their prayers for the last time before they surrendered and drink the water from the well... The request was granted. Thereupon, seventy-four women and girls entered the compound in which the well was located. They had their ceremonial bath and then began saying their prayers. Their Muslim captors impatiently shouted at them to hurry up. The leader of the women shouted back, "Come if you dare. You will never touch us alive!" And with that she jumped into the well, followed by the rest. This act of heroic sacrifice so touched the gangsters that they stood rooted to the spot, and with bowed heads departed one after another, leaving untouched the men and the children whom they had assembled for conversion. The Sikhs then entered the compound and brought out the bodies of the women who had jumped into the well. All except Sardar Pratap Singh's daughter were dead. At night they were attacked by another Muslim mob but a military patrol came to their rescue and escorted them to the Wah camp... The number of wounded coming to the hospital increased. A truckload of the nearly dead and dying arrived one day... One day, a report arrived of an impending attack on the camp. At night, the military came and took up position at strategic points commanding the camp. I had gone to bed dead tired. Some people came running to me. "Please get up. The attackers are coming." Wearily I replied, "Come and tell me when they are here." They stood dumbfounded for a moment and then went away. After a while, some social workers working with me in the camp compound shook me awake. "There is panic in the barracks." Military jeeps were on the move. There was a blaze of light from the sector where they were taking up positions. I felt worried. "Supposing an attack comes, how shall I protect these people? They had faith in Gandhiji and Gandhiji had placed them in my charge. He had said that I should die before any harm befell them. It was simple enough to die but would I get that opportunity? Would I be able to stand up to the test?" A companion asked me, "How do you expect them to defend themselves non-violently? What exactly should they do?" My reply did not carry conviction to him. Non-violent self-defence cannot be learnt at a moment's notice. If I could set an example by laying down my own life non-violently, that might help... When we reached the barracks, the men who had first brought the news of the impending attack were already there. They must have told them how they had found me sleeping in spite of the alarming rumour. That had served to reassure them. We talked with them for a while and then came back. There was no attack on the camp that night. When similar rumours led to military movement on the two subsequent nights, there was much less panic.'

In the last week of August, Patel received the following report from Sushila Nayyar through a Sikh military officer, who came from the Wah camp.

'We are completely cut off. No post comes or leaves this place. People here are living in hourly fear of certain death. I am trying my best to keep up their morale. They won't allow me to leave this place... The camp commander says that the camp was going to be attacked three or four days ago. But the attack did not come. You should send some reliable person to report on the exact situation here... Some Hindu refugees who have managed to reach here disguised as Muslims reported that Gujranwala, Wazirabad, Gujerat and Lalamusa are burning. Sialkot too is reported to be ablaze from yesterday. A similar report has come from Gujrakhan near Rawalpindi. It is said that the railway track on either side is strewn with the dead. The attack on village Sukhoke in Rawalpindi district was warded off by the presence of the military police the day before yesterday. Yesterday, 500 Muslims again launched an attack, killing 15 Hindus. The situation is deteriorating. It is difficult to say when the Muslim mass may again go out of control... It is feared that this camp will be attacked after non-Muslim troops are withdrawn. At Taxila station, a passenger train, it is reported, was stopped by pulling the alarm chain in the presence of the Muslim military and police. Two Sikhs were killed and another two or three wounded. At subsequent stations the military were heard to be congratulating the murderers... It is a question of how long the refugees can continue to remain in this camp. Their condition is anything but satisfactory. The civil surgeon visited the camp the other day. He told the refugees to go to the relief organizations. "They are your own kith and kin." Another officer, a Muslim, was heard to remark, "How long are we going to have these fellows on our hands?" There is no trace of sympathy for the refugees nor any feeling of shame over what has happened.'

Patel immediately took up the issue with Liaquat Ali Khan, and asked him to ensure the safety and well-being of the refugees at Wah. Khan instructed Ghaznafar Ali and the premier of West Punjab to take appropriate steps. Forwarding Sushila's report to Gandhi, Patel commented: 'I feel very concerned at your leaving Sushila behind. Today, a special military man has come with a letter from her. I send it to you. The Punjab situation has become very bad... Cities and villages are being burnt down. Men are being cut to pieces... Reports are coming in that the military and the police are involved in it. People in their thousands are fleeing and spreading panic wherever they go. Eighty five per cent of the police force are Muslims. It has become difficult to obtain accurate information as to what is happening in the Punjab. Hundreds upon thousands are fleeing. Today Jawaharlal has gone to Jullundhar and Amritsar. The League Ministers will also be there. But the masses seem to have gone out of their control. The situation is most difficult. It calls for very strenuous effort to prevent the Punjab situation from affecting other places. More and more fleeing refugees from the Punjab are pouring into Delhi. They allow no rest by day or by night. They are distraught with fury and panic and it is most difficult to make them pull themselves together.'

Patel again wrote to Gandhi on 27 August: 'Rajkumari Amrit Kaur had accompanied Lady Mountbatten on a three day tour of the Punjab. She returned today at 8 o'clock. She has brought a terrible report. She met Sushila, too. I had asked Lady Mountbatten to bring her back with her. Accordingly, Sushila had got ready. But the people in the camp began to weep and wail. She is, therefore, staying on there. This camp is not in danger. We have now made arrangements for some more supply of food, too. She is keeping quite fit. So there is nothing to worry. The rest of course is in God's hands.'

Patel had given up hope of a peaceful solution and the chance of co-existence in Punjab; he had decided that the only solution was in an exchange of populations. Naively, he believed that the large number of Hindus and Muslims trapped on the wrong side of the divided Punjab would be able to just get up and leave, Hindus to East Punjab and Muslims to West Punjab. Patel questioned Gandhi: 'What will you do by going to the Punjab? You can do nothing to put down the conflagration. It is not possible for the Hindus, Sikhs and Muslims to live together; Hindus might be able to stay there some time in future, not today. But one cannot imagine Sikhs and Muslims living together even in the remote future. The forces have been thoroughly infected. People in their lakhs are fleeing from either side of the border. Terror prevails in the camps. Those who are fleeing are set upon and done to death. There is no arrangement for their evacuation with safety.' Patel was forgetting that now it was the government's and its ministers' responsibility on both sides to provide security for their people.

On the 29th, Gandhi again wrote to Nehru: 'Herewith is a letter from one Sardar Ajit Singh. You will see he is insistent on my going to the Punjab without a moment's delay. You will judge what I should do. Will it be any use my going after life and property are destroyed to the saturation point? Will it not be a mockery? I put before you for consideration the thoughts welling up within me. I have three wires pressing me to go.' Nehru wired back the same day: 'I still think that the time has not come for you to visit the Punjab but feel your presence in Delhi very desirable so as to keep in touch with the Punjab situation and advise us.' The next day, Patel sent another report on the situation in the Punjab, but it was very clear that neither he nor Nehru were in favour of Gandhi going to the Punjab: 'Yesterday, there was a meeting at Lahore. The result was satisfactory. Jinnah and other Leaguers were present. All resolutions were passed unanimously. But it will take time to put out the conflagration. From today, Jawaharlal and Liaquat Ali have commenced touring the Punjab together. The tour will last for a week. Others too have commenced touring similarly. Everybody is trying hard. The rest is in God's hands.'

Gandhi was disturbed by the note of complacency in Patel's letter. His colleagues did not seem to understand the gravity of the situation. He did not wish to embarrass his colleagues by what they might consider unwanted interference. Nonetheless, he felt that he owed it to them to sound a final note of warning. On 30 August, he wrote to Nehru: 'About my going to the Punjab, I won't move without you and Vallabhbhai's wish. I want to say, however, that every day pressure is being put upon me to rush to the Punjab before it is too late… If I am not going to the Punjab, would I be of much use in Delhi as an adviser or consultant? I fancy I am not built that way. My advice has value only when I am actually working at a particular thing. I can only disturb when I give academic advice. Left to myself, I would probably rush to the Punjab and if necessary break myself in the attempt to stop the warring elements from committing suicide. From a letter I just have from Lord Mountbatten, I get the same impression. He would welcome my immediate going to the Punjab.'

Patel redirected Gandhi's letters to Nehru, who was touring both the Punjabs with Liaquat Ali Khan. What he saw there, coupled, perhaps, with Lord Mountbatten's advice, helped him decide. On 31 August he sent a wire to Gandhi: 'Punjab problem overwhelming in extent and intensity. I feel now that your presence in Punjab is desirable and would be helpful in curing insanity and bringing solace to this ruined and heartbroken province. I am returning to Delhi on 4th. After brief stay coming back to Punjab.' On 2 September, he followed this up with another wire: 'I feel sure now that you should come to Punjab as early as possible.'

It now seemed certain that Gandhi would leave immediately for the Punjab and strive to do what he had so far succeeded in doing in Calcutta. But fate decreed differently; Calcutta was about to erupt.

After the Direct Action Day riots, Hindu right-wing organizations, with the Hindu Mahasabha and the RSS at the forefront, had projected themselves as the protectors of the Hindus, and many had fallen under the spell of militant Hinduism. When the post-Partition riots erupted, these Hindu extremists set up recruitment centres in areas which were their strongholds and amongst the refugee camps. In the post-War scenario, arms and ammunition were easily available and so, just like the National Guard of the Muslim League, the fanatics of Hindu Mahasabha and the RSS, too, had armed and trained themselves. These groups, who had infiltrated Calcutta in large numbers, attempted to start trouble in Barrackpore and Kanchrapara but failed. Now they were exploiting the anger in the Punjabi and Sikh communities in Calcutta due to the reports of the massacre in Punjab. Leaders of the communities and heads of the Bengal Hindu Mahasabha had received bangles mocking their 'manhood'; this is a tactic still practised efficiently by these patriarchal fanatic organizations to provoke violence. By 1 September, their pent up anger was ready to explode.

Pyarelal Nayyar describes what happened at Hydari Mansion on that fateful night.

'Charu and I had gone out to the city on business. When we returned to Hydari Mansion, it was past ten. We had expected to find everybody asleep. Instead, we found the building in a blaze of light. Some youngsters at the gate tried to stop our car asking, "Who are you—Hindu or Muslim?" We came out of the car. Chucking the leader, Charu said that children were expected to be in bed at that hour. "In Noakhali our boys show more maturity. We enforce strict discipline in Gandhi Camps." The demonstrators had already broken their cordon in their eagerness to hear the dialogue and were clustering round us in a disorderly fashion. We brushed them aside and went in. Crowds were all over the place. Some rowdies were already inside the main hall. More were pouring in. It was only the next day that we were able to piece together the story. A little before 10 o'clock, a man, heavily bandaged, had been brought to Gandhiji's residence by some excited young men at the head of a procession. How they got hold of him and who had engineered the demonstration, will probably never be known. There were several conflicting versions. One was that he had fallen out of a tramcar. Another was that he was accosted by a drunken man on the street and asked to shout *"Pakistan Zindabad!"* on his refusing to do so a scuffle ensued, resulting in some minor injuries. Some communal fanatics, hearing of the incident, traced him to his residence and pulled him out of his bed. Another version claimed that he had been stabbed by Muslims in a Muslim locality. His assailants could not be traced. Later, the Chief Minister Dr Prafulla Ghosh, had the victim of the alleged stabbing examined. The doctor's report was that he bore no mark of stabbing. The details of the injury however did not matter. What really mattered was that these young men had taken the law into their own hands and had assumed the role of judge, jury and executioner rolled into one. Gandhiji had gone to bed.' "This was about 10:00 p.m. (Calcutta time). They began to shout at the top of their voices. My sleep was disturbed but I tried to lie quiet, not knowing what was happening. I heard the windowpanes being smashed. I had on either side of me two brave girls, Abha and Manu. They would not wake me up from my sleep, but without my knowledge, for my eyes were closed, they went among the crowd and tried to pacify them. Thank God, the crowd did not do any harm to them" ...The entreaties of the two girls apparently had no effect on the rowdies. They began to smash furniture, picture frames and chandeliers with hockey sticks and by hurling stones. There were two groups—one trying to incite, the other to pacify the rowdies. The sensible section tried their best to protect the two girls and entreated with them to go inside. One of Gandhiji's party was wearing pyjamas. He was mistaken for a Muslim and set upon'. To resume Gandhiji's narrative: "The old Muslim lady in the house, endearingly called Bi Amma, mother, and a young Muslim stood near my mattress, I suppose, to protect me from harm. The noise continued to swell. Some had entered the central hall, and begun to knock open the many doors. I felt that I must get up and face the ugly crowd. I stood at the threshold of one of the doors. Friendly faces surrounded me and would not let me move forward."'

Pyarelal resumes: 'The hefty Dr Dinshaw Mehta was in the house, but what could poor Dinshaw do? He did not know the language. Besides, "even the strength of a Hercules could not have availed much in such circumstances".

'Gandhiji addressed the rowdies: "What madness is this? Why don't you attack me? I offer myself for attack." He repeated it thrice and asked his Bengali grand-daughter-in-law, Abha, to translate his words. "All to no purpose. Their ears were closed against reason. I clasped my hands in the Hindu fashion. Nothing doing; more window panes began to be smashed," Gandhi recounts.

'"Where is the rascal Suhrawardy? shouted someone from the crowd. It seems they intended to lynch Suhrawardy. Luckily, he was not in the house. He had gone home to get ready to start with me for Noakhali. Not finding him, they turned their wrath on me. There was pandemonium." Just then, two Muslim members of the household, with whom Gandhiji was staying, came rushing in, pursued by the infuriated mob. One of them was bleeding profusely. He took shelter behind Gandhiji. Seeing him, someone aimed a massive brickbat at him. It struck a Muslim standing by. A heavy stick narrowly missed Gandhiji's head and crashed against the opposite wall without hurting anybody. If it had hit Gandhiji, that would have been the end. At last Gandhiji said in a husky voice: "My God asks me, 'Where do you stand?' I am deeply pained. Is this the reality of the peace that was established on 15 August?"

'Minutes later, the police chief and his officers came in and took charge of the situation. They appealed to Gandhiji to retire. In an aside, I requested them not to use force against the rowdies, knowing how it would effect Gandhiji. After a time they succeeded in getting the building cleared of the mob. Gandhiji called Charu and me to him and said: "My resolve to go to Noakhali collapses after this. You will agree I cannot leave for Noakhali or for that matter for anywhere else in the circumstances. I would like you to think it over and then tell me. I do not know what God has in store for me next. But Noakhali seems to be just now out of the question." Hardly had this talk finished when Dr Prafulla Ghosh, the chief minister, arrived. He asked Gandhiji, "Shall we arrest Hindu Mahasabha leaders?" Gandhiji: "No. Instead, you should put upon them the burden and responsibility of maintaining the peace. Ask them whether they want peace or fighting. Tell them you want their cooperation and wait for their reply." It was half past twelve when Gandhiji went to bed. But the crowd outside lingered on in the streets till long after that. Ultimately, the police had to use tear gas to disperse it. By the time quiet was fully restored, it was half past one in the morning. Not till two o'clock could everyone finally go to sleep.'

The news of the night's happenings swept through the city like wildfire. From early in the morning, a continuous stream of anxious visitors poured into Hydari Mansion. Charu Choudhuri and Pyarelal feared a very serious reaction in Noakhali if Calcutta erupted. They decided to approach the Hindu Mahasabha leaders and plead with them for their cooperation.

They met Hindu Mahasabha leader and Bharatiya Jan Sangh founder Dr Syama Prasad Mookerji first. They informed him that if the minority community in Noakhali, or for that matter in the whole of East Bengal, was not to be exposed to an incalculable risk, the situation in Calcutta would have to be immediately brought under control. Dr Mukherji listened to them with great attention. In the end, he said, 'I shall certainly issue an appeal and do anything besides that you might suggest.' He asked them to return in an hour when he would be ready with his statement. The two then went to the other Hindu Mahasabha leader, N.C. Chatterji's residence, but were unable to meet him. They returned to Dr Mookerji's home, where he assured them that he would try and convince Chatterji and handed his statement to them. When Choudhuri and Pyarelal returned to Hydari Mansion, Gandhi's face lit up when Pyarelal handed him Dr Mookerji's draft statement. With some minor changes, it was released to the press the next day: 'The continuance of peaceful conditions in West Bengal and East Bengal is essential for peace in India. Calcutta is the key to the situation. If it is at peace, it must influence East Bengal. Peace in the whole of Bengal must again affect the whole of the Punjab. The majority community in Bengal must realize, the senseless oppression of innocent members of the minority community does not pay and creates a vicious circle which one cannot cut through. The unity efforts of leaders of the communities must see to this.'

At about two in the afternoon, news came that violent communal conflagrations had broken out simultaneously in several parts of the city. Fresh reports of incidents poured in every few minutes. Gandhi wrote to Patel: 'Preparations for a fight are today in evidence everywhere. I have just returned after seeing the corpses of two Muslims. I have heard that conflagration has burst out at many places. What was regarded as the "Calcutta Miracle" has turned out to be a nine-day wonder. I am pondering what my duty is in the circumstances. I am writing this almost at 6:00 p.m. This letter will leave with tomorrow's post. I shall, therefore, be able to add a postscript to it. There is a wire from Jawaharlal that I should proceed to the Punjab. How can I go now? I am searching deep within myself.'

After a lot of deliberation and meeting with delegations, Gandhi knew what he was going to do. He sipped on a glass of hot water mixed with glucose and dictated the statement announcing his decision. When Rajaji came to meet him at ten that night, Gandhi showed him the draft statement. Rajaji commented, 'You don't expect me to approve of your proposed step?' He was referring to Gandhi's decision to begin a fast against the violence. Together, they discussed the issue threadbare. Rajaji advised him to watch the situation for a while, but Gandhi had decided. He said, 'The fast has to be now or never. It will be too late afterwards. The minority community cannot be left in a perilous condition. My fast has to be preventive if it is to be of any good. I know I shall be able to tackle the Punjab too if I can control Calcutta. But if I falter now, the conflagration may spread, and soon I can see clearly, two or three powers will be upon us and thus will end our short-lived dream of independence.'

It was past eleven when Rajaji left with the final statement; it was released to the press the same night. After referring to the disturbances at Hydari Mansion on the night of 31 August, it went on to state:

'What is the lesson of the incident? It is clear to me that if India is to retain her dearly won independence, all men and women must completely forget lynch law. What was attempted was an indifferent imitation of it. There is no way of keeping the peace in Calcutta or elsewhere if the elementary rule of civilised society is not observed. The recognition of the golden rule of never taking the law into one's own hands has no exceptions. From the very first day of peace, that is 14 August, I have been saying that the peace might only be a temporary lull. There was no miracle. Will the foreboding prove true and will Calcutta again lapse into the law of the jungle? Let us hope not, let us pray to the Almighty that He will touch our hearts and ward off the recurrence of insanity. Since this was written, some of the places which were safe till yesterday, 31 August, have suddenly become unsafe. Several deaths have taken place. I saw two bodies of very poor Muslims... I have told the friends who saw me, what their duty is. What part am I to play in order to stop it? The Sikhs and the Hindus must not forget what the East Punjab has done during these few days. Now the Muslims in the West Punjab have begun the mad career. It is said that the Sikhs and the Hindus of Calcutta are enraged over the Punjab happenings... Now that the Calcutta bubble seems to have burst, with what face can I go to the Punjab? The weapon which has hitherto proved infallible for me is fasting. To put an appearance before a yelling crowd does not always work. It certainly did not last night. What my word in person cannot do, my fast may. It may touch the hearts of all warring elements in the Punjab to end only if and when sanity returns to Calcutta. I shall, as usual, permit myself to add salt and soda bicarb to the water I may wish to drink during the fast. If the people of Calcutta wish me to proceed to the Punjab and help the people there, they have to enable me to break the fast as early as may be.'

Gandhi woke up Abha and Manu and informed them that, from 8:15 that evening, he had commenced a fast which would last as long as there was communal violence raging in the city. 'This will be "do or die". Either there will be peace or I shall be dead. On you two is going to rest the responsibility of looking after me during the fast. You should eat and take rest as usual. If you do not keep yourself fit, you will not be able to do justice to your duty.'

The communal frenzy that had gripped the city did not spare Gandhi's peace workers either. Gandhi had demanded the ultimate sacrifice from his workers: in their efforts to establish peace, two of them did. Sachin Mitra was a thirty-eight-year-old arts graduate from Calcutta University. He was a seasoned Satyagrahi and a dedicated Khadi worker. In Noakhali, he had won admiration by his fearlessness and dedication while working with Thakker Bappa in the Gandhi Peace Mission. On hearing of the conflagration in the city, Sachin met with some Hindu and Muslim friends and decided to intervene in the riots in an effort to stop them. They headed for the Nakhoda Mosque area, which was reported to be one of the most dangerous spots in the city. At the crossing of Chitpur Road and Canning Street, the group was surrounded and accosted by a hostile Muslim mob. Hindus were separated and beaten up. Sachin was repeatedly stabbed in the chest and abdomen. Eventually, the police managed to rescue them, but Sachin's condition had turned critical by then; he succumbed to his injuries before he could be taken to a hospital.

Smritish Bannerjee, also in his late thirties, was a dedicated peace worker. On hearing that a peace procession was under attack, he rushed to their rescue. What transpired is not known, but the procession came under attack and eyewitnesses reported that they saw Smritish escorting a group of girls to safety. They saw that his shirt was drenched in blood. Later, when his body was identified in the morgue, the cause of death was stated to be 'loss of blood due to five deep stab wounds on the chest and abdomen'. Gandhi refused to mourn their deaths. In a message to Angshu Rani Mitra, Sachin's young wife, he wrote in Hindi: 'Pyarelalji has just given me the news that your husband who was mortally stabbed in the course of protecting others has succumbed to his wounds today. Do not let this be an occasion for sorrow but only for joy. Sachin has become immortal. You must not grieve but lose yourself in service in emulation of him.'

Gandhi informed Patel on 2 September: 'Since writing to you yesterday, a lot more news has come. I was already pondering within me as to what my duty was? The news that I received clinched the issue for me. I decided to undertake a fast. It commenced at 8:15 last evening. Rajaji came last night. I patiently listened to all he had to say. He exhausted all the resources of his logic. But none of his arguments went down with me. Let no-one be perturbed, it won't help. If the leaders are sincere, the killing will stop and the fast end, if the killing continues what use is my life? If I cannot prevent people from running amok, what else is left for me to do? If God wants to take work from this body, he will enter into people's hearts, bring them round to sanity and sustain my body. In his name alone was my fast undertaken. May God sustain and protect you all. In this conflagration, others will not be able to help much.' To Nehru, he wrote: 'I would have started for Lahore today but for the flare up in Calcutta. If the fury did not abate, my going to the Punjab would be of no avail. I would have no self confidence. If the Calcutta friendship was wrong, how could I hope to affect the situation in the Punjab? Therefore my departure from Calcutta depends solely upon the result of the Calcutta fast. Don't be distressed or angry over the fast.'

The morning of 2 September dawned on a Calcutta set ablaze. Violence, arson, looting and murder continued unabated. A medical check-up by the naturopath Dr Dinshaw Mehta showed that Gandhi's heartbeat was erratic. The doctor advised him to drink a minimum of 4 lbs water daily. 'I shall try,' Gandhi replied. 'But if Ram's name is in my heart, I should not need even the help of water. You see how peaceful I am today. Before this I could hardly sleep even at night.'

Gandhi followed his well-laid-down routine and slowly sipped 8 ounces of plain hot water, which took him an hour. This time, he started weakening at a much faster rate. By afternoon, he displayed symptoms of growing weakness, his voice sank to a barely audible whisper. At half past one, after resting for about an hour, he again drank 8 ounces of hot water. At noon, a co-worker brought news that there was large-scale looting and gunfire in Zacharia Street. Armed police had entered a mosque and were harassing Muslims who had taken refuge there. The distant sounds of firing could be heard through the afternoon.

Prof. Nirmal Bose, who had served as Gandhi's interpreter in Noakhali, had been to meet nationalist leader Sarat Bose. The report he brought back claimed that the disturbances were largely the work of Sikhs and Biharis, the Bengalis had only now joined in the large-scale looting and arson. A hotel owned by a Muslim was set on fire near the Sealdah railway station. At places there were reports of the police slackening in their duties. According to Sarat Bose, the violence was not the work of ordinary hooligans. It seemed to be strategically planned and executed with the guidance and support of organizations like the RSS and the Hindu Mahasabha. Chief Minister Dr Prafulla Ghosh blamed the disturbances on the Sikhs. He suggested that an all-party meeting should be called immediately to formulate measures required to curb the present disturbances and normalize the situation as fast as possible. He was getting Gandhi's statement printed in Hindi, Urdu and Bengali; these would then be distributed widely in the city and its surroundings.

Sometime later, Sarat Bose came to see Gandhi. Ever since Gandhi had withdrawn his support for Bose's proposal for a united sovereign Bengal, the latter had nursed a grievance against him. This was their first meeting since Gandhi had come to Calcutta. Laughingly, Gandhi said that it took a fast on his part for Bose to visit him.

Bose replied, 'I had a feeling that you no more cared for me. But I will not tax your strength. Are you permitted to talk?'

Gandhi said, 'I have to, at least in the pursuance of the object for which I am fasting.'

Bose said, 'I have always been opposed to Partition. I have never made any secret of my views. I am a frank man. I did not come before because, as I have already said, I had a feeling that you had not much use for me.'

Gandhi went on to say, 'Representatives of all groups and parties have come and asked me why I did not send for you. Some of them said that they had a suspicion that Forward Bloc people were behind the disturbances. I told them that Sarat Bose knows that my door is always open to him. He will come whenever he thinks fit.' Gandhi's remark hurt Bose; he said, 'In your prayer address, you said that I was spending money like water, in corrupt practices.'

Gandhi replied, 'Was it not then your clear duty to come to me and clear my doubts, if they were ill-founded? It is the privilege of friendship to speak out one's mind unreservedly without the fear of being misunderstood. Otherwise what is friendship worth? Even your Suhrawardy (also well known for his spendthrift habits) has said you spend money like water. But if you had a grievance on that score, why did you not contradict it publicly? Or you could have written to me. I would have then either explained to you what I meant, or you would have removed the misconception under which I was labouring. I would have then withdrawn my remarks. That was what true friendship demanded.'

Bose told him to let bygones be bygones and asked Gandhi what his complaints were against the Forward Bloc.

Gandhi said, 'The Hindu Mahasabha people say Forward Bloc people are behind this holocaust. I owe it to you to place their allegation before you.'

Sarat Bose replied, 'You may believe it if you like. But I tell you, a number of Hindu Mahasabha people are behind this business. It is they who are inciting the Sikhs by telling them that it is unmanly on their part to passively look on while the Punjab is burning. The Sikhs were asked to wear bangles in place of their Kada. I could even mention names.'

Gandhi told Bose that mutual recrimination would lead them nowhere. He added that his fast was an appeal to people to make them introspect, and it was time they realized that they could not carry on much longer with the help of the police and the military.

Referring to Gandhi's remark about the police and the military, which was endorsed by Suhrawardy, Bose said, 'The deterioration in Bengal set in with the introduction by Suhrawardy of armed forces from the Punjab. Does he now want the British?' Gandhi ignored the jibe against Suhrawardy. He explained, 'No, he did not say the British. He only said mixed. But there I have a bone to pick with him too. If the hearts of our volunteers could be cleansed, peace would immediately return. For that, cleansing of the hearts on the part of the leaders is necessary. Then alone will they be able to give the masses a clear lead. This is lacking today. You should first declare what you stand for and then back it by appropriate personal example. If in the course of it some top ranking leaders are killed, I will not grieve… Peace processions by themselves will be an empty show if the basic honesty of intention on the part of the leaders and the rank-and-file workers is not there. If such a volunteer organization, wedded to non-violence and ready to make the supreme sacrifice for the achievement of unity and peace begins functioning, I will not mind if the entire police force in the city is withdrawn. And if in the result the whole of Calcutta swims in blood, it will not dismay me. For it will be willing offering of innocent blood. I know how to tackle such a situation… I shall be content if I get honest and whole-hearted cooperation of you all in this work. We shall then be able to control the situation in the Punjab too.'

Gandhi went on to say, 'I had the authorities withdraw the armed police guard that was posted at my residence. Unfortunately, it has again come back. I have suffered it to remain, not for mine but Suhrawardy's sake. He feels nervous. If on the night of 31 August, he had not luckily gone out to get ready for the journey to Noakhali, who knows what would have happened to him, and consequently to me? I have often asked why there should be any further trouble, now that the League and Jinnah have got what they wanted. If only Jinnah had accepted my offer embodied in the Rajaji formula, all this could have been avoided. I was prepared to go even further. If after the British had quitted, the collective wisdom and statesmanship of India were still unable to achieve a peaceful solution, I would have invited the Muslim League to take charge of the government. The Congress ministers would have made way for them if I had asked them to. Pandit Nehru and Sardar Patel had told me that they would carry out my orders if I took over command.'

As Gandhi finished speaking, Dr Prafulla Ghosh, accompanied by some of his ministers, walked in. 'You have been very unfair to the ministry in undertaking the fast without taking them into your confidence,' Ghosh complained.

Gandhi replied, 'Perhaps you are right. But the conflagration was spreading so fast that every moment counted. Any avoidable delay would have meant further loss of innocent lives.' It had been an hour since Gandhi had been speaking and he was now showing signs of fatigue. Noticing this, Ghosh said, 'I do not wish to prolong the argument,' to which Gandhi replied, 'That is just like you. I had expected nothing less of you.' Not one to give up, Ghosh said, 'One thing, however, strikes me. You have launched your fast at a time when a section of the Hindus have begun to look upon you as their enemy. They foolishly feel that by asking them to practice non-violence, when the other side has shed all scruples, you are being very unfair to them. I would have had nothing to say if you had declared a fast for anything wrong that the ministry did.'

Gandhi said, 'All this is way off the mark. Don't you see, this now gives me the right to fast against the Muslims, too. My fast is intended to serve both the communities. The moment the Hindus realize that they cannot keep me alive on any other terms, peace will return to Calcutta.'

Dr Ghosh said, 'Your fast weighs down on us more than anything else. How can we effectively set to work under the heavy weight of your fast?' However, Gandhi told him that this was the wrong way of looking at things. He said his fast was intended to strengthen the hands of the people. At this point, Suhrawardy intervened, saying that the representatives of both the Hindus and Muslims should be called for a joint meeting. It was decided that the meeting would be held at the chief minister's residence. After this, Ghosh briefed Gandhi about the strict warning his government had issued to the press: any paper indulging in inflammatory propaganda would be summarily suspended.

On 3 September, the second day of Gandhi's fast, Dr Mehta came to check on him. Even during such trying times, besides his regular routine, Gandhi worked at his daily lesson in Bengali. Gandhi told him that he had had a very peaceful night and added, 'I am not at all anxious to terminate my fast. At this rate, though the body might become weaker, I feel I could go on even for one month.'

It was reported that looting had continued in the city till past midnight, but had then subsided and since then all was quiet. Slowly, the efforts of the peace workers and the political leaders, spurred on by Gandhi's fast, began to make a difference. Students from Calcutta University formed peace committees and peace processions started thronging Hydari Mansion, but its occupant was steadfast that he would break his fast only when he was convinced that a true and lasting unity of the hearts had been established.

The evening, at half past six, a procession of Hindus and Muslims came to Hydari Mansion. Two members from each community were allowed into the room where Gandhi rested. One of the Muslims, an eminent member of the Bengal Muslim League, pleaded with Gandhi to break his fast saying, 'I worked with you during the Khilafat movement. I undertake that no Muslim in this area will again disturb the peace. Your mere presence in our midst is an asset to us. It is the guarantee of our safety. Do not deprive us of it.' The two Hindu members also gave Gandhi the same assurance. Gandhi replied, 'My word seems to have lost its power so far as they are concerned. My fast will now be broken only when the conflagration ends and the glorious peace of the last fifteen days returns. If the Muslims really love me and regard me as an asset, they can demonstrate their faith in me by refusing to give way to the instinct of revenge and retaliation even if the whole of Calcutta goes mad. In the meantime, my ordeal must continue.'

That evening, at quarter past seven, Rajaji brought news that compared to the previous day, the city was markedly peaceful and volunteers as well as the police were providing effective protection to members of both communities.

Thursday, 4 September, the third day of the fast, dawned with a fast deterioration in Gandhi's physical condition. His voice was barely audible, just a little louder than a faint whisper. His pulse was rapid and erratic, he felt giddy when he tried to stand up. That morning, Gandhi had a surprise guest. Police Superintendent Abdullah of Noakhali turned up at Hydari Mansion. On seeing him, Gandhi seemed a bit more cheerful as he said, 'What a curious coincidence! I was thinking of you, and wondering how we could meet and here you are!' This was Gandhi's last meeting with Abdullah, who returned to serve East Pakistan soon after. After Gandhi's murder, a memorial fund was established, and the first contribution of ₹1,000 came from Abdullah.

After chatting with him for a short while, Gandhi began editing the next issue of *Harijan*, which he had continued to do during his fast.

Then, as it had always happened, the tide began to turn. As the fast began taking a toll on the frail old man, it caused a deep impact amongst the people. At midday, a party of twenty-seven people, all residents of central Calcutta, came to meet him. They were members of what had come to be known as 'resistance groups': Hindus seeking revenge for the massacres during the Muslim League-sponsored Direct Action Day. They begged for Gandhi's forgiveness and pleaded with him to give up his fast. Gandhi paid no attention to their request or those from the several others who came to Hyadri Mansion.

At half past five, Gandhi received a note from Rajaji, which mentioned that tension had subsided in the city. Gandhi rested for a while; he woke up to find Suhrawardy, N.C. Chatterji and Sardar Niranjan Singh Talib waiting to meet him. They informed Gandhi that, having visited localities that had been ravaged by riots, they had found the areas returning to normalcy. They ended with a request to Gandhi to break his fast. He said, 'Before I can accede to your request, I want to ask you two questions: First, can you in all sincerity assure me that there never will be a repetition of trouble in Calcutta? Can you say that there is a genuine change of heart among the citizens so that they will no longer tolerate, much less foster, communal frenzy? If you cannot give that guarantee, you should rather let me continue this fast. It won't hurt me. When a man fasts like this, it is not the gallons of water he drinks that sustains him, but God; and second, if trouble breaks out—since you are not omnipotent or even omniscient—would you give me your word of honour that you would not live to report failure but lay down your life in the attempt to protect those whose safety you are pledging? You should remember, too, that if you break your pledge after giving it to me, you will have to face an unconditional fast unto death on my part... If you deceive me ... my death will be upon your head. I want a clear and straight answer. Your assurance must be in writing.'

It was quite clear to all those present in the room that Gandhi meant every word of what he was saying. Rajaji and Acharya Kripalani, who had arrived during the latter part of the discussion, proposed that they should leave Gandhi alone for a little while to confer among themselves. Just as the delegation was moving out of the room, a joint declaration signed by some forty representatives of Hindu and Muslim residents of Narkeldanga, Sitalatala, Maniktola and Kankurgachi areas was brought in. They pledged that no untoward incident would hereafter occur in their localities.

The strain of speaking had drained the last of Gandhi's energy. The leaders went to the adjoining room and prepared the draft of the peace pledge. The discussion was brief. Rajaji dictated the draft of the pledge which was signed first by N.C. Chatterji and D.N. Mukherjee of the Hindu Mahasabha, followed by Shaheed Suhrawardy as the leader of the Muslim League parliamentary party of West Bengal, R.K. Jaidka, the Punjabi leader and Niranjan Singh Talib, the Sikh leader. Immediately after its signing, the leaders returned to Gandhi's room where it was read out to Gandhi: 'We the undersigned promise to Gandhiji that now that peace and quiet have been restored in Calcutta once again, we shall never allow communal violence and shall strive unto death to prevent it.'

'But, Sir, is it any good my signing this document?' remarked Suhrawardy to Gandhi. 'I may at any time be called to Pakistan and then what happens to my pledge?'

'You must, in that event, have confidence that those whom you leave behind will deliver the goods,' replied Gandhi. 'Moreover, you can come back.'

Before breaking his fast, Gandhi said a few words to the gathering in Hindustani, 'I am breaking this fast so that I might be able to do something for the Punjab. I have accepted your assurance at its face value. I hope and pray that I shall never have to regret it. I would certainly like to serve India and humanity, but I do not wish to be duped into prolonging my life. I hope that I will not have again to fast for the peace of Calcutta. Let me therefore warn you that you dare not relax your vigilance. Calcutta today holds the key to the peace of the whole of India. If something happens here, its repercussion is bound to be felt elsewhere. You should, therefore, solemnly resolve that even if the whole world went up in a blaze, Calcutta would remain untouched by the flames. You have just heard the hymn "Ishwar and Allah are Thy name", may he be witness between you and me.'

At 9:15 p.m. on 4 September, seventy-three hours after he commenced, Gandhi broke his fast by slowly sipping a glass of diluted orange juice given to him by Suhrawardy. Before the relieved leaders could disperse, Gandhi called Rajaji to his side and whispered to him, 'I am thinking of leaving for the Punjab tomorrow.' Rajaji was worried: once Gandhi made up his mind it was difficult to deter him, but he was in no condition to travel. Suhrawardy sprang to his rescue by saying, 'Sir, you cannot leave Calcutta without giving its citizens an opportunity to join you in a public prayer of thanksgiving. If we tried tomorrow, it would be simply impossible to control the delirious crowd. At the earliest it can be the day after tomorrow.'

Gandhi held his first public prayer meeting after the fast on 6 September. He reiterated that his appeal for peace had to hold under all circumstances. He announced his plans of leaving for the Punjab the next evening. Suhrawardy seconded Gandhi's appeal and announced that he would be accompanying Gandhi in his peace mission to the Punjab. He had put himself unreservedly under 'Mahatmaji's' orders. Thereafter, he would carry out his bidding.

On 7 September, Gandhi boarded the train for Delhi at Belur, a station near Calcutta. He had decided to disembark in Delhi and spend a day there to consult with Nehru and Patel and then leave for the Punjab. The train rushed towards the national capital, bearing the apostle of peace to what was now being referred to as the 'city of the dead'.

XI

CITY OF THE DEAD

The wretches have created chaos in the whole city. What can we say to Pakistan now?

—Jawaharlal Nehru, lamenting the situation in Delhi

Gandhi arrived in Delhi on the morning of 9 September; he was fated never to leave. A grim and worried Patel received him at the railway station. Gandhi noticed that the usual crowd of ministers and Congress leaders was conspicuous by their absence. His arrival had been kept a secret.

In the car, rushing through the deserted streets of the capital, Patel told him that communal riots had erupted in the capital since 4 September. There was one more surprise awaiting Gandhi: he was not taken to Bhangi Colony, his usual residence in Delhi, but instead to the residence of Ghanshyamdas Birla on Albuqureque Road. Patel explained that Bhangi Colony had been occupied by refugees from West Punjab; they would have to be displaced if he insisted on staying there.

As Gandhi alighted from the car at Birla House, Nehru drove up. His face was furrowed by worry and the lack of sleep. He briefed Gandhi about the situation in the capital: a twenty-four-hour curfew had been clamped on the city; the military had been deployed in the most ravaged areas, but arson, looting and murder still continued unabated and the streets were littered with the corpses of the victims. Nehru was indignant. 'The wretches have created chaos in the whole city. What can we say to Pakistan now?'

'What is the use of being angry?' Gandhi asked.

Nehru replied, 'I am angry with myself. We go about with armed guards under elaborate security measures. It is a disgrace. Ration shops have been looted. Fruits, vegetables and provisions are difficult to obtain. What must be the plight of the ordinary citizens? Dr Joshi, the famous surgeon who knew no distinction between Hindu and Muslim but served both alike, was fired upon from a Muslim house while he was rushing to treat an ailing Muslim patient and killed.'

There was no respite for Gandhi. A conference with leaders followed and he was apprised about the situation in and around the capital. The atmosphere in Delhi had grown increasingly tense as hordes of refugees poured in from West Punjab. Fanatics had taken control on both sides of the border in the Punjab; minorities on both sides were being attacked; the administration and its various arms had abdicated and stood by merely as spectators and watched the situation deteriorate into anarchy. The very structure of civilized society was under threat. The refugees coming in to Delhi brought with them tales of gruesome savagery, of large-scale massacres of Hindus, of the loot of their wealth and possessions, of entire villages and communities having been wiped out, of the rape of their women, of their abduction and of them being distributed as 'bounty' amongst their captors, often sold to the highest bidder, of children flung alive into infernos and speared to death in cold blood, of attacks on fleeing refugee convoys and trains—with each telling, the tales became more and more gruesome. Large-scale conversions were done in West Punjab, Hindus and Sikhs were given two options—Islam or death. Many stories were vastly exaggerated and sensationalized to provoke people to seek revenge, but they were not baseless. The situation was the same in west Punjab, Muslims fleeing India had similar experiences, the only difference was that Muslims fleeing India were not offered the choice 'convert or perish', they were mercilessly murdered.

In India and Pakistan, the ministers blamed the British officers commanding the Boundary Force, of inaction and complicity. The British officers lamented that the troops under their command refused to fire on, or take action against, their co-religionists. On 29 August, the Joint Defence Council decided to abolish the Punjab Boundary Force from 31 August midnight. Responsibility for maintaining peace now rested on the respective governments. Mountbatten, his last executive responsibility having lapsed, left for Simla for ten days of rest, but was peremptorily called back by an urgent summons from Delhi. He arrived back in the capital on the afternoon of 5 September. The same day, the government constituted an Emergency Committee of the Cabinet, with Mountbatten as its chairman, to deal with the crises. A notification was issued by the Government of India, declaring the Delhi Province a dangerously disturbed area. Orders were issued to the police and the armed forces to shoot to kill. The notification permitted the infliction of the death penalty for offences like attempt to murder, kidnapping, abduction, arson, dacoity and looting.

Pyarelal writes: 'After the fury of the first slaughter had been brought under control in the East Punjab, a most dangerous problem arose in the capital itself, where at one stage every fourth person was a refugee. The administration was faced with a most difficult situation. In the tornado of primitive passions that had broken loose, individual wills seemed to count for nothing. Millions had been uprooted and thrown into an atomic turmoil, like forest leaves caught in a tropical hurricane. The biggest migration of population in recorded history was in progress. Almost ten million people were on the move in both directions across the border in the Punjab. The government had not anticipated an outbreak of such dimensions. The civil authority, in both the Punjabs, was paralysed.'

The Government of India had established a military evacuation organization, which took over the evacuation of the refugees from the civil authorities in the first week of September. All modes of transport were utilized for the purpose—trains, motor vehicles and aeroplanes. Between 27 August and 6 November, it was later computed, 673 trains were run carrying over 2,799,000 people inside India and across the border. Over 427,000 non-Muslims and over 217,000 Muslims were moved during the same period by motor transport using 1,200 military and civil vehicles. Nearly 27,000 evacuees were brought to India by government chartered planes on 962 flights between 15 September and 7 December. But these measures catered to a very small number of the displaced people. The most effective method of moving such a vast number of people was by route marches. Long caravans of refugees on foot going east and west crisscrossed the fertile plains of the Punjab.

To provide even the barest minimum of basic necessities to these uprooted millions was a mammoth task. There was the risk of epidemics breaking out due to the poor sanitation facilities and potable drinking water and paucity of medical staff and supplies. The risk of violent clashes erupting as refugee caravans moved in opposite directions was always present. Clashes between incoming refugees—who had arrived with deep resentment due to the grief and the privations they had suffered—and members of the minority communities who had stayed back on both sides created what seemed to be an insurmountable situation for the civil and administrative services. During the meeting of the Emergency Committee, Mountbatten had uttered the prophetic words, 'If we go down in Delhi, we are finished.'

The harried government and Congress leaders had only one hope: Gandhi. Would he be able to perform the miracle that he had performed in Calcutta? Now they all looked to him in desperation. At last he spoke, and declared that Delhi was not Calcutta. 'I find no one in Delhi who can accompany me and console the Muslims. There is no such person amongst the Sikhs or among the RSS either. I do not know what I shall be able to do here. But one thing is clear. I cannot leave this place until Delhi is peaceful again.' The assembled leaders heaved a sigh of relief. He had rescued them before, they were certain he could be relied upon once again.

In a statement released to the press that afternoon, Gandhi stated: 'Man proposes, God disposes, has come true often enough in my life, as it probably has in the case of many others. When I left Calcutta on Sunday last, I knew nothing about the sad state of things in Delhi. But since my arrival in the capital city, I have been listening the whole day long to the tale of woe that is Delhi today. I have seen several Muslim friends who have recited to me their pathetic story. I have heard enough to warn me that I must not leave Delhi for the Punjab until it has once again become its former peaceful self.

'I must do my little bit to calm the heated atmosphere. I must apply the old formula, "do or die" to the capital of India. I am glad to say that the residents of Delhi do not want the senseless destruction that is going on. I am prepared to understand the anger of the refugees, whom fate has driven from West Punjab. But anger is short term madness… Retaliation is no remedy. It only makes the original disease worse. I therefore, appeal to all those who are engaged in committing senseless murder, arson and loot, to stay their hands.'

At noon, news came in that refugees were about to attack the tuberculosis hospital opposite the Kingsway refugee camp, where a large number of Muslim patients were being treated. Dr Sushila Nayyar, who had been evacuated from the Wah refugee camp along with the refugees, had reached Delhi a few days back. Gandhi asked her to rush to the hospital with the instructions: 'On your way, stop at the Secretariat and inform the Sardar and Jawaharlal where I am sending you.'

At the Secretariat, Sushila could not find Patel but she saw Nehru, who asked her to accompany him in his car. At the town hall, he asked the deputy commissioner to rush a guard to the hospital; the deputy commissioner expressed his inability to do so as all the guards were out on duty. Nehru turned to him and said, 'All right then, I shall send Sushila to guard them.' With these words, he sent Sushila away in his car. On her way to the hospital, she saw a mosque in flames. She stopped to see if anyone was injured or trapped in the fire: 'The flames prevented us exploring all the rooms. As I stood there, a shower of bullets came from the building opposite.' It was a stronghold of the RSS. The bullets were aimed at Muslims who tried to escape the flames and anyone attempting rescue.

On reaching the hospital, Sushila found that the patients had been evacuated with the help of Lady Mountbatten, who had taken them to Jama Masjid. The hospital was being looted by refugees from the Kingsway camp. Sushila chased some of the refugees who were carrying away cots, beddings and other hospital materials. She found a policeman standing by the door of the hospital watching. 'What are you doing here? Don't you see they are looting hospital property? Can't you stop it?' she shouted at the policeman. He shrugged and replied, 'Bigger men than I cannot stop this. What can I do?'

Just then, Nehru reached the hospital. When Sushila told him about the looting, he became extremely angry. Getting in his car, he headed straight for the Kingsway refugee camp. Just as he reached the camp, a group of refugees loaded with loot were entering. He confronted them, 'I thought we were helping our suffering brethren. I did not know we were sheltering thieves and dacoits.' The crowd was incensed and a man asked him angrily if he knew what they had suffered. Nehru could not contain his anger any more and caught the man by the scruff of his neck.

Sushila became anxious, fearing that the crowd could get out of hand. The young man muttered, 'Yes, Panditji, go on. What better luck can I expect than to die at your hands?' At this, Nehru's anger melted away. He said, 'This is not the time for me to tell you how much I feel for you all and how my heart aches at your suffering. But what I say to you is: have these Muslims done you any harm? If not, then you must not injure them. We must be just. If justice requires it and it is necessary, we can go to war with Pakistan and you can enlist. But this kind of thing is degrading and cowardly.'

The next morning, less than a week after courting death with his fast in Calcutta, Gandhi set up a daily routine. He would visit the various Hindu and Muslim refugee camps and riot-affected areas of the city every day. He began with the Arab-ki-Sarai camp near Humayun's tomb, where Meos from Alwar and Bharatpur states were awaiting their removal to Pakistan. The refugees told Gandhi that none of them wanted to leave India but they had been driven out of their homes and were being forced to go to Pakistan. Gandhi promised to see what he could do for them. From Arab-ki-Sarai, he went to Jamia Millia Islamia, the Muslim National University at Okhla. A number of Muslim men and women from the neighbouring villages had taken refuge there. Pale, haggard and terrified, they were living under constant fear of death for the last two days.

Gandhi met the vice-chancellor of the university, Dr Zakir Hussain, who said that he was hopeful of the situation improving. Just a few days back, he had narrowly escaped a lynching at Jullundhar station, where, while returning from Punjab, he had been surrounded by a hostile mob of Hindus and Sikhs. He was saved by the timely intervention of a Sikh captain and a Hindu friend who recognized and protected him at risk of grave personal danger. He said that Gandhi's arrival in the capital had galvanized the administration.

At his next stop, the Devan Hall Hindu refugee camp, Gandhi was confronted by an angry crowd. The camp was overflowing with refugees from West Punjab, both Hindus and Sikhs, persecuted, hounded and driven out of their homes. Some of them accused Gandhi of hard-heartedness, of having more sympathy for the Muslims than for them. He was deeply grieved by these accusations. He said that they had a right to be angry as they were the real sufferers, but he could feel their anguish. He then went to the Wavell Canteen transit camp near the railway station, which was teeming with Muslim refugees waiting to be evacuated to Pakistan, The last stop on his day's itinerary, which had covered a distance of 41 miles, was the Kingsway refugee camp. Things there had considerably settled down since Nehru's visit the previous day.

That evening, addressing his prayer meeting audience, Gandhi said that he was anxious to go to Pakistan and test for himself the reality of Jinnah's professions. The Hindus of Pakistan were their brothers, Jinnah had proclaimed. Were these only empty words? But he could not go there owing to the disturbances in Delhi. Each dominion must bear full responsibility for the acts of those who lived in it. He declared that the same held true for the Indian Union. Were the Union ministers to declare their moral bankruptcy and shamelessly own to the world that the people of Delhi or the refugees would not voluntarily obey the rule of the land? It was in the hands of the people to send him to the Punjab by restoring normal conditions in Delhi. Why should there be curfew in Delhi? Why should Delhi be called 'the city of the dead'?

An anti-Muslim paranoia had gripped the capital. The bulk of Delhi's police force had been Muslim, and a number of them had deserted with uniforms and arms. Due to this, the integrity and loyalty of those remaining had immediately come under suspicion. Patel wired Bengal to send units of Gurkha policemen from West Bengal. The chief minister of central provinces sent a contingent of 250 constables and sub-inspectors of police. There were rumours of a coup d'état being planned by the Muslims to seize the administration. Searches of some Muslim homes by the police had revealed dumps of bombs, arms and ammunition. The Muslims claimed that arms had been planted in deserted Muslim homes to discredit the community and fan anger amongst the Hindus. In fact, similar caches of weapons had been found all over the country in Hindu homes and offices of the Hindu extremist organizations too. But in Delhi and Punjab, in some of the pitched battles fought between the Muslims and Hindus, and in some of the attacks on Hindus by the Muslims, these very weapons had been used. Muslims were to be blamed as well; many of them had been storing illegal weapons. Even when the British prohibited Indians from possessing arms after the first battle for freedom in 1857, the Muslims had stored illegal arms. Gandhi had been pleading with the community to voluntarily surrender their arms, but his plea was ignored.

The Sikhs were annoyed over the government's decision to prohibit, for reasons of security, the carrying of Kirpans with blades longer than 9 inches. Their representatives met Gandhi and complained that any such restriction was an interference with their religion. 'I do not see religion anywhere in evidence today,' replied Gandhi. 'And if it is just a religious symbol, the restriction as regards its size should not matter.' The Sikhs were not satisfied and cited, in support of their argument, an old judgment of the privy council, which interpreted the Kirpan as a sword of any size. Gandhi told them that it was wholly irrelevant and even improper to cite legal precedents to break up healthy restraints under which alone society could grow in a state of liberty. The Kirpan, which the Sikh religion enjoined upon its votaries to carry, was a symbol of purity and self-restraint. It was a weapon for the defence of innocent women, children and old and disabled persons against tyranny in the face of overwhelming odds, never a weapon of offence or to be used in retaliation against defenceless women and children. The Kirpan had, of late, been used for totally indefensible purposes, and he who used it wrongly forfeited the right to carry it.

On 12 September, a Friday, Gandhi visited the Jama Masjid, where 5,000 Muslims had taken refuge. Unmindful of the filth, Gandhi took off his slippers before entering. Thousands had gathered to offer the Friday namaz. Gandhi met some of the refugees and reprimanded them for being so unconcerned about cleanliness.

The same day, the city chief of the RSS came to meet Gandhi. It was common knowledge that it was the RSS that was behind the spate of killings in the capital, in East Punjab and in those parts of the country where vicious anti-Muslim campaigns were being carried out. The RSS head flatly denied these allegations, saying that the organization was set up to protect Hinduism, not to kill Muslims; they were not hostile to anyone, he said, the RSS stood for peace. This was downright dishonest. But Gandhi, with the boundless faith that he had displayed when trusting the claims of repentance from Muslim fanatics in Noakhali, felt that they should be given a chance to clear the air. The chief was asked to issue a public statement repudiating the allegations against them and openly condemning the killing and harassment of the Muslims that had taken place and that still was going on in the city. Not wanting to be pinned down into giving a statement, the chief suggested that Gandhi should do it and absolve the RSS of all the alleged wrongdoings. Gandhi agreed to this suggestion. Sushila Nayyar added that the RSS had done some good work at the Wah camp. They had shown discipline, courage and capacity for hard work. Gandhi cautioned her that behind the facade of service lurked a dangerous fanaticism, comparing the organization to the Nazis and Mussolini's fascists.

While welcoming Gandhi to their rally, the RSS leader described him as 'a great man that Hinduism had produced'. Gandhi admitted that while he was certainly proud of being a Hindu, his Hinduism was neither intolerant, nor exclusive. The beauty of Hinduism, as he understood it, was that it absorbed the best that was in all faiths. If Hindus believed that in India there was no place for non-Hindus on equal and honourable terms, and that Muslims, if they wanted to live in India, must be content with an inferior status or if Muslims thought that in Pakistan Hindus could live only as a subject race on the sufferance of the Muslims, it would mean an eclipse of both Hinduism and Islam. He was glad, therefore, he said, to have their assurance that their policy was not of antagonism towards Islam. He warned them that if the charges against them were proved, the organization would come to a bad end. Today, Mohan Bhagwat, the RSS supremo, attributes Gandhi's patriotism to his religion.

Purana Qila, the venue of the Asian Conference, had been converted into a transit camp for Muslim refugees. Almost seventy five thousand Muslims awaited their removal to Pakistan. As the Hindu refugee camps had been infiltrated by Hindu extremists, the Muslim camps too were infiltrated by fanatic Muslim Leaguers. They had established themselves as benefactors of their troubled co-religionists, while in reality pilfering rations meant for the refugees and selling them off on the black market for huge profits.

Some of the Muslim policemen who had deserted with their weapons had taken refuge in these camps. On the 13th, when Gandhi visited the camp, hundreds of angry refugees rushed towards his car and surrounded it. Anti-Gandhi slogans were raised, and some of them tried to pull Gandhi out of the car. The driver, panicked, pressed down on the accelerator and tried to flee. The car shot forward and could have run over the milling refugees. Gandhi ordered him to stop; he was determined to face the angry crowd. Gandhi stepped out, joining his palms, he requested the crowd to settle down. The refugees were bewildered by this act of fearlessness by an unarmed and unprotected old man. Was he challenging them or did he trust them not to do him any harm? Initially, some of Gandhi's comments elicited rude and angry jibes from the refugees. He entreated them to be calm and shed their anger and fear. On hearing the passion and the ring of honesty in his voice, and seeing his evident grief, the refugees realized that unlike other 'leaders' and 'sympathizers', here was a man who shared their suffering and empathized with them. He listened to them with deep sympathy and promised to do all in his power to remedy the wrongs. Although he did not offer any instant remedies or relief, they believed him.

That day, Gandhi visited two more Muslim refugee camps, one at Idgah and the other at Motia Khan. Gandhi was informed that the daughter and son-in-law of Dr Mukhtar Ahmed Ansari, a nationalist Muslim and one of the founders of Jamia Milia Islamia, had been driven out of their home in Daryaganj. Gandhi had often enjoyed the hospitality of the Ansari family at their Daryaganj residence in the past. Some Sikh refugees, instigated by local leaders, had laid siege to the house and, under threat to kill, forced the couple to abandon it and shift to a hotel. At the prayer meeting that evening, Gandhi said, 'Is it not a shame that the daughter of a pillar of the Congress and a ceaseless worker for Hindu–Muslim unity has been driven out of her house in such a manner? It hurts me that this historic city should have disgraced itself as it has today.'

Some Muslims invited Gandhi to shift to a Muslim quarter in Delhi as he had done in Calcutta, saying that if he stayed in their midst, they would feel safe. Gandhi agreed to their proposal and decided to move into prominent Congressman and lawyer Asaf Ali's house, which was situated in a locality that had witnessed continuous rioting. That morning, Patel had informed Gandhi that firing had continued all night long from the roof of a building quite close to Asaf Ali's residence. An armed police posse had unsuccessfully tried to storm the building four times. When finally they succeeded, the snipers escaped by jumping over the roofs of surrounding buildings. A large cache of arms and ammunition was found stashed on the roof.

The Muslim friends who had invited Gandhi were briefed about the situation. If a stray bullet killed Gandhi or even injured him, there would be a nationwide massacre of Muslims; were they willing to take the risk? The Muslims realized the gravity of the situation. For their protection, instead, they were offered an army contingent stationed in their locality. Even though Gandhi decided against going to Asaf Ali's residence, he was dissatisfied with the alternative arrangement made to protect the residents and how he was being thwarted from practicing his tried-and-tested methods. He reiterated that if he had his way, he would withdraw the entire police and military from the city and put the onus of establishing peace and harmony on the rioters.

Many in India felt that the best solution for the resettlement of refugees was to settle them in abandoned Muslim homes. The Hindu fanatics openly advocated this option, and incited the incoming refugees to not only occupy the vacant homes of Muslims but to drive out those who had stayed back and take over those as well. The same lobby of Hindu fanatics advocated a planned and compulsory transfer of non Hindus. Gandhi opposed this suggestion and warned that, once this principle was accepted, its application would not be confined to the Punjab and Bengal—it would be applied to both nations in their entirety. Then, if no Muslim could live in India and non-Muslim in Pakistan, the estrangement between the two dominions would become permanent, with a mutually destructive war as the inevitable result.

The Hindu and Sikh refugees argued, however, that since they had been driven out of Pakistan, no Muslim should be allowed to stay in India or at least in Delhi. Gandhi explained that he did not advise the Indian government to ignore the ill-treatment of Hindus and Sikhs in Pakistan. But for the Indian government to take up the cases of atrocities on minorities in Pakistan with the Pakistani government, they would be required to show that minorities in India were safe.

Gandhi visited the majority Muslim quarter of Daryaganj on the evening of 18 September. The residents complained to him of the partisan behaviour of the police and military personnel, which was likely to force them to flee their homes and the city of their birth. Gandhi advised them not to leave under any circumstances, saying, 'Even if the police and military should open fire upon you, you should face the hail of bullets and bravely die but not flee from your homes.' Gandhi gave similar advice to the residents of Kucha Tarachand, a Hindu pocket surrounded on all sides by a large Muslim population. The residents claimed that thousands of Pathans, armed to their teeth, had been smuggled in to massacre the Hindus. This is a bogey used to raise fear among Hindus even today. It has been used multiple times: in 1992-3 in Gujarat and Maharashtra, then again in 2002 in Gujarat and in almost all communal configurations by the communal Hindu organizations.

Gandhi appealed to both the Hindus and Muslims to surrender their arms. The following day, some maulanas visited him and presented a few rusty arms, claiming that Muslims had voluntarily surrendered these in response to his appeal. Gandhi rebuked them, saying that this was dishonest eyewash and did not signify any change of heart on the part of the community. 'Do not deceive yourselves,' he sternly warned them. 'My stay here will avail the Muslims nothing if they do not thoroughly cleanse their hearts.'

During a visit to the Muslim localities of Pul Bangash, Bada Hindu Rao, Khari Baoli and Chandni Chowk—some of the most congested localities of Delhi—Gandhi noticed that they were now nearly deserted. The Muslims gave him a rousing reception wherever he went; some young Hindu men staged a hostile demonstration and tried to attack the car he was travelling in. The police later informed Patel that the young men were hotheads of the local Hindu Mahasabha.

The ceaseless physical strain was now beginning to take its toll on Gandhi's health. He had developed whooping cough and it did not allow him to sleep well. The stress and his concern about the deteriorating situation added to his anxiety; he complained of nightmares, of a mob of Hindu young men rushing into his room. One of them started abusing him, and it seemed, wanted to assault him. 'I began chanting Lord Ram's name to calm them down.' On another occasion, when his sleep was similarly disturbed, he said that he had dreamt that he was surrounded by a angry Muslim mob while he was trying to bring home to them their duty. 'Waking or sleeping, I can think of nothing else,' he said. He instructed the doctors that he was not to be administered any alcohol or injections of any forbidden drugs. 'I will refuse to cooperate with life if anybody tries to do this. I do not wish to be kept alive anyhow. It would please me to die with my faith intact.'

2 October 1947 was Gandhi's first birthday in independent India. According to the Hindu calendar, Gandhi was born on the twelfth day of the second half of Bhadrapad. He observed his birthday, as always, by fasting, prayer and extra spinning. The fast, he explained was for self-purification and the spinning was a renewal of his covenant to dedicate his being to the service of the lowliest in the caste hierarchies and least provided for. He had turned his birthday into a celebration of the rebirth of the spinning wheel, commemorated as 'Rentia Baras'. The spinning wheel, to him, was a symbol of non-violence and rural renaissance and a tool of alleviating India's poverty.

From early morning, a continuous stream of visitors trooped into his room. When he emerged from his bath, a small party of dear friends comprising Patel, Nehru, Ghanshyamdas Birla, his host, and members of the Birla family in Delhi were all assembled to greet him. Lady Mountbatten arrived with a sheaf of letters and telegrams addressed to him from England. He requested all to pray that 'either the present conflagration should end or He should take me away. I do not wish another birthday to overtake me in an India still in flames.' Maniben, Sardar Patel's daughter, wrote in her journal: 'His anguish was unbearable. We had gone to him in elation; we returned home with a heavy heart.'

One of the messages from the high commissioner of Pakistan in India, Zahid Hussain, said: 'Today the people of India, in which I include Pakistan, are suffering untold miseries and privation resulting from hatred and conflicts. All eyes are turned to Mahatma Gandhi in this unparalleled crises which has overtaken the country. India is in many ways a key to the future of the human race and we all hope and pray that, inspired by the ideals of Mahatma Gandhi, she will play her part truly and well.' Present-day India needs a reminder of this message.

Gandhi made the plight of the refugees his special concern. Although he had cut down on his entourage and was now accompanied by the barest minimum of staff, Gandhi sent Dr Sushila Nayyar to organize medical relief for the refugee camp at Kurukshetra and also to educate the people about and to inculcate and implement proper sanitary practices there. The Kurukshetra camp housed one of the biggest concentrations of refugees from West Punjab.

'For method, planning and almost perfect sanitation, give me a military camp. I have never recognized the necessity of a military. But that is not to say that nothing good can come out of it. It gives valuable lessons in discipline, corporate existence, sanitation and an exact timetable with due provision for every useful activity. It is a city under canvas brought into being inside a few hours. I would like our refugee camps to approach that ideal. These camps can be made inexpensively, provided all the work, including building up these canvas cities, was done by the refugees themselves. You must be your own sweepers, cleaners, road makers, trench-diggers, cooks, washermen, etc. Then no refugee will be a burden to others wherever they go.'

Since winter was approaching, Gandhi appealed to the public for blankets and woollens for the refugees, and gave precise instructions on how these were to be sent. 'The clothes and blankets should be washed and mended before they are sent.' The response was immediate and overwhelming. Blankets, woollens, eiderdowns, satins and furs, costly rugs, silks, expensive shawls, embroidered stuff, silken curtains and bed covers poured in from as far as Kashmir, Ceylon and Burma.

Till this time, Sind had remained comparatively quiet and peaceful, but the troubles in both the Punjabs were beginning to have their repercussions there, too. 'The Marwaris and Gujaratis have all gone back to their respective homes outside Sind; where shall the poor Sindhi Hindus and Sikhs go?' Acharya Kripalani asked Gandhi. 'If I were asked, I would say, no-one should leave his hearth and home. This will put Pakistan on its trial.'

N.R. Malkani, a Congress leader from Sind, declared his creed after the establishment of Pakistan, thus: 'I do not reject Pakistan. I shall live in Sind and Pakistan, for Sind is my homeland. I shall, therefore, not be disloyal to Pakistan. I shall try and make it a good and strong state. I shall not try to weaken it and in no case shall I be its saboteur... Being a Sindhi and a Pakistani, I shall claim the full rights of citizenship for I have become a Pakistani as anyone else. If necessary, I shall fight for these rights as a Pakistani in Pakistan and a Sindhi in Sind... I shall no more hoist the Indian flag, old or new. I shall roll it up and keep it as a sacred memory in the secret recess of my heart. I shall accept the Pakistan flag as the State flag. But I will not hoist a flag on my house until it endears itself to me... If I am refused full rights of citizenship, I shall resist openly and when I find my resistance vain and life here dishonourable, then I will leave Pakistan and my Sind and induce others to do the same. I hope that evil day will never come.'

But circumstances proved too harsh for them to resist.

In a penetrating analysis of Muslim aspirations embodied in the Pakistan slogan, R.G. Casey, in his book *An Australian in India*, writes:

> The political leadership of the Muslim League ... had raised the demand for Pakistan only with one goal, to acquire political supremacy, prosperity and for the creation of personal fiefs. The minority community in their provinces were the easy targets. Where open communal flare-ups could be engineered, they did so in West Punjab and East Bengal, and successfully killed or drove out the minorities and then divided the booty left behind amongst themselves. But the situation in Sind was different, the local Muslim was not prepared to act against his fellow Sindhi Hindu or Sikh, so no 'popular' outburst could be engineered, but a systematic campaign of terror was unleashed with the help of refugees from East Punjab. Non-Muslim homes and properties were selectively requisitioned as requirement of the state. Refugees were encouraged to forcibly occupy non-Muslim homes and throw out the home owners. Threats, hooliganism and molestation were carried out systematically against the minorities, with the administration turning a blind eye, till the spirit of the minority community was at its nadir. Then the influx of the refugees from East Punjab did the trick. A large number of refugees from East Punjab were forcibly sent for resettlement to Sind. These refugees were seething with anger at first having been driven out of their ancestral homes in East Punjab and then not having been accommodated in West Punjab. They were kept in pitiable conditions and were told that, since there were a number of non-Muslims in Sind, the government was finding it difficult to settle them. This provided the spark required to ignite anger in the refugees. The refugees decided to take things in their own hands and, assisted by the administration, attacked non-Muslims with brutal fury. There were massacres in Karachi and

Hyderabad. A group of Sikhs who had taken refuge in a gurdwara were smoked out and killed to the last person. A large number of Hindus who had taken refuge in an educational institution in Hyderabad were similarly slaughtered. Non-Muslim businesses and commercial properties were torched. Houses were spared, their inhabitants were butchered. Those who survived, fled with whatever they could carry to India. This new wave of refugees reached India in October.

The worst off were the Harijans in Sind. They were required to wear symbols of their caste on their persons, similar to the badges Jews were forced to wear in Europe by the Nazis. This was for their own safety they were told, so that their Muslim protectors could identify them. What it achieved was that they became easily recognized targets. Many were butchered, and there were reports of forced mass conversions of Harijans in Sind. But even after converting to Islam, they were treated as outcasts.

As Hindus were mercilessly persecuted and massacred in Muslim-dominated Pakistan by the thugs of the Muslim League, so were Muslims in India by the Hindu fanatics. Hindu princely states were strongholds of the Hindu extremist organizations. In many places, they enjoyed the patronage of the princes; Gwalior was one such place. Several offshoots of Hindu militant groups found refuge and patronage there.

Shaheed Suhrawardy had joined Gandhi soon after he came to Delhi, to act as an emissary between him and members of the Muslim League government in Pakistan. He intended to initiate a dialogue which would ensure peace between the two states and the security of the minorities in both nations. Due to his old association with the Pakistan leaders, Suhrawardy possessed an advantage which he could exploit in the quest for peace. Gandhi warned him not to act in haste. He was categorical that Suhrawardy should only go to Karachi if his heart was free of all prejudice. His usefulness would depend upon his ability to get his old colleague, the Quaid-i-Azam, to face up to his own declaration with respect to the minorities. If Shaheed himself lacked conviction, or if his mind was clouded, his visit would do more harm than good.

Only after Gandhi was convinced did he send Suhrawardy to Karachi. Suhrawardy sent six despatches from Karachi to Gandhi, reporting on his dialogues with the Muslim League leaders: 'Both (Sir) Ghulam Mohammed and Liaquat Ali Khan agree with my draft. It now remains to promote a conference (after I have seen the Quaid-i-Azam) with him and Mountbatten, Nehru and Liaquat Ali, Baldev Singh, Tara Singh and Kartar Singh, Patel and yourself (Ghulam Mohammad thinks I should be there too), to draft the terms and condition and future conduct... I am glad to find that the two agree with the "contrition", no interchange of population (except for the Punjab where it has taken place, and no power on earth can stop it—I shall write later about it, as I think Hindus and Muslims can get together, the Sikhs appear to be impossible), and a determined effort to get back the refugees (except for the Punjab Sikhs).'

A few days later, in the first week of October, Suhrawardy made another trip to Karachi to meet Jinnah with his draft proposal which Gandhi had approved. At the meeting, Jinnah did a volte-face, telling Suhrawardy that he (Jinnah) had allowed himself to be bamboozled by Gandhi.

Gandhi said, 'Maybe. He has never done so in public. If only you could get Jinnah to do the right thing, peace between the two dominions might return.'

Suhrawardy replied, 'Jinnah says he never asked the Hindus to go out of Pakistan.'

Gandhi said, 'You surprise me. Why do you not speak out to Jinnah and Liaquat Ali? You know the facts. Does not your "peace mission" require you to uphold truth and justice fearlessly and courageously at any cost?'

Suhrawardy replied, 'You do not know how unpopular with the masses the Pakistan government has become. Some are even abusing Jinnah and Liaquat Ali.' Gandhi said, 'That shouldn't concern either of them.' He reminded Suhrawardy that his mission to Karachi was not to report who was abusing whom but to put the facts as he knew them before Jinnah and ask him what he proposed to do to implement the agreements the two dominions had entered into. 'The minorities on both sides should be able to live in their original homes. The main thing is to get the Pakistan government to square their declarations with their performance.'

In a letter to Jinnah on 11 October, Gandhi said: 'Shaheed Saheb has reported to me your reactions to my endorsement on the suggestions drafted by him. I am sorry to learn about it... In my opinion, some such agreement as suggested by Shaheed Saheb should precede any move for hearty cooperation between the two States. What is wanted no doubt is like mind, like word and like action between the two.' Jinnah did not bother to acknowledge or reply.

While Gandhi, with his influence, strove to bring about a rapprochement between the communities and ensure the safety of the Muslims in the Indian dominion, the leaders in Pakistan were still trying to derive political mileage from the situation. A statement issued by Jinnah seeking funds for rehabilitation exposed his and the entire Pakistani leadership's attitude: 'Sufferings that have been inflicted on our people in ... various ... parts of the Dominion of India have few parallels in their extent.' Jinnah did not express a word of regret or remorse for what the non-Muslim subjects of Pakistan had suffered and continued to suffer at Muslim hands. Pyarelal sums up the situation in *Mahatma Gandhi: The Last Phase, Vol. 10, Part II*: 'Quaid-i-Azam was already showing symptoms of that deep physical and spiritual ailment which within three months of the founding of Pakistan had robbed him of his debonair self-assurance and stamped him with a "paralysing inability to make even the smallest decision ... sullen silences ... striped with outbursts of irritation ... a spiritual numbness concealing something close to panic underneath". A liberal and progressive by temperament and conviction, he was fated to conform to the ways of orthodox fanatical Mullahs and political obscurantists about whom he used to confide to the elder Pandit, Pandit Nehru's father, Motilal: "Pandit, I believe in none of their nonsense but somehow I have to carry these fools along!"'

Suhrawardy failed in his peace mission due to his inability and unwillingness to stand up to Jinnah. After one of his abortive visits to Karachi in the last week of October, Gandhi on his day of silence scribbled this: 'I am at a loss to understand what Pakistan really wants to do, whether they want the Hindus to stay there or not... Please remember that to the minorities this is a life and death question. If you can get the Pakistan authorities to implement its declarations in action, you will have rendered the greatest service to the Indian Muslims. It is my claim that though many heinous things have happened in the Indian Union, the Union government has spread no effort to ensure complete security and protection to the Muslims... The Sardar and Pandit Nehru have worn themselves out in putting down lawlessness... You do not know how ill the Sardar is. Yet he carries on by his iron will. I do not know what the policy of the Pakistan government is, but I know what is happening to the minorities in Pakistan in the Punjab, in Sind and in the Frontier Province... But I have faith and hope.'

In a letter to Suhrawardy, written on 27 October 1947, Gandhi wrote:

> My Dear Shaheed,
>
> I address you frankly. I would like you, if you can, to remove your angularity. If you think you have none, I withdraw my remarks.
>
> Hindus and Muslims are not two nations. Muslims never shall be slaves of Hindus nor Hindus of Muslims. Hence you and I have to die in the attempt to make them live together as friends and brothers, which they are. Whatever others may say, you and I have to regard Sikhs and others as part of India. If any one of them declines, it is their concern.
>
> I cannot escape the conclusion that the mischief commenced with Quaid-i-Azam and still continues. This I say more to make myself clear to you than to correct you. I have only one course—to do or die in the attempt to make the two, one.
>
> Yours,
>
> Bapu

Gandhi again tested Suhrawardy's sincerity by asking him to condemn Pakistan's hand in the invasion of Kashmir by so-called tribesmen. Either Pakistan was behind it, as all circumstantial evidence showed, or it was not. If Pakistan was involved, was it not Suhrawardy's duty as an Indian national to proclaim his conviction? 'I suggest to you that it is your duty to ascertain the truth. Nothing would please me more than to find that I was wrong and you were right.' Suhrawardy agreed with all that Gandhi said, but did nothing.

After one of the many unfruitful meetings he had with Suhrawardy, Gandhi commented that although he was afraid that Shaheed was not being of any use to either India or Pakistan, he did not want to give up on him. 'He has undoubted talent. He could render great service to the

Indian Union, whose citizen he claims to be, and to the Indian Muslims if he had the will. But that will is completely lacking. I have, however, faith.' Gandhi was warned by many that he was allowing Suhrawardy to spy on him and the Union government. Gandhi replied that he did not mind being spied upon as he had no secrets; in fact, he wanted Suhrawardy to keep a close watch on him and on those who came to meet him and then report to Jinnah what he saw and heard.

While the northeast was smouldering and the northwest was an inferno, some other parts of the country were beginning to boil over as well. The situation in Junagadh—one of the three princely states which had not decided the question of accession when the transfer of power took place—was deteriorating. Junagadh was surrounded on all sides by the princely state of Kathiawad, which had acceded to India. The Muslim nawab ruled over a majority Hindu populace. His prime minister, a Muslim Leaguer Shahnawaz Bhutto, declared Junagadh's accession to Pakistan. The will of the people—predominantly Hindus—was ignored, as well as the principle of geographical contiguity which had been agreed upon by the leaders of both India and Pakistan. The Government of India immediately reacted and asked the Pakistan government to define its attitude vis-à-vis Junagadh's accession to Pakistan. After keeping silent despite repeated reminders, on 13 September, Pakistan declared that it had accepted Junagadh's accession to it.

During British rule, the sheikh of Mangrol and the principality of Babariawad were vassals of Junagadh. On 19 September, Mangrol broke away from his 'suzerain' and acceded to India. The diwan of Junagadh forced him to withdraw his accession within 24 hours. Having forced Mangrol to retract, Junagadh sent its military into Babariawad, which had acceded to India earlier. The use of force to coerce its neighbours, over whom its claim of sovereignty had ended with the lapse of paramountcy, led the other princes of Kathiawad to appeal to the Indian Union government to intervene. The Government of India wrote to Pakistan requesting it to order Junagadh to withdraw from Mangrol and Babariawad, which had acceded to India.

A movement to establish a provisional government on behalf of the people of Junagadh gathered momentum in Kathiawad in the third week of September 1947. Gandhi hoped that the movement would remain non-violent, and that once the people decided to refuse to acknowledge any authority that did not represent their will, the ruler would bow to their decision. 'What is more, Junagadh can, in this way, blaze the trail for the Kashmir National Conference to follow and thus provide an automatic solution to the Kashmir problem,' he said.

On 1 November, a week after the ransacking of Kashmir by Pakistan-backed tribesmen, Indian forces entered and liberated both Mangrol and Babariawad. The people's movement was spreading in Junagadh. The forces of the provisional government were on the move, capturing one position after the other. Shahnawaz Bhutto, sensing defeat, wrote to the Government of India on 8 November, requesting it to take over the administration of the state, pending the settlement of issues involved in the state's accession, in order to save it from complete anarchy. He also informed the prime minister of Pakistan that he had decided to ask for the Indian government's intervention with the support of the people's opinion, the authority of the State's Council and of the nawab himself, who had flown a few days prior to Karachi.

The Government of India accepted the diwan's request and asked the regional commissioner at Rajkot to take over charge of the state administration. Immediately after fleeing to Karachi, Bhutto made allegations of an illegal and forceful takeover of Junagadh by the Government of India. The Pakistan government termed the action taken by India as a clear violation of Pakistani territory and a breach of 'international law'. While accepting the nawab's sovereignty when he went against the wishes of his people and acceded to Pakistan, the Pakistan government now challenged his authority to bow to the will of his subjects, claiming that after acceding to Pakistan, the nawab or his diwan had no right to decide on their own or on behalf of their subjects on any issues, and hence refused to accept their decision to accede to India.

Gandhi made his stand on Junagadh clear. He said, 'In free India, the whole country belongs to the people, none of it belongs to the princes as individuals. Accession to Pakistan by the nawab of Junagadh was therefore, *ab initio* void. There is nothing unlawful in the actions of the provisional government on behalf of the people of Junagadh and nothing illegal about the actions of the Union government lending the services of its troops for the preservation of peace in Kathiawad. As for the question of the accession of Junagadh, it should be decided by a referendum.'

A plebiscite was accordingly held in February 1948, weeks after Gandhi's murder. The results showed that out of the total votes polled, 190,779 were in favour of accession to India; only 91 were for joining Pakistan. Pakistan till date refuses to accept the verdict of the plebiscite.

One of the fallouts of the Junagadh imbroglio was that extremist elements of the RSS and Hindu Mahasabha infiltrated the people's movement, and there was a spate of killing, looting and arson before they could be brought under control. This led to a partial exodus of the Muslim mercantile community of Kathiawad, which spilled over into Sind. Till then, the provincial government of Sind had protected the Hindu mercantile community because the government feared that without the Hindu business community's acumen, the economy of Sind would collapse. With the arrival of the merchants of Kathiawad, however, this need was fulfilled and the dependence of the Sind government on the Hindu mercantile community vanished along with their patronage. In its place there was persecution, harassment and attacks; a few examples were set to send the message that the Hindu merchants would have to leave or be driven out. Another wave of immigration of refugees from Pakistan ensued, adding to the already strained situation in the Indian Union.

Gandhi condemned the atrocities committed against Muslims in Kathiawad. Some people complained that he was 'jumping the gun' by commenting on unverified allegations. 'I am not unaware of the danger,' Gandhi replied, 'but that makes no difference to me. If I ignore the charges made in influential Pakistan journals backed by the Prime Minister of Pakistan,' he explained, 'my indifference would result in the Muslim world giving credence to the reports as if they are gospel truth. Now, the best Muslim mind is already sceptical about the truth... We should never make the mistake of thinking that we never make any mistakes. The bitterest critic is bitter because he has some grudge, fancied or real, against us. We shall set him right if we are patient with him and, whenever the occasion arises, show him his error or correct our own when we are found to be in error... In the present disturbed atmosphere, when charges are hurled against one another, it would be folly to live in a fool's paradise and feel that we can do no wrong... Nature has so made us that we do not see our backs; it is reserved for others to see. Hence, it is wise to profit by what they see.'

To the Muslims, he said that if their object was not to discredit the Hindus of Kathiawad and the Indian Union but to elucidate the truth and to protect Muslim life, honour and property, all that could be secured by the strictest adherence to truth. 'The workers in Kathiawad, who have no communal prejudice, are striving to reach the truth and seek redress of every wrong done to the Muslims, who are as dear to them as themselves. Will they (the Muslims) help the process?'

Gandhi sent two of his own trusted workers to Kathiawad on a fact-finding mission. These workers, along with workers from Bombay and Kathiawad, after comparing notes with local Muslims, wired Gandhi, admitting that some excesses had occurred, but most of the reports were gross exaggerations. This had an immediate effect on the local Muslim leaders, who had initially complained to Gandhi. They admitted that there had been much exaggeration and what had appeared about the situation in Kathiawad in the papers in Pakistan was incorrect: 'Our telegram was the result of unverified reports... No question of unimaginable wrong or wrong without parallel. Please do not be worried.'

This was a good example of Gandhi's technique in action. He pointed out the moral: False propaganda did no good; 'the proper thing is to trust truth to conquer untruth'. He wrote in *Harijan*: 'When it is relevant, truth has to be uttered, however unpleasant it may be... Misdeeds of the Hindus in the Union have to be proclaimed by Hindus from the housetop, if those of the Muslims in Pakistan are to be arrested or stopped.'

Kashmir was slowly becoming the cause for anxiety. In mid-July 1947, Mountbatten had tried to persuade the maharaja of Kashmir to make up his mind to accede to either of the dominions after ascertaining the will of the people, and to announce his decision before 15 August. The state department under Patel went out of its way to reassure the maharaja, that in case Kashmir decided to accede to Pakistan, the Union government would not regard it as an unfriendly act. But the maharaja failed to come to a decision by the appointed date. He said that he needed more time to decide; it was not merely to which dominion he should accede to—it was much more whether 'it is not in the best interest of both Dominions and of my State to stand independent'. The indecision cost him dearly.

Three days before the transfer of power, the maharaja entered into a standstill agreement for one year with Pakistan. He wanted to enter into a similar agreement with the Indian Union too, but Pakistan proceeded to force the issue by enforcing a virtual siege. The main line of communication and transport to Kashmir lay through West Punjab, now a province of Pakistan. The supply of essential commodities and the route for its timber and fruits exports was via Pakistan. The Pakistan government stopped the supply of essential items like sugar, salt, food grains, medicine and fuel to Kashmir through its territories. The prime minister of Kashmir, M.C. Mahajan, sent a wire to the Governor-General of Pakistan on 15 October:

'Ever since 15 August, even in spite of agreement to observe standstill on matters on which agreement existed on 14 August ... difficulties have been felt not only with regard to supplies from West Punjab of essentials but also with the working of the postal system. Savings bank accounts are refused to be operated. Postal certificates are not cashed, cheques on West Punjab banks are not honoured. Owing to the failure of remittances from the Lahore Currency Office, even the Imperial Bank is hard put to meet obligations. Railway traffic from Sialkot to Jammu has been discontinued... The Radio of Pakistan appears to have been licensed to pour volumes of malicious, libellous and false propaganda... The Kashmir government cannot but conclude that all this is being done with the knowledge and connivance of the local authorities. The Kashmir government considers these acts extremely unfriendly if not actually inimical. Finally, government wish to make it plain that it is not possible to tolerate this attitude any longer.... The Governor-General and the Premier are asked personally to look into the matter and put a stop to these inequities which are being perpetrated. Unfortunately, if this request is not heeded, the government would be justified in asking for friendly assistance and oppose trespass on its fundamental rights.'

The reply from Pakistan was:

We are astonished to hear your threat 'to ask for assistance', presumably meaning thereby assistance from an outside power. The only object of this intervention by an outside power secured by you would be to complete the process of suppressing the Musalmans to enable you to join the Indian Dominion... If this policy is not changed, the gravest consequences will follow for which you alone will be responsible.

In an editorial in *Dawn* published on 24 August, a dire warning was issued to the maharaja of Kashmir: 'The time has come to tell the Maharaja of Kashmir that he must make his choice and choose Pakistan.' Should Kashmir fail to join Pakistan, it warned, 'the gravest possible trouble will inevitably ensue'.

On 23 October, a large-scale invasion by a body of what were called tribesmen from the tribal province, led by Pakistani army regulars who were said to be 'on leave', occurred from Abbottabad-Mansehra. The invaders were armed with modern weapons, including Bren guns, machine guns, mortars and flame throwers. They were transported in one hundred trucks fuelled by petrol issued from Frontier Province and West Punjab rationed quota; they moved rapidly down the valley towards Srinagar, the capital. All along the way, they resorted to arson, loot and murder, and women were subjected to mass rape and abducted.

On the 24th, the Indian Army intelligence reported that the so-called tribesmen were being transported by the military up the Rawalpindi road. Muzaffarabad and Domel were captured by a band of over five thousand attackers on the 25th; Srinagar was only 35 miles away. The state forces were in full retreat, the situation was critical. The Kashmir government panicked. The maharaja approached the Indian government with a request for armed assistance to save the situation. The Government of India expressed its inability to oblige unless Kashmir acceded to India. V.P. Menon, secretary to the ministry of states, flew to Kashmir on the 25th to convey the Indian government's decision to the maharaja. He returned to Delhi the following day with a duly signed letter of Kashmir's accession to India. The maharaja had finally capitulated. Under the terms agreed to by the Partition Council, by signing a treaty of accession, Kashmir became a part of the Indian Union. The letter stated: 'With the conditions obtaining at present in my state and the great emergency of the situation as it exists, I have no option but to ask for help from the Indian Dominion. Naturally they cannot send the help asked for by me without my State acceding to the dominion of India. I have accordingly decided to do so and attach the Instrument of Accession for acceptance by your government.' The maharaja informed the Government of India that 'it is my intention at once to set up an interim government and ask Sheikh Abdullah to carry the responsibility in this emergency with my prime minister'.

On 29 September, the maharaja ordered the release of Sheikh Abdullah and other members of his Kashmir National Conference. Addressing a rally after his release, Sheikh Abdullah declared: 'I have never believed in the Pakistan slogan ... but in spite of it, Pakistan is a reality ... I am the President of the Indian State People's Conference, whose policy is clear. Pandit Nehru is my best friend and I hold Gandhiji in real reverence. It is also a fact that the Congress has greatly helped us in our movement for a democratic government in the State. Our choice of joining India or Pakistan would be based on the welfare of the four million people living in Jammu and Kashmir.' The National Conference and Sheikh Abdullah joined in the request to the Indian government to accept the accession and send in troops to repel the invaders. Thus, the accession was not only the action of the ruler but it had been ratified by a democratic organization with public opinion behind it.

While accepting the accession, the government of the Indian Union declared that it was their intention to ratify the maharaja of Kashmir's decision with the people of Kashmir: 'As soon as law and order have been restored in Kashmir, and her soil is cleared of the invader, the question of the state's accession should be settled by a reference to the people'. Early on the 27th morning, 330 officers and men of the First Sikh Battalion were airlifted to Srinagar to stop the hordes of tribesmen who, after sacking Baramulla, were reaching the outskirts of the capital, Srinagar. Now began one of the most well planned and executed military operations. The logistics were difficult, as there were no supply and communication lines. The only way of reaching men, supplies, arms and equipment was by air. Commandeering every military and civilian aircraft, a continuous supply link was established. Planes ferried men, arms and supplies to the only airstrip at Srinagar. The battle to drive back the invaders was being fought just over the perimeter fence of the airport; as troops disembarked, they joined the fight. Lord Mountbatten, the decorated hero of the Second World War, commented, 'As a military operation, the speed of the fly-in on 27 October left ... South East Asia Command's efforts standing.' It left the Pakistani war machine standing too.

The raiders were caught totally by surprise, but it had been touch and go; another twenty-four hours and all would have been lost. The raiders' downfall happened due to the time they had spent ransacking Baramulla. The arson and plundering had gone on for nine days. Neither Hindus nor Muslims were spared; the Kabalees, as the invaders came to be known, did not even spare the clergy. They sacked St Joseph's Convent, looted and burnt the Welfare Hospital, shot and wounded the mother superior and raped many of the nuns. These nine days, however, gave the workers of the National Conference time to organize the local people's militia for defence against the raiders. There was no administration in Srinagar. Under advice, the maharaja had shifted to his summer palace in Jammu. There were no troops, no police; electricity had failed since the burning of the power station at Mohor. And yet, remarkably, Srinagar functioned without panic. The leaders of the National Conference and their workers took charge; Hindus and Muslims of Kashmir united to defend their motherland.

Soon the raiders were on the run. Uri was recaptured, the Poonch garrison was relieved by the time a ceasefire was declared; Kashmir had been strategically secured and the threat to the valley was removed.

Jinnah, who had made the capture of Kashmir a personal ambition, had stationed himself at Abbottabad to make a triumphant entry into the capital of Kashmir on the festival of Eid, at the head of a procession reminiscent of the conquerors of the past. When news of India's military intervention and the subsequent rout of the infiltrators was conveyed to him, he was livid. He ordered an immediate intervention by the Pakistani army. General Gracy, the acting commander-in-chief of the Pakistan Army, informed Sir Claude Auchinleck, the supreme commander, of the involvement of Pakistani military regulars being a part of the invasion of Kashmir. Sir Claude advised Jinnah that the Indian Union was perfectly within its rights in sending the troops into Kashmir in response to the maharaja's plea for help. If Pakistan intervened with its army, it could trigger a war between the two dominions. He warned Jinnah that this would result in every British officer being withdrawn from both sides. Jinnah withdrew his earlier orders.

The Pakistan government denounced Kashmir's accession to India and alleged that it was engineered by 'fraud and violence'. In a meeting at Lahore on 2 November, Mountbatten pointed out to Jinnah that while Kashmir's accession had certainly been brought about by 'force and violence', the violence had come from the tribes for which Pakistan, not India, was responsible. Jinnah alledged that, in his opinion, it was India who had committed the violence by sending in its troops, but Mountbatten stood his ground that where the tribesmen were was where the violence lay. Finally, Jinnah could no longer conceal his anger at what he called 'Mountbatten's obtuseness'.

The Pakistan government categorically denied any complicity in the invasion of Kashmir; it was carried out by those they claimed were 'tribesmen'. They pleaded their inability to prevent their passage through Pakistan. The Pakistan prime minister said that the only way they could help pull out the invading tribes from Kashmir was if the Pakistan Army Regulars were allowed to enter Kashmir. When Mountbatten apprised them of the strength of the Indian Armed Forces in Kashmir, the projected build-up over the next few weeks and India's determination to hold on to Kashmir 'at any cost', Jinnah offered to 'call the whole thing off'.

Gandhi had been closely watching the developments in Kashmir and was pained at the way the matter was becoming a festering sore between the two fledgling nations. He had always maintained, as he affirmed in one of his prayer addresses, that the real rulers of all the states were their people. The Pakistan government had been coercing Kashmir to join Pakistan. When in distress, the maharaja, backed by Sheikh Abdullah, wished to accede to the Union and the Indian Governor-General could not reject their appeal. If the maharaja alone had wanted to accede, Gandhi said, he could not have defended such an accession. It was legitimate since both the maharaja and Sheikh Abdullah, speaking for the people of Jammu and Kashmir, had jointly asked for it.

Having previously taken the stand in the case of the accession of Junagadh that the ruler had 'full legal right to decide the issue of accession', the Pakistan government's objection to the ruler of Kashmir exercising the same prerogative with respect to his state was frivolous.

The defence of Kashmir exacted its toll of heroic sacrifice. Brigadier Usman, a Muslim officer of the Indian Army, fell fighting valiantly while commanding his troops at Naoshera. He is remembered as 'Naoshera ka Sher'—The Lion of Naoshera. Mir Maqbool Sherwani, a young Muslim leader of the National Conference in Baramulla, engaged in organizing the people against the raiders, was captured by the invaders when they took Baramulla. They asked him to repudiate the Kashmir National Conference and swear allegiance to the so-called Azad Kashmir government. Sherwani courageously refused to comply, telling the invaders that their triumph was short-lived since the Indian troops would shortly recapture Baramulla and drive them out. He was declared a traitor. The infiltrators tortured him mercilessly, finally nailing him to a wall by hammering nails through his palms and feet. Then, they used him as a live target. Every direct hit was acknowledged by a moan from Sherwani. He was shot fourteen times. The infiltrators then displayed their bestiality by mutilating his body and defecating on it. Sherwani's dying prophecy came true within forty-eight hours: liberating Indian troops drove the infiltrators out of Baramulla. Paying tribute to the young martyr's steadfastness and undaunted courage, Gandhi remarked: 'This was a martyrdom of which anyone, Hindu, Sikh, Muslim or any other, would be proud.'

Gandhi was not in favour of taking any Indo-Pak dispute to an outside organization for arbitration. It would only get 'monkey justice', he warned. 'Were the Union and Pakistan always to depend on a third party to settle their disputes?' he asked in his post-prayer address on 25 December. 'Could not the representatives of the Union and Pakistan sit down together and thrash out the Kashmir issue, just as they had already done in the case of many others? Alternatively, could they not select from among themselves good, true persons who would direct their steps? The first necessary condition for it was an open and sincere confession of past lapses. Hearty repentance broke the edge of guilt and led the way to proper understanding.'

Four days later, he again said, 'Will not the Pakistan government and the Union government close ranks and come to an amicable settlement with the assistance of impartial Indians? Or, has impartiality fled from India? I am sure it has not.'

On 30 December 1947, the Government of India made a formal reference to the UN Security Council in regard to Pakistan's aggression in Kashmir. Gandhi again made it public that his own views on the subject remained unchanged. Speaking on 4 January, Gandhi appealed to the Government of Pakistan to remain pure, 'Pak', as its name implied. He remarked that both Hindus and Muslims had resorted to cruel acts and made grievous blunders. He pleaded for amity and goodwill, which could enable the Union's representation to the UN to be withdrawn with dignity, which even the latter would welcome. The main thing, however, was a real change of heart. The understanding should be genuine. To harbour hatred would be even worse than war.

The issue of Kashmir's accession to the Indian Union became a decisive factor in the Indian Union's battle for the secular state ideal. Gandhi used it to bring home to the Indian people the vital necessity for a return to sanity. Many of the land routes to Kashmir from the Indian Union passed through Pakistan. There was a narrow strip which joined Kashmir to East Punjab. 'How could Kashmir have trade with India if Muslims could not safely pass through, much less live, in East Punjab? If the insanity continued in East Punjab,' he warned, 'Kashmir's accession to the Union would be rendered nugatory.' He hoped, however, that wisdom would dawn upon East Punjab.

Kashmir had not remained untouched by the fanatical communal insanity that had gripped the rest of the subcontinent. Following the upheaval in Punjab, in October 1947, Muslim evacuee convoys going out of Jammu were attacked and massacred by non-Muslims who were armed and guided by RSS cadres. The maharaja's army played a very disreputable part in these massacres. When these events were reported to Gandhi, he said 'the Maharaja, as the absolute ruler, could not be absolved from responsibility for the happenings'; he said that the maharaja was unfit to continue to rule and advised him to either abdicate or to remain only as a titular head 'even as the British King is', full power *de jure* and *de facto* being transferred to the true representatives of the people.

Some members of the Indian government were distrustful of Sheikh Abdullah's ultimate aims; they doubted the loyalty of all the Indian Muslims who had stayed back. They would rather place their faith, under the prevailing circumstances, in the Hindu maharaja. The Cabinet was vertically divided over the issue. Gandhi too had his misgivings, but added that it was far better to risk everything for the sake of a principle than to compromise one's principles for fear of a risk, however great.

'If Sheikh Abdullah is erring in the discharge of his duty as the chief of the Cabinet or as a devout Muslim, he should certainly step aside and give place to a better man. It is on Kashmir soil that Islam and Hinduism are being weighed. If both pull their weight correctly and in the same direction, the chief actors will cover themselves with glory and nothing can move them from their joint credit. My sole hope and prayer is that Kashmir should become a beacon light to this benighted sub-continent.'

A person posing as the president of the Kashmir Freedom League wrote to Gandhi from Lahore, saying that as Kashmir was the root cause of tensions between the two dominions, withdrawal of the 'aggressive' Indian troops from Kashmir and its handing over 'to whomsoever it rightly belongs' would help to bring about a rapprochement between the two countries and clear the way for the establishment of Hindu–Muslim unity, which was so dear to Gandhi's heart. The naïveté of the argument hurt Gandhi. He wondered if the Muslims would continue to distrust the Hindus and Sikhs and vice versa till the Kashmir issue was solved. 'The army of the Indian Union had not entered Kashmir on their own; they had gone there at the call of the ruler of the state and leaders of the Kashmir people. If the invaders, tribesman and others, withdraw and leave the issue to the rebels in Poonch and the rest of Kashmir without any aid from outside, it would be time to ask the Indian troops to withdraw.'

'The suggestion that Kashmir should go to whomsoever it rightly belonged,' he went on to observe, 'was perfectly true. Who were the rightful owners of Kashmir? The Maharaja was there, and the Indian government could not ignore him. Ultimately, it was for the people of Kashmir to decide their own fate. Hence, the Government of India had unilaterally decided to ascertain their wishes as soon as the requisite conditions for it were forthcoming.'

Some advocates of Partition, both in India and Pakistan, proposed the division of Kashmir. Their formula—surprisingly similar to the trifurcation implemented by the Bharatiya Janata Party government recently—was that Jammu, with a predominant Hindu population, would go to India; the valley of Kashmir, with a majority Muslim population, would accede to Pakistan. Gandhi characterized this proposal as 'fantastic'. He indignantly asked if it was not more than enough that India had been divided into two. 'One would have thought that it was impossible for man to divide a country which God had made one. Yet it had happened and the Congress and the Muslim League had both accepted it, though each for its own reasons. But that did not mean that the process of dividing should be further extended. If Kashmir was to be divided, then why not the other states? Where would this process stop?'

Before long, his fears with regard to the referral of the Kashmir issue to the UN proved true. After a series of denials and prevarications, Pakistan was ultimately driven to admit that its troops had participated in the invasion of Kashmir. The UN Commission put on record their findings that on Kashmir soil Pakistan had violated India's sovereignty. But the UN would not name Pakistan as 'aggressor'. Pakistan placed a series of counter-complaints against India, including one of 'genocide'. The British representative in the UN, in pursuance of the old British tradition of Anglo-Muslim League collaboration, sided with Pakistan. India was thus put in the dock.

Gandhi continued to make the refugee crisis his priority. On a visit to a Muslim refugee camp in Panipat, he was shocked to see the filthy living conditions. There were close to twenty thousand Hindu refugees from West Punjab, and their plight was pathetic too; the camps were disorganized, ill-equipped and filthy. That evening, in his post-prayer speech, Gandhi took the authorities to task. The chief minister of Punjab was a veteran Congressman and an old colleague, but if Panipat was a sample of his administrative abilities, Gandhi observed, 'it was a sad reflection on himself and the capabilities of his government. Why were the refugees dumped anywhere without notice? Why were arrangements for their reception inadequate? Why were the officers not informed in advance about who and how many they were to expect and provide for?' He was even more disturbed to find out that over a hundred and fifty thousand Muslims, who had been driven out of their homes and had been walking to Pakistan, were forced due to the winter to camp by the roadside on the outskirts of Gurgaon, with no arrangements for their stay or for their passage to Pakistan. They were faced with a 300-mile march in the bleak winter.

The AICC met after a gap of four months to chart their future; on their decisions would depend the path the newborn nation and its people take.

Two days later, on 8 November, Gandhi addressed the AICC for the last time. Pyarelal writes: 'Ever since its inception over a quarter of a century ago, it had been guided by him, whether he was present or not. A straight from the shoulder talk by the Father of the Nation, it was listened to by all sections of the House with the respect it deserved. Each period was a sledgehammer blow aimed at the anvil of their conscience, to strike the fire of the old Congress tradition and the ideals that had made the Congress a power without a rival in the land.

"'I have seen enough to realize that though not all of us have gone mad, a sufficiently large number have lost their heads… It is to me obvious that if we do not cure ourselves of this insanity, we shall lose the freedom we have won. You must understand and recognize the gravity of the plight we are in… You represent the vast ocean of Indian humanity. You will not allow it to be said that the Congress consists of a handful of people who rule the country. At least I will not allow it… When we were fighting for our freedom, we bore a heavy responsibility. But today, when we have achieved freedom, our responsibility has grown a hundred-fold… There are many places where a Muslim cannot live in security… I would not be satisfied if you said that it could not be helped or that you had no part in it… It is the basic creed of the Congress that India is the home of Muslims no less than that of Hindus … I do not need to quote the authority of the Congress Constitution to support my claim.

"'Some say that if we perpetrate worse atrocities on Muslims here than those perpetrated on Hindus and Sikhs in Pakistan, it will teach the Muslims in Pakistan a salutary lesson. They will indeed be taught a lesson, but what will happen to you in the meanwhile? The wicked sink under the weight of their own evil; must we sink with them? … I hold it to be an impossibility that three and a half crore (thirty five million) Muslims can be driven away to Pakistan. What crime have they committed? The Muslim League may have been culpable, but not every Muslim … it is your duty to call back all those Muslims who have been obliged to flee to Pakistan. India is big enough to keep them, as well as all the Hindu and Sikh refugees who have fled here from Pakistan. Of course, those Muslims who believe in Pakistan and wish to seek their happiness there are welcome to migrate. For them, there is no bar…

"'A hundred and fifty thousand Muslims near Gurgaon are about to be sent to Pakistan. It is said that they are no better than criminal tribes and had better be sent to Pakistan. I cannot understand the logic of this argument. There were criminal tribes in India during the British regime. Was there any talk of deporting them then? ... Our duty should be to reform them. How shameful it is for us that we should force them to trudge three hundred miles! I am against all such forced exodus... I know some people are saying that the Congress has surrendered its soul to the Muslims. Gandhi! Let him rave as he will. He is a wash-out. Jawaharlal is no better. As regards Sardar Patel, there is something in him. A portion of him is sound Hindu, but he, too, is after all a Congressman! Such talk will not help us ... will not save either Hinduism or Sikhism. Such is not the teaching of the Guru Granth Sahib. Christianity does not teach these ways. Nor has Islam been saved by the sword. I have heard many things about the RSS... You have to preserve your freedom.'"

Many of the resolutions passed by the AICC were extracted from Gandhi's speech. One assured the minorities that the Congress would always stand by them and ensure that they enjoyed equal privileges and security as every citizen of India. In another resolution, it warned the private militias to desist from mischief; the resolution identified and named the Muslim National Guard, RSS, Akali Volunteers and other such organizations and movements as actual and potential culprits under that category and called them 'a menace to the hard won freedom of the country'. It appealed to them to discontinue such activities and asked the central and provincial governments to take necessary steps to ensure this. Another resolution appealed to the citizens to help in creating an atmosphere where the evacuees from both the dominions would be induced to return to their former homes. Unfortunately, the AICC resolution had no effect: a fresh wave of refugees brought with them their tales of woe, and violence erupted once more.

On 17 December, a vicious riot broke out in Hyderabad, Sind, where non-Muslims were identified and targeted systematically. Under the pretext of housing refugees from East Punjab, the government began forcibly occupying educational institutions run by non-Muslims; even places of worship of the minorities were not spared. The government put many obstacles in the sale or transfer of non-Muslim property, the reason being to discourage migration of non-Muslims from the province.

Gandhi warned the Pakistan government that their actions would lead to grave consequences if they made it impossible for non-Muslims to remain in Sind as free citizens. He advised the government that the only way to check the exodus was to regain the confidence of the minorities. His advice fell on deaf ears.

On 6 January, riots broke out in Karachi, the capital of Sind. Nearly 70 per cent of the non-Muslim-owned property in Karachi—homes, shops and business premises—were looted. The combined population of Hindus and Sikhs in Karachi stood at 350,000 before Partition; by 13 January 1948, all the surviving Sikhs had fled and only 90,000 Hindus remained. The Pakistan government expressed its inability to cope with the situation and Gandhi advised them to quit if they were powerless to provide security to their citizens. 'That might make things worse for a while, but ultimately the things would improve,' he said. He gave identical advice to the Government of India.

Pyarelal writes: 'The exodus from East Bengal continued. To this was added still another from the State of Bahawalpur (Pakistan). It helped to swell the ranks of destitute refugees in Bombay, Kathiawad, the C.P., Delhi and the U.P. on one side and Bengal, Assam, Bihar and Orissa on the other. The incoming refugees did not come with any friendly feelings towards those whose co-religionists across the border had dispossessed them of their hearth and driven them almost naked and penniless from the land of their ancestors and birth which they dearly loved. A menacing situation thus began to develop in India generally, and in Delhi in particular.'

Many Muslim League leaders and supporters who did not subscribe to Jinnah's views had stayed back in the Indian Union. Here, they were under surveillance: once before they had betrayed the country and sided with the separatists, where were their loyalties now? Patel, the eternal pragmatist, warned them: 'I believe in plain speaking. I want to tell the Muslims frankly that, at this critical juncture, it is your duty to sail in the same boat and sink or swim together with us. You cannot ride on two horses. You must select one horse, whichever you like best.'

The leader of the Muslim League Party in the Constituent Assembly,

Khalik-uz-Zaman, told his erstwhile colleagues across the border to mind their own business and leave the Indian Muslims alone. The leader of the Muslim League Party in the Orissa Assembly appealed to the Indian Muslims: 'Let us now forget the two-nation theory and owe allegiance to the Indian Union... In spite of the platitudes by the Pakistanists, they cannot do anything for our safety and it would be futile for us to look to them for protection.'

During the riots in Delhi, many mosques had been vandalized and forcibly occupied by refugees. Some had been converted into temples. Gandhi drew Patel's attention to this and told him to ensure that such incidents did not occur again. Gandhi suggested that the department headed by Patel, on behalf of the Union government, should make an announcement that no sacrilege would be suffered in regard to mosques, and if any damage did occur, the repairs would be affected by the government. The Delhi administration issued a communiqué, giving seven days' notice to non-Muslims occupying mosques to vacate them, failing which the police would eject them by force.

Pyarelal writes: 'Muslims made grave allegations against Sardar Patel and his officers. The latter, they alleged, were turning a blind eye to the looting of Muslim shops. While making a pretence of taking action, they were actually telling the refugee crowds to come in their numbers so that the police could afterwards plead helplessness in the face of "superior numbers". Gandhiji arranged a meeting between their spokesmen and three of the senior members of the Cabinet to thrash out the whole matter in his presence. The meeting was repeated on 25 December, when the police chief of Delhi was also present. Gandhiji did not feel very satisfied with the result.

'"People expect much from me," he observed at one of his prayer meetings, "but they must realize that I am not running the government." Those at the helm of affairs were his friends, but he did not, he went on to say, want anyone to accept his advice merely out of friendship or regard for him. They should do so only if it went home.... The ministers had inherited the old machinery from the British rulers, they were trying to make the best of it. There were stresses and strains within the Cabinet too. The temperamental differences between Pandit Nehru and Sardar Patel had always been there... Both the Sardar and Pandit Nehru had by turns been allergic to Gandhiji's approach to sundry issues. But neither could do without Gandhiji, and Gandhiji had come to the conclusion that the country needed the services of them both in the government. In spite of their differences, the two had cooperated as disciplined soldiers and loyal friends and comrades for nearly thirty years during the struggle for freedom… But since independence, these differences had begun, more and more, to assume a practical shape and even to affect their personal relations. The delimitation of powers and functions of the prime minister vis-à-vis his Cabinet colleagues had never been clearly effected. Had the prime minister a special function as a "coordinator and supervisor" covering all the other ministries? If so, how was that function discharged without interference with the functioning of other ministries? This particularly affected the relations between Pandit Nehru and Sardar Patel. Gandhiji was afraid that the growing rift between the Congress leaders would be exploited by Pakistan. It almost seemed that Pakistan was banking upon a split and was only biding its opportunity. Even more painful to Gandhiji personally was the fact that the Governor General was being drawn into these bickering. "Why should we allow Mountbatten to take such interest in our family quarrels, his best intentions not withstanding?" he exclaimed to a Congress colleague. It was no reflection on Mountbatten the man. Gandhiji had the fullest confidence in him, but it was humiliating for India. Gandhiji had been trying in his own way to bridge these differences and from what he knew of the parties, he had not a shadow of a doubt as to the ultimate result. They were both patriots to the core… Soon after I had rejoined him in Delhi, Gandhiji remarked to me one day: "Each one of them—the Sardar, Pandit Nehru and Mountbatten—is playing his game with consummate skill, with the purest of motives and with the sole purpose of serving India according to his lights. As I am playing mine," he added, "and it alone is going to prevail in the end. There is no salvation for India except through my way. Mountbatten at least has seen this."

The situation in Kashmir was deteriorating by the day. Gandhi likened the situation in Kashmir to a glowing matchstick in a stack of hay. 'You never can tell when it may light up and the whole thing go(es) up in a blaze.' The question of special powers given to the maharaja post his accession was becoming a contentious and complicated issue. Gandhi wanted that the Union government should have no special agreements with any of the princes or provinces. He hoped that the Indian Union would stand by the principles it was founded on, where there was 'full justice and equal treatment to the minorities and punishment for the wrongdoers without fear or favour.'

To compound the chaos, every day brought with it a new complication. One of these was Pakistan's share of the cash balance of undivided India, which evolved into a long drawn out and acrimonious issue. Eventually, out of the ₹375 crores cash balance, Pakistan was paid ₹20 crores on the day of the transfer of power. Pakistan's share was to be decided after negotiations between the two governments. This agreement was signed between the representatives of the Pakistan government and senior leaders of the Union government, including Patel and Nehru, after both India and Pakistan had become independent nations. After prolonged negotiations, an amount of ₹75 crores being Pakistan's share was agreed upon. A bilateral treaty was signed between the two independent nations, by which India agreed to pay the balance ₹55 crores to Pakistan.

To force India's hand and to score brownie points with their people, the Pakistan leaders made a triumphal announcement to the media that they had 'forced India to agree to pay Pakistan its share'. This did not go down well with the people of India against the backdrop of the developments in Kashmir and the rehabilitation of refugees from Pakistani territories. To save face, the Indian leaders issued statements saying that they had insisted that the final settlement of the accounts and the payment of the balance amount would be done only after all issues were resolved between the two dominions. Pakistani leaders denied that any such conditions were imposed or accepted by them. The text of the treaty did not mention this either. Facing growing criticism, the Indian government decided unilaterally to defer the payment of the balance amount 'till all issues were resolved'. Pakistan immediately went on the offensive. The finance minister of Pakistan termed the move 'an act of aggression'. The Indian government justified their decision as their unwillingness to fund Pakistan's aggression against India in Kashmir. But when the agreement was signed, the aggression in Kashmir had already begun, but no such rider had been included in the agreement. Nehru issued a statement justifying the Indian government's actions: 'A State freezes the credit of the other party in such circumstances. We have not frozen anything in that sense. All that we said was that we accept this agreement but there must be an overall settlement and we shall honour it completely.' This was logical but should have been included in the treaty. Also, going by this agreement, when an act of aggression had already been committed, why was the treaty, agreement, whatever one may call it, signed?

On 12 January, while meeting Gandhi to discuss the overall situation in Delhi, Mountbatten voiced his concern about the government's stand. Gandhi asked Mountbatten for his frank and candid opinion. Mountbatten replied that it would be the 'first dishonourable act' by the Indian Union government if the payment of the cash balance claimed by Pakistan was withheld. After this conversation, Gandhi did refer to it and also said that by agreeing to the partition, a sin had been committed. By dishonouring an agreement, which was a moral commitment, India would compound the sin, and after that its word would be worthless. He did not question the legality of the Union government's decision. He agreed that he would not insist that the Union government go beyond what the strict letter of the law required and permitted them. But he expected that India would live up to its tradition of death before dishonouring a promise.

Thus, Delhi kept Gandhi occupied, keeping the peace between its people, and between the two senior-most ministers of the government. He responded in his ethical manner to all the shenanigans and provocations by the Government of Pakistan, ensuring that the Nation he had helped liberate remained on the path he had hoped it would never stray from. Circumstances were such that he was facing disappointment and betrayal on most of the fronts. His people were going insane in an orgy of hate and violence. His most trusted colleagues had abandoned him, his cherished ideal of non-violence was tarnished, there was betrayal and deceit all around and, in their midst, Gandhi was forced to walk alone.

BOOK 3

RED FORT TRIAL, APPEALS,
EXECUTION AND KAPUR COMMISSION

XII

RED FORT TRIAL

A film clip of the proceedings of the first hearing showed some of the accused chatting and smiling among themselves, a very tense, gloomy and frail Savarkar and the murderer Nathuram Godse with a very sombre expression on his face sat in the dock. Apte and the others merrily posed for photographers.

—Description of the first day's proceedings in court

Immediately after Gandhi's murder at 5:17 p.m. on the lawns of Birla House on 30 January 1948, his murderer, Ramchandra 'Nathuram' Vinayak Godse, was arrested on the spot. A member of Gandhi's entourage and an eyewitness to the murder, Nandlal Mehta, filed an FIR of the murder at the Tughlaq Road police station. The original FIR was recorded in Hindustani, written in the Urdu script. The following is its translation.

F.I.R. (First Information Report) & A.T.R. (Action Taken Report) of the Assassination of Mahatma Gandhi Police Station: Tughlaq Road, District New Delhi

F.I.R. No. 68 (*In the original in Urdu script, the numerals 14 precede the handwritten number 68*)*

1. Date and Place *(should be time)* of Occurrence: 30-1-1948; at 5:10 p.m. *(5:17 p.m.)*
2. Date and Hour when reported: 30-1-1948, 9:45 in the evening *(the time was when the FIR was filed)*
3. Name and Address of Informant & Complainant: Nandlal

---

*All bracketed italics by the author.

Mehta S/O. Nathalal Mehta, Community: Hindustani. Address: Connaught Circus, Lala Sarju Prasad Building, M Block, New Delhi
4. Brief Description of the Offence and Property Carried off if any: 302 IPC
5. Name & Address of the Criminal: (Nathuram Vinayak Godse)
6. Steps Taken regarding Investigation Explanation for Delay in recording Information: There have been no delays. Complaint Number 50, Note Book No. 1
7. Date and Time of Despatch from Police Station: Refer to Special Report

Signed D/O. ASI Dalu Ram

The statement of Nandlal Mehta S/O. Nathalal Mehta, Community: Hindustani, resident of Connaught Circus, Building Lala Sarju Prasad, New Delhi:

> I was present at the Birla House today. At about 10 minutes past 5 o'clock Gandhiji got up and left to go to the Prarthana Sthal from his room in the Birla House. He was accompanied by his 'sticks' Mrs Abhabehn Gandhi and Miss Manubehn Gandhi. Mahatma Gandhi was walking between the two sisters with his arms on their shoulders. Shri Brijkishan Chandiwala resident of No. 1, Narendra Palace, Parliament Street and Sardar Gurbachan Singh resident of Minarpur, Delhi, were walking a few paces behind them. Some women from the Birla Family and 2 or 3 members of his staff were also in the entourage. After passing through the garden, Gandhiji climbed up the stone paved steps to go to the Prarthana Sthal. As Gandhiji ascended the steps, the gathering at the Prarthana Sthal stood up and parted, forming a passage three feet wide through which Gandhiji could pass. Gandhiji folded his hands in greeting and started walking down the passage towards the dais. He had barely taken six or seven steps towards the Prarthana Sthal when a youth stepped out of the crowd and blocked his path, it was later learnt that the name of the young man was Narayan (*should be Nathuram*) Vinayak Godse, resident of Poona. The young man walked up to Gandhiji, when he was barely 2 to 3 feet away, he

whipped out a pistol and fired thrice in rapid succession at Gandhiji. The bullets hit Gandhiji in his stomach and chest, blood began to flow from the wounds. Gandhiji collapsed to the ground saying, 'Ram ... R...a...m ... R...a.....m.' The attacker was immediately caught along with the pistol. Mahatma Gandhi was picked up and carried, unconscious, to his room in Birla House. There it was discovered that Gandhiji was no more. The police took the murderer to the Police Station.

Signed N.L. Mehta, 30-1-48

Action Taken: 'On hearing the report of Gandhiji's murder, I immediately rushed to Birla House. Mahatma Gandhi's body was kept in a room in Birla House. I met Nandlal Mehta Sahib, who had given his eyewitness statement. The text of his statement was read out to him, after confirming that it was correct he signed it. A copy was given; on inquiring about the accused, I was told that ASI Dalu Ram had taken him to the police station. Since the offence was of IPC 302, the crime scene was investigated, evidence gathered, statements of eyewitnesses recorded and all this was filed at the Tughlaq Road police station as per due procedure. A special report must be forwarded to the concerned senior officials from the police station post haste. Signed.

Thus a file containing all the statements, investigation reports and copies of the relevant entries in the registers have been despatched to the office of DSP New Delhi, Jaswant Singh. The special report was despatched to the concerned officers on 30-1-1948 by ASI Dalu Ram.'

Written by SI Kuldeep Singh.

♦

The political fallout of Gandhi's murder was that the Union home minister, Sardar Patel, came under intense attack for the failure of the police department, which was directly under him, to save Gandhi. The Nehru loyalists in the Congress saw this as an opportunity to attack and weaken the Iron Man of India. The attacks were bitterly corrosive. It took a terrible toll, both on Patel's political as well as physical health. On 6 February 1948, in a special session to discuss Gandhi's murder, questions were raised in Parliament, and the home minister faced severe criticism.

(The following is a translation from Hindi by the author of the actual parliamentary proceedings.)

Balakrishna Sharma, member of Parliament (MP): Is it true that a superintendent of police was assigned to remain present during the prayer meetings, but on that unfortunate day, he was absent?

Hon. Sardar Vallabhbhai Patel: There were armed policemen in large numbers. But I have no information about whether a superintendent was not present. I cannot confirm whether the officer was present or not. But I will inquire.

BS: On the day of the bomb explosion, a search was carried out at Marina Hotel and some clothes were found with the laundry mark 'N.V.G.', Nathuram Vinayak Godse. .Armed with this information the police went to Bombay and asked the Bombay Police to find that person. The Bombay Police sent back the policemen from there saying that they would make inquiries. Is it true that Bombay Police failed to track down and arrest Nathuram Vinayak Godse?

SVP: It is difficult and also improper to speak about or reveal issues which are under investigation. I can only say that after the arrest and interrogation of the first person who exploded the bomb, an officer (actually two) from Delhi was immediately sent to Bombay to interact with the CID there. After consultations, it was decided that some people should be arrested, but it was felt that immediate arrest would be improper: this would alert others involved in the conspiracy, they would then abscond or, worse, go underground and continue their nefarious activities. That is why, after consultations, the Bombay Police and the Delhi CID decided that the matter should be discreetly investigated and the entire conspiracy should be exposed along with all who were a part of it before (the) arrests. It is true that the police were on the lookout for these people, but all of them were not in Bombay.

BS: If the information does not compromise the ongoing investigation, can I ask if it is true that Nathuram Godse came back to Delhi by plane?

SVP: I feel that it is improper to reveal details about a matter that is currently being investigated.

Deshbandhu Gupta, MP: If it is true that the person arrested first had confessed the name of the murderer, was it not possible for the Delhi CID to secure his photograph from Bombay? Then copies of the photograph could have been distributed amongst the people looking after arrangements at the prayer meeting and they could have detained the murderer in time to prevent the murder?

SVP: After getting the information, the Delhi Police did try to locate these people. But all the accused were not in one place and it was not possible to photograph them. (Rana, Chief of CID Poona had photographs of Godse, Apte and Badge in his hand on the early evening of 29 January, he did not inform either Bombay Police or Delhi Police. Rana was only questioned about this lapse during the Kapur Commission's cross examination, almost twenty years later.)

L. Krishnaswamy Bharati, MP: Is it true that this government had been informed by the Bombay Police that a 'criminal' involved in the conspiracy was on his way from Bombay?

SVP: This is not true.

H.B. Kamath, MP: Is the government aware that after the calamity that has befallen us, certain vested interests and people are putting the entire blame on the Hon. home minister and are thus trying to create a rift in the Cabinet and are sowing doubts in the minds of the people?

Speaker: Keep quiet. Second question.

Rohini Kumar Chaudhury, MP: Can I ask if the police seek the convenience of the person they are assigned to protect? The truth is that in the matter of security, the convenience of neither the governor nor the Governor-General is asked.

SVP: As far as the issue pertaining to the current matter, the concerned person was of a different category and in his case, it was impossible for the police to act without seeking his advice.

RKC: But in the wake of the incident, will the Hon. minister ensure and institute procedures so that in the matter of security arrangements, the police will be solely responsible?

Speaker: Quiet! Silence! Member, you have started arguing.

RKC: I am only suggesting that in future, all security decisions should be left to the discretion and ability of the police without interference.

Speaker: It is clear that this will largely depend on the concerned person.

BS: The Hon. home minister in person has informed the august house that in the matter of the security of our ministers, their concerns and wishes are taken into consideration. I would like to appeal that some of our ministers are such that their consent and wishes should not be considered, because...

Speaker: This is not a question nor an effort to get at the truth, you are being argumentative.

RKC: Sir, can I ask how did it transpire that Raghu Mali was the first person to catch the murderer? He grappled with the killer and brought him down. The police only reached the spot after some time. Where was the police at that time?

SVP: I cannot say whether the police reached first or the gardener. These are all unsubstantiated newspaper reports.

Deputy Prime Minister Sardar Patel's letter dated 27 February 1948 to Prime Minister Nehru indicating the involvement of Savarkar and a fanatical wing of Hindu Mahasabha under his command in Gandhi's murder: 'It was a fanatical wing of the Hindu Mahasabha directly under Savarkar that (hatched) the conspiracy and saw it through' (*Sardar Patel's Correspondence*, Volume 6, p. 56).

♦

After the murder, there was a spate of arrests all over the Union. Many unsubstantiated, sensational and speculative stories were published by the press, further compounding the confusion. This led to many reprisals against those who were alleged to be involved in the murder, and a potentially explosive situation developed. This forced many provincial governments to ban the publication of any news concerned with the murder investigation. Under the guise of avenging the murder, gangs vandalized properties of and murdered a few Brahmins in Bombay State and in the princely state of Kolhapur. Patel went on to issue a public appeal: 'In this moment of tragedy, if we succumb to the feeling of revenge and counter violence we will fail to be worthy of Gandhiji. I assure the people that the government will take severe action against people indulging in such activities… It is only proper for the people to leave the responsibility of investigation on the government… I appeal to all the people to maintain calm and remain steadfast and soon return to their work and profession. They must allow the law to do its duty and not commit acts of counter violence.'

♦

The Red Fort Trial

The trial of the accused in the Gandhi murder was the third trial to be held at the Red Fort in Delhi, the seat of the Mughal emperors constructed by Emperor Shahjahan in the seventeenth century on the banks of the Yamuna. A few hundred yards ahead, Gandhi's mortal remains had been consigned to flames at Raj Ghat. The structure in which the court was to sit was a British Army Barrack. In an adjoining barrack in the fort, the trials of the INA officers were conducted two years ago. The first trial had been that of the last Mughal Emperor, Bahadur Shah 'Zafar', the poet, after 1857.

A few months had passed since Gandhi's murder, and there was widespread speculation about the investigation and when the trial would commence. Finally, during the second week of April 1948, the news came that the district and circuit judge of Kanpur, H. Atmacharan, Indian Civil Services (ICS), would hear the case. Unconfirmed reports from Delhi suggested that it would begin in May and would be conducted in a special court. The Hindu extremists were hoping that the trial would not begin soon. They needed time to formulate a defence strategy. But as soon as the possibility of an early trial began to gain credence, they instituted a 'defence fund' which was to meet the cost of hiring the best defence team for the accused and meet the financial needs of the dependants of the accused. Donations were collected by the Hindu Mahasabha and RSS branches and members from their supporters and sympathizers. The Bengal Hindu Mahasabha took the lead in this activity.

On 8 May 1948, the government published a notification 'No. 54/1/48—Political, Government of India, Ministry of Home Affairs, dated 4 May 1948, under Section 10 and 11 of the Bombay Public Security Measures Act, 1947 as extended to the Province of Delhi' and the case was made over to the court for trial under 'Notification No. 54/1/48—Political, Government of India, Ministry of Home Affairs, dated 13 May 1948'.

A barrack in the Red Fort was declared a prison under 'Notification No. 54/6/48—Political, Government of India, Ministry of Home Affairs, dated 15 May 1948'.

The delay occurred because the prosecution were unable to decide whether they wanted to try Savarkar along with Godse and the others or separately. Eventually, all the accused were tried together. It was also decided to extend Sections 10 and 11 of the Bombay Public Security Measures Act, 1947, to the provinces of Delhi to facilitate a speedy trial. This empowered the presiding judge to skip the noting of detailed statements of the witnesses and similar time-consuming procedures. On 15 May 1948, the Union Government of India published a special gazette notification and proclaimed that the nine accused in the Gandhi murder case would be tried on behalf of the Government of India under Sections 109, 114, 115, 120B and 302 of the Indian Penal Code (IPC); Sections 3, 4, 5 and 6 of the Explosive Substances Act of 1908 and under Sections 19(D) and 19(F) of the Arms Act of 1878.

The nine accused to be tried were:

1. Ramchandra 'Nathuram' Vinayak Godse: Hindu, 37, Editor, *Hindu Rashtra,* Shaniwar Peth, Poona.
2. Narayan Dattatreya Apte: Hindu, 34, Director, H.R. Prakashan Ltd., 22, Budhwar Peth, Poona.
3. Vishnu Ramkrishna Karkare: Hindu, 37, Proprietor, Deccan Lodging and Boarding House, Pardeshi Aali, Ahmednagar.
4. Digambar Ramchandra Badge (Approver): Hindu, 39, Proprietor, Shastra Bhandar, 300, Narayan Peth, Poona.
5. Madanlal Kashmirilal Pahwa: Hindu, 20, (Punjabi Refugee), Visapur Refugee Camp, Ahmednagar.
6. Shankar Kistayya: Hindu, 20, Domestic Servant (Yellamma Peth, Sholapur), 300, Narayan Peth, Poona.
7. Gopal Vinayak Godse: Hindu, 27, Store Keeper, Military Ordinance Depot, Kirkee, Poona.
8. Vinayak Damodar Savarkar: Hindu, 65, Landlord, Savarkar

Sadan, Shivaji Park Road, Bombay.
9. Dattatreya Sadashiv Parchure: Hindu, 40, Medical Practitioner, Station Road, Gwalior.

Three more accused, from Gwalior, were named absconders:
1. Gangadhar Sakharam Dandavate
2. Gangadhar Jadhav
3. Suryadev Sharma and others.

◆

The Chargesheet

The following separate categories of charges were framed against the eight accused: (1) Nathuram Vinayak Godse, Narayan D. Apte, Vishnu Ramkrishna Karkare, Madanlal K. Pahwa, Shankar Kistayya, Gopal V. Godse, Vinayak Damodar Savarkar and Dattatreya S. Parchure were charged under Section 120B IPC. (conspiracy) read with Section 302 IPC 9 (murder); (2) Nathuram V. Godse, Narayan Apte, Karkare, Madanlal, Shankar Kistayya and Gopal Godse were also charged under Section 19(D), Indian Arms Act, and Section 19(D), Indian Arms Act read with Section 109 and 114 IPC, Section 19(F), Indian Arms Act, and Section 19(F) Indian Arms Act read with Section 114 IPC, 4(B), Explosive Substances Act read with Section 6 of the said Act, Section 5 of the Explosive Substances Act and Section 5 of the Explosive Substances Act read with Section 6 of the said Act; (3) Madanlal was separately charged under Section 3 of the Explosive Substances Act. Nathuram Godse, Apte, Karkare, Shankar Kistayya and Gopal Godse were also charged under Section 3 of the Explosive Substances Act read with Section 6 of the said Act; (4) Nathuram Godse, Apte, Karkare, Madanlal, Shankar Kistayya, Gopal Godse and V.D. Savarkar were further charged under Section 115 IPC read with Section 302 IPC; (5) Nathuram Godse and Apte were also charged under Section 19(C) of the Indian Arms Act; (6) Nathuram Godse, Apte and Dattatreya Parchure were further charged under Section 19(C) of the Indian Arms Act, read with Section 114 IPC; (7) Nathuram Godse was separately charged under Section 19(F) of the Indian Arms Act; (8) Apte and Karkare were charged under Section 19(F) of the Indian Arms Act, read with Section 114 IPC; (9) Apte and Karkare were further charged Section 302 IPC for the murder of Gandhi; (10) Apte and Karkare were further charged under Section 302 IPC (murder), read with Section 114 IPC (abetment by presence); (11) Madanlal, Shankar Kistayya, Gopal Godse, Vinayak Savarkar and Dattatreya Parchure were also charged under Section 302 IPC, read with Section 109 IPC.

◆

In the spirit of conducting a fair trial, the accused were offered legal aid. Savarkar made a personal appeal to senior advocate L.B. Bhopatkar, requesting him to take up his defence. Savarkar said that he trusted Bhopatkar explicitly and would feel he was in safe hands. Bhopatkar could not refuse the plea of an old friend and agreed to personally appear for Savarkar. Being the senior-most advocate for the defence, he was chosen to head the team of advocates defending the various accused. The Working Committee of the Maharashtra-region Hindu Mahasabha formed a legal aid committee and raised a legal aid fund. The defence committee was headed by Bhopatkar, with Rambhau Mandalik as convenor and G.V. Ketkar as treasurer.

The committee began work on 2 May 1948. On 6 June, it met once again in Poona and an all-India defence committee was formed with twelve members. The committee requested Dr Jayakar to defend Savarkar, but the former refused. The defence committee also appealed to the Bombay provincial government to pardon or parole Advocate Vasudev Balwant Gogate who was imprisoned in the Yerawada Jail, as Karkare had requested for him. The provincial government turned down the request.

The defence committee formed two subcommittees which were entrusted with the work of making arrangements for the transportation and accommodation needs of the defence counsels. The members comprised Joglekar of Chalisgaon, Babarao Kale and V.K. Mahendale of Barsi.

The following is a list of members of the all-India defence committee: (1) L.B. Bhopatkar, President; (2) Lala Narayan Dutt, Treasurer, 13 Barakhamba Road, New Delhi; (3) G.V. Ketkar (Tilak's grandson), Treasurer, Kesari Office, Poona; (4) Rambhau Mandalik, Convenor; (5) Jamunadas Mehta; (6) Devendrakumar Mukherjee; (7) Captain Keshavchandra; (8) Panchanathan; (9) Ganapati Aiyer; (10)

Lakshmishankar Verma; (11) Dr L.B. Paranjape, Nagpur; (12) R.A. Kanitkar, Buldhana.

◆

Preparations for the trial began in earnest. The historic Red Fort was once again the focus of the attention of the entire world. A room measuring 100 feet by 23 feet on the top floor of a twin-wing stone building was to house the special court. The building had previously served as the principal camp of the British military police. An 8-feet high barbed wire fence was erected surrounding the building. Two manned gates served as entry and exit points to the building. Barracks close by were commandeered to hold the accused. Reinforced iron doors and window grills were brought from the Delhi Central Jail and installed in the doors and windows of the cells. A raised wooden platform served as the seat of the judge and the court's reporter. Three wooden benches placed on the right side of the room constituted the dock, for the accused. The witness stand was to the left. Two hundred chairs were placed in the room to accommodate press reporters and special pass holders who wished to watch the proceedings. Chambers were provided in rooms along the corridors on both sides of the courtroom. The judge's chambers, court reporter's room, chambers for the defence and prosecution lawyers, police officer's room and a canteen were located here. The press room was equipped with two telephones.

On the ground floor, a big room was reserved for the Bombay Police. Next to it was the room for the female witnesses. The advocate general of Bombay State and his assistants were given an adjoining room. All other police personnel and witnesses were accommodated in a room in the adjoining wing. The court's registrar issued a notification on 19 May, stating that only those people who held a valid entry pass would be allowed to enter the court premises.

On 24 May, Godse, Savarkar and the other accused were brought to Delhi from Bombay by different planes, accompanied by a large contingent of the Bombay Police. They were directly driven from the airport to their cells in the Red Fort, which had been converted into a maximum security prison for the duration of the trial.

The Bombay Public Security Measures Act of 1947, also known as the 'Goonda Act', and some of its sections, which pertained to special courts, were extended to apply to Delhi to ensure a speedy trial. The Act was instituted in 1947 to enable the speedy trial of those accused in the communal riots that had erupted in the Bombay Province. The fifth part of this act deals with the rules for constituting special courts. The sections were:

Section 10: The government can institute a special court in any part of the Union after duly publishing a notification in the government gazette.

Section 11: The government can appoint any high court or any circuit court judge having a minimum of two years' experience to head such a court.

Section 12: By issuing special orders, the government can ask the presiding judge of such special courts to take up special trials.

Section 13 (1-2): Even if the matter has not been referred to the circuit court by lower courts, the special court can take up cases assigned to it. The court is permitted to note only pertinent portions of the statements of witnesses. If, after consultation with the accused, the court decides that a witness is not required to testify, it can refuse to call such a witness. If the presiding judge feels that it is not necessary to the dispensation of justice, he can, for any other reasons, refuse to adjourn the proceedings of the case.

Section 14: Apart from these two subsections and those covered by Sections 10 to 20, any other Penal Codes that are not contrary will be applicable to the special court. The court will be recognized as a circuit court. If the presiding judge so wishes, the statement of any witness will be recorded by a single person commission.

Section 15: Anyone accused of attempted murder may be sentenced to death by hanging and those accused of murder by stabbing may be sentenced to death by hanging or life imprisonment.

Section 17: The special judge is empowered to award any punishment prescribed by the law. In case of a fine being imposed, the court may issue warrants to impound, confiscate and sell any/all movable or immovable assets of the accused to raise the fine.

Section 18: A person sentenced by the special court may appeal to a higher court within fifteen days. In dealing with such appeals, the high court can ask for any/all documents pertaining to the trial and will have privileges of other appeal courts, but no court will have any powers to transfer the case from this special court to any other circuit court or to pass orders affecting the work of this special court. No court will be able to interfere in whatever way with the working of this special court.

Section 20: No jury or assessor will be appointed for the case before this special court.

By passing an ordinance, the government introduced some amendments to the Bombay Public Security Measures Act. The amendment empowered the special judge, hearing the trial before the special court, to grant a conditional pardon to any person directly or indirectly involved with the case and record their statements. The condition was that such a person would confess to everything he or she knew about the conspiracy and about those who were involved in it.

◆

First Three Preliminary Hearings

Finally, four months after Gandhi's murder, legal proceedings in the much awaited trial began on 27 May. The first three hearings on 27 May, 3 June and 14 June 1948 dealt with preliminary procedures.

The first day's proceedings did not reflect the kind of atmosphere, reverence, decorum and importance one would have expected in such a high-profile case. The loudspeaker system installed in the court for the benefit of the visitors and press was so bad that on the first day, the reporters were reduced to mere spectators; no one could hear what was being said either by the judge or by the lawyers. The proceedings were being conducted in a very informal manner. At one time, ten to twelve lawyers from both sides crowded around Judge Atmacharan and began speaking all at once. Since the courtroom was long, 24 feet wide and 100 feet long, it looked more like a passageway. It became impossible for those who were seated at the extreme end of the courtroom to comprehend the proceedings.

On request, Judge Atmacharan allowed photographers to take photographs of the court as well as of the accused. A film clip of the proceedings of the first hearing shows some of the accused chatting and smiling among themselves; a very tense, gloomy and frail Savarkar and the murderer Nathuram Godse with a very sombre expression on his face. Apte and the others merrily posed for the photographers. Photographs of the first day were widely published all over India and abroad. The atmosphere in the courtroom that day was more like a festive occasion than a sombre murder trial.

The continuous movements of drinking water servers compounded the chaos. With earthen pots balanced on their heads and metal glasses in hand, the servers constantly moved around the courtroom, serving the thirsty. The hot summer temperature of May was also adding to the 'heat' of the case being heard. The surroundings of the Red Fort were deserted, apart from the cordon thrown around the entry and exit points by 250–300 uniformed and plainclothes policemen. The Red Fort precinct was declared a high-security zone and guarded thus. It was difficult to enter the courtroom too: one required a special pass and there was a lot of checking and frisking before one could enter the court. The accused in the Gandhi murder were being protected much more efficiently than Gandhi himself had been.

On the first day, the court worked for only two hours, from 10:00 a.m. till noon. The accused were brought into the barracks, housing the courtroom, at 9:00 a.m. and brought into the courtroom at 9:50 a.m., ten minutes before the proceedings began. None of the accused were manacled or handcuffed. Nathuram was the first to enter the court. Wearing a pyjama and long-sleeved shirt, he occupied a spot in the centre of the bench in the first row in the dock. Apte and Karkare sat on either side of him on the front bench; Karkare was dressed in a silk shirt and dhoti. Apte and Gopal Godse were dressed like Nathuram. Savarkar, Kistayya and Parchure were wearing black topis, a part of the Hindu Mahasabha and RSS uniforms. Badge, Gopal Godse and Madanlal Pahwa entered next and occupied the bench in the second row. The bench in the last row was occupied by Kistayya, Savarkar and Parchure.

Bhopatkar requested the court that Savarkar was frail and keeping indifferent health so a comfortable, cushioned chair be provided for him. The court immediately ordered one to be brought in. Savarkar sat on this chair, outside the dock, for the duration of the trail. This also effectively separated him from the other accused. The strategy for Savarkar's defence, employed by Bhopatkar, was to separate him from the other accused and use every ploy to strengthen his argument that Savarkar was not involved in the murder or the conspiracy in any manner and had no connection with the other accused.

After the photo session, the chief prosecutor, Daftary, read out the chargesheet against all the accused. The charges were murder, attempt to murder, conspiracy to murder, assisting in murder, possessing illegal weapons, possessing and transporting explosives, etc. Next, the court asked the accused if adequate arrangements had been made for their defence. The accused were offered government assistance if they required. Godse and six of the accused informed the court that they would arrange for their defence with the help of Bhopatkar. Madanlal and Badge informed the court that they would not be requiring the services of a lawyer. Initially, Kistayya requested the government to arrange for his defence. But after some time, he too informed the court that he would arrange for his defence through Bhopatkar; he would again change his mind later.

Apart from Savarkar and Nathuram, all the others were seen smiling and joking with one another. A pensive Savarkar intently listened to the proceedings. Nathuram did not interact with any of the accused. Senior journalist Dr Krushnalal Shridharani, who was present in court that day, described the two thus: 'Nathuram Godse is the main protagonist in this drama. He is thin and bears a very intense and serious demeanour. He was wearing a dhoti and kurta. He looked fresh and clean, because he had availed of a shave and haircut the previous day. His chin is a reflection of his firm resolve and his nose is as sharp as a hawk's beak. There are dark circles under his small and beady eyes due to the prolonged incarceration. He spoke lucidly and his tone and behaviour did not reflect any regret or remorse. The second actor in this sordid drama was old Savarkar. He is so old and infirm that he had to be brought into court on an armchair. (This description varies from the court diary of another Hindi reporter whose daily record of the court proceedings was later published by Gyanmandal Press Limited of Benaras titled *Gandhi Hatyakand*, Gandhi Murder Conspiracy.) This was very astonishing. This brave patriot had accomplished many valorous deeds; at one time he was revered in every home. Today he stands in the dock amongst the accused, prosecuted by the first government of independent India. People plunge to such depths from dizzying heights in the course of their lives. Savarkar looked astonished.'

A situation developed in court with regards to the languages spoken and understood by the accused. Badge and Karkare informed the court that they could speak and understand only Marathi. Kistayya said that he spoke and understood only Telugu. Bhopatkar translated the court's questions into Marathi, while a Telugu-speaking press reporter translated for Kistayya.

After the reading of the chargesheet, Bhopatkar, counsel for Savarkar, told the court that according to the warrant proceedings of Section 21 of the Penal Code, initially on the basis of primary investigations, the charges should be proven and the matter should be entrusted to a circuit court, and only then would the proceedings begin. The judge informed him that, according to the provisions in Chapter 23 of the Penal Code, the trial was being conducted after the promulgation of a special law. Bhopatkar asked the court to suspend the hearing for two months, to allow the defence time for preparation. Judge Atmacharan denied the request but agreed to suspend hearings till 14 June.

♦

At the second sitting of the court, it functioned only for an hour and a few minutes. It enquired about the facilities provided to the accused and the arrangements for their defence and announced that the daily proceedings would commence from 22 June. Madanlal and Karkare appeared worried and downcast. Nathuram, who had remained stoic and serious on the first day, was relatively cheerful that day. The day's proceedings were initiated by Nathuram. Speaking in English, he complained that they were being treated like 'C'-class prisoners. He alleged that they were not given water for bathing for two to three days despite repeated requests. But he admitted that he was expecting, and was prepared for, much harsher treatment and displayed surprise at the civility shown to them. He demanded that those facilities which were guaranteed to prisoners in the jail manual should be provided to them.

Responding to the request for better facilities by the accused, Pettigara, a member of the prosecution counsel, informed the court that they had no objections to the demands made by the accused. They only requested the court to ensure that the accused were not permitted to meet or confer with anyone outside or with each other and not be allowed to receive outside food to prevent them from being poisoned. They should also not be allowed to shave; if required they were to use the services of the prison barber.

Nathuram enquired the court whether they were under police custody or judicial custody. The court passed an order that henceforth they were to be treated as 'B'-class or special class prisoners and receive all facilities entitled as such. Apte complained that the police had confiscated some money and personal items from them at the time of their arrests and requested that it be handed back to him. The court asked him to submit a written application to the jail superintendent. The court allowed the accused to wear their own clothes, get additional food items prepared in the prison according to their tastes and allowed them to receive letters, order newspapers, books and magazines. Bhopatkar requested the court to allow the defence advocates to freely meet the accused in jail. The court declared that a summary of the statements of 150 witnesses of the prosecution had been given to the defence. Pettigara informed the court that the prosecution would call upon five or six more witnesses; a summary of their statements would be given to the defence at an appropriate time. Pettigara requested the court to write to the presidency magistrate of Bombay, to send a Marathi and a Telugu translator to serve the court. He also requested the court to procure certain witness statements and investigation records from Bombay and Gwalior. It was also decided that the court's proceedings would be conducted and recorded in English. The statements of the witnesses would be written in the language spoken by the witnesses.

Judge Atmacharan asked Bhopatkar to submit a list of the defence lawyers. Bhopatkar asked for a week's time but Atmacharan responded that under the provisions of the law he would not provide any extension. However, he added that he would consider the plea to begin the court's proceedings from 21 June instead of 14 June. Pettigara informed the court that since Governor-General Mountbatten was leaving India on 21 June 1948, the police were likely to be busy with his security arrangements. The date for the hearing was then scheduled for 22 June 1948.

On the first day of the trial, Madanlal had refused the services of a lawyer, but he now requested Bhopatkar to fight his case. Kistayya, too, asked the court to appoint a competent lawyer to defend him.

♦

The final hearing for the preliminary proceedings took place on 14 June 1948 and lasted barely thirty minutes. Bhopatkar submitted the final list of defence lawyers and assured the court that all of them would be present on 22 June. He added that Barrister Oak would appear for Nathuram and Maniyar would defend Gopal Godse. Copies of the brief summary of the prosecution's witnesses' statements were handed over to the accused. Kistayya and Karkare, who did not understand English, were provided with translations.

♦

Special Court

The court was presided over by Judge H. Atmacharan, ICS, assisted by the following lawyers and officials:

Chandra Kishan Daftary, advocate general, Bombay Province, was chief prosecutor. He was assisted by, N.K. Pettigara, Bombay; N.G. Vyavharkar, Bombay; Raibahadur Jwalaprasad, Punjab; Pandit Thakurdas, Delhi and other court staff.

Jamshed Dorabjee 'Jimmy' Nagarvala, deputy commissioner of police, Bombay, was the special investigating officer.

♦

Defence Lawyers

The list of defence lawyers comprised principal defence counsel and counsel: for Savarkar, L.B. Bhopatkar, Poona; for Nathuram Godse, Barrister V.V. Oak, Bombay (later, under the section 'Recording of Evidence', it is stated that Nathuram argued his own case); for Narayan Apte, K.H. Mengle and G.K. Dua, Bombay; for Vishnu Karkare, Advocate Narhar Daji Dange and G.K. Dua, Bombay; Badge turned approver and was granted a judicial pardon; for Madanlal Pahwa and Puranchandra Bannerjee; for Shankar Kistayya, Hansraj R. Mehta, from the North-

The urns containing Gandhi's ashes.

U.P. Chief Minister G.B. Pant, Prime Minister Nehru, U.P. Governor Sarojini Naidu, Maulana Abul Kalam Azad and Sardar Patel along with dignitaries, await the arrival of the special train carrying Gandhi's ashes.

The urn in a special train on its way to Allahabad.

Prime Minister Nehru, Devadas Gandhi and Ramdas Gandhi, with urn in hand, heading to Triveni Sangam for the immersion.

Boats ferrying VIPs and media persons at the Triveni Sangam while millions throng the banks.

The stone ventilation grill in the wall behind where Gandhi sat during the evening prayers. On 20 January 1948, Badge was supposed to hide in the servant's room behind the grill and shoot at Gandhi from there, and then push a grenade through the grill at him.

The Beretta 9 mm semi-automatic used to murder Gandhi.

Bhillare Guruji, the man who saved Gandhi when Nathuram Godse attacked him at Panchgani.

Justice G.D. Khosla, member of the three-judge bench which heard the appeal in the Punjab High Court.

Justice A.N. Bhandari, the senior-most judge of the three-judge bench which heard the appeal in the Gandhi murder trial in the Punjab High Court.

Justice Achchruram, who jointly heard the high court appeal.

Chief prosecutor in the Gandhi murder trial, C.K. Daftary.

The lawyers and judge at the Red Fort trial.
First Row (sitting) from L. to R. Raibahadur Jwalaprasad (prosecution), C.K. Daftary (chief prosecutor), Judge H. Atmacharan, ICS (special judge), P.R. Das (defence), L.B. Bhopatkar (chief defence team).
Second Row (standing) from L. to R. K.H. Mengle (defence), Ganpat Rai (defence), N.D. Dange (defence), J.C. Shah (prosecution), Hansraj Mehta (defence), B. Bannerjee (defence), V.V. Oak (defence).
Third Row (standing) from L. to R. K.L. Bhopatkar (defence), P.L. Inamdar (defence), N.G. Vyavharkar (prosecution).

Police portrait of Nathuram Vinayak Godse, the murderer.

The Intelligence Bureau index card of Vishnu Ramkrishna Karkare.

A police portrait of Narayan D. Apte.

Conspirators and killers. (Sitting) from L. to R. Narayan Apte, V.D. Savarkar, Nathuram Godse and Vishnu R. Karkare. (Standing) from L. to R. Shankar Kistayya, Gopal Godse, Madanlal Kashmirilal Pahwa and Badge. The one missing member of the gang is Dr Sadashiv Parchure.

The accused in the dock. Front Row from L. to R. Nathuram V. Godse, Narayan Apte and Vishnu Karkare. Middle Row from L. to R. Ramchandra Badge, Madanlal K. Pahwa and Gopal Godse. Back Row from L. to R. Shankar Kistayya, V.D. Savarkar and a partially seen Dr Parchure.

1666-A

Madan Lal s/o Pishori Lal Ali Paluwa of Pakpattan Dist Montgomery West Punjab aged 20/21.

Refugee went to Bombay in middle of November

Contacted Mahasabha workers for employment

Met Karkare who appeared to be active worker or president of the sabha. Karkare also proprietor of a hotel — Deccan Guest House. Karkare having come to know that the accused was a member of RSS revealed a plan by them to kill Mahatma Gandhi who is enemy of hindus.

Came to Delhi with Karkare reaching here about 17.1.48

Stayed at Hindu Sharif Hotel Room No 2. Servant Ram Singh took his and Karkare's clothes for washing to a laundry. The accused gave Rs 15/- for sewing charges of pant and for washing charges.

Left the hotel on 19.1.48 in the evening. Karkare met Sham Deshpande in the Hindu Mahasabha Bhawan and got Room No 3 where they placed their luggage.

Translation of Madanlal's confession prepared by the Delhi Police.

were going to Paharganj with
5 Destitute to see some refugees to
make them create noise in prayer. &
One Bala was brought to the Sabha
by police.

3 marhattas came to the
Sabha. Karkare talked to them in
marhatti. They stayed with us.

On 20.1.48 Karkare left at
6.
                 with muffler
One man came to see
the 3 marhattas and took them
away at 12 noon.

Karkare took the accused
to Marina Hotel Room No. 40
where the man with Muffler
3 marhatti and one other man
who was called maharaj.

Then talked out.
                          the
Went in tanga for th Karkare
at about 1.45 from Marina Hotel
others proceeded in a Car.

4 Bomb burst & a Grenade
1st   one pistol   "   Karkare
2nd   "   man with
3rd   one pistol   muffler
Maharaja 2 grenades had to Signal   editor
{Car No. Bogus?}   of Hindu
  Chalis?   Rashtra
                                      or
                                    Agni A!

Copy of the translation of Madanlal's statement prepared by the Delhi Police.

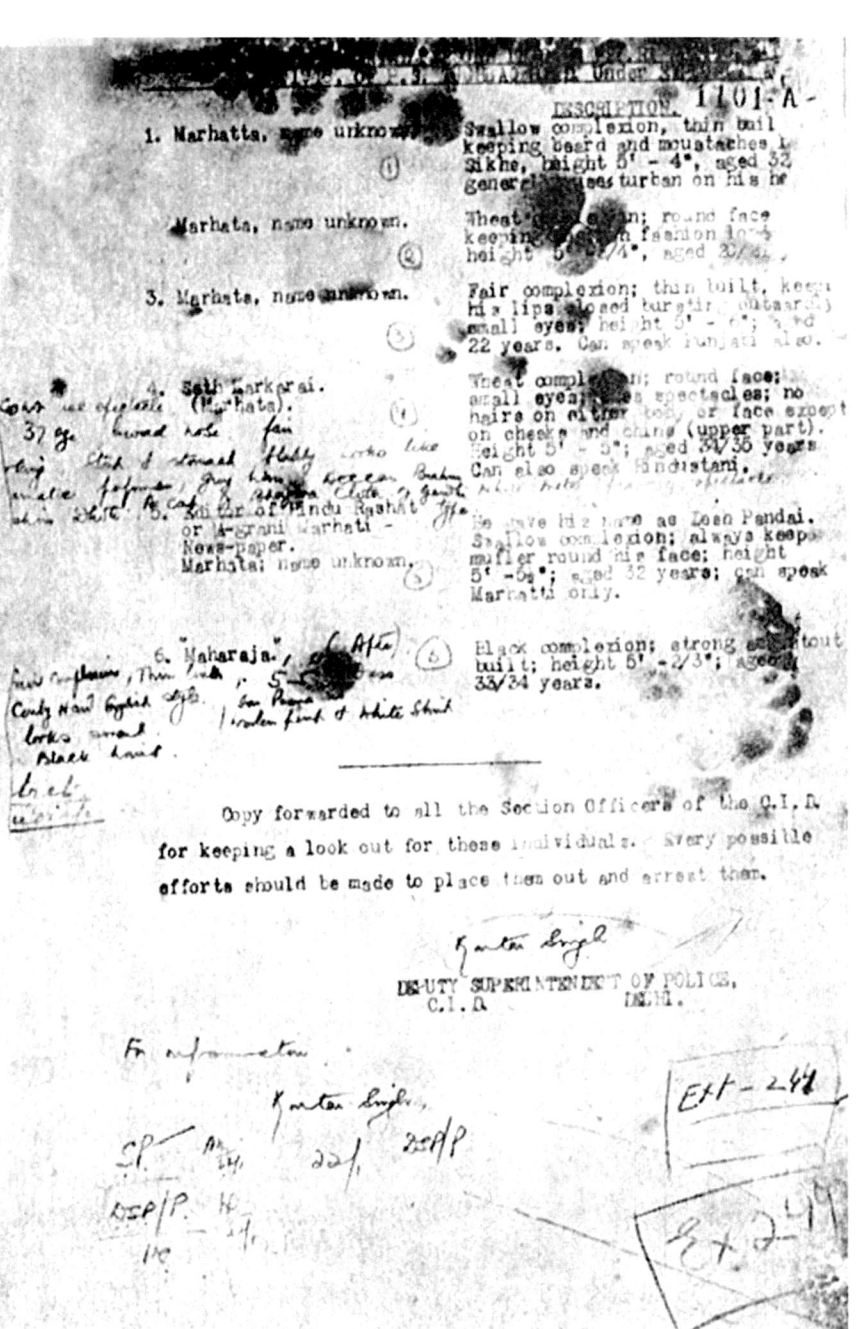

Ex. 24 Kapur Commission. A police translation of Madanlal's statement.

Precautionary measures to prevent assassination of Mahatma Gandhi.

notice question No. 864 put A.J. Doddameti.

Will the Hon'ble Minister for Home and Revenue be pleased to state –

(1) whether it is a fact that the plot for the assassination of Mahatma Gandhi and plans for the assassination of other high-ranking India leaders were hatched in the Bombay Province;

(2) whether reports regarding the existence of such a plot had reached Government, prior to the assassination of Mahatma Gandhi;

(3) if so, what precautionary measures were taken by Government to prevent the tragedy that followed;

(4) what is the number (district-wise) of the members of the R.S.S. so far arrested in the Province in connection with the assassination of Mahatma Gandhi?

Proposed reply.

(1) As the investigation into the alleged conspiracy ~~to assassinate Mahatma Gandhi and other Indian leaders~~ is still not complete, it is too early to give any information on the question asked in this clause.

(2) ~~No.~~ A report reached Govt on 21st Jan re. such a plot.

(3) ~~Does not arise.~~ [handwritten notes]

(4) Some persons have been arrested in connection with the assassination of Mahatma Gandhi. It is not possible to say at this stage how many of them are members of the R.S.S. Sangh.

[See para. 4.8]

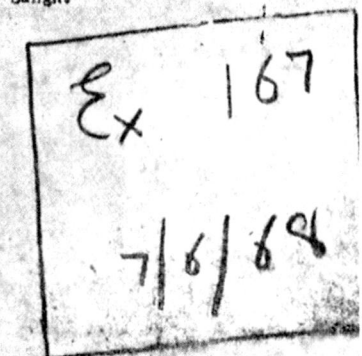

Copy of the answer filed in the Bombay Provincial Council during the debate on Gandhi's murder (Ex. 167, Kapur Commission).

From L. to R. Sindhutai Godse, Gopal Godse, G.V. Ketkar, Vishnu Karkare and Smt S. Karkare at the Satya Vinayak Puja.

(1) Gopal V. Godse,
(2) G.V. Ketkar,
(3) V.R. Thakur,
(4) V.R. Karkare,
(5) Smt S. Karkare,
(6) Smt D.H. Thatte at the Satya Vinayak Puja.

G.V. Ketkar addressing the meeting to felicitate Gopal Godse (L) and Vishnu R. Karkare (R).

West Frontier Province (appointed by the government); for Gopal Godse, Mohanlal B. Maniyar, Bombay; for V.D. Savarkar, L.B. Bhopatkar from Poona; Barrister Jamnadas Mehta, Bombay; Ganpat Rai, Delhi; Kunjbihari L. Bhopatkar, Poona, *(Gandhi Murder Trial* adds three more names to Savarkar's defence team: B. Bannerjee, J.P. Mitter and N.P. Aiyar. Later on, *Gandhi Murder Trial,* under 'Recording of Evidence', claims that P.R. Das of Patna argued on behalf of Savarkar.); for Parchure, P.L. Inamdar, Gwalior.

◆

Recording Evidence

Recording of the prosecution's evidence began on 24 June 1948 and continued till 6 November. One hundred and forty-nine witnesses were examined, 720 pages of their testimony were recorded. The prosecution brought on record 404 documentary and 80 material exhibits. Recording the statements of the accused began on 8 November and continued till 22 November, comprising 106 pages. All the accused except Shankar Kistayya filed written statements, amounting to 297 pages. The defence brought on record 119 documentary exhibits. The hearing of defences' arguments began on 1 December and continued till 30 December 1948.

◆

Trial Begins: Badge Declared Approver

Four months and three weeks after Gandhi's murder, the daily hearings in the Gandhi murder trial began. The proceedings began with the presiding judge asking all the accused if they had appointed or were provided with defence counsels. He then went on to read the six-page chargesheet. The Marathi version was read out by M.A. Navalkar, a translator working for the Bombay presidency magistrate's court, while the Telugu translation was read out by Ms M. Kamalamma of Bellary. A Punjabi and Hindustani translator, M.R. Handa, was also appointed. Every question and its reply was interpreted in English, Gujarati, Hindustani, Marathi, Punjabi and Telugu. This process prolonged the duration of the proceedings.

After reading the chargesheet, Atmacharan declared that Badge was now a 'witness for the prosecution' and announced that Badge had been granted a conditional pardon. He ordered that Badge be immediately removed from among the accused and placed in protective custody. A lot of hostility was directed towards Badge and the strategy of the defence lawyers also underwent a change. Although it was suspected that one of the accused had turned approver and was providing the police with all the information on which they had built the prosecution's case against the accused, there was only speculation about the identity of the 'rat'. Gopal Godse, Parchure and Madanlal Pahwa were suspected to be the most likely 'turncoats' by the defence. Because of his voluntary confession, Parchure was shunned by the defence lawyers; his statement was thought to pose the greatest danger to Savarkar. Lawyers of the defence committee had refused to defend Parchure. As soon as Badge was declared the approver, the defence team concentrated all their efforts on discrediting his testimony and proving that he was a habitual and incorrigible liar, thus his testimony could not be relied upon.

Atmacharan asked the accused if they had understood the charges filed against them and if so, would they plead guilty as charged or did they wish for the court to conduct a trial to prove their guilt or establish their innocence. All the eight accused claimed they were innocent. Nathuram Godse told the court, 'Try me.' Initially, Kistayya pleaded guilty, but after the charges were explained to him in Telugu, he said he would confess all that he knew and requested the court to conduct a trial to establish his innocence. Savarkar pleaded 'innocent', so did Apte, Gopal Godse and Parchure. Madanlal submitted a written statement to the court, which said: 'I consider myself innocent. There was no conspiracy to cause any harm to Mahatma Gandhi. I was never a part of any such conspiracy. The incident of 20 January was only to display the anger sweeping the nation due to the policy of Muslim appeasement practised by Mahatma Gandhi in those days. There was nothing more than this in it. No one else was involved in that incident apart from me.'

◆

Charges Framed

The detailed chargesheet is reproduced in Appendix 1. All the accused pleaded 'not guilty' and 'declared they wanted to be tried'; Parchure further pleaded that he was a subject of Gwalior State, thus not amenable to the jurisdiction of the court.

♦

Recording Testimonies of Prosecution's Witnesses

24 June 1948: Before the proceedings began for the day, Atmacharan, Daftary and Bhopatkar, along with Apte, Karkare, Madanlal and Gopal Godse, visited Birla House. Atmacharan minutely inspected the entire prayer ground and the room where Gandhi spent the last five months of his life. At 2:00 p.m., the court began examining and recording the statements of the prosecution's witnesses. With the consent of the prosecution and defence, it was agreed that Atmacharan would himself record the statements of the witnesses in English.

The first witness to be examined was a thirty-year-old Hindu Brahmin head constable from Gwalior State, Ishwardutt Mulchand.

After the tea break, Madanlal's lawyer Bannerjee submitted a request to the court that the prosecution should first prove the conspiracy charge and then the murder charge against his client. In an attempt to waste the court's time, he asked that the prosecution deal with the events in a chronological order and present witnesses right from 1944. The court rejected his arguments.

The next witness was Ramlal Dutt, the general manager of Sharif Hindu Hotel situated at Fatehpuri in Delhi. He told the court that three people had stayed in Room No. 2 of the hotel from 17 to late afternoon of 19 January 1948. Ramlal identified Madanlal and Karkare seated in the dock. The prosecution brought Shantaram Atmaram Amchekar into the courtroom; Ramlal identified him as the third person. Ramlal pointed to Gopal Godse, identifying him as the person who had visited the other three.

25 June 1948: Addressing Parchure's counsel Inamdar's application to the court, Atmacharan replied, 'You have requested that the charge of conspiracy be explained in greater detail. I feel that the charges have been framed with utmost clarity… I will not give any more clarifications…'

The court then called Shantiprakash, Ramlal's partner, who also identified Karkare, and Gopal Godse as the visitor.

Before the court adjourned for tea that day, the electricity failed twelve times in half an hour.

The proceedings continued with the questioning of Ramsinh, son of Mansinh. Ramsinh was a bearer and Khansama at the Sharif hotel. He identified Karkare and Madanlal. The next witness was thirty-year-old Amchekar. Amchekar was a resident of Hirloke in Sawantwadi in Bombay Province. He was a refugee from Karachi, where he was posted as a government employee. He described to the court his travel to Delhi by the Peshawar Express on 15 January, his meeting with Karkare and Madanlal, Karkare offering him hospitality in Delhi, and all the incidents in detail till he parted with Karkare and Madanlal, late in the afternoon of 19 January. He then returned to Bombay, having finished his work with the Government Transfers Bureau.

Before the court adjourned for the day, Nathuram requested that Badge and Kistayya should not be allowed to interact either with each other or with the other accused. His plea was accepted.

28 June 1948: The recording of Amchekar's statement continued.

Nathuram claimed that the identification of the accused in court was not correct. Their photographs had appeared in newspapers and films of the trial were being shown in many places. Under these circumstances, identifying the accused in court had become easy. The court overruled his objection.

After a short break, Madanlal's counsel informed the court that his client was unwell. The court allowed him to rest for a while in the adjoining room and a doctor was summoned. The next witness was Hiranandani, who worked as a clerk in the Transfer Bureau under the home department. He informed the court that Application No. 5286 was filed by a person named Shantaram Amchekar, and he had accepted and filed the application. Ramchandra and Narayan Singh, who both worked in Marina Hotel in Delhi were called next; both identified Nathuram and Apte, who had checked in as S. Deshpande and M. Deshpande. Madanlal was brought back to court. The prosecution then produced some clothes as exhibits, which were recovered by the police from Marina Hotel, a few of them bore the laundry mark 'N.V.G.'.

29 June 1948: The first witness to be examined was Mehar Singh, a sepoy in the forest department. He said that on the day when a bomb exploded in Gandhi's prayer meeting, he was patrolling in his sector with his colleagues Pyarelal and Kaptan at about 11:00 a.m. At this point, Daftary called for Badge; this was the first time he was being brought into court after he being declared an approver. Mehar Singh identified Shankar Kistayya, Gopal V. Godse, Narayan D. Apte and Digambar R. Badge as those he had seen on 20 January.

Search for a Bible

Next on the witness stand was C. Pacheko, manager of Marina Hotel. Daftary asked for a Bible so Pacheko could take oath. It was discovered that there was no Bible available in the courtroom. Nathuram said that he had seen a copy in the prison and a police officer was despatched to fetch it, holding up the court's proceedings for some time. In the meanwhile, two bearers, Govindram and Kelaram, working in Marina Hotel, testified. After a tea break, Pacheko was called back to the stand. He took oath on the Bible and recounted the events of the evening of 20 January. Pointing to Madanlal, Pacheko identified him as the man who was brought handcuffed to the hotel, he identified Nathuram and Apte, too.

30 June 1948: Surjeet Singh, a taxi driver from Delhi, was the first to be examined that day, and his testimony lasted for four hours. Atmacharan inspected the car in which the accused had travelled to Birla House on the 20th. The unique feature of the blue-green Ford was that it was the only car in Delhi at that time which was fitted with a luggage carrier. Pointing to Apte, Surjeet Singh said, 'He finalized everything with me. They agreed to pay me ₹12 for the round trip. Three people sat behind and the dadhivala, bearded man, sat in front with me.' He also identified Gopal Godse, Apte and Kistayya as the ones who had occupied the back seat. He said that on the return trip, another man had joined the group, pointing to Nathuram. He added, 'I remember the day Gandhiji was murdered. Three to four days after the murder I drove in my taxi to the Tughlaq Road Police Station, to finish some pending work I had with the police. Two Sikh officers called me and inquired if I had driven anyone to the Birla House on the 20th. I gave a statement to the police on that day. Four to five days later I was taken to the Delhi District Jail where I identified Nathuram and some days later I identified Apte. I was then taken to Bombay where I identified Gopal Godse and Badge.'

After a break, the judge informed the court that he had received a request from a Shivnarayan who wished to appear as defence counsel for Parchure.

1 July 1948: The proceedings began by recording Sulochana Devi's statement. She said that she clearly remembered where and when the bomb explosion took place at Birla House. At the time of the explosion, she was standing barely 14 feet away from the spot where the bomb exploded. The shockwave from the explosion had almost knocked her over, but fortunately, she had escaped injury. She had pointed to the man she had seen placing the explosive on the wall and lighting the fuse. The police had immediately caught him. Sulochana pointed to Madanlal and said 'It was him!' She also identified Badge, Apte and Gopal Godse as the people who had come in the car that day to Birla House. She informed the court that after the explosion she had seen four people rushing out of Birla House and get into the car and being driven away. She pointed to Nathuram and told the court that he was a part of the gang too. Daftary then took Sulochana outside the court and asked her to identify the car, which she did.

The next witness examined was Choturam, the car cleaner. He told the court, 'When the blast occurred, I was sitting (at) a little distance outside my quarter. One room separates Phulsinh's quarter from mine. There is an open ground behind Birla House, which is adjacent to the rear gate. I had seen the dark green car driving up and stopping at the roundabout. It was parked by the left side of the roundabout, there was a luggage carrier on its roof. When the car stopped, I saw four people getting out of it and enter the compound. Here they were met by three or four other men, after talking for some time they entered the prayer ground in groups of two and three. One of them inspected my quarters, twice or thrice. After this, three of the men went into the prayer ground and one man came and started talking to me. He said he wanted to take Gandhi's photograph through the ventilator grill. I told him to do so from the front. He wasn't carrying a camera on him. Finally, I asked him *'Camera kahan hai?'* (Where is your camera?) He was carrying a black cloth bag filled with something quite heavy. But there was no camera in it. The man ran towards the car as if he was going to fetch his camera. Then he came back and entered the prayer ground. I had seen a man placing something on the wall and then igniting it. There was a loud bang. I grabbed the hand of the man who exploded the bomb. Afterwards the man was sent to the police picket outside the Birla House. I had gone there myself. An officer frisked him and found a bomb (grenade) in his coat pocket. Some soldiers unscrewed the bomb and defused it. The bomb was placed in a tin and the tin was wrapped in a cloth. They sealed the packet with the Birla House seal.' He then stepped down from the witness stand and identified Madanlal, Karkare, Apte and Nathuram. He said that he had remained on the spot of the murder for twenty to thirty minutes after the tragedy, on the 30th. 'I found some of the spent bullets, two empty shells and a cloth that was draped around the shoulders. These things were scattered around the place where Mahatma Gandhi fell.' The exhibits were brought to the court and Choturam identified them.

2 July 1948: Choturam's cross-examination continued. He said that he used to attend Gandhi's prayer meetings regularly, but on 20 January, he could not. Pointing to Karkare, he said, 'He tried to bribe me with five or ten rupees to allow his friend to take a picture of Gandhi from my room, this made me suspicious about his intentions.'

The next witness was Bhursinh, a chowkidar, watchman, at Birla House, who narrated to the court all that he had witnessed on 20 January.

5 July 1948: The court resumed hearing Bhursinh's cross examination. Next on the witness stand was K.M. Sahni, a magistrate from Karnal and a refugee officer. The witness informed the court that he was present at the prayer grounds on 20 January at exactly 5:00 p.m. His wife had died in a car accident on 10 January, and he was grieving her loss. 'Gandhiji had requested me to meet him before I proceeded back to Karnal to join duty.' He said that he was seated exactly in front of Gandhi, hardly about four or five steps away. 'At a quarter past five, there was a terrible explosion while Gandhiji was delivering his post-prayer speech. Gandhiji would have long begun his prayers, but that day the loudspeakers had failed, delaying everything.'

Sahni went on to say that on the 20th, he had filed the report in his private capacity. 'I was with Gandhiji till almost 6:30 p.m. Gandhiji continued speaking even after the bomb exploded; there was a little disturbance, but Gandhiji calmed the people. No one was injured in the explosion.'

6 July 1948: The court recorded the statement of the manager of the Frontier Hindu Hotel, Ramprakash.

7 July 1948: The court cross-examined S.C. Rai from Agra, an explosive substances expert working in the Government of India's explosives factory. He described the unexploded hand grenades as extremely lethal explosives. They were British-issued anti-personnel grenades. The other packet contained an unexploded gun cotton slab, which he described as extremely lethal when used with shrapnel.

The next two witnesses were police photographer Kunvar Singh and the administrator of the telephone revenue department of New Delhi, P.R. Kailash. The latter informed the court that his office kept records of all the trunk calls made from Delhi. A note, which showed that on 19 January a trunk call had been made from the Delhi telephone number 8024 to Bombay number 60201 at 9:20 a.m., was presented in court. It was a person to person 'urgent' call for Damle or Kasiya (It should have been Kasar, Appa Kasar, a handyman and Savarkar's bodyguard). The Delhi number was registered in the name of the honorary office secretary of the Hindu Mahasabha on Reading Road. Since neither of the two persons requested for were available, the call was cancelled and a charge levied of two rupees and seventy-five paise. L.B. Bhopatkar, for the first time in the trial, rose to cross-examine the witness. The witness informed the court that the chit produced as evidence in court was prepared by the operator on duty at the Bombay exchange at the time the call was cancelled.

Bhopatkar examined the chit and then, handing it over to the judge, he said, 'Kindly look at the bottom of the chit, something has been cancelled out and overwritten.' The court examined the chit and found that 'Dalal' had been cancelled out and 'Demello' overwritten, the second name written appeared to be 'Kasiya'. The call had been booked for Damle and Kasar and the two wrong names were a result of misunderstanding. But the defence was able to create sufficient doubt to discredit the evidence.

Next on the witness stand was the ticket clerk working at the Old Delhi station, Lala Badrinath, He told the court that during his duty hours from 4:00 p.m. to midnight on 20 January 1948, he had sold only three first-class tickets to Kanpur: ticket nos. 614A, 614B and 615. He identified Nathuram in court.

8 July 1948: The first witness was the booking clerk of the Delhi junction station, Sunderlal, who identified Nathuram and Apte and said that the two had occupied the retiring room on 29 January 1948. He also identified Karkare as the one who had joined the other two. Jannu Mochi, the shoe-shine boy, confirmed that three men had occupied Room 6 of the Delhi junction station's retiring rooms. He pointed to Nathuram, Apte and Karkare.

9 July 1948: Eight witnesses were examined that day. Madanlal's counsel made a plea that the court should accept the book *Delhi Diaries* and give it legal validity as a standard reference for establishing the movements, discourses and writings of Gandhi during his last stay in Delhi. All the witnesses that day narrated eyewitness accounts of the bomb attack on the 20th and Gandhi's murder on the 30th. The first on the stand was Sgt Ramchandra of the RIAF. He was a regular at Gandhi's prayer meetings. He identified Madanlal as the man he had caught on 20 January after the bomb explosion.

Next was sub-inspector Amarnath of the Tughlaq Road police station, who was in charge of the security at Birla House during the prayer meetings. He said that on the day Gandhi was murdered, he was standing behind him. 'I heard one bullet being fired and I saw smoke emanating. I leapt at the murderer immediately and caught hold of him by his neck and shoulders. But by the time I caught him, he had already fired two more bullets. Sgt Devraj grabbed the murderer's wrist and disarmed him. We found that the pistol had four more bullets.' He then identified Nathuram Vinayak Godse as the man who had shot and murdered Gandhi.

Nandlal Mehta, a member of Gandhi's entourage, was questioned next. He said that after Gandhi had been shot and fell, he supported him and placed his head in Abhabehn's lap. 'Gandhiji breathed his last within a couple of minutes. While bathing his body, I discovered that there were three gunshot wounds on his upper torso. I signed the FIR prepared by the police.' Head Constable Kabul Singh, Constable Ratan Singh, and Assistant Sub-inspector Dhaluram from the Tughlaq Road police station, were called in next. The next two witnesses were Assistant Sub-inspector Parshuram and Head Constable Dharam Singh. Singh was on duty at Birla House on the 30th; he identified Nathuram as the man who had shot Gandhi.

12 July 1948: The first issue taken up by the court was Madanlal's lawyer's application about the *Delhi Diaries*. The prosecutor objected. The court ruled that such an application should be made when the relevant defence witnesses were being examined.

The first witness to be examined was the superintendent and civil surgeon of Irwin Hospital, Lt Col Dr P.N. Taneja. He had examined Gandhi's body at 8:30 a.m. on 31 January at Birla House. He informed the court: 'Gandhiji died due to shock suffered from internal haemorrhaging caused by gunshot wounds due to bullets fired from a pistol, from close range.' He added, 'Gandhiji's body had been examined by Dr Jivraj Mehta before me. I saw five wounds on his body, three entry wounds on his chest and two exit wounds on his back. There was a deep wound on the right side of his chest that had caused a depression oval in shape. There were two wounds on the left side. The entry wounds were 1/4" × 1/6" and on his back the corresponding exit wounds were 1/3" × 1/4" in dimension. The two wounds on his back had been caused when two of the bullets pierced his body, and came out of his back.' As per instructions given by Nathuram, the defence did not cross-examine the witness.

Witnesses from Gwalior

Jagdish Prasad Goel stated that he had known Parchure since 1941 and identified him. He said that Parchure was the supremo of the Hindu Rashtra Sena, a band of fanatic Hindu youth. He pointed towards Apte and Nathuram and said they were present at Parchure's home on 28 January.

Kulwant Kaur, a Sikh lady operator of the Delhi Telephone Exchange, was called to the stand. She was on duty at the switchboard at the time the call was attempted on 19 January. She informed the court that the persons who had been called were not available. At that time, a new operator was on duty in the enquiry section, Miss G. Phurness, who, by mistake, wrote 'cancelled' on the ticket. On being cross-examined by Bhopatkar, Kaur said that she did not know the name of the operator on duty in Bombay at that time. The last to take the witness stand was the twenty-six-year-old Anglo-Indian telephone operator G. Phurness. 'On realizing my mistake, I scratched out the word and signed under it. Also by mistake I wrote "12" and then tried to erase it. I don't remember who had scratched out the word "cancelled"'. The testimonies of the witnesses from the telephone department were handled very inefficiently by the prosecution, allowing Savarkar's defence to raise doubts about their veracity in the court's mind.

13 July 1948: The first witness was the fifty-year-old tonga driver from Gwalior, Gariba, who looked very intimidated by his surroundings; he said, 'Two to three days before Gandhiji's murder, I had ferried two people who wanted to go to Parchure's house from Gwalior station in my tonga at 11:30 p.m. The reins of my horse snapped on the way, so I sent them on in another tonga.' He identified both Nathuram and Apte. Five or six days after Gandhi's murder, Gariba picked up Sub-inspector Mandlik at the Gwalior station. 'Mandlik told me, that the allegation that the two people who had stayed at Parchure's home were involved in the conspiracy to murder Mahatma Gandhi, was a mere rumour. I told Mandlik that I had taken the two people in question halfway to Parchure's home.' The other tonga driver also identified Nathuram Godse and Narayan Apte.

The next to take the witness stand were three employees working at the Kanpur railway station, inspection clerks Shivpyarelal Dikshit and A.B. Saxena, and Angelina Colestone, who was in charge of cleaning the railway retiring room. All three had seen Nathuram and Apte at the Kanpur station on 21 January 1948.

14 July 1948: The next witness to take the stand was Manzar Ali who said, 'I remember that I had gone to the home of the accused Parchure on 27 February 1948. Police Superintendent Khijr Muhammad and CID Inspector Mandlik accompanied me. We first went to the Park Hotel near the railway station. A police officer brought Apte down. Apte told us that he could show us the wall in Dr Parchure's home at which shots had been fired to test their revolver. There were policemen from Bombay and Gwalior who accompanied me to Dr Parchure's home. We went from the Park Hotel to Dr Parchure's home in a special car. The car had dark tinted window glasses which were rolled up.'

The second witness that day was twenty-two-year-old Madhukar Keshav Kale, a clerk working for the Gwalior State administration. He said, 'I have been associated with the Hindu Rashtra Sena since 1940–1. I have known Parchure for the past five to seven years. On 28 January, I went to Parchure's home at around 12:30 in the afternoon. When I entered, I found him sitting with three other persons. One of them was Dandavate. I later found out that the other two were Nathuram Godse and Narayan Apte.'

Kale continued, 'At around six in the evening of 30 January, I met Parchure in front of the Maratha Boarding House. I had heard the news of Mahatma Gandhi's murder on the radio news bulletin. I told Parchure about Gandhiji's death. Parchure asked me if Gandhiji had died naturally or had been murdered.' He said that he learnt the following day that it was Nathuram who had killed Gandhi. 'On the 1st, I narrated the entire incident of the 28th to my mother and also my friends, Patwardhan and Pawar. The former pressurized me to give all the information to the Gwalior government. Patwardhan took me in his car to meet Home Minister Ghule.' Kale identified Parchure.

15 July 1948: Ramdayal Singh, a thirty-seven-year-old zamindar, landlord, and president of the Rajput Seva Sangh, was called to testify. He said that he learnt of the murder on the 30th itself and decided to organize a condolence meeting at the boarding house. 'Parchure came up to me and said, "At last a good deed has been done. An enemy of Hindu dharma has been killed. The man who murdered Gandhiji is our own man. The man who exploded a bomb a few days back was also our man. It is true, the gun used to murder Gandhiji was sent from Gwalior. The man who murdered Gandhiji, came from South India to Gwalior and then went on to Delhi." I did not react to the inflammatory talk, but my friend Jagunnath Singh shouted at Parchure, "Shut up and get lost from here!"'

Next to take the stand was Jagunnath Singh, a forest contractor operating from Gwalior. He corroborated Ramdayal Singh's statement.

16 July 1948: The court sat for only fifty minutes.

19 July 1948: The prosecution called on Magistrate First Class R.B. Atal of Gwalior. He said, 'On 17 February, Superintendent Thorat Patil brought me a letter. I was told that the letter was written by Inspector Balakrishnan of the CID. The letter requested that I record the statement of Dr D.S. Parchure, who was being held by the military at Gwalior Fort. I received the order on the evening of 17 January. I went to the Fort accompanied by Thorat Patil, Khijr Muhammad and a couple of other police officers. We were accompanied by the Fort Commandant Major Chatrey, when we went to the cell the accused was held in. I asked Parchure if he wanted to make a confessional statement. Parchure nodded his head and said, "Yes."' Atal then described the meeting in detail. He added, 'I carried Parchure's confession with me when I returned home. Two or three days later, I placed the confession statement in an envelope and sealed and stamped it with my personal seal. I then deposited the envelope in the Imperial Bank of India. On 6 April 1948, I handed it over to the secretary for external and political affairs of Gwalior state.' Atal identified Parchure.

Parchure's Confessional Statement

Then, Atal read out the confessional statement of Dr Dattatreya Sadashiv Parchure of Gwalior, accused number 9. Parchure in his statement had stated, 'For making this confessional statement, the police has not threatened me nor have they promised me any reward. I am making this statement of confession absolutely voluntarily, of my own free will.

'I have known Nathuram Vinayak Godse personally since 1941, but I had heard about Godse in 1939 itself. Godse accompanied by Apte came to my home at about 11 o'clock on the night of 27 January 1948. Godse told me that he had come on a very important mission. "I am going to perform a terrible deed before 2 February. I am going to murder Mahatma Gandhi."

'Godse possessed a revolver, but he could not use it and so he wished to procure a more modern and reliable handgun. I told him that under no circumstances would I give him my licensed pistol, but I promised to get him another. Next morning, I sent my son Neelkanth and servant Rupa to fetch Dandavate. When I returned home in the afternoon of 28 January, I saw that Godse, Apte and Dandavate were trying out a country-made revolver. They went into the courtyard to test it. I did not accompany them.

'Late in the evening, Dandavate came back to my home. He had an automatic pistol and approximately eleven or twelve bullets with him. I do not know where he got the pistol. He told us that the price of the pistol was ₹500. Apte gave Dandavate ₹300 and promised to pay the balance later. That night all three of them left in a tonga.

'On 29 January I told my brother that I had helped Godse and Apte procure a pistol with which they planned to murder Gandhiji. On hearing this, my brother was shocked. He asked me why I had involved myself in such a deed. On the evening of 30 January 1948, when I heard the news about the murder of Mahatma Gandhi, I ordered sweetmeats for Re. 1 and distributed them amongst my family members and friends. I also celebrated the murder of Mahatma Gandhi by distributing sweets to members of the Hindu Rashtra Sena.

'I don't know if Godse and Apte kept the revolver that they had brought to Gwalior with themselves or gave it to Dandavate in exchange for the automatic pistol. I also owned a STEN gun. I had left it with a friend of mine in Murar.' (Signed Dr Dattatreya Sadashiv Parchure)

Testimony of Badge, the Approver

On 20 July, the prosecution called upon the approver Digambar Ramchandra Badge to the witness stand. Badge was initially an accused but he later became, as he was referred to, 'Maafi Cha Sakshidar', an 'approver', and was granted a conditional pardon.

21 July 1948: Badge read out his entire confession and then identified all the accused.

In his testimony, Badge further informed the court that on being arrested on 31 January 1948, he had shown the police the homes of Harbans Singh, Deshmukh and member of Legislative Assembly, Kharat.

Badge Cross-Examined

Replying to a question from Bhopatkar, Badge said, 'We only received funds for our Delhi Yatra from one place in Kurla, which was from Kale. From another source we got ₹400, but that was due to my personal relations and to cover my individual expenses. The last convention of the

Hindu Mahasabha was held at Gorakhpur in December 1946. Savarkar did not attend the convention as in the past three or four years his health had deteriorated and he did not actively participate in the functioning of the Hindu Mahasabha.' He added, 'It was not true that Savarkar had not stepped out of his house since the past three years as he used to attend small private meetings and social meetings at his home or close by. He is a well-known writer and poet of Marathi literature. I don't only consider him a leader of the Hindus. To me he is God.'

22 July 1948: Badge continued, 'I was arrested on 31 January, a day after Gandhiji's murder. During the interim nine days after 20 January, I met no one. I bumped into G.V. Ketkar one afternoon. I was terrified of being arrested as I knew that Madanlal had been arrested. I realized that if I went to Kharat's home, he would inform the police and hand over both the packets of explosives I had kept with him, and the police would implicate me.

'On 31 January, a very angry and violent mob attacked my house and shop. They torched my shop. All my goods and account books were destroyed in the fire. An angry mob attacked the homes and offices of Hindu Mahasabha leaders and those who were believed to have been involved in Gandhi's murder.'

23 July 1948: Atmacharan informed the court that he had received an anonymous letter threatening to kill him. Daftary and B. Bannerjee said that they had received death threats too. The judge ruled that he would not order the curtailment or relaxing of any security procedures.

Badge continued, 'On the morning of 20 January, when I met Apte at the Hindu Mahasabha Bhavan in Delhi, I did not ask for any money. But I showed him a statement of accounts for the ₹350 he had given me. I had not informed my servant Shankar about the plan to kill Gandhiji till all of us had assembled at Marina Hotel on the afternoon of 20 January. After this, weapons were distributed to all of us. It was then that I told Shankar that I was going to shoot a man and then hurl a grenade him. "You must do exactly the same to the person as I do." I told him that the man we were going to kill was an old man, his name was "Gandhi". On the 20th, I escaped from Birla House within a few minutes of the bomb explosion, and so I cannot say what happened thereafter. I heard the explosion, I saw Madanlal being caught. As I have a very remarkable beard and long hair I am easily recognizable. I realized that if I did anything that evening, I would be caught. So I handed over the hand grenade I was carrying to Shankar and ordered him not to do anything till I signalled to him. If Nathuram, Apte, Karkare or Gopal Godse or any one of them had thrown the grenades they were carrying first, I would have signalled Shankar to throw the grenades he was carrying at Gandhiji. But as soon as Madanlal exploded the gun cotton bomb, the four rushed out of the prayer ground, got into the taxi and ran away. I realized their intentions. They planned to implicate Madanlal, Shankar and me, while they would get away scotfree.'

27 July 1948: Answering a question by Bhopatkar, Badge said, 'On returning from Delhi, I emptied my entire house. I did not wish to be caught with any incriminating evidence. I did not even contact my old friends. From 23 to 31 January, I remained confined in my house. The next day, I was arrested. Shankar was not arrested along with me. I saw Shankar in the Bombay prison during the second week of February. I was transferred to the prison in Bombay on 4 February and remained incarcerated there until I was brought to Delhi on 24 May. I was granted a conditional pardon at 5:30 p.m. on 21 June 1948.

He said that he was kept almost in solitary confinement in the Bombay branch of the CID till the recording of his statement was over.

28 July 1948: Replying to another question, Badge said that on the morning of 20 January, when Apte and he reconnoitred Birla House, no one had either reprimanded or confronted them. 'I used to be known as a Hindu Rashtra Sevak. Karkare is from Ahmednagar, he owns Deccan Guest House. On 9 January, Karkare did not tell me who Madanlal, Chopra and Omprakash were.'

29 July 1948: Badge continued, 'In the beginning of June, I had sought permission to meet J.D. Nagarvala, Deputy Commissioner of Police, Bombay. He was the Chief Police Prosecutor (Nagarvala was the Chief Investigating Officer). I told him that I wished to confess everything. He said that I would have to testify as a witness. But I insisted on making a confessional statement.'

Shankar's counsel Mehta then began his cross-examination of Badge. Badge said, 'I took part in the conspiracy to murder Mahatma Gandhi willingly and intentionally. I knew the consequences of my actions and was willing to face them.'

30 July 1948: It was expected that Badge's cross-examination would end that day. The court would then ask him to sign his testimony.

Not satisfied by his counsel's questioning of Badge, in a surprising move, Shankar Kistayya requested the court to allow him to question Badge. He asked Badge if he had been informed of the plan to kill Gandhi. Badge said Shankar was not informed while they were in Poona, and later in Bombay or Delhi. He was told about the gang's objective while coming down the stairs of the Marina Hotel on the afternoon of 20 January 1948. Then, Badge identified the bag in which he had carried the revolver and hand grenade to the prayer meeting.

31 July 1948: Recording of Badge's testimony (68 pages) and his cross-examination took nine days. The written statement was read out to the approver and he was asked to sign it.

2 August 1948: The director of the Scientific Laboratory of East Punjab, Dr D.N. Goyal, had analysed the recovered bullets, spent shells and the gun. He stated that the spent cartridges and bullets were from the same gun.

The next witness was Satyavan Bhilaji Rale, manager of the Sea Green Hotel, Bombay. He provided the court with all the details about the accused who had checked into the hotel under the names Narayanrao D. and V. Krushnaji. Rale then identified Apte.

3 August 1948: Glamour was added to the trial when actress Shanta Bhaskar Modak, popularly known as 'Bimba', took the witness stand. She told the court that she lived in Poona and had travelled to Bombay on 14 January by the Poona Express in a second-class coach. 'When I got on the train I was looking for a window seat. A gentleman occupying a window seat got up and offered me his seat. When the train started, another man came and occupied the seat next to the one who had given me his window seat. I felt as if both the men knew each other and were travelling together.' She then pointed to Apte and Godse, and identified them as her fellow travellers. She told the court that after getting off the train at Dadar, she and her brother had given the two a lift till Savarkar Sadan. She went to the police station to record her statement on 12 February 1948 in Poona. The police took her to Bombay to identify the accused.

The next witness was Kashmiri Lal, partner of the Elphinstone Hotel of Bombay. Next on the stand was Narasinh Bhagji, owner of Bombay Laundry of Poona. He identified Nathuram and his clothes which bore the laundry mark 'N.V.G.'. The next two witnesses were Gayaprasad Dube, manager of the Aryapathik Ashram, Bombay, and Govind Vishwanath Malekar, a servant working in the Elphinstone Annexe Hotel. The former said that he had known Apte for the past year and a half as he used to stay regularly at his hotel, sometimes accompanied by his lady friend. Dube and Malekar identified both Apte and Karkare.

5 August 1948: Candido Pinto, a clerk working for Pyrkes Apollo Hotel, Bombay, was the first to take the witness stand. He testified that two of the accused had checked into the hotel under the assumed names of R. Vishnu and N. Kashinath. He identified Apte and Kakare and stated that both of them were arrested at the hotel.

Testimony of Prof. Jagdish Chandra Jain

After a tea break, Jagdish Chandra Jain, resident of Shivaji Park, Bombay, and professor at Ramnarayan Ruia College, Bombay, took the stand. He spoke about his association with Madanlal Kashmirilal Pahwa, whom he had known since October 1947. He told the court that in the first week of January 1948, Madanlal had come to his home accompanied by a person he called 'Seth'. A few days later, Madanlal again came to visit him, and said, 'We have formed a Hindu commando group in Ahmednagar to protect the Hindus and are collecting arms and explosives for the same. Karkare Seth took me to meet Savarkar; impressed by my exploits, he patted me on my back and told me to continue doing good work.' Jain told the court, 'Then Madanlal told me "we have formed a group and our plan is to murder Gandhiji. Our plan is that I will explode a bomb at the evening prayer meeting conducted by Gandhiji to create terror and chaos, and taking advantage of this, the other members of our group will finish him off." I tried to dissuade Madanlal, I told him not to even think of doing such terrible deeds, but he left, promising to come back again. He came back to meet me one last time, saying that he was going to Delhi on an "important mission".'

Jain added, 'After reading the news of the bomb attack at Gandhiji's prayer meeting and the name of the arrested bomber Madanlal, I met the Prime Minister of Bombay Province B.G. Kher and Home Minister Desai at 4:00 p.m. on 21 January and told them everything I knew about the conspiracy.' (In fact, Kher had asked Jain to meet Desai since he was going out of town.)

5 August 1948: Jain continued, 'My first interaction with the police in connection with this conspiracy, was after the murder when they came to record my statement. Ten days after the police recorded my statement, it was again recorded in the presence of a magistrate.'

Testimony of Mahant Shri Krishnaji Jivanji Maharaj

9 August 1948: The head priest of the Mota Mandir, Bombay, Mahant Krishnaji Jivanji Maharaj, a.k.a., Dada Maharaj, was called on next. The witness was from the genetic lineage of the founder of the Vaishnava sect Valabhacharya. He stated that he knew Apte and identified him. 'I had heard that Apte was planning to blow up the Pakistan Constituent Assembly which was to meet in Delhi, so I went to meet him.' Apte told him that there were two mortar launchers available in Goa for ₹4,000. Pointing to Nathuram, Dada Maharaj said, 'He had accompanied Apte to my place and later I met him in Poona.'

10 August 1948: Maharaj went on to give the details of all his meetings with Godse and Apte, who had demanded that he get them a revolver. 'I had lost faith in them by then, so I refused to help them any more.' Replying to a question by Bhopatkar, Maharaj said, 'On 9 August, a few days before Independence Day, I had gone to Delhi to attend the Hindu Convention presided over by Savarkar. I don't remember if a resolution declaring support to the Nehru government was passed at the convention or not. I had gone to Noakhali after Diwali 1946 and performed the purification of over 4,000 persons who had been polluted by being force-fed beef. I performed purification rites and brought them all back into the Hindu religion.'

11 and 12 August 1948: As Kistayya was unwell, the court was adjourned on both days. Advocate N.H. Panchnathan submitted an application requesting to appear as a defence counsel.

13 August 1948: Lorna Bainbridge, an air hostess working for Air

India International Services, identified both Nathuram and Apte as having flown on 27 January 1948 under the names B. Narayanrau and N. Vinayakrau. 'I remember them because one of them had constantly kept asking for coffee and refreshments.'

Ruling on an application submitted by Bhopatkar regarding the testimony of Angad Singh, a broker from Bombay, the court ordered that it could be recorded under Section 157 of the Indian Evidence Act of 1872. Angad Singh admitted to knowing Prof. J.C. Jain and Madanlal, having met the latter on 26 October 1947. He then narrated the events that occurred in Jain's house on 10 or 11 January, where Madanlal was also present and when he had bragged about a plot to murder Gandhi.

16 August 1948: Before Angad Singh's cross-examination began, the court declared that it refused to accept the *Delhi Diaries* as a recognized original source for reference for the speeches, articles and statements made by Gandhi. Two witnesses were examined, a retired pensioner of the Imperial Bank of India's Bombay branch, Ganpatrao Bhimrao Afzulpurkar and businessman Charandas Meghji Mathuradas. Both of them admitted that they knew Badge as a fund collector for Hindu Mahasabha and told the court that he had come to collect funds from them in January.

17 August 1948: As Badge and Kistayya were unwell, the court was adjourned till 20 August.

Testimony of Raghu Mali, the Man Who Caught Nathuram Godse

20 August 1948: Ragunath Naik, a gardener, Mali, working at Birla House, informed the court that he was present at the prayer ground the day Gandhi was murdered. He described the events of that fateful evening to the court. He was carrying a sickle; he hit Nathuram on his head with the blunt side and grappled with him till others joined and disarmed Nathuram. On instructions from Nathuram Godse, the defence counsels did not cross-examine Raghu Mali.

Testimony of Dixit Maharaj

Goswami Dixit Maharaj was the younger brother of Goswami Krishnaji Maharaj, a.k.a. Dada Maharaj. He told the court that towards the end of

1946, he purchased daggers from Badge. He said that Apte had visited him on several occasions when they discussed the Hyderabad situation. He said, 'In the last week of January 1948, I participated in a meeting on the crisis in Jaisalmer; Godse (Nathuram) approached me at the meeting and inquired if I had made arrangements to provide them with the requested handguns. I replied in the negative. Seven days after the murder of Mahatma Gandhi, Dada Maharaj returned from Banaras. I asked him, "Do you know this man Godse who has been arrested for murdering Mahatma Gandhi?" Dada told me about his identity.'

Weapons Were Concealed in a Tabla and Dugga

Dixit Maharaj continued, 'During the August Kranti Movement, socialist leader Achyut Patwardhan stayed in Mota Mandir for three days. I used to live there myself. I do not agree with all the policies and beliefs of Hindu Mahasabha, but I agree with their philosophy of protecting Hindus.' Dixit Maharaj said that Badge used to bring the daggers concealed in tablas and duggas.

Nathuram Cross-Examines the Witness

After Dange was through questioning Dixit Maharaj, Nathuram requested the court to allow him to ask a few questions. Replying to a question asked by Nathuram, Dixit said, 'I have very close relations with many socialist leaders. I knew that they did not subscribe to the Hindu supremacists ideology and to the practice of militant Hinduism. I had never liked the idea of the vivisection of my motherland.'

23 August 1948: Madanlal's counsel, Bannerjee, submitted an application in court, which said, 'On 21 August, during the cross examination of Dixit Maharaj, certain statements alluding to my being a member of the Hindu Mahasabha were made, they are false.

'I was deeply hurt by the fact that Gandhiji had forced the government of India to pay ₹55 crores to Pakistan. I felt that Gandhiji could hear the isolated whispers of the Muslims of Delhi. But the ears of the Father of the Nation and the "Dictator" of the Government of India were deaf to the heart-wrenching cries of the millions of Hindu refugees. I exploded the bomb on 20 January, only to carry the refugees' cries to the selectively deaf ears of Gandhiji.'

Testimony of Home Minister of Bombay Province, Morarji Desai

Bhopatkar submitted an application objecting to the prosecution calling on Morarji Desai to confirm the testimony of Prof. Jain under Section 157 of the Indian Evidence Act. The objection was over-ruled. Desai stated, 'I am the Home Minister of the Government of Bombay province. I am in charge of the Home and Revenue departments. All the departments of criminal investigations come under the purview of the Home Ministry. I have only now come to know who Prof Jagdish Chandra Jain is. I had seen him for the first time on 21 January 1948, at approximately 4:00 p.m. when B.G. Kher summoned me to his chambers. Jain narrated the entire tale of what Madanlal had told him to me. I met and briefed Nagarvala at the railway station, before I left for Ahmedabad, that night. I gave him three specific orders: One was to arrest Karkare immediately, the second was to keep a close watch on Savarkar's home and his activities, and the third was to gather maximum information about those who were involved in the conspiracy.' Desai went on to say that he had informed Patel about the conspiracy on 22 January.

24 August 1948: Desai continued by saying that he did not reveal the identity of his informant to Nagarvala. 'Three or four days after Gandhiji was murdered. I introduced Jain to Nagarvala.' Desai was questioned by Bhopatkar, Mengle and Oak.

Vasant Joshi, a student and resident of Thana, was called next. He said that his father was the owner of Shivajee Mudranalaya. He said that he knew Karkare, Apte and Nathuram, as the three had come to his home on 25 January 1948. He gave the details of what had transpired at his home. He also claimed to know Gopal Godse. Vasant informed the court that Apte and Karkare had stayed at their home till 13 February, barring two days in between.

26 August 1948: Aitappa Krishna Kotian, a taxi driver, described in detail the events of 17 January and informed the court about the places he had driven the accused to, right up to dropping off Apte and Godse at Santacruz airport. He also informed the court that when finally he dropped Badge and Shankar, Badge asked him to give a receipt for ₹16.25.

30 August 1948: Gurbachan Singh, a Delhi-based businessman, took the stand. He was a regular at Gandhi's prayer meetings and was present on 30 January too. He said that there was no one to make a path for Gandhi through the crowd that day. 'I was trying to overtake Gandhiji to get in front of him and clear a path for him, but just as I caught up with him, as I reached his right side, I heard a shot being fired, then another shot and one more in rapid succession. There was a man standing in front of Gandhiji with a gun in his hand. I immediately hit him on his hand; I think he fired the third and last shot as my blow landed.' Singh then walked up to the dock and pointing to Nathuram Godse, said, 'This man is the killer, the murderer of Mahatma Gandhi.'

31 August 1948: The manager of Udyam Engineering Limited of Poona, Pandurang Vinayak Godbole, took the stand next. He worked for the company when Dattatreya Vinayak Godse, Nathuram's brother, was its proprietor. 'Eight or ten days before 30 January 1948, Gopal came to my house at half past nine or ten at night, saying that he wanted to leave a couple of revolvers and bullets at my home. The things were in a cloth bag, which I kept in a trunk. On 30 January, I heard the news that Nathuram Godse had murdered Mahatma Gandhi. I was terrified of being implicated in the case. That day my friend Govind Vishnu Kale came to my house. I told him about the weapons and we decided to immediately get rid of the bag. But I was very scared so I asked my friend to get rid of it. He did so.

'On 8 February, just as I was about to enter my home, I saw Gopal Godse alighting from a car with some police officers. He asked me what I had done with the bag containing the handgun and bullets. I told them that I had given the bag along with its contents to my friend Kale. On being asked, Kale said that he had thrown the bag by the roadside near Fergusson College. We went to the spot but the police could not find the guns or bullets there. We were detained under the Public Security Ordinance Act till the third week of June.'

The eighty-eighth witness was Govind Vishnu Kale, a resident of Sadashiv Peth, Poona. He told the court, 'I have known Pandurang V. Godbole for the past ten years. On 30 January, I went to his home, late in the evening. I spoke to him about the murder of Mahatma Gandhi. I saw that Godbole was very anxious, on the verge of panic. He told me that he had a revolver that he wished to throw away. I told him I would throw it away for him. He gave me a cloth bag, it contained a revolver and five bullets. I threw the bullets near Fergusson College Road on 3 or 4 February and the revolver on 7 February 1948. On 8 February, Godbole and Gopal Godse came along with policemen to my home. I told them that I had thrown it away just the day before. I took the police to the place where I had thrown the revolver and bullets, but we could not find them.'

2 September 1948: Ramanlal Desai, an employee of the Bombay Baroda and Central India Railway (BB&CIR), was called to take the stand. He explained in great detail the process of collecting tickets from passengers at stations and the process of accounting them and finally sending them to Ajmer where they were eventually destroyed. Desai went on to say that the ticket recovered from Apte was not punched and so it must have been removed after it was entered in the register, but before it was bundled and punched.

6 September 1948: Assistant accounts officer of the BB&CIR, Nathuram Agrawal took the stand. He said his department in Ajmer had received the collection report of the tickets collected from passengers at Vile Parle station on 30 January 1948.

Where Did the Collected Tickets Disappear?

Jayprakash Kudesia, a ticket collector working at Thana station, was called in next but Mengle raised an objection to his testimony. Daftary explained to the court that the accused had collected many such railway tickets, which should not have been with them. He said, 'The accused has collected train tickets from 30 January to 14 February to establish an alibi for himself to prove that on 30 January 1948, he was not present at the scene of the murder.' The court sustained Mengle's objection.

A Coat and Trousers with Unusually Large Pockets

8 September 1948: The 104th witness was Narayan Ganesh Dabke, proprietor of the Poona-based tailoring firm Dabke & Co. He informed the court, 'I know Apte because he gets all his clothes stitched from me for the past three years. His house is barely a minute away from my shop.'

A woollen suit was brought into the courtroom, Dabke recognized it immediately. He said, 'This was stitched in my shop. The order was placed on 19 November 1946 and the suit was delivered on 5 December 1946. We were asked to make large pockets both in the coat and in the trousers, which was unusual. Ten months ago, Apte had asked me to accompany him to Delhi to protest at and disrupt Gandhiji's prayer meetings.'

9 December 1948: Police Superintendent of Gwalior Dinkar Pandurang Thorat Patil was called to testify. He said, 'I am an employee of Gwalior state for the past eleven years. In January and February, I was the Police Superintendent of Lashkar. I know Dr Parchure; he was the president of the Gwalior Hindu Mahasabha and the convenor of the Hindu Rashtra Sangh. He was arrested on the morning of 3 February 1948.'

14 September 1948: CID Inspector Dasvanda Singh of the Delhi Police informed the court that on 20 January 1948, when he went to Birla House he saw Madanlal there. 'While searching him, I recovered a hand grenade from the right-hand pocket of the coat worn by Madanlal. I took him to the spot where he had exploded the bomb. A crack, 38 inches long and 19 inches deep, had formed on the wall due to the explosion.'

Dasvanda Singh continued, 'When I saw the accused Nathuram Godse, he did not have a bandage tied on his head. He was kept in a tiny cell at the Tughlaq Road Police Station. One head constable and four sepoys were posted to maintain law and order at the prayer ground. On 20 January, Head Constable Dharam Singh was on duty there.'

16 September 1948: The DSP of Delhi Police Sardar Jaswant Singh was called to testify. 'On 20 January 1948, I learnt that a bomb had been exploded at the prayer ground. I went to Birla House and questioned Madanlal in one of the rooms there.' Singh then gave further details of his visit to Marina Hotel and the Hindu Mahasabha Bhavan and the searches he conducted. He said that Madanlal had been sent to the Civil Lines Police Station where he was detained in solitary confinement till 3 February. 'I learnt that Gandhiji had been murdered at a quarter past five in the evening on 31 January 1948 (sic).' Singh then went around Birla House and said that he did not see Nathuram there. 'I saw him for the first time at seven in the evening at the Parliament Street station.

I had sent a medical officer to see Nathuram since he had given me a written complaint about the head injury he had suffered. At 9:30 a.m. on the morning of 31 January, Devadas Gandhi gave me a spent bullet at the Birla House.'

20 September 1948: Jaswant Singh continued his testimony, 'Madanlal was questioned by both, the Superintendent of Police, Delhi, P. Jagunnath and the Superintendent of Police, New Delhi, A.N. Bhatia.'

21 September 1948: The DSP of CID N.Y. Deulkar took the stand and said that he had received orders from the IG Bombay to investigate Gandhi's murder. 'I saw Nathuram Godse for the first time at the Tughlaq Road Police Station lockup on 8 February. On 11 February, when I saw Shankar Kistayya, he was accompanied by Nagarvala.' Deulkar stated that he had known Parchure.

Testimony of the Royal Astrologer

The astrologer of the royal family of Gwalior was the next to take the witness stand. Suryanarayan Vyas said, 'I am the family astrologer for the kings of Gwalior, Navanagar, Kashmir and Baroda and reside permanently at Ujjain.' He was shown an astrological chart, which he recognized it as being that of Parchure's father, Sadashiv Parchure of Gwalior.

The prosecution then called two witnesses whose testimonies helped in establishing that Godse and Apte had flown to Delhi on 17 and again on 27 January. Another witness from Poona presented evidence to prove that S.G. Parchure was a student of Deccan College.

27 September 1948: Inspector B.S. Haldipur of Bombay Police told the court, 'On 12 February, I had gone to Green Hotel (Sea Green Hotel) and made inquiries there, by the orders of Deputy Commissioner of Police Nagarvala.' He added that he had gone to Apollo Hotel to check the guest register and make some inquiries. He realized that of all the names in the register, two persons were not present in the hotel. He waited for them to arrive and arrested Apte and Karkare.

28 September 1948: Haldipur continued his testimony by saying that he had taken handwriting samples of the accused. 'On 28 January 1948, I was ordered to assist in the investigations of the bomb explosion case and on 31 January 1948, I was ordered to assist in the investigations of the murder case. I came to Delhi on 5 April 1948 or thereabouts, in connection with this case. I recollect that the accused were finally brought to Delhi in the third week of May.'

29 September 1948: Haldipur's cross-examination continued.

Next, the prosecution was to call a witness whose testimony would prove that Savarkar had ties with the other accused. The defence counsels questioned the credentials of the witness and raised objections. Daftary argued that the testimony was valid under Section 11 of the Indian Witness Act, and the witness was being called to demolish Savarkar's statement wherein he had stated that he had no relations with the accused.

Before this, Daftary submitted three applications. In his first application, he requested the court to show Karkare's counsel Dange some letters and goods seized from Karkare. In the second, he denied that the collector of Poona, S.G. Barve, had taken any goods or letters from Apte's home. The third application requested that Deulkar's statement, where he stated that Parchure had voluntarily expressed the desire to make a confessional statement and had not complained about any harassment or ill-treatment, be accepted by the court.

Bhopatkar submitted an application in which a clarification was made about Savarkar's statement, wherein he had claimed: 'I have never had contact in any form, with any of the accused.' Bhopatkar explained that Savarkar had a long-standing relationship with Godse, Apte, Parchure and Badge due to their work with the Hindu Mahasabha, but it did not imply that he had entered into a conspiracy with the accused to murder Gandhi.

30 September 1948: Ruling on the plea of Savarkar's counsel, Bhopatkar, regarding his objection to the correspondence between Savarkar and some of the accused being recognized as authentic evidence by the court, Judge Atmacharan ruled that the twenty-nine letters believed to have been written by Apte and Godse to Savarkar were relevant up to a certain extent and could be treated as authentic evidence. Next on the witness stand was CID Inspector A.R. Pradhan of Poona Police. The witness told the court that DIG of Bombay Province, Rana, had ordered him to assist Nagarvala in the investigations. On 21 February 1948, he was ordered to read the contents of the files seized from Savarkar's residence.

Mengle selected seven letters and submitted these to the court as prime evidence. B. Bannerjee informed the court that the letter written by Gandhi to Savarkar on his sixty-first birthday was also in the file. Godse had written a letter to Savarkar in October 1946, his last letter to his idol, mentor and patron, which was also in the file. Bhopatkar selected six letters written by Savarkar and ten by Nathuram and requested the court to admit these as prime evidence. The statement issued by Savarkar in 1942 on the arrest of the CWC and the condolence letter he had written to Gandhi on the death of Kasturba were also included.

The CID sub-inspector C.R. Pradhan now gave his testimony. He had been ordered by Nagarvala to keep a watch on Savarkar's home in Shivaji Park and some other establishments, and also ordered to arrest Karkare. He went to Poona on 8 February with Gopal Godse and Badge to locate the addresses of Godbole and G.P. Kale. 'On 20 January 1948 (sic) Nagarvala ordered me to arrest Karkare.'

The next witness to testify was CID Inspector Mandlik of Gwalior. He narrated to the court how he had heard from a tongawala that he had ferried two men wanting to go to Parchure's home on the night of 27 January.

Nagarvala's Testimony

The 132nd witness in the trial was the chief investigating officer, Deputy Commissioner of Bombay CID Jamshed D. Nagarvala. Taking the stand, he said, 'I joined the Indian Police Service on 2 February 1937. I received my police training from the Nasik Central Police Training School. I was posted in Sindh for three years in connection with the suppression of the "Hur Uprising".'

How the Police Uncovered the Conspiracy

Nagarvala said that along with his duties in Bombay, he had additionally been appointed a special police superintendent in Delhi too. He was to investigate the bomb explosion case and the Gandhi murder case. (This was not correct: the bomb explosion case was investigated by Director of Intelligence Bureau (DIB) T.G. Sanjeevi Pillai.)

Nagarvala then went on to give details of the investigation between 21 January and 30 January; these have been narrated in an earlier chapter in detail. He immediately ordered a very strict watch on Savarkar's home from 9:30 p.m. on 21 January and ordered Karkare's arrest. He said that he had enquired if the Ahmednagar Police had arrested Karkare.

'The Deputy Superintendent of Delhi Police Sardar Jaswant Singh and another inspector (Balakisan) came to Bombay to meet me, on 22 January 1948. They wished to arrest Karkare and his accomplices. They stayed till the afternoon of 23 January. During the interim period, they kept looking for Karkare and his accomplices. Before this, the Bombay police was not aware of Karkare's antecedents.'

He informed the court that Rana had come to Bombay on 27 January 1948 and had briefed Nagarvala about the situation and the ongoing investigation in Delhi. He said that on the 30th, the home minister of Bombay Province informed him that Gandhi had been murdered. 'On the morning of 31 January 1948, the police commissioner of Bombay informed me that Savarkar had asked for help. He immediately ordered me to proceed with a posse to Savarkar's home. Savarkar walked out of his room and met me as I entered his second floor residence. I was surprised when he came forward and said, "So you have come to arrest me for the murder of Mahatma Gandhi." He sounded very guilty; I also felt that he was only pretending to be ill. I told him that I had only come to conduct a search of his home. Savarkar definitely looked very crestfallen and also fearful,' said Nagarvala, and went on to give details about interviewing taxi driver Kotian and the actress Shanta Bhaskar Modak.

Apte Arrested

Nagarvala added that Apte and Karkare were arrested from Pyrke's Apollo Hotel after the police secretly tapped the telephone line of Manorama Salvi's father and listened in to the conversation between Apte and Manorama. He then said that all the accused, barring Savarkar and Parchure, were brought to Delhi on 24 May 1948. In accordance with Section 4 of the Prisoner Identification Act, a group photograph of all the accused was taken.

6 October 1948: Nagarvala's testimony continued. 'I sent a police party to Poona to search Apte's home to look for a pair of missing trousers, but they were not found. On getting information, I called three Panchas, and in their presence we searched the room where Apte was held. Apte opened his trunk and handed over the trousers to me. A recovery statement was prepared, which I signed.'

Nagarvala continued, 'I personally recorded Miss Modak's testimony in my room. When I received orders to investigate this case, I had, for my convenience, got the entire second floor of the new building of the CID office in Bombay vacated. A sentry was posted at the entrance to the elevator on the ground floor. I had warned the liftman not to bring any one to the upper floor without my orders. I used to meet very few persons in my room. The windows and doors of the rooms in which the accused were held were kept shut and locked. The doors of the rooms in which Gopal Godse and Narayan Apte were held were open but we had hung curtains across them.'

Nagarvala said that during the investigation, he had sufficiently satisfied himself that the telegram sent in Apte's name was neither sent by him nor was it his writing on the booking form. Manorama Salvi could have testified with regard to the telegram, but she had turned hostile.

8 October 1948: Nagarvala said, 'I suspended Lance Naik Kadam because he had smuggled a letter written by the accused Apte to Manorama Salvi out of the prison.' This completed Nagarvala's testimony. The court was adjourned till 18 October 1948 because of Navratra, Vijaya Dashmi and Bakri Eid.

18 and 20 October 1948: The proceedings of the court resumed on 18 October, after a ten-day vacation. However, after a short while, it was adjourned again as Atmacharan had to leave for Kanpur due to a bereavement in his family.

21 October 1948: The chief handwriting expert, Gajjar, of the Poona provincial CID unit, was called. He said that he had received orders on 17 March 1948 to analyse some documents related to the Gandhi murder case. Haldipur gave him some documents for analyses. The documents were in English and Marathi. On many occasions, the accused were asked to write on clean sheets of paper what Haldipur dictated to them. All these documents and papers were given to Gajjar for analysis.

Gajjar informed the court, 'The handwriting specimen of the accused was sent to me. The handwriting of an entry in the traveller's register, made on 21 January 1948 at Kanpur railway station, matched exactly with Nathuram's writing. So did the writing of the entry made in the guest register of Elphinstone Annexe Hotel, Bombay on 24 January 1948.'

25 October 1948: Gajjar continued, 'The entries in the guest register of Sea Green Hotel on 2 February 1948, were written by Karkare, so were those in the name of G.M. Joshi in the register of the Frontier Hindu Hotel on 20 January 1948 and in the name of B.M. Vyas in the guest register of Sharief Hindu Hotel on 17 January 1948; these were all examined minutely by me. I observed that the method of holding the pen, the characteristics of strokes, nib angles and the formation of letters were all exactly like those found in the handwriting specimen provided by Vishnu Karkare. The two insurance policies of the Oriental Government Security Life Insurance bear Nathuram's signature. The signature appearing in the box marked as witness is definitely that of Narayan Apte.'

Replying to a question from Oak, Gajjar said, 'While analysing Nathuram's writing, I came across a recurring characteristic. When he writes "I", the vertical stroke is always tilted, never straight. Of course, there are slight variations, which is natural. The "I" in Nathuram's writing is very distinctive.'

27 October 1948: Replying to a question asked by Gopal Godse's counsel Inamdar, Gajjar said, 'I have compared the handwritings in the documents in question with the handwriting specimen of the accused obtained by the police. I gave my opinion after thoroughly analysing and satisfying myself about my inferences.'

Testimony of CID Inspector Pinto

The CID Inspector Charles Anthony Pinto of Bombay Police was called to testify next. He said that he worked in the special branch of the Bombay CID since 29 January 1948. His first task was to find both Badge and Karkare. He arrested Gopal Godse on 5 February from Uksan but did not find any incriminating evidence on him. A day after, Apte and Karkare were handed over to the authorities of the district jail.

28 October 1948: Pinto said that when he brought Nathuram to Delhi on 5 April 1948, Apte and Karkare were not with him. He assisted Nagarvala in investigating the case and had no recollection of when the police learnt of Karkare's name and his address.

29 October 1948: Witness No. 139 in the Gandhi murder trial was a seventy-eight-year-old retired major from Gwalior, Dadabhai Manekjee. He said, 'I went to Gwalior in 1895, and enrolled in the Gwalior Army that very year. I also served on the personal staff of the late king of Gwalior. I have known Sadashiv Gopal Parchure, I used to call him "Master Saheb". He was either a lecturer or professor in the Mahadev College of Ujjain. S.G. Parchure had five sons and one daughter. After serving in many positions, he ended his career as the DIG in the education department. I had met him on the day he died. I remember that he had requested for a loan from the late monarch to purchase a house. I have neither met nor spoken to Parchure, the accused.'

The editor of the newspaper *Jiyajee Pratap*, published from Gwalior, Ramprasad, was the last witnesses in the trial. The process lasted four months. One hundred and forty-three witnesses testified and almost five hundred items were accepted by the court as authentic evidence.

5 November 1948: Additional witnesses were presented in court by the prosecution. The chief clerk of Bombay University, Vinayak Raghunath Darshethkar, submitted the university calendars of the years 1880–1, 1884–5 and 1885–6 and the 'result sheets' of the 1876–7 metric exam and the 1881–2 and 1891–2 B.A. exams to the court. He examined and confirmed the seal of the Bombay University on the certificate which was conferred, in 1886 on S.G. Parchure, father of the accused Dattatreya S. Parchure. Another witness was the superintendent of the records department of Gwalior, Raghavan. He presented the Military and Civilian Record of Gwalior in which there was a mention of S.G. Parchure, along with his signature. There was the station in-charge of the Lashkar police station of Gwalior State, Keshav. He had seized the birth chart of S.G. Parchure, a photograph and six land revenue receipts. Some of the seized documents were presented in court as evidence. An old resident of Gwalior, Shyam Bahadur, said in his testimony, 'On 29 and 30 October, and on 2 and 3 November, when Parchure's home was searched, I was present.'

With this, the cross-examination of the witnesses finally came to an end.

◆

Statement of Nathuram Vinayak Godse: 'I Alone Murdered Gandhiji.'

On 8 November, when the proceedings of the court began, Chief Prosecutor Daftary informed the court that the prosecution would not be presenting any more witnesses. The court asked prime accused Nathuram Godse if he wished to say anything to the court. Nathuram replied that he wished to read out a ninety-three-page long statement.

Nathuram began reading his statement at 10:15 a.m. Before reading his statement he said, 'I have divided my statement into six parts. The first deals with the conspiracy and related matters; the second part will throw light on Gandhiji's politics (initial phase); part three will focus on his politics (final phase); part four deals with Gandhiji and Indian independence; part five with the shattering of the dream of independence; and the last part deals with the zenith of the anti-national policy of appeasement.'

At 11 o'clock, while reading his statement, Nathuram began feeling giddy and collapsed. After being revived and resting for a while, he continued. It took him almost five hours to read the entire statement. Through it, he sipped water and chewed cloves. He ended his statement by shouting '*Akhand Bharat Amar Rahe! Vande Mataram!*' (Long live undivided India! Hail the Motherland!).

After Nathuram finished reading his statement, Daftary raised objections, saying that many parts in the statement were inconsequential to the trial and should not be incorporated in the court's record. He cited as an example the part in which Nathuram stated, 'I have no respect for the current Government of India, because it is partial towards the Muslims.' Atmacharan replied that he could not order certain parts of a written statement to be deleted. They could be irrelevant for the lawyer but for Nathuram they may be essential. He added that written statements were always accepted in important trials in the United Provinces.

Although the statement was attributed to Nathuram Godse, he had never displayed such mastery over English previously. He was known for his very abusive and rabid language. The statement was a cleverly written afterthought to justify Gandhi's murder. It smacked of the penmanship of V.D. Savarkar, a co-accused in the Gandhi murder case, who was cloistered with Nathuram since the time when all the accused were brought to Delhi and were held in the specially designated jail in the Red Fort. Savarkar had realized that Nathuram would be given his time in court to read his statement. This was an opportunity they would not miss, to justify their deed and garner sympathy for the cause of radical Hinduism, which is today called 'Hindutva'. Savarkar and Nathuram succeeded spectacularly in their objective. Today, the cult of Nathuram worship and Gandhi hate is entirely due to this statement written by V.D. Savarkar and read out by Nathuram in court first during the Red Fort trial and again during the appeal in the Punjab High Court.

The courtroom was almost packed to capacity that day.

The Government of India, at the time of the trial, in a knee-jerk reaction, banned the publication of Nathuram's statement after it was melodramatically narrated in front of the press, in a packed courtroom. The government's action added credibility to a rabid account of a zealot, which twisted facts, based its arguments on incidents taken out of context, and exploited the emotions of the people and was liberally embellished with lies.

I have written about the last years of Gandhi's life in Book Two, which shows how false this campaign, carried out by the Hindutva gang, is.

Judge Questions the Accused

9 November 1948: The judge asked Nathuram 28 questions; the accused answered all of them standing in the dock.

Nathuram denied all the conspiracy charges: he kept asserting that he had acted as a lone wolf in the murder of Gandhi and refuted all the charges of conspiracy brought against him by the prosecution.

Godse accepted the fact that he had fired thrice at Gandhi. He described graphically his mental condition, a few minutes before and a few minutes after killing Gandhi.

Godse said, 'Just as Gandhiji approached the verandah at the prayer place, I leapt in front of him. I had decided that I would shoot Gandhiji in such a way that no one else would get injured. I greeted Gandhiji with folded palms, I had hidden the pistol between my folded palms. I had disengaged the safety catch. I imagined that I had fired twice, later I found out from the police that I had fired thrice. I became agitated and shouted "Police! Police!" repeatedly. After I had fired the shots, I found that the people were frozen with shock. I remember that first I was caught hold of by a police constable. Later, another one came. Then someone snatched the pistol from my hand.' Godse continued, 'One man came up from behind me and hit me on the back of my head and I started bleeding from the wound. I told him that I had done what I had set out to do and had no regrets about what I had done. I warned the person who had snatched the pistol from my hand that it was an automatic and that I had disengaged the safety catch so he better handle it carefully otherwise it may go off and hurt or kill someone else. The person turned to me and said, "I will shoot you!" I told him—"Shoot me, I am ready to die."' In the end, Nathuram Vinayak Godse said, 'Gandhiji definitely died as a result of the bullets I fired at him, from the pistol in my hand.'

10 November 1948: Godse was questioned further by the judge and he continued to deny every charge.

The second accused, Narayan Dattatreya Apte, read out his twenty-two-page long statement in court. He proclaimed his innocence and refuted all the charges the prosecution had brought against him. 'I am innocent. I was not present at the scene of crime at the time of the murder. I deny outright the charges levelled against me, of being an accomplice in the murder of Mahatma Gandhi and of encouraging, planning and assisting in his murder.'

In the end, Apte said, 'The prosecution has failed to prove any of the charges levelled against me. I am absolutely innocent, and so I must be released, post haste.'

11 November 1948: Apte was questioned by Judge Atmacharan, and he denied all the charges.

15 November 1948: Reading his thirty-seven-page long statement in Marathi, the third accused in the Gandhi murder conspiracy, Vishnu Ramchandra Karkare, claimed that he was absolutely innocent and should be honourably discharged from the case. '*Me neerdosh aahe, hya kataat maza hath nahin, mala phasavla gela ahe.*' (I am absolutely not guilty, I have been framed.) He said that the conspiracy charge was very unclear and vague, and challenged the powers and jurisdiction of the court to prosecute him.

Like Apte, Karkare too said that he was not present at the time of Gandhi's murder and that he was not, in any way, involved in the conspiracy. He said that he heard about it from some people and then read about it in the newspapers.

After Karkare finished reading out his statement in Marathi, the court asked him some questions. Karkare too denied all accusations and claimed that he was innocent and was being framed by the police and the prosecution lawyers.

Madanlal's Statement

Next, the fourth accused in the Gandhi murder trial, Madanlal Kashmirilal Pahwa, rose to make his statement in court. 'I accept that on 20 January 1948, when Gandhiji was conducting his evening prayer meeting at Birla House, I exploded a bomb made of gun cotton explosive.'

Madanlal read out his twenty-one-page statement in court and accepted the fact that he had exploded a bomb in Gandhi's prayer meeting but claimed that it was only to register his protest. It was his form of Satyagraha against the anti-Hindu stance of Mahatma Gandhi. He had no intention to hurt Gandhi and he was definitely not part of any conspiracy or group of people conspiring to murder Gandhi as claimed by the prosecution.

At the end of his statement he said, 'There was no conspiracy to murder Mahatma Gandhi. Even if there was one, I was in no manner involved in it.'

After he finished reading his statement, the judge questioned Madanlal, who also refuted all charges brought against him by the prosecution and maintained that he was not guilty.

18 November 1948: Judge Atmacharan began questioning the fifth accused, Shankar Kistayya, to ascertain his involvement in the conspiracy.

Shankar was unlettered so, unlike the first four accused, he had not prepared any written statement to accept or refute the charges levelled against him by the prosecution or to accept or dispute the testimonies of witnesses. He could only speak Telugu and bits of broken Marathi, therefore, a translator was used to explain to the court what he said.

Shankar informed the court, 'I am about twenty years old. I am a domestic servant, a resident of Sholapur. I only obeyed my master's orders. Apart from that, I know nothing.'

Before his questioning began, responding to a plea by Bannerjee, the court ordered the removal of approver Badge, Shankar's employer, and the jail authorities from the courtroom.

'I was Badge's servant. That is why I went with them to Delhi. I know nothing about the conspiracy. I do not wish to produce any witnesses to refute the claims of the prosecution or to support my statement.'

In his statement, the sixth accused, Gopal Vinayak Godse, denied that Gandhi's murder was the result of a plot or conspiracy.

He read out his fifteen-page statement. He too, refuted all charges brought against him by the prosecution and claimed to be innocent; he requested the court to set him free.

On being questioned, Gopal denied any knowledge of Nathuram nominating his wife on his insurance policy. To all further questions from Judge Atmacharan, Gopal claimed that the testimony of witnesses was false and refuted the charges brought against him by the prosecution.

20 November 1948: 'I say with absolute sincerity and heartfelt honesty that I am innocent of the charges levelled against me by the prosecution. I am not involved in any plot or conspiracy in any manner whatsoever; neither did I have any prior knowledge about any such illegal actions or plots. I have done nothing, as has been alleged in the charges filed against me, there was no reason for me to get involved in such a conspiracy either as a participant or as a patron.' These were the opening remarks of the statement of the seventh accused in the Gandhi murder trial, V.D. Savarkar.

Reading his fifty-seven-page statement in court, Savarkar gave a detailed account of his life, so that he could state his position with absolute conviction. Then he began talking about the Hindu Mahasabha. He denied all charges brought against him by the prosecution and claimed that he was being framed due to political vendetta.

In the end, Savarkar presented the press announcements he had made, condemning the arrests of Nehru in 1940, and Gandhi and Nehru in 1942, to the court. He submitted the plea he had made to Gandhi to abandon his fast in 1943, and criticizing the attempt on Jinnah's life. He also produced the statement where he had in very clear terms and strong language condemned Gandhi's murder. 'It is evident from these statements made by me from time to time, how much I respect the leaders of the various parties. I consider it a privilege I have remained alive to see the liberation of my motherland.' Savarkar continued in this vein for the remainder of his statement. 'The prosecution has failed to substantiate any of the charges levelled against me. Thus, the order for my release must be given post haste.' It took Savarkar nearly two-and-a-half hours to read his statement.

After his statement, the court asked him some questions. Savarkar dismissed most of the questions as based on blatant lies.

Next, the eighth accused, Dr Dattatreya Sadashiv Parchure, read out his fifteen-page statement in court. Denying his association with the conspiracy to murder Gandhi, Parchure claimed that he was a citizen of the princely state of Gwalior and so could not be prosecuted. He claimed that his arrest and court proceedings against him were illegal.

'Neither on the basis of any facts nor on the basis of any incidents can this special court prosecute me. I am a patriotic citizen of the government of the princely state of Gwalior. I was born in Lashkar and studied there. I have not stayed in British India ever in my life. Thus the proceedings against me are illegal.'

1 December 1948: The third phase of the Gandhi murder trial began on this day. The chief prosecutor, C.K. Daftary, began his summing up.

'This special court and Special Judge Atmacharan are empowered to try this case. By a special ordinance, the special judge was given the powers to grant a conditional pardon to the approver. The ordinance has now been converted into an Act.'

Referring to the charges framed by the prosecution against all the accused, Daftary said, 'The murder of Mahatma Gandhi is not an action of Nathuram Godse individually. He was induced and encouraged and a conspiracy was hatched. Badge had an association with Apte since 1947. He would meet Apte in the office of *Hindu Rashtra* and sell him weapons, bombs and explosives. Badge's servant Shankar also used to be present then. Madanlal met Prof Jain along with Karkare on 10 January; he had introduced Karkare to him as "Seth". Two–three days later, Madanlal again met Prof Jain, and narrated his exploits in Ahmednagar. At that time, he told Jain about the conspiracy to murder Mahatma Gandhi.' Daftary then established the entire chain of events leading up to Gandhi's murder and established every instance with the testimony of corroborative witnesses presented by the prosecution to prove the existence of the conspiracy and the involvement of all the accused.

Finally, concluding his eight-day summation, Daftary said, 'Looking at the case from any perspective and keeping in mind the fact that the prosecution has produced irrefutable evidence and credible witnesses, the court must accept that the prosecution has proven the guilt of all the accused. All charges against them have been proven beyond reasonable doubt. The court must declare the accused guilty as charged, my Lord.'

10 December 1948: Arguments by the defence began with Apte's counsel, Mengle.

'I hope to safely take the defence's ship to harbour, by navigating the minefield laid by the prosecution. It must be remembered that the defence has only called on 149 witnesses from the 250 originally listed in the chargesheet. In a criminal matter, the onus of proving a charge rests on the prosecution. The prosecution has alleged that the statements of the accused have been fortified by adding several afterthoughts, in an effort to strengthen their defence.'

Mengle went on to try and discredit the prosecution's witnesses against the accused in a bid to sow enough doubts about the case presented by the prosecution.

Next, Shankar Kistayya's defence counsel Mehta began his arguments. Mehta said, 'Shankar was Badge's faithful servant. When all the accused used to meet, Shankar was always left out, so it is possible that he may not have known of the said conspiracy. He used to transport weapons, bombs and explosives, but only on the orders of his master. My client does not possess any political thought or subscribe to a political philosophy. The prosecution has failed to reason why Shankar would want to murder Mahatma Gandhi.'

Ending his arguments, Mehta said, 'It may be possible that Shankar is guilty, but while considering his guilt, it must be kept in mind that Shankar is Badge's servant.'

Nathuram Godse expressed a desire to defend himself, but only on the condition that it would not have any implications on the status of his defence counsel. Atmacharan said that this would be decided by his defence counsel, V.V. Oak.

Nathuram Godse did not challenge the murder charge against him, but completely rejected Badge's testimony as a pack of lies and unsubstantiated accusations. He claimed that the prosecution had completely failed in proving the conspiracy charge.

Nathuram concluded his arguments with the oft-repeated litany of having performed a deed to save the motherland and Hindu Dharma. 'Looking at the situation which developed after the vivisection of Mother India, and the vacillating attitude of the Government of India which capitulated under pressure from Gandhiji, after deciding to withhold payment of ₹55 crores to Pakistan; under these circumstances, although in the eyes of the law I am a criminal, but the Indian people, the future generations and honest historians of the future will agree that it was necessary to kill Gandhiji.'

'Since I showed no mercy towards the person I murdered, I have forfeited the right to seek mercy. I have achieved my objectives by murdering Gandhiji, I have nothing further to say. A time will come when the world will ridicule patriotism much in the same manner as they ridicule religious pride today.'

Having grandly declared, in his concluding remarks, that he did not intend to beg for mercy, the self-proclaimed martyr did exactly this after his sentencing, right up to the highest authority of that time, the privy council of England.

Arguments by Karkare's Counsel

Next, Karkare's defence counsel, Dange, began his arguments. He said, 'The testimony of only 46 prosecution witnesses concern my client Karkare. Out of these, 26 testimonies are totally irrelevant. The prosecution did not summon any Muslim citizen of the Indian Union, as a witness. Badge is not a very important witness. From those who testified in court, only five witnesses are important to the case. The testimonies of the witnesses from Marina Hotel have no bearing on the charges framed against my client Karkare.' He too based his defence by alleging that all the evidence and witness testimonies presented in court by the prosecution were insufficient to establish his client's guilt.

Objections against the Statement of Sardar Patel

Inamdar, defence counsel for Parchure and Gopal, drew the attention of the court to a newspaper report which stated that while speaking at the Congress convention in Raipur, the Union home minister, Sardar Patel had said that the pistol used to murder Gandhi had been purchased in Gwalior. Inamdar said, 'Till such time as the trial is in progress, such statements should not be made in public.'

Concluding his arguments, he said, 'My client has committed no crime, he must be given the benefit of the doubt and immediately released.'

Das Argues in Defence of Savarkar

Next, P.R. Das began arguments in defence of V.D. Savarkar. He began, 'There are two things we must think about. First, whether there was any conspiracy to murder Mahatma Gandhi. Second, if there was a conspiracy, to what extent was Savarkar involved? According to the statements of the prosecution, the final decision to murder Mahatma Gandhi was taken in Room 40 of Marina Hotel on the afternoon of 20 January 1948. The defence has stated that there was no conspiracy to murder Mahatma Gandhi, and if it is alleged that there was one, it would be such a sad conclusion because the other accused had only planned to stage a peaceful demonstration during the prayer meeting. The event of 30 January was an individual action of Nathuram Godse. If there was a conspiracy, why was Gandhiji not murdered on 20 January itself? The prosecution has not said that after the failed attempt on 20th, the conspiracy continued till 30 January.'

The judge asked, 'If a conspiracy fails on a particular day, does it cease to exist? Jain's testimony has been branded as full of exaggeration. If it was so, he would have fallen prey to his exaggerations during the cross-examination.' Das continued to refute the existence of a conspiracy to murder Gandhi and denied that Savarkar had any role to play, even if one was to for even an instance believe that a conspiracy existed.

'I have no doubt that Savarkar will be declared innocent and released. But the court must also declare that he is being released with his honour and reputation unblemished,' Das concluded.

Arguments by Madanlal's Counsel

Next, Madanlal's defence counsel, Bannerjee, began his arguments. He reiterated his demand that the court should include the text of Gandhi's speeches and articles written by him in the court's record, as well as the 'fact that the government was forced to pay ₹55 crores to Pakistan because of Gandhi.' Then, Bannerjee, like all other defence counsels, went on to attempt to discredit the prosecution's case against the accused.

Concluding his arguments, Bannerjee said, 'Very serious charges have been filed against the accused. For generations, lawyers and judges will argue and debate the ruling of this court, it will come in for criticism and for praise, it will be read by hundreds of thousands of people.'

Arguments by Gopal Godse's Counsel

Next, Inamdar, the defence counsel for Gopal Godse and Dr Parchure, began his arguments.

Inamdar said, 'The way the prosecution has built a case against my client Gopal Godse leads me to believe that it was done as an afterthought.' Speaking of the charge of trafficking of illegal weapons and explosives, he said, 'From all the testimonies of the witnesses produced by the prosecution, I could not find even a sentence, which could prove that my client, Gopal Godse, illegally transported an unlicensed revolver to Delhi.' Inamdar then challenged the authority of the court to hear the case against the accused based on the powers vested in it. 'Till such time it is not established that my client transported an unlicensed revolver, the accused have the right to get the case dismissed and be released.'

Inamdar then went on a spree of discrediting the prosecution's witnesses over minor discrepancies in their testimony. Inamdar concluded his arguments by stating that since Parchure was a bonafide citizen of the Gwalior principality, his arrest was illegal and the court did not have the right to prosecute him.

Some of his startling and, to an extent, astute observations were:

1. Madanlal is an idiot and braggart, that is why he disclosed the conspiracy to Prof. Jain.
2. Prof. Jain is an even bigger idiot.
3. Morarji Desai and Sardar Patel are unfit for their posts.
4. Nagarvala is also incompetent because he did not record the statement of Prof. Jain on 21 January itself.

In conclusion, Inamdar said: 'Parchure's father, S.G. Parchure came and settled in Gwalior. The accused Parchure was born in Gwalior, and since his birth he has lived there. Thus, there is no doubt about the fact that Parchure is a citizen of the princely state of Gwalior.... The prosecution's entire case is doubtful and suspicious.'

With this ended the arguments of the defence counsels.

Judge Congratulated by Prosecution and Defence

Daftary, on behalf of the prosecution, and Bhopatkar, on behalf of the defence, thanked and congratulated the judge for patiently hearing the matter.

Thus concluded the hearings in the Gandhi murder trial. Judge Atmacharan promised that he would deliver judgment within a month.

The recording of the testimonies of the prosecution's witnesses went on for eighty-four days. The testimonies ran into 696 pages. Every question and answer was written in English and translated into Telugu, Marathi and Hindustani. Some witnesses had given their testimonies in Gujarati and Punjabi too.

The prosecution submitted 354 documents in court and the defence submitted 118. Eighty other articles relating to the trial were deposited in court.

A notable aspect was that the entire argument of the defence was based on proving that there was no conspiracy and that the act was entirely that of Nathuram Godse, committed due to the outrage he experienced—an act of momentary insanity. The accused and their defence counsel used the trial to continuously harp on the RSS–Hindu Mahasabha litany that Gandhi was responsible for the partition of India, that Gandhi was responsible for his own murder, that Nathuram, his killer, was helpless. The strategy was to create sympathy and support for the murderers of Gandhi and for the Hindu supremacist ideology of the Sangh and Mahasabha.

Judgment

On 10 February 1949, at 11:30 a.m., Judge Atmacharan delivered the judgment in the Gandhi murder trial.

He sentenced Gandhi's murderer Nathuram V. Godse and his accomplice Narayan D. Apte to death by hanging.

Vishnu R. Karkare, Madanlal K. Pahwa, Shankar Kistayya, Gopal V. Godse and Dr Dattatreya S. Parchure were sentenced to life in prison. (In India, this meant a maximum of fourteen years in prison minus permissible remissions.)

The judge found Vinayak Damodar Savarkar 'not guilty'; he felt that the prosecution had not proven his guilt as efficiently as with the other accused and ordered his immediate release. It is essential to remember that when the investigation in the Gandhi murder was going on, the chief minister of Bombay Province, accompanied by commissionaire of police, Bombay, and Investigating Officer Nagarvala, had gone to Delhi and briefed Home Minister Sardar Patel about the investigation. They had requested that they wanted to arrest Savarkar and charge him. Sardar told them that they should not implicate Savarkar in the case and arrest him, thinking it will please the Congress government. They should charge Savarkar of being an accomplice in the Gandhi murder only if they were certain that they would be able to get a conviction. Sardar was assured by the three that they had sufficient evidence to get Savarkar convicted. Surprisingly, in the trial, the evidence produced against Savarkar by the prosecution was very weak and the defence very easily discredited it, raising sufficient doubts in the judge's mind about Savarkar's involvement. It was only much later, after Savarkar's death, that the Kapur Commission concluded that Gandhi's murder could not have happened without the involvement of Savarkar and, hence, Savarkarites and Sanghis have been desperately trying to discredit the Kapur Commission's report and attempting to subvert it.

Badge, the approver, was also released in accordance with the conditional pardon granted to him.

Each accused rose as his sentence was read out. Before being removed from the dock, all the accused raised slogans in court: '*Hindu Dharm Ki Jai!*' (Hail the Hindu religion!), '*Tod ke rahenge Pakistan, Hindi Hindu Hindustan!*' (We will destroy Pakistan, Hindustan for and of Hindi and Hindus only!), till they were taken away.

The judge informed the accused that they were free to appeal against their sentences within fifteen days in a higher court. He also recommended that Shankar Kistayya's sentence should be reduced from life imprisonment to seven years' rigorous imprisonment.

Description of the Scene in Court

The court was packed to capacity. The vicinity of the Red Fort was declared a restricted area and a large force of policemen and soldiers were deployed to maintain law and order. At 11:20 a.m., the doors of the room adjoining the dock were opened, and led by Nathuram Godse, the eight accused entered. Only Savarkar bore a very serious expression. The other accused, especially Godse, Apte and Karkare, looked cheerful and kept smiling and nodding at their family and acquaintances present in court.

Judge Atmacharan, wearing his regular black suit, entered the courtroom at exactly 11:30 a.m. All in the courtroom rose. The judge first called Nathuram Godse; he stood up and heard the judge pronounce his sentence and punishment. Then Apte, Karkare, Madanlal, Shankar Kistayya, Gopal Godse and Dr Parchure were called and sentenced. In the end, Judge Atmacharan called V.D. Savarkar; the judge declared that he found Vinayak D. Savarkar 'not guilty'. It took the judge twenty minutes to read out the sentences.

The judgment was 204 pages long; Judge Atmacharan left the court after informing the accused that they should take a copy of the judgment which was available with the court's clerk. Two minutes later, the accused were removed from the dock.

After the court arose, it was declared that the Delhi district magistrate had promulgated the Public Security Ordinance in the Delhi Province. He had ordered that Savarkar be kept in Red Fort for the time being to maintain law and order.

All the confiscated arms, ammunition, explosives and bombs were to be preserved. The pistol used to murder Gandhi and the recovered spent bullets were also to be preserved. The judge ordered that no decision could be made about these without consulting the Union government. They could be required for display in a national museum.

On the evening of 10 February 1949, in accordance with the Punjab Public Security Act, the Delhi district magistrate ordered V.D. Savarkar to leave Delhi immediately and not to return for the next three months.

Judge Atmacharan Reprimands Police

Judge Atmacharan drew the attention of the Union government to the almost criminal negligence displayed by the police in preventing the tragedy. He wrote in his judgment, 'I draw the attention of the Union government to the shocking inefficiency and the lack of initiative displayed by the police in investigating the matter between 20–30 January 1948. After the arrest of Madanlal, the Delhi Police had detailed information about the existence of a conspiracy to murder Gandhiji, in a very comprehensive statement made by Madanlal. Dr J.C. Jain had informed the Honourable Minister, Morarji Desai, about the existence of a conspiracy to murder Mahatma Gandhi, and the Bombay Police were immediately given all the information. On the basis of these two statements, contact was immediately established between the Delhi and Bombay Police. But the police failed in extracting any benefit from these two statements. If at that time investigations were carried out with due diligence and a bit of enterprise, it is possible that this tragedy could have been averted.'

This was a very severe indictment of the police by a presiding judge and was made part of a judgment. Surprisingly, none of the policemen were taken to task. Sanjeevi and Rana were allowed to retire honourably; others were rewarded with promotions. Jamshed D. Nagarvala retired as India's top cop, his bungling the investigation in the bomb attack case was thereby rewarded. Till his death, Nagarvala maintained that he was convinced that without the help and active involvement of Savarkar in the conspiracy to murder Gandhi, the murderers would not have succeeded.

XIII

APPEALS AND EXECUTION

It seemed to me that I was taking part in some kind of melodrama or in a scene out of a Hollywood feature film. Once or twice I had interrupted Godse and pointed out the irrelevance of what he was saying, but my colleagues seemed inclined to hear him and the audience most certainly thought that Godse's performance was the only worthwhile part of the lengthy proceedings.

—Justice G.D. Khosla, commenting on
Nathuram Godse's performance in court

I can not, in all conscience, agree to anyone being sent to the gallows… once a man is killed, the punishment is beyond recall or reparation. God alone can take life, because He alone gives it.

—M.K. Gandhi, *Gandhiji, His Life and Works*, p. 381

All those convicted in the Gandhi murder trial appealed to the Punjab High Court within four days of their sentencing by the special court. The Government of India did not appeal against the acquittal of V.D. Savarkar. The Chief Justice of Punjab High Court constituted a three-judge bench to hear the appeal of the accused, comprising Justice A.N. Bhandari, Justice Achchruram and Justice G.D. Khosla.

I have described the proceedings in the Punjab High Court from the book *The Murder of the Mahatma* written by Justice G.D. Khosla, from the chapter 'Crimes of Nathuram'. Describing the preparation for the trial, Justice Khosla writes, and I quote: 'An appeal in a murder case is, according to High Court Rules and Orders, heard by a Division Bench consisting of two judges, but owing to the unique position which the deceased had occupied, the complexity and volume of the evidence which would have to be considered and appraised and the unprecedented interest aroused by the case, the Chief Justice decided to constitute a bench of three judges to hear the appeal by Godse and his accomplices. The judges were Mr Justice A.N. Bhandari, Mr Justice Achchruram and myself. The Punjab High Court was, at that time, located at Simla, where it had been hurriedly set up during the autumn of 1947, because at no other place was suitable accommodation available. The Government of India had placed at our disposal "Peterhoff", a large manorial building which was formerly the summer residence of the Viceroy. It was a picturesque house standing in pleasant surroundings and commanding a view of the distant hills with their snow-covered peaks. But it was scarcely suitable for a high court. The viceregal bedrooms, stripped of their opulent furnishings and silver-plated fittings, gave an appearance of mock austerity, but even the largest of them was not commodious enough for a courtroom in which, besides the judge and his reader, half a dozen lawyers and their clerks spent several hours a day. There must be a table for the judge, another for his reader and stenographer, a separate table for the lawyers on which they can place their briefs and the law books they cite. And when a few bookshelves to hold law reports and other books of reference were placed along the walls, there was no room left for the public. We had a constant feeling of being cramped. Fortunately, the non-litigant public of Simla was incurious about High Court proceedings, and we seldom had any visitors. But the hearing of the appeal in the Gandhi murder case was expected to arouse widespread interest and bring large numbers of lawyers, pressmen and spectators to court each day, and there was not a single courtroom which could accommodate even the persons actually engaged in dealing with the appeal. The ballroom on the ground floor was being used as a passage, giving access to the courtrooms on the first floor; the large hall was cold and draughty. However, with a few minor alterations and the addition of a dais at one end, it became an admirable courtroom, and the generous teak wood staircase which came down to the specially constructed dais displayed a dignity worthy of the robed and bewigged judges who day after day for a period of six weeks marched down it, preceded by ushers resplendent in their scarlet and gold liveries and carrying tall silver-mounted staffs, symbols of the triple embodiment of law. Such splendour and glory had not been witnessed in the refugee High Court since it had been forced to abandon its old seat in Lahore. The staffs had been put away in a storeroom, even the wigs had ceased to be worn because many of the advocates had left them behind in Lahore in their stampede to safety; at Simla they had made a formal request that the dress regulation be relaxed in this respect. Their reappearance on the opening day of the appeal was, therefore, all the more impressive. The hearing began on 2 May 1949. It was a bright day with the gold of the sun lying in a thin layer on the lawns of "Peterhoff". There was a slight chill in the air, the ballroom was warmed by a dozen or so electric fires. Policemen stood guard at the entrance, admission to the courtroom was regulated by passes issued by the registrar. When we took our seats on the dais, I saw that the room was full to capacity. All the black-coated and gowned lawyers who were not engaged in arguing their cases before other judges had spread themselves over the privileged front rows in a large inky splash. Behind them sat the members of the gentry of Simla. There were separate seats for pressmen and reporters, and to the right of the dais a score or so of chairs had been reserved for the V.I.P.s. At a long table in front of the dais sat an impressive row of advocates representing the appellants and the King. There was Mr Bannerjee, a senior advocate from Calcutta, for Apte and Madanlal Pahwa, Mr Dange for Karkare, Mr Avasthi of the Punjab High Court, engaged at public expense to represent Kistayya, who was too poor to pay counsel's fees, and Mr Inamdar from Bombay (Inamdar, counsel for Parchure and Gopal Godse, was from Gwalior) for Parchure and Gopal Godse. Nathuram Godse had declined to be represented by a lawyer, and had made a prayer that he should be permitted to appear in person and argue his appeal himself. His prayer was granted, so he stood in a specially constructed dock. His small defiant figure with flashing eyes and close-cropped hair offered a remarkable and immediately noticeable contrast to the lawyers who represented his accomplices. *The plea of poverty on which Godse had based his request to be present in person was only an excuse, the real reason behind the manoeuvre was a morbid desire to watch the process of his disintegration firsthand and also to exhibit himself as a fearless patriot and a passionate protagonist of Hindu ideology. He had remained completely unrepentant of his atrocious crime, he had sought this opportunity of displaying his talents before he dissolved into oblivion.* On the right-hand end of the front row sat four lawyers who were appearing for the prosecution—Mr Daphtary, Advocate General of Bombay, Messrs Petigara and Vyavaharkar, also from Bombay, and Mr Kartar Singh Chawla of our own High Court.

'There was a falling out between the three judges on the very first day of the hearing, which is mentioned in Justice Khosla's book. Thus, the decision to appoint a three judge bench proved futile. The cleft in the bench was so deep and wide that separate judgements were delivered in the appeal trial. The cause of the rift in Justice Khosla's words: I have made it a rule never to make a deep study of any case before the actual hearing begins. I usually read the judgment appealed against to acquaint myself of the salient facts and get an overall impression of the matter I have to deal with. I have always been of the view that too close a pre-study of the evidence and a mastery of the details involved hinder a fair and impartial hearing. This builds up an unconscious resistance against the arguments of counsel, for though judges are perpetually advertising the remarkable fluidity of truly judicial minds and their capacity for remaining open till the last word in a case has been uttered, eminent judges are notoriously obstinate and difficult to dislodge from their beliefs and convictions. I have known judges who come to court even more fully prepared than the lawyers engaged by the parties. I have a suspicion that they do this partly from a sense of their high duty, but also because of their desire to make an exhibition of their industry and erudition. No matter how learned and experienced the judge, if he has made a deep study of a case, he will inevitably have formed an opinion regarding its merits before he comes to court. So, he will start with a bias and it will be difficult to displace him from his position, for his subconscious mind will refuse to admit that something important escaped his close study of the case or that a certain piece of evidence was erroneously interpreted. A truly liquid mind is a very rare commodity among high judicial dignitaries. My friend and colleague Mr Justice Achchruram has always been a very industrious lawyer. He commanded an extensive and lucrative practice at the Bar before he was raised to the Bench, and he brought with him his inimitable capacity for hard work and his deep knowledge of Civil Law. Criminal Law and procedure had remained comparative strangers to him, though he had often sat on a Bench dealing with criminal matters.

For weeks before the appeal of Godse and his accomplices came up for hearing, he had been studying the bulky volumes in which the entire evidence, oral and documentary, was contained. There were in all 1,131 printed pages of foolscap size and a supplementary volume of 115 pages of cyclostyled foolscap paper. He had taken pains to look up a number of reported cases dealing with some legal aspects of the trial, and had made a note of these rulings. So, when he came to court on the morning of 2 May, he showed a complete understanding of the facts of the case as well as of the points of law raised in the memoranda of appeals. I have always had the profoundest respect for my colleague, both as a lawyer and as a judge, and I shall continue to respect his learning, but his habit of industry had a most unfortunate consequence on the first day of the Godse appeal. The case was opened by Mr Bannerjee, who started by putting forward an argument that a charge of conspiracy could not survive the consummation of the purpose of the conspiracy, and the conspirators could not be tried on multiple charges of conspiracy to murder Mahatma Gandhi and also of actually murdering him. They should have been tried for murder and abatement (sic) of murder. Mr Bannerjee's argument was that owing to this serious irregularity the trial of all the appellants was vitiated. It was, as lawyers say, a nice point, and much could be said for and against it; but no sooner had Mr Bannerjee uttered a few sentences than Mr Justice Achchruram cut him short by drawing his attention to a number of reported rulings from the various High Courts of India. Mr Bannerjee tried, in vain, to expound the law on the subject according to his own understanding of it. The merest reference to a decision which supported his argument was repulsed by a volley of rulings to the contrary. My friend Mr Justice Bhandari, as the seniormost judge of the bench, felt that he should be the one to guide and control the proceedings, which during the course of the day resolved themselves into an animated dialogue, with Mr Bannerjee being allowed to utter only a few brief and minor speeches. Justice Bhandari was greatly concerned about the unusual turn which the hearing had taken, and thought that the bench was making a far from dignified exhibition of its judicial attitude in a case which was drawing very widespread attention. He feared we might convey the impression that we had already made up our minds about the whole case and had no wish to examine the merits of any argument advanced on behalf of the convicted persons. After the day's proceedings were over, he came to my chamber and confided to me his irritation over the day's proceedings and his misgiving about the future conduct of the case. He asked me how he should deal with the situation. I agreed with him that the day had been a very unusual one, and, if the faces of the large audience were any indication, we seemed to have provided a great deal of entertainment for the gallery.

"'But he won't let the case proceed. Gopal, we can't go on like this. The lawyer should be allowed to argue his case."

"'Hm, yes. But, you know, some judges like to talk. They just can't help chipping in when counsel is arguing. It happens even in England."

"'Don't you think I should speak to him? You see, we have spent five hours over the case and we haven't advanced a single step forward."

"'Well, you might mention it to him. He won't like it."

'Mr Justice Achchruram didn't like it. In fact, he greatly resented it, and for the next few days relations between two of the members of the bench were far from cordial. They hardly spoke to one another, and each greeted the other with a scowl.' (Emphasis mine)

The entire procedure of the hearing of the appeal lasted for twenty-six sittings. Banerjee began the proceedings for the defence. He raised objections to the publication of the book *Bapu Ko Na Bacha Saka* (*I Could Not Save Bapu*) by Prof. J.C. Jain. He claimed that by writing and publishing the book, the author had committed contempt of court. He argued about the non-admissibility of a conspiracy and the double charges of accomplice in murder as well as conspirator in murder. His arguments continued till 4 May. Bannerjee was indisposed on 5 May, so Nathuram was asked to make his statement. Instead of writing or commenting on what Nathuram said in court, I quote from Justice Khosla's book: 'The highlight of the appeal before us was the discourse delivered by Nathuram Godse in his defence. He spoke for several hours, discussing, in the first instance, the facts of the case and then the motives which had prompted him to take Mahatma Gandhi's life. He had pursued the same line in the long written statement which he had filed in the trial court, the following passages taken from this statement will give some indication of his opinions and attitudes:

"'Born in a devotional Brahmin family, I instinctively came to revere

Hindu religion, Hindu history and Hindu culture. I had been intensely proud of Hindudom as a whole. Nevertheless, as I grew up, I developed a tendency to free thinking, unfettered by any superstitious allegiance to any 'ism', political or religious.

"'I have read the works of Dadabhai Naoroji, Vivekananda, Gokhale, Tilak, along with the books of ancient and modern history of India and of some prominent countries in the world like England, France, America and Russia. Not only that, I studied tolerably well the current tenets of Socialism and Communism too. But above all I studied very closely whatever Veer Savarkar and Gandhiji had written and spoken, as to my mind, these two ideologies had contributed more to mould the thought and action of modern India during the last fifty years or so, than any other single factor had done.

"'All this reading and thinking brought me to believe that, above all, it was my first duty to serve the Hindudom and the Hindu people, as a patriot and even as a humanitarian. For, is it not true that to secure the freedom and to safeguard the just interests of some thirty crores of Hindus constituted the freedom and the well-being of one-fifth of human race?

"'In 1946 or thereabouts the Muslim atrocities perpetrated on the Hindus under the government patronage of Suhrawardy in Noakhali, made our blood boil. After coming to Delhi, Gandhiji began to hold his prayer meetings in a Hindu temple in Bhangi Colony and persisted in reading passages from the Koran as a part of the prayer in that Hindu temple, in spite of the protest of the Hindu worshippers there. Of course he dared not read Gita in a mosque in the teeth of Muslim opposition. He knew what a terrible Muslim reaction there would have been if he had done so. But he could safely trample over the feelings of the tolerant Hindu. To belie this belief I was determined to prove to Gandhiji that the Hindu too could be intolerant when his honour was insulted.

"'Just after that, followed the terrible outburst of Muslim fanaticism in the Punjab and other parts of India. The Congress government began to persecute, prosecute and shoot the Hindus themselves who dared to resist the Muslim forces in Bihar, Calcutta, Punjab and other places. Our worst fears seemed to be coming true; and yet how painful and disgraceful it was for us to find that 15 of August 1947 was celebrated with illuminations and festivities, while the whole of the Punjab was set by the Muslims in flames and Hindu blood ran in rivers. The Hindu Mahasabhaites of my persuasion decided to boycott the festivities and the Congressite government, and to launch a fighting programme to check Muslim onslaughts.

"'Five crores (fifty million) of Indian Muslims have ceased to be our countrymen; virtually the non-Muslim minority in Western Pakistan has been liquidated either by the most brutal murders or by a forced tragic removal from their moorings of centuries; the same process is furiously at work in Eastern Pakistan. One hundred and ten million people have been torn from their homes, of which not less than four million are Muslims, and when I found that even after such terrible results Gandhiji continued to pursue the same policy of appeasement, my blood boiled and I could not tolerate him any longer. I do not mean to use hard words against Gandhiji personally, nor do I wish to conceal my utter dissent from and disapproval of the very foundation of his policy and methods. Gandhiji in fact succeeded in doing what the British always wanted to do in pursuance of their policy of 'Divide and Rule'. He helped them in dividing India and it is not yet certain whether their rule has ceased.

"'The accumulating provocation of 32 years, culminating in his last pro-Muslim fast, at last, goaded me to the conclusion that the existence of Gandhiji should be brought to an end immediately. 'A Satyagrahi can never fail' was his formula for declaring his own infallibility and nobody except he himself knew who a Satyagrahi was. Thus, Gandhiji became the judge and the counsel in his own case. These childish inanities and obstinacies coupled with a most severe austerity of life, ceaseless work and lofty character made Gandhiji formidable and irresistible. In a position of such absolute irresponsibility Gandhiji was guilty of blunder after blunder, failure after failure and disaster after disaster. No one single political victory can be claimed to his credit during 33 years of his political predominance.

"'So long as Gandhian method was in the ascendance (sic), frustration was the only inevitable result. He had constantly boosted his Charka, non-violence and truth. The Charka had, after 34 years of the best efforts of Gandhiji, only led to the expansion of the machine-run textile industry by over 200 per cent. It is unable even now to clothe even one per cent of the nation. As regards non-violence, it was absurd to expect 40 crores of people to regulate their lives on such a lofty plane and it broke down most conspicuously in 1942. As regards truth, the least I can say is that the truthfulness of the average Congressman is by no means of a higher order than that of the man in the street, and that very often it is untruth, in reality, masked by a thin veneer of pretended truthfulness.

"'Gandhiji's inner voice, his spiritual power and his doctrine of non-violence, of which so much is made of, all crumbled before Mr Jinnah's iron will and proved to be powerless. Having known that with his spiritual powers he could not influence Mr Jinnah, Gandhiji should have either changed his policy or could have admitted his defeat and given way to others of different political views to deal with Mr Jinnah and the Muslim League. But Gandhiji was not honest enough to do that.

"'Those who personally know me, take me as a person of quiet temperament. But when the top-rank leaders of the Congress with the consent of Gandhiji divided and tore the country—which we consider as a deity of worship — my mind became full with the thoughts of direful anger. Briefly speaking, I thought to myself and foresaw that I shall be totally ruined and the only thing that I could expect from the people would be nothing but hatred and that I shall have lost all my honour, even more valuable than my life, if I were to kill Gandhiji. After having fully considered the question, I took the final decision in the matter but I did not speak about it to anyone whatsoever. I took courage in both my hands and I did fire the shots at Gandhiji, on 30 January 1948, on the prayer grounds in Birla House. I fully and confidently believe that if there be any other court of justice beyond the one founded by the mortals, my act will not be taken as unjust. If after death there be no such place to reach or to go to, there is nothing to be said. I have resorted to the action I did purely for the benefit of the humanity. I do say that my shots were fired at the person whose policy and action had brought rack and ruin and destruction to lacs of Hindus.

"'May the country properly known as Hindustan be again united and be one, and may the people be taught to discard the defeatist mentality leading them to submit to the aggressors. This is my last wish and prayer to the Almighty.

"'My confidence about the moral side of my action has not been shaken even by the criticism levelled against it on all sides. I have no doubt honest writers of history will weigh my act and find the true value thereof on some day in future." Godse had, while talking to Apte and Karkare, claimed a measure of competence in the arts of writing and public speaking. He made full use of his talents during the trial and at the hearing of the appeal. Before us, he reiterated the arguments he had advanced before the trial judge and supplemented them with some fresh points which he had not thought of before. His main theme, however, was the nature of a righteous man's duty, his dharma. He ended his peroration on a high note of emotion, reciting verses from the Gita. The audience was visibly and audibly moved. There was a deep silence when he ceased speaking. Many women were in tears and men were coughing and searching for their handkerchiefs. The silence was accentuated and made deeper by the sound of an occasional subdued sniff or a muffled cough. *It seemed to me that I was taking part in some kind of melodrama or in a scene out of a Hollywood feature film. Once or twice I had interrupted Godse and pointed out the irrelevance of what he was saying, but my colleagues seemed inclined to hear him and the audience most certainly thought that Godse's performance was the only worthwhile part of the lengthy proceedings. A writer's curiosity in watching the interplay of impact and response made me abstain from being too conscientious in the matter. Also I said to myself: "The man is going to die soon. He is past doing any harm. He should be allowed to let off steam for the last time." I have, however, no doubt that had the audience of that day been constituted into a jury and entrusted with the task of deciding Godse's appeal, they would have brought in a verdict of "not guilty" by an overwhelming majority.'* (Emphasis mine)

(One must also realize that most of the people present in court that day were those who were affected by Partition, many of them having to flee their homes as refugees, and so, it was understandable that Nathuram's statement, masterfully written by his patron Savarkar, would have made them emotional.)

Nathuram had cleverly exploited the benevolence displayed by the judges to once again propound his philosophy of hate and intolerance. This self-anointed patriot refused to acknowledge that the non-Hindus who had, for centuries and generations, lived in India were also a part of the Indian nation, and to carry on a campaign of hate against them was tantamount to treason. But Nathuram was a fanatic and a bigot and did not posses the capability of understanding any other viewpoint which digressed from his belief. That his statement was a cleverly engineered compilation of lies and half-truths merged with highly exaggerated accounts of real incidents, made it into a very volatile diatribe against a person who was not alive to defend himself. But when one studies the history of Gandhi's last four years, one can immediately see through Godse's lies.

Godse's statement lasted till 11 May; after this, B. Bannerjee continued his arguments, and Kistayya's counsel Avasthi concluded his arguments on 24 May. On 25 May, Daftary argued the prosecution's case, followed by Dange's argument. Finally, after the replies given by Bannerjee, the hearing of the appeal came to an end on 6 June.

Since the rift between the presiding judges had failed to heal, it was impossible to arrive at a unanimous judgment. Justice Achchruram delivered his judgment separately from Justice A.N. Bhandari and Justice G.D. Khosla. Parchure was acquitted because the high court justices refused to accept his confessional statement as a voluntary statement. Kistayya was acquitted since the justices believed that he merely acted as Badge's servant and so could not be held guilty as an accomplice. This had been suggested even by Judge Atmacharan, although he had recommended a lighter sentence. The high court justices recommended that the government show leniency towards Gopal Godse due to his youth. The sentences of Nathuram V. Godse, Narayan D. Apte, Vishnu R. Karkare and Madanlal K. Pahwa were upheld. The judgment was delivered on 21 June 1949.

Although the high court was only hearing an appeal against the ruling of the special court, Justice Achchruram took it upon himself to embellish the tarnished image of the investigating police and absolved them of all wrongdoings and ruled that the critical comments made by Judge Atmacharan were not called for. While on the one hand Achchruram and Bhandari absolved the police of all wrongdoings and praised them for performing beyond the call of duty, in the case of Dr Parchure, Achchruram compared the police to demons from hell and criticized them for using draconian methods to terrify Parchure into signing a confession. Ironically, the justices issued the police a certificate of merit and condemned them as Nazis at the same time. The justices refused to accept Parchure's confession as being voluntary and acquitted him, ignoring the fact that without his help, Nathuram Godse and Narayan Apte would not have been able to acquire a gun from Gwalior. If Parchure was not guilty of helping in acquiring the murder weapon, who was?

The 315-page long judgment of Justice A.N. Bhandari and Justice G.D. Khosla was read out in court by Justice Bhandari.

◆

Appeal to the Privy Council

The convicts Nathuram Godse, Narayan Apte, Vishnu Karkare, Gopal Godse and Madanlal Pahwa appealed to the privy council against the judgment of the Punjab High Court. The appeal was made under the 'Paupers Act', instituted to provide facilities to those who could not spend money to avail of the justice system. The gang of self-proclaimed patriots appealed for mercy to their colonial masters. John Mega appeared for the accused. The main argument of the appeal was: (1) The judicial pardon granted to the approver was given illegally and improperly. Thus, all the witnesses corroborating the testimony of the approver must be termed illegal and rejected; (2) According to the law, the charge of conspiracy was unsustainable. Various charges were clubbed together, which went against the tenets of criminal law. Many testimonies were recorded, which were in violation of the Indian Witness Act; (3) The courts in India had not followed proper procedures of establishing guilt in a criminal matter; (4) The conspiracy charge against Madanlal was unsustainable, since he was held not guilty in another charge related to the conspiracy.

The judicial committee of the privy council refused to hear the appeal and returned it on 12 October.

◆

Appeal to the Governor-General

After the privy council rejected their appeal, Special Judge S.S. Dulaar of Delhi issued a death warrant for Nathuram V. Godse and Narayan

D. Apte on 26 October. The execution was set for 15 November 1949, at Ambala Jail.

Nathuram Godse's parents appealed for mercy for their son to the Governor-General; so did Narayan Apte and his wife. At 11:30 a.m. on 7 November, the Governor-General's office issued a one-line press statement, which said that 'the Governor General has declined to intervene in the matter.' The fates of Nathuram V. Godse and Narayan D. Apte were sealed. They would now be 'hanged by their necks till dead', as sentenced. Gandhi's sons Manilal and Ramadas appealed to the prime minister of India and to the Governor-General to commute the death sentence, terming it to be in violation of Gandhi's belief in non-violence and his ideology of 'punishing the sin, not the sinner'. Their appeal was ignored.

◆

Execution

I do regard death sentence as contrary to Ahimsa. Only He takes life who gives it.

—M.K. Gandhi, *Harijan*, 19 March 1937

Justice G.D. Khosla has narrated an eyewitness account of the execution of Nathuram Godse and Narayan Apte in his book *The Murder of the Mahatma* in the chapter 'Crimes of Nathuram'. I have reproduced his description of the execution verbatim, below, and I quote:

'The final chapter of this sad story takes us to the Central Gaol, Ambala, where Nathuram Godse and Apte were executed on the morning of 15 November 1949. After the conclusion of the trial, they had been sent there to await the decision of the appeal preferred by them. The two condemned prisoners were led out of their cells with their hands pinioned behind them. Godse walked in front. His step occasionally faltered. His demeanour and general appearance evidenced a state of nervousness and fear. He tried to fight against it and keep up a bold exterior by shouting every few seconds the slogan "*Akhand Bharat!*" (Undivided India!), but his voice had a slight croak in it, and the vigour with which he had argued his case at the trial and in the High Court seemed to have been all but expended. The desperate cry was taken up by Apte, who shouted "*Amar rahe!*" (May live eternally!). His loud and firm tone made an uncanny contrast to Godse's, at times, almost feeble utterance.

'The Superintendent of the gaol and the District Magistrate of Ambala who had come to certify the due execution of the High Court's order observed that, unlike Godse, Apte was completely self-possessed and displayed not the slightest sign of nervousness. He walked with a firm step with his shoulders thrown back and his head held high. Taller than Godse by several inches, he appeared to dominate over him. It was said afterwards that Godse had, during his last days in gaol, repented of his deed and declared that were he to be given another chance he would spend the rest of his life in the promotion of peace and the service of his country. Apte, on the other hand, maintained an unrelenting attitude. Till the very end, he refused to admit his guilt, nor did he plead his innocence in the cringing tones of a beaten adversary.

'A single gallows had been prepared for the execution of both. Two ropes, each with a noose, hung from the high crossbar in parallel lines. Godse and Apte were made to stand side by side, the black cloth bags were drawn over their heads and tied at the necks. After adjusting the nooses, the executioner stepped off the platform and pulled the lever to release the trap doors under the feet of the condemned men.

'Apte died almost at once and his still body swung in a slow oscillating movement, but Godse, though unconscious and unfeeling, continued to wriggle and display signs of life in the shivering of his legs and the convulsing of his body for fifteen minutes.

'The dead bodies were cremated inside the gaol, the ground where the pyres had been erected was ploughed up and the earth and ashes taken to the Ghaggar River and secretly submerged at a secluded spot.'

Thus, what begun as a tragedy ended in a tragedy, with the waste of two young lives. The fate that befell Nathuram Godse and Narayan Apte would not have met with the approval of their victim. The barbaric practice of avenging a murder with officially sanctioned murder was enforced, disguised as justice.

Vishnu Karkare went back to Ahmednagar after his release, where he spent the rest of his days as a hotelier and patron of the performing arts. He died on 4 April 1974; his wife died in 2003. The Deccan Guest House is run by his adopted daughter in Ahmednagar.

Madanlal Pahwa lived in Mumbai and ran a small business as a dealer in cotton and paper waste, supplying to the paper and board mills. Anytime he found someone who would buy him a few drinks and kababs, Madanlal would narrate his colourful exploits in Gwalior and his role in the murder of Gandhi. He died in the year 2001; he was survived by his wife, but her fate is not known.

Badge was given a tenement in the campus of the police commissioner's office in Bombay, where he lived under protection till his death. Badge continued making chain mail vests and tiger claws for his patrons. What happened to Badge, his wife and children is not known.

Dattatreya Parchure, after his acquittal, returned to his medical practice in Gwalior. He died in the eighties after suffering from Parkinson's disease. After his acquittal, he denied having been involved in the conspiracy till his death. The Parchure Vada still stands in Gwalior.

Shankar Kistayya disappeared into the obscurity of the impoverished Indian masses after his acquittal. Nothing is known about his life after he was acquitted by the high court in 1949.

Gopal Godse, Nathuram's hero-worshipping younger brother, was the last surviving member of the gang of murderers; he lived in Pune with his family. After his release from prison, he was once again imprisoned in the mid-sixties. After languishing in obscurity till the nineties, Gopal become a mascot of the resurgent Hindu right-wing organizations of the Sangh Parivar. He enjoyed a brief innings under the limelight. Gopal died of old age on 26 November 2005.

Nothing is known about Manorama Salvi, Narayan Apte's lover, not even whether she delivered his child or not. If she did, what happened to it? How did the unfortunate Manorama survive the ignominy of being an unwed mother? Narayan Apte, as was his wont, had left behind a lot of loose ends in his personal life too. The Apte family has adopted anonymity.

V.D. Savarkar, the Hindu Mahasabha ideologue, father of radical Hinduism and definitely the inspiration and patron of Gandhi's murder, was acquitted because the prosecution did not vigorously pursue the case against him. Acquitting him in the case was also a political necessity.

Patel had admitted that the government had 'annoyed the Muslims, we could not afford to anger the Hindus too.' The investigating officer Nagarvala refused to accept that Savarkar was not involved in the murder conspiracy. The then police commissioner Bharucha, after meeting Savarkar, told the home minister of Bombay, Morarji Desai, that 'Savarkar behaved very guiltily' in the aftermath of Gandhi's murder. Limaye, who had been detained earlier, told Nagarvala that if Nathuram Godse was the murderer, Apte must have been with him and that they must have consulted Savarkar. V.D. Savarkar continued to propagate his version of fanatic Hinduism till his death on 27 February 1966. The Sanghi government has installed Savarkar's portrait in Parliament, where it gazes at Gandhi's statue.

The 9 mm Berretta semi-automatic pistol no. 606824 remains locked in a sealed cupboard in the premises of the Gandhi National Museum, Raj Ghat, New Delhi; its career of dispensing death is over. From its birth in Italy, it had made a long journey through Europe, Africa and Asia to finally lie rotting in a cupboard. In its short working life, it participated in one of the most gruesome wars of the last century, the Second World War, passed through many hands, and finally landed in the hands of a fanatical murderer on 28 January. On 30 January, three bullets emerged through its short barrel and hit Gandhi at point blank range. After this, the gun was fired by forensic experts and then packed, sealed and mothballed.

XIV

KAPUR COMMISSION[*]

Conspiracy is a black, vicious enigma, elusive and deluding like a shadowy spectre, easy to assert, difficult to prove.

—Tapan Ghosh, compiler and editor of
The Gandhi Murder Trial

On 12 October 1964, Gopal V. Godse, Vishnu R. Karkare and Madanlal K. Pahwa were released from prison after serving life sentences for their role in the murder of Gandhi. When the three reached Poona, their friends decided to welcome them as heroes. A function was planned to felicitate them and to commemorate their deed.

A Satya Vinayak Puja was organized at Udyan Mangal Karyalaya on 12 November 1964. The invitations were sent out in the name of M.G. Ghaisas. The following is an English translation of the Marathi invitation: 'Shri Gajanan Prasanna. In respect of love—To rejoice the release from jail of Shri Gopalrao Godse, the brother of Deshbhakt, Patriot, the late Shri Nathuram V. Godse, Shri Vishnupant Karkare and Shri Madanlal Pahwa, we their friends are going to perform Shri Satya Vinayak Puja and congratulate them by inviting them here: You are therefore requested to remain present for this ceremony along with your friends. Yours, M.G. Ghaisas. Time: Thursday, 12-11-1964 5:30 p.m. To 7:30 p.m., Place: Udayan Karyalaya, 61 Shaniwar Peth, Poona-2.'

---

[*]To ensure authenticity and to maintain the sanctity of the Kapur Commission's report, the language of the extracts has not been corrected. The numbers appended to the extracted paragraphs reproduced here are as they appear in the commission's published report.

In an affidavit filed in the Bombay High Court, M.G. Ghaisas, who was detained as a consequence of the function, said that about fifty invitations were sent out, but intelligence reports stated that between 125 to 200 persons attended the function.

G.V. Ketkar, grandson of 'Lokmanya' B.G. Tilak, former editor of *Kesari* and *Tarun Bharat* and Hindu Mahasabha ideologue, presided over the function. While speaking after the puja, after Gopal Godse and Karkare had narrated their prison experiences, Ketkar revealed that he had been aware of the plan to kill Gandhi much in advance and that he had been told about this by Nathuram Godse himself. He said that Godse had indicated his intention at a public meeting held at Shivaji Mandir, when he referred to Gandhi's oft repeated wish to live to the age of 125 years. Nathuram had said in Marathi, '*Pan tumhala tevdha jagu denaar kon?*' (Who will allow you to live till then?) Ketkar claimed that he, along with another veteran Balukaka Kanitkar, heard this part of Nathuram's speech and were perturbed by it. Ketkar assured Balukaka that he would confront 'Nathya' and find out if he implied that Gandhi would be killed and if that is what he meant, he would dissuade him from proceeding with any such plans. In the meantime, he suggested that Balukaka should write to the government and inform them. Gopal Godse interrupted Ketkar and asked him to be careful of what he was saying, but there was no holding back Ketkar. He went on to say, he had confronted Nathuram and asked him whether what he meant was that Gandhi should be killed. Ketkar said that Nathuram had replied in the affirmative and had said that he would ensure that Gandhi did not cause any more trouble. Ketkar also said that he was acquainted with Badge and after the bomb attack on Gandhi on 20 January 1948, he had met Badge who told him that Apte, Godse, Karkare and Badge were involved in the attack, that the plan was to kill Gandhi and that Godse and Apte were on their way back to kill him. Badge had told Ketkar that they were very determined to achieve success.

This meeting and Ketkar's speech were extensively reported in the Bombay newspapers. The correspondent of the *Indian Express* in Poona interviewed Ketkar and filed a detailed story which was published. It was reported that people garlanded Nathuram's photograph. A Gita and a Bhagva Zenda, the Hindu Mahasabha's saffron pennant, were displayed, which were claimed to have been held by Nathuram when he ascended the gallows and a dhoti allegedly worn by him at the hanging was displayed at the meeting too. Ketkar, it is said, took off his dhoti and put on the one allegedly worn by Nathuram as a mark of his respect for Gandhi's murderer.

The bragging, on Ketkar's part, got him and Gopal Godse into a lot of trouble. Ketkar, Ghaisas and Gopal Godse were arrested and imprisoned. There were debates in the Maharashtra Assembly and in Parliament. As a result, the Union government constituted a commission of inquiry on 22 March 1965, headed by Gopal Sawrup Pathak, MP, On 21 November 1966, on Pathak being appointed as a minister in the Union Cabinet, retired Justice J.L. Kapur of the Supreme Court of India was appointed in his place to head the inquiry. The terms of reference of the commission were, to ascertain: (a) whether any persons, in particular Shri Gajanan Viswanath Ketkar, of Poona, had prior information of the conspiracy of Nathuram Vinayak Godse and others to assassinate Mahatma Gandhi; (b) whether any of them had communicated the said information to any authorities of the Government of Bombay or of the Government of India, in particular whether the aforementioned Shri Ketkar had conveyed the said information to the late Bal Gangadhar Kher, the then-premier of Bombay, through the late Balukaka Kanitkar; (c) if so, what action was taken by the Government of Bombay, in particular by the late Bal Gangadhar Kher, and the Government of India on the basis of the said information.

This notification was amended by notification No. 31/28/68 PII.I(A) dated 28 October 1968, making clause (c) read as follows: (c) if so, what action was taken by the Government of Bombay, in particular by the late Bal Gangadhar Kher, and the Government of India and by the officers of the said governments on the basis of the said information

To assist the commission, G.N. Vaidya was engaged by the Government of Maharashtra and K.S. Chawla, barrister-at-law, was appointed by the Government of India. The latter replaced their counsel and engaged B.B. Lal, advocate, who appeared before the commission from 10 February 1968. When G.N. Vaidya was raised to the bench, R.B. Kotwal took his place. The commission examined 101 witnesses, and 407 documents were produced by the two governments and the witnesses who appeared before the commission. The examination of the witnesses took 162 days at various places where the commission sat for the convenience of the witnesses: Bombay, New Delhi, Dharwar, Nagpur, Poona, Baroda and Chandigarh.

The report is in six volumes. The evidence recorded by the commission is contained in five volumes and the documents produced before it are contained in another five volumes. Besides this, the record of the proceedings before Judge Atmacharan had also to be perused as some of the statements were made part of the evidence before the commission. The case diaries of the Delhi Police's investigation into the bomb case and the murder case and the crime report of the Bombay Police, as also some of the files produced by the Government of India, director of the Intelligence Bureau and inspector-general of police, Delhi, have been made part of the records. Chapter II of the commission's report, the section headed 'Inquiries – Delhi,' Para 3.3, states: 'After the funeral, a meeting was called at a very short notice at the house of the Home Minister in the evening of 31 January 1948. According to R.N. Bannerjee's statement before Pathak, as witness No. 17, the following were present: Prime Minister Nehru, Deputy Prime Minister Sardar Patel, B.G. Kher, Premier of Bombay, Rajagopalachari, Governor of West Bengal and Bannerjee and Sanjeevi. D.W. Mehra's note Ex. 10-A dated 1 February 1948, besides these names included the names of Rajkumari Amrit Kaur, Morarji Desai, the Chief Commissioner and himself.'

At the meeting, Sanjeevi read out the confessional statement of Madanlal Pahwa and said that he had sent a copy to Bombay with two police officials who were flown from Delhi to Bombay on 21 January 1948. Sanjeevi complained that the two police officers returned after two or three days and complained that the Bombay Police had asked them to return to Delhi.

(This was what the director of Intelligence Bureau told the prime minister and home minister of the Union of India in the presence of the then- premier and home minister of the province of Bombay. This was a serious allegation by a senior policeman against a subordinate police officer. The police officer at the receiving end was Jamshed 'Jimmy' Nagarvala, assistant commissioner of police and head of CID, Bombay. Nagarvala in his testimony before the commission denied that Madanlal's confession was given to him. At the time when the commission began proceedings, Sanjeevi had died. Nagarvala and U.H. Rana, another senior police officer from Poona, appeared before the commission to defend their actions.)

At the meeting, it was revealed that Sanjeevi gave no information regarding the investigation post 20 January to either the deputy commissioner of Delhi or to Bannerjee. Bannerjee commented: 'I will put it to gross incompetency and lethargy on part of Sanjeevi that he did not care to inform either me or to remind the Bombay Police as to what action they had been taking.'

Deposing before the commission, Bannerjee stated that besides the gentlemen he had named before, Shankarrao Deo was also present at the meeting. He said, 'This was the first intimation that we, from Pandit Nehru downwards, got that there was a confessional statement and certain information was contained in it which if properly utilized would have resulted in the arrest of those persons who were participants in the murder of Mahatma Gandhi. In the statement, the particulars and haunts of some of the persons who were subsequently accused and convicted of murder were given. If the police had been vigilant, it should have been possible for them to have arrested those persons.'

Bannerjee continued, 'None of us knew about the particulars of this conspiracy. Sanjeevi never gave us any information about it. When he was asked why he had not done so he just said, "he was sorry he just did not do it". I put this due to the incompetency and lethargy of Sanjeevi not to have informed or to have ordered the Bombay Police to send their men here or to have reminded the Bombay Police in regard to the information which was sent to them.'

(This is a very surprising statement by a senior official. The dispute between Sardar Patel, the Union home minister and Jawaharlal Nehru, the prime minister, had arisen because it was alleged that Nehru used to constantly interfere in the affairs of the home ministry. Patel complained about this to Gandhi too. Surprisingly, after the bomb attack on 20 January, till 30 January, the Prime Minister's Office did not enquire about the progress in the investigation or try to find out what had been learnt from the arrested man even once. As home minister, neither did Sardar enquire about the progress in the bomb attack case.)

Writing about the inquiry carried out by Nagarvala in Bombay, the commission states in Para 2.34: 'The scene now shifts to Bombay where on an information given by Prof Jain investigation was carried on between 21 January and 30 January 1948. This is an unfortunate chapter of opportunities missed, errors committed and of assuming exaggerated notions about one's self. After the explosion of the bomb Prof Jain of the Ruia College got a little unnerved because Madanlal had disclosed to him before going to Delhi that he and his companions were going to murder Mahatma Gandhi which he (Jain) had considered to be a mere boast though in fact he did not take the matter so lightly. But he was hesitant, dithering and failed to give this information to any authority'.

2.36: What Nagarvala did on being given the information Prof Jain had given to Morarji Desai: 'Nagarvala promptly got into touch with his contacts and his informers, instructing them to locate Karkare and his associates. He learnt from Ahmednagar that Karkare was not there.' (Neither did Nagarvala speak to police officers in Ahmednagar nor did he care to brief them about the information he had got from either Morarjee Desai or what Sanjeevi or Rana had told him. He asked his brother, who lived in Ahmednagar, about Karkare's whereabouts.)

2.37: It is not necessary at this stage to give a resume of what Nagarvala did or what steps he took. But briefly stated, he learnt that one Balraj Mehta and Avtar Singh of the Sher-e-Punjab Hotel, of Bombay, were in the conspiracy. Information from Ahmednagar was that Badge of Poona, a dealer in illicit arms, was a close associate of Karkare; and his contacts informed him that Savarkar was the real instigator of the conspiracy and his illness was feigned. Savarkar's house was kept under watch. Nagarvala's informants told him that there were many other conspirators, about 20 Punjabis and Maharashtrians, with a large following. Efforts were made to find out the haunts of those persons. From 22nd onwards the Police tried to find out the whereabouts of Karkare and Badge, particularly in Hindu Mahasabha Bhavan at Parel. Watch was kept on the Arya Pathik Ashram where two suspicious looking Punjabis were staying. They were suspected to be associates of Balraj Mehta. (After the failed attempt on the 20th, Godse and Apte had stayed at Arya Pathik Ashram for two days. During that stay, Apte had spent two nights with Manorama Salvi there too.)

2.38: Rana the D.I.G. (CID) arrived in Bombay on the 27th and stayed with Nagarvala who told him of the steps he had taken up to then and both of them had a long distance talk with Sanjeevi, the D.I.B. and then gave him full details of what had been done uptill then. Rana had taken with him the statement of Madanlal, which he showed to Nagarvala who read one or two pages, but Rana took it back from him saying it was too long and promised to send him a copy from Poona, which he never did.

2.39: After the murder when Nagarvala learnt the name of Nathuram Godse, he arrested the various suspects and interrogated Savarkar's secretary Damle and his bodyguard Kasar. Limaye who had been detained earlier told the police that if Nathuram Godse was the murderer, Apte must have been with him and that they must have consulted Savarkar.

Bannerjee was cross-examined by Vaidya, counsel for Government of Mahrashtra, and Bannerjee said that when they came back from the cremation, a meeting was called at a very short notice where everybody was in a mournful mood, the Sardar (Patel) asked Sanjeevi what had happened and he came out with the allegation that the names had been sent to Bombay police and nothing was done there. It was that part which was emphasized by Sanjeevi there. Bannerjee added, 'Sardar Patel was in great anguish and so were we all but I told Sardar Patel that he could not have done anything more than to ask the police to be vigilant.'

In Para 3.9, Bannerjee said that after 30 January, the government felt rather guilty about not having taken preventive or punitive action against the RSS; an informal decision at the post-funeral meeting was that the RSS should be banned immediately and secret instructions were passed to provincial governments the same night, but somehow or the other the news of the ban leaked out and the leaders of the movement went underground.

(This was an indication how far up the government and administration Hindu extremists had infiltrated that a decision taken in a closed-door meeting attended only by some very senior ministers and senior home department and police officials also leaked out.)

Questions were raised in the Bombay Provincial Council. Members grilled Home Minister Morarji Desai. A member asked the home minister whether the police had lost track of Nathuram Godse. The minister replied saying that after the arrest of Madanlal a copy of his statement was taken to the Bombay CID. The arrest was not made because it was considered inexpedient as by doing so the other conspirators would have gone underground. Therefore, after consultations between the Bombay and the Delhi Police, it was decided that for the moment no arrest should be made. The Bombay Police was on the track of the conspirators but they were not all in Bombay.

Asked if photographs could have been procured of those persons, the reply was that all of them were not at one place. However, photographs of Narayan Apte, Nathuram Godse and Vishnu Karkare were on police records then. (On the 29th, when briefed about Madanlal's confession, Rao Saheb Gurtu of Poona Police immediately pulled out Nathuram, Apte and Badge's police files and their photographs, and gave them to Rana twenty-four hours before Bapu's murder.)

These were the questions and answers given in a Provincial Assembly. (They very clearly show that Desai was misleading the House. The Bombay Police had stated that they were in the dark about the identities of the conspirators till after the murder.)

Nagarvala vehemently denied that the two police officers showed him Madanlal's statement. He claimed that they only showed him a chit bearing some words scribbled in Urdu. He also denied that Rana had given him the report. (On the 27th, when he met Nagarvala, Rana was carrying an English translation of Madanlal's confession. Nagarvala learnt Nathuram Godse's identity for the first time after the murder. But the home minister had claimed in the Assembly that the police was on the track of the conspirators. What made him say so?)

After Judge Atamacharan made adverse remarks against the police in his judgment, the Government of India called for an explanation from the condemned police officials. The replies show the course of investigation of the bomb case both in Delhi and in Bombay and what the police had to say in reply to the learned judge's criticism. The commission first dealt with Sanjeevi's explanation and then with what Nagarvala had to say as to the investigation process in Bombay.

(The Kapur Commission examined many confidential records to investigate and find out which police department had slipped up in exposing the conspirators in time to prevent the murder. Looking at its findings, a shocking scenario emerges. All the departments involved in the investigation after the bomb attack on 20th committed blunders and showed a distinct lack of efficiency and intelligence in investigations: their approach was lackadaisical, to say the least. All the four concerned departments were guilty of criminal negligence and unacceptable blunders; the three senior officials handling the investigation were most guilty: Sanjeevi, who had come to Delhi after building a very formidable reputation in Madras Province, Nagarvala who was the blue-eyed boy of the home minister of Bombay and a cop with a formidable reputation in Bombay Police, and U.H. Rana, a senior officer of Poona CID. The findings of the Kapur Commission paint a very sorry picture of the police, especially these three officers.)

In his note to the Union home ministry, Sanjeevi claimed that the Delhi Police had done all that they could have and blamed the Bombay Police for all that had gone wrong. Para 3.34 states: 'Sanjeevi himself visited the scene of occurrence and made inquiries from the Police Superintendent of New Delhi. The next day he ordered 2 Police officers to fly to Bombay "to contact Nagarvala, Deputy Commissioner of Police Bombay, and Rao Saheb Gurtu, A.D.I.G. (C.I.D.) Poona". They took with them Ex. 5-A which officers of the Law Commission, after some effort, found with the original case diary of the bomb (attack) case lying somewhere in the Delhi District Record Room.' (Exhibit 5-A is the translation of the first confession made by Madanlal Pahwa on the night between 20 and 21 January 1948.)

The commission's report, Para 3.35: The Delhi Police continued with its investigation and ordered its C.I.D. to be on the look out for the conspirators whose descriptions were given in a document Ex. 244 which is a bundle of corrections, contradictory descriptions and a mere look at it will show its worthlessness.

3.37: The note then proceeds to state the steps taken at Bombay. It mentions that the two officers with all the information furnished to the Delhi Police by Madanlal flew to Bombay and stayed at the Universal National Restaurant and met Nagarvala the next day and gave him all the information that they possessed. Nagarvala told them that he also had received information about the case and had deputed special men to locate the wanted persons. He warned them that nobody should know about their presence in Bombay and so they should not stay in the city because if the suspected persons came to know of their arrival the whole plan of their arrest would be 'ruined'. He ordered the police officers to go about in Mufti (plain clothes). When the two officers met Nagarvala at his office, they claim that they gave him the facts of the case and also showed him the note of Madanlal's statement from which Nagarvala took extracts, Nagarvala vehemently denied this. 'The Delhi Police Officers told him that one of the accused was the editor of the *Agranee* or the *Hindu Rashtra* newspaper. The description of all the accused persons as disclosed by Madanlal, was communicated to him.' The Police Officers again met Nagarvala and he told them, 'his information was that there were more persons in this conspiracy. He said that there were about 20 persons. He added that he had made special arrangements for Karkare in Bombay, Poona and Ahmednagar. About the other persons connected with this case, he said that he had located three or four.' He also disclosed to them the scheme to locate all the offenders and to carry out their simultaneous arrests, his reason being that if only a few were arrested, the others would go underground. He also told them that he would accompany them to Ahmednagar as soon as he got the necessary information and asked one of his inspectors to arrange their lodging so that nobody should know about their presence. He also told them not to give their Delhi address at the hotel, and that he would consult his Home Minister and will take further action against the accused (at that time there were no accused except Madanlal, the others were suspects). The same day again they went to the Bombay C.I.D. Office where they were told by an Inspector that their presence was no longer required. The Inspector also told them that Bombay Officers had been deputed to arrest the other suspects who had not been located till then. In regard to Karkare and the editor of *Agranee* or *Hindu Rashtra*, he told them that an Inspector from Ahmednagar was arriving the next day at Bombay, and they would then arrange for their arrest.

3.39: The next day, i.e. 23 January 1948, the note says, the Delhi Police officers went to the Deputy Commissioner's office but could not meet him. A C.I.D. Inspector told them that the inspector from Ahmednagar had arrived and he had been told to search for the editor of *Agranee* or the *Hindu Rashtra*, which again appears to be a wrong statement or misunderstanding by the Delhi Officers. Deputy Superintendent Jaswant Singh then asked for information regarding Karkare and his associates and the Bombay C.I.D. Inspector gave him the following name as being Karkare's associates: i) Badge of Poona. ii) Avtar Singh, Punjabi Sikh of Amritsar. iii) Talwar of Karachi, then in Bombay. iv) Balraj Mehta of Lahore, then in Shivaji Park in Bombay.

3.40: Nagarvala who arrived at about 12:30 p.m. told the Police Officers that he was doing his best to arrest the wanted persons and that the presence of the Delhi Police was not required at Bombay and he ordered them to return. On this Jaswant Singh, Deputy Superintendent of Police, Delhi, drew Nagarvala's attention to Madanlal's statement regarding Karkare and the editor of *Agranee* or the *Hindu Rashtra* and asked that as soon as they were arrested, they should be sent to Delhi. The Delhi Officers handed over to the C.I.D. Inspector a brief note on the case, with the names and the description of the accused wanted, as far as I knew then. (Of the handing over of this note, there is no evidence except this cryptic reference. No questions were put to Nagarvala, although he was questioned at length and was examined for a good few days. In a subsequent affidavit in reply to the commission's questionnaire, Nagarvala denied any such document having been given to his officers.)

The Delhi officers returned to Delhi and complained to Sanjeevi about the treatment they received in Bombay. V. Shankar, secretary to the Union home minister, in a note, expressed surprise that the Delhi officers did not stay back in Bombay to assist in the investigation there. In his statement before the commission, Rai Sahib Rikhikesh, superintendent of police, CID, stated that these officers stayed in Bombay too long and should have returned earlier.

3.42: The Deputy Inspector General of Police, (C.I.D.) Poona, U.H. Rana was in Delhi, he was summoned by Sanjeevi in the presence of the Superintendent of C.I.D., Delhi. The D.I.G. was given the report of the two Delhi Police Officers and his attention was drawn to the importance of locating the absconding accused. A copy of the detailed statement of Madanlal was given to him. Both he and Sanjeevi went over it, and the D.I.G. was asked to fly to Bombay but he did not, as he could not. (If he could not, one would have thought that another officer could have been sent by air to deliver the statement to Nagarvala.) He left by train via Allahabad (and wasted 24 hours in Allahabad) and reached Bombay only on 27 evening.

3.43: This acquiescence in this circuitous route is corroborative of Rana's statement that 'no one expected the conspirators to strike so soon, certainly not Sanjeevi'. (So according to senior police officers the killers did not play fair by making another attempt so soon after their failed attempt!)

(On 27 evening, most probably inspired by the knowledge of the lavish hospitality provided by Jimmy Nagarvala, on arriving in Bombay, Rana went straight to his home.) Sanjeevi describes the phone call he received from Rana and Nagarvala. 'On 27th evening Rana rang me up from Bombay and told me that he had seen Nagarvala, and that Nagarvala would give me an explanation for what had happened to the two Delhi Police Officers at Bombay. Nagarvala told me that he had good reason for not allowing the two Delhi Police Officers to move about freely in Bombay. He told me of the information that he and the Bombay Police had of a conspiracy to kidnap Mahatma Gandhi. He told me that it was a very big organization with about 20 principal conspirators, each assisted by 20 persons and in possession of considerable quantities of firearms and other lethal weapons. I asked him about the absconding accused whose names or descriptions were given to the Delhi Police by Madanlal. Nagarvala told me that he would send a detailed note on the investigation made at Bombay City and elsewhere in the Province by air the next day.'

(The report was on Sanjeevi's desk on 31 January morning, the day after Gandhi was murdered.

This note does not state whether Sanjeevi asked if Nagarvala had been given the names and descriptions of the persons named by Madanlal. Nagarvala also does not make any reference to this beyond saying that he would send a progress report by air the next day. There is nothing to show that Sanjeevi pressed Nagarvala to tell him if he had done anything to trace those who were named by Madanlal, he also did not show any anxiety about their arrest or even tried to find out who they were or whether they had been located at all. On the other hand, Patel's replies in the Constituent Assembly made on 6 February 1948 show that the Bombay and Delhi police were in accord on the steps taken and on the question of the proposal to make simultaneous arrests to prevent some of the accused going underground. Who was providing false information to the Union home minister? Or was he protecting his policemen?)

3.45: The note then goes on to say Nagarvala did not write to Sanjeevi. On the 30th he sent a letter which reached Sanjeevi on 3 February, a copy of that letter was received through an officer who came by air from Bombay on 1 February.

Para 3.50 of the commission's report deals with Para 11 of Sanjeevi's note. (It is now definitely known that from 23 to 28 January, Godse was in Bombay. He flew from the Bombay aerodrome to Delhi on the 28th morning. The window of 22 to 28 January was a long enough period for the Bombay Police to find out who the editor of *Agranee* or *Hindu Rashtra* was. As long as the Delhi Police did not have full information in regard to the identity and correct description of this person, they could not possibly spot him when he arrived in Delhi. He had completely changed his clothes, and on 30th evening, was wearing a military khaki jacket, and went into the prayer grounds with the large crowds that congregated there.) 'In these circumstances, the Delhi Police did all that was possible. In his observations the Judge has, unfortunately, not distinguished between the Delhi and the Bombay Police. He was not aware of the real position. He did not know that the Bombay Police had not taken all the action necessary on the information conveyed from Delhi. Even on the evidence that he had before him, his observations against the Delhi Police cannot be justified'.

If T.G. Sanjeevi Pillai had shown the same zeal in saving the life of Gandhi as he did in defending the reputation of his department, history would have been different. The Kapur Commission's report states, 'Sanjeevi is unfortunately dead and this is the only record of what he did or did not do in regard to Mahatma Gandhi's life and safety.'

H.V.R. Iyengar, secretary to the Ministry of Home Affairs, wrote in a note on receipt of the explanations he received from Sanjeevi and Nagarvala: 'Secondly, while it is clear that Bombay Police took all possible steps to arrest Karkare and Badge, they do not appear to have taken any notice of Godse. Admittedly his name was not mentioned in Madanlal's statement but there was a description of him as the editor of the *Hindu Rashtra* or the *Agranee*. According to D.I.B.'s (Sanjeevi) report the investigating officers from Delhi took with them to Bombay on 21 January a statement (Annexure V to D.I.B.'s report-Slip 'T') which mentioned the editor of this paper. Nagarvala says that these officers did not give him any information other than that they wanted Karkare. Here is a discrepancy which cannot be reconciled without further examination.'

Iyengar continued, 'I have put to the D.I.B. the view that as soon as it became clear that there was a conspiracy among certain Maharashtra Brahmins from Poona, Ahmednagar and the neighbourhood to commit assassination, plain-clothesmen from that part of the Bombay Province should have been summoned to Delhi, on the chance that they might have been able to identify these persons if they came to Birla House. Sanjeevi says that as the Bombay Police did not take the idea of conspiracy to assassinate very seriously, the responsibility was really theirs. Personally I do not accept this view and that there was a failure in Delhi to insist on this precaution. It may not have been successful in preventing the assassination, but it was certainly worth trying.

'I think the Bombay Police are to blame more seriously because they refused to take note of the idea of a conspiracy to assassinate seriously, although every rule of common-sense pointed in that direction'.

(This was a very severe comment from one of the senior-most bureaucrats serving the Union government, indicting both the police departments severely.)

The two letters of Nagarvala, dated 30 and 31 January, one on the day of the murder and the other a day after, make for interesting reading as they show how an obstinate mind refuses to acknowledge reality.

'The first letter shows that Madanlal's statement in the Press showing (sic) that "he had come from Bombay" led to the initiation of investigations in Bombay. In the course of preliminary investigations names of Balraj Mehta, Karkare, Talwar, Badge, Avtar Singh (proprietor of the Sher-e-Punjab Hotel), Chavan and Somnath Kapoor transpired, of whom Avtar Singh and Chavan were under detention. Balraj had been identified and a tail put on him. Karkare and Badge were the two Maharashtrian companions of Balraj and Somnath Kapoor who were both Punjabis, Badge had been seen in Ahmednagar three days earlier.' (This illustrates how careless the investigation conducted by Nagarvala and his subordinates was. Badge was at that time hiding in Poona. During the Red Fort Trial, Nagarvala had said that they were looking for Badge since the 24th but he was hiding in Poona.) 'On the 27th and arrangements had been made to bring informants from Ahmednagar to Bombay who knew both Karkare and Badge, the object being to get them (Badge and Karkare) identified and to arrest them. Karkare's rendezvous in Bombay was known to the police and if he came to Bombay he would be arrested but Talwar had not been identified and inquiries were going on.'

'From investigation it appears that there were 21 Punjabis and Maharashtrians in the conspiracy and they had 20 workers under each one of them. The object of the gang was to drive out Muslims from the Indian Dominion. With that object they had collected arms and ammunition and it was also learnt that Col. Mohan Singh of the INA had organized the gang and he had the support of the Akali leader Master Tara Singh. But the information had not yet been corroborated. There was also a suggestion that one of the Sikh refugees had been sent by the gang to the Speaker of the Uttar Pradesh Assembly Shri Purshotamdas Tandon for further consultation as to their plan. The opinion amongst the members of the gang was that it was easy to win over the Delhi Police and their object was to kidnap Gandhiji. But the letter made it clear that this was only an information which had been gathered, it as to be seen if it was correct. Nobody had been arrested but a fair amount of progress had been made in the investigation.

'The general policy which Nagarvala proposed to follow was (and Rana agreed with him) that they might arrest Karkare and Badge which was not likely to (a) rouse any suspicion because Karkare had been named by Madanlal and Badge was always with Karkare and they were known to the police to be good friends. Rana agreed with Nagarvala that arrest of others should wait till the Information collected by the Delhi Police, Poona Provincial C.I.D. and the Bombay City C.I.D. was pooled together. The Home Minister of Bombay and Rana had entrusted the case to him (Nagarvala) for the Province of Bombay and Nagarvala was hoping to produce concrete results.

'The letter of 31 January, said that Nagarvala had arrested Balraj Mehta, Somnath Kapoor, Kasar, bodyguard of Savarkar and Damle, his secretary. It had also transpired that Godse had seen Savarkar along with one Apte on the eve of their departure to Delhi. Kasar and Damle had not stated what conversation these two had with Savarkar during their

40 minutes interview but they had admitted that these two had access to the house of Savarkar without any restriction.' If Madanlal was brought to Bombay, they would be able to 'drag out Madanlal and get all facts and details out of him'.

A detailed analysis of Nagarvala's letter has been made and the discrepancies therein highlighted, in the Kapur Commission's Report.

'That after the statement of Madanlal appeared in the Press about his being from Bombay, investigations were taken up. There is no mention of either the orders of Morarji Desai or of what Jain had told Desai.

'It does mention Madanlal's statement where in Karkare was mentioned.

'It mentions that Karkare and Badge were two Maharashtrian companions of Balraj and Somnath Kapoor, and the former two were good friends.

'It then states that Badge was seen at Ahmednagar about 27 January but he had left that place and that two informants had been called from Ahmednagar who would identify and help in the arrest of Karkare and Badge. Now if Badge belonged to Poona and Karkare to Ahmednagar, even if they were friends, one would have expected that informants would have been called from Poona also.

'The letter mentions that a large number of Punjabis and Maharashtrians being in the conspiracy which was being organized by Col Mohan Singh of the I.N.A., this gentleman was examined by the Commission (Witness No. 86) he denied any knowledge about this gang, it is difficult to imagine that Col Mohan Singh would be a party to encouraging either the assassination or the kidnapping Mahatma Gandhi and it would be still more astonishing if the then Speaker of the Uttar Pradesh Assembly, Shri Purshottamdas Tandon, could be persuaded to join the plan. Even if the objective was eviction of the Mohammedans, the Speaker was unlikely to give his blessings to any such action.

'Although the letter mentions that the plan was to arrest Karkare and Badge, there is no indication as to what tangible steps had been taken to carry out the plan.

'The most important omission is the non-mention of either the editor or the proprietor of the *Agranee* or the *Hindu Rashtra* because that seems to have been emphasized again and again in the note of Sanjeevi. This would show that either these persons were never mentioned till then or Nagarvala was deliberately omitting them. The latter possibility appears likely in the circumstances.

'There is no indication in the note that in the telephonic talk with Nagarvala, Sanjeevi mentioned either of these two persons. All he says in the note is, "I asked him about the absconding accused whose names or descriptions were given to the Delhi Police by Madanlal and Nagarvala promised to send a detailed note." One should have imagined that if the editor of the newspaper had been mentioned, Sanjeevi would have made pointed inquiries about the editor and/or the proprietor.

'Further there is nothing in this note that when Nagarvala mentioned the conspiracy to kidnap Mahatma Gandhi, Sanjeevi ticked him off or told him that the very theory or idea was absurd.

'Commission has been unable to discover any reason why Nagarvala in his letter made the Press report of Madanlal's statement the basis of his investigation rather than the information or order given to him by Morarji Desai, the factum of which is not denied and was accepted by both the trial court as well as the High Court in the Conspiracy Case. Unfortunately, this matter was not put to Nagarvala before the Commission.

'The omission of references to names, descriptions, avocations or places of residence of Madanlal's co-conspirators has remained unexplained.

'The letter of the 30th by Nagarvala to Sanjeevi was top secret and there could not have been any inherent danger in disclosing to Sanjeevi the factum of information given by Morarji Desai or the order he passed'.

The correspondence between the inspector-general of police, Bombay, N.M. Kamte, and the DIG, CID, U.H. Rana describes the extent of bungling by Rana. In a letter written on 6 February 1948 to Rana, Kamte wrote that he had carefully read Madanlal's statement which showed that there was sufficient indication to make out that there was a plot to kill Gandhi by certain Poona men and he wanted information on two matters from Rana: (1) What steps were taken by him to arrest them immediately and (2) What steps were taken to send men to Delhi to comb out Delhi and arrest them there.

Rana replied to this letter on 24 February 1948, mentioning the sequence of events and the action taken by him. There is a very astonishing claim by Rana; he says that 'on 21st morning when two Delhi Police Officers met him and gave him the information they had up to then, he (Rana) told them at once that the gang must be followers of V.D. Savarkar and suggested that two officers be sent to Bombay to contact Nagarvala at Bombay and Rao Saheb Gurtu at Poona.' This claim does not hold water: in the investigation report, it is very clearly stated that Rana was brought into the picture by Sanjeevi after the two officers sent by Sanjeevi to Bombay returned to Delhi and complained about the non-cooperation by the Bombay Police and the obstinacy of Nagarvala. Rana further said that 'By the time the Delhi Policemen arrived in Bombay, the Bombay Police had already got some information about Karkare and some inquiries had been made' or as he put it, 'this information had already been worked out by the Bombay City Police'. The Delhi Police officers went and stayed at the National Hotel which was in the vicinity of the Sher-e-Punjab Hotel whose proprietor, Avtar Singh had been detained by the Bombay City Police and whose name had transpired as one of the conspirators to kill Mahatma Gandhi'. (At that time, Nagarvala believed the conspiracy was to kidnap, not murder.)

Instead of giving an explanation about his actions, as desired by Kamte, Rana gave a detailed description of the actions of the Bombay Police. About his own actions, Rana said that he left for Poona on the 28th and asked the DSP, Poona, to spare his L.I.B. Inspector Angarkar. On the 29th, he was informed that Angarkar was down with fever. Rana then sent a wireless message to recall DSP Deulkar, who was in Colaba district at the time. Deulkar returned on the night of the 30th. Immediately four officers were sent by plane, as there was a lurking suspicion that these men would attack other ministers in the central Cabinet. From the facts which were revealed later, the culprits had slipped out on the morning of the 28th from Bombay.

Rana's reply to Kamte smacks of obfuscation and excuses and an attempt to take credit for actions initiated and executed by others. Kamte caught him out, in a reply dated 6 March 1948. In this letter, Kamte restated the two questions he had asked to which, according to him, Rana's reply was not satisfactory.

He then asked Rana to give his replies on certain specific matters which were: (1) What did the two police officers tell him (Rana) on the 21st which was not quite clear from the letter?; (2) Why did he not ask his own CID to make inquiries because two officers from Delhi were not going to make much headway in Bombay or Poona?; (3) The object of contacting Nagarvala by these police officers was not stated; (4) The statement of Madanlal was given to him (Rana) on the 25th. What action did he take till the evening of 27th? (What actions would he have taken? He was on his leisurely sojourn to Bombay via Allahabad, including a halt there.); (5) The information that Nagarvala learnt through a source about associates of Madanlal was not correct because all he had come to know was Karkare's name and the other information was very vague. But in Madanlal's statement, pp. 7, 16, 18 etc., the description given therein showed that the other accused were Godse, Apte, Badge, etc. Why was there no attempt made to arrest them from the 25th evening onwards?; (6) Although on 27th, he (Rana) had telephoned the DIB about taking precautions for Gandhi's protection, he could very well have deputed his own men to Delhi because Madanlal's statement showed that there was a plan to kill Gandhi by men from the Bombay Province; (7) Kamte could not subscribe to the proposition that the Bombay Police had done all that they could in the matter of precaution. The best thing which Rana could have done on 29th was to have sent for Rao Saheh Gurtu and get that officer on the move; (8) Sending men by air to Delhi was done at Kamte's suggestion and not Rana's, for which Rana could not take any credit.

(This letter makes some telling points of criticism: (a) why Rana did not send his own CID to make inquiries rather than send Delhi Police officers; (b) why he did not send his own CID to Delhi to protect Gandhi and (c) why he did not get hold of Gurtu even on 29th January.)

'Rana did not take any further action because he presumed that the gang must have been located in Bombay and he had one C.I.D. Head Constable Yadav in Delhi who was directed to move about in Delhi and visit railway stations and try to locate Karkare whom the Head Constable knew was a communist from Ahmednagar.' (This is another erroneous description; Karkare was not known to be a communist; he was known to be a fanatical communalist.) Rana did not think it necessary to send a special man from Bombay to Delhi. Rana's explanation for not doing anything further was that he had given instructions to the Delhi Police officers in regard to what was to be done in Bombay and Poona. This is again untrue. Investigation records showed that Rana did absolutely nothing from the time he was handed the copy of Madanlal's detailed confession till the 30th; his claim that he had on his own briefed Delhi police on the 21st was untrue, it is surprising he was not questioned and reprimanded.

'En route from Delhi to Bombay, Rana got fever. He went straight to Nagarvala who showed him what investigation had been done and Rana showed the statement of Madanlal which tallied with the information of Savarkarvadi (pro) group. Rana told him that he would send him a copy of Madanlal's statement immediately after reaching Poona to enable him to start further investigations in Bombay, Nagarvala asked him to send Poona Police Officers to help him identify those people, he specifically asked for Angarkar. But Rana could not go to Poona because he had developed fever.'

Rana claimed that since the telephone lines were considered to be unreliable he did not use it to inform Nagarvala or Sanjeevi about his information (given to him by Rao Saheb Gurtu on 29th evening). He cites the example that when after the murder on 31st he was speaking with Nagarvala they had heard the operators giggling as they listened to the two cops speaking.

Rana's litany of excuses continues: 'It was incorrect that I knew about the names of Godse, Apte and Badge and that that fact was also known to Nagarvala. The fact is, as far as I am concerned, I did not know till I reached Poona who the editor and proprietor of *Hindu Rashtra* was.' (This statement itself shows how incompetent Rana was as a chief of CID based in Poona: he did not know the identity of persons who were actively being watched by his own department. Then also if he came to know the identity of the editor and proprietor of *Agranee* and *Hindu Rashtra* on reaching Poona, why did he sit on the information? He had reached Poona on the evening of the 28th, more than forty hours before Gandhi was murdered. There was ample time to send Rao Saheb Gurtu and any other officer from Poona to Delhi who could have been present in Delhi by the morning of the 30th and would have had the opportunity of spotting Nathuram, Apte and Karkare who had gone to Birla House twice on the 30th, before the murder.)

The Kapur Commission's report states: 'As far as the Commission has been able to see, Rana made no effort to find out their identity or to take action to get them apprehended.'

In the last paragraph of his letter, Rana justifies his inactions: 'He (Rana) had got his officers on the move on 29 January 1948 within a short time that he had at his disposal. However, I will make it more clear. Rao Saheb Gurtu was there when DSP Poona was called and the names of Apte, Godse and Badge were known from Rao Saheb Gurtu. I also asked him if Angarkar knows all three to which his reply was in the affirmative. There was no question of getting Gurtu and others in Poona on the move because the culprits were hiding in Bombay and the Bombay Special Branch were on their watch.' The letter ended by saying: 'It is really disgraceful in that we have not been able to prevent this, and now I wonder if really we can justify our existence as CIDs.' (But the remorseful Rana who suddenly realized how incompetent he was, did not act upon his remorse by resigning.)

Kamte continued his criticism of Rana: 'If telephone conversations were considered undesirable, the D.I.G. should have sent Civil Cipher Code Telegram.'

Kamte writes: 'The D.I.G. cannot be absolved of his failure to contact the Poona C.I.D. giving instructions to arrest the persons whose names or descriptions were known from Madanlal's statement, it was no use finding fault with Delhi Police Officers. The D.I.G. should have immediately informed Rao Saheb Gurtu. Even if the D.I.G. had fever, he could have sent a code telegram to Rao Saheb Gurtu and his telephoning to the D.I.B. was not the point at issue.'

(The 'only fact' was that he failed to take action immediately after receiving the statement of Madanlal. When he reached Poona, Rana should have asked the assistant DIG to arrest the persons whose names and descriptions had been disclosed in Madanlal's statement.)

After severely criticizing Rana for his acts of negligence and sheer incompetence, Kamte suddenly goes soft in his conclusion: 'But what follows takes away the force of the criticism because it says, "He was being corrected for not realizing this so that in future he may not commit these mistakes again."' Justice Kapur adds: 'Unfortunately, there cannot be Gandhis over and over again, at least not in the very near future, and therefore this admonishing was wholly fatuous.'

'In the opinion of the Commission, the assessment of Kamte was correct, had the D.I.G. taken only the most elementary step of asking his C.I.D. Poona about the identity of the associates of Karkare or Madanlal, he would most probably have found out who they were. At any rate if officers could be flown from Poona after the murder to protect the Ministers in the Central Cabinet, the same course could have fruitfully been adopted after the bomb was exploded and Madanlal's statement of the 24th or 25th January had become available.'

A fourth inquiry was in the form of a cut motion introduced in the Bombay Provincial Assembly. Morarji Desai replied to questions and gave a report of the actions of the Bombay provincial government. He informed the assembly about what Prof. Jain had told him on 21 January 1948 but denied that Prof. Jain had told him that he had given this information to Jayprakash Narayan too. Jain's name was not disclosed to the police till the 30th because Jain had requested him not to do so. He then said that whatever information he had received he had conveyed to Patel at Ahmedabad. There are two discrepancies in Desai's statement. One was that while testifying before the Kapur Commission both Shankar, Patel's secretary, and Manibehn, Patel's daughter, said that they did not recall Desai having informed Sardar about Jain's information. Second, Desai did not rush to Ahmedabad to inform Patel, the trip was for another purpose. Patel had gone to attend the foundation stone-laying ceremony for a hospital in Ahmedabad. Desai was a trustee of the trust which was building the hospital. One wonders what made him mislead the assembly. Desai then claimed that he had also informed Gandhi about the threat to his life and had requested him to allow the police to take appropriate measures to protect him, but Gandhi had refused. Desai then went on to defend his police officers. He said: 'I told the police officer to take action against everybody who came under suspicion. Jain had not said that he gave me names of two other persons who ultimately were found to be in the conspiracy and who had nothing to do with the offence.... I have stated what steps were taken by the police force. I know all that because I was inquiring of the police officer constantly as to what was being done not only before the incident, but even afterwards when the offence was being investigated, because I wanted to give him the benefit, of my views and knowledge. I found that they were constantly on the move. Even at midnight I found that they were on duty. I found that police were not even caring for their meals. They had so much concentration on their work. That is why I cannot say that they failed in their duty.' (The fact is that for all their 'industriousness' as claimed by Desai, their efforts amounted to naught as far as saving Gandhi's life was concerned.)

When the Kapur Commission summoned Manu Gandhi to testify, Desai called her and instructed her to say that since she was very young at the time of Gandhi's murder she could not remember anything. Manubehn told him that she was 'Bapu's daughter and would only tell the truth, nothing less and nothing more.' What was Desai apprehensive about, Manu revealing to the inquiry commission?

Nagarvala was asked to explain his actions. His explanation was sent to the Government of India by Dehejia with his letter dated 25 March 1949. Nagarvala sets out the steps taken by him in the investigation, if one may so call it, which he conducted in Bombay after Desai gave him information about Karkare, etc. It is really a copy of the crime report from 20–30 January 1948. With this letter, he attached his letter to Sanjeevi, dated 30 January 1948. He also attached certain other documents: a list of places watched and names of persons watched during that period; his statement in court and portions of statement of Inspector Pinto and DSP Jaswant Singh.

'When his explanation was received in the Secretariat, there were certain notings on it which were adverse to what Nagarvala had done. The office pointed out the various infirmities in the investigation which were worth mentioning.

'(1) Badge was well known to D.S.P. Poona. Why was he not contacted and why was Karkare made the central figure and the case started with Madanlal? (2) Why did the Delhi police not bring Madanlal's statement on 22 January 1948? (3) What efforts were made to establish contact with Delhi and what action did Rana take on Madanlal's statement? (4) Did Nagarvala spot an editor with initials N.V.G. from Poona who was Madanlal's companion? (5) Did Nagarvala go to Ahmednagar to look for Madanlal's links there? Who was handling the investigation at Ahmednagar and Poona? If Badge was seen in Ahmednagar three days before and he was suspected, why was no action taken?'

When this note went to Morarji Desai, he held a discussion with his secretary and finally it was decided that it would be sent along with all the attachments to the Government of India.

Nagarvala raised objection to the commission and challenged its jurisdiction to make an inquiry into the conduct of the police, i.e., its shortcomings, its inaction or its acts of commission or omission, its negligence in the matter of investigation of the bomb case. Nagarvala's main contention against the jurisdiction of the commission was based on the ground that after the strictures passed by Judge Atmacharan, the high court came to different conclusions and that once a court or a competent tribunal has come to the conclusion on a point in controversy in a criminal matter that becomes *res judicata* and cannot be reopened. The decision is binding and conclusive in all subsequent proceedings between the parties to the adjudication. (This seems to be a desperate attempt by Nagarvala to avoid being cross-examined by the Kapur Commission. Answering Nagarvala's contentions, Justice Kapur cited precedents and previous judgments to establish the legality of the commission's jurisdiction.)

7.5: During the trial, or at the appellate stage, whether the police investigated a matter properly or not could not be a matter materially and substantially in issue because on the efficient investigation of a case does not depend the acquittal or otherwise of an accused person, although it has been ruled in certain jurisdictions that evidence improperly collected or illegally obtained cannot sustain a conviction. In the inquiry before this Commission, the matters in controversy are (1) whether the investigation in the bomb case was proper or improper; (2) whether as a consequence of it or even without that matter being taken into consideration, the police had given proper protection to Mahatma Gandhi; (3) whether by improper or negligent investigation the accused were allowed to return to Delhi and commit the murder; and (4) whether murder could, by adequate measures being taken by the police, have been prevented. This may depend upon whether the investigation which was carried on from the time that the bomb was exploded at 4:15 p.m. (this is an error, Madanlal detonated the gun cotton slab at 5:15 p.m.) on 20 January to 30 January 1948, was efficient or not; and upon the question whether the police by its inaction, improper investigation, allowed the persons in the conspiracy to escape and remain undetected. In the opinion of the commission that matter was not before the High Court and any decision given by the High Court is not *res judicata* within the rule laid down by the Supreme Court in Pritam Singh's case. Besides there is no *lis* before a Commission of Inquiry.

7.6: Investigation by the police and the conduct of the inquiry or trial in a case are two separate compartments treated in the Code of Criminal Procedure and the Courts except to the extent so provided in the Code have no jurisdiction on police investigations which was pointed out by the Privy Council in Khawaja Nazir Ahmad's Case. 71 I.A. 203; A.I.R. 1945 P.C. 18.

7.7: Judge Atmacharan had found the police guilty of inaction and therefore, guilty of not having prevented the death of Mahatma Gandhi. The High Court held that those remarks were not justified although no petition had been filed before the High Court for the expunction of those remarks.

7.8: It may be remarked that *res judicata* in criminal cases has the effect of preventing double jeopardy, i.e., the person acquitted cannot be again tried for the same offence. But there is nothing to prevent the sovereign from satisfying himself by collateral proceedings that the conviction was not improperly obtained, in order to exercise its powers of mercy or paying compensation to the wrong man. Similarly, if an accused has been acquitted by improper means, the sovereign may try to find out the illegality.

7.9: In the High Court after dealing with the question of negligence or otherwise of the police, Justice Bhandari said: 'The evidence on record satisfies me (a) that no opportunity was afforded to the police to explain the circumstances which prevented them from apprehending Nathuram before 30 January and there by saving the life of Mahatma Gandhi; (b) that Madanlal failed to supply the names of the conspirators to the police; (c) that even if those names were supplied it was extremely difficult, if not impossible, for the police to arrest Nathuram who was going about from place to place under assumed names and who was determined to assassinate Mahatma Gandhi even at the risk of losing his own life.'

Justice Achchruram said: 'Before concluding I want to advert some remarks made by the learned Special Judge as to the slackness shown in the investigation during the period between 20 and 30 January 1948 but for which in the view of the learned Judge, the tragedy could have been prevented. I must say that I have not been able to discover any justification at all for these remarks which in my judgement were wholly uncalled for.'

Justice Khosla said: 'I concur with the conclusions arrived by my learned brothers Bhandari and Achchru Ram J.J.'

The Kapur Commission's report gives a detailed summary of why Justice Bhandari absolved the police; Justice Achchruram did not give any new reasons.

7.12: This Commission is not sitting as a Court of Appeal against the High Court nor is it open to find fault with the findings of the High Court, still less to re-adjudicate on matters already dealt with by it. But this principle applies to matters which deal with the guilt or innocence of the accused or matters so connected with the decision of that question as to be part of it, but not to matters wholly subsidiary which do not affect the merits of the case e.g. the commission of the offence and those who committed it. Therefore, it is open to the sovereign or the State to find out through the agency of a Commission whether its protective and investigational machinery was properly geared to the protection of the Mahatma. In the opinion of the Commission the finding of the High Court about the quality of investigation is not binding on it, because it was not a matter materially and substantially or even collaterally in issue at the trail which falls within the rule of *res judicata* as stated in Sambasivam's Case.

7.13: As has been said, the rule *res judicata* is inapplicable and there is no rule of propriety or fairness which would bar such an inquiry.

7.14: The objection on the ground of want of jurisdiction is, therefore, overruled.

8.3: It is further alleged that the police acted inefficiently, ineptly and unskilfully and the Home Minister of Bombay was complacent and even if he did convey the information given by Prof Jain to the Police, he was bound and required to supervise the investigation and keep a watchful eye on it and that the ineptitude of the police in the matter of investigation made the Minister responsible, and further that the Minister should have ordered the arrest of the persons named by Madanlal and by Prof Jain and seen to it that they were arrested and their associates were quickly found and arrested. And if the Police bungled, the responsibility is of the Minister, at least the failure of the Police falls under what is called the 'Ministerial responsibility to the Legislature'.

The commission had cited comments of two witnesses on this issue, one the eminent statesman and constitutional lawyer, K.M. Munshi, and the other R.N. Bannerjee, ICS, who was home secretary to the Government of India.

8.15: The Commission's Report states: 'The opinion of K.M. Munshi may be quoted in *verbatim:*

"If as a Minister, I get a report about somebody's life being in danger, the first thing that I would do would be to pass on the report to the Inspector-General of Police to look into its trustworthiness and ask him to take such steps as the law allows. If, on inquiry, he finds that the report is baseless, he can do nothing. If he finds that there is something in the report, then he can take action and keep the Minister informed.

"If the Minister ordered arrests of persons on reports, that would be the end of law and order in the country. I would not do it. The Home Minister can only put his police in charge of the case; he cannot do anything more except to use the instrument of the police machinery to verify and take action."'

8.16: R.N. Bannerjee's opinion is as follows:

'If any information had been given as it is now stated that it was given by Prof Jain, then proper directions should have been given to the Secretary or to the Head of the Police and he should have been asked to submit his report within a short but specified time and the progress of the investigation should have been watched and more interest taken as to what the police was doing.

'As far as I can see, Bombay Government had great faith in the ability of Nagarvala. If the Home Minister had given him instructions then it would be right in saying that he had done what he should have done i.e. in leaving the matter in the competent hands of an officer of the ability of Nagarvala.'

8.17: He (Bannerjee) was asked by the Commission if he did not think it necessary to call up the police officers to whom the information had been given in Madanlal's case and ask them what they were doing, his answer was:

'Those were the days when the Ministers had just come. To the best of my recollection I must have prepared a note suggesting close attention to the matter. I have not the record with me and therefore I cannot say what exactly I wrote. But it is correct that we relied upon the efficiency of the police which proved wrong.'

8.20: In reply to a further question as to why sufficient interest was not taken in finding out the progress of the bomb case as it was done after the murder case. Banerjee replied:

'My assessment of that is that they did not take the case so seriously then and they trusted the high police officials who were in charge of the investigations and they were under the impression that such high police officials would do their duty.'

Nagarvala was asked by the commission (8.30):

'Q. What power has the minister to order the arrest of any one?'

'Ans. If a minister gave an order for arresting any particular person and I on considering the matter thought that it was a reasonable order under the circumstances, I would unhesitatingly carry it out.'

Chapter IX of the Kapur Commission's Report deals with the previous attempts on Gandhi's life. (Since I have dealt with these in a previous chapter I will not repeat these here except for a few select extracts.) While dealing with the attack at Panchgani the commission has cited an extract from *Agranee*.

9.29: Ex.52 is an extract from the *Agranee* of 23 July 1944. There also the incident given is that of demonstration organized by Hindus against Rajaji's 'unpious formula of Pakistan in this land of Shivaji'.

'Apte says: "Gandhiji you have committed an offence of stabbing the nation, by giving your consent to Pakistan formula. You have already confessed that you have no right to speak on behalf of Hindus. Today we are demonstrating peacefully our protest on behalf of Hindu Youths. You bear in mind that if you do not change your behaviour more difficult situation and ill fame await you. We will treat them as traitors who will try to vivisect our motherland. We, by this statement call on national minded people to treat Gandhi-Rajaji formula in this manner."'

Although the Kapur Commission concluded that the attack in Panchgani was not life threatening but a mere demonstration, a similar instance throws light on the attitude of Godse and Apte towards those who held diverse opinions. This was narrated during Badge's cross examination during the Red Fort Trial. Bhopatkar the chief defence counsel, was present in court. Neither Nathuram nor Bhopatkar challenged Badge's story. This would lead one to believe that what Badge had narrated was true. (At the Red Fort Trial, Badge had stated that at a meeting of the Hindu Rashtra Dal, he had witnessed Nathuram rushing to attack Bhopatkar when the two had disagreed about something Nathuram had said, Nathuram was disarmed and subdued before he could assault Bhopatkar.)

The Kapur Commission relied on police testimonies to arrive at the conclusion that both the attack at Panchgani and at Sevagram were mere protests and not murder attempts. It must be remembered that at that time the police were under the British and not likely to be too concerned about what Indians did to each other. It would have been very convenient for the British if an Indian did away with Gandhi; they would then be rid of the irritant and they would face no blame for it.

Chapter X deals with the attack at Wardha and Chapter XI deals with the derailment of the Gandhi Special Train. (I have dealt with this in another chapter and the Kapur Commission's report states nothing different so I will not delve on these incidents again.)

Volume II, Chapter XII of the report deals with conditions in Delhi; 'Partition of India', the events leading up to it and the aftermath of the partition'. (I have dealt with this in detail previously so I will only reproduce some pertinent excerpts.)

Dr Sushila Nayyar was called by the Kapur Commission; she was witness No. 53. Her testimony is as follows:

12A.29: Dr. Sushila Nayyar, Mahatma's Personal Physician (witness No. 53) has described the conditions before and during the fast thus: Mahatma Gandhi blamed persons who were guilty of violence and advised the majority community to behave properly towards the minority which caused a certain amount of discontent among the refugees who shouted slogans outside the Birla House. Mahatma Gandhi undertook a fast because the atmosphere became too oppressive on account of both sides exaggerating matters and the Mahatma was anxious that proper protection should be accorded to minorities here so that in Pakistan also the minorities could feel safe. He said that he could not ask Pakistan to behave until India herself behaved in a proper manner. 'Evil is not weighed in golden scales.' Continuing she said: 'When Mahatmaji undertook the fast, for the first two or three days the refugees were not affected thereby. On the other hand they began shouting, "*Gandhiji ko marne do, ham ko ghar do!*" (Let Gandhiji die, give us home.) But after four or five days when Gandhiji's health deteriorated there was a complete change in the mentality of both the Hindus and the Muslims of Delhi. Long lines of persons used to come to ask Gandhiji to give up his fast; they had tears running down their cheeks. There were men, women, Hindus, Muslims, Muslim women in burqas, refugees and non-refugees. It made a tremendous impression on the whole of the Delhi populace.'

12A.30: She added that the refugees were in an angry mood when the Mahatma undertook the fast. About the precautions taken she said that after the bomb there were more plain-clothes policemen round about the Birla House but she did not know if they also attended the prayer meetings. There was one policeman who said, 'What difference does it make if an old man dies. Why make a fuss.' She said that she was not consulted about the security arrangements.

12A.56: At pages 685–686 of the same book, Pyarelal has said that the Mahatma had become irritable and that he was trying to keep it down. Suddenly he used to say, 'Don't you see. I am mounted on my funeral pyre?' Sometimes he would say, 'You should know it is a corpse that is telling you this.'

12A.77: J.N. Sahani, a well known journalist, further stated that people like Dr N.B. Khare, Prime Minister of Alwar, made provocative speeches likely to incite violence and other people from Poona also were making similar kind of speeches. Most of them were Marathi newspapers. He learnt this as a member of the editor's conference. 'There were,' he said, 'some Punjab papers also which were writing in the same strain and those matters were also reported to the conference. It was being openly discussed in those days that there were about six lakhs volunteers forming a part of a secret organization plotting to stage a *coup d'etat*. This organization had secret cells in different parts of India - Punjab, Southern India, Maharashtra, etc.'

12A.85: Sahni's attention was then drawn to page 223 of the book as follows:

'Q. Now I draw your attention to Maulana Azad's book, *India Wins Freedom*, page 223, wherein he has said that Jayaprakash Narayan had accused Sardar Patel that the Home Minister of the Government of India could not escape the responsibility of the assassination of Mahatma Gandhi.'

'A. I do not remember exactly these words. But I do remember that there was quite a feeling in responsible circles that Government could not escape the responsibility for not having taken proper precautions to avert this tragedy especially after the bomb incident.'

12A.92: There was a meeting of All India States Hindu Mahasabha at Bombay on 29, 30 November and 1 December 1947 (Ex. 275-A). One of the speakers was Master Tara Singh, the Akali leader. He made a spirited speech saying that hundreds and thousands of Sikhs were killed in Punjab by Muslims and still the government was protecting the interests of Muslims while Hindu and Sikh refugees were dying of cold in Delhi. 'Gandhi had no feeling for them. He cared more for the Muslims and he was requesting them not to leave India. He said that the English had left the eternal enmity between Hindus and Muslims... Jinnah had said that as long as Islam remained they would not allow a single Sikh to live in Pakistan. He (Master Tara Singh) retorted that as long as Hindu Dharma lived, they shall not allow a single Muslim to live (loud cheers).' 'Nowadays,' he said, 'many Muslims were calling themselves nationalists but no Musalman could ever be a Hindu-loving man. He would always be a Muslim at heart although he might pretend to be a nationalist.' He added that they would allow all religions to continue to live in India but they could not allow their necks to be cut by Musalmans. He wanted all Musalmans to be sent to Pakistan.

12A.93: Savarkar (also at that meeting) drew the attention of the public to the danger from Muslims who were joining the Congress. 'How could a Muslim Leaguer become a nationalist overnight?' The Musalmans wanted to create another Pakistan in India. He said that Rajaji was their next enemy and that Congress' repressive policy towards the Hindus would rouse Hindutva in the hearts of the masses.

12B.10: Under the heading 'Hindu Affairs', it was stated that the orthodox Hindus were criticizing the Congress for their policy of appeasement. V.G. Deshpande, Mahant Digvijay Nath and Professor Ram Singh at a meeting held on 27th at Connaught Place under the auspices of the Delhi Provincial Hindu Sabha said that Gandhi's attitude had strengthened the hands of Pakistanis. They criticized the communal policy of the Government of India and the measures taken by Gandhi to coerce the Indian Cabinet to pay ₹55 crores to Pakistan. Mahant Digvijay Nath exhorted the gathering to turn out Mahatma Gandhi and other anti-Hindu elements. Professor Ram Singh also opposed Gandhi's policy.

12C.7: Some Socialist leaders like Jayprakash Narayan, Dr Ram Manohar Lohiya and Mrs Kamaladevi Chattopadhyay issued a statement at a press conference in which they said that 'the assassin was not one person but there was a wide conspiracy and organization behind it'. They laid blame on the Hindu Mahasabha, RSS and the Muslim League and such like bodies for the assassination of Mahatma Gandhi. They accused the Government for not protecting the Mahatma against a 'prowling assassin'. They then asked for reconstitution of the Government and demanded that the Home Ministry must be entrusted to a person who will have no other portfolio and who will be able to curb the cult and organizations of communal hate and there should be no place in the reconstituted Government and, in particular, the Home Minister must push through at top-speed the programme of purifying Government services of all communal elements and of educating them into a national citizenship.

12C.19: Further, the evidence of police witnesses that Bombay Provincial Police from Poona should have been called, is based on good common-sense and the Commission is of the view that that should also have been done although according to D.W. Mehra, witness No 23 and U.H. Rana, witness No. 3, both D.I.Gs., it would have been inefficacious.

12C.22: It would be fair to add that the conditions in Delhi from after the Partition right up to the time the fast was undertaken were most disturbed and disturbing. There were Hindu–Muslim riots in the old city and there were disturbances even in the area around about the city. According to V. Shankar, witness No. 10, the time of the District Magistrate was mostly taken up with the law and order problems, and M.S. Randhawa who was then the District Magistrate, has also emphasized this aspect of the state of affairs in the capital.

Next, the commission examined principal witnesses who at the time of the bomb explosion and Gandhi's murder were connected with the home ministry. These witnesses were V. Shankar, ICS; Patel's private secretary, R.N. Bannerjee, ICS, secretary of the Ministry of Home Affairs; Miss Manibehn Patel, MP, daughter of Patel.

12D.2: V. Shankar, witness No. 10 stated that from the intelligence reports as well as from the discussions between the Bombay Premier and the Home Minister, the Sardar knew that there was a move to assassinate Mahatma Gandhi and also that perhaps the centre of that movement was at Poona, but the witness did not know about any particular individual who had given that information. At that time there were vague rumours and suspicions but the bomb incident was the first concrete piece of evidence on which action could be taken.

12D.5: The general instructions were that the suspects 'should be particularly kept under watch and the first concrete evidence on the basis of which any effective action could be taken was the confessional statement of Madanlal. Before that there were only rumours. The Sardar, Kher and Morarji Desai knew that there was a conspiracy but not as to who was in it. Even a man like N.C. Kelkar was being mentioned.

12D.12: Shankar was examined by this commission on 10 April 1967. He did not know anything about Ketkar's giving information through Balukaka Kanitkar but there was information of the existence of a hostile camp at Poona known as the 'Kesari School' which was against Gandhi, Savarkar was its inspiration. But their activities were watched by the Bombay Special Branch which since British days used to deal with political matters and it was not the ordinary C.I.D. The witness said that the Sardar must have seen the statement of Madanlal made on 25 January. Even earlier, a gist of the statements of Madanlal made from time to time were conveyed to him by the D.I.B. and the witness distinctly remembered that the Sardar had ordered to keep persons mentioned by Madanlal under surveillance.

12D.17: R.N. Bannerjee, ICS (retired) was the Home Secretary of the Central Government at that time was examined by Pathak on 22 January 1966.

12D.18: Further at the meeting (on the evening of 31 January

1948) everybody was disgusted with the police inaction and Bannerjee described his own version in an article in a book called *The Civil Servants in India* by K.L. Punjabi where he said the following:

'All the same a great deal of temporary disintegration occurred in Secretariat administration. In Delhi Province (which never had a proper full-time inspector-general of police ever since its creation in 1912) the police force got ill-organized and weak; and minimum liaison between the Chief Commissioner and the Home Department on the one hand and the district administration on the other could hardly be maintained. Mahatma Gandhi's assassination on 30 January 1948 was partly a by-product of this confused state of affairs. After the cremation there was a meeting at Sardar Patel's residence in the evening of the 31st and it was disclosed for the first time that by the early morning of 21 January the Delhi Police had in their possession statement made by Madanlal (who detonated a hand grenade [actually an improvised explosive device]) at Mahatma Gandhi's prayer meeting at Birla House on the 20th evening and made a confession to the police overnight, in which the full history of the conspiracy was set out. The Delhi Police did function in one respect, namely that they sent Madanlal's statement to the Bombay Police on 21 January evening but the papers lay with the Bombay Police. Both Godse and Apte could have been found and nabbed in one of their two Bombay haunts on the 23rd (January). Unfortunately nobody took any action on this statement of Madanlal and the Delhi police did not even remind the Bombay police. The Delhi Magistracy and the Home Secretariat remained ignorant of the statement (as the head of the Delhi Police never kept them informed).'

12D.22: Asked as to what should have been done if information was given to the Bombay government as early as July 1947 that Gandhi's life had been threatened, Bannerjee said the government should have ordered to keep those persons under surveillance and should have also informed the Delhi Police.

12D.32: Regarding the RSS, the witness complained that when decisions were taken in regard to the banning of RSS, the news leaked out and appeared in the press the next morning and thus the tall poppies of RSS went underground in the early forenoon of 1 February.... In Mahatma Gandhi's case the Minister and the Secretariat started issuing directives to the police and the magistracy because it realized that the police had not functioned properly.

12D.37: The next witness whose testimony is relevant in regard to the Government of India is Miss Manibehn Patel, daughter of Sardar Patel, witness No. 79.

12D.44: 'We did know that Mahatma's life was in danger and whatever precautions could humanly be taken were taken. But this much I can say that I had no idea that there was a conspiracy to murder Mahatma Gandhi. At that time at least I thought that the danger to Mahatma Gandhi's life was more likely to come from Muslims...'

12D.45: She did not know anything about things happening and speeches being made in Poona or Ahmednagar indicative of violence against Mahatma Gandhi. She did remember that a fortnight before the murder a newspaper editor from Poona, from whose paper security had been demanded, came to see her father at 5:00 a.m. but she would not be able to recognize him because it used to be dark at that time. But she could remember that he talked about the demand of security payment from his paper. He complained that Morarji Desai had been unfair to him. (This has to be Nathuram Godse since his was the only paper from which security had been demanded by the Government of Bombay Province. In court, too, during the Red Fort Trial, when Morarji Desai appeared as witness, Nathuram had shouted angrily at him alleging that Desai had vindictively harassed him. This means that just a few days before the bomb attack, Nathuram Godse had met Union Home Minister Sardar Vallabhbhai Patel. In light of this statement of Maniben Patel, if Sardar Patel had been kept informed about the confessions of Madanlal, and by Morarjee Desai about information provided by Prof. Jain, Sardar would definitely recollected the identity of the editor from Poona who had met him a few days back and would have provided this information to the investigating officers. Or he too decided to remain silent? Highly unlikely.)

12D.46: Before Mahatma Gandhi was assassinated her father went to see him. She had accompanied him. They talked on various matters but he did not broach the subject of searching of persons coming to the prayer meetings. The news of the murder was conveyed to them by Brij Kishan Chandiwalal soon after they returned home.

12D.48: She added that her father was publicly accused for being responsible for the murder at a meeting by Jayprakash Narayan. Maulana Azad was present at the meeting but he did not protest, this was a great shock to her father.

12D.49: She could not remember if there was any talk between her father and Balasaheb Kher after the murder about earlier information about danger to Mahatma Gandhi's life.

'Q. Do you remember if at any time Balasaheb Kher mentioned it to your father that it was weighing on his mind that some information conveyed to him earlier was not taken much note of?'

'A. I can definitely say that nothing of that kind happened. Balasaheb did not either blame himself for being negligent nor was any blame against my father. Balasaheb I knew very well and at no stage did he ever blame himself for being negligent in the matter of handling of the information of danger to Mahatmaji's life.'

12D.53: She characterized the allegation absolutely false that her father was not protecting Mahatma Gandhi because of his attempts to remove him from office. On the other hand, she said that her father did not want to stay on in the Cabinet and had sent his resignation to Mahatma Gandhi. As a matter of fact Gandhiji opposed the presence of policemen in Birla House in order to maintain the reputation of the State.

12D.54: Gandhiji made a speech (post prayer) which was published in the *Harijan* of 25 January 1948 where he said: 'I wonder if with a knowledge of this background to my statement anybody would dare call my fast a condemnation of the police or of the Home Ministry. If there is any such person, I can only tell him that he would degrade and hurt himself, never the Sardar or me...'

12D.56: The Sardar said that Brajkishan and Aruna were also in league in his removal and that Jayaprakash had started attacking him in Bombay and at Surat.

12D.57: On the following day i.e. 5 March, Sardar Patel had a heart attack. At 4:00 p.m. that day he told Sushila Nayar that he had to go with Gandhiji who had gone ahead alone.

12D.58: The diary shows that the Sardar was saying that he must die and go to Gandhi.

12D.62: On 2 February 1948 Sanjeevi warned Sardar Patel that he should not go out for a walk in the mornings as there was danger to his life and that of Panditji.

12D.63: On 3 February 1948 a man came with his daughter who was employed in the telephone office and she gave a number in Alwar and repeated what she had heard on the telephone. Sanjeevi was called and asked to inquire into the matter at Alwar. (Unfortunately, nothing is mentioned about what she overheard, nor are supportive documents to be found amongst the documents of the Kapur Commission to find out the information reported by the telephone operator. Alwar was a hotbed of the Hindu fanatics and of rabid anti-Gandhi activities.)

12E.2: Evidently the Home Secretary of the Central Government who has always been the recognized pivot of the administration concerning law and order and security was kept ignorant and there is nothing to show that the seriousness of the offence was indicated to him or he kept himself informed of the progress of the investigation or what the Delhi Police were doing or what information was coming in to the Home Minister or his private secretariat.

12E.6: Morarji Desai also said that the danger to Mahatma Gandhi was from the RSS and from the Hindu Mahasabha. He put the matter thus:

'I could not say who the exact person were who would do harm to Mahatma Gandhi. But from the information I had I could say that they were likely to be either the refugees or the RSS and Hindu Mahasabha, but not necessary from Poona. It was also possible that they could be Muslim Fanatics and this class of people was dispersed all over the country and they were more in the North than in Bombay.'

12E.7: Khadilkar, witness No. 97, stated that danger to the Mahatma was from the Hindu Rashtra Dal. According to V. Shankar, Sardar Patel knew of the danger to Mahatma Gandhi from RSS.

12E.8: V. Shankar, witness No. 10, has stated: 'My impression is that there was information of the existence of a hostile camp in Poona which was then known as the Kesari school of thought against Gandhiji and Savarkar was the inspirer of the school and as far as I know their activities were kept under watch by the Bombay Special Branch', showing thereby that the Poona school was against Gandhiji and was a potential source of danger. According to J.N. Sahni, witness No. 95, there were two schools of thought in Delhi, one for banning communal organization and the other against it. B.B.S. Jetley, witness No. 55, when recalled on 14 January 1969 stated that there was a list of 600 to 700 cases against the RSS in a couple of months after independence, the charge against them being of collecting arms, attacking villages and assaulting individual, and he recommended that the RSS should be banned. He actually went to see the C.I.D. Chief at Lucknow and also Govind Vallabh Pant who was then the premier of U.P. and Lal Bahadur Shastri who was the Home Minister of U.P., and recommended to them that RSS be banned. They agreed with him but said that they will have to consult Sardar Patel. This organization was banned, but only after the murder. He (Sardar Patel) also said that it was difficult to ban RSS because the Muslims were already against them and he did not want a section of the Hindus also to be against them.

12E.9: Dr Sushila Nayyar, witness No. 53, has given the reaction of Mahatma Gandhi regarding the RSS thus. When she praised before the Mahatma the work of RSS volunteers at Wah, (a refugee camp near Rawalpindi), he said that she did not know them. 'They are like the Black Shirts, like the Fascists and the Nazis'.

12E.12: Rajaji in his book *Gandhiji's Teachings and Philosophy* published by the Bharatiya Vidya Bhavan at pages 20–22 has stated as follows: 'When on 30 January 1948, Gandhiji was assassinated by Godse, Sardar Vallabhbhai Patel felt that the conspiracy to kill Gandhiji was due to Hindu anger against him on account of the advice of his to pay a huge sum of money to the Pakistan Government when it was organizing and carrying out a wicked military campaign against us. Our folly in helping the enemy with fifty crores (should be ₹55 crores, ₹550 million) rupees at that juncture was thought to be inexcusable and the small militant anti-Gandhi Maharashtrian group felt this as a climax of Gandhiji's disservice to the nation and decided to put and end to this "foolish saint" whom the nation could not otherwise get rid of. So great was his influence and so foolishly did the people venerate and obey him that these conspirators thought, according to the Sardar, that there was no way out other than assassination.'

(In the wake of the murder, Patel continuously harped about the fact that the insistence of Gandhi to pay Pakistan was the main reason that he was murdered. Patel conveniently seemed to have forgotten that the agreement, by which the joint capital of undivided India was to be shared by India and Pakistan, was signed by him and Nehru, Gandhi was neither a part of the negotiations nor a signatory to the bilateral treaty. Becauseof the inexcusable inefficiency of the police department under his ministry, Patel was forced to cloud the real issue by diverting attention by making baseless allegations. The final fast of Gandhi was not to force the payment to Pakistan, if it were so he would not have continued his fast for four more days after the Indian Cabinet declared that it would pay the money. Gandhi fasted to bring about peace in Delhi and in the northwestern and eastern provinces of India.)

12E.16: Next witness No. 18, M.S. Randhawa, the Deputy Commissioner of Delhi at the time of the murder, was examined. He stated that from September 1947 to 20 January 1948 it never came to his knowledge that Gandhi's life was in danger. He had even taken Gandhi to a village to open a Panchayat Ghar without taking any special precautions.

12E.18: Randhawa referred to his letter of explanation, Ex. 140(7) dated 7 February 1948 in which he explained the reason why he allowed Mehta Puran Chand, advocate, to interview Madanlal on 24 January 1948. He then said, 'I must mention a serious lapse on the part of Superintendent of Police, New Delhi that he did not keep me informed of the progress of investigation of this case and I did not receive a single report from him which could give me an indication that Madanlal, accused was involved in a conspiracy to murder Mahatma Gandhi.' A special report regarding the bomb incident was cyclostyled on 26 January and a copy was sent to his office on 27 January. 'I was under the impression that Madanlal had exploded a cracker or a bomb simply as a protest against Mahatma Gandhi's views and was not involved in a conspiracy to murder case...' His explanation was not accepted by the Home Ministry and was characterized as 'obviously unsatisfactory'.

(Here is another interesting blunder. Madanlal, the only lead to the conspiracy to murder Gandhi, who was being interrogated by the Delhi Police, was allowed to be interviewed, while in police custody, by an advocate. The man could have been a decoy and could have killed

Madanlal to protect the others involved in the conspiracy. He could have also passed on instructions to Madanlal to enable him to feed misleading information to the police.)

12E.20: When asked what he would have done if he had known about the conspiracy, he said that he would have gone to the Home Minister and would have called a meeting of the emergency committee to devise means for doing something appropriate. He was shown a copy of Ex. 84, Special Report of the Superintendent of Police, but he said that neither could he remember whether he read it or not, nor whether it did reach him at all.

12E.23: He said, 'I would have stopped the prayer meetings whether Mahatma Gandhi liked it or not because his life was very important and I personally had a great respect for him as a leader.'

He added that he had saved the life of M.A. Jinnah and other Muslim League leaders when they were attacked at the Imperial Hotel by Khaksars. It was probably in May 1946. He further added, 'I would have controlled people who were coming to the prayer meetings.'

12F.1: Brij Krishan Chandiwala, witness No. 11, stated that the refugees were in an angry mood. Once, they called names to Gandhiji's face. On another occasion a procession came to Birla House shouting slogans, *'Khoon ka badla khoon se lenge.'* (We shall avenge bloodshed by shedding blood, or murder by murder.) When Gandhiji broke his fast, the people's minds and 'hearts were not clean' and that is why 'a hand-grenade burst with a great sound on 20 January 1948 after his finishing prayer and Gandhiji had a narrow escape. Arrests were made after this incident. About 2 or 3 persons were arrested. From that day we became very vigilant and took great care about Gandhiji. Three or four days later a police officer came to see me and informed that the incident of 20th was a conspiracy to murder Gandhiji and the names of 9 persons have come to our knowledge who were involved in it.... I thought that police will at once arrest those persons and there was no reason to fear left. Gandhiji's opinion was also that it was a conspiracy to kill him.' He added that 'he could not imagine that the police could be so careless that after knowing about the conspiracy Gandhiji would be murdered'. 'After we came to know that the police was looking into the matter, we did not do anything.'

12F.4: They never suspected that any kind of outrage would be committed by Poona people. They were suspecting other persons. Although Chandiwala had come to know that Madanlal had thrown the bomb he never tried to find out who was behind the offence.

12F.8: Dr Sushila Nayyar, witness No.53, was questioned next. She stated that nobody in the Ashram (Bapu's entourage) could imagine that anybody would do harm to Mahatma Gandhi. They took the fatalistic attitude that as long as God wanted the Mahatma to serve the country, he would. There were rumours that the Mahatma's life may be in danger and that is why security men in plain clothes were stationed in Birla House and the plainclothes policemen had to hide themselves behind bushes to keep themselves out of Mahatma's sight.

12F.12: Pyarelal, witness No.54 said, 'When the Mahatma learnt about the bomb he at once said that there was a conspiracy to murder him.' Previous to that he had thought that it was just a military practice.

12F.14: He knew that Madanlal had been arrested and Gandhiji had said that he (Madanlal) should not be harassed.

12F.15: 'Mahatmaji was convinced that there was a conspiracy but he did not know its extent or its nature.' The witness had never been able to reconcile himself to the failure of the police to trace the people mentioned by Madanlal in time. Either it was inefficiency or there was a lack of will.

(These three testimonies of persons very close to Gandhi reveal yet another lapse that facilitated his murderer. This time, it was the ones he trusted the most who let him down. As per the testimony of the persons living with Gandhi or in charge of the arrangements, whenever he went to attend the prayer meeting, he would be encircled by a chain of volunteers. The sturdier Ashramites and volunteers would walk ahead of him, clearing a path; the rest would form a impenetrable ring around him so that the crowds, in their eagerness to touch him and receive his blessings, would not hinder his progress or trip him. Inexplicably, after the bomb attack, the Ashramites and volunteers scaled down this arrangement, till only Chandiwala and Gurdayal Singh would walk in front of Gandhiji, clearing a path. On the fateful day, both Chandiwala and Gurdayal Singh were not even doing this. Nathuram Godse could, without a hitch, get close to Bapu and shoot him from less then 3 feet away. There was never a satisfactory answer as to why a practice which had not been objected to by Gandhi was suddenly discontinued.)

The next witness was Manuben Gandhi, granddaughter of Gandhiji's brother. Manuben was one of the girls who had come to be known as Gandhiji's 'walking sticks', and was one of the persons nearest to Mahatma Gandhi at the time of his murder. There is an interesting tale. When the Kapur Commission summoned Manuben, Morarji Desai called her and told her, 'Manu you must only tell the Commission that you were very young at the time of Gandhiji's murder and too much time has passed since, so you do not remember anything.' Manuben replied, 'I am Gandhiji's daughter, I have been taught to tell the truth by him and I will only tell the truth.' (This incident was narrated to me [the author] recently by a person who was present in the room when Morarji Desai spoke to Manuben.)

12F.16: Manuben Gandhi, witness No. 99, stated that they had no knowledge of danger to the Mahatma's life till after the bomb attack.

12F.17: The members of the Mahatma's party did feel that there was a danger for about two or three days after the bomb incident but after that everybody thought it was alright. Mahatma did not agree to special protection and he only allowed guards to be put there to satisfy the Sardar. He believed in the protection of God. She also said that the Mahatma's reaction to search of visitors was that he would have rather died than allowed it.

12F.18: This evidence does not show that the inmates of the Birla House and those who were around the Mahatma were quite alive to the danger to his life so much so that one of them even did not know whether Madanlal had been arrested or not, or whether it was one man who was arrested or more than one man, and they never found out if he had made any statement or what statement he had made. As far as they were concerned, they took no precautions of any kind to protect the Mahatma.

12F.22: Assuming though not deciding that the police was negligent, extremely negligent, even inefficient, this simple precaution (of four to five people flanking him) should in any case have been taken, if for nothing else than to prevent the people who were over-zealous. It is still more surprising that even the Congress volunteers (Seva Dal) were told that it was no longer necessary for them to look after the safety of the

Mahatma which in the opinion of the Commission was a serious lapse.

12F.38: Witness No. 11 Brij Krishan Chandiwala said that once a young man came to him in an agitated mood and said that he wanted to see the Mahatma and if he was not allowed to do so the witness would be sorry for it. He (Chandiwala) could not say who he (the young man) was; it might be that the man wanted to tell Gandhiji that his life was in danger or he might have become a murderer himself. The witness reiterated that he could not imagine that the police would become so careless as not to protect Gandhiji.

12F.41: The statement of this witness does not show that the inmates of Gandhiji's camp realized the danger to Mahatma Gandhi's life. It also appears that they were not getting correct information which is shown by the witness saying that two or three persons were arrested on the 20th and that later on a policeman had told them that the names of nine persons had been ascertained and they were being traced.

12F.56: Pyarelal Nayyar, witness No. 54, said that Sardar Patel did say that Muslims could stay in India and they will get protection but they must not have divided loyalties. Mahatma Gandhi exhorted the Muslims to condemn the abduction of Hindu women and he asked the Muslims to make a public statement that those women should be restored to their families but no organized Muslim society issued any such appeal as far as the witness could remember, but individuals might have done so. Mahatma Gandhi said that he would not be surprised if in spite of all the homage paid to him by leaders, they would say one day, 'We have had enough of this old man; why does not he leave us alone?' This was in connection with the general fall of standards which had come in Congress ranks and growing corruption which Mahatma Gandhi found in Congressmen and their deviation from the path of non-violence.

12F.77: Witness No. 3 Vishwanath Shah, deposing before Pande said that a woman in Birla House told him that some people used to roam about the Birla House whom she suspected. She was the wife of a driver. The witness told the police about this. The woman identified Madanlal Pahwa and said that he and his companions used to roam about Birla House. (He must be referring to Sulochana Devi, who had identified Madanlal as the man who had exploded the bomb on 20 January and told the police that she had seen him confer with four or five of his accomplices, some of whom she had seen running away from Birla House after the blast.)

12F.79: Manuben Gandhi, Witness No. 99 told the commission: 'When we mentioned to the Mahatma about the danger to his life, he just laughed and said, "If God wishes that I should live, I shall live and if he does not wish me to live then He would take me away." After the bomb was exploded, Lady Mountbatten came to congratulate the Mahatma. The Mahatma said to Lady Mountbatten, 'On this occasion I have shown no bravery. If somebody fired at me point-blank and I faced his bullet with a smile, repeating the name of Rama in my heart, I shall indeed be deserving of congratulations.'

12F.82: The most important part of this witness' statement is her deposition about the visit of Nathuram Godse on 30 January 1948. Manuben claimed that, at about noon Nathuram Godse came to Birla House. Nobody stopped him because people used to come like that 'and we did not think that it was anybody special who had come'. He must have come by the back door; quite a number of people used to do so. The Mahatma, at the time when Nathuram came, was sleeping outside in the sun and if he wanted he could have shot him there. She was certain it was Nathuram Godse who came because when he fired the fatal shots she was present and she recognized him to be the same person who had come on that day. Her feeling was that when he came at noon he was overawed by the very presence of the Mahatma.

12F.85: She was asked whether the Mahatma was miserable about what was happening around him, her answer was 'Yes'. When asked whether the Mahatma was unhappy because of what was happening in the country or because of the consequences of the Partition, her answer was 'because of both; both these affected him'. She was asked whether the Mahatma was unhappy because the Government misbehaved or the people were misbehaving or both were misbehaving. Her answer again was: 'because of both'.

12F.88: She was asked if the Mahatma used to receive threatening letters in January 1948, her reply was in the affirmative.

12F.89: She stated that she was surprised, rather annoyed to see the same man stopping the Mahatma because he had been there in the morning, but she did not think there was any danger from the man because he had folded both his hands and she thought he was going to pay respects to the Mahatma. Nathuram Godse in his statement in court had stated he had his revolver in his folded hands. If that is so, it is surprising why nobody spotted it in the audience, not even those leading the procession. (Nathuram's claim seems doubtful. I have held the Beretta semi-automatic pistol used by Nathuram. There is no way a person could hide the pistol in their folded palms: it is too big and too heavy to be held that way. The likely scenario is that Nathuram first folded his palms, then lashed out at Manuben and in the same action pulled out the gun from his pocket and shot Gandhi.)

12F.91: Manuben is rather an important witness. She was closely related to the Mahatma and was closely associated with him. She was one of the two girls who used to conduct him to prayer meetings and was slightly ahead of the Mahatma at the time of the murder. And when she makes a statement, no doubt after 21 years, that Nathuram came to Birla House unchecked and was shown the places where Mahatma slept, worked and had his meals and actually saw him sleeping in the grounds, the commission should be reluctant to disregard it.

12F.96: The Mahatma came to realize that the Congress was paying lip service to non-violence and he was considered as a burden. Pyarelal, whose power of observation and exactness is shown by the clarity of the narrative in his book, felt that in the Delhi Police there was infiltration of anti-Gandhi feelings and of pro-RSS elements.

12G.3: After the bomb incident, the number of policemen was increased and a larger force was stationed at Birla House. Ex.10 also shows that after the bomb incident, the number of policemen was immediately increased to one assistant sub-inspector, two head constables and sixteen foot constables. In addition to this, there were plain-clothes men, one sub-inspector, four head constables and two foot constables who were all armed with revolvers. Three plain-clothes men were stationed on the path leading from Birla House to the place where the prayer meetings were held, and a small detachment of troops for moving patrol all round the compound was also stationed.

12G.7: D.W. Mehra, D.I.G. Delhi, was personally present with Gandhiji when the latter started his fast and Gandhiji talked to him about the steps to be taken to improve Hindu–Muslim relations. Because of the mental anxiety on account of Gandhiji's fast and four months of constant arduous labour, Mehra fell ill with an attack of influenza on 16 January 1946 and was in bed for four days. In spite of that he went to Mahatmaji on 21 January and he resolved to attend all his prayer meetings. He again fell ill on the 24th and went to Birla House on the 30th after the great tragedy had taken place.

12G.8: It had also been decided that Superintendent of Police A.N. Bhatia should personally attend Mahatma Gandhi's meetings, he continued to do so but on the fateful day, 30 January, he was also absent due to the threatened strike of the CPWD.

12G.17: M.S. Randhawa, witness No. 18, has also stated: 'On account of the departure of Muslim police to Pakistan in very large numbers, the police organization in Delhi was seriously depleted and policemen had to be hastily recruited from the rural areas to fill the gap. They were not trained properly.'

12G.23: M.K. Sinha, when asked about the action which should have been taken after the statement of Madanlal, said: 'I still think that if adequate and prompt action had been taken to locate the persons described in Madanlal's statement, then the assassination could have been prevented. I had heard rumours when I was here that whispers about the conspiracy were current in Bombay and were even known to officials.'

12G.31: Examined before this Commission, Bannerjee deposed to certain important matters which might be enumerated thus:

1. Neither Sanjeevi nor Mehra had ever complained to him regarding inaction of the Bombay Police. It was at that meeting (on 31 January 1948) that Sanjeevi had stated that he had sent to Bombay the confessional statement of Madanlal the substance of which was that Apte and Godse must have gone back to one or the other of their two or three haunts in Bombay.
2. Bannerjee said that even under the prevailing practice, Sanjeevi should have discussed with him the bomb case but unfortunately the first time a copy of the statement of Madanlal was placed before him at the meeting after Mahatma's funeral. Bannerjee himself had no detailed information regarding the grave offence of Madanlal before the meeting and it was for that reason that the Home Secretariat remained inactive.

12G.32: When recalled, R.N. Bannerjee stated that the news of the bomb explosion reached him in Delhi the same evening when the bomb exploded and it was in the newspapers the next morning. His own reaction was that it was an act of an individual fanatic and it never occurred to him that there was anybody behind it, although he did see in the newspapers that Madanlal's companions had escaped. Although they thought that the bomb was a serious matter, he did not interfere in the investigation, because it had been left in the hands of a very senior and high police officer who had come from Madras with a high professional reputation.

12G.34: Bannerjee said: 'It may be said that it was really the procedure, the working of the Home Ministry which made it difficult for me to question Sanjeevi in regard to the progress of the investigation.' This passage from his evidence shows that there was something wrong in the working of the Home Ministry which had made the kingpin of the ministry, that is, Home Secretary, rather ineffective. If the Home Secretary could not question Sanjeevi in regard to the progress of the investigation it is difficult to imagine anybody else being able to do so.

12H.4: G.K. Handoo, witness No. 48, stated that as the Hindu Mahasabha was influential all over the country and the Partition had produced communal feelings, he would, if he had been in charge of security, have got C.I.D. policemen from all the provinces where Hindu Mahasabha was strong and he would have stationed them on a special look-out in the prayer meetings.

12H.11: On 30 January 1948 Police Superintendent A.N. Bhatia was absent. Assistant Sub-Inspector Amar Nath came on duty at 4:30 p.m. The statement of Raghunath Naik P.W.76 in Court, who was a gardener, shows that the assailant was caught hold by him, by an army man and two police constables, showing that the police was present at that time.

12H.18: B.B.S. Jetley was questioned by the Commission as to how the Viceroys used to be guarded when they went to a district or into a police range. He replied that the local police was not able to cope with the arrangements and plain-clothes and uniformed policemen had to be imported and deployed at all strategic points and the place where he was staying had to be heavily guarded. He also said that he went to Mahatma Gandhi and showed him the weapons which he had seized from the RSS and told the Home Minister that something serious might happen from the RSS. What he meant was not particularly something happening to Mahatma Gandhi but even to the Central ministers like Jawaharlal Nehru and Sardar Patel.

12H.20A: The statement of G.K. Handoo that Godse admitted to him that their next target would have been Prime Minister Nehru and the statement of J.N. Sahni that Nehru's life was also in danger find corroboration from an anonymous letter in Hindi to Godse while he was in police custody in Delhi. It bore the postmark of Bara Bazar, Calcutta, no doubt, of a date after the murder. It is in the Intelligence Bureau File Ex. 224A at pp 77-78. It praises Godse for having murdered Mahatma Gandhi and is strongly anti-Nehru who was therein dubbed as a 'crusher of the Hindu community'. It ended 'May God, Jawaharlal Nehru finishes'.

12H.23: He was asked what arrangements should have been made after the bomb was exploded at Birla House. His reply was that protections of the nature given in the blueprint should have been given i.e. an inner ring and an outer ring should have been formed along with the spotters, searchers from Bombay province for identifying any likely assailants. When asked what he would do in the case of Mahatma Gandhi who would have gone on a fast, he said, 'Why should he (Mahatma) have known anything about it? The police would have come from Bombay. The inner and outer rings would have been dressed exactly like Congress volunteers who would be around Mahatma and spotters could have been dressed as Malis and other domestic servants and nobody would have known about it.' He also said that he would have made arrangements for a watch to be kept at railway stations, the air terminals, terminal routes, Dharamshalas and other places where people are likely to come and stay.

12H.25: With regards to the Mahatma he said as follows:

'In case of Mahatma Gandhi and his security—it appears that no well-defined or carefully planned security measures whether physical or internal had been made by the Delhi Police or Intelligence Bureau. Admittedly the main responsibility for asking and for detailed and careful security measures to be instituted was by the Congress Party but if they failed to judge the seriousness and danger of the situation it was undoubtedly the business of the Delhi Police or the Intelligence Bureau to do so— particularly after the exploding of the gun cotton slab by Madanlal on 20 January 1948, at Gandhiji's prayer meeting. Further—in view of Madanlal's statement made soon after the incident—it became imperative for the Delhi Police to immediately wireless Bombay and Poona (the I.G. Police Bombay and the D.I.G., C.I.D. Poona) to send over immediately a plain-clothes squad of intelligent and knowledgeable police officers who would help in identifying the Maharashtra youths who had conspired to kill Gandhiji.

'What again is most unfortunate—is the fact that the Bombay Police in spite of the knowledge they had of the danger to Gandhij's life and even after Madanlal's arrest—failed to offer sending their knowledgeable plain-clothes staff to help in identifying any of the Maharatta (this is how Maharashtrians were referred to by north Indians in those days) youth who had been described by Madanlal. If the Bombay or Poona policemen had arrived—and if they had been utilized by the Delhi Police properly and carefully in batches at the railway stations, hotels, Dharamshalas and political party headquarters as also at the entrance and exits of Birla House and the actual prayer meeting, it would possibly have made it much more difficult for the assassin to succeed and after all security is never fool-proof but is always an intelligent and strenuous attempt to make it more and more difficult for the assassin.'

12I.5: Rajagopalachari had added that whether the assassination was due to the payment of ₹550 million or it may be the result of a more ancient grudge but Gandhiji insisted that India should carry out its agreement and not start its career of independence by breaking promises. India would have lost moral power, Gandhiji would have died of a broken heart instead of by a Hindu's revolver, ₹550 million given away saved India's moral status and added to it.

Chapter XIII of the Kapur Commission's Report deals with the investigations in Alwar.

13.1: There was a very strong rumour across the country that Savarkar and his Kesari group amongst the Hindu fanatics had reached an agreement with many of the erstwhile princes of India to forge an alliance which would stage a *coup d'etat* and overthrow the democratic government and declare India a Hindu Rashtra. The princes would then form a council which would rule as the protectors of the Hindu Rashtra, Gandhiji's murder was to be the trigger. The Princes of Alwar, Bharatpur, Bhopal, Baroda and Gwalior were said to be a part of this conspiracy. (The intelligence reports talked about a 600,000-strong cadre prepared to rise in revolt. Nagarvala's theory about a core group of twenty each supported by twenty plus volunteers spread across the nation also ties in with this scenario. Many of the rajas, smarting over the strong arm tactics used to force them to accede to the Indian dominion, would have backed any scheme which would have ensured that they clung on to their feudal authority and control over their fiefs.)

13.2: Ex. 96 dated 10 February 1948, contains a case diary of U.C. Malhotra who was appointed Chief Police Officer of Alwar State. The Case Diary No. 2 dated 8 February 1948, contains the following information: (1) A printed poster in Hindi a handwritten copy of which is Ex. 105, incited the public to murder Mahatma Gandhi; to cut him into pieces and feed his flesh to dogs and crows. This was an anonymous poster and it was not discernible as to where it was printed. (2) One Nathuram Shukla from Nagpur had visited Alwar towards the end of December 1947, he delivered speeches from the Hindu Mahasabha platform. His description is given as being 5'6" in height, wheat complexioned, small moustache, a good speaker in Hindi. This evidently does not fit in with Nathuram Godse's description. (It must be noted that there was strong suspicion that this person was indeed Nathuram Godse. He could have used a disguise or a sympathetic policeman could have written down a misleading description. What gives credence to the belief is that the police were never able to trace Nathuram Shukla; it was as if he had dissolved into thin air after delivering hate speeches in Alwar.) (3) A foreigner disguised as a Sadhu, Ascetic, came to Alwar and stayed with Girdhar Siddha, the secretary of the local Hindu Mahasabha. He had brought an envelope containing a printed letter giving the news of assassination of Mahatma Gandhi. This news was out at 3 p.m. on 30 January, at Alwar whereas the assassination actually took place at 5:17 p.m. at Delhi. (4) Sweets were distributed: Prime Minister Khare had addressed meetings pouring upon Gandhiji abuse and a curse of a Brahmin. The Hindu Mahasabha and RSS were encouraged by Dr Khare.

13.4: One Rikhi Jaimuni Kaushik, an editor of a newspaper, produced a printed article which contained the following information: (a) Anti-Gandhi Front party in Alwar distributed a pamphlet in which Hindus were requested to fast and pray for the death of Mahatma Gandhi. (b)

The RSS at Alwar had distributed sweets and held picnics on Mahatma's assassination day. (c) A few days before Mahatma Gandhi's assassination, Dr Khare had said that he was an Anti-Gandhi Front man.

13.16: Dr Khare was examined by the Commission, he said that he was anti-Gandhi i.e., against his philosophy but not anti-Gandhi qua his person. He did not know if one of the Ministers extended full facilities to the RSS. The head of the RSS, Golwalkar, did visit the State when he was the Prime Minister and he attended his meetings because he was a Nagpur man (The term 'Nagpur man' means he is a member of the RSS or a supporter/sympathizer of the fanatic organiztion.) He might have addressed the meeting also. He condemned Gandhism at the meetings and 'Guruji' (Golwalkar) also did the same. When asked whether he had allowed the RSS volunteers to be trained in the 'Samant Infantry', he replied he had no recollection.

13.24: Pannalal Choube, witness No.47, is now living in Mathura. He was an informer of the C.I.D. right up to 1952. He stated that three months before the assassination Hakim Rai, the Home Minister of Alwar, called Parchure and Godse to Alwar. There was a private meeting at which he (Pannalal) was present. Dr Khare was also present and he said that he had been unfairly treated by Mahatma Gandhi and in his opinion Mahatma Gandhi was a danger for India and something should be done in regard to him. Dr Khare was President of All India Hindu National Front Alwar, which was vituperative and against Mahatma Gandhi.

13.26: Godse and Parchure visited the arms museum in the palace as they wanted to take away pistols from there. The curator helped in getting them an old Mauser Pistol. It was taken but as it was useless it was returned by Godse and Parchure.

13.29: The conspiracy to assassinate was hatched at Alwar in which Dr N.B. Khare took a prominent part. Dr Parchure said that it was not in the interest of the country that the Mahatma should live and that Godse alone could assassinate Gandhi, Godse replied, 'Don't bother, I shall do the whole thing.'

13.32: Hakim Rai told him (Pannalal) that Godse and Parchure were big leaders of the Hindu Mahasabha.

13.33: He did not think that Godse and Parchure would actually assassinate Mahatma Gandhi.

13.34: He did not inform anyone about Godse and Parchure except the police.

13.36: He met Godse twice—once at the meeting which was for three hours and another time he met him in Delhi at the house of Prof Ram Singh about one and half months before the assassination.

13.42: The Inspector General of Police of Rajasthan has in reply to the questionnaire stated that there was nothing to show in the record that Pannalal Choube was working as a police informer in Alwar State but sometimes he used to get money from Inspector General and later on actually from some other police officers. Pannalal Choube was associating with Hindu Mahasabha but the police does not know that he was also associating with Raizada Hakim Rai. (Informers generally have an anonymous relationship with an individual officer or a couple of them and, thus, it is possible that no record or dossier is maintained about them.)

The Kapur Commission disbelieved the testimony of Pannalal Choube. Its contention was that he was a police informer, so the commission thought that he could not have been trusted by the Hindu Mahasabha leaders to be able to sit in when such important topics as the murder of Mahatma Gandhi was being discussed. (Informers are valuable because they have the ability to report on organizations and individuals being investigated, by gaining their confidence and so it is not surprising that Pannalal was able to infiltrate the Hindu Mahasabha and RSS and gain their trust. The fact that he was reportedly being paid by a very senior officer of the rank of inpsector-general, shows how important he was and how much the police trusted him.) The fact remains that the testimony of a witness in Alwar states that Parchure and Godse were in Alwar in December 1947 looking for a handgun. When, in the last week of January, Nathuram failed to procure a reliable handgun, Savarkar reminded him of Parchure and suggested he go to Gwalior, where he succeeded in procuring one of the most efficient handguns for close range murder. The Berretta was bought with the help of Parchure. The incidents in Alwar and Gwalior cannot be brushed away as unconnected coincidences. It must also be remembered that the Gwalior part of the conspiracy was least investigated because the police were satisfied after obtaining Parchure's detailed confession. (And the bungler Rana was heading the inquiry in Gwalior.)

The commission next examined M.L. Hooja, witness no. 59. He was the assistant director of Intelligence Bureau in 1948 and had submitted a report on the activities of the RSS in the Alwar principality.

13.50: Hooja concentrated his investigation on two points (1) Possible connection of the local people in the conspiracy to assassinate Mahatma Gandhi and (2) patronage and assistance by the state to the RSS organization.

13.51: There was considerable evidence of patronage and aid by the state to the RSS. Full facilities were provided for the training camp and rally in May–June 1947 of RSS officers. This was given under the direct orders of the Prime Minister Dr Khare and the Home Minister Raizada Hakim Rai, apparently with the knowledge of the ruler. Both Prime Minister and Home Minister took prominent part in RSS activities and the Prime Minister was in constant touch with all its local activities and extended fullest patronage to it.

13.55: The investigation into the conspiracy leading to Mahatma Gandhi's assassination revealed that one Nathu Ram Shukla of Jabbalpur (elsewhere in the report, he is stated to be from Nagpur) had come and stayed under state patronage and toured various parts of the State. It was suspected by people that he really was Nathuram Godse.

13.56: Investigation was unfortunately hampered by the fact that the local police was unreliable and even the I.G.P. was a 'staunch Rajput'. (In other words, likely to be a fanatic Hindu or supporter of the idea of Hindu Rashtra.)

13.58: Another report of M.L. Hooja dated 23 February 1948 restates that Nathu Ram Shukla was suspected to be, Nathuram Godse.

13.68: The Commission appreciates the misgivings of the Government of India in regard to Alwar where all these activities were carried on which had a communal colour and an anti-Congress and anti Praja Mandal (People's Council) leanings. Besides these, Dr N.B. Khare himself had been rather intemperate in condemning Mahatma Gandhi, so much so that he resorted to the ancient cult of cursing and he did so against Mahatma Gandhi by issuing 'A Brahmin's Curse' on him, Ex. 88 dated 12 October 1947. He has stated that he was opposed to Gandhiji's politics not his person. (Issuing a 'Brahmin's Curse' on Gandhiji shows that it was aimed not at his politics but at his person. It is akin to a practitioner of black magic piercing a doll with a nail but claiming it is not intended to harm the person but as a protest against his actions.) He denied any association of Godse or Parchure with Alwar. But police reports containing information no doubt collected after the murder have a different story to give (sic).

13.70: Other documents show that on the Dussehra day on 3 October 1938 Dr Khare hoisted a flag of open rebellion against Gandhiji and uttered a curse upon him and on his philosophy.

13.73: All this evidence put together shows that an atmosphere had been created in Alwar State which was anti-Congress and also anti-Gandhi; whether it was a purely anti-Gandhi movement is not easy to decide. However, Dr Khare's antecedents and his encouragement to the RSS and to the militant Hindu Mahasabha leaders were indicative of conditions being produced which were conducive to strong anti-Gandhi activities.

Chapter XIV deals with the investigations in Gwalior. Here it needs to be noted that the investigating officer sent to Gwalior was the infamous U.H. Rana. Even after his bungling of the bomb attack investigations, Rana was given the responsibility to investigate the murder, his lapses and carelessness had helped in succeeding.

14.1: Gopi Krishna Katarey who claims to have been an active political worker in Gwalior for about 30 years stated in his affidavit, Ex. 91, that a month or two before the assassination of the Mahatma there was a leading article in a weekly, which was the mouthpiece of the Hindu Mahasabha, that Mahatma Gandhi and Pandit Nehru should be murdered, and that the Hindu Mahasabha received the full patronage of the Government of Gwalior. He also said that about a fortnight before the murder of Mahatma Gandhi a cheque of ₹65,000 was given to one of the accused in the Gandhi murder case to regroup Goondas and purchase arms to launch a murderous attack on the Congress workers who were demanding a people's government in Gwalior and that it was out of this fund that the pistol with which the murderer shot Gandhiji was purchased. (The donor was the ruler of Gwalior Jiajirao Scindia.) When these matters came to light Sardar Patel hushed them up because the Maharani of Gwalior 'beseeched him for forgiveness' and promised obedience hence forth. He added that it was a tragedy that the real criminals who masterminded the murder were not tried.

14.4: The cheque referred to by him (Katarey) was given to Dr Parchure. The Maharaja thought that the National Movement was a danger which should be fought. He, Katarey, had told Leela Dhar Joshi after he became the Premier of the state about the cheque and he said that he would consult Sardar Patel before doing anything. Subsequently, he was told that since the Maharaja had acceded, no action was called for. The witness was externed for some time and after he returned met a person who was anti-Congress and was doing anti-Congress propaganda. He had got Godse's statement published and he said that it was financed by Sardar Angre's son. His name was Gokhale and he was from Poona.

14.7: Jetley, D.I.G., witness No. 55, had investigated the Gwalior matters. He had gone to Gwalior because it had gone around that the Maratha Princes had something to do with the Maratha clique responsible for Gandhiji's murder. ('Maratha' here refers to how Marathi speaking people were referred to by north Indians and not the Maratha caste.)

Chapter XV deals with Poona. The commission had carried out a very detailed study of the situation in Poona from 1947. Poona was described as a stronghold of the Hindu Mahasabha and Savarkarites. Out of the eight accused in the Gandhi murder case, the principal four accused belonged to Poona; V.R. Karkare was their close associate and V.D. Savarkar, their mentor and inspiration.

15.14: The Bombay Provincial Weekly Letter, Ex. 155, of 5 July 1947, shows that there was a bomb explosion on 26 June 1947 in Poona city. The matter went up to the premier, B.G. Kher, and on 9 July 1947 his remarks were, 'was not the Editor of *Agranee* arrested? I would like to know progress.' On what basis the *Agranee* was brought in is shown by the statement of Morarji Desai that there was some information indicative of the editor's connection with such subversive activities. Upon this the Home Department, Bombay, sent an express letter, dated 12 July 1947, to the District Magistrate, Poona, Ex. 156, asking for progress of the investigation. It enquired whether the editor of the *Agranee* was also arrested in connection therewith, adding that the Government should be kept informed as to the investigation into the matter. After a fortnight or so of the letter, the District Magistrate, on 29 July, sent his reply, Ex. 157, about the bomb explosion and enclosed therewith a report of the D.S.P. Poona, dated 23 July 1947, Ex. 157A, in which the details of the bomb explosion of 26th June were given which were to the effect that N.R. Athawale, Secretary of the Poona City Hindu Mahasabha was arrested in connection with the bomb explosion; that he had made a confessional statement under Section 164 Cr.P.C. to the effect that the bomb (hand grenade) had been given to him by N.D. Apte of the *Agranee*; that he (Athawale) threw the bomb from the second storey of the library; that Athawale's house was searched but nothing incriminating was found; and that against Athwale and Apte information was laid under section 4 of the Explosives Substance Act (Exs. 157 and 157A) and their trial was awaited.'

15.17: On 3 September 1947, the District Magistrate, S.G. Barve, gave sanction for the withdrawal of the case against Athawale and Apte under Section 494, Cr.P.C. The public prosecutor was directed to put in the application for withdrawal which he did and the case was thus withdrawn.

(This case is very important in connection with the Gandhi murder conspiracy. Later on, in the chapter dealing with Ahmednagar, it is stated that the hand grenade used in Poona by Athawale who confessed that it was given to him by Apte was from the same batch of hand grenades exploded at Kapda Bazaar in Ahmednagar in which the involvement of Vishnu Karkare and Madanlal Pahwa was suspected. Thus, an association between Godse and Apte of Poona and Karkare and Pahwa of Ahmednagar was established, much before the failed attack on Gandhi on 20 January, the police were aware of the identity of those alluded to in Madanlal's statements and the information provided by Prof. Jain. The bomb case also established the fact that Godse and Apte of *Agranee* were known to employ firearms and explosives in their protests. There is one more association going back by about over a decade, which links this bomb explosion more closely to Mahatma Gandhi. Athawale, in his confession, had said that he was asked to toss the grenade from the second story of the library. In 1934, a hand grenade was thrown from an upper floor on the motorcade bringing Gandhi to the Corporation Auditorium in Poona. The modus operandi in both the cases is the same and a person convicted in the murder of Mahatma Gandhi was an accused in the incident. This was indicative of a larger conspiracy and the involvement of many more persons in the conspiracy and that of militarist organizations like the RSS.)

15.18: The Commission had before it the DSP of Poona as witness No. 38, it is not very happy about his evidence. He stated that the *Agranee* or the *Hindu Rashtra* did not preach violence and he had no knowledge if the *Agranee* was stopped. It never came to his knowledge that either Apte or Nathuram Godse preached violence or indulged in any illegal activities. But there is nothing on record to show what energetic steps, if any, were taken to make a thorough investigation into the origin, possession and use or misuse of the bomb. (It is surprising that a very senior police officer wasn't aware of the antecedents of the editor and publisher of *Agranee* and later *Hindu Rashtra*, while the provincial government was actively prosecuting and fining them for a campaign of hate.)

(After this, the commission made a very startling charge, showing the attitude of officialdom towards the Kapur Commission.) At the end of Para 15.20 of the report, it is mentioned: 'And although officers of the Commission were able to make a successful search in the Record Rooms of the Delhi Collectorate, they were unable to do so in Poona and Ahmednagar.' (It is very surprising that a commission established by the Union government to inquire into hitherto not known detailes of the Gandhi murder conspiracy was being thwarted by government officials in a province state ruled by a Congress government. They were still attempting a cover up).

15.28: In two issues of the *Agranee* and the *Hindu Rashtra* there is a clear indication of incitement to violence. In Ex. 233-A the issue of *Agranee* dated 12 April 1947, one of the captions is 'Mahatma Gandhi, Commit Suicide' and epithets like 'his cowardly philosophy', 'his cowardly and worthless non-violence' were used towards him. He was also called 'Sokaji' (a derogatory term used to insult) and it was suggested that 'he should commit suicide', if not he should 'bid good-bye forever to Indian politics'.

15.29: In the same issue of the *Hindu Rashtra*, Ex. 233 of 7 September 1947, it was said, 'And if anyone has really the urge for Akhand Hindustan (lit. Undivided India) and if a feeling of sacrificing one's own life for its sake has been created, then do not strike at a wrong place! The flood of Indian bravery will in no time integrate the whole India into one.'

15.30: All this shows that the writings in the *Agranee* or the *Hindu Rashtra* were strongly anti-Gandhi but were so cleverly worded in Marathi, so that they did not come within the purview of the Indian Penal Code, i.e. Incitement to Murder.

15.31: There were some speeches made which were also inflammatory. Dr Parchure in his speech, Ex. 131, said, 'Gandhiji and Nehru will surely reap the fruits of their sins in a short time if the attitude assumed by them is continued.'

15.32: At another meeting on the following day, i.e., 3 December 1947, Ex. 206, G.V. Ketkar presided, he said that they should consider Gandhiism-cum-False Nationalism as their enemy No.1. This speech by Ketkar also shows his attitude towards Gandhi's philosophy though it need not be termed as being against Gandhi himself.

Hindu Rashtra Dal

15.34: In 1942 an organization known as the Hindu Rashtra Dal was formed with V.D. Savarkar as its dictator (Ex. 34 dated 1 August 1944) and its original organisers were Date, Gogte, N.D. Apte and N.V. Godse. The aims and object of the movement were the furtherance of the Hindu Sabha activities. This document also shows that in May 1943 Apte and Godse organized its second annual training camp at which volunteers from various Maratha districts, Bombay city and Maratha ruled Indian states such as Sangli, Miraj and Indore were present. It also shows that Savarkar was the chief architect and force behind the Dal. He laid down the policy and exhorted its volunteers to show and give implicit allegiance to him as the sole director.

15.36: On 22 May 1947, ex. 54, a document which deals with the Hindu Rashtra Dal was issued by Rao Saheb Gurtu, for D.I.G., C.I.D. Poona to all D.S.P.s and district magistrates, the objective of this document was to warn the district authorities against the attempts to revive and to revitalize the Dal. There was a meeting on 3 July 1947 in the Tilak Samrak Mandir (Ex.112) under the auspices of the Poona City Hindu Sabha, where about 5000 persons were present to observe the anti-Partition Day as a 'Kalaa Divas' (Black Day). L.B. Bhopatkar of Poona presided. The speakers included G.V. Ketkar and N.V. Godse besides other local leaders of the Hindu Sabha movement. Ketkar expressed his gratification at the successes of the observance of the Black Day and Godse said that the time for action had arrived.

15.38: On 8 August 1947 a letter, Ex. 113, was issued by the government to the D.I.G., C.I.D., Poona and the commissioner of Police, Bombay asking for the list of officers and members of the RSS and leaders of Hindu Mahasabha organizations and directing them to keep a strict watch on the operations of these two movements and send reports regarding that matter. This appears to be based on the note of B.G. Kher and Desai, Ex. 177, dated 7 August 1947. Pursuant thereto a list was prepared and sent on 19 August 1947, Ex. 114.

15.39: Likewise a similar list, Ex.114A, was prepared about Ahmednagar, which is a very important document. Amongst the Hindu Sabha workers at Poona there were N.V. Godse, N.D. Apte, the latter shown as potentially dangerous and a staunch Savarkarite organizer of the Hindu Rashtra Dal, the activities of the former were of a similar nature. Other members were G.V. Ketkar, also a staunch Savarkarite, editor of the *Maratha* and a trustee of the Kesari Maratha Trust and described as the brain behind the Hindu Sabha activities. Another member was N.R. Athawale shown as a co-worker of N.D. Apte, potentially dangerous, who was arrested under Section 3 of the Explosives Substances Act. Another person was D.R. Badge who is shown as proprietor of the Hindu Shastra Bhandar dealing in unlicensed weapons, a staunch Hindu Mahasabhaite, against whom there were two prosecutions under the Arms Act and who was considered to be potentially dangerous. There is also another list of the Poona District Hindu Mahasabha leaders. That also includes N.V. Godse, N.D. Apte, G.V. Ketkar, N.R. Athawale and several other Maharashtrians.

15.40: Even at the expense of repetition it may be stated that this is a document which would show the close association of Apte, Godse, Badge and others with an active Savarkar group which is really repetitive of what the documents relating to 1942 and 1944 showed. The association was thus old and longstanding.

Jayprakash Narayan's Speech

15.44: On 26 November 1947, a meeting was held in Kirkee Bazaar attended by about a thousand persons. It was addressed by Jayprakash Narayan, the Socialist leader (Ex.122). In this speech, Narayan wanted the arsenal and ammunition factory workers to know the then prevailing politics. He said that the Muslim League had achieved Pakistan at the cost of the poor Muslims and that the rich capitalist Mohammedans had run away to Pakistan. He exhorted others not to drive away the Muslims and thus create more enemies and that it was the rulers of Indian States, the Rajas and Maharajas, who were trying to create trouble amongst Hindu and Muslim labourers in order to strengthen their own position. Further that the Army personnel were citizens of the country and had a right to take part in politics. He described the evil of communalism which according to him was still prevailing in the Army which he deduced from rioting and killing which was being done by the Armed forces. This is a matter upon which the Commission is not called upon to express its opinion but perhaps the Defence Forces would not relish this accusation against them.

Parchure's Speech

15.45: There was a meeting in the Tilak Samrak Mandir, Poona on 2 December 1947 (Ex.131). The Chief Speaker was Dr D.S. Parchure of Gwalior who was convicted in the Gandhi Murder Conspiracy Case but was acquitted on appeal. He was described as a second Savarkar and that so great was his influence that on every mosque in Gwalior flew the Bhagva flag. In his speech Dr Parchure, after referring to the state of affairs in Gwalior, advocated the use of force to achieve whatever they wanted. He also said that Gwalior Army was full of Muslims who were in a majority and that the State was increasing the Muslim elements and that the adviser Srinivasan had advised the Ruler that Parchure and his followers 'were like dogs'. The trend of the speech was anti-Congress and extremely anti-Muslim. He criticized Pandit Nehru's policy as regards Kashmir and pointed out the quiescence of Hindus in the face of Mohammedan aggressiveness. In the end he made a significant remark, the importance of which was perhaps not then appreciated: 'Gandhi and Nehru would surely reap the fruits of their sins in a short time.' This speech was made in Hindi and because there was no Hindi shorthand reporter in the police, it could not be taken down verbatim and was reproduced from memory by the police reporters who were present. When a report of this went to Government they wanted a more authentic report of the speech but there could be nothing better because of the speech not being in Marathi.

Ketkar's Speech

15.46: On 3 December 1947, there was a meeting presided over by G.V. Ketkar (Ex. 206). In this speech he described Gandhism as enemy No. 1 showing thereby that his attitude of mind was not very different from that of the other members of the Savarkar group in regard to Gandhian philosophy. Of course, it does not mean that he was equally a votary of violence or protagonist of murder.

15.47: An abstract of intelligence (Ex.121) dated 27 December 1947, shows that on 18 December the Poona Police raided the house of R.J. Deshmukh who had close contact with R.S. Khanolkar and recovered from there STEN gun cartridges, rifle cartridges, revolver cartridges, bombs and hand grenade shells and also a bottle containing arsenic trichloride, an explosive substance. In connection with this find five persons were arrested and investigations made but the second paragraph of the report states that the collection of arms and ammunition was to facilitate the people in the Hyderabad struggle which, it appears, was a handy cover for the collection of arms by this group of people to which Godse etc. belonged and was an easy façade to hide their real intentions and objectives.

15.49: On 22 March 1947 on the eve of New Year's Day, (Hindu Calendar) Gudi Padva, an objectionable pamphlet, Ex. 265A, advocating terrorism of Savarkar type was distributed at the Railway Stations, Shivaji Nagar and Dehu but the police could not discover where they were printed and who distributed them.

Gopal Godse

15.50: Gopal Godse, witness No. 33, has published certain articles regarding the murder of Mahatma Gandhi. In Ex. 56 in the monthly journal, the *Painjan*, of August 1966, he said that it was difficult for the officials to think that a person who had failed once to assassinate Gandhiji would not dare to make another attempt because of the arrest of one person and the likely arrest of others within a few days and a strong cordon of security men around Gandhiji. He has added that there was complacency shown by security police in carrying out investigation between 20 and 30 January 1948. 'The police miserably failed to derive any advantage from the statements, of Jain and Madanlal. If only they had shown keenness in investigation the tragedy would have been avoided. In spite of all the precautions there are things such as luck, chance or suitability of circumstances. A person gets an opportunity many a time just by luck.'

15.51: Ex. 57, issue of that journal of September 1966, deals with the subject when the plot could have been hatched. The issue of November-December, 1966 of that journal is Ex. 55 under the heading 'Gandhi Murder and Maulana Azad'. Gopal Godse has said that Nathuram Godse did not like the murder of Gandhiji and both he and Apte would have laid down their lives to prevent Partition and to protect the life of Gandhiji. He blamed Maulana Azad for creating trouble between Sardar Patel and Pt Nehru through, as it were, Gandhiji. He blamed Maulana Azad for being the author of the conditions which were laid down by Mahatma Gandhi for breaking his fast.

Reply to Jayprakash Narayan's Speech

15.53: Ex. 71 is the report of the proceedings of the meeting of the Hindu Mahasabha at Shivaji Mandir held at 6:30 p.m. on 28 November 1947, where about 2000 people were present and the speakers were V.B. Gogte and N.V. Godse, the subject on which speeches were made was 'Hindu Nation and Jayprakash Narayan'. The speakers twitted Jayprakash Narayan about his socialism and ridiculed his attack on the Hindu Mahasabha and the RSS and accused the Socialists of hypocrisy and also spoke about atrocities of Muslims on Hindu women and accused the Socialists of helping in the creation of Pakistan and the partition of India and its consequences.

15.54: They also protested against handing over Kashmir to Sheikh Abdullah and taking it away from a Hindu king. It was also said there that the RSS and the Hindu Mahasabha were accused of conspiracy to murder Pt Nehru. There was also a reference to Mahatma Gandhi.

Statements of Witnesses in Poona

15.63: N.M. Kamte, retired Inspector General of Police witness No. 4 was examined thrice by the Commission and once before Pathak. He stated that Hindu Mahasabha movement did exist in Poona but he could not say if it was a strong movement. Its aims and objectives were to unite the Hindus and protect their interests, there was antagonism between the Hindu Mahasabha and the Congress. The Hindu Rashtra Dal in Poona was led by Chitpavan Brahmins.

15.64: Although the Hindu Mahasabha was not very much excited about the Partition, it was excited when the news of what was happening in western Punjab came.

15.67: He read about the bomb attack in the newspapers. Nobody informed him about that fact. He could not connect Madanlal with any person in Poona nor could he say if the Poona Police knew that Madanlal was living in Ahmednagar. Kamte did not know Prof Jain. Between the exploding of the bomb and the murder of the Mahatma he did not know who the conspirators were and he had no reason to suspect Poona people being involved in it. The first time he came to know about this fact was when Sanjeevi telephoned him about the murder on 30 January 1948 in the evening.

15.69: The Poona Police were not associated in the investigation from 20 to 30 January 1948 excepting that Rana was in Delhi and had been given certain information and also a copy of Madanlal's statement dated 24 January 1948 which was shown to him (Kamte) by Rana a day or two after the murder.

15.74: Immediately after he got information about the murder he sent for Rana and asked him for the statement of Madanlal which Rana showed him. Kamte then asked him why he had not taken immediate action, come to Poona and informed Gurtu. Rana's reply was that he was waiting for Inspector Angarkar who was then on leave. Kamte did not belive that the Poona Police was sympathetic towards the conspirators or the RSS.

15.78: He (Kamte) first said that he did not know that the intention of the conspirators was to kidnap Mahatma Gandhi. He knew nothing about the facts contained in Nagarvala's letter to Sanjeevi dated 30 January 1948. Ex. 8. Then Kamte added that he had a faint recollection that Nagarvala may have told him about the theory of kidnapping. He thought that it was a fantastic theory.

In answer to another question he said: 'The vigilance will depend on the suspicion against the persons concerned. In this case, the suspicion was not of murdering Mahatmaji but the suspicion was that there were people in Poona who were against Mahatmaji's idea of giving 55 crores (550 million) to Pakistan. If Gurtu had learnt about Madanlal's statement, he could easily have come to the conclusion that these are the people who were conspiring to murder Mahatmaji.'

15.82: Had he (Kamte) known that the people in the conspiracy were from Bombay province he would have placed 20 or 25 persons from Bombay around Mahatma Gandhi to see that the conspirators did not get anywhere near him. Godse etc. were known to the Poona C.I.D. There must have been good reason why they were not shadowed. Once a man was in a list called the Black List, he was shadowed for 24 hours. As the names of Godse etc. were not in the List it means C.I.D. did not know that they were dangerous.

(This seems to be a very curious stand. Less than six months before this, Apte was an accused in a bomb attack in Poona. Godse was known to be a close associate of Apte and yet all the policemen kept saying that they did not think that these persons were potentially dangerous.)

15.84: In cross examination he (Kamte) said if the statement Ex. 1 had been shown to him earlier, he would have got those persons mentioned there shadowed and kept them under constant watch. If the statement showed that there was a conspiracy to murder, he would have asked the police to arrest them at once and had he been told that one was an editor of the *Hindu Rashtra,* Poona and the other the owner of Shastra Bhandar, he would have been able to find out at once through his subordinate staff as to the identity of those persons. Before the murder he had not heard of Apte or Nathuram Godse. If he had arrested them, he might or might not have put shadow on their close associates.

1.87: In his letter to Sanjeevi dated 20 April 1948, Ex. 97, Kamte had complained about Rana's bungling. He said that his intention was to make Rana realize the desirability of taking steps immediately. He got a copy of Madanlal's statement and his desire was that Rana should not commit a mistake like that again. It shows that in the opinion of Kamte, Rana bungled in not making any use of the statement of Madanlal which had been handed over to him in Delhi on 25 January 1948. But will there be another Gandhi to be protected?

U.H. Rana, Wit. 3

15.90: U.H. Rana, D.I.G., CID witness No. 3 when examined on 7 February 1967, stated that he was called by Sanjeevi on the day following the explosion and was told that Madanlal had given certain information showing that his companions were from Bombay side but it did not disclose where they belonged to. He had not stated that they belonged to Poona but he had mentioned Savarkar. Rana was also told that Madanlal had said that one of them was a Sadhu with a beard and another was his servant named Shankar and the third was an editor of a newspaper but he did not say where the newspaper was published. Since Savarkar was mentioned, Rana at once concluded that they must be Savarkarites.

15.94: During the time that he was D.I.G., C.I.D., Poona, he did not hear the story of Godse and others going to Panchgani. Nothing of importance came to his notice about the activities of Nathuram Godse or of Apte or of Badge or of their group, nor that they were directed towards violence. The police reporters whose duty it was to report proceedings or the speeches of the meetings addressed by politicians did not make any such report. These persons were not on the Black List to be shadowed. Nor did he know that the Kesari Group was a militant group. He did not know that G.V. Ketkar, Bhagwan and others were connected with the Hindu Mahasabha.

15.97: He had no knowledge of Karkare and Madanlal having been ordered to be detained. When asked if he had seen the report of Sub Inspector Balkundi dated 4 January 1948, Ex. 66, about Karkare and Madanlal, he replied that he must have seen it because there was his endorsement dated 14 January on it. But it was not within his powers to recommend or not to recommend detention. They were not persons with provincial 'reputation'. He was not camping at Ahmednagar in January, the A.D.I.G. (Crime) was.

15.99: Rana was then examined in regard to various bomb incidents at Ahmednagar. He said that he had seen the reports and sent Inspector Razak on 12 December 1947, to investigate them. If written reports were sent in regard to Ahmednagar incidents and his initials are on them, then he must have seen them. He was shown the report of Inspector Razak about the activities of Madanlal etc. but he said that it did not come to his notice but it might have come to his office. Nor did he know that Karkare was holding conferences with Apte and Godse. According to what he knew, neither Godse nor Apte were of provincial or inter provincial importance. It was not reported to him that Godse and Apte were meeting Karkare in Ahmednagar.

15.100: He had not seen Ex. 67, the report of Sub-Inspector Balkundi dated 29 January 1948 about the identity of Madanlal. If the D.S.P. had received any information in regard to Madanlal in the ordinary course he should have sent it to him. There were violent activities in Poona and Ahmednagar but there was nothing to show that they were anti-Gandhi. They were anti-Muslim.

15.106: When asked about the statement of K.M. Munshi about the Poona School of thought led by Savarkar, he said it did exist but there was no information that its violence would be directed against Mahatma Gandhi, nor did he know that the Kesari group was against Mahatma Gandhi.

15.110: Rana said: 'I saw Sanjeevi at about 9:30 a.m. or 10:00 a.m. He said that Madanlal had started talking and the latter stated that he came from Bombay, that he had met Savarkar; and also gave the name of one Karkare and mentioned one Sadhu who had a servant. Sanjeevi did not give me the name of the *Agranee* or its proprietor or editor or the name of *Hindu Rashtra*, its proprietor or editor. I would like to repeat that he

(Sanjeevi) did not mention the names of either newspaper—*Agranee* or *Hindu Rashtra*—or that of their proprietors or editors.'

15.112: In the statement of Madanlal which he brought to Bombay, the name of the *Agranee* or the *Hindu Rashtra* was mentioned. There was also mention of the editor and the proprietor. There appears to be some confusion in the witness' mind as the name *Agranee* is not there. He did not telephone to Poona from Nagarvala's house because Nagarvala told him that there was a big organization and they wanted to make simultaneous arrests, also that Nagarvala's information was that they wanted to kidnap Mahatma Gandhi. Therefore, he did not inform his office in Poona to take any precautions in regard to the Editor of the *Agranee*. Besides, he was going to Poona next morning, he thought he would take action when he reached there.

15.114: He did not think that the culprits would return immediately to put their design into operation. Sanjeevi was also of the same opinion more particularly because one of them had been arrested.

15.117: Rana was asked a specific question whether the culprits were known to the Poona CID as being persons who were likely to take part in violent activities. He replied: 'I can now say that amongst them Apte, Godse, Karkare, Athawle and Badge were the potential mischief makers who were taking part in violent activities.'

15.118: He was then asked if the sending of Bombay Police would have averted the catastrophe. He replied that there were too many assumptions in the question, that the same person would commit the offence, that they would select the same place or that the men sent there would be able to identify them. He said that up to 22 January he did not know that Madanlal had named any other persons excepting Karkare and Savarkar. He was not told that Madanlal had made a statement to the police on the midnight of 20 January 1948. Sanjeevi did tell him that Madanlal had other associates on Bombay side and one of them was a Sadhu wearing a beard but he did not say that amongst them one was a manager or editor of the *Rashtra* newspaper nor did Sanjeevi say that Madanlal had given descriptions of six companions as his co-conspirators.

15.121: He did not leave Madanlal's statement with Nagarvala because (1) Nagarvala already had the information from Home Minister, (2)

He had been informed about Karkare and Savarkar, (3) Nagarvala had nothing to do with Poona, and (4) He himself was going to Poona the following day and he would take action himself.

(The next day, Rana conveniently developed fever and so he decided to postpone his return to Poona.)

15.128: He (Rana) went to see the home minister on the 28th morning. His object was to find out who his informant was which Nagarvala had not been able to get. If the identity had been given, it is possible that they might have been able to find out something more. He reached Delhi after the murder on 2 February. He did not know anything about Sathe who was mentioned by Mrs Barve.

15.129: In cross examination he (Rana) said that when he went to Sanjeevi on the 21st there were some other police officers one of whom was Rikhikesh and the other was Bhatia who were investigating officers in the Bomb Case. Neither of them had a statement of Madanlal with them and the talk was oral, no document was referred to and nobody mentioned the editor of *Agranee* or *Hindu Rashtra* or any newspaper nor was he asked by Sanjeevi to find out about any newspaper nor was he asked by Sanjeevi to find out about the editor or publisher of a newspaper. He was told that Madanlal had mentioned three persons, Karkare, a Sadhu and his servant, and the other companions were Marathas from Bombay side. As soon as Marathas of Bombay were mentioned, he (Rana) suspected Savarkar and his group. He mentioned Bombay to Sanjeevi because Savarkar resided there and Poona because it was the stronghold of the Hindu Mahasabhaite group. He had not heard that the officers going to Bombay had taken a précis of Madanlal's statement. He was told that Madanlal's statement was in Urdu; it was being translated to help him and the Bombay Police in the investigation in Bombay.

15.131: From the fact that Sanjeevi knew that he (Rana) was travelling by train, he must be under the impression that because one of the conspirators had been arrested, the others were not likely to come back soon to commit any further offences. Sanjeevi told him that it would be sufficient if he took necessary action on reaching Bombay and Poona and that he should proceed cautiously and secretly and round up the whole lot in one sweep. On the 25th Sanjeevi told him that one of the conspirators was an editor of a newspaper, but he did not mention the name of the person or the place of publication of the paper.

15.136: Nagarvala also told him that he had made inquiries from Ahmednagar and was told that Karkare was no longer there and he had posted his men to be on the look-out for Karkare in Bombay and he also wanted some Police officers from Poona to identify Badge, a known trafficker in illicit arms. Nagarvala told him that his theory was that the attempt was to kidnap Mahatma Gandhi. He had concluded this on the basis of the information he had from his informers. Nagarvala told him that there were 20 principals and each one of them had a lot of persons working under them and Nagarvala believed that information to be correct.

15.137: Rana: 'When Nagarvala was speaking and I was listening to him and asking him some questions also about it. I did not think this theory to be fantastic; on the other hand I asked him to inform the D.I.B. on telephone.'

15.141: When he went to Poona he asked for Angarkar but he was ill. Then he asked for Deulkar but he also was not available being away in Alibaug and he was called back immediately by wireless. Rao Sahib Gurtu knew the names of all the culprits mentioned by Madanlal. Other officers were available in Poona but he (Rana) only wanted Angarkar or Deulkar because they were the only ones who knew the names of the associates of Karkare and their hide-outs. He did not ask anyone about the presence of those persons in Poona. Subsequent inquiries showed that when he reached Poona, Apte and Godse were not there and he himself did not know the whereabouts of Badge. He learnt that Karkare was called Maharaj. After the murder, Sanjeevi asked Kamte to send some Police Officers from Bombay and they were sent by military plane on 31 January but he did not know who they were.

(That was because there was a fear that Central Cabinet Ministers would also be attacked. When Rana was sent back to Delhi to supervise the investigation, he stayed with Sanjeevi, and on the morning of the third day, they had a talk with each other but Sanjeevi did not tell him that after the bomb attack Nagarvala had proceeded on an absolutely wrong line of investigation and ignored information provided to him.)

Rao Sahib Gurtu, Wit. 22

15.146: Rao Sahib Gurtu, witness No. 22, was the assistant D.I.G., C.I.D. at Poona. He stated that the D.S.P. Ahmednagar made a reference towards the end of 1947 or thereabout about Madanlal who had addressed a meeting of refugees which had resulted in disturbances. The witness also knew about Karkare who was a prominent Hindu Mahasabha leader in Ahmednagar.

15.147: Reports used to come in about the communal activities of the group consisting of Nathuram Godse, Karkare, Apte and Badge and several other persons whose names he could not recollect, but they went under the name of Hindu Sabha Movement. There were reports that bombs were being prepared by some of the workers of the Hindu Mahasabha Movement but not that they intended to murder Mahatma Gandhi.

15.153: The witness was shown an intercepted letter of Karkare (Ex.43) which was addressed to various newspapers in Poona for publication. He said he must have come to know about it as it bore his endorsement. He knew about the orders for the detention of Karkare but could not say why they were passed.

15.154: Activities of Godse were also being watched by the police but it was not a continuous watch so as to prevent his eluding it. If any name had been given to Poona Police, it would have taken steps to apprehend them. He could not remember having any talks with Nagarvala during the period from 20 January to 30 January 1948. If the witness had been told that one of the persons mentioned by Madanlal was the editor of *Agranee* or the *Hindu Rashtra*, he would have arrested him at once. When he was asked how he would have arrested persons named by Madanlal when warrants on Karkare could not be effectively served, his reply was that that was being done by the District Police and not by the CID.

15.155: In his cross examination he (Gurtu) stated that reports were sent every week to amongst others, the D.I.B. by the D.I.G. compiled from the reports received by the D.S.P.s and that these reports contained the names of Godse, Apte, Karkare, Savarkar and Dr Parchure of Gwalior. Although from 15 August 1947, a watch was kept by the local police on certain Hindu Mahasabha and RSS workers, the watch was discontinued in November 1947,

Pravinsinhji Vijaysinhji, Wit. 38

Witness No. 38, Pravinsinhji Vijaysinhji, was D.S.P. of Poona between July 1947 and May 1949 and subsequently rose to be the Inspector General of Police of Bombay. His deposition shows that in mid 1947 communal violence in Poona City was running very high because of the Partition and the feeling against Muslims. The prominent Hindu Mahasabha workers then included Bhopatkar, Abhyankar, Apte, Nathuram Godse and G.V. Ketkar but their activities were confined to being anti-Muslim. There was no overt attack against the Muslim League or against the Muslims; although they carried on propaganda against the Congress because it agreed to the Partition and there was strong feeling against Mahatma Gandhi as being the main architect of the Partition. There was no overt attack against them.

15.165: A specific question was put to the witness about the July speech of Nathuram Godse in which he said that secret organizations should be formed and revolutionary methods resorted to and he had hinted that the time had come to do away with the top ranking Congress leaders or that Gandhiji and Nehru being thorns in the establishment of Hindu Rajya should be removed. The witness' reply was that it did not happen during his time. He was a reader of the *Kesari* and he heard nothing about the activities of Apte or his taking part in the bomb explosion. At no time did it come to his notice that Nathuram Godse or Apte were indulging in illegal activities.

15.167: This witness knew nothing about Sathe who was mentioned in the statement of Mrs Barve. If Barve had the information that Poona people had gone to Delhi to murder Mahatma Gandhi, he would certainly have passed it on to him (the witness). The Police was quite vigilant and tried to keep itself informed of the activities of every person who was likely to resort to violence. But it had no knowledge about what Apte and Godse were doing.

15.170: Coming to Hindu Rashtra Dal, the witness stated that a circular was issued to watch its activities and the activities of its members but he could not remember who its members were.

It must be noted that Pravinsinhji Vijaysinhji characterized the bomb explosion in Poona, in which Athawale and Apte were detained, as unimportant since, according to him, it was not targeted at any specific person. The fact that the bomb injured a young boy, damaged a vehicle and was exploded in a central part of the city did not seem to concern him.

G. P. Angarkar, Wit. 68

15.187: Deputy Superintendent of Police G.P. Angarkar, witness No. 68, was in the Intelligence Branch during the relevant period from July 1947 to end of January 1948. Police shorthand reporters sent the proceedings of meetings to him and he sent them on to higher officers. Amongst those whose speeches had to be reported were some Hindu Sabha workers but there were no RSS workers in the list. Amongst the former were Barrister Savarkar and L.B. Bhopatkar. Savarkar was the President of Hindu Mahasabha, Nathuram Godse was a kind of a bodyguard of him but was not particularly prominent. Apte was at one time a Government servant and an honorary recruiting officer in the Indian Army in Ahmednagar. (Apte was actually an honorary recruiting officer for the RIAF in Poona during the Second World War.) Badge had a Shastra Bhandar which was raided several times. Reports were sent to other districts also in regard to Badge when he sent any arms to those districts. But he was not considered dangerous and, therefore, his absence from Poona was not noticed.

15.196: The policy of the *Agranee* was anti-Gandhi and anti-Congress and the paper was pronouncedly a communalist paper.

15.199: After the Partition there was Hindu Muslim tension in Poona also. He could not say whether the recovery of arms had anything to do with the Hindu Mahasabha. After the arrest of Baba Saheb Paranjpe the witness came to know that the weapons were being sent to Hyderabad. They came to know about the connection of the Hindu Mahasabha with the arms when an account book was found in a raid. Apte and Godse were not arrested because they were not in the house where the raid was conducted.

15.203: List of dangerous persons who were to be watched was made by Government or by the C.I.D. They kept a watch also over persons whom they thought dangerous but were not in the list. Badge was one of them. He was watched because he was dealing in arms. One man stationed to watch his movements was to watch the movements of others also. He used to find out who visited him and where the subject went.

15.204: Badge had a distinguishable appearance. He had a long beard and long hair. His house was searched a number of times. He was considered dangerous in the context of Hindu Muslim tension.

15.205: Apte's house was searched twice in 1947 and Nathuram Godse's once.

15.206: If he had known that the editor of the *Agranee* was in the conspiracy of bomb explosion at the Birla House, he would certainly have arrested him and if he was not in Poona he would have tried to find out his whereabouts and then tried to follow him. If he had known that he had gone to Bombay he would have trailed him there. He would have tried to trace him wherever he was and even followed him to New Delhi. If he had known that Godse was one of the associates of Madanlal, he would at once have connected Apte with him because they were great friends. Athawale would also have been considered as an associate.

15.207: Khadilkar, M.P. had stated before the Commission that Inspector Angarkar used to be 'amongst them', i.e., he was quite friendly with them and knew everything and, therefore, he did not make any report to the police about the danger to Mahatma Gandhi's life.

15.214: He had no information in the period July–August 1947 that Gandhiji's life was in danger. Khadilkar may say so but the witness had no such information.

K.M. Munshi, Wit. 82

15.218: K.M. Munshi, an eminent Advocate, who has held every kind of high office in the Government and become a well known Congress leader, stated in his deposition (witness No. 82) that there was a group of political thought against Mahatma Gandhi, compendiously known as the Kesari Group.

15.219: This group was led by Savarkar who advocated violence ever since he was a student and believed in political assassinations.

15.211: A C.I.D. report at page 18 of I.B. file No. 8/CA/48-II shows that the Kesari Group were something different from what may be called the Savarkar Group. This document shows that when by August 1943 something like ₹219,514/- were collected as a purses for V. D. Savarkar, the Kesari Group became apprehensive that Savarkar may ultimately eclipse Lokmanya Tilak.

15.222: As a result of this conflict in political methods in the 'Kesari' school of thought in Maharashtra, personal prejudices against Mahatma Gandhi resulted. But due to a flood of emotional patriotism resulting from Gandhiji's 'Quit India' Movement and the inability of anyone to withstand its influence, nobody was prepared to take the odium of anti-Gandhism. But Savarkar never lowered his flag; he continued to believe in political assassination. However, he remained quiescent and retreated into the background while the country was being swept by the 'Quit India' Movement of Gandhiji. There was in the Kesari School of thought a certain section of people who genuinely believed that Hindus required a strong organization to meet Muslim aggressiveness and were apprehensive of the weak kneed policy of the secularity group.

15.223: The witness further stated that Partition was inevitable due to the circumstances created in the country; but Gandhiji was opposed to it resulting in strained relations with Jawaharlal Nehru and Sardar Patel. Munshi was of the opinion that had India not been divided at that time, there would have been civil war at all levels resulting in street fighting in every town and also amongst the Defence Services and the police; but in North India the feeling continued to exist amongst the Hindus in general that Mahatma Gandhi was responsible for the Partition. The feeling of the Hindus throughout was that if the Mahatma had not appeased the Muslims by conceding Pakistan, Hindus would have been spared the miseries to which they were subjected.

15.224: This is, in the opinion of the Commission, a fair and correct assessment of the political thought at the time in the country as a whole in general and in Maharashtra in particular and also in northern Provinces of India. This has been discussed at this stage with the happenings in Poona because Poona was the centre of the Kesari Group and of the activities of the extreme Hindu views which existed in the Maharashtrian districts round about Poona. The Commission will have very much more to say and other evidence to discuss both oral and documentary in this connection. But it would suffice to say that there was a strong anti-Gandhi feeling amongst the hands of the Kesari group. In that case,

Savarkar was tried as a member of the conspiracy but was acquitted. It has been stated before the Commission that the inspiration came from Savarkar and he even patted Madanlal for what he was proposing to do.

(The current practitioners of this ideology still use murder as a weapon to silence opposing opinion; the murders of Dabholkar, Pansare, Kalburgi and Gauri Lankesh prove this.)

Mrs Sarla Barve, Wit. 39

15.225: Mrs Barve, witness No. 39, in her written statement, Ex.72, said that her husband who was the District Magistrate of Poona did come to know about the illegal activities of the Hindu Mahasabha members and that is why a watch was kept on their activities. She accused the authorities of not taking any proper notice of the threat and the activities of those suspected of plotting to murder Gandhi. The exploding of the bomb on 20 January 1948 was, according to her, a precursor of something very serious, e.g. murder. She also stated therein that her husband did know something about the impending trouble at Delhi and for that reason he telephoned Morarji Desai and informed him about it.

15.226: She stated that two or three days before the murder of Mahatma Gandhi a man called Sathe came to their house but as her husband was not present he told her that some Poona people had gone to Delhi to take the life of Mahatma Gandhi. She had repeated that story to her husband. She asked Sathe where he lived and he said, 'Sadashiv Peth' and that he was a retired schoolteacher.

15.227: On 27 January 1948, she found her husband rather restless. He telephoned Kamte, Inspector General of Police, after asking her to go out of the room. A little while later she told her husband what Sathe had told her which made her husband even more restless, worried and serious and thereafter he was telephoning most of the time.

Gopal Godse, Wit. 33

15.229: Gopal Godse in his deposition before the Commission stated that, Nathuram Godse and Apte were collecting arms for the Hyderabad trouble which had the approval of the Provincial Government.

15.236: If a strict watch had been kept and Police from Ahmednagar, Poona or Bombay had closely watched the movements of Nathuram or Karkare or Apte, it is possible that this murder may not have been committed by them.

15.244: Nathuram and Apte used to go to Ahmednagar.

15.245: All the conspirators walked out of the prayer meeting within five minutes of the gun cotton slab exploding. There were a number of policemen at the Birla House on the 20th but nobody tried to stop the taxi in which the conspirators escaped.

15.246: Other witnesses who have deposed to the state of affairs and conditions in Poona are Messrs S.R. Bhagwat, Witness No. 69, R.K. Khadilkar, M.P., Witness No.97, G.V. Ketkar, Witness No. 1. Besides there are the statements of Balukaka Kanitkar, Ex. 81, recorded by the police and his writings, Ex.11, his letter to H.E. the Governor General of India and his writings in the *Purushartha* Ex. 166. (They have been discussed in different chapters wherein they appropriately fall.)

R.K. Khadilkar, Wit. 97

15.247: As G.V. Ketkar, witness No. 1, had stated that he had talked to R.K. Khadilkar about what he observed and what he heard and about what Godse had told him, the Commission thought it necessary to examine Khadilkar who readily consented to appear before the Commission, his statement on this matter is very revealing.

15.248: When questioned about what Ketkar said about his talking to him, Khadilkar's reply was that he had no recollection of his travelling with Ketkar or Ketkar informing him of what Godse had said.

15.250: He has deposed that there were rumours even before the first attempt on 20 January 1948 of a conspiracy being hatched in Poona to 'attack' Gandhiji. The rumours were to the effect that something will happen to Gandhiji. People were decrying him and saying, '*Ata Vaachnar Nahin*'. (Now he will not survive.)

15.253: The atmosphere in Poona was highly poisonous and antagonistic towards Mahatma Gandhi and people thought that if he continued to live he would barter away the country to appease Pakistan. Khadilkar repeated: 'The Poona police intelligence was "With them" (the radical fanatics).' The attention of this witness was drawn towards what Dehejia, Secretary of the Bombay Home Department had stated, that the violent propaganda in Poona was anti-Muslim. To this his reply was that it was incorrect that the Muslims were the targets of this resentment or enticement to violence; it was more correct to say that the sullenness and resentment was directed more against the Congress and particularly against Mahatma Gandhi.

S.R. Bhagwat, Wit. 69

15.257: S.R. Bhagwat, witness No. 69, in a letter, Ex. 115A, to M.G. Kanitkar said that the late Balukaka Kanitkar had informed the late B.G. Kher and the late Sardar Patel about the plot to murder Mahatma Gandhi but no one believed him.

15.258: Bhagwat, before this Commission, said that Balukaka Kanitkar in one of his speeches said that the relations and friends of Nathuram Godse were saying that Mahatma Gandhi was in favour of Muslims and was not protecting the Hindu interests. He must, therefore be 'removed'. He should not be given any place or position where he could influence the decisions in regard to Pakistan but he did not say that people were saying that the Mahatma should be murdered.

15.260: He (Bhagwat) met B.G. Kher before the murder, but Kher told the witness that he did not believe that Gandhiji's life was in danger and that 'I was imagining'.

Conclusion

15.265: Broadly speaking, there was a strong school of political thought in Poona which was associated with the Hindu Mahasabha, a part of it and yet ideologically different. This school has compendiously been called by K.M. Munshi as the Kesari Group led by Savarkar. By Kamte it was called a group of Chitpawan Brahmins but it was not really anti-Gandhi. Even in this group there were some people who were willing to resort to political assassination and there were others whose activities might have consisted of strong anti-Muslim propaganda but they would not go so far as to commit a murder of political opponents. (If the continuous and vicious hounding of Gandhi by this group and the several failed attempts on his life were not indicative of this group's murderous intentions, I fail to understand what greater indication of their intentions were required.)

15.266: (1) The Hindu Mahasabha was strong in Poona; (2) there were bomb incidents; and (3) there were collection of arms in regard to which a number of searches were carried out and persons arrested.

But all these activities were directed against Muslims in order to drive them out of India and force them to go away to Pakistan.

15.268: Gopal Godse had gone even further and said that even if Nathuram Godse, Apte and Karkare had been arrested, there would have been others who would have taken their place and would have 'finished' Mahatma Gandhi, showing though not saying so that conspiracy to murder Mahatma Gandhi had larger ramifications than police investigation showed or were brought out at the trial in Judge Atmacharan's court and confirmed the involvement of organizations.

15.269: The group which actually took part in the conspiracy to murder was the most militant group among the Hindu Mahasabha workers. They had formed a separate organization called the Hindu Rashtra Dal which from the evidence produced before the Commission was perhaps more militant than the RSS and had implicit faith in the ideology preached by V.D. Savarkar which consisted of 'tooth for Tooth and Eye for Eye'. (This also confirms the patronage this group received from Savarkar and his involvement in Gandhi's murder.)

Chapter XVI deals with the situation in Ahmednagar.

16.1: Documentary evidence regarding Ahmednagar shows that Karkare even in the beginning of 1947 was prominent among the Hindu Mahasabhaites. He went to Noakhali and was making provocatory speeches on Noakhali happenings. So much so that the District Magistrate issued orders under section 144 Cr. P.C. against him and another. There is a letter showing that he was importing arms.

16.2: The order passed by the Government of Bombay Province for the compiling of the list of Hindu Mahasabha and RSS leaders was applicable to Ahmednagar also. Ex. 114A relates to that District and V.R. Karkare was one of the names therein mentioned. This was up to August 1947.

16.5: Ex.266 dated 22 January 1948, is an extract from the Weekly Confidential Report of the District Magistrate. It shows that V.R. Karkare had gone to consult the Hindu Mahasabha leaders about the future line of Hindu Mahasabha work and to complain that the local Hindu Mahasabha workers did not cooperate with him on account of his activities amongst the refugees. (This appears to be an incorrect report because there is other evidence to show that Karkare had vanished from Ahmednagar before 10 January 1948, and had proceeded to accomplish the nefarious task of murdering Mahatma Gandhi and not consulting the leaders about the future line of Hindu Mahasabha work.) Ex. 227 dated 31 January shows that Karkare had been out of Ahmednagar for the last 12 or 13 days, he was reported to have paid a visit to the Refugee Camp at Chembur and was moving about in Bombay. Ex. 228 is an innocuous kind of a report showing that Karkare had not been arrested under the Detention Order as he had absconded from Ahmednagar.

16.6: Ex. 67 dated 29 January 1948 is Sub-Inspector Balkundi's report to the D.I.G., stating that Madanlal appeared to be the same person who was operating in Ahmednagar and that he had left with V.R. Karkare ome 15 days back and had not returned to Ahmednagar. Madanlal was known to be a staunch RSS member. But this report whatever its authenticity was a belated document. (It must be noted that in the Kapur Commission's repport all the accused in the Gandhi murder are proven to be active members of the RSS too, thus establishing the involvement of the RSS in the Gandhi murder too.)

16.7: On 26 January 1948 Inspector Razak sent a report to the D.S.P.s of Ahmednagar and Poona including therein a list of persons named by S.V. Ketkar and other persons. These names had been obtained with the help of Inspector Savant of the C.I.D. presumably during the investigation. This report attached to ex. 58–Razak's letter has the names of 25 persons amongst whom were S.V. Ketkar, V.R. Karkare, R.S. Rekhi, and D.V. Godse. Amongst them Ketkar, Karkare and Rekhi were considered to be persons holding extreme views, whatever that word may mean. Two of them D.V. Godse and Chandekar were stated to be from Poona. S.V. Ketkar and Rekhi were connected with Karkare's guest house and D.V. Godse was a brother of Nathuram Godse, and the others were members of Karkare's amateur dramatic troupe.

16.13: Madanlal came into contact with and was helped by Vishnu R. Karkare, who was also an accused in the conspiracy to kill Mahatma Gandhi. Karkare owned and ran a hotel in Ahmednagar, Deccan Guest House which still exists in the Kapdabazar locality. and used his position and influence to the fullest extent in inciting the refugees to take out processions and indulge in anti-Muslim activities. His strategy was to terrorize and drive out Muslims of Ahmednagar and hand over their homes and businesses to the refugees. He had thus grabbed several Muslim owned stalls in the fruit market and even given one to Madanlal.

16.23: The evidence of the witnesses and the documents produced before the Commission show that four bombs were thrown in Ahmednagar town between 24 November 1947 and 26 December 1947.

In connection with these bombs, information was being sent by the District Authorities to Government. On 8 December 1947, the District Magistrate wrote a letter to the Chief Secretary to the Bombay Government giving details of the bomb explosion in Vasant Talkies and the extent of damage done. A copy of the letter had been sent to the D.I.G. C.I.D., Poona. Thereupon Inspector Razak of the C.I.D., witness no. 34, was sent to Ahmednagar to investigate or to help in the investigation into the bomb incidents. By then there had been two explosions. Inspector Razak came and conducted his investigation and his evidence shows that the bomb explosions were caused by the workers of the Hindu Mahasabha but nobody had been arrested although Karkare and Madanlal who were both accused in the Gandhi Murder Case and were suspected to have been involved in these explosions. On 18 December 1947, he made a report (ex. 61) stating that the bombs excepting one that was thrown in Kappad Bazar which was different, were of the same type, similar to the bombs which had been found on 3 June 1947, in a bomb factory owned by Vassen Puspasen in Bombay which had been unearthed by the Bombay C.I.D. and one of which was brought to Poona by a police officer, inspector Ranbhice, in connection with that find some Gujaratis were arrested. This according to him showed a common source and a common agency operating. On 24 December 1947 (Ex.62) the houses of the Secretary of the Muslim League and the Captain of the Muslim National Guards were searched but nothing incriminating was found. The report of this is Ex. 62. This document also shows that the lives of the Congress leaders including the local secretary Saptarshi were threatened and that the bomb attack on the Moharram procession in Ahmednagar was similar to the attack in Shanivar Peth in Poona.

(Madanlal Kashmirilal Pahwa worked at the Vassen Puspasen Fireworks factory, in the clandestine part of the factory manufacturing hand grenades. He had managed to escape barely a few minutes before the police raid. The knowledge of an imminent police raid on the factory was one of the reasons why he shifted to Ahmednagar. He was known to have carried a significant quantity of hand grenades with him.)

16.33: On 5 January 1948, Raosaheb Patwardhan (an eminent Congress leader) was addressing a public meeting in Ahmednagar, to promote Hindu Muslim unity. Madanlal Pahwa arrived there with several Hindu Mahasabha workers and disrupted the meeting. According to his own statements during the Gandhi Murder trial he had caught hold of Raosaheb Patwardhan by the scruff of his neck and dragged him off the stage. Police reports of this incident are conflicting. According to S.I. Rane, Madanlal was hot tempered and was shouting slogans during the meeting and threatening to disrupt it. S.I. Balkundi stated that Madanlal and his companions created disturbances during the meeting but it was not correct that Madanlal had caught hold of Patwardhan and tried to attack him with a knife. Karkare also arrived there and he too started shouting and demanded that he and Madanlal should be allowed to speak. They tried to snatch away the mike from the rostrum. After the meeting ended and when the audience had dispersed Madanlal and two others were arrested. Madanlal was kept in the lockup for some time and then allowed to go, it was added that Madanlal used to create trouble all the time. Inspector Razak has added that both Madanlal and Karkare were brought to the Police Station and interrogated there but nothing useful was found. Madanlal on that occasion gave an undertaking not to take part in violent movements so he was let off. S.I. Balkundi deposed that on or about 6 January 1948 both Madanlal and Karkare disappeared from Ahmednagar and the police had no information where they had gone. S.I. Deshmukh was on the look out for the duo.

16.34: From the testimony of another witness Sub-Inspector L.N. Joshi (witness 36) who was a Police Shorthand Reporter in Ahmednagar at the time, it appears that Madanlal had told him that he was going to Delhi to get married. This was on or about 10 January 1948.

16.36: On 9 January, Inspector Razak advised Deshmukh to recommend the detention of both Madanlal and Karkare. S.I. Balkundi has stated that he recommended that Madanlal and Karkare be detained or externed.

16.37: On the report dated 8 January 1948 S.M. Dalal made an endorsement on 11 January and V.T. Dahejia on 12 January, and on the same day the Home Minister Morarji Desai issued an order that the persons mentioned in the report should be arrested. He inquired why the District Magistrate had not done so earlier?

(Based on these facts, it is unbelievable that the policemen, the home minister and the intelligence sleuths developed collective amnesia barely ten days later. When Prof. Jain informed Morarji Desai about Madanlal's confessions, Desai did not recollect that he had signed detention orders for both Madanlal and Karkare of Ahmednagar barely ten days earlier.)

16.41: The statement of the D.S.P. is that it did not strike him that the Madanlal arrested at Delhi was the same person from Ahmednagar, but he had a faint recollection that Inspector Razak and S.I. Deshmukh had mentioned to him their suspicions about the identity of Madanlal. He told them that if that was so Madanlal must have been interrogated by the Delhi police who would find out everything. He told Deshmukh that if he wanted to go to Delhi he could do so and also told Razak that on his return to Poona he might as well tell the D.I.G., C.I.D., about this suspicion. Surprisingly enough, this gentleman too did not think it expedient to telephone the D.I.G., C.I.D., and give him the information nor did he bother to inform the District Magistrate.

16.48: From the evidence before the Commission, it does appear that S.I. Balkundi was aware of the activities of Karkare and Madanlal. It also appears that he did suspect that Madanlal, who had exploded the bomb, was the same who had been operating in Ahmednagar, but for some reason he did not put his suspicion in writing, when he did so its utility was nil. It also appears that it was this witness who gave the particulars of Karkare to Poona C.I.D. and the photograph which was on the I.B. file was supplied by him too.

16.50: Sub-Inspector Balkundi has stated that both Nathuram Godse and Apte used to come to Ahmednagar, they met Karkare and that he and his staff were watching the activities of both these persons although nothing emanated from this surveillance. He also stated that he did not know if Karkare was sending any money to Godse and Apte. But he did know that Karkare was acting under the aegis of the Hindu Mahasabha. He further stated that when Madanlal and Karkare had left Ahmednagar in or about the second week of January 1948 as the place had become too hot for them, he thought that they might have gone to Kolhapur to stay with one Jere who was one of the paid workers of the Hindu Mahasabha. Now this is an important piece of evidence because in explanation dated 6 February 1948, also he has said that Karkare, so it was learnt, had gone to Kolhapur and was likely to have taken shelter with one Jere who had previously been working at Nagar (Ahmednagar) and that this information also had been passed on to Inspector Razak who was working on it, but unfortunately this was on 7 February 1948.

16.51: After Madanlal had exploded the bomb, a letter addressed to Karkare was intercepted by Sub-Inspector Deshmukh. The writer of the letter could not be traced but in that letter it was written that a building had to be constructed in Bombay which was not possible without Karkare's help. Deshmukh took this letter to the D.S.P. and told him that it meant much more than what appeared on the surface. In other words, it was in code. A copy of that letter was sent by the D.S.P. to the D.I.G., C.I.D. requesting that inquiries be made in Bombay. Deshmukh suggested to the D.S.P. that he (Deshmukh) should go to Bombay and Poona to find out about the whereabouts of Karkare and he left for Bombay on the pretext of purchasing a rectophoto machine, taking with him Sub-Inspector L.N. Joshi, because Joshi belonged to Poona and knew Apte and Godse. They went to the *Agranee* Press and made inquiries about Apte and Godse. This was on 29 January 1948. They were told that neither of them was in Poona. They then went to Apte's house under some pretext and asked Mrs Champatai Apte about her husband's whereabouts. She told them Apte had gone to Gwalior. Joshi remained in Poona and Deshmukh went to Bombay to find out about Karkare's brother who was working in a mill in Dadar. He made inquiries about Karkare till about 9:00 pm on 30th when he learnt about the murder of Mahatma Gandhi.

16.52: An extract of the weekly diary of Deshmukh shows that he arrived at Poona on 28 January 1948 and made confidential inquiries till 11:00 p.m. On 29 January he made more confidential inquiries and left Poona at 11:30 a.m., he arrived at Bombay at 4:00 p.m. and went to Kurla and made inquiries there and then returned to Dadar. On the following day, i.e., 30 January, he moved about in Byculla, V.T., Kalbadevi, Dadar and Parel areas and made confidential inquiries there. In this report it is not stated as to what confidential inquiries he was making or about whom? But one or two important matters emanate from this portion of the testimony of this witness. (1) That Deshmukh had gone to Poona to look for Karkare; if that was so it is difficult to imagine why he should have gone to the *Agranee* press and asked about Karkare and when there he made inquiries about the whereabouts of Apte and Godse. It is still very surprising that Deshmukh and L.N. Joshi should have gone to Mrs Apte to find out where her husband was and then this witness (Deshmukh) should have left for Bombay to look for Karkare. The whole thing does not fit in or appear to be very logical. If Karkare was being looked for then the witness should have stated that they went to find out about him from the *Agranee* press and from Mrs Apte which he has not stated. And this connection between Karkare and the *Agranee* press or Mrs Apte should appear somewhere at least in the evidence before the Commission. (2) It shows that the witness was connecting Karkare with Apte and Godse. Why? Is not clear. He has nowhere stated in his evidence that according to his knowledge, Godse and Apte were associating with Karkare in Ahmednagar although Sub-Inspector Balkundi has stated that both Godse and Apte used to meet Karkare in Ahmednagar. (3) If Karkare had taken shelter in Kolhapur with Jere, why was he being looked for in Poona? Besides, why was the police in Kolhapur not contacted about him? (4) It is difficult to find out any cogent reason for the inquiries made by these witnesses about Apte and Godse and not about Karkare. As has been said above, the events do not fit in properly and the picture seems to be out of focus as it were. Either these witnesses had information about the association of Karkare and Apte and Godse or they had not. If they had, one would have expected that they would have informed the authorities about this matter and when Karkare disappeared from Ahmednagar, they might have looked for him at places where Apte and Godse were or they had no knowledge about this association.

16.53: But this much is clear that Sub-Inspector L.N. Joshi did know Mrs Apte. As a matter of fact, he has stated that he had helped Karkare to start his business and Karkare was helping Apte in his publication work. He has also stated that Deshmukh had (a) suspicion that Apte and party had gone to Delhi but he does not seem to have mentioned the fact to anybody nor informed the D.S.P. he has further stated that Mrs Apte had no suspicion when he made inquiries about Apte because they had known each other for some time. This previous acquaintance of Joshi with Apte and Karkare can have a sinister meaning and yet may be more or less innocuous. Joshi has stated that he had no sympathy for the Hindu Mahasabha. L.N. Joshi has also stated that he accompanied Deshmukh because he knew friends of Karkare in Poona and went to the *Agranee* office for that reason. In the circumstances, it was, perhaps, not very wise for Deshmukh to have taken L.N. Joshi with him.

16.54: But the reason of his going to Poona and Bombay remains a mystery in view of his previous knowledge about Karkare hiding in Kolhapur with Jere.

(The Kapur Commission has mildly hinted at a nexus between certain officers of the Ahmednagar Police and Karkare and the Apte–Godse gang. After the murder, Pyarelal wrote that there was sympathy for the Hindu Mahasabha and RSS amongst several police officers and bureaucrats and that the administration was largely infiltrated by members of these fanatic organizations. When the decision was taken to ban the RSS and Hindu Mahasabha, the news was leaked out and the top leadership of both organizations went underground. In one instance, a senior police officer advised RSS and Hindu Mahasabha cadres in his jurisdiction to lie low for some time till the heat subsided. It would not be surprising if the two police officials from Ahmednagar were actually on a trip to warn Karkare, Apte and Godse that the police were closing in, rather than to arrest them.)

16.85: Witness No. 36, Lakshman Narayan Joshi is a D.S.P. attached to the C.I.D., Bombay. He was working as a Sub Inspector in the C.I.D. Ahmednagar in 1947-50 under D.S.P. Ahmednagar.

16.86: On 10 January, Madanlal had told him that he was going to

Delhi to get married. When the news of bomb explosion at Gandhiji's meeting came on the radio or was published in the newspapers it struck the witness that it was the same Madanlal who was in Ahmednagar and he talked to the sub-inspector about his suspicion. But evidently no use was made of this information, if indeed it was given. Secondly, when detention orders against Madanlal were passed and he absconded, this witness gave information of the absconding; or his going to Delhi assuming he knew of the detention orders. He also was searching for Madanlal. Sub-Inspector Deshmukh had a similar suspicion and he went to speak to the D.S.P. about the identity of this Madanlal. This was on or about the 24 January 1948. They both went to the D.S.P. but Deshmukh did the talking, Inspector Razak was also there. According to him the D.S.P. said that the Delhi Police should be coming to enquire and that they should not bother themselves about it but should arrest Karkare and get all the details of Madanlal. What that meant the witness did not know.

16.87: On the 27 or 28 January, Deshmukh asked the witness to accompany him to Poona. Why it was five days or so later, he could not say. As he knew some friends of Karkare in Poona, that is why they went to Poona. They visited *Agranee* press and some of Deshmukh's friends. While Deshmukh made inquiries, this witness stood outside.

(He does not know whether they went to Nathuram Godse's house but they did go to Apte's house, Anand Ashram, at about 3:30 or 4:00 p.m. The witness went in and asked Mrs Apte about the whereabouts of Karkare. She said she did not know about Karkare but Apte had gone to Nagpur for publish Savarkar's literature and from there he might have gone to Gwalior.)

16.89: The statement of this witness is rather important. Although he knew that Madanlal had gone to Delhi, he gave no information to Sub-Inspector Deshmukh. If the movements of Madanlal and Karkare were being watched and the witness knew Madanlal, as he says he did, it is difficult to believe that he did not know that the movements of Madanlal were being watched. Besides he took his meals at Karkare's hotel and so did Madanlal.

16.94: The witness says that he did not know about the activities of Karkare though he was friendly with him since 1937. He did not know that Karkare's house was searched in connection with the bomb explosion and yet in the next breath he says that he knew that Karkare's house was being searched in connection with the bomb explosions, and that Inspector Razak had come in that connection. He has admitted that he knew Mrs Apte and her husband since long and that his friend wanted to get insurance of Apte but he does not know what company his friend was an agent for. He did hear Razak and Deshmukh talking about the detention of Karkare.

16.95: This witness was friendly with Karkare. He had helped him to start the Hotel. He had been friendly with Karkare for ten years and it is difficult to believe that he did not know about his (Karkare's) activities. He also knew Apte and was aware of the fact that Apte and Karkare were friends. He knew that Karkare was out of town and yet he gave no such information to the police when the police were looking for him. He also knew that Madanlal was leaving for Delhi, this information he did not give to his colleagues in the police force. He had gone to Poona to find out Karkare, some of whose friends he knew there.

16.96: Police Deputy Superintendent Anant Shamrao Balkundi, witness No. 37, is now the Deputy Superintendent of Police C.I.D. Aurangabad. From July 1945 to July 1948 he was a Sub-Inspector, C.I.D., at Ahmednagar.

16.98: When on the 20 January a bomb was exploded at Birla House at Mahatma's prayer meeting and the matter was reported in the press, this witness suspected that Madanlal therein described was the same person who had been carrying on activities in Ahmednagar. He conveyed his suspicions to Inspector Razak who in turn informed the D.S.P. but what orders the D.S.P. gave, the witness does not know.

16.101: The next piece of evidence which is of importance in connection with this witness is his explanation dated 9 February 1948 (Ex.69). He stated therein (1) that he was not aware of the D.I.G.'s camp at Ahmednagar; (2) that he could not make arrangements for interrogation of Ved Prakash on 1 February 1948 because of disturbances in the city; (3) that the D.S.P. informed him that he, the witness, was wanted at Poona with full details regarding the relatives and servants of Karkare and the collection of that information had kept him busy and he had handed over the information along with Karkare's photograph to deputy Superintendent Chaubal; (4) that he was constantly reporting about the movement of Karkare and Madanlal through weekly and special reports and had finally reported about the detention of both of them on 4 January 1948; (5) that after the meeting of Raosaheb Patwardhan on 6 January 1948 the atmosphere at Ahmednagar had become too hot for Karkare and Madanlal and therefore they had disappeared from Ahmednagar; (6) that Karkare had written to his wife that he would be arriving during the course of the week and strict watch was being kept at the Railway Station and motor stands; (7) that Karkare had gone to Kolhapur where he was likely to take shelter with someone named Jere.

16.103: Another important piece of evidence which emanates from the statement of this witness is that Godse and Apte both used to come to Ahmednagar and meet Karkare and that this witness and his staff were watching the activities of both Apte and Godse in Ahmednagar although nothing emanated from this attempted intelligence. The witness did not know if Karkare was sending any money to Godse and Apte. And he had no information about any plot being hatched in Ahmednagar.

16.136: The evidence from Ahmednagar shows that had efforts been made earlier either by the Delhi Police or the Bombay Police the complete record of Karkare as well as of Madanlal would have been available and if a photograph had been published in the newspapers, the police of Ahmednagar would have come to know about him and would have been in a position to give the information. Commission would like to add that issuing photographs of arrested persons is not always a very wise mode of investigation because of the fear that identification parades or identification by witnesses might be held to be valueless. Nevertheless the Delhi Police should have sent a photograph of Madanlal to all Police stations and especially to the police stations of the places mentioned by him, this was a serious lapse.

Morarji Desai, Wit. 96

Morarji Desai was the Home Minister of Bombay Government when the Congress party again took office in November 1946 and held that office during the period with the happenings of which this Commission is concerned and particularly from after August 1947 till 1949 covering the tragic events culminating in the murder of Mahatma Gandhi and the trial and conviction of his murderers.

18.12: Desai then said that the Hindu Mahasabha and its press were indulging in highly inflammatory communal propaganda, in consequence of which action had to be taken against the latter under the Press Emergency Powers Act. He could remember that there was a newspaper called the *Agranee* of which the editor was Nathuram Godse, whom he knew, and the proprietor was Apte.

18.14: Morarji Desai was then asked about the bomb explosion at Poona, particularly in the heart of the city. Exhibit 155 relates to this incident showing that a bomb was thrown from the top of and near the city library in Poona city on 16 June 1947 resulting in injuries to 'a boy' and damage to a motor truck. One N.R. Athawale, a Hindu Mahasabhaite was arrested and he made a confessional statement before a Magistrate under S. 164 Cr.P.C. that the bomb (grenade) had been given to him by N.D. Apte of '*the Agranee*', with the instructions to throw it from a height and he admitted that he had thrown it on the road from the second floor of the City Library. Apte was arrested on 4 July 1947 but a search of his house showed nothing and nothing incriminating was recovered.

18.15: It may be remarked that the similarity between this case and the case of recovery of a large quantity of arms and ammunition from the house of V.R. Ketkar of Ahmednagar is significant. In both cases the persons arrested made confessional statements involving prominent Hindu Sabha workers, Apte in the Poona case and Karkare in the Ahmednagar case. In both cases the persons named escaped without a scratch and in one case even the self confessed bomb thrower could not be prosecuted. In both cases the confessions were retracted and the police found no other evidence against the prominent workers. The parallel is striking if not indicative of a pattern of Hindu Mahasabha's *modus operandi*.

18.16: On 9 July, Kher wrote a note on the file, when the matter of the Poona bomb went to him after passing through the various Secretariat *echelons,* wherein he said 'was not the editor of the *Agranee* arrested? I would like to know the progress.' Morarji Desai was asked how the editor of the *Agranee*'s name came to be mentioned when there was nothing in exhibit 155 (the bomb matter) to show any connection between the

Agranee and the throwing of the bomb, his reply was that the name of the *Agranee* must have been mentioned in one of the weekly letters.

18.17: When the papers came to Morarji Desai for sanction for prosecution under the Explosive Substances Act he recorded a note on 5 August that his information was that the confession had been retracted and if that was so what was the evidence to prove the guilt of the accused persons? On this Kher wrote: 'This matter must be treated more seriously. We must impress it upon the D.S.P. that he is to investigate the case thoroughly. The *Agranee* has stated that it is a matter of high honour that the Hindu Sabha should be accused of throwing a bomb—H.D. is returning his security. Is terrorism to be allowed to be openly encouraged? I would like to see Secretary H.D.'

This is demonstrative of Kher's anxiety in relation to the incidents of bomb throwing.

18.19: Desai was next asked about exhibit 177, dated August 1947, an order of Kher about preparing a list of and keeping a strict watch on the operations of the members of the Hindu Mahasabha organisation and of the RSS. To this order Desai had added that this be done within 10 days showing need for expedition. He has also said that Hindu Mahasabha and RSS were working together.

18.21: Morarji Desai was then examined and closely questioned in regard to the letter which G.V. Ketkar claims to have got sent to Bombay Government through Balukaka Kanetkar. He was asked:

'Q. Did Balasaheb Kher ever talk to you about this letter?'

'A. I think, he did but as far as my memory goes, no names were mentioned in that .... I do not think I saw the letter. Balasaheb told me of the contents of the letter. As far as I can recollect, no names were given.' He added, 'From my recollection I can say that the letter seemed to show that the atmosphere was very tense and there was danger to the life of Mahatma Gandhi which several other people were saying and which also felt because of the atmosphere which refugees had created.'

The witness emphasized that Nathuram Godse's name was not mentioned by Balukaka Kanetkar.

18.22: He was then asked about Balukaka's article in *Purshartha* (Exhibit 166) wherein there is an alleged reiteration by Balukaka of informing the authorities that Nathuram Godse had said that Mahatma

Gandhi should be killed; Morarji Desai said that he had not seen it.

18.24: Desai said that Balukaka Kanetkar talked to him also and he told him that the atmosphere in Poona was very tense and there was danger to the Mahatma as also to the life of Congress leaders generally but he never mentioned any names of the likely assailants and never mentioned the names of Godse or Apte.

'I do not agree that there was any complacency or the matter would have been taken lightly even if the names of these persons had been given. Even otherwise people were worried and all of us including Sardar Patel, myself and my chief Balasaheb Kher, were worried about it and we mentioned the matter to Gandhiji about the danger but we could not do anything more than what we did, i.e., to keep some plain clothes men around Mahatma Gandhi.' (They were all absent on 30 January evening.)

18.25: But the danger, according to him was not confined to Poona; it was from all over the Country. Morarji Desai did not accept the claim of Balukaka Kanetkar that he was the only person who for six months had been trying to prevent the tragedy which ultimately overtook the country. The first time any names were mentioned to him was when Prof Jain talked to him on 21 January 1948.

18.31: Prof Jain did tell Morarji Desai that Madanlal had disclosed to him that he (Madanlal) and his companions were going to kill Mahatma Gandhi but he had not involved Savarkar in it.

18.34: When asked why the Inspector General of Police, Kamte and the Commissioner of Police Bharucha were not taken into confidence, the witness replied that Nagarvala was in charge of the C.I.D. (Special Branch) and the information could not be dispersed among so many officers. Besides he did not consider Bharucha to be very competent and Kamte was in Poona; and he had no real control or jurisdiction over Bombay City. It may be remarked that as things turned out later and in the light of the disclosures as to the names of the conspirators which later transpired, perhaps Kamte's assistance with his control of the Provincial Police would have been helpful.

18.41: Gadgil's article disclosed that a friend of his a Jedhe, M.C.A. came to Delhi from Poona on 15 January 1948, he (Jedhe) knew that Godse and others had chalked out a plan in Poona and send-offs were being given to them. If Jedhe could come to know about it, it should have been possible for the Provincial or Local Intelligence also because according to Khadilkar, the Intelligence Officer Inspector Angarkar was 'with us'. This fact of the feasting was deposed to by Gadgil. As a witness he said: 'Godse and his friends were being feted as they were to go and murder Gandhiji, there was a function at Tilak Smarak Mandir.'

18.42: Morarji Desai did say that Police Intelligence was weak and weakness still continues but surely it could not be so weak and so inept that if feasting was done to felicitate people who were going to murder Mahatma Gandhi the police should have known nothing about it unless it was done in a very secret manner as is usual in the case of conspiracies. In that case it should have been impossible for Jedhe to know of it unless he was close friend or a clever sleuth.

18.48: Morarji Desai had a faint recollection about Purushottam Trikamdas witness No. 15 having seen him but could not remember who the man with him was. When the statement of Purushottam was read out to him, he said he could not remember who the man was nor what he had said if he had said that the conspiracy was to murder Mahatma Gandhi he must have referred the man to the Police. Desai said that the real cause of the murder was that the Hindu Mahasabha was strongly opposed to the Mahatma, considered him to be enemy of Hinduism and therefore they viewed everything from that angle. He agreed with Kamte about his suggestion as to what he would have done if the information had been given except that no case could be registered and the Bombay Police could not be sent to Delhi unless the Delhi Police asked for them.

18.51: Kidnapping Theory—Morarji Desai stated that he did not agree with the kidnapping theory which as a matter of fact was never mentioned to him and if it had been, he would never have accepted it because it was an impossible proposition.

18.53: From the talk he had with Balukaka and from other information which he got, 'It was not possible for me to locate anybody in particular as the likely assassin of Mahatma Gandhi.' If he had the slightest inkling about the persons in the conspiracy, he would have put it down by all means at his command. 'I could not say who the exact persons were who would do harm to Mahatma Gandhi but from the information I had. I could say that they were likely to be either the refugees or the RSS and

Hindu Mahasabha. Not necessarily from Poona.'

18.64: In Morarji Desai's opinion, Nagarvala did all that could possibly be done.

18.65: In answer to questions by Commission, he said that Nagarvala did not tell him that the Delhi Police officers had mentioned the editor of *Agranee*. On the other hand, he was complaining that they were not very cooperative. As said earlier this must have been after the murder. Before the murder there was not even inkling of Godse and Apte being in the conspiracy. When the murder took place, Desai could not imagine that it had been committed by someone from Poona. He knew Nathuram Godse as the editor of the *Agranee*.

18.66: Desai said, 'I have heard from Counsel portions from the evidence of Nagarvala as to what he was doing *qua* "Kidnapping Theory" but that would not impair the values of the investigation which was being carried out under my instructions. But during the investigation Nagarvala never told me anything about kidnapping as far as I remember.' Nagarvala had not told him that Delhi Police officers had asked him to arrest the editor of the *Agranee*. Had this name been mentioned even the most incompetent officer would have arrested him.

V.T. Dehejia. Wit. 84

18.79: Another important witness as to the events preceding the exploding of the bomb and the murder of Mahatma Gandhi is V.T. Dehejia, I.C.S. (Retired)—witness No. 84. At the relevant time, i.e., from about August 1947 to sometime after the murder, he was the Home Secretary in the Home Department of Bombay Province.

18.80: Under the directions of the Premier, Kher, and subsequent discussions with the Home Minister and the Secretariat officials, a direction was sent to the Provincial C.I.D. and the Commissioner of Police to compile a list of officers of the Hindu Mahasabha and the RSS. The list prepared for Poona was ex. 114 and for Ahmednagar Ex. 114-A which was sent to the Government from Poona. By a letter to Dehejia, Ex. 113-A, dated 19 August 1947, Rana D.I.G., C.I.D., said that arrangements had been made to keep a watch on the activities of the RSS and the Hindu Mahasabha and periodical reports would be sent. It seems that later Rana suggested that as secret weekly reports were being sent, it was perhaps not necessary to send special reports which had been ordered; on which Dehejia wrote that they were necessary. The matter was put before a meeting of the Provincial Cabinet and it was decided to discontinue the periodical reports on these two organizations and Rana was informed accordingly.

18.81: Dehejia was examined on all these matters in detail in regard to the special reports, he has stated that as there was apprehension of violence which was indicated by rabid speeches made on the anti-Pakistan observance day and also as there was apprehension that there might be trouble on 15 August 1947, Independence Day, the witness thought that the continuance of special reports on these organizations to be necessary in spite of what Rana had suggested.

18.82: When asked why special reports were necessary, his reply was that there was a report of the proposed observance of the 'Anti Pakistan Day', in order to check the trouble on that day the special reports were necessary but evidently the danger had passed and therefore the authorities thought that the special reports were no longer required.

18.83: The Commission then examined him in regard to the statement of G.V. Ketkar about the hostile sentiments allegedly rife in Poona against Mahatma Gandhi, he replied that these sentiments appeared to come in waves. After the Partition they were directed against the Congress and Mahatma Gandhi and again when he undertook the fast, similar sentiments were against him. The hostile sentiments were largely ignited by the Hindu Mahasabha and RSS.

18.87: When his attention was drawn to Dr Parchure's speech about 'Nehru and Gandhi reaping the fruits of their sins in a short time' he said that if he had learnt about it he would have been put on guard but he would not have concluded there from that Gandhiji and Nehru were going to be murdered but he would not let the speech pass without any further inquiry.

18.87-A: As a matter of fact the District Magistrate was asked by the Government about this speech of Dr Parchure but his reply based on the report of the D.S.P. was that the report of the speech was based on the police reporter's memory as the speech was in Hindi and there were no Hindi shorthand reporters in Poona Police. That might perhaps be the reason for the immobility of the police or the quiescence of the Bombay authorities but the sentence is so telling that the police reporter would not have put in unless some such words were said. Commission of course presumes that the reporter knew Hindi and did not have a mind which could imagine or make up things.

18.92: Although the noting of Secretariat files of this witness has shown clear grasp of the problems which arose at different times indicating a vigilant mind the Commission is unable to accept some of the statements of this witness particularly that there was no atmosphere of violence discernible from the newspapers and from the speeches made by various people in Poona. The evidence of Messrs Ketkar, Khadilkar and the late N.V. Gadgil and the documents which have been produced shows not only a general atmosphere of violence but a particular slant directed against Congress leaders in general and Mahatma Gandhi in particular. The intensity of feelings against Mahatma Gandhi was the consequence of what was considered to be the appeasement of Muslims at the cost of the Hindus, of which the Partition, the post-prayer speeches of Gandhiji and the giving away of ₹55 crores were outward manifestations. On a matter like this the people who are non-official, who move in non-official circles and are generally in touch with the general state of affairs of a town and sentiments of the citizen have a better knowledge than the officials. Even though they happen to be clever, vigilant and wide-awake. This is particularly so in the case of non-official gentlemen who take a prominent part in politics whatever colour of the spectrum it may assume.

Kanji Dwarkadas, Wit. 7

18.93: Kanji Dwarkadas witness No.7 is a Labour leader, a follower of Mrs Besant and a Socialist. He deposed that two days before the murder, B.G. Kher went to Mahatma Gandhi and told him that Poona Brahmins were committed to kill him but as it was his day of silence, Mahatma Gandhi wrote on a piece of paper, 'If I have to die, I shall die. I do not want any police protection'. Kher also told the witness that Nathuram Godse was running a rabid Hindu Mahasabha paper and that he knew that these people were after Gandhiji and that the Delhi C.I.D. did not take the

Bombay Police into confidence, otherwise they would have immediately come to know about Nathuram Godse. He had also said that from the recovery of a shirt in the Marina Hotel which had a Dhobi mark (N.V.G.) 'Nathuram Godse' the police should have been able to trace him.

18.94: The Communist paper *People's Age* had been saying since August 1947 that the Mahatma was going to be murdered, that the Delhi Police was infiltrated by RSS people and that the Deputy Commissioner of Delhi, Randhawa, was behind the movement thus they were not keen to protect the life of Mahatma Gandhi.

18.95: He further stated that a Doctor friend of his, Dr. X from Alwar state, went to Mahatma Gandhi in the middle of December 1947 and told him that Alwar and Bharatpur States were in the conspiracy. Acharya Jugal Kishore had also warned Gandhiji about it. The Doctor above mentioned had sent a leaflet to Acharya Jugal Kishore that said that Gandhiji must be murdered and the Acharya wrote back to the Doctor that he would place the leaflet before Gandhiji and Panditji.

Jaypraksh Narayan, Wit. 98

18.102A: Jayprakash Narayan, witness No. 98, stated that he had no recollection of sending a man to Purushottam with the information regarding danger to the life of Mahatma Gandhi.

'I have no recollection if I had sent a man to him. If I had sent a man to him that would mean that I had taken the information seriously, which I did not. That may be wrong on my part but this is exactly what happened and I am stating so.'

18.102B: He added, 'At that time it must have appeared very incredible to anyone to whom this information was given.'

18.102C: He also did not speak to Gandhiji about this information nor to Sardar Patel. He had a great deal of respect for Sardar Patel although they did not see eye to eye on political matters. He (Narayan) did blame the police for not being vigilant. He was surprised that any Indian could have committed the murder of Mahatma Gandhi. It made no difference as to where he came from. He was not aware that there was a party of militant people who would commit violence against the person of Mahatma Gandhi. There was a strong antagonism between the group of Tilakites and Gandhiites, the Kesari Group and the Savarkarites but that was all on political level. He could not imagine anyone would commit murder of Mahatma Gandhi whatever be the differences.

(Jayprakash Narayan's testimony before the Kapur Commission is very surprising. Previously, both Sardar Patel's secretary Shankar and his daughter Maniben have testified that immediately after Gandhi's murder, Jayprakash Narayan carried out a very public campaign against Sardar Patel for his failure to protect Mahatma Gandhi, insinuating that he held Sardar Patel responsible for Gandhiji's murder and demanding that Sardar Patel be sacked from the Union Cabinet. Before that, he is reported to have criticized the Hindu Mahasabha and RSS at Kirkee and other places for their campaign of violence and their attempt to destabilize the Indian Union. As compared to these facts contained in the Kapur Commission's report, Jayprakash Narayan's testimony appears to be very diluted. It is also very unlike Jayaprakash Narayan. It would have been illuminating to find out what brought about such a dramatic change in him. Alas, J.P., as he is famously remembered, is no more to shed light on the issue. Later, J.P. granted the RSS political legitimacy by including them in the post-Emergency Janta Party government. The dominance of the RSS via the BJP on Indian politics today is due to his benevolence.)

J.D. Nagarvala's Statement

18.103: As the conduct of J.D. Nagarvala, the then Deputy Commissioner of Police, Bombay, has come in for serious criticism at the hands of counsel, the Commission thinks it necessary to set out the salient points of his statement which are relevant to the course of the investigation or inquiry which he conducted after the information given by Prof Jain had been relayed to him by Morarji Desai. The evidence of Nagarvala comes to this.

18.104: There was communal tension due to influx of refugees into Bombay. Arms and ammunition were left by the British with certain communities and transmitters left by the Royal Air Force were being used for transmission of news to Pakistan.

18.105: The Hindu Mahasabha believed in political assassination as a means of achieving political ends. (This practice continues by Sanghis even today as illustrated by the murder of Dabholkar, Pansare, Kalburgi and Gauri Lankesh.)

18.107: The Bombay City Police had not heard of Madanlal or of Godse or Apte before the bomb was thrown, and the Bombay City Police could not have started any investigation from mere press reports unless it was therein given that Madanlal had migrated to some locality in the city of Bombay. On 21 January there was no communication from Delhi about the bomb incident. Normally, the practice was that if any information had to be sent by the police of one province to that of another, it would communicate with the Inspector General of Police or the D.I.G. or the D.S.P. direct, and in the case of Bombay city with the Commissioner or Deputy Commissioner of Police.

What Desai Told Nagarvala

18.108: Officially Nagarvala got information about the bomb on 21 January when the Home Minister called him and conveyed to him the information which Professor Jain had given him without disclosing to him the name of Professor Jain. He was asked what information was given to him by Morarji Desai.

'Q. Did he tell you anything?'

'Ans. Yes, he did. He told me that the man, Madanlal, who had exploded the bomb in Delhi prayer meeting of Mahatma Gandhi was companion of one Karkare from Ahmednagar and I should try and arrest Karkare.'

Desai also suggested to him that he might keep a watch on Barrister Savarkar's house. Whatever Morarji Desai told him was correctly recorded by him in his Crime Report No.1 as follows:

'I was told by H. M. that he had received definite information that the attempt on the life of Mahatmaji on 20-1-48 at the prayer meeting at Birla House, Delhi, was made by one Madanlal along with his associates, Karkare and others. He also told me that Karkare and Madanlal had met Savarkar immediately before their departure to Delhi to attempt on the life of Mahatmaji. He also ordered me to apprehend and arrest this man named Karkare who hailed from Ahmednagar and whose arrest he had already ordered in connection with other incidents of anti-Muslim nature at Ahmednagar. He also ordered me to inquire and apprehend the associates of Madanlal and Karkare.'

18.109: Nagarvala also stated that he had kept a note about the information given by Desai but he did not take down a First Information Report as he was not making an investigation. He said:

'I was not an Investigating Officer. They were orders given to me by the Government on the basis of which I started my inquiries.'

18.116: Nagarvala was not told who had sent those police officers to Bombay. All he knew was that they had come to arrest Karkare and belonged to Delhi Police.

(Even if one were to believe Nagarvala that the Delhi Police had kept him in the dark, when he found out that they were looking for Karkare, why did he not inform them that the home minister had issued orders for his arrest? One must remember that while most of the other police officers involved in the bungling of the investigations between 20 and 30 January 1948 got an opportunity to save their skins by appearing before the Kapur Commission, Sanjeevi had passed away before the Kapur Commission was constituted. So, he could not put forth his side of the story and all his colleagues got a convenient posthumous scapegoat to pin the blame on. I hold no brief for Sanjeevi but he was the only incompetent bungler who did not get a chance to make excuses and blame someone else.)

18.117: Nagarvala was questioned whether he asked them about any statement made by Madanlal, his reply was: 'No I did not ask them but during the course of conversation I gathered that they had no knowledge of what Madanlal had said or done.'

He did not ask them about the antecedents of Madanlal because the Home Minister had told him that he and Karkare were together and Bombay Police was already looking for Karkare. Nagarvala repeated 'the officers could not have told me anything because they knew nothing more'.

18.118: When asked if he had got the Delhi Police diaries translated into English, he said that he did get them translated, he went through the English translation of the case diaries of the bomb case. When his attention was drawn to paragraph 15 of case diary No.1 and that Deputy Superintendent Jaswant Singh and Inspector Balkrishna were present when the statement of Madanlal was made and therefore they must have known what statement he made, his reply was that that may or may not be so. All the information they gave him about Karkare was that they had come to arrest him. He did not ring up Delhi to find out what the officers had been sent for, as it was not for him to do so. The investigation was by Delhi Police. It was for them to ask for help. Assuming that in a strictly procedure wise this position is understandable, yet because the matter concerned the safety of a person of the stature of Mahatma Gandhi, one expected at least a display of more inquisitiveness to get out all what those Delhi Officers knew. A bland procedural response at that stage was no credit to the Bombay 'Inquiry'. And if the Delhi Police officers could give him no information, a long distance call to Rana or to the New Delhi Superintendent of Police could have been helpful.

18.120: Knowledge of Madanlal's statement—He came to know about Madanlal's statement after the murder. Rana did not tell him what statement Madanlal had made but he told Rana what he had done up to then in the way of investigation.

18.121: He came to know that the conspirators were from Poona only during the investigation, post murder, and not before. The Home Minister had told him that Karkare and his associates wanted to murder Mahatma Gandhi.

'Q. Were these associates according to your information Maharashtrians or refugees from Pakistan?'

'Ans. The information that we had in this connection was as recorded in my case diary and my reply to Government which would show that predominant suspicion of the Bombay City Police was on people who had migrated to Bombay and who might be classified as refugees.'

He did not learn from Ahmednagar about the associates of Karkare. His information was that Karkare was not in Ahmednagar during the last few days. He did not know that Madanlal had migrated to Ahmednagar or had been living there. All he knew was that Karkare belonged to Ahmednagar. But this is not in absolute accord with the first Crime Report. He further said that he did not think necessary to find out from Ahmedmagar Police about the associates of Karkare. That in the opinion of the Commission was an erroneous approach.

18.122: It was only after the murder that he came to know that amongst the associates of Karkare were Poona people like Godse, Apte and Badge. About Badge he knew that he was a trafficker in arms but he did not connect him as an associate of Karkare and Madanlal. He said that he must have ordered a watch to be kept at railway stations which would also include the airport.

(Here Nagarvala has resorted to a blatant lie. When he did not know whom to look for, why would he have ordered a watch and for whom? He has confessed that he did not investigate Karkare's whereabouts after the home minister had told him that he had ordered his arrest, so his own statements condemn Nagarvala.)

18.123: It is difficult for the Commission to find on the evidence as to what watch was kept at Air or railway terminals but if any watch was kept it must have been most ineffective because Karkare, Apte and Godse used both rail and air without any detection during the period from 23 to 27 January 1948. The watch could not but be futile, as no one seemed to know these people as the statement of Rana shows.

18.124: On his return from Delhi on 27 January, Rana stayed with Nagarvala and the later explained to him what all he had already done, and they decided to let the D.I.B. know about it. In the presence of Rana, Nagarvala told the D.I.B. on the telephone as to what he had done.

18.125: Nagarvala did not ask Rana as to the contents of the statement of Madanlal because Rana appeared to be satisfied with what he (Nagarvala) had already done. This is a rather peculiar statement because Nagarvala was working out the information given by Professor Jain which had been conveyed to him by Morarji Desai and Madanlal's statement at Delhi would have been helpful in working out the information. Rana had brought valuable information from one of the co-conspirators, the Commission has been unable to find any reason why the content of Madanlal's statement were not given by Rana to Nagarvala and why the later did not ask Rana as to what the statement contained? Particularly when Nagarvala later stated that he would have liked Madanlal to be brought to Bombay.

18.126: According to the statement of Nagarvala, Badge could not be considered a member of the Savarkar group because he was trafficking in arms and Nagarvala was looking for him not as a conspirator but as a trafficker in arms.

18.128: He was asked why he persisted with his theory of conspiracy of kidnapping and not of murder? His reply was that that was not his theory but that is what he learnt during the course of investigation. He added, 'What I mean to say is that I was working on the information given to me by the Home Minister and at the same time telling the Home Minister the result of my enquiries.'

18.129A: He emphasized that he had not seen Ex. 5A before. He was asked whether the reading of Ex. 5A would not have disclosed to him the class of persons who were in the conspiracy though not their identity. His reply was that it was possible to get a clue as to who those persons were. More so, from the reference to Karkare as proprietor of Deccan Guest House and member of the RSS. Nagarvala tried to clarify the matter in regard to conspiracy to murder or the conspiracy to kidnapping Mahatma Gandhi. He said:

'On 21 January 1948, the information that was given to me by the Home Minister, Bombay, is recorded in Crime Report No.1 dated 30-1-1948 contained in document called file of crime reports which is marked as Ex.185 by which number the whole book will hereinafter be referred to. The first crime report Dt. 30-1-1948 contained in Ex, 185 reads: "Before the Home Minister talked to me all I had was the report of the newspaper which I had read." I started no activity or enquiry till I received instructions from the Home Minister. In other words, the information to me was attempt on the life of Mahatma Gandhi. What I recorded on that occasion was this: "I was told by the Home Minister that he had received definite information that the attempt on the life of Mahatmaji on 20-1-1948 on (sic) the prayer meeting at Birla House, Delhi, was made by Madanlal and his associate Karkare and others."

'All that was conveyed to me by the Home Minister was that an attempt had been made on the life of Mahatma Gandhi on 20-1-1948 by Madanlal, Karkare and others. During the course of my enquiries what I learnt was that at no stage it was contemplated that we should go on with the theory of kidnapping and forget the original information. The information of kidnapping transpired during the course of enquiries in connection with the information furnished by the Home Minister. I did not ask the Home Minister as to who his informant was. I would not do so because if the Home Minister wanted to tell me the name of his source he would have done so. The stage at which the Home Minister gave me the information, the question of conspiracy did not arise in the legal sense. If I were to register this case in the Tughlaq Road Police Station as F.I.R., I would have put it under section 307, I.P.C. At this stage I would not have added section 120-B. The investigations or the enquiries which the police would be conducting would have been on the same lines whether or not section 120-B were added or invoked.'

(This statement of Nagarvala is a masterful act of obfuscation and evasion. He has completely clouded the issue and evaded answering the simple question put to him by the commission.)

18.134: The evidence before the Commission, however, shows that the Ahmednagar Police had a full record of Karkare's doings or misdoings in Ahmednagar, and had Nagarvala asked for this information, the District Police would have given him something valuable, e.g., connection of Karkare with Apte which Sub-Inspector Balkundi furnished to the Deputy Superintendent Chaubal soon after the murder when this information was called for from him by the Poona C.I.D. Sub-Inspector Deshmukh, witness No. 32, has stated that all this information was with him.

18.135: Nagarvala got the full statement of Madanlal on 5 February 1948.

18.139: Bombay Police not investigating the Bomb Case—'The Bombay Police,' Nagarvala said, 'Was not investigating the bomb case but it was making enquiries on information received from the Home Minister. The offence was committed in Delhi and the investigation was in the hands of the Delhi Police. The Bombay Police had neither been asked by the Delhi Police to make any investigation nor did the Delhi Police come to do it. An investigating officer had to ask for help, if that had been done in the bomb case, the Bombay Police would have given it willingly. It was not for the Bombay Police to interfere *suo motu* with the investigation of the Delhi Police and Sanjeevi's note that Bombay Police had to do any investigation was not correct.' (Once again Nagarvala was calling a dead man a liar to save his own skin.) He further stated that he was not under any duty to inform D.I.G. Kamte of the information given to him by the Home Minister but he did disclose to the Commissioner of Police the information given by the Home Minister on 22nd in the Tea Room over tea which was usual practice where matters of this kind were discussed. When the attention of Nagarvala was drawn to Ex. 8 where it was stated that the investigation was entrusted to Nagarvala, he replied that the word was loosely used.

(No wonder Nagarvala was Morarji Desai's blue-eyed boy: he had the knack to twist and turn everything to suit his purpose and possessed the quality of self righteousness in excess which was a quality Morarji Desai also possesed in abundance.)

18.140: The position taken by Nagarvala is not correct. On the facts of this case, Nagarvala was making an investigation, which has been dealt in a chapter headed 'Bombay Investigation'. But assuming he was making an inquiry to work out the information, he was acting as a police detective whose duty it was to obtain intelligence concerning the commission or design to commit a cognizable offence. A part of the conspiracy was entered into in Bombay city and even if it was the commission of an offence outside, Nagarvala as the head of the detective agency was performing a statutory duty otherwise it would be officiousness on his part and his order of arresting Badge on 24th would be wholly without jurisdiction.

18.142: Trunkcall to Sanjeevi must have been made by Nagarvala and Rana after 7 o'clock when both Rana and Nagarvala talked to Sanjeevi. The most important part of the talk was that Nagarvala told Sanjeevi that the situation was serious and effective steps should be taken to protect the life of Mahatma Gandhi, he told Sanjeevi that there was a gang whose objective was to kidnap Mahatma Gandhi. He gave this information to Rana also. Ex.8 dated 30 January, 1948, is a letter confirmatory of what he had talked on telephone with Sanjeevi. (It is very strange that Sanjeevi, who outranked both Nagarvala and Rana, did not tick them off for propagating nonsensical theories. Sanjeevi knew more than both these officers because by then Madanlal had made an extensive confession to officers interrogating him. What prevented him from ordering Nagarvala and Rana to stop wasting time and get on with the investigation will never be known.)

18.152: Nagarvala claimed that Morarji Desai did not give him any information about the editor of the *Hindu Rashtra* or the *Agranee*. For the first time, he heard the name Godse, was when the B.B.C. broadcast the news about Gandhi's murder at 7:30 p.m. IST on 30 January 1948.

18.153: In regard to Badge, Nagarvala said that he was hiding in

Poona jungles because that is the information his contacts had given him. When his attention was drawn to the statement of Badge that he was attending to his normal work in Poona and that he was staying in his house from 23 to 31 January, Nagarvala replied that it would not be in the 'case diary' that his contacts in Bombay had informed him that Badge was hiding in the jungles of Poona.

18.156: After Morarji Desai's orders, when he started making inquiries, a lot of information was coming from numerous sources. In that context, Badge was being looked for. The names of Karkare and Badge appeared prominently in the first Crime Report. Karkare's connections were seen and they were looking for Badge. After 20 January, Badge had completely disappeared from the conspiracy. In view of all that, information about Badge had to be verified. Nagarvala said that he was treating Karkare as (an) associate of Madanlal but there was nothing to show that Badge was also an associate.

18.161: When asked if Rana had discussed the statement of Madanlal with him, he replied that Madanlal's statement was given to him and hardly had he read one or two pages when Rana took it back from him. He also told Rana that he was in touch with Ahmednagar and every effort was being made to locate Karkare. But the statement of Madanlal was not discussed after the telephone call nor before.

18.162: Nagarvala said that reading of the statement of Madanlal, Ex.l, would have made no difference as whatever had to be done in regard to it was to be done at Poona which was outside his jurisdiction. As far as he remembered, the statement which Rana brought was a typed copy on a slightly coloured paper, it was pinkish.

18.164: 'The culprits,' he said, 'were not residing in Bombay; they came to Thana and escaped from Santa Cruz by air but they were not identified by the Police there.' Karkare had left by train from Kalyan in Thana district and he (Nagarvala) himself was operating only within his jurisdiction.

(It may be mentioned that Karkare did not leave from Kalyan but took the train for Delhi from Bombay Central railway station and the other two, Apte and Godse, were staying in Bombay hotels up to the morning of the 27th, both well within Nagarvala's jurisdiction. Once again, Nagarvala was lying to the commission.)

18.166: The Crime Report also showed that inquiries had been made about Badge also but Badge never came to Bombay, so the question of his identification never arose. Nagarvala discussed with Rana what he had already done but Madanlal's statement was not discussed. He kept a small diary in which he had some names which were the names mentioned in the Crime Report. Badge's name was also there. When a portion of Rana's letter addressed to Kamte was read out to Nagarvala, he said that it was incorrect that persons mentioned by Madanlal were hiding in Bombay. He said that he had done his job and he was quite satisfied with what he had done.

(Nagarvala could not be bothered that his satisfaction with having done his job had been largely responsible for helping Nathuram Godse murder Gandhi, but then according to Nagarvala's way of reasoning, the deed was done in Delhi which was outside his jurisdiction.)

18.169: The Commission would like to remark that Badge was arrested on 31 January after the murder and his house was searched. The order for his arrest on 24th apparently was because he was suspected to be connected with Karkare. It would have been fruitful if at that stage the aid of Poona Police had been sought. An earlier arrest should have been more useful.

18.171: Nagarvala said that it was correct that he wanted the Delhi Police Officers to interrogate Avatar Singh but they were not prepared to do so. He could not force them because they were not prepared to do so. He could not force them because they were not subordinate to him. He got the statement of Madanlal on 5 February 1948. He also said that the house of Savarkar was kept constantly under watch and he could not say where Bharucha, the Commissioner of Police, Bombay, got his information from that the conspirators visited the house of Savarkar and still they were not detected.

(Nagarvala claimed that Savarkar's home was continuously under watch. On the 31st, after the murder, when it came under attack, where were his watchers? Since his department did not know who to look out for, how would they have known whether Madanlal's accomplices had visited Savarkar's home or not?)

18.178: Nagarvala stated that from their police statement it appears that both Nathuram Godse and Apte were staying in the Elphinstone

Hotel, and Arya Pathik Ashram under assumed names as from 23rd when they arrived in Bombay by Calcutta Punjab Mail, till the 27th when they left Bombay for Delhi by air but at that time he had no knowledge of their being in the conspiracy.

18.179: It therefore, appears that after the bomb was exploded and N.D. Apte returned to Bombay he stayed in the Ashram under an assumed name although the owner of the Ashram knew what his correct name was. It is surprising that he was allowed to do so with the knowledge and connivance of the owner.

18.181: At this stage Counsel for the Government of India made a statement saying that his case was not that Karkare was at Ahmednagar during the period 21st to the time of his arrest but his case was that if information had been given to Ahmednagar Police the whereabouts of Karkare could be more effectively found out. The Commission wholly disagrees with this view. Ahmednagar Police knew nothing about Karkare's whereabouts and cared less. But they did have a full record of his activities and knew that he was an associate of N.D. Apte and that could have been available to the Bombay Police.

18.185: When asked about finding out from Ahmednagar Police as to the associates of Karkare. He said that he found out from Ahmednagar Police that Karkare was not there thus he did not make any further inquiries there but continued his inquiries in Bombay about Karkare and his associates. He did not ask his brother for the names of Karkare's associates. 'Question of associates would have arisen if he would have got Karkare because people who came and saw Karkare did not become his associates.' He said that the D.S.P., Ahmednagar could not have thrown more light on Karkare. Those were names of persons who were anti-Mahatma Gandhi and might kidnap him and do harm to him. One of the main objects of writing the Crime Report at that stage was that it might not later on be said that associating the name of Savarkar with the conspiracy was an after thought.

18.188: During the course of his inquiry and from the information received he had reason to believe that there was a gang which was likely to kidnap the Mahatma. He was not obsessed by any theory much less kidnapping theory. He added that if information regarding kidnapping persistently came in and was credibly correct, howsoever much one might disagree with it one had to work on it. The purpose of kidnapping as far as he knew was that if Mahatma was not there the 55 crores would not have been paid to Pakistan.

18.189: In Ex.7, paragraph 8, Sanjeevi had stated:

> 'I asked him about the absconding accused whose names or descriptions were given to the Delhi Police by Madanlal. Nagarvala told me that he would send me a detailed note on the investigation made at Bombay City and elsewhere in the Province by air the next day.'

Nagarvala was given an opportunity to reply to this matter and his reply was that the statement in Paragraph 8 was not correct and that Sanjeevi in his telephonic talk never asked him about any absconding accused. In his conversation with Sanjeevi, Nagarvala had mainly referred to the information which he had received about the conspiracy to kidnap Mahatma Gandhi by a large gang. It was his practice to confirm by letter the substance of a telephonic talk and he, therefore, sent a confirmatory letter on 30 January 1948 summarizing the talk which he had with Sanjeevi on the telephone and the letter is a correct record of the talk, he said.

18.192: He did mention about the kidnapping theory to Morarji Desai and if the latter says that he did not then it must be a lapse of his memory. (One thing that no one could accuse Morarji Desai of was a lapse in memory. Till his death, at the age of ninety-eight, the man possessed a remarkably efficient memory. He recollected events in the minutest detail, and was not in the habit of embellishing them.) He met the Home Minister several times between the 20 and 30 January in connection with the information which the Home Minister had given him.

18.197: Evidence has been produced before the Commission contained in Intelligence Bureau file No. 13/HA(R)/59-II, Ex.224-A which contains certain documents which if they had been obtained earlier might have been of great assistance in the investigation or inquiry which was going on at Bombay. Chaubal of the office of the D.I.G., C.I.D. sent to Nagarvala after the murder a document giving the list of relatives and associates of Karkare, amongst them was N.D. Apte, the next document of importance is a letter with which were sent three copies of photographs of V.R.

Karkare and his descriptive role. Along with this photograph of Karkare were three copies of the photograph of Apte so that reference to the D.I.G., C.I.D. Poona would have been most useful even for Nagarvala's inquiry or working out the information given to him by the Home Minister.

18.199: The evidence of police witnesses from Ahmednagar shows that they had a complete dossier on the activities of Madanlal and Karkare. As a matter of fact it was S.I. Balkundi who furnished the information to Dy. Supdt. Chaubal about Karkare and his association with Apte. If the District police of Ahmednagar had been asked it seems not only possible but probable that the information and photograph of Karkare supplied after the murder would have been supplied earlier.

18.201: The Commission has been thinking as to how the idea of kidnapping came to be considered the objective of the conspirators by Bombay Police. One explanation may be (the) faulty understanding of the Punjabi language by the contacts and informers because many Punjabi words sound alike though they are different words and some times same words have different meanings in different contexts e.g. 'Dus' meaning 'ten' and also 'to show'. This may be highly conjectural an explanation but the theory of kidnapping was so astounding that some such mistake must have led to its being considered respectable.

J.S. Bharucha's Statement-Wit. 22

18.202: J.S. Bharucha, IP, was Commissioner of Police, Bombay, witness No. 22, during the period with which the inquiry is concerned.

18.204: His information was that the Delhi Police did come to Bombay but they did not do very much and Nagarvala told him that they were not of much use. After the murder, he (Bharucha) asked Nagarvala as to why he did not tell him anything about Professor Jain? His reply was that Morarji Desai had asked him to keep the whole thing confidential. Morarji Desai dealt with the police directly, although the orders to the police should have come through the Home Secretary.

18.205: He was shown Ex5-A and asked if he would be able to make anything of it. His reply was 'yes', he would be able to do so particularly in regard to the editor *Hindu Rashtra* and *Agranee* and also Karkare. From Ex. 5-A it should have been possible for the Bombay Police to find out from the Poona Police as to who the conspirators were. He was for two months D.S.P. of Poona and at that time he must have known something about Nathuram Godse. If he had been told that Nathuram had met Savarkar, he would have got in touch with the Poona Police and tried to locate the companions of Madanlal. He did not think that Poona Police was pro-RSS. If there was cooperation between Bombay Police and Poona District Police and C.I.D. Poona, arrest of conspirators would not have been difficult, and if Bombay Police had got in touch with Angarkar and Gurtu and Kamte, it would not have been difficult to nip the controversy in the bud.

18.208: Rana, when he returned from Delhi did not meet this witness and, therefore, he never came to know about the statement of Madanlal. He was asked about what he should have done knowing that a bomb had been exploded at Mahatma Gandhi's meeting. His reply was as follows:

'Q. When you came to know that a bomb had been thrown at Mahatma Gandhi's meeting by a person who was a refugee from West Punjab but then living in Bombay, would it not have been your ordinary duty to find out who this man was, who his other co conspirators were and how serious the matter was?'

'A. From the information that I had, I did not think it was serious enough for me to initiate any investigation myself. I remember I did not do anything. Nobody thought it to be so serious as it turned out to be.'

18.209: In cross-examination he stated that he could not remember if during the time that he was D.S.P., Poona he came to know anything about the conspiracy to murder. He surprisingly replied, 'I do not remember.' He could not remember if Apte was arrested during his term of office. During the investigation of the bomb case he had no information about the conspiracy to kidnap Mahatma Gandhi, nor that the Deputy Commissioner was working on it. He could not exactly remember what Nagarvala told him about the visit of the Delhi Police officers.

18.210: He did not know at that time that Savarkar's house was being watched. As it was an important matter, information should have been given to him. After the murder, he met Savarkar, who told him (Bharucha) that he had nothing to do with Gandhiji's murder. From that Bharucha concluded that there was something wrong. He immediately went and met Morarji Desai and told him that he suspected Savarkar and also told him what Savarkar had said to him. Morarji Desai said to Bharucha, 'Why do you not arrest him?' At that time Savarkar was really ill and Bharucha told Morarji Desai about it. Nagarvala had deposed that Savarkar was feigning illness.

Chapter XIX of the Kapur Commission's report deals with the communal Hindu organizations, Hindu Mahasabha, RSS and the Hindu Rashtra Dal.

19.19: R.K. Khadilkar, witness No. 97, said that they felt at the time that the kind of fanaticism they were having in Poona among the Hindu Sabha circles would lead to violence. The danger to Mahatma Gandhi, he added, came from Hindu fanatics i.e. the small section of Hindu Rashtra Dal which was part of Hindu Mahasabha and RSS.

19.21: R.S. Gurtu, witness No. 22, stated that reports came to him about the communal activities of Nathuram Godse, Karkare, Apte, Badge and several others. They carried on propaganda against Gandhiji's policies *qua* Muslims but he could not remember if there were any propaganda for doing harm to Mahatma Gandhi, least of all murdering him. There were reports of their preparing bombs but that they were not meant to be used against Mahatma Gandhi. When he heard about the bomb explosion at Birla House, he had a vague suspicion that it might be the work of Hindu Mahasabha and RSS group. But he had no idea that it was the work of Godse group.

19.27: Another document which is demonstrative of the attitude of Nathuram Godse, is Ex. 71 which is a Marathi record of the proceedings of a meeting of the Hindu Mahasabha held at Shivaji Mandir on 28 November 1947, at 6.30 p.m. The audience was about two thousand and the speakers were V.B. Gogte and N.V. Godse. The subject of the speeches was 'Hindu Nation and Jayprakash Narayan', and was a quick reply to J.P. Narayan's speech made in Poona. The speakers ridiculed Jayprakash Narayan about his socialism and accused the socialists of helping in the creation of Pakistan and the partition of India and its consequences. At that meeting Nathuram Godse said: 'Allegations have been made that the Sangh and the Hindu Sabha have hatched a conspiracy to murder Pandit Nehru because he said that he would brandish his sword on behalf of the British Government for finishing Subhash Babu as he was a traitor.'

There was some reference to Mahatma Gandhi also and that Socialism was the unclaimed progeny of Gandhism. The speech ended with: 'The Hindu Mahasabha and the Sangh have been subjected to criticism. The main reason is that they saw Kansa.'

Activities of Hindu Mahasabha in Delhi

19.32: The Abstract of Intelligence dated 31 January 1948, Ex. 136, also gives the activities of the Hindu Mahasabha. It shows that a procession was taken out on 25 January in connection with Arya Samaj Anniversary. Swami Dharmananda said that the fast undertaken by Mahatma Gandhi has spoiled 'the show to remove Muslims from Delhi.'

19.35: Prof. Ram Singh was examined by the Commission as witness No. 75. He put the position of Hindu Mahasabha as follows: 'It was opposed to the Partition and was trying to undo the disadvantages thereof. It was in favour of all Hindus being brought safe to India from Pakistan. It was opposed to the policy of Mahatma Gandhi of placating the Muslims and keeping them in India and getting the mosques vacated which had been taken possession of by Hindus and Sikhs, who had placed their deities and religious symbols there. It was also opposed to keeping Muslim houses vacant when Hindus and Sikhs were without shelter and pregnant Hindu women were giving birth to children and had nowhere to go to. It was also opposed to 55 crores being placed at the disposal of Pakistan to continue its Kashmir war.' He said that he was not in favour of murder of Mahatma Gandhi and no Hindusabhaite was. The Hindu Mahasabha was not in favour of assassination of leaders, they were not responsible for shouting 'Madanlal Zindabad!'

The RSS in Bombay Province

19.42: The activities of the RSS and the Hindu Mahasabha must have come to the notice and been under the consideration of the Bombay Government in 1947; because we find that in confidential secret document Ex 177 B.G. Kher, the then Premier, made three suggestions regarding these bodies, that (1) complete list of officers and members of the RSS be collected by the police and submitted to Government; (ii) similar order as to the leaders of the Hindu Mahasabha organizations, and (iii) strict watch be kept on the operation of the two organizations. There was no date on this order but on 7 August 1947, Morarji Desai issued an order to the D.I.G., C.I.D. and to the Commissioner of Police, Bombay to get the requisite information within 10 days; the information should be discretely obtained and must be correct and complete in all respects.

19.45: It does not appear that any separate list was prepared of the RSS by the D.I.G., C.I.D., nor does this list show that the various persons whose names are given in this list were members of the RSS. But there is evidence to show that many RSS members were members of the Hindu Mahasabha. This list contains the names of Nathuram Godse who is known as a staunch Savarkarite, of N.D. Apte who is shown as potentially dangerous, of G.V. Ketkar shown as a staunch Savarkarite and the brain behind Hindu Sabha activities and influential, N.R. Athawale also shown as potentially dangerous and staunch Savarkarite, and D.R. Badge is also shown as potentially dangerous and a dealer in unlicensed arms.

19.46: To this is added another list, Ex.114-A, which is of Ahmednagar. It mentions V.R. Karkare as a smuggler of arms, co worker of N.D. Apte and potentially dangerous. But both Ex. 114 and Ex. 114-A are provincial lists. The district list of Ahmednagar does not give all this elaborate information.

19.55: We may take up the evidence relating to the activities of the RSS at Delhi. Bannerjee, witness No 19 has stated:

'Some of the activities of the RSS were considered to be anti-social and objectionable and the feeling was that Government was showing itself rather tardy in dealing with this organization.'

19.64: On page 687 of his book Pyarelal has said the following:

'The RSS was a communalist, para-military, Fascist organization, controlled from Maharashtra. The key-positions were held almost exclusively by the Maharashtrians. Their declared object was to set up Hindu Raj. They had adopted the slogan "Muslims clear out of India". At the time they were not very active, at least overtly, but it was being darkly hinted that they were only waiting for all the Hindus and Sikhs in West Pakistan to be evacuated. They would then wreak full vengeance on the Indian Muslims for what Pakistan had done.'

19.67: On or about 12 September 1947 the head of the RSS called upon Gandhiji and told him that they were not for killing of Muslims, but for protection of Hindus i.e. they were a protective and not destructive force and that RSS stood for peace. But when the Mahatma asked them to openly repudiate the allegations and condemn killings and harassment of Muslims they said that Gandhi could do it himself. A few days later the leaders of the RSS took Gandhiji to attend one of their rallies which they were holding at the Sweeper's Colony. They welcomed Gandhiji and called him a great man that Hinduism had produced. In reply Gandhiji said that he was proud of being a Hindu but his Hinduism was not intolerant nor exclusive.

19.72: According to the diary of Manibehn Patel dated 1 February 1948, members of the RSS came and said to Sardar that 'their organization was not involved in the murder.' (The RSS has a reputation of disassociating with deeds after they are done at their behest or in which they are involved.)

(This is a strange revelation since on the evening of 31 January immediately after the funeral, a meeting of senior members of the Cabinet, bureaucrats and police was held and a decision was taken to ban the RSS and Hindu Mahasabha, and yet the Union home minister's daughter reveals that her father received members of the RSS at his official home the next morning.)

19.75: The criticism by communist workers, socialists etc. had sent the local Hindu Mahasabha members 'in high dungeon'. There was an increased activity on the part of the RSS workers and their meetings were addressed by many prominent Hindus calling upon the people to strengthen the RSS. It also shows that the RSS and Hindu Mahasabha leaders at Poona were, 'to say the least, alike to each other'. (In other words one and the same.)

Activities of the Hindu Rashtra Dal

19.82: A brief history. On 15 May 1942, V.D. Savarkar, President of the Hindu Mahasabha addressed the volunteers at the training camp of the organization at Poona and emphasized the necessity of forming a volunteer organization for clandestine activities, as that could not be undertaken by the Mahasabha. As a consequence of this Hindu Mahasabha leaders such as S.R. Date, V.V. Gogte, N.D. Apte and N.V. Godse founded the Hindu Rashtra Dal at Poona with the object of assisting the Hindu Mahasabha's activities. But they made no effort in popularizing the movement of the Dal or to increase its membership.

19.83: In May 1943, N.D. Apte and N.V. Godse organized a second annual training camp of the Dal at Ahmednagar. 70 volunteers from Marathi speaking districts of Bombay Province and Marathi speaking Indian Princely States attended the camp. Volunteers were trained in the use of firearms, and indoctrinated with Savarkar ideology.

19.84: On 29 May 1943, V.D. Savarkar held private discussions with the Hindu Rashtra Dal in Anandashram, Poona (Apte's home). He required the volunteers to owe an implicit allegiance to him irrespective of who the President of Hindu Mahasabha was, the Dal was to remain a distinct body, its primary duty being to protect Hindudom and render help to every Hindu institution in their attempt to oppose encroachment on their rights and religion. Savarkar's ideology was attainment of Hindudom, opposition of Pakistan and indivisibility of India.

19.85: Membership of the Dal: There were 150 members of the Dal at Poona. Its office bearers were (1) N.V. Godse, editor of *Agranee*, Chief Organiser. (2) Kashinath Limaye, Sangli. (3) N.D. Apte, Secretary. (4) Prof R.S. Jog of Ferguson College, Organiser.

19.86: The activities of the Dal were confined to maintaining order during Hindu Mahasabha meetings and enrolling of Hindu Mahasabha members. On 22 June 1944, 15 Hindu Rashtra Dal volunteers led by N.D. Apte staged demonstrations against Gandhiji at Panchgani. During that demonstration an armed Nathuram Godse made an abortive attempt to assault Mahatma Gandhi.

19.88: The object of the Dal was stated to be the propagation of 'Hindu Rashtra Vad as propounded by Vir Savarkarji' called Savarkarism. (Today, it is called Hindutva.)

19.89: Savarkar as the dictator nominated—S.V. Modak of Satara and P.V. Gothaskar as the next dictator and General Secretary. Savarkar spoke about Muslim atrocities in the Punjab, Bengal and N.W.F.P. and said that they would not stop until the Hindus retaliated in the same spirit including raping Muslim women and destroying mosques, etc. if

Hindu women and Hindu places of worship were treated in that manner. Savarkar advised the Dal volunteers to oppose the Constitution to be framed by the Constituent Assembly if it was against the interests of Hindus and Hindudom.

19.92: Nathuram Godse's statement, in Court, also shows that on 16 January 1944, Godse and Apte decided to start a newspaper to give publicity to the work of Hindu Mahasabha. ₹15,000/- were given as a loan by Savarkar, the first issue of *Agranee* appeared on 25 March 1944. It ceased publication under this name in July 1947 because of the demand of ₹5,000/- as security deposit on 3 July 1947 under the Press Emergency Powers Act and soon after on 15 July 1947, it restarted under the name of the *Hindu Rashtra*, which cannot be a credit to the efficacy of the Press Act. N.V. Godse was the Editor of both these papers. N.D. Apte was the proprietor of the *Agranee,* the *Hindu Rashtra* was owned by a private company of which the shareholders were N.D. Apte and N.V. Godse, this continued to be published till 31 January 1948. Godse was arrested on the 30th, i.e. a day before.

19.93: The following extracts, translated into English from Marathi, of the editorials published in the *Agranee* and the *Hindu Rashtra* reflect the anti-Gandhi policy of these newspapers, and the mentality of its editor, Nathuram V. Godse:

The Agranee, dated 12 April 1947: 'The thirst for blood of the advocate of non-violence has not been quenched.'

'Gandhi who cherishes (lit. taken to heart) as his life time ideal to annihilate the mentality of resistance of the Hindus by advocating unilateral non-violence, has now clearly stated in his post-prayer speech that he is anxious to see (Barrister) Jinnah adorn the Presidential chair (lit. Presidentship) of Independent India. Gandhi had already revealed his pro-Islam slavish mentality, at the beginning of his political career (lit. life) by inviting the Amir of Afghanistan to invade India under the gorgeous pretext (lit. name) of achieving independence. After that by raising the issue that some imposter's rule might be established in India as a result of anarchy due to war, this false (lit. nominal) devotee of freedom and his hypocritical worship of truth and non-violence was eager to place the crown of India's sovereignty on the head of the Nizam and to pay respects to (lit. to wave the five lamped platter round the face of) such a Nizam.

Gandhiji had already tried to entrust power again to Jinnah through the mouth of Rajaji by offering (Ba)rrister Jinnah the Prime Ministership of the interim Government, and now feeling definitely that independence is knocking at the door, this "quisling" of the Hindu nation is openly wooing (Jinnah) saying (Barrister) Jinnahbhai why do you demand only Pakistan, that is India's one third or one fourth? Why do you not accept when this humble servant is prepared to offer at your feet the whole of India? From this, we are constrained to say that the thirst for Hindu blood which this "Mohatma", (which means a 'lustful soul', the editor is parodying the honorific title Mahatma) is feeling has not yet been satisfied.'

'Mr Gandhi, Commit Suicide.' 'It is the height of (lit. to reach the height of) shamelessness that the coward who cannot do without taking the aid of the police and soldiers so that no harm is done to his person, the touch of whose feet converts many an Ahilya occupying Minister's post into Shurpankha's, who can not step forward in carrying on the administration without bombs, cannons and British soldiers, should advice (the Hindus) to sacrifice themselves without offering resistance. Does the Sultan blinded by power consider the blood of the Hindu people as not worth a pie (penny), so that this Bania who is a traitor to his community (meaning Mahatma Gandhi) should despite the flowing of several rivers of it, devise fresh means of satisfying the blood thirst of these monstrous aggressors. Does he not think the bloodshed at Noakhali, Punjab and Bihar (in Bihar Hindus massacred Muslims) as adequate? We clearly tell Gandhi that if the rivers of Hindu blood that he has made to flow or the encouragement that he has indirectly given to such outrages, by the advocacy of which cowardly philosophy, is at least to be partially undone, then Gandhiji should accept the defeat of his cowardly and worthless non-violence and should, for the defence of his self-respect (if any is left of it) commit suicide; if not, he should bid goodbye for ever to Indian Politics. Does this Sokaji who has been so generous about the lives of others consider lakhs of his countrymen? Is it not the duty of the people to determine from this the real worth of this hypocritical patriot?'

Hindu Rashtra, dated 7-6-1947: 'Hindu Rashtra Sevak Badge Arrested', Poona, dated 6-6-1947. 'The Police (B. Sub) arrested tonight at 8:30 under 19F of the Arms Act, Hindu Rashtra Sevak, H.N. Badge, the Manager of the Maharashtra Shastra Bhandar here. He was immediately released on bail. Now the prosecution is launched (lit. started) against Badge for the second time.'

Hindu Rashtra, dated 3-7-1947. 'The *Agranee* has received several letters (requesting) "Write something about this day-to-day and send more copies". That means the object is that they want something like curses on (lit. abuses to Congressmen and opposition to the Muslims). But what have today's young men done so that the devotees of Hindutva who have tolerated today for years together the timid rule of the Congress, should be glorified.'

'This today's youth (?) who is devotee of Hindutva reads everyday the news that today the Congressmen arrested more Hindus, Jawaharlal killed Hindus only; Vallabhbhai tolerated the molestation of a Hindu woman and Gandhi (lit. and what of Gandhi) he is always eager to start for a tour in order to annex every day a new province to Pakistan.'

'After reading this news what else has the youth who is devotee of Hindutva done beyond saying that the Congressmen are cowards and anti-Hindu?'

'If you cannot do anything else, you should remain bearing silently that which is in existence. You should not at all make a tom tom of your devotion to Hindutva!'

Translation of Bhalji Pendharkar's (a pioneering and acclaimed maker of Marathi films) message on the observance of the Black Day, 3 July, appearing in the *Dainik Agranee, Hindu Rashtra* dated 6 July 1947.

'My sad, distressed and perhaps despondent Hindu brothers! This is such a black day, forced on us by those who have black marketeered in the nation (as a commodity) that every Hindu, every patriot should protest against it at the top of his voice until the threat gives way and the chest bursts. And it is a matter of great shame that some weaklings accidentally (lit. by mistake) born in Maharashtra, should come and justify this Partition in this capital of the Chhatrapati.... The partitioner's of *Akhand Bharat* be condemned a hundred times.' These are the remarks touching the hearts of every Hindu, made by Bhalji Pendharkar in a letter sent from his sick bed on the occasion of the Kolhapur 'Black Day'.

Dainik Hindu Rashtra, Dt. 6 September 1947: 'Non-resisting tendency (which is) accomplished easily by animals. The strenuous nature (of the effort) made by Gandhi and his followers (lit. Gandhi people) to make the Hindu community assimilate the revengeless and non-violent tendency like that which sheep and goats have made their own is understood. There is no reason to blame them (Gandhi and his followers) for it. But when even Dr Shyama Prasad following in the footsteps of an imbecile Prime Minister like Pandit Jawaharlal issues a statement and when persons who call themselves the leaders of the Hindu Sabha like Barrister Chatterjee the President of the Bengal Hindu Sabha and Devendranath Mukerji, the Secretary, feel agonised at the fast of Gandhi which has an ill will against the Hindus, we are inclined to say this much that it is necessary that the Hindusabha should give more serious consideration to its health, (lit. constitution).

Dainik Hindu Rashtra, dated 7 September 1947: 'The Swaraj which the Congress has got is engaged in taking out tours with Liaquat Ali, while (Mahatma Gandhi the deity of its Swaraj, is busy showing the scene (by way) of drinking lime (lit. musambi) juice in Suhrawardy's cup.

'And if anyone has really the urge for Akhand Hindustan (lit. undivided India) and if a feeling of sacrificing one's own life for its sake has been created, then do not strike at a wrong place! Remove these obstacles (lit. bolts)! The flood of Indian bravery will in no time integrate the whole of India into one.

'Of course all this (will be done) by peaceful ways of elections, meetings, propaganda, etc! What more than that can we tell?'

Dainik Hindu Rashtra, dated 16 December 1947: 'Pakistani Reward for Congress Betrayal of the Hindus'. 'Gandhi, father of all these wicked conspiracies, is openly propagating that Hindi should not be the National Language. Power is an intoxicating substance. Similarly, the support of the majority too is an intoxicating influence. The Congressmen have become intoxicated today with this drug.'

19.94: There are some other extracts from the *Agranee* which also show the trend of opinion of its editor. Ex. 152 is of the issue of 6 July 1947, which refers to the arrest of Athawale, Secretary of the Hindu Mahasabha in connection with the bomb outrage. The significant portions of the article are these: 'that it is gratifying to know that the Government suspects Hindu Mahasabha workers to be members of bomb conspiracies, that other workers are likely to be involved including Godse, that the

Congress Government seeks the satisfaction of obstructing Hindu Sabha Movement by these arrests. That the *Agranee* may stop but the Black Day observance of 3 July is the beginning of the fight of Hindutva.'

In Chapter XX, the Kapur Commission's report deals with G.V. Ketkar and others.

20.1: G.V. Ketkar, witness No. 1 is a prominent citizen of Poona. He is a grandson (daughter's son) of the great Indian leader the Late Bal Gangadhar 'Lokmanya' Tilak. He was the editor of the *Kesari*, Tilak's paper, and was at one time the President of the Provincial Congress Committee of Bombay Province and took part in the Salt Satyagraha, Dandi Kooch in 1930.

20.30: A very significant part of his statement showing his association with Nathuram Godse, rather a close one at that, is at page 15, Vol. I, in an answer to a question, 'Have you anything more to say about these matters (terms of reference)?

'A. I do not think I have to add anything to these matters. I was told that some letters were sent by Nathuram Godse before his execution to his relatives and friends. Those letters were never sent to the addressees. I wrote to the jail authorities in March 1965, and I was told that they were sent to the Inspector General of Prisons. I want the letter addressed to me, if any, to be given to me or to the Commission because that would, I am sure, corroborate my statement that I tried to dissuade them from committing this murder.'

20.35: When asked why he did not report or inform anyone about Apte and Godse after his meeting with Badge when previously on the basis of a mere speech with sinister words he had asked Balukaka to inform Government of the intention of Godse, his answer was, 'I was editor at that time. I had no time to go and see Balukaka, Badge said to me that bomb attempt itself was an attempt to murder and that they were going again. As I had abused him, he (Badge) ran away.'

When asked what inference he drew from the talk he had on the three occasions above referred to, his answer was, 'Mahatma Gandhi was alone to be killed.... I did not know the place where the attack on Mahatma Gandhi would take place.' He added, 'I knew that Godse was going to kill Mahatma Gandhi because he himself told me and Apte was going to be the helper. I did not know what means they were going to adopt to kill.... I did not infer from the talks I had that there was a conspiracy to murder Mahatma Gandhi. I was under the impression that only Godse was going to commit murder.'

20.36: This was his information up to 22 January 1948. It was after he met Badge that he (Ketkar) discovered that more than one person were going to take part in the murder.

20.50: In paragraph 33, of the review petition filed by Ketkar regarding his detention after the disclosures he made about the conspiracy at the function held to felicitate Karkare and Gopal Godse on their release, Ketkar mentioned that when, on the midday of Sunday, 22 November 1964, he was showing some Americans round Poona city and was near the Jain Mandir Bus Stop when some boys collected around him and put a garland of shoes round his neck and told the Americans that he (Ketkar) was a traitor, indicating there by that there was a violent propaganda against him.

20.51: Three things emerge from this petition (1) Three months before the murder, N.V. Godse disclosed to Ketkar his idea of murdering Mahatma Gandhi and Ketkar admonished him and tried to dissuade him. We shall leave the story of discussing pros and cons of murdering Mahatma Gandhi. (2) A few months before that Godse made a speech about Mahatma living 125 years, etc. Ketkar met Balukaka Kanitkar and urged him to warn the Government which Balukaka did. He spoke to Balukaka about the speech and the corroborative private talk he had with Nathuram Godse. (3) Badge met Ketkar after the bomb explosion and disclosed the names of the participants in that bomb throwing and also that they were returning to Delhi to commit the murder.

20.54: Ketkar was asked to explain what he meant by saying in his letter to this Commission dated 14 September 1965, Ex. 19, 'About the fearful and disastrous consequences that would result if Godse carries out the idea.' His reply is significant; he says, 'What I meant was that there would be public agitation. Political parties, i.e. the Congress and non-Congress parties would fight amongst themselves and Brahmin and non-Brahmin controversy may flare up.' He has used the word, 'Bhayankar!', which means 'awfully disastrous'.

20.60: In his cross examination, Ketkar told the Commission that he knew of the intention to murder but not the plan, and that there were three occasions when he came to know of this. He did not know about Apte's being in it till Badge told him. He knew Apte only by name and sight which, in the opinion of the Commission, is the anti thesis of truth, as is shown by the fact that he stood surety for Apte in the Library Bomb Case.

20.61: After Ketkar's petition to the reviewing authority was dismissed, he filed a petition under Section 491 of the Criminal Procedure Code in the High Court of Bombay but this petition was also dismissed by a judgement of the Bombay High Court dated 21 July 1965. Some facts stated in the petition and the findings of the Bombay High Court are relevant and may usefully be set out here: (1) The learned Judges have said, 'According to him (Ketkar), the two Governments felt themselves embarrassed, because the petitioner had disclosed that he had informed B.G. Kher, the then Chief Minister of Bombay, about the "plan" to murder Mahatma Gandhi and yet no action was taken to prevent the commission of the offence.' Significantly the judgement has used the word 'plan', and not 'intention'.... (3) In the affidavit filed by the District Magistrate in reply to Ketkar's affidavit, he said that Ketkar was invalid because he belonged to the group of persons who believed that Nathuram Godse had been of service to India by assassinating Mahatma Gandhi, and that all the persons who gathered at the function shared that view which was reflected in the speeches delivered there. (4) The speech delivered by Ketkar showed, according to the affidavit of the District Magistrate, a pre-knowledge of the conspiracy which had been hatched to murder the Mahatma.... (6) In all probability, the correspondent of the *Indian Express* was also present, and the fact that a number of photographs of persons on the dais, including Ketkar, were taken at the time and produced before the High Court was corroborative of the function being attended by persons other than invitees. These photographs are before the Commission and show that publicity was given to the meeting and its proceedings, and whatever else it might have been, it was not private. (7) Ketkar had prior knowledge of the Nathuram Godse's 'idea', plan or intention to murder Mahatma Gandhi, and that even if he did write through Balukaka Kanitkar the statement of Ketkar in his affidavit was vague, and that on the material, on the record the Court could not hold that Ketkar made it clear to the audience that he 'did not like the idea of Nathuram Godse contemplating the murder of Mahatma Gandhi.'

(8) 'According to the District Magistrate, the speech delivered by the petitioner was objectionable and in a sense inflammatory. To refer to Nathuram Godse as a Deshbhakt patriot and to eulogize him for the act committed by him cannot be treated as a legal or innocuous activity. It may be that it is possible to make a distinction between the eulogy of the assassin for his individual qualities and the eulogy for the act done by him or the praise of the act itself. But that distinction can be made by people of intelligence, ability and subtlety. It is difficult for the ordinary people to understand the subtle distinctions between the two positions. Now, if as a result of indiscriminate praise of Nathuram Godse, the assassin of Mahatma Gandhi, the District Magistrate apprehends that breach of the peace was likely. (9) The Court rejected the submissions by the counsel for Ketkar that the order passed was mala fide and was the result of questions asked in the Assembly and in Parliament or that they were the result of any direction given by the Central Government or the State Government or was the consequence of any pressure.

On these grounds the High Court dismissed Ketkar's *habeas corpus* petition.

Statement of Balukaka Kanitkar

20.102: The next document that is relevant in this connection is Ex. 81, dated 10 May 1948, which is Balukaka Kanitkar's statement made to the Police in the Gandhi Murder Case. He stated that in the second week of July 1947, in a meeting under the Presidentship of N.D. Apte, in Shivaji Mandir in Poona, Nathuram Godse delivered a lecture at which thousands of persons were present including Balukaka himself. In that Nathuram Godse stated that constitutional methods had failed, Hindu Mahasabha had no money and organisers to fight elections. He suggested that they should form secret organizations and take to revolutionary methods and he also hinted that the time had come to do away with the leadership of some of the top ranking Congressmen. There were a number of RSS volunteers there and after the meeting was over, Balukaka Kanitkar heard some of them say that Nathuram was right and that Gandhiji and Nehru were thorns in the establishment of Hindu Raj and hence they should be removed from the path, but Balukaka

Kanitkar did not know who those volunteers were and would not be able to identify them. As in Balukaka's view the matters might take an ugly turn, he sent a registered letter to B.G. (Balasheb) Kher, who was in Delhi then, giving him the information of the above meeting and also about the atmosphere developing in Bombay. In that letter he suggested that protective measures should be adopted to safeguard the lives of top ranking Congress leaders, particularly Gandhiji.

Cross-Examination of R.K. Khadilkar

R.K. Khadilkar was an MP of the Peasant's and Worker's Party.

20.135: Khadilkar was quite outraged by the fact that while a Congress Government was in power an attempt was made on the life of Mahatma Gandhi, because nobody whether Communist, leftist or politician of any other hue, wanted Gandhiji to be injured, much less killed.

20.137: Before the bomb was exploded the atmosphere was poisoned and after the attempt there was alarm. 'The local police intelligence were almost with us, they knew everything', and, therefore, Khadilkar and his party did not inform the authorities of what was happening. This, in the opinion of the Commission, is an inexcusable alibi.

20.144: When asked why he did not convey the true feelings of the people to the authorities, he said that he was at that time a protestant against the Congress and he thought that they would not take him seriously.

20.145: They all sensed danger to Gandhiji from the camp which was advocating Hindu fanaticism and which was in Poona. He was put a specific question whether he connected the movement with Poona, Nagpur, Allahabad, Delhi or some other place, his reply was 'Poona'. He did not agree with Morarji Desai that the danger to Gandhiji was from three quarters e.g. the Hindu Fanatics, the refugees and the Muslims. As far as his knowledge went, the danger was from a small section of Hindu fanatics belonging to Hindu Rashtra Dal. It was the Hindu Mahasabha papers which were bitterly criticizing Gandhiji in Poona. These papers were the *Kal*, the *Trikal*, and the *Agranee* or the *Hindu Rashtra*.

20.161: On the first term of reference, therefore, the finding of the Commission is that some persons, including G.V. Ketkar, had prior knowledge of the danger to Mahatma Gandhi's life, but with the exception of G.V. Ketkar nobody had any information in regard to the conspiracy of which the architect was Nathuram Godse. No other witness, excepting Ketkar, has deposed to the likelihood of any danger to the life of Mahatma Gandhi from Nathuram Godse, still less of any conspiracy.

Chapter XXI deals with the issue 'If any one had prior knowledge about the murder'. The Commission has relied upon the statements of many witnesses. (I am not repeating all the statements only some which have not been previously mentioned have been reproduced here.)

1.32: Evidently the Home Minister, Sardar Patel, and his personal staff were being misled by stories of trailing and special groups being on their heels. Brij Kishan Chandiwala stated before the Commission that a police officer had informed him that there were nine conspirators in the bomb case and the police had been able to find out their identity. But what really happened was that the conspirators were eluding all precautions or trailings if there were any.

N.V. Gadgil, Wit. 6 (P)

21.34: The evidence in regard to previous knowledge of N.V. Gadgil really consists of nothing more than what he was told by Keshavrao Jedhe, a member of the Constituent Assembly, and as Gadgil was a member of the Central Cabinet, the Commission has thought it proper to include his evidence under the head 'Knowledge of Central Government'.

21.35: The late N.V. Gadgil affectionately called Kaka Gadgil was a Minister in the Central Government. He was a prominent resident of Poona. Before he became a Minister he was at the Bar at Poona and was the Secretary of the District Congress Committee, Poona, and was intimately connected with local affairs as he was at one time Vice President of the Municipality.

21.36: Keshavrao Jedhe used to stay with him. One day Jedhe said to Gadgil: '*Kaka, Punyatli loka kahitari bhayanak ghadvun aannaar ahet, japun raha.*' (Kaka, some people in Poona are out to do something [dangerous] beware!) Unfortunately, Kakasaheb Gadgil never asked him to elaborate, though he says he should have done so. That is because he never thought that Poona people would do anything that would go against Gadgil himself. Jedhe came to Delhi on 15-1-1948 from Poona.

He knew that Godse and others had chalked out a plan in Poona and send-offs were being given to them but unfortunately Jedhe told Kaka Gadgil this only on the night of 30th and when Kakasaheb asked him why he did not tell earlier, Jedhe's reply was that he thought that Kaka knew this before. He then disclosed names of three or four persons as well as names of some places but he did not disclose this information to him before 30 January. There is nothing to indicate that Gadgil conveyed this information to the Police.

21.37: Another portion which is rather important is that within one or two days after 30 January 1948 Gandhiji was to have gone to Wardha because Sardar's idea was that Gandhiji should be persuaded to stay at Wardha and should be spared from the daily complaints from Muslims and the Maulanas.

21.38: Fortunately, Gadgil before his death was examined by Pathak as witness No. 6. He had stated then that when Jedhe warned him about being cautious, he had thought that it was something against him personally and thus he had replied, 'What have I done to raise their anger?' Jedhe replied: 'All right, I have told you what I heard in Poona.' After that the witness had heard nothing from Jedhe. It is unfortunate that Gadgil did not pursue the matter further with his guest; did not ask him what he meant by the cryptic information that he had given and that he should have left the matter there. But that is what happened, another link in the chain of unfortunate omissions.

21.39: Gadgil further stated that at 8:30 p.m. after the murder on 30 January 1948, Jedhe met the witness on the veranda of the witness' house in New Delhi and said: 'What I had warned you about has happened!' The witness asked Jedhe to give him the details, his reply was: 'Godse and his friends were being feted as they were leaving to murder Gandhiji. There was a function at Tilak Smarak Mandir.' Thereafter the witness kept quiet and nothing could be done. Gadgil also stated that beyond what Jedhe told him, he had no other information.

21.40: Gadgil further said that Sardar Patel 'right up to 5:20 p.m. on the 30 of January (Gadgil is mistaken here: Sardar's meeting with Gandhi got over at nine minutes past 5 p.m. on 30th, Bapu was murdered at seventeen minutes past 5 p.m.) was trying to persuade the Mahatma to allow search at least some visitors to the prayer meeting before they attended the meeting but Mahatma refused. "No! It is God's house and nobody can search!"'

21.49: *The Statesman* of 21 January 1948, Ex. 106A shows that the newspaper had given out the story as follows:

'Present inquiries tend to show that there was a formidable plot on the life of the Mahatma. A police Inspector said, "The bomb was intended to create confusion even though it was powerful enough to kill many people. The hand grenade (recovered from Madanlal after his arrest) was apparently to be used against the Mahatma himself."'

Even other newspapers had said that four men drove away in a small green colour car parked at the rear of Birla House showing that there were more than one person who were involved in the exploding of the bomb. (See the *Times of India*, 21 January 1948)

21.57: Commission drew the attention of J.N. Sahni to a pamphlet, Ex. 105, which is a document in Hindi, published in Amritsar and alleged to have been distributed in Alwar. This document as produced before the Commission was hand written. It is undated and starts by saying '*Gandhi Murdabad!*' (Dishonourable death to Gandhi!). It is an anti Gandhi leaflet accusing Gandhiji of helping Muslims and Pakistan and that people should pray to the Almighty that Gandhi should die. It also accused Gandhiji of his fast being a farce and called him 'Neechatma' (a low down evil soul). Sahni's reply was as follows—

'I would not say that this was the attitude of mind of the Hindus and the Sikhs from Punjab because whatever else might not have happened they could not forget the services rendered by Gandhiji whenever Hindus and Sikhs were in trouble in the Punjab. Jalianwala Bagh and Guru Ka Bagh are examples. They would rather like to convert Gandhiji and use his influence rather than to kill him.'

'The document,' he said, 'was in line with the political secret movement which was being helped by the Princes through their chieftains creating a fifth column in India to take over when the British power withdrew, at least in their respective states which would become free. I am particularly mentioning states like Jaisalmer, Jodhpur, Baroda, Alwar, Bharatpur, Gwalior and Bhopal. This movement was led by Golwalkar from Nagpur and Bhopatkar, a staunch Savarkarite from Poona. The concentration of the leadership was in Nagpur and Poona.'

The Bakshi Ram Episode

21.64: One Bakshi Ram was arrested in the last week of January 1948 for robbery; under S. 394 I.P.C., he was lodged in Agra Central Jail. He claimed to be a one-time associate of Bhagat Singh and Batukeshwar Datt, the well-known Lahore revolutionaries. This arrest was affected by Senior Superintendent of Police Agra, G.K. Handoo, witness No. 48, for some reason Bakshi Ram showed some confidence in Handoo. According to the statement of Handoo, on or about 23 January, Bakshi Ram went on a hunger strike and insisted on seeing Handoo. When Handoo did see him, Bakshi Ram told him that Mahatma Gandhi was certain to be murdered very soon and that he had read in the news papers that Madanlal had been arrested in connection with the explosion of Gun-cotton slab, he further told Handoo that Madanlal was an intermediary between him and about seven Maratha young men. (Here, Maratha is being used as a collective noun for Marathi-speaking persons and not the Maratha community.) Madanlal had asked Bakshi Ram to give instructions to those Maratha young men in pistol shooting, which Bakshi Ram did at Gwalior. That was some time in December or a little earlier. These Maratha young men never called each other by name but by military ranks like Subedar, Jamadar, etc. (Readers should note that in one of the attacks on Mahatma Gandhi's life at Sevagram, Thatte had pointed to Nathuram and referred to him as their 'Jamadar'.) Bakshi Ram had gathered from the cross talk between these young men that they were learning to shoot with small arms to commit a political murder of a very high ranking person in Delhi. So when Bakshi Ram read in the papers about Madanlal exploding the bomb he felt convinced that the victim was going to be Mahatma Gandhi and here was a conspiracy to murder him.

21.65: Handoo then cross-examined Bakshi Ram and found his story to be consistent. He recorded Bakshiram's statement and sent copies of it to the D.I.B., New Delhi, Inspector General of Police, U.P., B.N. Lahiri and to the D.I.G. Meerut Range B.B.S. Jetley who was on tour at Agra at that time. He did not hear anything further and then Mahatma Gandhi was murdered. In that communication to the Police officers, Handoo gave the descriptions which Bakshi Ram had given him. Bakshi Ram had also told him that one of those young men who was the leader of the group was a 'Patrakar', journalist from Poona but he neither knew his name or the name of his newspaper.

21.76: Paragraphs 7 and 9 of Ex. 133, report of Inspector Bannerjee, stated:

'Should Bakshi Ram be released, as suggested and would the risk be worth it? Personally, Jetley does not mind if the Dacoity case goes down provided it brings to light the conspiracy which has been hatched in the States of Gwalior, Bharatpur. etc... He recommends that unless the Police, here have anything definite at this end, the possibilities of the information given by Bakshi Ram should be investigated....

'Jetley is of the opinion that Bakshi Ram is genuinely pained on Mahatmaji's murder and is anxious to give out all he knows. He fasted for 13 days after Mahatmaji's death and is very much moved and, if suitably tackled, would probably lead to something very definite.'

21.93: G.K. Handoo, a high ranking Police Officer, was empathic that Bakshi Ram had given him information before the murder.

21.94: Bakshi Ram wanted to appear before this Commission and was asked to put in an affidavit of what he wanted to depose but that he has not done.

(What Bakshi Ram said may not have been of importance in the investigation between the 20 and 30 January 1948. But the senior police officer, G.K. Handoo, who had initially recorded Bakshi Ram's statement, stuck to his claim that Bakshi Ram had made an initial statement before the murder: this is important. Bakshi Ram may have been trying to swing a deal and also exploring a way to escape punishment, but a senior police official, Jetley, felt that if Bakshi Ram could help in exposing the conspiracy, releasing him from jail was worth the risk. Sanjeevi and Rana along with Nagarvala had committed a series of blunders during the ten days between the bomb attack and the murder. Unfortunately, Sanjeevi and Rana were in a position to scuttle the initiative shown by Jetley. Bakshi Ram may not have proven to be of much use but it must be noted that he named Dr Parchure and Gwalior before it had become public knowledge about their role in the conspiracy. This factor alone makes Bakshi Ram's statement important. The other fact that Bakshi Ram hailed from the Montgomery district of the Punjab, links him with Madanlal who also hailed from that district, Madanlal had also been active in

Gwalior for some time after crossing over to India, this lends further credibility to Bakshi Ram's statement. It is very difficult to believe that sitting in jail Bakshi Ram could have cooked up a story which had so many credible and verifiable links to facts. Alas, like many other missed opportunities and ignored leads this one too will remain an enigma.)

Chapter XXIII of the Kapur Commission's report deals with the investigations at Delhi. These are the investigations of events happening between 20 and 30 January.

Case Diary No. 3-A

23.32: We have then the most important entry in the case diary, No. 3-A, of Deputy Superintendent Jaswant Singh purporting to be from Bombay. This begins on 22 January at 8:00 a.m. and closes at 8:00 p.m. It states that at 9:10 a.m. these officers met Nagarvala at his house. He said that he had already been apprised of the full facts of this case and that he had already had a talk with higher authorities of Delhi on phone and that he had posted special officers of the C.I.D. at strategic points. He had made proper arrangements for the tracing of the alleged suspects and had posted men on the railway station.... Nagarvala also told them that he did not want them to stay where they were staying because he did not want their presence to be known to others which would frustrate the arrest of persons and he ordered them to get into mufti and meet him at the C.I.D. Office. At 10:30 a.m. the entry in the diary is as follows:

'At this time I along with Inspector reached the office of C.I.D. by taxi and contacted Nagarvala and again acquainted with full facts on the case and an English note, which incorporates the précis of Madanlal's statement with the note of the Superintendent of Police, New Delhi, at its foot, was handed over to Nagarvala Sahib who read this note carefully and kept it. He returned a written note covering this case, which is attached. Nagarvala Sahib was also acquainted with the facts concerning Kirkree (Karkare). It was also brought to his notice that Madanlal accused had stated that he did not know the name of his associates but had said that he was editor of *Hindu Rashtra* or *Agranee* Newspaper, who was of light complexion, aged 33/34 height 5'6". It is not known whether this editor belongs to Bombay or Poona. Apart from this, he was also acquainted with the descriptions of the three other Mahrattas (Marathas) and one "Maharaj" who according to the accused were his companions. Special stress was laid on the immediate apprehension of the Editor of *Hindu Rashtra* or *Agranee* Newspaper, and Kirkree of Ahmednagar, whose mention was specially made by the accused in his statement, so that they may be interrogated ("*Taake unse daryaft amal mein lai jaaye.*").

The point to be noted in regard to this diary is that besides the name of Karkare which was written as 'Kirkree' the editor of *Hindu Rashtra* or the *Agranee* newspaper with his description and of his belonging to Poona was also mentioned as also the description of the 3 other 'Marathas and Maharaj' who, according to Madanlal, were his co-conspirators, and special stress was laid on the immediate apprehension of the editor of the *Hindu Rashtra* or the *Agranee* and Karkare of Ahmednagar.

23.35: At 7:30 p.m. they were informed by their host, Inspector Kargaonkar, and two other officers that they had traced the suspects and men had been posted and he was confident that the whole matter will end usefully. But regarding 'Kirkree' he said that an Inspector of Police was coming from Ahmednagar and after getting information of the full address of Karkare and of the editor of *Agranee* or the *Hindu Rashtra*, a report about their arrest would be sent. This diary closes at 8:00 p.m. at which time the two officers 'Went off to sleep', 'Shab Bash' literally retired for the night.

Case Diary No 4-B Of 23-1-48 from Bombay

23.40: Case Diary No. 4-B is by Deputy Superintendent Jaswant Singh purporting to be from Bombay. It is marked Ex. 39. It begins at 10:00 a.m. of 23 January 1948. It shows that Nagarvala gave Jaswant Singh a list of passengers who had travelled from Bombay to Delhi between January 13 and 20 but Jaswant Singh did not find anything useful in that list. The entry of 12:00 noon is that Inspector Kargaonkar had informed them that a Police Inspector from Ahmednagar had come and had contacted Nagarvala and informed that 'Kirkree was not present in Ahmednagar'. But the C.I.D. had been instructed to search for the Editor.

23.41: The next entry is that inquiries were made about Kirkree (Karkare) from Inspector, C.I.D., Bombay, he was requested to inform them about the suspects who were responsible for the occurrence. The inspector had disclosed to the Deputy Superintendent Jaswant Singh that the real name of 'Kirkree' was V.R. Karkare and he was the owner of the Deccan Guest House in Ahmednagar and was a zealous worker of the Hindu Mahasabha; and his co-workers were Badge of Poona, Avtar Singh of Amritsar, Talwar of Karachi, Balraj Mehta of Lahore, who were also Hindu Mahasabha workers.

23.42: Thus this Police Diary makes some very significant assertions; one, that the Delhi Police Officers were informed that Karkare was the owner of the Deccan Guest House, four of his associates were mentioned, Nagarvala directed these officers to return to Delhi; and that they again informed Nagarvala that Madanlal had named Karkare and had mentioned the editor of the *Agranee* or *Hindu Rashtra*. This is a re-assertion of the mention of the editor of the *Hindu Rashtra* or *Agranee* to the Deputy Commissioner.

Lacuna No. 1

23.135: The first failure on the part of the Delhi Police was not to send for Bombay Police to Delhi for stationing them to guard Mahatma Gandhi and to act as watchers and spotters. Sanjeevi did not get into touch with the Bombay Provincial C.I.D. direct. To his credit it must be said that he got in touch with Rana in Delhi but it turned out to be futile as Rana proceeded at a snail's pace and was as complacent as Sanjeevi, he did not requisition his C.I.D. force or put them into immediate action against the proprietor of the *Hindu Rashtra* whose identity he failed to discover, a failure for which he must share the blame with a much more experienced and senior officer, Sanjeevi, who had come to occupy the top police job in India—of Director Intelligence Bureau. If this name had been discovered earlier it could have been that the whole case would burst and the conspirators would have been nabbed before they got to Delhi.

Lacuna No. 2

23.136: It was argued that Madanlal should have been sent to Bombay, Poona and Ahmednagar, with the Delhi Police after his statement made on 24 January 1948. He could have been confronted in all these places and could have been interrogated by the police there. Crime Report No. 6 shows that during the interrogation of Madanlal by the Bombay Police on 4 February 1948, Badge was brought from Poona, at first he denied all knowledge of the conspiracy. When he was confronted with Madanlal accused, who identified him as the 'Sikh' Maratha referred to by him, and after he was subjected to searching interrogation, Badge broke down and made a clean breast of the whole conspiracy and the persons involved therein. He confessed that the attempt on Gandhiji's life on 20 January 1948, was in pursuance of this conspiracy. It was rightly submitted that what was done after the murder should have been done after 24 January, if not after 20th, when Ex.6 according to the Delhi police was made.

23.137: Amar Nath Bhatia, Police Superintendent of New Delhi, witness No. 17, said that he did not know anything about Sanjeevi's order for Madanlal to be taken to Bombay, but D.S.P. Kartar Singh, Wit. 26, said that he had a distinct recollection that before the murder it was proposed by Sanjeevi that Madanlal should be flown to Bombay so that the Bombay Police could interrogate him and arrangements were made to put that proposal into effect but Sanjeevi countermanded his previous orders and Madanlal was not sent.

23.140: The course of investigations in Bombay after the murder and the comparatively quicker and successful results of the investigation in Bombay leads one to the conclusion that if this course had been adopted, the course of events might have been different. It cannot be overlooked that we are looking at the matter 21 years after its occurrence.

Lacuna No 3

23.141: In Ex. 1 which is the fuller statement of Madanlal dated 24 January, the name of the newspaper *Hindu Rashtra* of Poona was given and also its proprietor was mentioned. Although it should have been possible for Sanjeevi to find out the identity of the proprietor, he did not do so. A reference may be made to Exs. 198, 199, 199-A and 201. Ex. 198 is an extract from the Bombay list of newspapers and their proprietors and editors and relates to *Agranee* where the names of Apte and Godse are given as proprietor and editor, respectively. Ex. 199 also relates to the *Agranee*. Ex. 199-A is an extract relating to *Hindu Rashtra* a Marathi Daily of Poona, wherein N.V. Godse is shown as the printer and publisher and the paper is described as a Savarkarite group paper. Its proprietor is N.D. Apte and editor N.V. Godse. Ex. 201 shows that a copy of this list of newspapers called the Annual Statement of Newspapers was sent to the Government of India, Home Department, Government of India, Information and Broadcasting Department.

M.K. Sinha, Deputy Director, Intelligence Bureau, has stated before the Commission that the names of the editor and proprietor of a paper could have been available to the police at Delhi from the C.I.D.

Lacuna No. 4

23.142: The Delhi Police and the Intelligence Bureau failed to use the Intelligence Bureau records because that contained important information regarding Madanlal. Inspector Balkundi of Ahmednagar had sent a report dated 7/10 December, 1947 to the Intelligence Bureau. This is Ex. 195. This was addressed to the Assistant Director (P), I.B., Ministry of Home Affairs. There are endorsements on it showing Hooja dealt with it on 14 January and M.K. Sinha, the Deputy Director, also on the same date. The report of Inspector Balkundi regarding Madanlal in the Intelligence Bureau had a seal put on it with the word 'Indexed'. This word 'Indexed' was stamped on the Provincial C.I.D. report from Ahmednagar which is separately marked as Ex. 66-A. In this report the complaint against Madanlal was in regard to his leading a procession of refugees and shouting slogans against Muslims and '*Vir Savarkar Ki Jai*!' (Hail brave Savarkar!) showing that the procession which had been taken out had a Savarkarite association and complexion.

23.143: M.K. Sinha witness No.44, was asked about this indexed document. He said, 'We in the bureau did not connect this Madanlal with the Madanlal Kashmirilal.... The name of Madanlal Kashmirilal is misleading and it would not be possible for the Bureau to at once connect a particular name with the name indexed in the Bureau.' He was further examined on this matter and he stated as follows:

'Q. From the fact that Madanlal was from Bombay should it not have struck the members of the bureau to look into their indexing system?'

'A. If I were the in charge of the Investigation, I would at once have asked my own office as well as the offices of the various provincial C.I.D. to see whether the names which transpired from the various statements were or were not in the index cards.'

23.145: In reply to another question, it was said that when a card is prepared for an individual his identity is indicated and very briefly reasons are also indicated on the card. Madanlal's card shows that he was a refugee and led a procession of refugees in Ahmednagar. The exact date is not given. At any rate, this much is clear that the name of Madanlal had been sent up by the Ahmednagar Police in connection with his activities in Ahmednagar, this document was seen in the Intelligence Bureau by high officials and his name was indexed.

23.146: In the *Times of India* of 21 January 1948 Ex. 106, the name Madanlal was given out as the person who exploded the bomb and it was stated that his companions had escaped in a car but they had not been apprehended till midnight. Madanlal stated that he was from Montgomery and had migrated to Bombay and had returned to Delhi and was staying at the railway station.

23.147: In the *Daily Statesman* of 21 January (Ex. 106-A) the name given was Madanlal who was carrying a ration card in the name of Balbir Singh, it was stated that three of his companions had escaped in the confusion and that policemen have been posted at all exits from the city. Besides this, it was stated that there was a formidable plot on the life of Mahatma Gandhi; and the hand grenade found on the person of Madanlal was to be used against Mahatma Gandhi himself.

23.148: In the *Hindustan Times* of 21 January, Ex. 106-B, account is given of the arrest of Madanlal. This news is given on the front page but in a comparatively unimportant place with an unimportant heading 'Bomb Goes Up (sic) Near Prayer Ground'. There also the bomb explosion was taken as an attempt on the life of Mahatma Gandhi. In that newspaper the statement of Madanlal as given does not disclose that he had gone to or was connected with Bombay.

23.149: Therefore, one would expect the Director of the Intelligence Bureau to get his own records searched for any clues regarding the bomber and one would also expect that the name Madanlal would tingle in the memory of two high officials like the Deputy Director and an Assistant Director; yet there are matters which the Commission cannot loose sight of (1) that the name Madanlal Kashmirilal could easily confuse officer in Northern India, where father's name is not so appended; (2) there was nothing to connect the arrested Madanlal with Ahmednagar at least not to the knowledge of these two officers. But all this hardly excuses the Delhi Police and the Director of the Intelligence Bureau who was also the Inspector General in charge of the investigation of a case of that importance from seeking information from any possible source known to them or they could reasonably have been expected to think of, Sanjeevi should have had his own records searched.

Lacuna No. 5

23.150: Kotwal emphasized that it was the duty of the Delhi Police to apprehend the accused persons and they could ask the outside police for their cooperation. He referred to the reply of the Government of India to Question 8 of the questionnaire.

'It would be the responsibility of the Delhi Police to ensure that the persons named were apprehended or prevented from coming to Delhi, if they were not already there. To the extent such action related to persons residing outside the jurisdiction of the Delhi Police. It would have been also the responsibility of the other police authorities concerned to extend necessary assistance and cooperation to the Delhi Police.'

Lacuna No. 6

23.151: It was suggested by Kotwal that Rana was in Delhi from the 20 January to 25 January 1948, and if he had been asked to be present at the time of Madanlal's interrogation, Madanlal would have been more informative and the very presence of Rana would have been a help in this direction. This he based on the fact that Madanlal in his statement Ex. 1

at Page 29 stated that on one occasion in Ahmednagar he led a procession of 500 refugees through the town of Ahmednagar where various slogans were raised. Thereafter, a meeting was held in Aarti Bazar in which high officials participated, amongst whom was the D.I.G. of Police, C.I.D., Poona, Rana, and a few others. They promised to help the refugees within a few days when a demand was made that Municipal officials should allot sites for fruit shops to refugees.

23.152: Rana, witness No.3, when recalled at Baroda stated that he was not present at the meeting. As a matter of fact he was not in Ahmednagar on that day. But he was in Ahmednagar on the 18, 19 and 20 December, 1947 and visited Visapur Camp. This is a very slender basis for saying that association of Rana with the interrogation of Madanlal would have produced more information. At the most it is speculative and that by itself cannot be taken to be a failure on the part of Sanjeevi in his investigational process.

Lacuna No. 7

23.153: The Delhi police officers were sent to Bombay on 21 January. They returned from there on the 24 January and met the Superintendents of Police of Delhi on the morning of 25 January. Sanjeevi's note, Ex.7, in Paragraphs 5 and 6 sets out what the Delhi Police Officers on their return reported to Delhi. In these paragraphs emphasis is laid on the Police officers telling Nagarvala that one of the accused mentioned by Madanlal was the editor of the *Agranee* or the *Hindu Rashtra* and that C.I.D. Inspector there told them that Inspector of Police from Ahmednagar had arrived and he had been told to make a search for the editor of the *Agranee* or the *Hindu Rashtra* and that some names were given to Deputy Superintendent Jaswant Singh when he asked for information in regard to Karkare and his associates. Those names were Badge of Poona, Avtar Singh of Amritsar, Talwar of Karachi and Balraj Mehta of Lahore. Paragraph 6 also mentions that Delhi Police officers handed over to the Inspector, C.I.D., a brief note on the case with the names and descriptions of the accused wanted as far as known then, a point on which Nagarvala was not questioned though he was cross-examined at length.

23.154: It is surprising that after this complaint was made to the

D.I.B. he never took the trouble to find out from Nagarvala as to what had happened. It is true that he did tell U.H. Rana of the complaint by the Delhi Police Officers but he never found out from Nagarvala himself what had happened. As submitted by Kotwal, from 21 January, 1948 to 27 January, 1948, the D.I.B. who was also the Inspector General of Police, Delhi, did nothing and even after the fuller statement of Madanlal a copy of which was given to Rana on 25th, he took no steps to get in touch with the Provincial C.I.D., Poona, or find out as to who the proprietor of the *Hindu Rashtra* was. The Commission is not overlooking the fact that Rana was himself the D.I.G. (C.I.D.), Bombay.

23.155: Even when Rana and Nagarvala rang him up on the 27th evening and Rana told him that Nagarvala had good reasons for not allowing Police Officers to move about in Bombay, and Nagarvala gave the information in regard to his theory of kidnapping of Mahatma Gandhi, there is nothing in Paragraph 8 to indicate that Sanjeevi demurred in any way to or reacted sharply or even mildly against this rather unusual theory on which Nagarvala was working. All that he said in paragraph 8 is, 'I asked him about the absconding accused whose names or descriptions were given to the Delhi Police by Madanlal.' This paragraph does not go further and say which names or what descriptions had been given to Nagarvala by the Delhi Police officers. Nagarvala has denied any such question having been put to him.

23.156: If, as is claimed, Madanlal had indicated in his statement of the 20 January, Ex. 6, the proprietor of *Hindu Rashtra* or the editor of the *Agranee* to be one of his companions, the Commission is unable to find any reason why the D.I.B. did not at once find out who the persons were and direct either Nagarvala or Rao Saheb Gurtu to apprehend those persons immediately, and get some Maharashtrian Policemen over to keep a watch both at the railway station and air terminal and at Birla House so as to spot those persons as and when they come to Delhi.

Lacuna No. 8

23.158: Rana and Nagarvala on the evening of 27 January 1948 spoke to Sanjeevi on the long distance telephone and gave all information in regard to kidnapping theory. Sanjeevi is not shown to have found fault with that theory or rejected it nor did he violently react against it.

23.160: In Ex. 7-B it is stated that two police officers of Delhi were flown to Bombay and they contacted Nagarvala and 'put him in full possession of all the facts known to them so far'. These officers were not allowed to make any inquiries nor move about freely, that was because Nagarvala feared that the presence of police officers from Delhi would be a set back to his efforts in tracing the absconding men.

23.161: Commission finds little validity in this complaint. These two police officers had precious little knowledge of the City of Bombay which is a vast metropolis with the then population of three millions and a half. How these officers, even if clever and experienced, were to look for and spot Karkare in Bombay is beyond one's comprehension. In the matter of investigational utility their value was practically nil. Then why this complaint?

23.162: The two police officers returned after two days. On 25 January, Sanjeevi gave a copy of the statement of Madanlal made on 24th to the D.I.G., C.I.D., Poona, Rana. This was a detailed statement. On arrival, in Bombay, Rana and Nagarvala contacted Sanjeevi on the telephone and Nagarvala promised to send a letter by air next morning with a copy to Rana, but no letter was received excepting the one sent on 30th which contained no information about the assassins.

23.163: Unfortunately, Sanjeevi from 25th to 30th morning did nothing to find out as to what had been done in regard to the persons mentioned in the fuller statement of Madanlal; it is still more unfortunate that the statement of 20 January purported to have been made by Madanlal containing descriptions, names and mentioning the editor of the *Agranee* or *Hindu Rashtra* was sent through the police officers of Delhi and yet no contact was made by the D.I.B. or by any other high ranking police officer in Delhi with Nagarvala to find out from him as to what he had done or was doing in regard to that information and why he was not asked as to why no credence was given to the information alleged to have been given by the Delhi police to him.

23.164: It is indeed a very perplexing situation. According to Delhi Police they took the document which contained the name of Karkare; and mentioned the editor of the *Agranee* or the *Hindu Rashtra* which fact is flatly and emphatically denied by Nagarvala and it is still more perplexing that the name *Agranee* is not mentioned in the fuller statement of Madanlal made on 24 January and a copy of which was given to Rana on 25 January 1948, nor was it mentioned in his police statement at Bombay after the murder. In spite of the name of *Hindu Rashtriya* having been mentioned, it is astounding that the Delhi police made no effort to find out the identity of this person. It is still more astounding that the names of *Hindu Rashtriya* was admittedly given to Rana though it is doubtable whether it was to Nagarvala or not, and yet no effort should have been made by him on his reaching Bombay or even Poona to find out as to who this person was and to warn both the Bombay Police and the Delhi Police to be on the look-out for him. It would be unbelievable if that thing did not happen as it did, that U.H. Rana should have gone through the statement of Madanlal along with Sanjeevi, as Sanjeevi's note shows and neither of them should, on 25 January, have taken the slightest trouble to find out from the intelligence Bureau or the Press Information Bureau or the C.I.D. as to who the proprietor of the *Hindu Rashtra* was. Admittedly, there was mention of it in the statement of Madanlal of the 24th.

23.165: U.H. Rana denies that Sanjeevi told him about the editor and proprietor of either *Agranee* or *Hindu Rashtra*, he was emphatic that the names of these papers were never mentioned to him. He does mention that the statement of Madanlal was made available to him and it was on that day that he came to know about the mention of the editor of the *Hindu Rashtra* daily and the proprietor of the Shastra Bhandar, Poona and Karkare of Ahmednagar. It appears that there is some mistake in the mind of Rana because the statement, Ex. 1, does not mention the editor of *Hindu Rashtra*, although it does the proprietor of the *Hindu Rashtra*. Due to the maze of documents which he had to study and on account of the lapse of over 20 years he might have been led into this confusion. The correct position appears to be that on the 25 January Rana did come to know of the complicity of a person who was the proprietor of the *Hindu Rashtra* mispronounced by Punjabees as *Rashtriya*. The question again arises, why was no effort made there and then to find out the identity of this person and why his full particulars were not called for from Poona as they were after the murder and even his photographs were obtained from there as shown by I.B. file No. 13/HA(R)/39-11, Ex. 254-A.

Lacuna No. 9

23.166: R.N. Bannerjee as witness No. 19 before this Commission stated that he did not know of the conspiracy to murder Mahatma Gandhi prior to 30 January 1948, the first time he came to know about it was on the 31st at the post-cremation meeting. Normally, the police should have informed him of the conspiracy in his capacity as Secretary of the Home Ministry, as Sanjeevi was in constant touch with him. He added that Sanjeevi had not informed the Deputy Commissioner of Delhi either.

23.167: According to the Punjab Police Rules, No. 24.15, special reports were to be sent by the Inspector General of Police, to the Government of India, Ministry of Home Affairs, but evidently, none were sent to Bannerjee. In reply to question No. 27 of the interrogative questionnaire to the Government of India regarding the duties of the Director of Intelligence Bureau *vis-à-vis* the Home Ministry, the position was described thus:

'It would be the duty of the Director, Intelligence Bureau, to keep the Home Minister and the Ministry of Home Affairs informed about the threat or danger to important persons like Mahatma Gandhi. It would also be his duty to caution officers and officials working under him to remain vigilant about such a threat or danger and to take such other measures necessary to collect further intelligence thereon. He would also warn the State CIDs about such developments and impress upon them their importance and urgency. In all these matters he would keep the Ministry of Home Affairs informed.'

23.168: Bannerjee stated that if he had known anything about the matter, he would have taken as much meticulous care in regard to what police was doing in regard to the Bomb Case investigation as he did after the murder.

23.169: It was also argued and rightly that if the Director, Intelligence Bureau, could send his own officers to Alwar, Agra, Gwalior after the murder why could he not have done this earlier after the bomb throwing?

23.170: M.K. Sinha said that if the information which Madanlal had given in his statement had been given to him as an I.B. officer, he would have got into touch with the C.I.D., Bombay, on the secraphone and would have told them what had happened and requested them to try and arrest the persons whose descriptions had been given by Madanlal. He would also have got in touch with the Inspector General of Police and the C.I.D., at Poona and would have been constantly in touch with them to find out the progress of the investigation.

Lacuna No. 10

23.172: It cannot be called a failure on the part of Sanjeevi himself but is a matter which does concern the conduct of the Delhi Police. In the noting made in the Government of India Secretariat on the explanation given by Sanjeevi and Nagarvala, Ex. 14, there is a remark by Sardar Patel that it was a mistake to have sent a Deputy Superintendent of Police to Bombay, with which the Commission agrees particularly after having seen the whole course of conduct of the two respective forces, Bombay and Delhi Police. But that fact alone was no justification for Nagarvala not trying to find out from the officers what they knew or why they had been sent.

23.173: There is one matter which has not been explained and for which explanation could not be sought from Deputy Superintendent Jaswant Singh because he is dead and as Inspector Balakishan was rather ineffective. And that was why did the two police officers who went to Bombay, besides giving the information which they allege they gave to Nagarvala and which they have incorporated in their police diaries No. 3-A and No. 4-B, not orally tell Nagarvala what was within their knowledge besides what was contained in Ex. 5-A. The two offices should have told Nagarvala that they were themselves present during Madanlal's interrogation. They should have apprised Nagarvala of the facts. The explosion of the bomb, the recovery of a hand grenade, and the association of Savarkar, were all pointers to attempted political assassination by Savarkar's followers rather than kidnapping by Punjabis even if directed by General Mohan Singh of the I.N.A. which that gentleman has strongly repudiated in his statement before the Commission which statement the Commission accepts.

Chapter XXIV of the Kapur Commission's report deals with whether Delhi Police had given the Bombay Police Madanlal's statement Exhibit 5-A.

(Since this has been covered in details previously except for a few new fact, I have not reproduced much from the report.)

24.23: Case Diary No. 3-A. The next diary of Jaswant Singh is 3-A dated Bombay 22 January 1948, in paragraph 3 of which it is stated that the two police officers 'contacted' Nagarvala at the C.I.D. office where he was 'again' apprised of the full facts of the case 'and an English note, which incorporates a précis of Madanlal's statement with a note of S.P. New Delhi at its foot was handed over to Nagarvala Sahib who read this note carefully and kept it. He returned a (the?) written note covering this case which is attached'.

'Jinhon ne is yadasht ko baghor parah aur apen pas yadashat rakhi. Tahriri note mutliqa muqadama haza wapis di joke laf haza hai.' The document attached is Ex. 5-A.

24.24: The translation of diary No. 3-A seems to be slightly inaccurate; it should read—

'He read the memorandum carefully and kept an extract from it. He returned the written note (the memorandum) regarding the case above referred to, which is attached herewith.'

This document Ex. 5A is undated and unsigned. It is a disjointed account of events alleged to have been given by Madanlal. It is scrappy and is written in two distinct handwritings and distinct inks on both sides of a foolscap size sheet of paper.

Ex. 5-A When Written and by Whom?

24.27: In this context it is very necessary to see when Ex.5A came into existence and why it was scribed; because if it was not in existence on 21 January it could not have been taken to Bombay. It is necessary therefore to examine the evidence dealing with the authorship of Ex.5A and the date of its being scribed. The important witnesses on this point are Nos. 42 R.C. Bhatia who at the time was Inspector in charge of Parliament Street Police Station. No. 13 Rai Sahib Rikhikesh who at the time was Superintendent of Police, C.I.D., New Delhi and No. 17 Amar Nath Bhatia who at the time was Superintendent of Police New Delhi, i.e. the two Police Superintendents of Delhi and the Station House Officer of the Parliament Street Police Station. A Photostat copy of Ex. 5-A is attached.

R.C. Bhatia, Wit. 42

24.28: The account of witness R.C. Bhatia as to how Ex.5A came into existence was this that during the course of interrogation of Madanlal, he could not remember when it was, he was asked to 'take down'. It might have been three or four days after the arrest of Madanlal. The document was shown to him and he said that it was in his hand writing only up to the words 'plan chalked out.... Went in tonga.' i.e. up to the middle of the back of the page. The rest of the document beginning with the words 'with Karkare at about 3.45 p.m. from Marina Hotel' are not in his handwriting nor that portion of the document at the back which was enclosed within a red pencil line: (this was done by the Commission). The portion other than what R.C. Bhatia admits to be in his hand is in a different handwriting and in different ink. And this, according to R.C. Bhatia, is in the handwriting of Police Superintendent Amar Nath Bhatia with whose handwriting he is familiar. He also said that it is not in the handwriting of Deputy Superintendent Jaswant Singh.

24.29: Madanlal, he said was interrogated several times, it was on one of these occasions that the notes were dictated to him. He was not sure whether what was contained in Ex. 5A was repeated to him during interrogation. He could not say why the note was prepared. The dictation, he said, must have been seen by Superintendent Amar Nath Bhatia but he was not sure. But looking at the portion which was in the handwriting of Amar Nath Bhatia, this witness said that the dictation must have been by him. When his attention was drawn to the diary of Deputy Superintendent Jaswant Singh, the witness said it must have been dictated before Jaswant Singh left for Bombay. The statement of this witness is vague as to the sequence of events as to dates and even as to the occasion relating to scribing of Ex. 5A but after the lapse of twenty years it would not be unexpected.

Rai Sahib Rikhikesh, Wit. 13

24.30: The next witness in this connection is Rai Sahib Rikhikesh who was Superintendent of Police, C.I.D. at the time. Unfortunately, he is in failing health and is unable to see as he has practically lost his eye-sight but happily he readily appeared before the Commission, though at great personal inconvenience.

24.31: On 21 January 1948 Madanlal was taken to Civil Lines Police Station where R.S. Rikhikesh interrogated him for about 3 or 4 hours but he disclosed no names. He only gave descriptions of persons. All this the witness took down on a piece of paper which was handed over to Deputy Superintendent Jaswant Singh when he was leaving for Bombay. This was done under the orders of the D.I.B. Sanjeevi. The police case diaries No. 2 and 2-A show that interrogation was by Inspector Jai Dayal under orders of the Deputy Superintendent of Police. When Ex. 5 which is a copy of Ex. 5A was read out to the witness, his reply was that that was not what he had written nor did he send it to Bombay. The original of the document could not be shown to him because unfortunately he is unable to see. He said he had written down the descriptions of the conspirators as given by Madanlal which was something like what was read out to him from the police case diary No. 1, page 13, paragraph 15 which is marked Ex. 36. The statement was marked Ex. 6 by Pathak. Rikhikesh remembered that Madanlal had said that the leader of the party was a Maratha who was the editor of a Hindu newspaper, probably *Hindu Rashtra* but he could not remember if Madanlal had also mentioned the *Agranee* but he did not say that the man was from Poona. He was told by the D.I.B., to give a typed copy of whatever Madanlal had stated up to that time which he did.

24.32: He was asked how it was that in spite of Madanlal's arrest and his mentioning Karkare and the editor of the Poona journal no effective steps were taken to prevent the murder. His answer was:

'We did our level best. The conspirators came from Maharashtra. It was very difficult for us to make out who was who. Many officers from different parts of India came here and mentioned names of many suspects. Some of them we arrested and interrogated; others we just interrogated. But we did not succeed in getting any useful information about these persons. It should have been possible for the Bombay Police to have arrested the editor of the Poona journal because they knew his identity. Similarly there should have been no difficulty in arresting Karkare who had a shop in Ahmednagar.'

(This indicates clear information of the identity of two persons: (i) an editor whose particulars the Bombay Police should have known and (ii) the other Karkare of Ahmednagar, both of whom the Bombay Police could easily have arrested.)

24.33: The witness has deposed that during the course of the interrogation of Madanlal he got the following names: (1) Servant of Karkare, but not the name of Karkare whose business was mentioned. (2) The head of the conspiracy was the editor of a newspaper from Poona. (3) Another person mentioned was a discharged Army Officer. (4) A fat Maratha who financed the conspiracy and had a shop at the Chauk at Ahmednagar dealing in arms and ammunition. (5) Shankar. But it may be pointed out that that name is neither in the first statement of Madanlal, Ex. 6, nor in his fuller statement, ex. 1.

24.34: It appears that this witness has confused the names and descriptions. Shankar's name is neither in Ex. 6 nor in Ex. 1. The discharged Army Officer also was mentioned by Godse after his arrest on 30 January 1948 and is not mentioned in either of the two statements of Madanlal. The name of Karkare was mentioned by Madanlal in both his statements. As a matter of fact, that is the only name mentioned by Madanlal. But his description in the statement Ex. 1 and 6.

24.35: The name 'Shastra Bhandar' is mentioned in Ex. 1 but not in Ex. 6. The description 'fat Maratha' is nowhere to be found.

24.36: All this shows is that this is a case of *lapsus memoriae* which is not unnatural or unexpected after the lapse of twenty years, even if the physical ailments which afflict this police officer are ignored.

24.43: In cross-examination by Chawla this witness said that he did not give a covering letter for Nagarvala. He was sitting at Sanjeevi's house when Jaswant Singh came. When Jaswant Singh was leaving, he, Rikhikesh, gave him instructions as to what he was to do in Bombay.

24.44: He (Rikhikesh) interrogated Madanlal for about 6 hours. He started at about 4:00 or 5:00 p.m. and went on till late at night. Madanlal had given full description of his co-conspirators and the places where they were likely to be found. But this seems to be inaccurate because this information so elaborately stated is not even in the fuller statement, Ex. 1. The witness took down the descriptions and the addresses as there was no time to do anything more elaborate. The witness did not give the full statement to Jaswant Singh but descriptions and addresses of the conspirators. The object of sending the officers by air was to take immediate action and effect arrests. He added that he must have given the usual instructions to Jaswant Singh to explain the facts of the case to Nagarvala and also tell him on behalf of Sanjeevi that the matter was urgent and that he should report back any progress made in the case which seems to have been ignored altogether.

A.N. Bhatia. Wit. 17

24.45: The next witness relevant to this matter is witness No. 17, Amar Nath Bhatia, who was then the Superintendent of Police, New Delhi and is now an Advocate. He stated that Madanlal was interrogated at the Parliament Street Police Station, where he made the statement, Ex. 6. He named only one person, Karkare, but gave descriptions of six persons.

24.46: Deputy Superintendent Jaswant Singh and Inspector Balakishen of the C.I.D. were sent to Bombay under his directions but the decision was of the D.I.B. and of Police Superintendent Rikhikesh. When asked what instructions he gave to Deputy Superintendent Jaswant Singh, he said:

'We gave to Deputy Superintendent Jaswant Singh a list of persons who were suspected. By a list of persons I mean the description which we had gathered from the statement made by Madanlal. I gave to Jaswant Singh whatever we had. I could not give him more than what we had. We had also told Jaswant Singh that they were to seek the assistance, cooperation and instructions from the officers in Bombay who would know more about the Maratha accused than we did.'

'Q. Did you tell them as to whose assistance they should seek?'

'Ans. As far as I know, Rana had taken upon himself to do everything which was necessary.'

'(By Commission) Q. Would you be surprised to learn that Rana had not left Delhi for Bombay till 25 of January? How could he then have taken upon himself to do everything that was possible?'

'Ans. I only know this much that Rana had taken upon himself to do everything which was possible. I do not know when he left Delhi for Bombay.'

24.48: He was then asked how he could have ordered Jaswant Singh to get persons arrested in Bombay whose names and places of residence he did not know because up to the time the officers left for Bombay, Madanlal had only given the name of Karkare and some description of others, his reply was: 'Our anxiety only was to get those persons arrested whose description had been given by Madanlal.'

When reminded that the descriptions were inadequate, his reply was that whatever description they could get from Madanlal were sent to Bombay and his opinion was that with the cooperation of the Bombay Police it would be possible to arrest those persons.

24.50: A.N. Bhatia admitted that whatever was said or was given to Jaswant Singh should have been mentioned in the case diary. His attention was drawn to diary No. 2B of Jaswant Singh dated 21 January 1948, which does not contain any reference to the statement of Madanlal or to a synopsis thereof. His reply was that he could remember about Nagarvala but could not say anything about Gurtu, which was hardly a reply relevant to the question asked.

24.51: His attention was next drawn to the case diary No. 3-A of Jaswant Singh of 22 January and he was asked if he had any recollection about the matter. He said that some kind of endorsement might have been made on one of those documents by him but he could not recollect what exactly it was.

24.52: He was recalled on 17 October 1967 and was questioned about Ex. 5A. He was asked as to when the document was prepared. He said he could not remember. He said: 'I personally did not have a précis of the statement of Madanlal prepared. I do remember that such a précis of the statement was prepared. Whatever was happening was known to me because I was being constantly told of what investigation was going on. I was asked my advice which I gave and I also gave directions where I thought necessary and in this way the subordinate police officers had the advantage of my advice.'

24.53: The witness was shown the document Ex. 5A and asked, 'Have you seen this document?'

Ans. 'I must have seen it at about the time it was prepared and may have seen it later also during investigation but I have not seen it since.'

24.54: His attention was drawn to the portion, 'Met Karkare who appeared to be active worker or President of the Sabha' and to the portion relating to 'S. Deshpande, Om Baba and with Karkare left at 6.00 on 20

January 1948' they are not in the police diaries and the answer of the witness was, 'I cannot say anything about it.'

24.56: In Cross-examination by Mr Vaidya, he said, '.... And after looking at the case diary No. 1, I can now say that I asked the Inspector to prepare in English a précis of the statement of Madanlal. Because it was incomplete I added a few words, those words I have already indicated.'

24.61: A.N. Bhatia proved endorsement of Rai Sahib Rikhikesh, Ex. 1-A, on the copy of the full statement of Madanlal, Ex. 1 which was attached to Sanjeevi's note, Ex. 7. It may be mentioned that the copy of Ex. 5 which was attached to Sanjeevi's note, Ex. 7, and is marked Annexure V therein has the following endorsement—'True copy. Inspr. CID, N.D.' But the Inspector's signature is not there; and underneath it is signed 'T.G. Sanjeevi' dated 20-2-49. Which Inspector certified the original to be a true copy, the Commission has not been able to discover.

24.62: Cross-examined by B.B. Lal, A.N. Bhatia said that the document must have been prepared by Ram Chand (R.C. Bhatia) under his orders he must have prepared it from the case diaries. The witness himself got the information contained in portion A-Al of Ex. 5A from the officers who were interrogating the accused. He added, 'Really speaking what is given in the portion A-A1 is a gist of what Ram Chand had written in the two pages and something from my own knowledge.'

'I prepared this small note A-A1 so that I could at once tell any officer who made enquiries from me.'

He put the document on his table. He could not say when his reader or stenographer handed it over to Jaswant Singh but it must have been before 25 January. He did not miss the document because he had no occasion to use it. He was emphatic that this document could not have been taken by Jaswant Singh when he went to Bombay nor could Sanjeevi have sent it.

24.63: Examined by the Commission, A.N. Bhatia said if he had anything to do with the sending of the papers he would not have sent that document. No officer would have done it. He could give no explanation why Jaswant Singh falsely introduced this document into the file before 25 January 1948.

24.64: As far as A.N. Bhatia could recollect whatever had been got from the statement of Madanlal had been sent to Bombay. He never showed the document Ex. 5A to Sanjeevi.

The commission examined many witnesses—Inspector Balakishan, Deputy Superintendent Jaswant Singh, Sardar Patel's Secretary V. Shankar, Union Home Secretary R.N. Bannerjee, Sardar Patel's daughter Maniben Patel, the infamous U.H. Rana and many more—to ascertain whether Ex. 5A and a few other documents which the Delhi Police claimed were sent to Bombay were true or fabricated.

Chapter XXV of the Kapur Commission's report deals with investigations in Bombay.

25.3: In between the period from 22nd to the 30th two things happened. Two Delhi police officers came to arrest Karkare and to seek the aid of Nagarvala. The second fact is that U.H. Rana reached Bombay on the 27th evening. He had with him the fuller statement of Madanlal, Ex. 1, which amongst other things made mention of the proprietor of the *Hindu Rashtra* as one of the conspirators. Both Rana and Nagarvala did not read this statement. To say the least, this was rather surprising conduct because if Nagarvala was even making an inquiry, the information which was contained in Ex. 1 should have been of the greatest importance to him.

25.11: To Nagarvala, Morarji Desai gave the whole story but did not ask him to arrest Savarkar because there was no evidence against him. 'I had a very strong feeling,' he said, 'that Savarkar was behind the conspiracy and that is the reason why I asked his house to be particularly watched.' Morarji Desai considered the story of Jain to be genuine.

25.13: It was argued by Kotwal that if these were the facts, i.e. Madanlal and Karkare were from Ahmednagar, dump of arms was also at Ahmednagar, the proper person to be informed of these facts and proper person who should have been asked to take action would be Kamte, Inspector General of Police and not Nagarvala, because Kamte's jurisdiction extended over the whole of the Province of Bombay, while Nagarvala's was confined to only within the City of Bombay and because Nagarvala could not have taken any action in regard to the conspiracy which was formed outside the city of Bombay i.e. at Ahmednagar. There may be some justification for not disclosing the name of Jain who had requested Morarji Desai not to do so because he lived in a dangerous locality, if his name was given out he was likely to be murdered. (Prof.

Jain lived in the Shivaji Park area, a stone's throw away from the Savarkar residence. Dadar and Shivaji Park were considered to be Hindu Mahasabha bastions.) But it would in the opinion of the Commission be difficult to blame Desai for choosing Nagarvala rather than Kamte to take over the investigation or inquiry. At this distance of time after knowing all the facts and identity of the conspirators it may be said that Kamte would perhaps have been better, but could the same thing have been said on 21 January 1948 when the two names were of the 'Seth' Karkare or as reported 'Kirkree' of Ahmednagar, and V.D. Savarkar; and which of them was more important? That is where the choice lay. (Here, I differ from the commission's view: Desai could have also brought in Kamte, who could have dealt with the provincial police while Nagarvala dealt with the investigation in Bombay city. History shows Nagarvala didn't do much justice to the faith reposed in him by the home minister of the province.)

25.15: When asked whether Morarji Desai was right in passing on the information to the Deputy Commissioner of Police, K.M. Munshi, Wit. No. 82 replied 'that is the only way that a Minister can act. He is not expected to do the investigation himself'. Munshi gave an instance of a similar case when he was the Governor of United Province. Information was received about a conspiracy at Jhansi to murder Prime Minister Jawaharlal Nehru. He passed on the information to the Home Minister, who asked the Inspector General of Police to make inquiries, which showed that the information was without substance.

25.16: Kotwal referred to the provisions of the City of Bombay Police Act, 1902 (No. IV of 1902), henceforth referred to as the 'Bombay City Act', to buttress his argument that entrusting the investigation to Nagarvala was a mistake. According to the aforementioned Act Nagarvala could not have taken any action either to get intelligence regarding the crime or to prevent the commission of the crime because of the limited nature of the powers given by the Bombay City Act. Kotwal cited many Sections and codes of procedures in support of his contention.

The Kapur Commission did not accept Kotwal's arguments.

25.26: The Commission is unable to accept the contention of Kotwal so broadly stated. If his contention is correct, then it would lead to some extraordinary results. If information was received by an officer of the City of Bombay Police that certain persons within his jurisdiction had armed themselves to go and murder the members of the Government of another Province or of the Centre, then the Bombay City Police officer need and even can take no notice of the information given and may twiddle his thumbs and remain totally indifferent and inactive and allow persons in his jurisdiction to make preparations, collect arms and to allow them to proceed from Bombay to wherever they were going to commit the offence. Taken to its logical conclusion, if there was an espionage ring having its base in Bombay but operating outside the city of Bombay, it would be free to operate outside Bombay, it could steal any secret and confidential information that it wanted, it could commit acts of sabotage, it could do the most dangerous, the most treacherous acts but as long as its operative filed was outside the City of Bombay, the Bombay City Police would be helpless even when after doing all these acts the spies returned to Bombay and were hiding there to the knowledge of the Bombay Police and even when attempting to cross the seas or the skies. (But this is what Nagarvala's investigation in the bomb attack case amounted to, almost exactly like the scenario illustrated by the commission above.)

25.34: Two salient features of the information given by Morarji Desai were: the complicity of V.R. Karkare of Ahmednagar and the suspicion of V.D. Savarkar of Bombay also being a participant in the conspiracy which had resulted up to then in the explosion of the bomb and an attempt to murder Mahatma Gandhi. The Police may not have known much about V.R. Karkare but they were fully aware of the political philosophy of Savarkar, whose followers though not active in the City of Bombay were quite active in Poona. Karkare's activities could have been obtained from Ahmednagar if an effort had been made.

25.36: The combination of Karkare, of Savarkar, and some association of Badge and the evidence of exploding of a bomb were not proof of attempting to kidnap and thereby immunize Mahatma Gandhi from his activities which were considered as pro-Muslim and anti Hindu by the Savarkar school of thought. But the group had given enough proof of their intention to murder. In the opinion of the Commission, efforts should have been made by the Special Branch to get whatever information it could from Ahmednagar and also to make full use of the Provincial C.I.D. which could be a source of useful information both in regard to

Karkare as well as in regard to Badge. If Dy. Supdt. Chaubal of Poona and Gurtu, the A.D.I.G., C.I.D. Bombay Province could supply useful information after the murder, they could have done so before the murder also. (On the evening of 29th, Gurtu had provided the names, police records and photographs of Apte, Godse and Badge to Rana who sat on the information and did not share it with Nagarvala or Sanjeevi.) Evidence shows that the Provincial C.I.D. sent, on 1 February 1948, to the D.I.B., Delhi, photographs of Karkare and Apte, and also evidence of association of Karkare and Apte. Nagarvala was then investigating as a Delhi Officer. The same information would have been available to him as a mere C.I.D. fact-collecting officer under S. 32(1)(b) of the Bombay City Act as also if he was acting under Chapter V of that Act.

25.38: But the main error of Nagarvala was to pursue the theory of kidnapping which led him to suspect a different group of persons and thus led him into a *cul-de-sac*.

25.46: After receiving directions from the Home Minister to inquire into the matter and apprehend the associates of Madanlal and Karkare, Nagarvala got in touch with his informants and contacts and instructed Police Officers to locate Karkare and his associates.

25.47; By the 22 January 1948, the information was that one Balraj Mehta of Shivaji Park was an active member of the conspiracy. Orders were given to watch him and contacts at Ahmednagar were also asked to try and locate Karkare if he was there.

25.52: On 23 January reports received were that Karkare and Badge were not in Bombay, and that they were both staunch Hindu Mahasabhaites and if they came to Bombay they would be at Parel Hindu Mahasabha office and that that place was already being watched. Balraj Mehta, it was learnt, used to meet his associates at the India Coffee House at Mahatma Gandhi Road. A watch was organized at that Coffee House also but without any tangible results.

The same was in case of Savarkar's home. It was also learnt from Ahmednagar that Karkare was not there and his whereabouts were not known.

25.54: On 25 January 1948 it was learnt from sources that two Punjabis living in Arya Pathik Ashram, Room No. 27, were close associates of Balraj Mehta and were dealing in arms; the description of these two Punjabis is given. In view of this it was decided to keep a watcher in room No. 26. The watchers reported that a suspicious looking person came in car No. BYF 2744 to the Ashram but the watcher did not know whom he visited. The watcher also said that the driver of the car also looked suspicious. (Apte and Godse had only the previous evening shifted from the Arya Pathik Ashram to the Elphinstone Annexe Hotel; the police informers who gave information about the suspicious Punjabis failed to recognize them.) It was also learnt that Karkare's brother was working as a jobber in one of the textile mills of Bombay and lived in Naigaum. A watch was organized on his house also. It was discovered that Balraj Mehta was holding long conversations with two persons in Parekh Chambers, Shivaji Park, one of whom was a Sikh and the other a Punjabi. But the attempt to overhear the talks proved futile, because they were talking in Punjabi and the watcher could not understand it. The behaviour of these persons appeared to be suspicious.

25.61: On 31 January 1948 it was learnt that if Nathuram Godse was the assailant of Mahatmaji, then the plot would be known to Savarkar and also to Damle his secretary and Kasar his bodyguard, who both lived at Savarkar Sadan. This information was as a result of the interrogation of Chavan and Limaye who were already under detention.

25.62: Some very useful information was gathered from N.V. Limaye, detained under trial, who said that Savarkar must be fully aware of the facts and Nathuram Godse must have consulted him before undertaking his mission. W.B. Chavan told the police that Savarkar must have got the offence committed and that Godse must have been accompanied by his associate N.D. Apte because Godse never did anything without taking Apte with him. Thereafter Damle and Kasar were interrogated and Savarkar's house was placed under strict surveillance. Others interrogated were Balraj Mehta, Rameshwar Singh Thakur, Trilok Nath Mehra, Fakirchand Chopra, L.G. Thatte and Prahlad Dutt. As a matter of fact Dutt had been injured during the police raids and had been sent to the hospital. From Damle and Kasar it was learnt that Godse and Apte had seen Savarkar twice or thrice before the bomb was exploded and it appeared from their story that on these occasions the plan to murder Mahatma Gandhi was finalized. They also disclosed that Karkare was an active Hindu Mahasabhaite and had also come to see Savarkar. He was accompanied by a young Punjabi whose name later was learnt to be Madanlal. They had an hour long talk with Savarkar. But neither of them was prepared to depose to anything which took place at the meeting at Savarkar's house. They also disclosed that Badge also used to come to see Savarkar. As a matter of fact Apte and Godse had free access to Savarkar and could come without any appointment or having to wait downstairs. (They told the commission that Godse and Apte had met Savarkar on 28 January before leaving for Delhi.)

25.63: No information could be obtained from Balraj Mehta, Avtar Singh and others, but Thatte disclosed that Apte and Godse were the two main organisers of Savarkar's Hindu Rashtra Dal whose members believed in Savarkar and his ideology. On the basis of this the police decided to search Savarkar's house. When the police arrived Savarkar significantly asked Nagarvala whether he had come to arrest him in connection with Gandhiji's murder. But when he was told that it was only a search in connection with Gandhiji's case, Savarkar pretended to be ill and went inside the room and lay down. A mob started attacking his house, it was only the timely arrival of a large police squad which saved him and his property. He mentioned to the Police that the mob fury was likely to be repeated and he asked for police protection. Poona and Ahmednagar Police were contacted because of Karkare, Badge and others being accused, with instructions to carry out searches at their places of residence and to arrest them.

Several Hindu Mahasabhaites who were anti-Gandhi were rounded up and their homes searched but nothing important was recovered. Several other persons were arrested. They were all RSS or Hindu Mahasabha workers.

Nagarvala's investigations between 21 and 30 January in the Bomb Case came under severe criticism from Lal.

25.83: Lal argued that when Morarji Desai had mentioned the name of Savarkar in conjunction with Karkare and had also told Nagarvala that there was a conspiracy to murder Mahatma Gandhi, he should have directed his attention to Maharashtrian Brahmins, to Savarkar and his followers who were mostly in Poona and Ahmednagar and not followed his will-o'-the-wisp of Punjabis and the theory to kidnap. He had also criticized Nagarvala for not mentioning the kidnap theory in his Crime Report at all and he wanted the Commission to infer there from that what had been stated in the Crime Report was not a correct representation of facts and that it was a false document. From the fact that the kidnapping theory is not mentioned in the Crime Report, no inference can be drawn that the Crime Report is a false document. By the time the Crime Report came to be written, Mahatma Gandhi had been murdered so that the theory which Nagarvala was working on had been proved to be wrong if not *ignis fatuus*. He had by then been appointed a Special Officer of the Delhi Police to investigate in to the murder. It was unnecessary at that stage to mention the tangential investigational line which for some reason or another perhaps wrongly Nagarvala had hitherto pursued.

(For all his bungling in investigating the bomb attack case and exposing the conspiracy to murder before the actual murder, it must be said that Nagarvala carried out a very efficient investigation of the Gandhi murder case and managed to build a case which withstood very severe attacks from the defence counsels in the Special Court. It must be mentioned here that Nagarvala's investigation was facilitated by the very visible trail left by the conspirators and by the very detailed confessional statement given by Badge almost immediately after his arrest.)

25.104: The Commission would like to emphasize that the difference between the two theories, the theory of conspiracy to murder and of conspiracy to kidnap was this; that in the former case the emphasis would have been on Savarkarites of Poona who believed in political assassination, and in the later the emphasis could and would have been on a mixed crowd as indeed it was in the present case.

25.106: All these facts taken together were destructive of any theory other than *the conspiracy to murder by Savarkar and his group* and, in the opinion of the Commission, Nagarvala tripped because perhaps he was badly served by informants and contacts on whom he had every right to rely, or there was some erroneous conclusion. Of course, he does say that this was merely an information which had yet to be verified; but did it deserve to be so seriously considered under the circumstances? (Emphasis mine)

25.114: Another lapse in the investigational processes in Bombay can justifiably be attributed to Rana. He reached Poona on 28 January, his evidence shows that he called the D.S.P. of Poona and asked for Inspector Angarkar on the 29th. Rao Saheb Gurtu was also there and according to Ex. 30, Rana's letter to Kamte, the names of Apte, Godse and Badge were known from R.S. Gurtu. In his testimony before the Commission, Rana stated that when asked Gurtu gave the names of the editor and proprietor of the *Agranee* and the *Hindu Rashtra* and of the proprietor of the Shastra Bhandar to be Godse, Apte and Badge respectively and he gave these names from memory. This is indicative of the fact that even on the 28th no effort was made to find out where the companions of Madanlal were nor any efforts made to arrest Badge whom Nagarvala was looking for. By then Madanlal's statement, Ex. 1 was with Rana, if not with Nagarvala and Rana could have as he should have warned Delhi as well as Bombay about them and flown watchers and other alert policemen to Delhi as he did after the murder. Here were future murderers on the prowl and no effort was made at the Poona end to warn Delhi or to take preventive measures. Of course by the 28 January Apte and Godse were in Delhi (they actually reached Delhi on the 29th) and Karkare who was from Ahmednagar was also at Delhi. Photographs of the latter two could also have been flown to Delhi. Some effort should have been made in that direction even if it was rather late. But the Police could not divine that the murder will take place on 30th.

Conspiracy to Kidnap

25.119: The theory of conspiracy to kidnap Mahatma Gandhi which has been variously described as fantastic, fatuous and even incredible, was sought to be given respectability by Kotwal. He argued that it was no fault of Nagarvala if during the course of his investigation the evidence disclosed a conspiracy to kidnap Mahatma Gandhi and he tried to investigate into the correctness or otherwise of the information.

25.120: Nagarvala in his statement before the Commission has stated that as a police officer if he learnt something about a gang wanting to kidnap Mahatma Gandhi he was duty-bound to diligently inquire into the matter. He added that his mind was open and he was not obsessed by anything. When asked by the Commission as to whether he seriously believed in the kidnapping theory, his reply was that he did and he added that a police officer does not allow his likes or dislikes to interfere and affect his inquiries.

25.122: There is evidence, submits Kotwal, to show that other people had given credence to this theory. He referred to the evidence of Prof Jain who stated that Madanlal had told him that he would throw a bomb at a prayer meeting and thus cause confusion which would enable them to 'overpower' Gandhiji.

25.124: In his semi-official letter, Ex. 8, dated 30-1-1948, Nagarvala wrote to Sanjeevi that a large number of persons had joined hands to oust the Muslims and for that purpose had collected weapons of all sorts including bombs, and that his opinion was that this gang thought it would be easy to win over the Delhi Police and to kidnap Mahatma Gandhi.

25.125: Kamte, the then Inspector General of Police when recalled stated, 'If I had the information which Professor Jain gave to the Home Minister and the Minister passed on to Nagarvala in regards to the kidnapping theory of Mahatma Gandhi, I would have worked on that theory.' But as far as the Commission has been able to see, the Minister never gave any information to Nagarvala in regard to kidnapping.

25.126: Morarji Desai when examined on this point stated that Jain did not inform him about kidnapping, that the idea of kidnapping was fantastic but even the kidnapping theory could not have impaired the course of investigation.

25.129: Even Sanjeevi had not taken any objection to this theory of kidnapping. Nagarvala had deposed that he told Rana about this theory and a long distance telephone call was made to the D.I.B. to whom the theory of kidnapping was repeated but he did not say anything showing that he thought it to be absurd nor did he disapprove of it or deprecate it. Nagarvala has stated that everyone was satisfied in regard to the kidnapping theory. Rana also said that when the theory of kidnapping was conveyed to Sanjeevi on the long distance telephone he did not say anything in disapproval of this theory. Further Nagarvala told Sanjeevi that security arrangements regarding Mahatma should be strengthened.

25.132: Kamte Inspector General of Police of Bombay, said that he had no knowledge that the intention of the conspirators was to kidnap Mahatma Gandhi. In his opinion it was a fantastic theory.

25.134: This track of investigational procedure, i.e., of conspiracy to kidnap ignored the definite information given by Madanlal to Prof Jain and relayed through Morarji Desai to Nagarvala that Madanlal and his companions were going to murder a big leader was none other than Mahatma Gandhi, that his financier Karkare had formed a party in Ahmednagar which indulged in violence, that there was a dump of arms with the party and finally that Savarkar had patted Madanlal on his back appreciating his actions. Further, if Jain's name had been disclosed to Nagarvala, his interrogation by trained and experienced police officers of the Bombay Police would, in all probability, have weighed the scales heavily in favour of the murder theory and would have enfeebled the theory of kidnapping if not jettisoned it. One can quite appreciate the desire of Jain not to have his name disclosed but he could have been given protection in some other manner and even Nagarvala could have been asked to keep his name secret. Besides, if Jain was anxious to go to Delhi to get more information out of Madanlal which would have unveiled his identity he should not have been afraid to appear before Nagarvala.

25.135: As already remarked, another big difference in the consequences of pursuing the two theories was this. In the conspiracy to kidnap, the suspected participants amongst others were a large number of Punjabis, names of some of whom are given in the Crime Report, and in the letter of Nagarvala to Sanjeevi; and in the investigation of the conspiracy to murder theory, the suspect participants were different, i.e., people coming from a particular section of the Maharashtrian community of Poona and Bombay. Of course, they could also have been very many more than those put up for trial. As far as the Commission can see from the evidence before it, the emphasis would in the case of murder conspiracy be directed against the comparatively smaller set of Maharashtrians rather than a large number of persons, a mixed crowd of Savarkarites and of Punjabi Hindus having a grievance on account of the aftermath of Partition of the country. In other words, in case of the murder theory, the investigational energies would have been directed against the disgruntled, antagonistic Maharashtrian Savarkarites, who because of strong idealistic and fundamental differences with Mahatma Gandhi would unhesitatingly end 'the Gandhian menace' once for all, which in their view was the only way to ensure a 'Hindu Hindustan' in contrast to a secular India.

25.136: The Commission on the facts placed before it is unable to find that the attempt to give respectability to the kidnapping theory has, in the circumstances, succeeded.

Interrogation of Savarkar's Personal Staff

25.161: The statement of Appa Ramchandra Kasar, bodyguard of V.D. Savarkar, Ex. 277, which was recorded by the Bombay Police on 4 March 1948 shows that even in 1946 Apte and Godse were frequent visitors to Savarkar and Karkare also sometimes visited him. During the period when the question of partition of India was being discussed all these three used to visit Savarkar and discussed with him the question of the Partition and Savarkar was telling Apte and Godse that Congress was acting in a manner detrimental to the Hindus and they should carry on a propaganda through the agency of the *Agranee* against the Congress, Mahatma Gandhi and his 'dictatorial policy'.

25.162: In August 1947 when Savarkar went to Poona in connection with a meeting, Godse and Apte were always with Savarkar and were discussing with him the future policy of the Hindu Mahasabha, Savarkar told them that he was getting old and that they would have to carry on the work.

25.163: In the beginning of August 1947, on the 5th or 6th, there was an All India Hindu Convention at Delhi and Savarkar, Godse and Apte travelled together by plane. At the Convention the Congress policies were strongly criticized. On 11 August Savarkar, Godse and Apte all returned to Bombay by plane.

25.164: In the month of November 1947 there was a conference of All India State Hindu Mahasabha at Mahim. Dr Parchure and Surya Dev of Gwalior attended that meeting.

25.165: In the middle of December 1947, Badge came to Savarkar to inquire after his health but he could not see him. But two or three days later he again came and had a 15 minute talk with Savarkar. Karkare, Apte and Godse also met him during that month twice or thrice.

25.166: On or about 13 or 14 January 1948, Karkare came to Savarkar with a Punjabi youth and they had an interview with Savarkar for about 15 or 20 minutes. On or about 15th or 16th, Apte and Godse had an interview with Savarkar at 9:30 p.m. After about a week or so, may be 23 or 24 January 1948 (most likely 28th), Apte and Godse again came to Savarkar and had a talk with him at about 10:00 or 10:30 a.m. for about half an hour.

25.167: When the news of Mahatma Gandhi's murder was announced on the radio at about 5:45 p.m. Kasar went and informed Savarkar who said that it was bad news and then kept quiet. The same night at 2:00 a.m. both Damle and Kasar were arrested and brought to the C.I.D. office. Kasar said that he did not know anything about the assassination.

25.168: Gajanan Vishnu Damle, secretary of Savarkar, was also examined on 4 March 1948 by the Bombay Police. He said that he had known N.D. Apte of the *Agranee* for the past four years. Apte started a rifle club at Ahmednagar and also was an Honorary Recruiting Officer during the war. Apte was a frequent visitor to Savarkar's house and sometimes came with Godse. Savarkar had lent Rs.15,000 to Apte and Godse for the newspaper when security had been demanded from the *Agranee*. That paper was stopped and a new paper called the *Hindu Rashtra* was started. Savarkar was one of its Directors and Apte and Godse were the Managing Agents. He knew V.R. Karkare who was a Hindu Mahasabha worker at Ahmednagar for about three years and occasionally visited Savarkar. Badge was also known to him for the last three years. He also used to visit Savarkar.

25.169: In the first week of January 1948, Karkare and a Punjabi refugee boy came to see Savarkar and they both had an interview with Savarkar for about half an hour or 45 minutes. Neither of them came to see Savarkar again.

25.170: Apte and Godse came to see Savarkar about the middle of January 1948 late at night. Last time that Badge paid a visit to Savarkar was in the last week of December 1947. Several prominent Hindu Mahasabha leaders like Dr Moonje used to come and see Savarkar.

25.172: When the news was announced on the radio, Damle immediately went to report to Savarkar who said that he would give a statement to the press next morning. The same night Damle and Kasar were arrested.

25.173: The statements of both these witnesses show that Apte and

Godse were frequent visitors to Savarkar at Bombay and at conferences and at every meeting they were shown to have been with Savarkar. In August 1947 they were travelling with him both to and from Bombay to Delhi. This evidence also shows that Karkare was also well known to Savarkar and was a frequent visitor. Badge also visited Savarkar frequently. Dr Parchure visited him too. All this shows that the people who were subsequently involved in the murder of Mahatma Gandhi were all congregating sometime or the other at Savarkar Sadan and sometimes had long interviews with Savarkar.

Investigations Showing Association of Karkare and Apte

25.174: Intelligence Bureau file No. 13/HA(R)/59-11, Ex. 224-A, contains some important and revealing documents. At page 11 of this file there is a forwarding letter No. C/3 dated 3-2-1948 from G.S. Chaubal, one of the Deputy Superintendents of Police of the C.I.D. in the office of the D.I.G., C.I.D., Poona and is addressed to J.D. Nagarvala, Deputy Commissioner of Police with a copy to M.K. Sinha, Deputy Director, I.B. in the Ministry of Home Affairs. To this letter was attached a document giving a list of relatives and associates of Karkare and his description. Among the friends and associates at No. 10 was N.D. Apte of Poona. This letter was received in the Intelligence Bureau on the 6 February and was seen by M.K. Sinha, Deputy Director on 9 February 1948. These delays in the receipt of important letters are both astounding and not an uncommon feature of the investigation.

25.175: The next document is at page 13 and is addressed by Chaubal to the Inspector General of Police, Delhi, with a copy to the Deputy Director, I.B., Government of India. It is dated 1 February 1948. It says that four Head Constables were being sent to watch the activities of Maharshtrians, especially N.D. Apte who is considered to be inseparable from N.V. Godse and is also the person referred to in Madanlal's statement as proprietor of the *Hindu Rashtra* of Poona. Their duty will be to point out to the police at Delhi these persons with a view to prevent further outrage. The Constables sent were Head Constable Kulkarni, Constable Mahajan, Head Constable Jadhav and Head Constable Kadam.

25.178: Another letter at page 21 dated 3 February 1948 is from D.I.G.,

C.I.D., Poona to the Inspector General of Police, Bombay, with copies to the Deputy Director, I.B. New Delhi and Deputy Commissioner of Police, Bombay. This was also received in the I.B. Office on 9 February 1948. The report attached to this letter is dated 3 February 1948 and shows what action was taken at Poona and Lonavala (near Poona) showing that the police had started taking diligent interest in the investigation. If the information about Karkare and his association with N.D. Apte and the photographs of both Karkare and Apte were in the possession of the D.I.G., C.I.D., it is surprising why nobody asked for it earlier and it is more surprising that Rana should not have directed his office to send these photographs at least of Karkare whose name was known and the names of his associates to Nagarvala at Bombay or Sanjeevi at Delhi. Nagarvala also could have easily asked for this information from the office of the D.I.G., C.I.D., Poona which is equally applicable to the D.I.B. at Delhi who was also Inspector General of Police at that time. The sending of the Head Constables from Poona if it had been done earlier as was suggested in the statement of N.M. Kamte and R.N. Bannerjee, might have averted the catastrophe. Of course it is only a 'might have'.

25.181: At various pages of that file, there is a mention of different persons who were arrested and interrogated but at page 52 is the statement made before a Magistrate under section 164 Cr. P.C. of one Devendra Kumar, who was originally a resident of Goa and had joined the Hindu Rashtra Dal in March 1937. He stated that he met N.V. Godse who was 'Captain' of the Dal. The statement shows how the deponent was taught to manufacture bombs and to use guns from bicycles and cars and how to use pistols and revolvers. He was also training others. Among other things he disclosed that it was planned that Mahatma Gandhi, Nehru, Sardar Patel, Maulana Azad and Baldev Singh should all be killed as they were standing in the way of the Rashtra Dal. The party was waiting for a chance to execute this programme. He then added:

'We were creating hatred against these leaders in the minds of the public and it was planned that as soon as the public was ready the leaders should be killed one by one.... When I heard of the sad incident about Gandhiji, I became unnerved. I dropped a letter to Savarkar threatening to expose the conspiracy if he did not desist from the execution of the rest of the programme....'

25.182: Among the names of the conspirators to assassinate Mahatma Gandhi he named Deshpande, Apte, Godse, A. Chavan, Modak, Jog, Damle and Kasar, secretary and bodyguard of Savarkar respectively. Keskar, Joshi, Jogulkar and Chandrashekhar Aiyer. He gave a list of the manufacturers of bombs and amongst them was D.R. Badge of Narainpeth, Poona. This statement may in the context of the offence mean nothing but it does show that after the murder the police throughout the country became active. Devendra Kumar was examined by a Magistrate at Mirzapur in U.P. and the investigation was done by officers of Benaras and Lucknow. This Devendra Kumar was brought to Delhi and was examined by the police there and his statement shows a fair amount of knowledge of the working of the Hindu Mahasabha and the Rashtra Dal and that among the prominent workers of the Savarkar group were Kasar, N.D. Apte, N.V. Godse, Karkare and several others with whose names we may not be concerned. The statement also mentions a session of the Hindu Mahasabha at Barsee where Nathuram Godse made a very fiery speech and raised most objectionable slogans against the Congress Government like, 'Down with Maulana Gandhi!', 'Down with Gandhism!'. Godse also advocated the collection of arms and ammunitions to fight the Congress and declared that the main targets were 'Maulana Gandhi', Pandit Jawaharlal Nehru, Sardar Patel, Maulana Azad and Baldev Singh. This was at a meeting of the Hindu Rashtra Dal at Jogeshwari Mandir at which Godse, Apte, Karkare, Kasar and several others were present.

Chapter XXVI of the Kapur Commission's report deals with its findings on the terms of reference of the commission. The chapter deals with in details all the findings of the commission, but since I have reproduced the investigations in detail, it is not necessary to go into all the details again except for some which are revealing.

26.3: The following gentlemen from Poona must be held to have had prior knowledge; Balukaka Kanitkar, S.R. Bhagwat, R.K. Khadilkar, Keshavrao Jedhe, Member Constituent Assembly and G.V. Ketkar. In this category one may include N.V. Gadgil who was given some information by Jedhe, in language which was full of conundrums and which, therefore, makes it almost valueless. Besides these gentlemen, Purshottamdas Trikamdas, Barrister-at-Law of Bombay, has deposed that a man came to him whose name he could not recall and told him about the threat to the life of Mahatma Gandhi. Trikamdas took him to B.G. Kher and then to Morarji Desai who has no recollection of this. Kanji Dwarkadas has also given evidence of some information which B.G. Kher had but the Commission is unable to derive much benefit from his testimony.

26.4: If the word 'Conspiracy' is read in its technical sense, then the only persons who before the bomb was exploded at Birla House had any knowledge of the conspiracy were Prof Jain and his friends Angad Singh and Prof. Yajnik and after the bomb was exploded G.V. Ketkar also had this information. The others can not be said to have had any knowledge about the conspiracy. But the former (Prof. Jain) did not have any knowledge of Nathuram Godse whereas G.V. Ketkar had that knowledge.

26.5: As regards the second question the Commission has found in the discussion in the Chapter 'sub-nominee' G.V. Ketkar and Balukaka Kanitkar, i.e. under the first term of reference (a), that G.V. Ketkar whose name has been particularized in the first term of reference, did have, according to his own statement, knowledge of danger to the life of Mahatma Gandhi, knowledge that Nathuram Godse was determined to murder him and also the knowledge of the conspiracy to murder Mahatma Gandhi in which besides Nathuram Godse, there were other participants e.g. Badge and Apte.

Terms of Reference (C)

26.76: There is also evidence to show that there was a group of persons mostly Punjabis who had joined together with the object of turning out Muslims and forcing them to go to Pakistan. Amongst them were Avtar Singh of Sher-e-Punjab Hotel who had been detained, Balraj Mehta, Somnath Kapur, one Chavan who was also under detention. They had under them a number of other Punjabis and followers of Savarkar and members of the RSS. They had an easy access to military arms and ammunition and had support and backing of disgruntled rich Punjabis. There was one other in this group, N.V. Limaye, who was also arrested and detained in connection with bomb outrages in Greater Bombay. Thus, there was an organization which was subsequently suspected by Nagarvala of being involved in the bomb outrage on Mahatma Gandhi, but their communal activities had come to the notice of the Bombay

Special Branch earlier and some of them were detained and activities of others were being watched. Thus, in Bombay also there was an organization which was anti-Muslim whose object was to oust the Muslims; and they had collected weapons of all sorts including bombs so much so that even ex-Col. Mohan Singh of the I.N.A. was suspected though wrongly of being in it, (Nagarvala had also claimed that this group had contacted the speaker of the Assembly of the United Provinces Purshottamdas Tandon) and that was at the bidding of Master Tara Singh, the well known Akali Leader. But it has not been proved that this group had anything to do with the Delhi bomb or anti-Gandhi propaganda much less with attempt to murder him.

26.102: In spite of the erroneous line of investigation adopted by Nagarvala, he was far sighted enough to warn the D.I.B. on 27 January to be careful about the safety of Mahatma Gandhi. That was on the basis of 20X20, i.e., 400 would be kidnappers and if proper precautions were taken in Delhi, the assassin might not have been successful or left unwatched.

26.117: Bannerjee has rightly said that the police was guilty of lethargy and inefficiency and the Commission is of the opinion that in the circumstances those precautions should have been taken, which were deposed before the Commission and in their depositions suggested by police experts. But its result might not be predictable.

26.118: The Commission is unable to hold that the failure of the Bombay Police or their non-cooperation or their wrong investigational tracks, was any justification for the inefficiency shown by the Delhi Police. That however does not exonerate the Bombay Police of the blemishes in their investigation or of rigidness.

26.119: The three principal lacunae of Delhi Police were the failure to provide unobtrusive protection to Mahatma Gandhi and the failure to get Bombay Police to guard and act as watchers and spotters and the failure to get the identity of the proprietor of the *Hindu Rashtra* and put the Poona Police on to trace him and his associates.

Findings Summed Up

26.120: The findings of the Commission on the three terms of reference are as follows:

Terms of Reference (a)—

(i) G.V. Ketkar of Poona did have prior information about danger to the life of Mahatma Gandhi in October or November 1947. (ii) He did have information of the conspiracy of Nathuram Godse which he learnt from his talk with D.R. Badge on or about 23 January 1948. (iii) Up to the time he met Badge, he did not know that Apte and Badge were in the conspiracy to murder Mahatma Gandhi; but he must have known about Nathuram Godse's complicity as Nathuram had told him in October or November of his intention or plan to assassinate the Mahatma.

That is the finding of the Commission on the first term of reference.
26.121: Its finding on the second i.e. (b) are as follows:

Terms of Reference (b)—

(i) G.V. Ketkar did not communicate any information to the Government of Bombay or to the Government of India or any of its authorities. (ii) In particular, Ketkar did not get any information conveyed to the late B.G. Kher through the late Balukaka Kanitkar. This claim made by him is not established. Balukaka Kanitkar conveyed the information of danger to the life of Mahatma Gandhi and other top leaders of the Congress, on his own and out of his own volition.

26.122: The findings of the Commission on the third term i.e. (c) are as follows:

Term of Reference (c)—

(i) On the basis of the information conveyed to the Government of Bombay, and in particular to B.G. Kher, no action to try and get the information checked is proved to have been taken by the Government of Bombay or by B.G. Kher. Or by any authority under that Government. The information, in the opinion of the Commission, was vague, misty, nebulous and obscure but the matter should have been referred to the Police C.I.D. and got properly vetted and confirmed. It must be added that it will be highly speculative and conjectural on the part of the Commission to say what the result of this investigation would have been. It might well have been as unproductive, sterile and fruitless as was the result of investigation following definite information given by Prof Jain or the confessional police statement of Madanlal. (ii) There is no evidence from Delhi Secretariat or official records or from evidence of Delhi witnesses to show that the information given by Balukaka Kanitkar to B.G. Kher was conveyed to Government of India, i.e. Sardar Patel, Balukaka Kanitkar in a subsequent letter, Ex. 11, did say that B.G. Kher told him that he had conveyed the information to the Sardar. But there is no corroboration of this bald statement either in the evidence of Sardar's Private Secretary V. Shankar or of R.N. Bannerjee or of Maniben Patel. Morarji Desai had stated that Sardar already knew about it from his own sources. (iii) The information of Balukaka Kanitkar was neither conveyed to any officer of the Government of Bombay nor to any officer of the Government of India. (iv) There is evidence of Morarji Desai that information given by Balukaka was taken into consideration when the threat relating to welcome to and felicitation of Daji Joshi was discussed. At that meeting Messrs Kher and V.T. Dehejia and Morarji Desai were present. (v) There is evidence of V. Shankar that whatever information Sardar had in regard to danger to the life of Mahatma Gandhi whether conveyed to him by Morarji Desai or received through his own sources was communicated to and discussed with the Provincial Government which, in the opinion of the Commission, was the proper thing to do under the Constitution. (vi) The precautions taken at Birla House and the adequacy thereof have been discussed in sub chapters (G) and (H) of Chapter XII. (x) The investigation of the Delhi Police after the arrest of Madanlal was not of a high professional order and it lacked investigational skill and drive which one should have expected from a trained police force and particularly in the case of threat to the life of a person of the eminence of Mahatma Gandhi taking into consideration the knowledge of the factum of a conspiracy to murder Mahatma Gandhi which information Madanlal after his arrest gave to the Delhi Police. (xi) The D.I.G., C.I.D., Poona, U.H. Rana seems to have ignored the importance and utility of Madanlal's fuller statement, Ex.1, wherein the mention of the proprietor of the *Hindu Rashtriya* was a very valuable clue, which if pursued would have disclosed the identity of Apte and with a little more diligence also of Godse. Whether they could have arrested them or not would still be speculative. (xii) It is unfortunate that Nagarvala was not allowed an opportunity to read and study Madanlal's statement, Ex.1, and it is surprising why he did not evince any interest in that statement and insist on reading it through to find out what Madanlal had disclosed. This action is quite at variance with his later action after the murder, when he got Madanlal over to Bombay and interrogated him at great length. No doubt, then he was the principal investigator and previously he was what he calls, working out an information. It might be that his inquiry was complementary to the investigation by the Delhi Police, but a study of Madanlal's statement should have been as helpful then as it was after the murder. (xiii) The powers of the Police to move in a case like the present where information was given to the Bombay Police of a conspiracy to murder Mahatma Gandhi at Delhi have been debated before the Commission. It was argued that in such cases the Bombay Police, as then constituted, was helpless and had no power to investigate and take action. (xiv) Evidence shows that Godse and Apte were staying at different hotels under assumed names. Where the hotel keeper had no means of knowing that the names being given are false, there may be no easy remedy. But where, as in the case of the Arya Pathik Ashram, the manager, Gaya Shankar Dubey, P.W. 68, was aware that Apte had given a false name and yet he allowed that to be done without demur, the law should be made stringent and should make the hotel keeper liable in such cases to higher penalty than merely a small fine. (xv) In considering the measures taken by the authorities this crucial fact has to be kept in view that the Congress Governments had just come into power after several years of struggle by the Congress and its helpers against the British Government, in which the strictness of police interference with the liberty of the subject played a very important part. The Congress Governments could not suddenly adopt or allow the adoption of strict measures by the police, a tail put on by them on and keeping, as it were, under surveillance citizens of India even if they happened to be rather bad citizens.

J. L. Kapur,
Commission of Inquiry,
Mahatma Gandhi Murder Conspiracy.
Shastri Bhavan,
New Delhi,
September 30, 1969.

The Kapur Commission was hampered by its restrictive 'Terms of Reference' which limited its scope in finding out whether there was pre-knowledge of the conspiracy to murder Gandhi, whether provincial or Union governments or any of their ministers had been warned about the murder plot. Because of this, although in the course of its investigations it discovered evidence of the active involvement of 'organizations' like the RSS and Hindu Mahasabha, its leaders and of the undeniable involvement of V.D. Savarkar in the conspiracy to murder Gandhi, the commission was restrained from stating this emphatically in its report. Today, the RSS and Savarkarites have gone to great lengths to condemn the report and try and get it officially dismissed since in its investigation, the Kapur Commission not ony discovered evidence of both the organizations' involvement in the Gandhi murder but also about their sinister and treacherous conspiracy to subvert the nation in its infancy. The self-proclaimed patriots do not wish to have their treacherous anti-national activities come to light.

With the submission of the Kapur Commission's report, the curtain finally fell on the final chapter in the sordid saga of the murder of Mohandas K. Gandhi, Father of the Nation, Mahatma.

EPILOGUE

The Establishments Associated with Gandhi's Murder

Delhi

Birla House was acquired, after paying the market value, by the Government of India from the Birla family in the late sixties and converted into Gandhi Smriti. K.K. Birla sold it to the government after extensive negotiations in 1966. The Government of India paid ₹5.4 million and also gave 7 acres of prime land in Delhi as compensation. It was due to the efforts and pressure put by Shashi Bhushan, Krishna Kant, who later became the vice president of India, Mohan Dharia and Chandrashekhar, who, for a brief period, was the prime minister, that Birla House was finally acquired. Eventually, Shashi Bhushan sat on a Dharna (sit in) and fast to hasten the process of acquiring it. K.K. Birla drove a hard bargain. According to one version, while deciding the sale price of the family mansion, he even added the value of the fruit-bearing trees and all the saplings that had been planted to the price tag. Thus, it was a generously profitable deal by any consideration. Unfortunately, in recent years a misconception has gained currency that the Birlas magnanimously donated their family home, so that it could be converted into a monument to Mahatma Gandhi. This is not so.

Many changes have been made to Birla House; successive caretakers have recklessly added structures in recent times and demolished significant parts of this historic monument in their quest for personal glory. Instead of preserving history, they have successfully obliterated it. Gandhi Smriti today is distinctly different from the way it was when Gandhi lived his last days here from September 1947 till 30 January 1948. Visitors today do not get a feel of the historic significance of Birla House. All signs of the historic events that took place here during the month of January 1948 and especially on 20 and 30 January have been erased.

On a visit to Memphis, I went to see the motel where Reverend Dr Martin Luther King was murdered. The motel has been preserved exactly the way it was at the time of Dr King's murder. Even the cars in its parking lot are replicas of the ones that were parked there on that fateful day. Albuquerque Road is now named Tees January Marg. The servants' quarters at the rear were unfortunately demolished in 2014. The roundabout behind the erstwhile Birla House, where the murderers had parked the taxi which brought them to Birla House on the evening of 20 January 1948, now has a canteen.

Several changes have been made in the interior of Birla House, and an interactive museum has been installed on the top floor. The beautiful display of large bromide prints of photographs from the last year and his last stay at Birla House especially the photographs by Henri Cartier Bresson immediately after Gandhi's murder have been removed and replaced by big digital television screens displaying randomly moving digital images of the old photographs; the text describing the history depicted in the photographs has also been removed and this is tragic. Visitors now fail to comprehend the significance of the events that took place here during that fateful January of 1948.

The taxi used on the 20th by the conspirators is today owned by a vintage car collector in Meerut. It is wrongly called the 'killer car', as it was used on the 20th and not on the 30th January. Various Gandhi museums have on several occasions appealed to the owner to present the car to them, but their appeals have gone unheeded.

Hindu Mahasabha Bhavan, I think, has been enlarged and expanded, but the old wing where the gang stayed in January 1948 exists. The South Indian School next to it is still there. The woods behind it, where the guns were tested have survived time. I have visited all three places and walked into those woods.

Marina Hotel on Connaught Circus now houses offices.

I have no idea about the fate of the Frontier Hotel and the Sharif Hotel. They might have been turned into offices or shops or made way for new development.

The Regal Cinema still stands on a rapidly changing Connaught Circus. How long it will remain, only God knows.

The waiting rooms at the Old Delhi railway station may still exist. I don't think the Old Delhi station has been drastically renovated. The murderers Godse, Apte and Karkare stayed in the first-class waiting room on the night of the 29th and left to murder Gandhi from the second-class waiting room on the afternoon of 30 January 1948.

I have no idea if the structure housing the special court, and the barracks, which were converted into a specially notified prison to hold the accused during the Gandhi murder trial, in the historic precincts of the Red Fort, survive. Fortunately, the Red Fort does.

Raj Ghat has changed many a times and now does not resemble the humble cremation ground of a simple man.

The Tughlaq Road police station is the same as it was in January 1948. The cell in which Godse was held is still in use. The record room of the police station has the FIR of the Gandhi murder framed on its wall. I have visited this too and spent a few minutes in the cell in which Nathuram was held after the murder.

Poona

Poona is now known as Pune.

495, Shanivar Peth, where the *Hindu Rashtra* office, Shivaji Printing Press and the office of *Agranee* was located was attacked by a violent mob in the wake of Gandhi's murder. The press and office were vandalized and burned down. I am not sure if the Godse or Apte family ever reclaimed it.

In the early seventies, I visited Gopal Godse's home with my parents and grandmother. I think it still survives. Gopal built a shrine and has placed what he claims were the ashes of his brother Nathuram Godse in it. On Nathuram's death anniversary, a band of admirers gathers to worship the murderer, whom they consider a martyr. This has now become a big public function.

Badge's Shastra Bhandar at 300, Narayan Peth has disappeared. It was attacked and torched in the aftermath of Gandhi's murder.

Narayan Apte's family home Anandashram was situated at 22, Budhwar Peth. I have no idea whether it exists. If it does, does it belong to the Aptes? I have not tried to find out.

Ahmednagar

Vishnu Karkare's Deccan Guest House still stands in the Pardeshi Aali in Kapda Bazaar area of Ahmednagar.

Gwalior

Dr Sadashiv Parchure, till his death, lived in his joint family home, Parchure Vada on Station Road in the Lashkar area of Gwalior. In the seventies or eighties, the late Madhur Valluri interviewed a terminally-ill Parchure at the Parchure Vada. Most probably, Parchure Vada still exists and is owned by Parchure's descendants.

Bombay

Bombay is now called Mumbai.

Sea Green South and Sea Green North hotels still exist. They are still hotels, bearing the same names and are situated on the scenic Marine Drive.

Pyrke's Apollo Hotel on the junction of Landsdowne Road and Colaba Causeway, a stone's throw away from Regal Cinema is still there; it still is a hotel.

Arya Patheekashram, situated in the area adjoining Sandhurst Bridge, is listed in the Brihanmumbai Municipal Corporation's guide to Bombay of 1962, as situated on Vallabhbhai Patel Road. When this book was first published in 2007, it existed.

Elphinstone Hotel on Gunbow Street off Hornby Road, which are now named Rustam Sidhwa Marg and Dadabhai Naoroji Road respectively, was also listed in the BMC Guide to Bombay 1962. I got its number from MTNL directory inquiries. When I called the number, I was told that I had reached the Residency Hotel, they had no idea about any Elphinstone Hotel. Its sister concern, the Elphinstone Annexe Hotel, on Carnac Road has also disappeared.

The Hindu Mahasabha office is located in Parel above the Damodar Hall.

Mota Mandir in Bhuleshwar still survives. It was in the news in 2006 because of a dispute between its trustees and some shopkeepers and warehouse owners who are tenants. I don't know if the descendants of Dada Maharaj and Dixit Maharaj still live there.

Savarkar Sadan was built by V.D. Savarkar in 1938. It is situated a building away from Balmohan Vidyamandir in the lane now named Dr Madhukar B. Raut Marg. This is the first left turn while going towards Shivaji Park from Shiv Sena Bhavan. V.D. Savarkar's son lives there. He now owns only one-third of his father's home; the other two-thirds are owned by two other families, one of them my acquaintances. While looking for an office for Mahatma Gandhi Foundation, this acquaintance offered to let me temporarily use a ground floor room as an office. It would have led to an ironic address: Mahatma Gandhi Foundation, Savarkar Sadan!

It is sad that although Savarkar is venerated by many, none of his worshippers ever thought of preserving his home. They have erected a grand memorial to him across at Shivaji Park.

The CID headquarters from where Nagarvala ran his investigation and where all the accused, accept Parchure, were held in custody, stands in the police headquarters campus opposite Crawford Market, which is now named Mahatma Jyotiba Fule Market. It is said that after the Gandhi murder trial, Badge, the approver, was allotted a tenement in the campus, where he lived till his death.

The presidency magistrate's court still functions from the same building. It was in this court that many statements of witnesses were recorded and identification parades carried out. The presidency magistrate's court is popularly called Qilla Court.

Madanlal Pahwa, after his release, settled in Bombay. It is believed that he lived somewhere in Dadar. Records of where he lived, or if he left behind any progeny, aren't available.

On 17 January and 27 January 1948, Apte and Godse boarded the Air India flight to Delhi from the airport gate near the Military Camp in Kalina. In those days, passengers boarded flights from here. For many years the area was called 'Old Airport'. This part of the Mumbai Airport has now been converted into a terminal for private and chartered flights. The gate from which Apte and Nathuram entered the airport is now the gate of the Air Force Station, entry is restricted.

APPENDICES

APPENDIX 1

CHARGESHEET

REX VERSUS NATHURAM GODSE AND EIGHT ACCUSED.

'I, Atmacharan, am charging you Nathuram Godse *(37)*, Narayan Apte *(34)*, Vishnu Karkare *(37)*, Madanlal Pahwa *(20)*, Shankar Kistayya *(20)*, Gopal Godse *(27)*, Vinayak Savarkar *(65)* and Dattatreya Parchure *(49)*:

I. Firstly, that you, Nathuram V. Godse, Narayan D. Apte, Vishnu R. Karkare, Madanlal K. Pahwa, Shankar Kistayya, Gopal V. Godse, Vinayak D. Savarkar and Dattatreya S. Parchure between December 1, 1947, and January 30, 1948, at Poona, Bombay, Delhi and other places agreed and conspired among and between yourselves and Digambar R. Badge, who has been tendered a pardon. Gangadhar S. Dandawate, Gangadhar Jadhav and Suryadev Sharma, who along with others not known are absconding, to do or caused to be done an illegal act, *viz.*, to commit the murder of Mohandas Karamchand Gandhi more popularly known as 'Mahatma Gandhi' that the same act, *viz.*, the murder of Mahatma Gandhi' was done in pursuance of the said agreement and conspiracy at Delhi on January 30, 1948, and thereby committed an offence punishable under Section 120(B) of the Indian Penal Code read with Section 302 of the Indian Penal Code and within the cognisance of the Court;

II. Secondly, that in pursuance of the said agreement and conspiracy between January 10, 1948 and January 20, 1948, you Nathuram V. Godse, Narayan D. Apte, Vishnu R. Karkare, Madanlal K. Pahwa, Shankar Kistayya and Gopal V. Godse along with Digambar R. Badge:

A (1) transported without a licence to Delhi arms and ammunition, viz., 2 revolvers with cartridges, in contravention of the provisions of Section 10 of the Indian Arms Act and thereby committed an offence punishable under Section 19(d) of the Indian Arms Act and within the cognisance of the Court;

(2) Abetted each other in the commission of the above offence and thereby committed an offence punishable under Section 19(d) of the Indian Arms Act read with Sections 109 and 114 of the Indian Penal Code, and within cognisance of the Court;

B (1) at Delhi, had without a licence in your possession under your control arms and ammunition, *viz.*, 2 revolvers with cartridges, in contravention of the provisions of Section 14 and 15 of the Indian Arms Act and there by committed an offence punishable under Section 19(f) of the Indian Arms Act and within the cognisance of the Court;

(2) at Delhi, abetted each other in the commission of the above offence and thereby committed an offence punishable under Section 19(f) of the Indian Arms Act read with Section 114 of the Indian Penal Code and within the cognisance of the Court;

III. Thirdly, that in pursuance of the said agreement and conspiracy between January 10, 1948 and January 20, 1948, at Delhi you Nathuram V. Godse, Narayan D. Apte, Vishnu R. Karkare, Madanlal K. Pahwa, Shankar Kistayya and Gopal V. Godse along with Digambar R. Badge:

A(1) had in your possession and under your control explosive substances, *viz.*, 2 gun-cotton-slabs and five hand grenades with detonators and wicks, with intent to endanger life by means thereof or to enable any other person to endanger life thereof and thereby committed an offence Punishable under Section 4(b) of the Explosive Substance Act and within the cognisance of the Court;

(2) abetted each other in the commission of the above offence and thereby committed an offence punishable under

Section 4(b) of the Explosive Substances Act read with Section 6 of the Act and within cognisance of the Court;

B(1) had in your possession and under your control explosive substances, *viz.*, 2 gun-cotton-slabs and 5 hand grenades with detonators and wicks, under such circumstances as to give rise to a reasonable suspicion that you did not have them in your possession or under your control for a lawful object and thereby committed an offence punishable under Section 5 of the Explosive Substances Act and within the cognisance of the Court; abetted each other in the commission of the above offence and thereby committed an offence punishable under Section 5 of the Explosive Substances Act read with Section 6 of the Act and within the cognisance of the Court;

IV. Fourthly, that in pursuance of the said agreement and conspiracy on January 20, 1948, at Birla House, Delhi, you A(1) Madanlal K. Pahwa unlawfully and maliciously caused an explosive substance, viz., a gun cotton-slab, to explode, which explosion was of a nature likely to endanger life and to cause serious injury to property and thereby committed an offence punishable under Section 3 of the Explosive Substances Act and within the cognisance of the Court;

(2) Nathuram V. Godse, Narayan D. Apte, Vishnu R. Karkare, Shankar Kistayya and Gopal V. Godse along with Digambar R. Badge abetted Madanlal K. Pahwa in the commission of the above offence, and thereby committed an offence punishable under Section 3 of the Explosive Substances Act read with Section 6 of the Act and within the cognisance of the Court;

V. Fifthly, that in pursuance of the said agreement a conspiracy on January 20, 1948 at Birla House, Delhi, you Nathuram V. Godse, Narayan D. Apte, Vishnu R. Karkare, Madanlal K. Pahwa, Shankar Kistayya, Gopal V. Godse and Vinayak D. Savarkar along with Digambar R. Badge abetted each other in the commission of an offence, *viz.*, to commit the murder of 'Mahatma Gandhi' which offence is punishable with death or transportation for life and which offence was not committed in consequence of the abetment and thereby committed an offence punishable under Section 115 of the Indian Penal Code read with Section 302 of the Indian Penal Code and within the cognisance of the Court;

VI. Sixthly, that in pursuance of the said agreement and conspiracy between January 28, 1948, and January 30, 1948, you

A (1) Nathuram V. Godse and Narayan D. Apte brought without a licence from Gwalior to Delhi arms and ammunition, viz., automatic pistol No. 606824 with cartridges, in contravention of the provisions of Section 6 of the Indian Arms Act and thereby committed an offence punishable under Section 19 (c) of the Indian Arms Act and within the cognisance of the Court;

(2) Nathuram V. Godse, Narayan D. Apte and Dattatreya S. Parchure abetted each other in the commission of the above offence punishable under Section 19(c) of the Indian Arms Act read with Section 114 of the Indian Penal Code and within cognisance of the Court;

B (1) Nathuram V. Godse at Delhi, had in your possession and under your control arms and ammunition, viz., automatic pistol No.606824 with cartridges, in contravention of Section 14 and 15 of the Indian Arms Act and thereby committed an offence punishable under Section 19(f) of the Indian Arms Act and within the cognisance of the Court;

(2) Narayan D. Apte and Vishnu R. Karkare at Delhi, abetted each other in the commission of the above offence and thereby committed an offence punishable under Section 19(f) of the Indian Arms Act read with Section 114 of the Indian Penal Code and within the cognisance of the Court;

VII. Seventhly, that in the pursuance of the said agreement and conspiracy on January 30, 1948, at the Birla House, Delhi you:

A (1) Nathuram V. Godse did commit murder by intentionally and knowingly causing the death of Mahatma Gandhi' and thereby committed an offence under Section 302 of the Indian Penal Code and within the cognisance of the Court;

(2) Narayan D. Apte and Vishnu R. Karkare abetted Nathuram V. Godse in the commission of the above offence, which offence was committed in your presence, and thereby committed an offence punishable under Section 302 of the Indian Penal Code read with Section 114 of the Indian Penal Code and within the cognisance of the Court;

(3) Madanlal K. Pahwa, Shankar Kistayya, Gopal V. Godse, Vinayak D. Savarkar and Dattatreya S. Parchure along with Digambar R. Badge abetted Nathuram V. Godse in the commission of above offence and thereby committed an offence punishable under Section 302 of the Indian Penal Code read with Section 109 of the Indian Penal Code and within the cognisance of the Court.

H. Atmacharan, I.C.S., Judge, Special Court. 22 June 1948, Red Fort, Delhi

APPENDIX 2

THE JUDGMENT

Charge I: Offences and Sentences 'That you Nathuram V. Godse, Narayan D. Apte, Vishnu R. Karkare, Madanlal K. Pahwa, Shankar Kistayya, Gopal V. Godse, Vinayak D. Savarkar and Dattatreya S. Parachure between December 1, 1947, and January 30, 1948, at Poona, Bombay, Delhi and other places agreed and conspired among and between yourselves and Digambar R. Badge, who has been tendered a pardon, Gangadhar S. Dandvate, Gangadhar Jadhav and Suryadev Sharma, who along with others not known or absconding, to do or cause to be done an illegal act. *viz.*, to commit the murder of Mohandas Karamchand Gandhi more popularly known as "Mahatma Gandhi" and that the same act viz., the murder of Mahatma Gandhi, was done in pursuance of the said agreement and conspiracy at Delhi on 30 January 1948, and thereby committed an offence punishable under section 120-B of the Indian Penal Code and within the cognisance of the court.

'It has already been held established that there was a "conspiracy" to commit the murder of Mahatma Gandhi, that the conspiracy was definitely in existence in the beginning of January 1948 and continued till 30-1-1948. The "conspiracy" took place at Poona, Bombay, Delhi, Gwalior and other places and that among the conspirators were at least Nathuram V. Godse, Narayan D. Apte, Vishnu R. Karkare, Madanlal K. Pahwa, Shankar Kistayya, Gopal V. Godse and Dattatreya S. Parachure along with Digambar R. Badge. These accused joined the "conspiracy" at different places and at different times. The offence of Nathuram V. Godse, Narayan D. Apte, Vishnu R. Karkare, Madanlal K. Pahwa, Shankar Kistayya, Gopal V. Godse and Dattatreya S. Parachure, in the circumstances, clearly falls within the purview of Section 120-B of the Indian Penal Code read with Section 302 of the Code.

'Nathuram V. Godse, Narayan D. Apte, Vishnu R. Karkare, Madanlal K. Pahwa, Shankar Kistayya, Gopal V. Godse, and Dattatreya S. Parachure thus are clearly 'guilty' under Section 120-B of the Indian Penal Code read with Section 302 of the Code.'

Charge II: 'That in pursuance of the said agreement and conspiracy between January 13, 1948, and January 20, 1948 you Nathuram V. Godse, Narayan D. Apte, Vishnu R. Karkare, Madanlal K Pahwa, Shankar Kistayya, Gopal V. Godse, along with Digambar R. Badge A (1) transported without a licence to Delhi arms and ammunition viz., 2 revolvers with cartridges, in contravention of the provisions of Section 10 of the Indian Arms Act and thereby committed an offence punishable under Section 19(d) of the Indian Arms Act within the cognisance of the court;

(2) abetted each other in the commission of the above offence and thereby committed an offence punishable under Section 19(d) of the Indian Arms Act read with Section 109 and 114 of the Indian Penal Code and within the cognisance of the court;

B(1) at Delhi, had without a licence in your possesssion and under your control arms and ammunition, viz., 2 revolvers with cartridges, in contravention of the provisions of the Section 14 and 15 of the Indian Arms Act and thereby committed an offence punishable under Section 19(f) of the Indian Arms Act read with Section 114 of the Indian Penal Code and within the cognisance of the court;

(2) at Delhi, abetted each other in the commission of the above offence and thereby committed an offence punishable under Section 19(1) of the Indian Arms Act read with Section 114 of the Indian Penal Code and within the cognizance of the court.

"The two revolvers said to have been transported to Delhi and tried out in the jungle behind the Hindu Mahasabha Bhawan have been recovered and have not been produced before the court. It could not in the circumstances, be held as to what was real nature of the "article" so transported to Delhi and so tried out in the jungle behind Hindu Mahasabha Bhavan. It would accordingly be unsafe to hold the charge established as against Nathuram V. Godse, Narayan D. Apte, Vishnu R. Karkare, Madanlal K. Pahwa, Shankar Kistayya and Gopal V. Godse.'

Charge III: 'That in pursuance of the said agreement and conspiracy between January 10, 1948, and January 20, 1948 at Delhi, you Nathuram V. Godse, Narayan D. Apte, Vishnu R. Karkare, Madanlal K Pahwa, Shankar Kistayya and Gopal V. Godse along with Digambar R. Badge A (1) had in your possession and under your control explosive substances viz., 2 gun-cotton-slabs and 5 hand-grenades with detonators and wicks; with intent to endanger life by means thereof or to enable any other person to endanger life by means thereof and thereby committed an offence punishable under Section 4 (b) of the Explosive Substances Act read with Section 6 of the Act and within the cognizance of the court;

B (1) had in your possession and under your control explosive substances, viz., 2 gun-cotton-slabs and 5 hand-grenades with detonators and wicks, under such circumstances as to give rise to a reasonable suspicion that you did not have them in your possession or under your control for a lawful object and thereby committed an offence punishable under Section 5 of the Explosive Substances Act and within the cognizance of the Court;

(2) abetted each other in the commission of the above offence and thereby committed an offence punishable under Section 5 of the Explosive Substances Act read with Section 6 of the Act and within the cognizance of the Court.

One gun cotton slab and four hand-grenades out of the two gun cotton slabs and the five hand-grenades said to have been in possession of the accused at Delhi have been recovered, and the evidence in regard thereto led before the Court. Out of the explosives recovered one hand-grenade had been recovered from the possesssion of Madanlal K. Pahwa and one gun-cotton-slab and three hand-grenades had been recovered at the instance of Shankar Kistayya from behind the Hindu Mahasabha Bhawan.

'The findings arrived at above are that the accused were in possesssion of two gun-cotton-slabs and five hand-grenades at Delhi on 20-1-1948. One of the gun-cotton-slabs was exploded at the Birla House by Madanlal K. Pahwa. The subject matter of the charge in regard thereto is Charge IV. It has already been mentioned above that my general impression is that it was really intended to make Digambar R. Badge enter the room of Choturam and throw the hand grenade in his possesssion through an opening in the trellis-work of the window therein at Mahatma Gandhi. Digambar R. Badge, however, could not be persuaded to enter the room. The offence of Nathuram V. Godse, Narayan D. Apte, Vishnu R. Karkare, Madanlal K. Pahwa, Shankar Kistayya and Gopal V Godse in regard to that hand-grenade, in the circumstances, clearly falls within the purview of Section 4(b) of the Explosive Substances Act read with Section 6 of the Act and in regards to remaining explosives clearly falls within the purview of Section 5 of the explosive Substances Act in the alternative u/s 5 of the Explosive Substances Act read with section 6 of the Act.'

Charge Established

Nathuram V. Godse, Narain D. Apte, Vishnu R. Karkare, Madanlal K Pahwa, Shankar Kistayya, and Gopal V. Godse thus are clearly 'guilty' u/s 4(b) of the Explosive Substances Act read with Section 6 of the Act and u/s 5 of Explosive Substances Act in the alternative u/s 5 of the Explosive Substances Act read with Section 6 of the Act.

Charge IV: 'That in pursuance of the said agreement and conspiracy on January 20, 1948, at the Birla House, Delhi, you A(1) Madanlal K. Pahwa, unlawfully and maliciously caused an explosive substance, viz., a gun cotton slab, to explode, which explosion was of a nature likely to endanger life and to cause serious injury to property and thereby committed an offence, punishable under Section 6 of the Act and within the cognizance of the Court.'

(2) Nathuram V. Godse, Narayan D. Apte, Vishnu R. Karkare, Shankar Kistayya and Gopal V. Godse along with Digambar R. Badge, abetted Madanlal K. Pahwa in the commission of the above offence, and thereby committed an offence, punishable under Section 3 of the Explosive Substances Act read with Section 6 of the Act and within the cognizance of the Court.'

The findings arrived at above are that Madanlal K. Pahwa exploded a gun-cotton-slab over the back compound wall of the Birla House on 20-1-1948. His act in doing so was certainly unlawful and malicious. The explosion was also of a nature likely to endanger life. In the circumstances the offence of Madanlal K. Pahwa clearly falls within the purview of

Section 3 of the Explosive Substances Act and the offence of Nathuram V. Godse, Narayan D. Apte, Vishnu R. Karkare, Shankar Kistayya and Gopal V. Godse u/s 3 of the Explosive Substances Act read with Section 6 of the Act.

Thus Madanlal K. Pahwa is clearly 'guilty' u/s 3 of the Explosive Substances Act and Nathuram V. Godse, Narayan D. Apte, Vishnu R. Karkare, Shankar Kistayya and Gopal V. Godse are clearly 'guilty' u/s 3 of the Explosive Substances Act read with section 6 of the Act.

Charge V: 'That the said agreement and conspiracy on January 20, 1948, at the Birla House, Delhi, you Nathuram V. Godse, Narayan D. Apte, Vishnu R Karkare, Madanlal K Pahwa, Shankar Kistayya, Gopal V. Godse and Vinayak D. Savarkar along with Digambar R. Badge abetted each other in commission of an offence, viz., to commit the murder of "Mahatma Gandhi" which offence is punishable with death or transportation for life and which offence was not committed in consequence of the abetment and thereby committed an offence punishable under Section 115 of the Indian Penal Code read with Section 302 of the Indian Penal Code and within the cognizance of the Court.'

First Attempt Fails

'The findings arrived at above are that though an effort was made to commit the murder of Mahatma Gandhi at the Birla House on 20-1-1948 but it ultimately failed as Digambar R. Badge would not agree to enter the room of Choturam. The offence of Nathuram V. Godse, Narayan D. Apte, Vishnu R. Karkare, Madanlal K. Pahwa, Shankar Kistayya and Gopal V. Godse, in the circumstances, clearly falls within the purview of Section 115 of the Indian Penal Code read with Section 302 of the Code.

'Nathuram V. Godse, Narayan D. Apte, Vishnu R. Karkare, Madanlal K. Pahwa, Shankar Kistayya and Gopal V. Godse thus clearly "guilty" u/s 115 of the Indian Penal Code read with Section 302 of the Code.

Charge VI: 'That in pursuance of the said agreement and conspiracy between January 28, 1948, and January 30, 1948, you A(1) Nathuram V. Godse and Narayan D. Apte brought without a licence from Gwalior to Delhi arms and ammunition. Viz., Automatic Pistol No 606824 with cartridges, in contravention of the provisions of Section 6 of the Indian Arms Act and thereby committed an offence punishable under Section 19(c) of the Indian Arms Act within the cognizance of the Court;

(2) Nathuram V. Godse, Narayan D. Apte and Dattatreya S. Parachure abetted each other in the commission of the above offence and thereby committed an offence punishable under Section 19(c) of the Indian Arms Act read with Section 114 of the Indian Penal Code and within the cognizance of the Court;

B(1) Nathuram V. Godse at Delhi had in your possesssion and under your control arms and ammunition, viz., Automatic Pistol No 606824 with cartridges, in contravention of Section 14 and 15 of the Indian Arms Act and thereby committed an offence punishable under Section 19(f) of the Indian Arms Act and within the cognizance of the Court;

(2) Narayan D. Apte & Vishnu R. Karkare at Delhi, abetted each other in the commission of the above offence and thereby committed an offence punishable under Section 19(f) of the Indian Arnis Act read with Section 114 of Indian Penal Code and within the cognizance of the Court.

The findings arrived at above are that Nathuram V. Godse and Narayan D. Apte brought without a licence from Gwalior to Delhi arms and ammunition, viz., Automatic Pistol No 606824 with cartridges during the period between 28-1-1948 and 29-1-1948. The offence of Nathuram V. Godse and Narayan D. Apte, in the circumstances, clearly falls within the purview of Section 19(c) of the Indian Arms Act or in the alternative under Section 114 of the Indian Penal Code read with Section 19(c) of the Indian Arms Act.'

Scope of Indian Arms Act

Whatever Dattatreya S. Parachure is said to have done in the matter he did from Gwalior. The Indian Arms Act extends to the whole of India, and does not stand extended extra-territorially. Datiatreya S. Parachure, in the circumstances, cannot be held liable for abetting the commission of the offence punishable under Section 19(c) of the Indian Arms Act.

The findings arrived at further are that Nathuram V. Godse was in possesssion of automatic pistol No 606824 with cartridges on 30-1-1948 and that day Narayan D. Apte and Vishnu R. Karkare were along with

Nathuram V. Godse at Delhi Main Rly. Station. In the circumstances of offence of Naturam V. Godse clearly falls within the purview of Section 19(f) of the Indian Arms Act and the offence of Narayan D. Apte and Vishnu R. Karkare clearly falls within the purview of Section 114 of the Indian Penal Code read with Section 19(f) of the Indian Arms Act.

Thus Nathuram V. Godse is clearly 'guilty' under Section 1(c) of the Indian Arms Act or in the alternative under Section 114 of the Indian Penal Code read with Section 19(c) of the Indian Arms Act and under Section 19(f) of the Indian Arms Act, Narayan D. Apte is clearly 'guilty under Section 19(c) of the Indian Arms Act or in the alternative under Section 114 of the Indian Penal Code read with Section 19(c) of the Indian Arms Act and under Section 114 of the Indian Penal Code with Section 19(f) of the Indian Arms Act and Vishnu R. Karkare is clearly 'guilty under Section 114 of the Indian Penal Code read with Section 19(1) of the Indian Arms Act.

Charge VII: 'That in pursuance of the said agreement and conspiracy on January 30, 1948, at Birla House, Delhi, you A (1) Nathuram V. Godse did commit murder by intentionally and knowingly causing the death of "Mahatma Gandhi" and thereby committed an offence punishable under Section 302 of the Indian Penal Code and within the cognizance of the court.

(2) Narayan D. Apte & Vishnu R. Karkare abetted Nathuram V Godse in the commission of the above offence, which offence was committed in your presence and thereby committed an offence punishable under Section 302 of the Indian Penal Code read with Section 114 of the Indian Penal Code and within the cognizance of the court;

(3) Madanlal K Pahwa, Shankar Kistayya, Gopal V. Godse, Vinayak D. Sarvarkar & Dattatreya S. Parachure along with Digambar R. Badge abetted Nathuram V. Godse in the commission of the above offence and thereby committed an offence punishable under Section 302 of the Indian Penal Code read with Section 109 of the Indian Penal Code and within the cognizance of the court.'

The findings arrived at above are that Nathuram V. Godse intentionally and knowingly caused the death of Mahatma Gandhi on 30-1-1948. The offence of Nathuram V. Godse, in the circumstances, clearly falls within the purview of Section 302 of the Indian Penal Code.

The presence of Narayan D. Apte and Vishnu R. Karkare at the time of the murder of Mahatma Gandhi at Birla House has not been established on behalf of the prosecution. The only evidence forthcoming on their behalf is to the effect that Narayan D. Apte and Vishnu R. Karkare were along with Nathuram V. Godse at the Delhi Main Ry. Station till about mid-day on 30-1-1948. The offence of Narayan D. Apte and Vishnu R. Karkare, in the circumstances, clearly falls within the purview of Section 109 of the Indian Penal Code read with Section 302 of the Code.

Madanlal's Position

"The position of Madanlal K. Pahwa and Shankar Kistayya, however, stands altogether on a different footing. Soon after the explosion incident Madanlal had been arrested by the police on 20-1-1948, and was thereafter throughout in custody. The very evidence produced on behalf of the prosecution goes to show that Digambar R. Badge after what had taken place at the Birla House on 20-1-1948 became disgusted, and came back along with Shankar Kistayya to the Hindu Mahasabha Bhawan. Digambar R. Badge asked Shankar Kistayya to throw away all the "stuff" that they had in the room. Nathuram V. Godse and Narayan D. Apte then came to the Hindu Mahasabha Bhawan and asked him what had happened. Digambar R. Badge abused them, and asked them to get out. There was thereafter no communication whatsoever in regards to the "conspiracy" between Digambar R. Badge and Shankar Kistayya on the one hand, and Nathuram V. Godse, Narayan D. Apte, Vishnu R. Karkare and Gopal V. Godse, on the other.

On these facts it may safely be inferred that Digambar R. Badge and Shankar Kistayya had completely dissociated themselves from the "conspiracy" after what had taken place at the Birla House and that the conspiracy for them had come to an end on 20-1-1948, Madanlal K. Pahwa and Shankar Kistayya, in the circumstances, cannot be held liable for abetting the commission of the offence punishable u/s 302 of the Indian Penal Code.

'There is nothing on the record of the case to justify the inference that Gopal V. Godse had dissociated himself completely from the "conspiracy" after the explosion incident at Birla House on 20-1-1948. The evidence on the record of the case, on the other hand, goes to show that Gopal V. Godse had visited Naturham V. Godse and Narayan D. Apte at Bombay on 24-1-1948 and that Nathuram V. Godse, Narayan D. Apte, Vishnu R. Karkare and Gopal V. Godse had met together at the house of G.M. Joshi at Thana on 25-1-1948. Dattatreya S. Parachure joined the "conspiracy" on 27-1-1948 when he agreed to get a pistol procured for Nathuram V. Godse and Narayan D. Apte. The offence of Gopal V. Godse and Dattatreya S. Parachure, in the circumstances, clearly falls within the purview of Section 109 of the Indian Penal Code read with Section 302 of the Code.

'It has already been held above that Dattatreya S. Parachure is a "British subject domiciled in India". Even if it be taken for granted just for argument's sake that he is a subject of the Gwalior State, then still he is triable at Delhi in view of the fact that the offence of murder was completed at Delhi 13 Cr. L.J. 426 and 29 Cr. L.J. 1089 are in support of this view.

"Thus Nathuram V. Godse is clearly "guilty" u/s 302 of the Indian Penal Code and Narayan D. Apte, Vishnu R. Karkare, Gopal V. Godse and Dattatreya S. Pachure are clearly "guilty" u/s 109 of the Indian Penal Code read with Section 302 of the Code.

'Nathuram V. Godse accordingly is "guilty" (1) u/s 120-B of the Indian Penal Code read with Section 302 of the Code. (2) under Section 19(c) of the Indian Arms Act or in the alternative under Section 114 of the Indian Arms Act, (3) under Section 19(1) of the Indian Arms Act, (4) under Section 5 of the Explosive Substances Act or in the alternative u/s 5 of the Explosive Substances Act read with Section 6 of the Act, (5) under Section 4(b) of the Explosive Substances Act read with Section 6 of the Act, (6) under Section 3 of the Explosive Substances Act read with Section 6 of the Act; (7) under Section 115 of the Indian Penal Code read with Section 302 of the Indian Penal Code and (8) u/s 302 of the Indian Penal Code.

Narayan D. Apte accordingly is "guilty" (1) under Section 120-B of the India Penal Code read with Section 302 of the Code, (2) under Section 19(c) of the Indian Arms Act in the alternative under Section 114 of the Indian Penal Code read with Section 19(c) of the Indian Arms Act,

(3) under Section 144 of the Indian Penal Code read with Section 19(f) of the India Arms Act, (4) under Section 5 of the Explosive Substances Act or in the alternative under Section 5 of the Explosive Substances Act read with Section 6 of the Act, (5) under Section 4(b) of the Explosive Substances Act read with Section 6 of the Act, (6) under Section 3 of the Explosive Substances Act read with Section 6 of the Act, (7) under Section 115 of the Indian Penal Code read with Section 302 of the Code and (8) under Section 109 of the Indian Penal Code read with Section 302 of the Code.

Vishnu R. Karkare accordingly is "guilty" (1) under Section 120-B of the Indian Penal Code read with Section 302 of the Code, (2) u/ s 114 of the Indian Penal Code read with Section 19 (1) of the Indian Arms Act, (3) u/s 5 of the Explosive Substances Act or in the alternative u/s 5 of the Explosive Substances Act read with Section 6 of the Act, (4) u/s 4(b) of the Explosive Substances Act read with Section 6 of the Act, (5) u/s 3 of the Explosive Substance Act read with Section 6 of the Act, (6) u/s 115 of the Indian Penal Code rea with Section 302 of the Code and (7) u/s 109 of the Indian Penal Code read with Section 302 of the Code.

Madanlal K. Pahwa accordingly is "guilty" (1) u/s 120-B of the Indian Penal Code read with Section 302 of the Code. (2) u/s 5 of the Explosive Substances Act or in the alternative u/s 5 of the Explosive Substances Act read with Section 6 of the Act, (2) u/s 4(b) of the Explosive Substances Act read with Section 6 of the Act, (4) u/s 3 of the Explosive Substances Act and (5) u/s 115 of the Indian Penal Code read with Section 302 of the Code.

'Shankar Kistayya accordingly is "guilty" (1) u/s 120-B of the Indian Penal Code read with Section 302 of the Code, (2) u/s 5 of the Explosive Substances Act or in the alternative u./s 3 of the Explosive Substances Act read with Section 6 of the Act, (3) u/s 4(b) of the Explosive Substances Act read with Section 6 of the Act, (4) u/s 3 of the Explosive Substances Act read with Section 6 of the Act and (5) u/s 115 of the Indian Penal Code read with Section 302 of the Code.

'Gopal V. Godse accordingly is "guilty" (1) u/s 120-B of the Indian Penal Code read with Section 302 of the Code, (2) u/s 5 of the Explosive Substances Act read with Section 6 of the Act, (3) u/s 4(b) of the Explosive Substances Act read with Section 6 of the Act, (4) u/s 3 or in the alternative u/s 5 of the explosive Substances Act read with Section 6 of the Act, (5) u/s 115 of the Indian Penal Code read with Section 302 of the Code and (6) u/s 109 of the Indian Penal Code read with Section 362 of the Code.

'Dattatreya S. Parchure accordingly is "guilty" (1) u/s 120-B of the Indian Penal Code read with Section 302 of the Code and (2) u/s 109 of the Indian Penal Code read with Section 302 of the Code.

'The main offences established against the accused are u/s 120 B of the Indian Penal Code read with Section 302 of the Code, u/s 115 of the Indian Penal Code read with Section 302 of the Code and under Section 302 of the Indian Penal Code or under Section 109 of the Indian Penal Code read with Section 302 of the Code. The subsidiary offences established against the accused are under Section 19 of the Indian Arms Act and under Section 3, 4(b) and 5 of the Explosive Substances Act.

'Chapter V-A comprising Section 120-A and 120-B was enacted by the Indian Criminal Law Amendment Act of 1913 and was enacted to assimilate the Indian to the English Criminal Law. According to the English Criminal Law a conspiracy to commit felony merges in the felony, if committed. The contention, as such, on behalf of the defence is that the accused cannot be convicted under Section 120-B of the Indian Penal Code read with Section 302 of the Code as well under Section 109 of the Indian Penal Code read with Section 302 of the Code.'

Harrison in his *Law of Conspiracy* (Edition 1924) on page 73 lays down as follows:

'If a conspiracy to commit a crime is actually carried out, the conspiracy is not merged in the crime, and it is technically possible for the accused to be indicted twice, once for the conspiracy and once for the crime (as explained by Lord Campbell in O'Connell v. Reg. (1844) II Cl. And F. 155) but this is discouraged by Judges as being unfair to the accused (see R.V. Boulton (1871) 12 Cox 87). This rule does not, however, apply to conspiracies to commit a felony, and if the agreement is carried out and the felony is actually committed, then the conspiracy is merged therein, by virtue of the statute 14 and 15 Vict. c. 100, s.12.'

No such law has been made applicable to India. The rulings, on the other hand, forthcoming on behalf of the prosecution go to show that the practice so far adopted by the courts in India has been to convict one or both in regards to the offence of conspiracy as well as in regards to the offence of abetment by conspiracy but to pass the sentence in regard to the latter offence only. 35 Cr. L.J. 322 and 39 Cr. L.J. 452 clearly go to show that an accused could be convicted both for conspiracy and abetment of conspiracy but a separate sentence for conspiracy is not called for. The defence have drawn my attention to 39 Cr. L.J. 266 which lays down as below:

Section 120-B, Penal Code, only applies where no offence has been actually committed and it is only in latter rare case where no crime has been committed in pursuance of a criminal conspiracy that sanction to initiate proceedings is necessary as some safeguard against frivolous prosecution. Where, however, the matter has gone beyond the stage of mere conspiracy and offences are alleged to have been actually committed in pursuance thereof. s.s.120-A and 120-B, are wholly irrelevant. Conspiracy is one form of abetment and where an offence is alleged to have been committed by more than two persons, such of them as actually took part in the commission should be charged with the substantive offence, while those who are alleged to have abetted it by conspiracy should be charged with the offence of abetment under S. 109, Penal Code.'

This is a single Judge ruling of the Madras High Court, while the ones cited on behalf of the prosecution are the Division Bench ruling of the Lahore High Court and the ruling Privy Council. The Court is thus bound by 35 Cr.L.J. 322 and 39 Cr. L.J.452.

Some of the accused have been held guilty under Section 120-B of the Indian Penal Code read with Section 302 of the code and under Section 115 of the Indian Penal Code read with Section 302 of the Code, and some of the accused have been held guilty under Section 120-B of the Indian Penal Code read with Section 302 of the Code, Under Section 115 of Indian Penal Code read with Section 302 of the Code and under Section 109 of the Indian Penal Code read with Section 302 of the Code. Separate sentences, in the circumstances, need not be passed under Section 120-B of the Indian Penal Code read with Section 302 wherein a person stands convicted under Section 120-B of the Indian Penal Code read with Section 302 of the Code as well as under Section 109 of Indian Penal Code read with Section 302 of the Code. On the same principle, in my opinion, separate sentences also need not be passed wherein a person stands convicted under Section 115 of the Indian Penal Code read with Section 302 of the Code as well as under Section 109 of the Indian Penal Code read with Section 302 of the Code. However, an altogether different position arises wherein a person stands convicted under Section 120 B of the Indian Penal Code read with Section 302 of the Code as well as under Section 115 of the Indian Penal Code read with Section 302 of the Code, The minimum punishment that could be awarded under Section 120-B of Indian Penal Code read with Section 302 of the Code is "transportation for life", but maximum punishment that could be awarded under Section 115 if the Indian Penal Code read with Section 302 of the Code, wherein no hurt is caused, is "seven years".

A Deliberate Act

'The act of Nathuram V. Godse in committing the murder of Mahatma Gandhi was a deliberate and a calculated one. No extenuating circumstances have been pointed out nor could have been pointed out on his behalf. The only sentence, in the circumstances, that could be passed on him under Section 302 of the of the Indian Penal Code is the sentence of death.

"The act of Narayan D. Apte in abetting the offence of the murder of Mahatma Gandhi is in no way less heinous. He throughout took the lead at each stage of the crime and at the most crucial moment either just ran away from the scene or just absented himself from the scene of the crime. Had it not been for his brainwork the murder of Mahatma Gandhi probably would never have been committed. The only sentence, in the circumstances, that could be passed on him under Section 109 of the Indian Penal Code read with Section 302 of the Code is the sentence of death.

"So far as Vishnu R. Karkare, Gopal V. Godse and Dattatreya S. Parachure are concerned, it would, in my opinion, meet the ends of justice if they are sentenced each to undergo transportation for life under Section 109 of the Indian Penal Code read with Section 302 of the Code. This is the minimum sentence awardable under Section 109 of the Indian Penal Code read with Section 302 of the Code.

Now the question is what sentences should be awarded to Madanlal

K. Pahwa and Shankar Kistayya under Section 120-B of the Indian Penal Code read with Section 302 of the Code under Section 115 of the Indian Penal Code read with Section 302 of the Code. It would, in my opinion, meet the end of justice if they are sentenced each to undergo transportation for life under Section 120-B of the Indian Penal Code read with Section 302 of the Code. This is minimum sentence awardable under Section 120-B of the Indian Penal Code read with Section 302 of the Code. There is nothing on the record of the case to show as to why a lenient view at all be taken in regard to the offence punishable under Section 115 of the Indian Penal Code read with Section 302 of the Code. Madanlal K. Pahwa and Shankar Kistayya, in the circumstances, should be sentenced each to undergo seven years' rigorous imprisonment under Section 115 of the Indian Penal Code read with Section 302 of the Code.'

Leniency For Shankar

'Shankar Kistayya is the servant of Digambar R. Badge, whatever he did more or less in obedience to the orders of his master Digambar R. Badge. Unless it was for Digambar R. Badge he would never have been approached by the other accused to join the conspiracy. Shankar Kistayya, in the circumstances, certainly deserves some leniency. I would accordingly recommend that his sentence of transportation of life under Section 120-B of the Indian Penal Code read with Section 302 of the Code may be commuted to seven years' rigorous imprisonment under Section 401 and 402 of the Code of Criminal Procedure.

'It would, in my opinion, meet the ends of justice if Nathuram V. Godse and Narayan D. Apte are sentenced each to undergo two years rigorous imprisonment under Section 19(C) of the Indian Arms Act or in the alternative under Section 114 of the Indian Penal Code read with Section 19(c) of the Indian Arms Act, if Nathuram V. Godse is sentenced to undergo two years' rigorous imprisonment under Section 19(f) of the Indian Arms Act and if Narayan D. Apte and Vishnu R. Karkare are sentenced each to undergo two years' rigorous imprisonment under Section 114 of the Indian Penal Code read with Section 19 (1) of the Indian Arms Act.

'It would, in my opinion, meet the ends of justice if Nathuram V.

Godse, Narayan D. Apte, Vishnu R. Karkare, Madanlal K. Pahwa, Shankar Kistayya and Gopal V. Godse are sentenced each to undergo three years rigorous imprisonment under Section 5 of the Explosive Substances Act or in the alternative under Section 5 of the Explosive Substances Act read with Section 6 of the Act five years' rigorous imprisonment under Section 4(b) of the Explosive Substances Act read with Section 6 of the Act, if Nathuram V. Godse, Narayan D. Apte, Vishnu R. Karkare, Shankar Kistayya, Gopal V. Godse are sentenced each to undergo seven years' rigorous imprisonment under Section 3 of Explosive substances Act read with Section 6 of the Act and if Madanlal K. Pahwa is sentenced to undergo ten years' rigorous imprisonment under Section 3 of the Explosive Substances Act.

Confirmation by High Court

"Now the question is whether the sentences of death are subject to confirmation by the Hon'ble High Court. It has already been stated above that the trial of the case has been under provisions of the Bombay Public Security Measures Act as extended to the Province of Delhi. Section 16 of the Act lays down that 'a Special Judge may pass any sentence authorised by law.' Section 19 of the Act lays down that the provisions of the Code and of any other law for the time being in force, in so far as they may be applicable and in so far as they are not inconsistent with the provisions of Section 10 to 20 shall apply to all matters connected with, arising from, or consequent upon, "a trial by Special Judge appointed under Section 11." Section 31 of the Code of Criminal Procedure lays down that "a Sessions Judge may pass any sentence authorised by law." A sentence of death passed by a Special Judge thus is not subject to confirmation by the High Court.

'This provision of the Code thus is inconsistent with the provisions of Section 16 of Bombay Public Security Measures Act as extended to the Province of Delhi, which just lays down that "a Special Judge may pass any sentence authorised by law." A sentence of death passed by a Special Judge thus is not subject to confirmation by the High Court.

"There is yet another way of looking at the matter. Section 18(3) of the Bombay Public Security Measures Act as extended to the

Province of Delhi, which just lays down that "no Court shall ... save as herein otherwise provided, have jurisdiction of any kind in respect of proceedings of any Special Judge." Section 18(2) of the Act gives power to the High Court in respect of the proceedings of any Judge only under Sections 423, 426, 427 & 428 of the Code of Criminal Procedures. Power to confirm a sentence of death under Section 376 of the Code of Criminal Procedure is not there. Had a sentence of death been subject to confirmation such power would certainly have been there. No doubt, the marginal note against Section 18 of the Act speaks of "appeal, revision and confirmation," but the marginal note could not be referred to for purposes of construing the Act.'

Final Order

Nathuram V. Godse 'He is found 'guilty' under Section 120-B of the Indian Penal Code read with Section 302 of the Code, under Section 19(c) of the Indian Arms Act or in the alternative under Section 114 of the Indian Penal Code read with Section 19(3) of the Indian Arms Act, under Section 19(f) of the Indian Arms Act, under Section 5 of the Explosive Substances Act or in the alternative under Section 5 of the Explosive Substances Act read with Section 6 of the Act, under Section 4(b) of the Explosive Substances Act read with Section 6 of the Act, under Section 3 of the Explosive Substances Act read with Section 6 of the Act, under Section 115 of the Indian Penal Code read with Section 302 of the Code and under Section of the Indian Penal Code is convicted thereunder and is sentenced (1) to two years' rigorous imprisonment under Section 19(c) of the Indian Arms Act, (2) to two years' rigorous imprisonment under Section 19(f) of the Indian arms Act, (3) to three years' rigorous imprisonment under Section 5 of the Explosive Substances Act read with Section 6 of the Act, (4) to five years' rigorous imprisonment under Section 4(b) of the Explosive Substances Act read with Section 6 of the Act, (5) to seven years' rigorous imprisonment under Section 3 of the Explosive Substances Act read with Section 6 of the Act and (6) to death under Section 302 of the Indian Penal Code—*he is to be hanged by the neck till he is dead:* the sentences of imprisonment shall run concurrently.

"He is found 'not guilty' of the remaining offences as specified in the charge, and is acquitted thereunder.'

Narayan D. Apte 'He is found "guilty" u/s 120-B of the Indian Penal Code read with Section 302 of the Code, u/s 19(c) of the Indian Arms Act or in the alternative u/s 114 of the Indian Penal Code read with Section 19(1) of the Indian Arms Act, u/s of the Explosive Substances Act or in the alternative u/s 5 of the Explosive Substances Act read with Section 6 of the Act, u/s 4(b) of the Explosive Substances Act read with Section 6 of the Act, u/s 115 of the Indian penal Code read with Section 302 of the Code, u/s 109 of the Indian Penal Code read with Section 302 of the Code, is convicted thereunder and is sentenced (1) to two years' R.I. u/s 19(c) of the Indian Arms Act or in the alternative u/s 114 of the Indian Penal Code read with Section 19(1) of the Indian Arms Act, (2) to two years' R.I. u/s 114 of the Indian Penal Code read with Section 19(f) of the Indian Arms Act, (3) to three years' R.I. u/s 5 of the Explosive Substances Act read with Section 6 of the Act. (4) to five years' R.I. u/s 4(b) of the Explosive Substances Act with Section 6 of the Act, (5) to seven years' R.I. u/s 3 of the Explosive Substances Act read with Section 6 of the Explosive Substances Act and (6) to death u/s 109 of the Indian Penal Code read with Section 302 of the Code-*he is to be hanged by the neck till he is dead*: the sentences of imprisonment shall run concurrently.

'He is found 'not guilty of the remaining offences as specified in the charge, and is acquitted thereunder.'

Vishnu R. Karkare "He is found "guilty" u/s 120-B of the Indian Penal Code read with Section 302 of the Code, u/s 114 of the Indian Penal Code read with Section 19(f) of the Indian Arms Act, u/s 5 of the Explosive Substances Act or in the alternative u/s 5 of Explosive Substances Act read with Section 6 of the Act or in the alternative u/s 5 of the Explosive Substances Act read with Section 6 of the Act, u/s 4(b) of the explosive Substances Act read with Section 6 of the Act, u/s 3 of the Explosive Substances Act read with Section 6 of the Act, u/s 115 of the Indian Penal Code read with Section 302 of the Code and u/s 109 of the Indian Penal Code read with Section 302 of the code, is convicted thereunder and is sentenced (1) to two years' R.I. u/s 114 of the Indian Penal Code read with Section 19(f) of the Indian Arms Act, (2) to three years' R.I. u/s 5 of the Explosive Substances Act or in the alternative of the Act, (3) to five years' R.I. u/s 4(b) of the Explosive Substances Act read with Section 6 of the Act, (4) to seven years' R.I. u/s 3 of the Explosive Substances Act read with Section 6 of the Act and (5) to transportation of life u/s 109 of the Indian Penal Code read with Section 302 of the Code; the sentences of imprisonment shall run concurrently and concurrent with the sentence of transportation for life.

'He is found "not guilty" of the remaining offences as specified in the charge, and is acquitted thereunder.'

Madanlal K. Pabwa "He is found "guilty" u/s 120-B of the Indian Penal Code read with Section 302 of the Code, u/s of the Explosive Substances Act or in the alternative u/s 5 of the Explosive Substances Act read with Section 6 of the Act, u/s 4(b) of the Explosive Substances Act read with Section 6 of the Act, u/s 3 of the Explosive Substances Act and u/s 115 of the Indian Penal Code read with Section 302 of the Code, is convicted thereunder and is sentenced (1) to transportation of life u/s 120-B of the Indian Penal Code read with Section 302 of the Code, (2) to three years' R.I u/s 5 of the Explosive Substances Act read with Section 6 of the Act, (3) to five years' R.I. u/s 3 of the Explosive Substances Act read with Section 6 of the Act, (4) to ten years R.I. under section 3 of the Explosive Substances Act and (5) to seven years' R.I. u/s 115 of the Indian Penal Code read with Section 302 of the Code; the sentences of imprisonment shall run concurrently with the sentence of transportation for life.

He is found "not guilty" of the remaining offences as specified in the charge, and is acquitted thereunder.

Shankar Kistayya 'He is found "guilty" u/s 120-B of the Indian Penal Code read with Section 302 of the Code, u/s 5 of the Explosive Substances Act or in the alternative u/s 5 of the Explosive Substances of act with Section 6 of the Act under Section 4(f) of the Explosive Substances Act read with Section 6 of the Act, u/s 3 of the Explosive Substances Act in the alternative u/s 5 of the Explosive Substances Act read with Section 6 of the Act and u/s 115 of the Indian Penal Code read with Section 302 of the Code, is convicted thereunder and is sentenced (1) to transportation for life u/s 120-B of the Indian Penal Code read with Section 302 of the Code, (2) to three years' R.I. u/s 5 of the Explosive Substances Act or in the alternative u/s of the Act (3) to five years' R.I. u/s 4(b) of the

Explosive Substances Act read with Section 6 of the Act, (4) to seven years' R.I. u/s 3 of the Explosive Substance Act read with Section 6 of the Act and (5) to seven years' R.I. u/s 115 of the Indian Penal Code read with Section 302 of the Code with the recommendation that the sentence of transportation for life u/s 120-B of the Indian Penal Code read with Section 302 of the Code may be commuted to seven years' R.I. u/s 401 and 402 of the Code of Criminal Procedure : the sentences of imprisonment shall run concurrently and concurrent with the sentences of transportation for life.

'He is found 'not guilty' of the remaining offences as specified in the charge and is acquitted thereunder.'

Gopal V. Godse 'He is found "guilty" u/s 120-B of the Indian Penal Code read with Section 302 of the Code, u/s 5 of the Explosive Substances Act or in the alternative u/s 5 of Explosive Substances Act read with Section 6 of the Act, u/s 4(b) of the explosive Substances Act read with Section 6 of the Act, u/s 3 of the Explosive Substances Act read with Section 6 of the Act, u/s 115 of the Indian Penal Code read with Section 302 of the Code and u/s 109 of the Indian Penal Code read with Section 302 of the Code, is convicted thereunder and is sentenced (1) to three years' R.I. u/s 5 of the Explosive Substances Act or in the alternative u/s 5 of the Explosive Substances Act read with Section 6 of the Act, (2) to five years' R.I. u/s 4(b) of the Explosive Substances Act read with Section 6 of the Act, (3) to seven years R.I. u/s 3 of the Explosive Substances Act read with Section 6 of the Act and (4) to transportation for life u/s 109 of the Indian Penal Code read with Section 302 of the Code; the sentences of imprisonment shall run concurrently and concurrent with the sentence of transportation for life.

'He is found "not guilty" of the remaining offences as specified in the charge, and is acquitted thereunder.'

Dattatreya S. Parchure 'He is found "guilty" under Section 120-B of the Indian Penal Code read with Section 302 of the Code read with Section 302 of the Code and u/s 109 of the Indian Penal code read with Section 302 of the Code, is convicted thereunder and is sentenced to transportation for life u/s 109 of the Indian Penal Code read with Section 302 of the Code.

'He is found "not guilty" of the remaining offences as specified in the charge, and is acquitted thereunder.

Vinayak D. Savarkar 'He is found "not guilty" of the offences as specified in the charge, and is acquitted thereunder. He is in custody and be released forthwith unless required otherwise.

'Digambar R. Badge has fulfilled the condition of his pardon, and be released from custody forthwith unless required otherwise.

'Nathuram V. Godse, Narayan D. Apte, Vishnu R. Karkare, Madanlal K. Pahwa, Shankar Kistayya, Gopal V.Godse, and Dattraya S. Parachure are informed that, if they want to appeal from this order they should do so within fifteen days from today. Copies of the Judgement are ready and may be had on application just now.

'I may bring to the notice of the Central Government the slackness of the police in the investigation of the case during the period between 20-1-1948 and 30-1-1948. The Delhi Police had obtained a detailed statement from Madanlal K. Pahwa soon after his arrest on 20-1-1948. The Bombay Police had also been reported the statement of Dr. J.C. Jain that he had made to the Hon'ble Morarji Desai on 21-1-1948. The Delhi Police and the Bombay Police had contacted each other soon after these two statements had been made. Yet the Police miserably failed to drive any advantage from these two statements. Had the slightest keenness been shown in the investigation of the case at that stage the tragedy probably could have been averted.

'My thanks are due to the counsel for the prosecution as well as the counsel for the defence for the cooperation they showed throughout with the court. Had it not been for their absolute cooperation the case of the nature could not have been disposed of in this time.

My thanks are also due to the staff of the Court. They came from different districts in the United Provinces, and worked splendidly throughout their stay at Delhi.

'All arms, ammunition and explosives and the articles connected therewith brought on the record of the case are confiscated to the Crown u/s 527 of the Code of Criminal Procedure Exs 14, 28, 29 and 30 are the shells of the hand-grenades that had been distributed at the Marina Hotel on 20-1-1948. Ex. 39 is the automatic-pistol with which Mahatma Gandhi was shot dead on 30-1-1948. Exs 9, 10, and 55 are the empty cartridge-case for the cartridges that had been fired at Mahatma Gandhi on 30-1-1948. Exs. 11 and 12 are the spent bullets that had passed right through the body of Mahatma Gandhi on 30-1-1948. No action in regard thereto be taken without first consulting the Central Government. They may perhaps be required for the National Museum.'

(sd) ATMACHARAN,
I.C.S.,
Judge, Special Court Red Fort, Delhi February 10, 1948

Appendix 3

TRANSLATION OF URDU DIARY ENTRY OF BRIEFING TO NAGARVALA

Rana Safvi

10½ بجے دن - نمبر 3 - اِس وقت معہ انسپکٹر صاحب دفتر پولیس
سی - آئی - ڈی بسواری ٹیکسی پہنچے - مسٹر نگروالا صاحب کی خدمت میں
پیش ہوئے - جن کو پھر دوبارہ جملہ حالات مقدمہ ھذا بتلائے گئے - ایک یادداشت
انگریزی جس میں مختصر بیان مدن لال ملزم انگریزی میں درج ہے - اور
اِس کے نیچے یادداشت S. P. صاحب نیو دھلی کی درج ہے - جناب نگروالا
صاحب کی خدمت میں پیش کی گئی - جنہوں نے اِس یادداشت کو بغور پڑھا
اور اپنے پاس یادداشت رکھی - تحریری نوٹ متعلقہ مقدمہ ھذا واپس دی - جو کہ
نف ھذا ہے - جناب نگروالا صاحب کو Karkra کے متعلق تمام حالات واضح کئے
گئے اور مزید یہ بھی عرض کیا گیا کہ مدن لال ملزم نے یہ بھی بتلایا تھا
کہ ہمراہی ملزمان میں سے ایک ملزم جس کا نام نہیں جانتا - ھندو راشٹریہ
یا اگرنی اخبار کا ایڈیٹر تھا - جس کا رنگ سانولہ ، عمر 33/34 سال - قد تقریباً
5'6" بیان کرتا تھا - یہ معلوم نہیں کہ وہ ایڈیٹر بمبئی یا پونہ کا ہے - اِس کے
علاوہ دیگر تین مرھٹہ و راجہ صاحب جو کہ اپنے ہمراہی ملزم بیان کرتا تھا - کے
حلیئے بتلائے گئے - ایڈیٹر ھندو راشٹریہ یا اگرنی اخبار اور Karkra ساکن احمدنگر
کے متعلق مسٹر نگروالا صاحب کی خدمت میں خاص طور پر زور دیا گیا - کہ
اِن کا ذکر ملزم کے بیان میں صاف طور پر آ چکا ہے - اِن کی گرفتاری کی
پہلے کوشش کی جاوے - تاکہ اِن سے دریافت عمل میں لائی جا سکے -

Diary entry at 10:30 a.m., Day 3: Along with inspector sahib, they reached police CID office in a taxi. They were presented in front of Mr Nagarvala.

They were once again explained the conditions and status of the case.

A brief memo with the statement of accused Madan Lal recorded in English, and below that a memo of SP sahib, New Delhi, were recorded and presented to Janab Nagarwala sahib.

He read it attentively and kept it with him. He gave them a written note regarding the proceedings of the day which are as follows:

Janab Mr Nagarvala was told all the facts relating to 'Karkra' and he was also told that the accused Madan Lal had said that from the co-accused—one accused whose name he doesn't know—was editor of *Hindu Rashtra* or *Agrani* newspaper, his complexion is on the darker side (*sanwla*) and is thirty-three or thirty-four years of age, with his height approximately 5'6".

He doesn't know whether this editor is from Bombay or Pune. Apart from that, there were three Maratha and a 'Raja sahib' whom he says were co-accused and were with him, and he described their appearance.

Mr Nagarvala was specially requested to prioritize the arrest of the editor of *Hindu Rashtra* or *Agrani* newspaper and 'Karkra', a resident of Ahmednagar, who have been clearly mentioned by the accused, so that they can be interrogated.

ACKNOWLEDGEMENTS

There are many who have contributed in enabling me to take on the task of writing this book, so first I would like to thank all those who, in their own way, helped me, knowingly or unknowingly.

First, I thank my parents Appa and Ma, my grandmothers Ba and Aijee and my sister Archana 'Bai'—that's what I grew up calling them—for bringing me up the way they did; but for all of them, I would have been incomplete. I'm grateful to Sonal, Vivan and Kasturi, my love and my life, for bearing with all my foibles and me, and for pushing me to write; Hariji, Paritosh and Anish for being patient; Punam, who was more of a friend than brother-in-law (Be happy wherever you are my friend, you have left a void in all our hearts); my parents-in-law Rohitbhai and Medhaben for having faith in me; Rajan, Devangi, Rashika and Adit for being there; all my relatives, Mashruwalas and Ambegaonkars—near and far—who continuously encouraged me; Krishna, for taking care of my home and children; Prabhubhai and Dhanuben, my teachers, who moulded me and instilled in me an insatiable quest for knowledge and learning, and many of the values that I did not realize; all my teachers at Adarsh Bal Mandir and Adarsh Vinay Mandir, Jaishreeben in particular. Thanks to my very close friends Bharat, Pankaj, Vijay, Raju, Janak, Mehul and Susheel, who have always been there for me; my friend Bhimsingh Yadav, who drove me around Delhi many a times, tracing the route taken by the killers from the Regal Theatre in Connaught Place to the roundabout behind Birla House and at other times too and, with sorrow in my heart, my childhood friend Arjav, who alas is no more.

I thank Venkatnarasimhan, who faces the brunt of my tantrums at work; Sudhir Gattawar for retouching the photographs published in the book and Dipankar Sadekar and Mahesh Baikar for scanning them and to Nipun, Sameer, Amol and Anoop, who worked with me at Mahatma Gandhi Foundation when I began writing the book.

I'm grateful to Mr Kanwal Rekhi, Mr B.V. Jagadeesh and Mr Harish Mehta for making it possible for me to be able to write with their generous help and my friends Kanakasabahpathy Pandiyan, Meeheer Mafatlal and Vijay Mukhi, who believed in me and stood by me.

Thanks to R. Sriram, who told me to just write and also introduced me to Jaypriya Vasudevan, who has been incredibly patient while waiting for me to finish writing so that she could sell the book; everyone at Jacaranda Press, especially Ashwati, whom I kept disturbing on her holidays; the team at Rupa that reduced my humongous manuscript into shape—I wish they were able to perform the same magic on me!

I am sincerely grateful to Mani Bhavan Gandhi Sangrahalaya for allowing me to keep the books from its library for as long as I wanted them; Dr Y.P. Anand, former director of Gandhi National Museum and its library, for helping with the research and to all the writers who wrote on this subject before me: Manohar Mulgaonkar, Advocate Inamdar, Justice Khosla, Tapan Ghosh and the two unknown reporters who wrote *Gandhi Murder Trial* and *Gandhi Hatyakand*—I have internalised much of their writing. Special thanks to Pyarelal Nayyar, Bapuji's secretary and biographer, who wrote *Mahatma Gandhi: The Last Phase Volume X, Parts I and II*, which have been invaluable. I would also like to thank Navjeevan and Pyarelal Foundation for allowing me to use text from the book; the late Jagan Phadnis, whose book in *Marathi, Mahatmya Chi Akher*, was what inspired me to write this book and Y.D. Phadke, whose book *Nathuramayan* gave me a different insight.

I am indebted to my friend Atul Tiwari for helping me with meanings of some very tough Hindi, Hindustani and Urdu words and phrases and Anil Nauria for sharing his article, which provided me with additional information that I have incorporated in this edition, and for telling me about books written by K.L. Gauba—*The Assassination of Mahatma Gandhi* and *Friends and Foes*, where I found additional information. Thanks to National Gandhi Museum and its director Dr Annamalai for providing me with a digital copy of *The Assassination of Mahatma Gandhi*. I am also grateful to my friend Rana Safvi for helping me with translations of documents in Urdu; Sharada Dwivedi for helping me with some of the establishments in Bombay used by the murderers and Kamal Haasan, my friend, and the gracious Sarika for making me a part of

Hey Ram (2000). I thank the team involved with the play *Me Nathuram Godse Boltoy* for twisting and manipulating history, and thus hardening my resolve to tell the truth; all those who, from time to time, provided references, which threw light on the many hidden aspects associated with the conspiracy and murder; the late Madhur Valluri, whom I never met; his mother, who was blessed with a tireless spirit and indomitable will, who gave me a book of Madhur's writings where I found an interview he had done with Gopal Godse, Madanlal Pahwa and Dr Sadashiv Parchure and Mandaliya, who brought me rare books and magazines, where I found some interesting titbits.

Last but not the least, I thank my publishers Rupa Publications for taking on a first-time writer like me and, thirteen years later, agreeing to publish this updated and edited edition; Mehta Publishers for publishing the Marathi translation and agreeing to publish this freshly translated, updated and edited edition and Kautilya Publications for publishing the Hindi translation. I also extend my gratitude to Dr Jagdish Patil for translating this updated and abridged edition into Marathi. I am grateful to Shri Bijuraj ji for translating this version of the book into Malyalam and my dear friend Sethu Das and Friends of Tibet for facilitating this. I deeply appreciate the design teams for designing the cover for this edition; Gandhi Research Foundation, Jalgaon, for always helping with reference material and Kinnari Bhatt of Sabarmati Ashram for her kind help with research material. Thanks to all those who heard that I was writing this book and encouraged me and to all the Sanghis: due to your lies, my resolve to keep writing the truth strengthens.

A big thank you to you, my reader. I am indebted. *Namostute, Shukriya, Karam, Meherbani*.

Cover

The Painting 'Death of Gandhi' by Tom Vattakuzhy: I am grateful to artist Tom Vattakuzhy of Kerala, for gifting me his painting Death of Gandhi. The painting depicts, quite realistically, the last moments of Gandhi's life after Nathuram Godse shot him. Tom's painting appropriately embellishes my book. Thank you very much, Tom. Post the printing of the current edition of the book, I intend to gift the painting to the National Gandhi Museum for them to display it in the museum dedicated to Bapu's death.

Tom Vattakuzhy
Born in 1967, Kerala, India

'If one asks me what I paint, I would shrink away from answering, as I do not have a straight answer. I do not work to give myself a political or ideological tag, and also do not consciously align myself with any 'isms' or trendy fashions in art. For me, art is a meditative solitary journey. I am concerned with exploring the psychological moods and feelings that I experience. I do not have any words to describe it. At best, what I can say at this moment is that I am a painter of interiors—of lives I see around, lives of the silenced, the marginalized and the alienated.'

Education: 1999 U.G.C. Net; 1998 M.F.A. (First Class) Faculty of Fine Arts, M.S. University of Baroda, Gujarat; 1996 B.F.A. (First Class) Kala Bhavan, Viswa Bharati University, Santiniketan, West Bengal.

Awards: 1998 AIFACS (All India Fine Arts and Crafts Society) Award, New Delhi; 1997 AIFACS (All India Fine Arts and Crafts Society) Award, New Delhi; 1997 Kerala Lalita Kala Academy Award, Govt. of Kerala; 1996 Highly Commended Certificate, Kerala Lalita Kala Academy, Govt. of Kerala; 1996 National Scholarship, Ministry of Human Resource Development, New Delhi; 1995 Haren Das Award, Academy of Fine Arts, Calcutta; 1992-1996 Merit Scholarship, Kala Bhavan, Vishwa Bharati University, Santiniketan.

Lives and works in Kerala, India.
tomvattakhuzy8809@gmail.com

Cover design by: Design And People. www.designandpeople.org